# Principles *of* Macroeconomics

# Principles *of* Macroeconomics
## The Way We Live

Susan K. Feigenbaum
*University of Missouri – St. Louis*

R. W. Hafer
*Southern Illinois University Edwardsville*

**Worth Publishers**

Senior Publisher: Catherine Woods
Executive Editor: Charles Linsmeier
Executive Marketing Manager: Scott Guile
Developmental Editors: Marie McHale/Amy Ray
Senior Media Editor: Marie McHale
Associate Managing Editor: Lisa Kinne
Supplements Project Editor: Edgar Bonilla
Editorial Assistant: Mary Walsh
Photo Editor: Bianca Moscatelli
Production Manager: Barbara Anne Seixas
Composition: MPS Limited, a Macmillan Company
Printing and Binding: Quad/Graphics

ISBN-13: 978-1-4292-2020-0
ISBN-10: 1-4292-2020-1

Library of Congress Control Number: 2011933854

Worth Publishers
41 Madison Avenue
New York, NY 10010
www.worthpublishers.com

To Professors Anne Carter, Barney Schwalberg, Ronald Teeples, and Burton Weisbrod for treating me like an economist long before I knew I was one. And to my husband, Jay Pepose, and our children, David, Max, Sam, and Morissa, who bore much of the opportunity cost of my writing this book. — S. K. F.

To Gail and Cait for the unending patience, support, and help they provided me during the writing of this book. — R. W. H.

# ABOUT THE AUTHORS

**Susan Feigenbaum** is Professor and former Chair of the Department of Economics at the University of Missouri in St. Louis. She has been the recipient of several National Science Foundation research and curriculum innovation grants and has received both the Governor's and Chancellor's Awards for Teaching Excellence. She has published extensively in such areas as public versus private provision of goods and services; the economics of science; and the economics of health care finance.

**R.W. Hafer** is the Distinguished Research Professor of Economics and Finance in the Department of Economics and Finance at Southern Illinois University Edwardsville. Prior to joining the SIUE faculty he worked as an economist with the Federal Reserve Bank of St. Louis. In addition to SIUE, he has taught at Washington University in St. Louis and at Erasmus University in Rotterdam, the Netherlands. He has published widely on monetary policy and financial markets in academic and non-academic publications, including the *Journal of Monetary Economics*, the *Journal of Finance*, and the *Wall Street Journal*.

# BRIEF CONTENTS

# CONTENTS

# Part 2: An Introduction to Macroeconomics

# Part 3: The Economics of the Long Run

# Part 4: Explaining Business Fluctuations

# Part 5: Policy Debates

# PREFACE

Our experiences in the classroom and our many years of working with students and talking to colleagues played a major part in our decision to write this book. Many principles of economics texts introduce students to economics as if it were a foreign language, one that they have never encountered. Economics is hardly foreign to anyone: day in and day out, we all make decisions—some that have significant effects on our economic well-being—that are consistent with basic economic principles.

Our goal in *Principles of Macroeconomics: The Way We Live* is to help students cultivate an appreciation for and an ability to use their economic "instincts." Unlike other books, our approach uses common experiences to demonstrate to students that they already engage in economic reasoning. This serves two purposes. First, it demystifies economics: for example, we show students how the cost and benefit calculations they make, even subconsciously, can be generalized to create an economic model that predicts human behavior. Second, it shows students that the economic principles upon which their own decisions are based are the very same principles used to gauge the success of decisions made by politicians and other policy makers. We achieve this goal by building up our economic system. First we explore the economics of individual decision making. Then we branch out to economic decision making and exchange within households; and only then do we expand our analysis to economy-wide phenomena. Throughout our book, we exploit the natural linkage between microeconomics and macroeconomics that other texts often fail to capitalize on.

Another difference between our book and others is that it reflects our belief that the language of economics should enhance learning, not be an impediment to it. We don't give short shrift to key economic concepts and theories, but we do not get bogged down in an unreasonable amount of technical economic jargon. Our approach is to offer an accessible, applied introduction to modern macroeconomic thinking that is concise, is extremely readable, and builds on everyday events to highlight the theory. The analytical tools students learn in this book are relevant to their everyday lives, and they can use them to understand macroeconomic phenomena—such as inflation and unemployment, economic growth, and recession—and to evaluate the costs and benefits of public policies. We continually benchmark macroeconomic theories against real-world events and data to show just how well they "fit" reality.

## What Makes This Book Different?

When you are considering adopting a principles of economics text, do you find yourself asking at least some of the following questions?

- Is my job to teach students an entirely new way of thinking, or can I successfully teach economics by building on the way students already approach their everyday decision making?

- Why is it that most books do not apply economics in a way that students would find useful in their everyday lives?

- Why do I cringe every time I ask my students to buy into assumptions that they—and I—know are unrealistic simplifications of the world around them?

■ Have I grown irritated with the overwhelming amount of technical apparatus that I must cover with my students, promising them that "down the line" they will see the relevance?

■ Why do I find that macroeconomics is becoming increasingly more about the model and less about how the economy works?

■ Do I wish that my text provided a better micro foundation for its macro discussion and models?

If you answered a resounding "Yes!" to any of these questions, then this textbook is a good choice for you.

Early readers of this book, even in manuscript form, often described the approach as an "inverted" one. That is, the book tends to describe a real-life situation, propose an economic explanation for observed behavior, and only then broaden the example to a more generalized theoretical result. This approach contrasts with other books that approach economics by first presenting an often obscure conceptual construct and then offering (sometimes) relevant examples. Our goal is to motivate students to want to use economic theory because it helps them to understand what is going on around them every day.

We have consciously adopted a writing style that involves the student in a dialogue. It strives to be both accessible and engaging. We have woven and rewoven certain themes throughout the book to reinforce student learning. One such theme is opportunity cost and the weighing of marginal costs against marginal benefits. Unlike some books that introduce these basic ideas at the outset and then jettison them as the discussion turns to macro issues, we highlight their applicability throughout the text. Concepts such as the production possibilities frontier (PPF) are used to bridge the analysis from earlier micro-foundation chapters to later ones that focus on macroeconomic issues. Family production decisions, first introduced in the introductory chapters, are reinforced within a macro context in the chapters on economic growth and short-run economic fluctuations. And throughout, we attempt to bring in international examples that help move students beyond a U.S.-centric perspective.

## How the Book Is Organized

This book is organized in a way that carries our approach throughout the book, from introductory chapters through the last. The following walk-through highlights the concepts and examples presented in each chapter.

### Part 1: The Economic Costs and Choices Facing Individuals

*Chapter 1, Economics as a Framework for Making Life's Decisions,* fosters student buy-in to the course by helping them realize that economics is an essential part of their everyday environment. The chapter stresses that the same concepts that explain why we trade with each other also can be used to explain why the prices of goods rise, unemployment rates fluctuate, and some countries grow faster than others. Economics is a dynamic social science that tries to predict human behavior, and that is how we approach it.

In *Chapter 2, The Benefits and Costs of an Activity: Specialization and Exchange,* the student is introduced to the basic framework of choice: the weighing of marginal costs versus benefits arising from the alternatives we face. The chapter opens up a world of questions that economics can help to answer: Why do people form habits? Can the decision process that couples go through when deciding on the number of children to have be cast in economic terms? How does a couple decide who will enter the labor force and who will engage in household production? In the end, economics tells a story about human behavior—the behavior of individuals, families, and the entire economy. As we cover such standard topics as opportunity cost, marginal benefit and marginal cost, production possibilities, and willingness to pay, our persistent drumbeat is that these concepts are present, and revealed, in everyday behavior.

We think it's important to use the demand-and-supply apparatus that students encounter in the introductory chapters later in the macroeconomic chapters. Many of today's macro texts review this important micro-foundation in an early chapter and then dismiss it in their race to cover macroeconomic theories. In *Chapter 3, The Demand for and Supply of Economic Goods,* we develop the supply-and-demand model within a context of events familiar to the student. The examples used vary from the demand for secondhand shirts and the effects of changing property rights on driving habits, to the effect on supply of outsourcing accounting jobs overseas and the effects of technology changes on animated movies. By covering a wide variety of familiar examples, the end result is that the student will understand not only how observed market outcomes come about but also why such outcomes reflect the behavior of rational individual decision makers like themselves. This foundation is built on later to develop the short-run macro model. In addition, we introduce property rights as a prerequisite for exchange, a notion that is central to our later analysis of economic growth. Because of the recurrent use of supply and demand in the macro chapters, we think that this chapter is essential for macro analysis.

*Chapter 4, Applying the Supply-and-Demand Model,* contains a wide array of applications designed to enhance the student's appreciation for the predictive power of this simple model. For the instructor who is looking for a variety of unique applications, this chapter fits the bill. We selected our examples not only with an eye toward the real trade-offs that students face but also with future chapters in mind. For example, the supply-and-demand model is used to explain labor-market dynamics, to show how taxes affect the allocation of goods, to investigate the impact of tariffs and quotas, and to see how interest rates are determined. Together with the previous chapter, Chapters 3 and 4 provide a solid foundation of basic economics that will enable the student to better understand the principles of macroeconomics.

## Part 2: An Introduction to Macroeconomics

When addressing the question "What is macroeconomics?" we emphasize that it is an extension of the micro foundations and issues students have already learned about but on a larger scale. *Chapter 5, What Are the Big Issues: A Macroeconomic Overview,* places the major concepts of macroeconomics into a context that once again taps into the student's experiences. The idea of price inflation, for example, is introduced by examining something students are familiar with: grade inflation across universities. The subject of economic growth begins with a question about why the average Dutch person is getting taller than the average American. Unrelated? Not at all if we are trying to explain why some countries are experiencing faster economic growth—or are "growing taller"—than others. Approaching macro concepts by looking at them from an individual perspective is a hallmark of our book's approach.

In *Chapter 6, Measuring a Nation's Price Level,* we fully develop the first macroeconomic concept—the price level. After we've completed the introduction of a price index, we take pains to show that a price index isn't just a mathematical computation but a useful device for answering important questions, including the following: How do oil price increases affect your cost of living? Is there anything the government can do about such price increases? Can government policies cause the price level to rise and thereby reduce your economic well-being? Seeing how a price index actually is measured also gives us the opportunity to expose the types of bad economic analysis students encounter every day. Our treatment of relative price changes, for instance, not only ties back to individual demand decisions but also sets the stage for discussions of policies to combat inflation. Inflation caused by higher food prices, for example, has different roots than inflation caused by a general increase in all prices, and each leads to very different policy implications. As in most of our other chapters, international examples are introduced to expand the student's awareness of how applicable economics is on a global scale.

Our recurrent theme is that economics always boils down to the choices that individuals make. In *Chapter 7, Output and Income,* we open with a story that relates firm-level production (in this case, handmade guitars) and income to the same concepts that explain output and income for the entire economy. Throughout the chapter, we stress that the reason we measure economic output is to gauge whether our overall well-being is rising or falling. Recognizing the limitations of the data, knowing whether the economy is expanding or contracting, and knowing the level of per capita income are important inputs into making policy decisions that affect our lives.

We introduce students to the economics of the labor market in *Chapter 8, The Labor Market and Unemployment.* Unlike other texts, unemployment first is treated in a much broader fashion than that of idle workers. We trace the concept of unemployment back to the production possibilities frontier (PPF) introduced in an earlier chapter, a linkage that broadens the notion of what unemployment—in an economic sense—really is. We also use the supply-and-demand framework to provide a complete treatment of unemployment in the labor market, once again highlighting how valuable this model is. Throughout the discussion, we stress micro-based causes of unemployment both here and abroad, such as education levels, minimum-wage laws, and unemployment compensation.

In *Chapter 9, The Global Economy,* we build on the concept of individual exchange: trade between people in a household or between people separated by an ocean is premised on the same fundamental economic principles. On the larger scale, external factors play a more important role. In addition to trade, this chapter introduces foreign exchange rates, again using supply and demand to understand their movements. Our goal is to demystify the material so that students realize that international trade and the determination of exchange rates are not exotic concepts but are simply examples of the economic models they have already learned about.

## Part 3: The Economics of the Long Run

Economic growth is a critical aspect of modern macroeconomics. *Chapter 10, The Basics of Growth Economics,* opens students' eyes to the fact that the benefits—and costs—of economic growth are all around us: wood-burning stoves have given way to microwave ovens; "books" are read on Nooks and Kindles; our eyes can be surgically corrected to eliminate the need for thick glasses; and people are living much longer than the generation before. If these are the positive outcomes of economic growth, how did we get here?

The now-familiar PPF is used to create a platform upon which a simple production function is built. This stepwise approach enables us to flesh out the roles that labor, capital, and knowledge play when it comes to determining an economy's economic growth. Concepts introduced earlier to explain trade between individuals— such as the principle of diminishing marginal returns—are resurrected to explain why some countries have succeeded economically while others have lagged behind. We emphasize that output per person, rather than total GDP, is the measure that really counts when gauging the well-being of members of a society. Using real-world data and a basic analytical tool (the scatter diagram) we show how well the macroeconomic story we tell fits with reality.

*Chapter 11, Other Aspects of Economic Growth: Why Isn't Everyone Rich?,* offers a wide-ranging exploration of current research on how social and institutional differences can affect the economic growth of countries. The approach of this chapter is both topical and data-based. It shows why economists recognize that "noneconomic" factors—things other than labor, capital, and knowledge—also can play an important role in predicting economic success. For example, we examine how a country's legal structure can affect its economic growth, tying this back to our earlier discussion of the importance of property rights in trade. This chapter also suggests determinants of economic growth that students might not have thought about, such as population growth, the health of the population, and education levels. In the end, this chapter gives instructors the flexibility to pick and choose the topics that best suit the objectives of their course.

*Chapter 12, Inflation: What It Is, and Why It's Bad,* explains to students who haven't personally experienced bouts of high inflation why it is economically harmful. Inflation is treated as a longer-term phenomenon, rather than something caused by short-term oil price spikes or bad harvests. This idea references our earlier treatment of relative price changes. Supply and demand are used again, this time to explain price-level changes as a function of money supply and money demand. Combined with the Quantity Theory of Money, we pose an important policy question: Is inflation a monetary phenomenon? The data presented indicates that, as the supply-and-demand model and the Quantity Theory predict, the answer is unequivocally "yes." Knowing why inflation occurs gives rise to the question of what inflation costs us. Not only does it create lost purchasing power, but inflation also affects interest rates that ultimately impact the ability of individuals and firms to borrow money for homes, college tuition, and so forth. In this way, students become aware that inflation-related policy decisions can have significant effects on their lives.

## Part 4: Explaining Business (Short-Run) Fluctuations

The important concept of potential GDP, developed in Part 3, lays the groundwork for analyzing short-term fluctuations in economic activity, the focus of Part 4. The model developed and "tested" in this part of the book tries to answer the question left open in the long-run growth discussion: If labor, capital, and knowledge explain *long-run* trends in output, what explains *short-term* deviations in real GDP around that trend? More to the point: Why are there recessions?

In Chapter 7, students were introduced to the different spending components that make up GDP. *Chapter 13, Aggregate Expenditures and Real Output,* uses that aggregation scheme to model total expenditures. The role of consumer spending, business investment, government purchases, and foreign trade as components of total expenditures are discussed. As a prelude to later policy chapters, we also introduce the real rate of interest and why it is often thought to be a key determinant of several components of total spending. By streamlining the approach while still preserving relevant economic content, we develop a dynamic aggregate demand curve—one that relates spending to inflation, not the price level—and apply it. In our introduction to aggregate demand, we use it to analyze the economic impact that monetary and fiscal-policy actions have, with an eye to the actions actually taken in the past few years.

Macroeconomics and related policies are most often discussed within the context of growth rates. Given this, why build a model that relies on the price level and the level of real GDP? In our book, we analyze business fluctuations as a dynamic process, relating changes in inflation and inflationary expectations to deviations in output from potential output. To get to this result, we construct a story about inflation expectations. *Chapter 14, Inflation Expectations and Their Effects on the Economy,* tells that story. In keeping with our commitment to emphasize macroeconomics' micro foundations, the supply-and-demand model is used to show how changes in individuals' inflation expectations can affect both the labor and goods markets to eventually impact the macro-economy. This approach produces a dynamic macro model that tells a plausible story of why business fluctuations occur. With the GDP gap as our output measure rather than the usual level of real GDP, our discussion once again exploits the students' understanding of unemployment (via the PPF) and their understanding of economic growth. The combination yields a modern macro model that students find not only accessible, but one they can readily use to explain short-term changes in output as well as longer-term changes in the rate of inflation.

The last chapter in Part 4 puts the model to work. *Chapter 15, Can Economic Fluctuations Be Predicted? Using the Aggregate Demand and Inflation Expectations Model,* "tests" whether the model's theoretical predictions mesh with reality. To do this, we must first address some previous definitional gaps, including the following: Is it business "cycles" or "fluctuations"? How are business cycles dated? Do they occur concurrently across countries? Most importantly, we test-drive the AD-IE model using several "case studies" of recessions in the United States, Mexico, and Canada. After relating the events leading up to each recession, we see whether the actual behavior of inflation and the GDP gap support the model's predictions. Our "test" of the theory uses graphs that are unique to our book. We find that students appreciate the usefulness of the model after they see that it really can explain movements in output and inflation. Based on our own classroom experience, this chapter brings the AD-IE model alive for many students. They not only come away with a much better appreciation of the AD-IE model's worth—but also recognize its limitations.

## Part 5: Policy Debates

This part of the book takes the foundation previously established and uses it to explore what we believe is the most interesting (and daunting) aspect of macroeconomics: policy applications. We open this discussion with *Chapter 16, Fiscal Policy,* which is a dual-purpose chapter. The chapter introduces students to the fundamentals of fiscal policy: what the deficit is, how it has changed and why, and what the debt is, how the debt and deficit are related, and so forth. It also covers fiscal-policy analysis within the confines of our macro model—automatic stabilizers and discretionary (both spending and tax) policy. After that, we depart from the norm by seeing if fiscal policy "works."

As we do throughout this book, real-world evidence is used to help students appreciate what fiscal policy can, and cannot, do. For example, instead of merely suggesting that crowding out exists and what the implications are, we provide evidence to assess whether the predictions hold true. We also explore whether fiscal-policy actions have, in general, led to more economic stability. And we examine the nature of the spending multiplier—not only its definition but also the actual estimates of its value. Our approach is not to reject any one theory but to open students' eyes to the possibility that some policy approaches they have heard about—for example, policies to reduce unemployment—may not be as credible as some might have them believe.

The final two chapters introduce and examine the role of monetary policy in the economy. *Chapter 17, Money, Banking, and the U.S. Federal Reserve System,* opens with a traditional nuts-and-bolts view of the money-supply process. Money is introduced by considering the cost of something students routinely do: barter. We also have them imagine the cost of using a type of money that is not easily divisible, such as a chicken, and help them understand why their credit cards are not really money. As before, we use personal examples to illustrate the important ideas of why money exists and its functions.

We opt for a streamlined—the number of T-accounts is kept to a minimum—yet fully functional treatment of the banking system's role in the creation of money. With the banking system covered, a brief overview of the institutional structure and history of the Federal Reserve is provided. Based on this prelude, we then explain how, primarily through open-market operations, the Fed's actions affect interest rates and the money supply. This is a more detailed version of the brief story hinted at in several earlier chapters. Recognizing that open-market operations are not the only policy option for the Fed, the chapter concludes with a section on quantitative easing.

The purpose of *Chapter 18, Monetary Policy,* is to make clear to students that economists' insights into how monetary policy making should be conducted continue to evolve. Part of this evolutionary development is the rise of policy transparency and the problems of time inconsistency, two relatively new ideas that have significantly altered the current conduct of monetary policy around the globe. An important goal of this chapter is for students to appreciate the fact that experience affects theory, and that policy makers are not infallible. As in Chapter 16, we want to see if monetary policy "works."

To drive home this point, we outline the rise and fall of important policy rules that the Fed used to guide its actions over the past 50 years. This treatment is typically absent in most books. By demonstrating the dynamic, evolving nature of macroeconomics, our approach should help students understand why equally informed and well-meaning individuals often disagree over appropriate policy actions. To illustrate this, we choose the monetary-policy debate surrounding the Great Recession of 2007–2009 as our case study.

## Supplements and Media

### For Instructors

#### Instructor's Resource Manual with Solutions Manual

The *Instructor's Resource Manual*, written by Gail Heyne Hafer (St. Louis Community College, Meramec), is a resource that provides materials and tips to enhance the classroom experience. The *Instructor's Resource Manual* provides the following:

- Overview of each chapter
- Chapter-by-chapter learning objectives
- Chapter outlines
- Teaching notes
- Outline of the principle concepts students will learn in each chapter
- Activities that can be conducted in or out of the classroom
- Solutions manual with detailed answers to all of the end-of-chapter problems from the textbook

### Printed Test Bank

The Test Bank provides a wide range of questions appropriate for assessing your students' comprehension, interpretation, analysis, and synthesis skills. The Test Bank offers questions designed for comprehensive coverage of the text concepts. Questions have been checked for continuity with the text content, overall usability, and accuracy.

The Test Bank features include the following:

- To aid instructors in building tests, each question has been categorized according to its general *degree of difficulty*. The three levels are easy, moderate, and difficult.
  - *Easy* questions require students to recognize concepts and definitions. These are questions that can be answered by direct reference to the textbook.
  - *Moderate* questions require some analysis on the student's part.
  - *Difficult* questions usually require more detailed analysis by the student.
- Each question has also been categorized according to a *skill descriptor*. These include fact-based, definitional, concept-based, critical-thinking, and analytical-thinking questions.
  - *Fact-based questions* require students to identify facts presented in the text.
  - *Definitional questions* require students to define an economic term or concept.
  - *Concept-based questions* require a straightforward knowledge of basic concepts.
  - *Critical-thinking questions* require the student to apply a concept to a particular situation.
  - *Analytical-thinking questions* require another level of analysis to answer the question. Students must be able to apply a concept and use this knowledge for further analysis of a situation or scenario.
- To further aid instructors in building tests, each question is conveniently cross-referenced to the appropriate topic heading in the textbook. Questions are presented in the order in which concepts are presented in the text.
- The Test Bank includes questions with tables that students must analyze to solve for numerical answers. It contains questions based on the graphs that appear in the book. These questions ask students to use the graphical models developed in the textbook and to interpret the information presented in the graph.
- Questions have been designed to correlate with the questions in the textbook.

### Computerized Test Bank

The printed Test Banks are available in CD-ROM format for both Windows and Macintosh users. With the Diploma program, instructors can easily create and print tests and write and edit questions. Tests can be printed in a wide range of formats. The software's unique synthesis of flexible word-processing and database features creates a program that is extremely intuitive and capable.

### Lecture PowerPoint Presentations

These presentations, created by Eric R. Nielsen (St. Louis Community College), consist of PowerPoint slides that provide graphs from the textbook, tables, and bulleted lists of key concepts suitable for lecture presentation. Key figures from the text are replicated and animated to enhance class lectures. These slides incorporate concept-based questions that may be used along with i>clicker. The slides may also be customized by instructors to suit their individual needs and can be accessed on the instructor's side of the Web site or on the Instructor's Resource CD-ROM.

Instructor's Resource CD-ROM

Using the Instructor's Resource CD-ROM, instructors can easily build classroom presentations or enhance online courses. This CD-ROM contains all text figures (in JPEG and PPT formats), PowerPoint lecture slides, and detailed solutions to all end-of-chapter problems. Instructors can choose from the various resources, and then edit and save them for use in the classroom. The Instructor's Resource CD-ROM includes the following:

- **Instructor's Resource Manual** (PDF): An overview of each chapter, chapter-by-chapter learning objectives, chapter outlines, teaching notes, outlines of the principle concepts students will learn in each chapter, and notes on activities that can be conducted in or out of the classroom.

- **Solutions Manual** (PDF): Detailed solutions to all of the end-of-chapter problems from the textbook.

- **Lecture PowerPoint presentations** (PPT): PowerPoint slides, including graphs, data tables, and bulleted lists of key concepts suitable for lecture presentation.

- **Images from the textbook** (JPEG): A complete set of textbook images in high-resolution and low-resolution JPEG formats.

- **Illustration PowerPoint slides** (PPT): A complete set of figures and tables from the textbook in PPT format.

## For Instructors and Students

Companion Web Site:

www.worthpublishers.com/feigenbaumhafer

The companion Web site is a virtual study guide for students and an excellent resource for instructors. The tools on the site include the following:

**Student Resources**

- **Quizzes:** Provides a set of quiz questions per chapter with appropriate feedback and page references to the textbook. All student answers are saved in an online gradebook that can be accessed by instructors.

- **Key term flashcards:** Students can test themselves on the key terms with these pop-up electronic flashcards.

**Instructor Resources**

- **Gradebook:** The site gives you the ability to track students' work by accessing an online gradebook.

- **Lecture PowerPoint presentations:** These PowerPoint slides are designed to assist instructors with lecture preparation and presentation by providing bulleted lecture outlines suitable for large lecture presentation. Instructors can customize these slides to suit their individual needs.

- **Images from the textbook** (JPEG): A complete set of textbook images in high-resolution and low-resolution JPEG formats.

- **Illustration PowerPoint slides** (PPT): A complete set of figures and tables from the textbook in PPT format.
- **Instructor's Resource Manual** (PDF): Files provide materials and tips to enhance the classroom experience.
- **Solutions Manual** (PDF): Files provide detailed solutions to all of the end-of-chapter problems from the textbook.

### EconPortal

EconPortal marries our rich content and customizability with a user interface that proves that power and simplicity aren't mutually exclusive. The features include the following:

- **Clear, consistent interface:** The eBook, media, assessment tools, instructor materials, and other content are integrated and unified to a degree unparalleled by other online learning systems.
- **Everything is assignable:** All course materials are assignable and computer-gradable: eBook sections, videos, flashcards, discussion forums, as well as traditionally assignable items such as quizzes. Studies show that assigning activities and making them part of students' grades is the most effective way to make online learning activities translate into higher student performance.
- **Everything is customizable:** Instructors can rearrange chapters or sections of the eBook and/or supplement or delete questions from the premade quizzes and homework assignments that come prepackaged in EconPortal.
- **Easy course management integration:** EconPortal is simple to integrate with existing learning-management systems.

EconPortal provides a powerful, easy-to-use, completely customizable teaching and learning-management system complete with the following:

- **Robust, interactive eBook:** The eBook enables a range of note-sharing options, highlighting, graph and example enlargement, a fully searchable glossary, and a full text search.
- **LearningCurve—personalized, formative assessments:** Learning Curve incorporates adaptive question selection, personalized study plans, and state-of-the-art question–analysis reports in activities with a game-like feel that keeps students engaged with the material. Integrated eBook sections provide students with one-click access to additional exposure to the course text. An innovative scoring system ensures that students who need more help with the material spend more time quizzing themselves than students who are already proficient.
- **Powerful online quizzing and homework:** EconPortal includes a state-of-the-art online homework and testing system. Instructors can use precreated assignments for each chapter or create their own assignments. Assignments may be created from the following:
  - **Complete Test Bank for the textbook:** Provides a wide range of questions appropriate for assessing students.
  - **End-of-chapter problems from the textbook:** The end-of-chapter problems will be available in a self-graded format—perfect for quick in-class quizzes or homework assignments. The questions have been carefully edited to ensure that they maintain the integrity of the text's end-of-chapter problems.

- **Graphing questions:** EconPortal provides electronically gradable graphing problems using a robust graphing engine. Students will be asked to draw their response to a question, and the software will automatically grade that response. These graphing questions are meant to replicate the pencil-and-paper experience of drawing graphs for students.

### Blackboard and WebCT

These WebCT and Blackboard e-Packs enable you to create a thorough, interactive, and pedagogically sound online course or course Web site. The e-Packs, provided free, give you cutting-edge online materials that facilitate critical thinking and learning, including Test Bank content, preprogrammed quizzes, links, activities, animated graphs, and a whole array of other materials. Best of all, this material is preprogrammed and fully functional in the WebCT or Blackboard environment. Prebuilt materials eliminate hours of course-preparation work and offer significant support as you develop your online course. The result is an interactive, comprehensive online course that allows for effortless implementation, management, and use. The files can be easily downloaded from our Course Management System site directly onto your department server.

## Further Resources Offered

### Faculty Lounge

Faculty Lounge is an online community of economics instructors. At this unique forum, economics instructors can connect, interact, and collaborate with fellow teachers and economics researchers, sharing thoughts and teaching resources. Instructors can upload their own resources and search for peer-reviewed content to use in class. Faculty Lounge is a great place to connect with colleagues nationwide who face the same challenges in the classroom as you do. To learn more, ask your Worth representative or visit www.worthpublishers.com/facultylounge.

### i>clicker

Developed by a team of University of Illinois physicists, i>clicker is the most flexible and reliable classroom response system available. It is the only solution created *for* educators, *by* educators—with continuous product improvements made through direct classroom testing and faculty feedback. You'll love i>clicker no matter your level of technical expertise because the focus is on *your* teaching, *not the technology*. To learn more about packaging i>clicker with this textbook, please contact your local sales rep or visit www.iclicker.com.

### *Financial Times* Edition

For adopters of the textbook, Worth Publishers and the *Financial Times* are offering a 15-week subscription to students at a tremendous savings. Instructors also receive their own free *Financial Times* subscription for one year. Students and instructors may access research and archived information at www.ft.com.

### Dismal Scientist

A high-powered business database and analysis service comes to the classroom! Dismal Scientist offers real-time monitoring of the global economy, produced locally by economists and professionals at Economy.com's London, Sydney, and West Chester offices. Dismal Scientist is *free* when packaged with the Feigenbaum-Hafer text. Please contact your local sales rep for more information or go to www.economy.com.

*The Economist*

*The Economist* has partnered with Worth Publishers to create an exclusive offer that will enhance the classroom experience. Faculty members receive a complimentary 15-week subscription when ten or more students purchase a subscription. Students get 15 issues of *The Economist* at a huge savings. Inside and outside the classroom, *The Economist* provides a global perspective that helps students keep abreast of what's going on in the world, and gives insight into how the world views the United States. *The Economist* ignites dialogue, encourages debate, and enables readers to form well-reasoned opinions—while providing a deeper understanding of key political, social, and business issues. Supplement your textbook with the knowledge and insight that only *The Economist* can provide. To get 15 issues of *The Economist,* go to www.economistacademic.com/worth.

## Acknowledgements

A book like this would not be possible without the assistance of many people, whom we gratefully acknowledge. First, the renowned team at Worth has spared no effort to help us; their experience and skill in publishing economics textbooks were invaluable. Numerous individuals have been involved with producing this book. The project was initiated by Craig Bleyer and guided to completion by our sponsoring editors Charles Linsmeier and Sarah Dorger. Through it all, the manuscript was improved endlessly by our development editors Marie McHale and Amy Ray. We are greatly in their debt. We would also like to thank Professor Sang Lee, at Southeastern Louisiana University, who did an amazing job ensuring the accuracy of the text. And we gratefully acknowledge the financial support of the National Science Foundation's Undergraduate Curriculum and Course Development Program; the programmatic support of Myles Boylan, our Program Officer; and the NSF grant reviewers who understood the significance of our approach to teaching economics in terms of attracting underrepresented groups into this field of study.

A number of our colleagues were very helpful in providing their reviews of earlier versions of the text. We wish to thank the following for their insights:

Anca Alecsandru
*Louisiana State University*

Michael Applegate
*Oklahoma State University*

Clare Battista, Ph.D.
*California Polytechnic State University*

Michael Brandl
*The University of Texas at Austin*

Bill Burrows
*Lane Community College*

Lisa Citron
*Cascadia Community College*

Amlan Datta
*Cisco Junior College*

Irene R. Foster
*Tennessee State University*

Eugene W. Gotwalt
*Sweet Briar College*

Eran Guse
*West Virginia University*

Denise Hazlett
*Whitman College*

Mark L. Healy
*William Rainey Harper College*

Terence Hunady
*Bowling Green State University*

Deborah Kelly
*Palomar College*

Dimitris J. Kraniou
*Point Park University*

Jacob Kurien
*Rockhurst University*

Sang Lee
*Southeastern Louisiana University*

Michael L. Marlow
*Cal Poly, San Luis Obispo*

Larry T. McRae
*Appalachian State University*

Heather Micelli
*Mira Costa College*

Ida Mirzaie
*The Ohio State University*

Andrew Ojede
*California State University, Long Beach*

Chris Phillips
*Somerset Community College*

Dennis Placone
*Clemson University*

Nishith Prakash
*University of Houston*

Joseph R. Radding
*Folsom Lake College, Los Rios Community College District*

Lynda Rush
*California State Polytechnic University, Pomona*

Ahmad Saranjam
*Bridgewater State College*

Todd P. Steen
*Hope College*

Jesus M. Valencia
*Slippery Rock University*

Jennifer VanGilder
*Ursinus College*

Jim R. Wollscheid
*Texas A&M University—Kingsville*

Last, but certainly not least, we thank our families, especially our spouses, Jay and Gail, for their sustained support during the time we devoted to writing this book.

Susan K. Feigenbaum
R.W. Hafer
December 2011

# PART 1

## The Economic Costs and Choices Facing Individuals

In Part 1, we begin by looking at the choices we make as individuals to improve our well-being as well as the constraints we face when doing so. Having explored economic decision making from an individual perspective, we move on to economic interrelationships that arise between people. We introduce the notion of gains from trade and how buyers and sellers meet face-to-face, online, or through representatives to voluntarily exchange rights to an economic good in the marketplace. The basic economics are the same whether that market is a physical place, such as a store or the New York Stock Exchange; electronic, such as the NASDAQ; or a Web site like eBay.

With the supply-and-demand framework firmly established, we then devote a chapter to showing how it is used. Our applications of supply and demand provide insights into the workings of several different markets, including the labor and capital markets, as well as the market for credit, thus introducing the idea of interest-rate determination. These models lay the foundation for Part 2.

# 1

# Economics as a Framework for Making Life's Decisions

*"You can't always get what you want."*

*Mick Jagger,*
*Rock music legend*

If you ask ten people what economics is about, you will probably get a dozen different answers. Most often, people will immediately think of business, Wall Street, and how to make money. Others will mention taxes, recessions, inflation, unemployment, or the weak dollar. Older respondents might recollect the "home economics" class that was offered in high school that focused on mastering such household tasks as cooking, sewing, and budgeting. Pushed further, people will likely embellish their answers with such descriptions as "complicated," "hard to understand," "complex," and even "mysterious." As we will see throughout this book, Mick Jagger aptly summarized what economics is really about—the choices we make when we can't get everything we want. The rest is simply commentary.

## 1.1 Exactly What Is Economics?

What is economics? The answer is simple. Economics is the study of the trade-offs we face in our lives. Because each decision we make requires us to choose between two or more options, we face **trade-offs** in just about everything we do.

> **TRADE-OFFS** Opportunities we pass up when we make one choice versus another choice.

> **EXAMPLE** When Mick Jagger decided to become a musician, he gave up the opportunity to become an economist.

> **EXAMPLE** When you chose to take this economics class during this time slot, you gave up the opportunity to take another class at the same time.

We each owe our very existence to choices made by our adoptive or biological parents. As we shall see, even decisions as basic as whether or not to have children are economic in nature. By observing the choices that people make, we find that individuals *act as if* they have weighed the trade-offs they face, whether it is deciding which movie to see or whether to have children. Economist and Nobel Laureate Friedrich von Hayek put it this way:

> Many of the greatest things man has achieved are not the result of consciously directed thought, and still less the product of a deliberately coordinated effort of many individuals, but of a process in which the individual plays a part which he can never fully understand.

In other words, humans are "hardwired" to act—not just consciously but also subconsciously—according to economic fundamentals. Whether this hardwiring is due to "nature" or "nurture," we don't know. What we do know, however, is that economists and biologists have discovered a similar pattern of behavior in many other species as well.

If, in fact, people make choices that are consistent with economic principles, then we can predict with some accuracy what their decisions will be when they face certain opportunities. To be more specific, economics provides a framework that helps us predict how people's choices will change when the trade-offs they face change. Although it might take a crystal ball to predict which horse will win the Kentucky Derby, economics does quite well when it comes to predicting how people react to changes in the price of gasoline, for example.

## 1.2  Living in a World of Scarcity

Why do we face trade-offs when we make choices? Why must we choose between alternatives and be forced to forgo some opportunities? To answer these questions, we must appreciate the reality that we—as well as the world around us—are constantly in a state of **scarcity**.

**SCARCITY** A situation in which only limited resources are available to meet people's unlimited wants.

**EXAMPLE** Seats to popular concerts are scarce, leading to ticket scalping.

**EXAMPLE** Certain sections of some courses are scarce, resulting in waiting lists.

**EXAMPLE** The talent required to land a job that pays $1 million-plus is scarce.

Because of scarcity, we "can't have it all." We have limited amounts of money to spend on a seemingly unlimited number of goods and services. We have limited amounts of time to work and enjoy activities from which we gain pleasure. Students who work and go to school or who are raising families and holding down jobs know just how scarce their time is. How often do we say to ourselves, "I wish I had another 10 hours in a day" or "I wish I had an extra weekend"? Time can become increasingly scarce as we age, particularly when we reach "middle age" and realize that more than half of our life has already been lived.

The degree to which a resource is scarce can vary over time. For example, parking spots at commuter colleges are at their peak scarcity during early morning and evening hours: students are more apt to attend classes during these times so that they can also hold down jobs. At other times, like midafternoon, parking spots may be relatively plentiful.

In some sense, our time has become more abundant over the past century because of the introduction of time-saving technologies that have expanded the number of activities we can perform during a 24-hour period. The microwave oven and washing machine have reduced the time that household chores demand and allowed the primary homemaker—traditionally a woman—to engage in other pursuits, including paid employment outside the home. Online shopping opportunities have reduced drive times and freed more time for leisure activities. The Internet allows students to research term papers 24 hours a day, rather than only when their campus libraries are open.

Technology is a tool that can loosen the bonds of scarcity. Because of new technology, drinking water can now be produced from ocean water at relatively low cost. New technology has also increased crop yields, led to new energy supplies, and put recycled materials to new uses. But technology itself is scarce. We must choose how much of the scarce resources we now have to invest in seeking innovations that may lessen the degree of scarcity we face in the future. Generally speaking, wealthier nations are in a better position to make this sacrifice, whereas poorer nations that function at subsistence levels cannot. This is the reason that the pharmaceutical discoveries used to treat AIDS, river blindness, and smallpox have taken place in the United States and Europe, despite the huge benefits they bestow on inhabitants of poorer countries.

Are there any resources that aren't scarce? Is sunshine, for example, scarce? Ask people who live in one of the Great Lakes states in December. Clearly, sunshine is a scarce resource to them, as evidenced by all of the license plates from northern states that populate Phoenix and Sarasota in the winter. At various times and in various locations, people are willing to sacrifice something (like buying a new MP3 player?) to purchase an airline ticket that will bring them to sunshine.

Is air scarce? Certainly, clean air is scarce, as is air in pressurized cabins under the sea or in an airplane at 37,000 feet. "Air" is a scarce resource from a legal standpoint when it contains a panoramic view that a new house will have or a view that a new building will block. People are willing to devote their scarce time and money to acquire "air rights" to unimpeded views and access to buildings with clean indoor air.

Are opinions scarce? Certainly, good ones must be, given the amount of money people are willing to pay stockbrokers, financial consultants, and TV commentators. Are children a scarce commodity? You need only look at the amount of scarce resources that some couples spend on infertility treatments or on adoption to answer this question.

To the extent that we are willing to give up our scarce resources to obtain something else, the object of our pursuit must also be scarce. Put this way, it is difficult to think of many things in our world that are not subject to some degree of scarcity. Even love requires some investment of scarce resources, not to mention the cost of going on dates and membership fees for online matchmaking services!

We use our scarce resources in ways that improve our sense of **well-being**.

**WELL-BEING** A person's happiness, benefit, or pleasure.

**EXAMPLE** Saving money for the proverbial "rainy day" may increase a person's sense of well-being by reducing anxiety about the future.

We call any scarce resource, product, service, or other source of well-being an **economic good**.

**ECONOMIC GOOD** Any scarce resource, product, service, or other source of well-being.

**EXAMPLE** Household pets increase a pet owner's sense of well-being.

If an economic good were offered free of charge to everyone, there would not be enough of the good to fulfill everyone's "wants." Some people would walk away empty-handed or with less than they would like to have. Notice that we refer to what people "want" rather than "need." We make this distinction because "needs" are generally subjective in nature. Beyond the most basic needs to stay alive—oxygen, water, and basic sustenance—to what extent are our "needs" truly necessary?

The perceived "needs" of people living in the twenty-first century in the United States (think about indoor plumbing, central air-conditioning, and color television, for example) are very different from their great-grandparents' "needs" of only a century ago. As a country's standard of living increases, so do the "needs" of its people. To avoid having to subjectively evaluate economic goods according to some "neediness" scale, we instead focus on people's "wants" to express their priorities for advancing their own well-being.

If, as we have argued, the condition of scarcity applies to virtually everything in our world, then economic principles—which deal with decision making in the face of scarcity—must be relevant to nearly every aspect of your life. Perhaps this is why economists believe that practically anything people do—whether it is time spent brushing their teeth or the choice of a college major—can be better understood and predicted using a basic economics framework.

Economics is therefore sometimes referred to as the "science of scarcity"—that is, it is the study of how people choose to use the scarce resources at their disposal. For this reason, economists are often cast as realists in discussions about the use of scarce resources in society. For example, economists remind policy makers that new health-insurance programs must be paid for by sacrificing resources currently used in some other economic activity. We encourage business leaders to consider what they will give up—in terms of potential clients—when they locate their retail operations in one place versus another. We are the persistent, nagging reminder to policy makers, business leaders, and individuals that there is no such thing as a "free lunch." Each and every choice costs us something in terms of forgone opportunities.

## 1.3 Economic Resources: Physical and Human

There are two types of scarce economic resources that we generally talk about: **human capital** and **physical capital**.

> **HUMAN CAPITAL** A person's physical and mental capabilities, including his or her health, education, skills, entrepreneurial ideas, and risk tolerance.

**EXAMPLE** The *Guinness Book of World Records* is filled with people's extraordinary feats that are, by their very nature, scarce talents cultivated by years of training (like the ability to eat 53.5 hot dogs and buns in 12 minutes).

**EXAMPLE** Tiger Woods has become one of the all-time great golfers by building his human capital through years of rigorous training.

> **PHYSICAL CAPITAL** Land and other natural resources, machinery, and technology.

**EXAMPLE** The United States is blessed with many natural resources, including fertile agricultural land and oil reserves.

**EXAMPLE** France has invested heavily in the development of nuclear energy.

The word *capital* is used in both cases because we are referring to a stock of resources—an accumulation that can be depleted over time or increased by investing scarce resources.

In most modern-day societies, slavery has been outlawed. This means that our human capital is *inalienable:* it cannot be bought or sold. Only the flow of services that our human capital generates—which we refer to as people's work or labor—can be bought and sold. In societies that permit the ownership of private property, people can buy and sell their physical capital, although such sales may come with restrictions. Land sales, for example, are frequently subject to zoning restrictions that limit what the buyers can do with the land. For example, factories cannot be built in the middle of residential neighborhoods.

Individuals differ in how much human and physical capital they possess. These differences arise partially because people's endowments (how much they start with) aren't the same. Someone who inherits thousands of acres of land from her parents has an initial endowment of physical capital that is substantially greater than what most of us have. Similarly, there are people born with genetic characteristics that substantially increase their odds of living to 100 years old. Other differences in human capital arise because people have not invested the same amount of scarce resources in the past to supplement their initial endowments. Both Mozart and Beethoven were wonderfully gifted musicians, but many musicologists argue that Beethoven's works are far superior because he worked much harder than Mozart.

Like people, geographic areas such as states and countries have different initial endowments of physical capital. The southwestern United States, for example, has a bountiful amount of sun but very little water. Saudi Arabia enjoys an abundance of crude oil but a limited amount of arable farmland. By investing in technology, the constraints that these initial endowments impose on people can be significantly lessened. For example, irrigation systems have turned the central and southern portion of California's arid land into some of the most productive agricultural regions in the nation.

The stock of human capital in a country can also be increased by investing in people's skills and health, or by encouraging migration of skilled foreigners to a country. The most immediate way to increase population is by encouraging migration to a particular region or country. Both the United States and Australia followed this course of action to quickly populate their countries, offering immigrants free land and even paid passage to move to their respective countries. More recently, the late Senator Edward Kennedy led the fight to relax U.S. immigration quotas for foreigners who have skills that are in demand or money to invest in new business enterprises.[1]

Governments that invest in education, public highways, water- and sewage-treatment facilities, and medical care increase the human capital of their residents. People who are healthier and better educated tend to be more productive. Investments in technology may not only increase a country's physical capital but also its human capital. A striking example of this is the rise of computer technology and advances in software applications. Both have made assembly-line equipment and workers "smarter," thereby increasing the value of the human and physical capital in industries where such computers are used.

Virtually every economic good is produced using both human and physical capital. In some instances, one type of capital can be substituted for another: checkout

· · · · · · ·

[1]Linda Greenhouse, "Redefining the Boundaries: Who May Come In; Pro & Con: What Price An Anarchist." *New York Times,* April 10, 1988.

scanners in supermarkets (physical capital) have replaced cashiers (human capital). Generally speaking, the mix of human and physical capital used in production will depend on the methods of production that are currently available and their cost relative to one another. The success of oceanic shipping once depended on a captain's skill (human capital) in navigating by the stars and crude maps. However, the invention of the sextant and, much later, radar and GPS systems (physical capital) substantially devalued these human capital skills.

## 1.4 Economics as a Predictive Science

Economists attempt to identify factors that systematically influence how people allocate their scarce resources. To the extent we are successful, we are then able to predict (1) the mix of economic goods produced in a society, (2) the way in which these goods are produced, (3) how these goods are distributed among people, and (4) how changes in the **economic environment** will affect people's trade-offs and the choices they make.

**ECONOMIC ENVIRONMENT** Prices, wages, laws, and social norms that serve as external constraints on the choices that we make; external factors that dictate the trade-offs we face.

**EXAMPLE** The price of gasoline in the United States is less than half the price in Europe. Therefore, the trade-off between driving an automobile and taking public transit will be different in these two locales.

How do declining interest rates affect home ownership? How does an increase in the minimum wage affect full-time college enrollments? How does the introduction of a particular piece of tax legislation change the way that people allocate their time between work and leisure? We can use an economic framework to predict how people will respond to such changes in their economic environment. We use the term "prediction" in a very specific way here. We are not predicting future unknowns like who will win the lottery or who will live to be 105 years old. We focus solely on people's responses to changes in the trade-offs they face.

The key to making such predictions is to identify these trade-offs and then make sense of how people choose between these opportunities. The difficulty that can arise is that one person's trade-off may not be the same as another's. A person who is allergic to peanuts would never consider a peanut butter sandwich to be a reasonable alternative to a grilled cheese sandwich.

Economists have long debated whether economics is supposed to predict people's behavior or explain it. Indeed, even though we are able to accurately predict behavior, economists usually refrain from explaining exactly why people act the way they do—that is, why they have the preferences they do. For example, economists (and those who study population statistics) have predicted with great reliability that the birthrate rises nine months after extended electrical blackouts. However, they have not explained why this is the case—that is, beyond the obvious loss of electricity-based activities, why do people use their time during a blackout the way they do?

It turns out that making predictions about people's choices—as difficult as that may be—is a far easier task than explaining the complexities of human behavior. As a result, economists evaluate the usefulness of economic models based on their ability to predict actual outcomes rather than explain why they occur. This approach is used to evaluate the goodness of one economic theory of behavior versus another. As more information becomes available about our economic environment, new theories arise that improve our predictive abilities. The "explanation part" of human behavior is left to psychologists, philosophers, and sociologists.

This means that economic analysis starts with individual preferences as a given and predicts behavior based on the trade-offs people face. This approach allows us to sidestep a detailed description of someone's personal preferences. It also permits people to have different preferences that affect the choices they make. For example, a vegan will not eat a steak even if its price drops, whereas a "steak and potatoes" kind of person might not reduce his meat purchases much, even in the face of substantial price increases. Our religious beliefs, education, and family upbringing can greatly influence our preferences. What this means is that we may make different choices than others, even when we face the same economic environment. This is an important result that deserves emphasis: economic prediction does not require everyone to make the same choices when faced with the same opportunities.

As we build our economic models of behavior, you will quickly find that simpler models are better than more complex ones. As long as our model can deliver accurate predictions, there is no reason to make it overly complicated. Sometimes you might think these models are too simplistic. For example, when we talk about a person's decision to go to college or not, the discussion will ignore which college he ultimately chooses because that is not the decision we are interested in. Of course, we could easily pursue another analysis to predict whether a person decides to go to a public or private four-year college, to go to school full-time versus part-time, and so on.

As economists, we ignore details that do not contribute to our ability to predict people's behavior. Instead, we indicate under what conditions our economic predictions will be valid. To appreciate the benefits of keeping models simple, think about the way in which you give someone directions to your house. Most likely, you focus on main streets and landmarks, not on every street and every traffic light. Similarly, economists strive to be minimalists. We rely only on the basic "landmarks" to achieve our goal of predicting responses to changes in the economic environment. Depending on where you live, directions to your home can be quite complex, or they may require only a few simple instructions. Similarly, in economics there are situations in which we can predict people's behavior based on a few simple economic principles.

*More of a good thing is better than less* is one such economic principle. This leads us to predict that if a person were offered more of something she desires, free of charge, she will take it and feel she is better off than before. However, we must qualify this prediction with the phrase "within reason." This qualification recognizes that a moviegoer might refuse a fifth free bucket of popcorn on the grounds that it will make her violently ill. In other words, at some point, too much of a good thing can become a bad thing.

Simplifying our approach to economic behavior permits us to use a variety of "languages" to build our predictive models. Sometimes we use words; at other times, we use graphs and mathematical equations. (A review of these tools is provided in the Appendix.) Whatever language we use, we are involved in a delicate balancing act: we're trying to capture all of the essential elements required to make accurate predictions while ignoring the extraneous complexities of life.

In reality, economic predictions about the decisions people make are rarely 100 percent correct. After all, we are talking about people, not balls rolling down a slope in a frictionless state. It's possible that predictions based on economic theory are less than perfect because people sometimes make mistakes when they make decisions. Even if we are hardwired to assess the trade-offs we face before making a choice, we sometimes have only limited information about our alternatives, resulting in a subpar choice. This is why economists prefer to talk about a person's *tendency* to make a particular decision when faced with a specific trade-off. In other words, we can think of our predictions as being accurate *on average*. This is why so-called hard scientists (like the chemist who combines elements and gets the same chemical every time) sometimes scoff when economics is referred to as a science.

Economists also know that no matter how good their predictions are, the expected outcome might not occur immediately. This is because people are sometimes bound by the old choices they have made for a while, even when the trade-offs they face have changed. In other words, their short-run behavior might not be what they would prefer to do in the longer run. A couple that is locked into a one-year apartment lease might find it too expensive to break the lease. As a result, they will postpone their purchase of a home—even if mortgage interest rates have fallen to their lowest level in a decade. When gasoline prices rise precipitously, a college student who commutes to school will not immediately transfer to a university closer to her home; she will first complete the semester or academic year. In other words, in the short run, these people are constrained by previous decisions: they are "stuck." Even though we can predict what they will do in response to a change in interest rates or gasoline prices, it may take some time for them to do it. Thus, our predictions about people's behavior will tend to be more accurate in the long run as people slowly adapt to their changing circumstances.

Predictions tend to be more accurate over time for another reason. As we just discussed, people sometimes make mistakes in their decision process and only later correct their errors. Information is itself an economic good, one that is scarce and can be costly to obtain. Unfortunately, in some situations, an error in judgment is the lowest-cost way to get the information you need to avoid mistakes in the future. Suppose you see two new energy drinks at a convenience store and wonder which one you should buy. You could go home and research the matter at eopinions.com or spend time surveying your friends. But that would take more time than it's worth. Instead, you will probably go ahead and buy one of the drinks. If it tastes bad, you won't make the mistake of buying it again. So, sometimes we use our scarce resources in ways that we later regret. On the next go-round, we use our scarce resources differently. Such errors could be thought of as "intelligent mistakes" because we learn from them.[2]

As you can probably tell, accurately predicting the choices people make when they have only limited information about the alternatives they face is a challenge for economists and their theories.

## 1.5 Positive versus Normative Analysis

As we move forward in developing predictive models of behavior, it is important that we distinguish between **positive analysis** and **normative analysis**.

**POSITIVE ANALYSIS** The evaluation of a situation based on facts and theories, leading to testable implications and validation.

**EXAMPLE** When elementary school students eat breakfast, they perform significantly better, on average, on in-class tests given before lunch.

· · · · · · ·

[2]Alina Tugend, "The Many Errors in Thinking about Mistakes." *New York Times,* November 24, 2007.

**NORMATIVE ANALYSIS** The evaluation of a situation based on one's values, religious beliefs, and opinions.

**EXAMPLE** Parents should be responsible for feeding their kids breakfast before sending them to school, rather than depending on their schools to feed them.

Consider the following situation. The federal government asks an economist to predict what would happen to the amount of money people would save if a national sales tax replaced the current income-tax system. People would only pay taxes when they purchase something. In contrast, they currently have to pay income taxes anytime they earn money, regardless of whether or not they save it. If a national sales tax replaced the income tax, then we would predict that people would buy fewer goods and save more money. This hypothesis is readily testable, perhaps using data from countries that have made such a switch in their tax system. The following is a positive statement related to the situation: "When savings are not taxed, more income is saved." A positive statement can be analyzed and validated.

Compare this to a normative statement: "We ought to promote saving by making sure that it is not taxed." This statement does not lend itself to analysis; it is simply an opinion. *Normative statements* are opinions about how the world *ought* to be or how people *ought* to behave. Scientific analysis cannot validate these opinions. Economists can do no more to settle conflicting normative positions than any other opinionated individuals. They can only speak to these issues as individuals, not as economists. After all, everyone is entitled to his or her own opinion, even an economist.

Let's now look at some positive statements that economists *can* make: most economists agree that legalizing trade in human organs—permitting kidneys to be bought and sold, for example—would increase the number of organs available in the marketplace and thereby reduce the amount of time people have to wait for kidney transplants. Similarly, economists largely concur that legalizing trade in illicit drugs would reduce the street prices for these drugs and, consequently, the amount of street crime. These are positive predictions based on economic principles.

Economists differ, however, in their opinions about whether buying and selling human organs or illicit drugs should be legal. They do so because of differences in their personal views. Therefore, it shouldn't surprise you that economists often disagree about whether or not different government policies are necessary and ought to be adopted.

Many of the issues we will discuss in this book can be, and often are, the subject of intense normative debate. However, it doesn't matter what an economist believes, for example, about how household chores ought to be divided among husbands and wives; or whether or not employers should hire job applicants with tattoos; or which applicants should be admitted by elite, private colleges. Instead, economic analysis takes a positive approach to these questions. Adopting a positive approach means that we can talk about how household chores are actually divided between household partners, the extent to which employers discriminate against applicants with tattoos, and how colleges actually fill their admission spots. Moreover, economic analysis can be used to identify determinants that influence each of these outcomes.

When we conduct a positive analysis, we must refrain from judging the choices people make. Economics has nothing to say about whether a particular choice is moral or immoral, ethical or unethical. Our responsibility throughout this book is to focus solely on how economics can be used to predict people's choices in the face of changing trade-offs.

## 1.6 Economic Rationality?

Although economic analysis doesn't pass judgment on people's choices, it does assume that people make choices that they believe advance their own well-being. In other words, they exhibit **economic rationality**.

**ECONOMIC RATIONALITY** A decision process whereby individuals make choices they believe will advance their own well-being.

**EXAMPLE** A college student goes to a review session for the final exam because she thinks it may improve her test performance, even though she already feels quite comfortable with the material.

Economic rationality is often referred to as the pursuit of one's self-interest. The term self-interest is, quite possibly, the most misunderstood term in economics. You might be tempted to think it's the same as selfishness or greed. It is not. There is a big difference between being self-interested and being selfish. As it turns out, economic theory predicts that self-interest will often motivate people to behave charitably. Your parents may make charitable donations to the local food pantry or homeless shelter because they derive an immense amount of satisfaction, or well-being, from doing so. Sometimes this sense of well-being increases if the contribution is publicized (say, for example, when a university building is named in their honor) or if the donation is tax-deductible. In any case, people engage in acts of kindness and charity because they believe it is in their self-interest. Others may benefit as well. To reiterate, self-interest—the drive to advance one's own well-being—underlies all of the decisions we make. This is, however, not the same as selfishness.

## 1.7 Free Markets or Central Planning?

One reason for studying economics is to better understand how markets work and how markets differ. As you may have learned in other courses you have taken, capitalism is distinctive from other economic systems, such as socialism and communism, where there is more central planning. Under capitalism, private entities rather than the government or a community own most of the physical capital used in production. As a result, scarce resources are allocated to alternative uses largely through voluntary trades between individuals and firms in the market. The owners of human and physical capital decide on how they want to use the capital at their disposal. By contrast, in more centralized or planned economies, the government, not individuals, assumes a greater role in deciding what gets produced, who gets the goods, and what prices will be charged.

Which type of system is the best? Keep in mind that no economy is completely capitalistic or socialistic. Most have some elements of each. For example, in the United States, the government uses the taxes it collects to provide its citizens with mail service, national defense, public education for children, health care for the poor, and so forth. In a purely capitalistic society, you personally would have to contract individually with providers for these services. Still, the United States tilts much more toward free-market exchanges than, say, China, in which central planning by the government still dominates. However, most observers agree that China would not have enjoyed the rapid economic growth it has experienced over the past two decades if its government had not begun to allow more market-based exchange to occur.

One problem with central planning is that those making allocation decisions in the government often aren't knowledgeable about the intricate web of relations between buyers and sellers in the economy. In other words, because of well-intentioned but inaccurate guesses, decisions by central planners may push resources to the production of goods for which there is no demand. In free markets, private producers would soon realize this and move on to producing goods for which there is a demand. Unlike planned economies, in market-based economies competition drives inept producers out of business. But their loss is the gain of consumers who buy less costly goods and enjoy better service by the surviving firms. After all, do you keep going to a restaurant that has bad food and poor service just to keep it in business? Probably not.

Free markets don't always perform as we might like, however. For example, when there is only one seller in a market, we tend to see higher prices and fewer goods available than when there are many sellers. When markets don't work as well as they should, governments try to provide some "rules of the game" or regulations. In addition, distrust for the way in which free markets allocate scarce resources can spike during times of economic distress. In times such as these, people tend to wonder if they are getting their fair share of the economic pie. For example, during the banking crisis and economic downturn of 2007–2009, many people argued that more government regulation was the only way to ensure that such a crisis would not happen again. The backlash was so bad that the president of France, Nicolas Sarkozy, even went so far as to proclaim that capitalism was "finished."

He was wrong. As the downturn abated, calls for abandoning free-market exchange in favor of more government-directed exchange quickly waned. The fact is that most economists (and individuals) realize that even though there are winners and losers in free-market economies, that does not mean that capitalism is fundamentally flawed and should be replaced by wholesale central planning. All systems have winners and losers. But how much regulation should a government impose without impeding the success of the market system of exchange? That is the million-dollar question—one that economists, politicians, and you will continue to evaluate and debate. Fortunately, the study of economics gives you a framework you can use to do so.

**ECONOMIC FALLACY**    Economics is the science of capitalism.

**False.** Economics provides a systematic, objective framework for predicting people's behavior no matter what type of economic system they operate in. For example, using economic principles, we can predict who will stand in line the longest when scarce goods are rationed on a "first-come, first-served" basis. Economics can even make predictions about how politicians in various political systems will finance and distribute goods such as education and medical care.

## 1.8 Micro- versus Macroeconomic Analysis

When the term *micro* is used, it brings to mind something very small. Microbes and microchips are things that are so small that they are virtually invisible to the naked eye. **Microeconomics** is the study of how individuals, households, and producing organizations allocate their scarce economic resources to maximize their own well-being. Each and every one of these decision makers is virtually invisible in the economy as a whole. But in aggregate, their choices dictate market outcomes, including the prices that goods sell for. And when these choices change in response to changes in the economic environment, this can have a significant impact on market outcomes and resource allocation.

**MICROECONOMICS** The study of how individuals, households, and producing organizations choose to use their scarce economic resources to maximize their own well-being.

**EXAMPLE** Microeconomists are employed by telephone companies to analyze customer cell-phone usage and create pricing plans that will improve profitability.

In this way, microeconomics is the foundation of all economic analysis: it all begins with the individual decision maker.

**Macroeconomics** is a newer branch of economics that focuses on the study of economywide events, such as the factors that influence the overall growth rates of national economies, the rate at which the general level of prices rises, or what causes the unemployment rate to rise and fall. Macroeconomics tries to make sense of why the rate of inflation is 15 percent or 2 percent and why recessions happen.

**MACROECONOMICS** The study of economywide events, such as economic growth, inflation, and business cycles.

**EXAMPLE** The Environmental Protection Agency retains macroeconomists to assess how alternative policies to lessen industrial air pollution will affect economic growth and employment in the United States.

The following examples will further distinguish between these two fields of economic analysis. Whereas a microeconomist would evaluate the effects of gas price increases on new SUV purchases, a macroeconomist would be concerned about whether higher gas prices will lead to greater price inflation in the overall economy or even to a recession. A microeconomist would examine how increases in the minimum wage affect hiring in the fast-food industry, while a macroeconomist would study the effects of wage policies on the overall unemployment rate. Even though there is some overlap, macroeconomics is really focused on big-picture issues compared with microeconomics.

Whether we are discussing a micro or a macro issue, economists agree that there are core elements common to any type of economic analysis. We identify these building blocks in the next few chapters.

## 1.9 Economics and the Decisions You Make in Life

In a nutshell, this book will give you the tools to cultivate an extraordinary self-awareness about factors in the world around you that influence the decisions that you make. You already systematically absorb and process changes in your economic environment, responding in such a way as to maximize your sense of well-being. When gas prices rise, you are likely to drive less and may even substitute online shopping for trips to the mall. When tuition rises, you may take fewer classes and become more serious about studying so you don't have to retake a class. When your household partner loses his job, you shift more of the household tasks to him. When the price of movies goes up, you stay home and watch DVDs more often.

The bottom line is that this book will *not* teach you to think like an economist— you already think this way. What it will do is provide you a framework that permits you to better understand how remarkable your decision-making abilities are already. You will see why it makes perfect sense that college students like yourself tend to have children later in life than people who do not go on to college. And why two people in a household sometimes both go to work and, at other times, one person stays home. You will also appreciate why people who take big risks as investors or entrepreneurs are sometimes rewarded quite handsomely; and why items such as new music CDs and brand-name electric guitars, sold through online auction sites like eBay, tend to sell for the same price (including shipping and handling).

You will surely encounter new terminology and analytical tools in this book. Nevertheless, the economic principles you learn should "ring true" in terms of your life experiences and those of your friends and family. After all, economics is about the way *all* of us live.

## WHAT YOU SHOULD HAVE LEARNED FROM CHAPTER 1

- That economics is the study of the choices we make.

- That trade-offs are the opportunities passed up when we make one choice versus another choice.

- That we live in a world of scarcity because there are limited resources to satisfy unlimited wants.

- That capital is more than just physical (land, machinery, technology); it is also human (our time, education, skills, and health).

- That a positive statement is readily testable, whereas a normative statement is an opinion, or judgment, that cannot be scientifically validated. Economics focuses solely on the analysis of positive statements.

- That we make choices we believe are in our self-interest. Because we do not always have perfect information about the alternatives we face, in hindsight we regret some of our decisions and learn from them. We call these decisions intelligent mistakes.

- That self-interest is not the same as selfishness.

- That microeconomics deals with the decisions of individuals and producing organizations, whereas macroeconomics is concerned with big-picture economic events such as the unemployment rate.

## KEY TERMS

| | |
|---|---|
| Trade-off, p. 3 | Economic environment, p. 8 |
| Scarcity, p. 4 | Positive analysis, p. 10 |
| Well-being, p. 5 | Normative analysis, p. 10 |
| Economic good, p. 5 | Economic rationality, p. 12 |
| Human capital, p. 6 | Microeconomics, p. 13 |
| Physical capital, p. 6 | Macroeconomics, p. 14 |

## QUESTIONS AND PROBLEMS

1. Suppose everyone had the same preferences, values, and incomes. In such a world, could we conclude that all individuals would buy the same economic goods in the same amounts?

2. Charities depend on people to donate their money or volunteer their time. Predict how a person's mix of money and time donated to a charity changes as he:
   a) gets a raise in his hourly wage.
   b) gets married and has children.
   c) retires from his job.

3. True, false, or uncertain: it is economically rational for a student to cheat to improve her grades if she knows with certainty she won't get caught. Explain your answer.

4. Education and exercise are two ways we can increase our human capital. Give two examples of choices we can make that will *decrease* our human capital.

5. We all make rational mistakes during our lifetime. Can you think of an example or two? Have you ever made an irrational mistake—that is, a mistake that you haven't learned from?

6. Suppose an animal is on the brink of extinction. How should we as a society determine the amount of resources to commit to preserving the species? Explain your answer.

7. When you use MapQuest.com to get driving directions between point A and point B, MapQuest asks whether you want the shortest route in terms of (a) mileage or (b) time. What is the opportunity cost to you of choosing (a) or (b)? Explain your answer.

8. The director of the central planning agency that oversees university enrollment decides that there are too many nurses. To solve this problem, nursing programs across the country are closed. Students currently enrolled are told to find alternative majors. Based on this decision and action, who benefits, and how? Who is harmed, and how? What are the effects of this decision if ten years from now an aging population requires more nursing care than today?

9. In the movie *Wall Street,* the character Gordon Gecko proclaims, "Greed is good." Does he mean greed or self-interest? Explain your answer.

10. To solve the problem of poverty, I think government should impose a tax on home owners and give the money to the poor. Is this an example of a positive or a normative analysis? Explain.

# Appendix 1A Basic Graphing and Math Skills Used in Economics

## GRAPHING

The purpose of a graph is to illustrate the relationship between two variables. For example, you could examine how much a family spends each year (one variable) relative to its annual income (the other variable). As **Table 1A.1** shows, this information can be arranged in a table with expenditures as the y (**dependent**) variable and income as the x (**independent**) variable.

| Table 1A.1 The Relationship between Two Variables | |
| --- | --- |
| y<br>Expenditure ($/Yr) | x<br>Income ($/Yr) |
| 20,000 | 10,000 |
| 25,000 | 20,000 |
| 30,000 | 30,000 |
| 35,000 | 40,000 |
| 40,000 | 50,000 |
| 45,000 | 60,000 |
| 50,000 | 70,000 |

The data in the table can now be plotted on a graph as in **Figure 1A.1**. The graph allows us to visually see the relationship between income and expenditures.

The line running from left to right across the bottom is referred to as the *horizontal axis* or the *x-axis*. The line running up and down the left side of the graph is called the *vertical axis* or the *y-axis*.

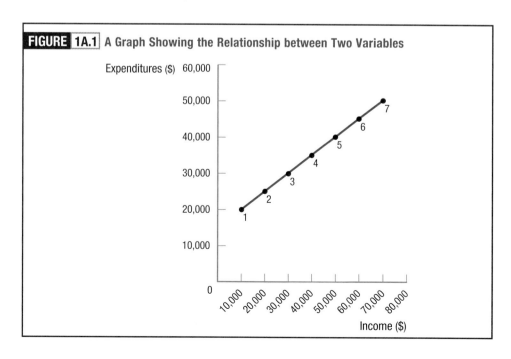

FIGURE 1A.1 A Graph Showing the Relationship between Two Variables

On the graph, each combination of $x$ and $y$ values is represented by a point on the graph. For example, point 1 shows that when income is $10,000 per year (measured on the $x$-axis), expenditures are at $20,000 per year (measured on the $y$-axis). This combination can be written (10,000, 20,000). In the same manner, point 7 on the graph can be written (70,000, 50,000). More generally, points can be expressed as $(x, y)$.

### CALCULATING THE SLOPE OF A LINE

The **slope** of a straight line is the change in the $y$ variable associated with the change in the $x$ variable as we move from one point on the line to another. The slope is often described as the "rise over run." Its mathematical formula is $\Delta y/\Delta x$. **Figure 1A.2** shows the slope of a line.

Using Figure 1A.2 as an example, we can find the slope of the line between different points. To find the slope of the line between points 4 and 6, we use the formula $\Delta y/\Delta x$.

$\Delta y$ = the change in $y$ = the value of $y$ at point 6 minus the value of $y$ at point 4
$= 30 - 20 = 10$

$\Delta x$ = the change in $x$ = the value of $x$ at point 6 minus the value of $x$ at point 4
$= 6 - 4 = 2$

Therefore, the slope of the line between points 4 and 6 = $\Delta y/\Delta x = 10/2 = 5$.

The line depicted in Figure 1A.2 shows a positive relationship between two variables; it has a **positive slope**. Any increase in $x$ is associated with an increase in $y$. Graphs in economics do not always have positive slopes. Consider **Figure 1A.3** and **Figure 1A.4**.

The line in Figure 1A.3 has a **negative slope**: as $x$ increases, the value of $y$ decreases. Conversely, as $x$ decreases, the value of $y$ increases. It can also be said that the two values are **inversely** related. The line in Figure 1A.4 has a slope of zero: as $x$

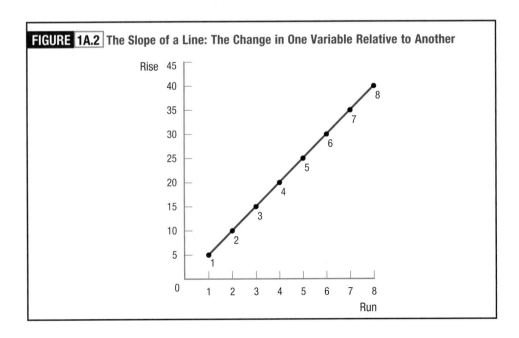

**FIGURE 1A.2** The Slope of a Line: The Change in One Variable Relative to Another

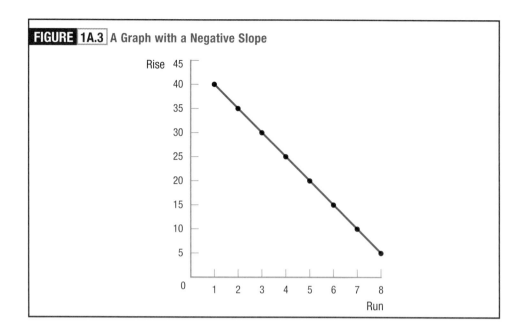

FIGURE 1A.3 A Graph with a Negative Slope

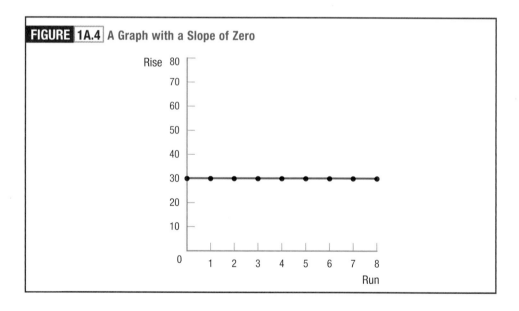

FIGURE 1A.4 A Graph with a Slope of Zero

increases or decreases, the value of $y$ remains constant at $y = 30$. **Figure 1A.5** shows a line with a slope that is undefined: the $x$ value does not change even as the value of $y$ increases or decreases. ($\Delta x$ equals zero between all points on the graph.)

## FINDING THE Y-INTERCEPT OF A LINE

Looking at **Figure 1A.6**, note that the line crosses the $y$-axis at the point $x = 0$, $y = 15$. Therefore, 15 is considered the **y-intercept** of the line. More technically, the $y$-intercept of the line is the point at which the line intersects the $y$-axis. This is the value of $y$ when the value of $x$ is zero.

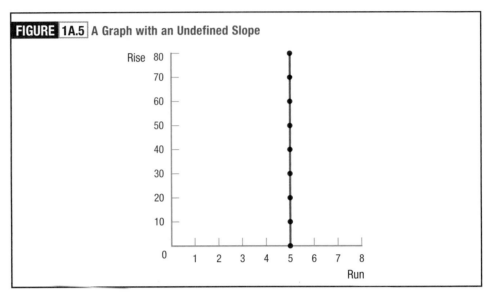

**FIGURE 1A.5** A Graph with an Undefined Slope

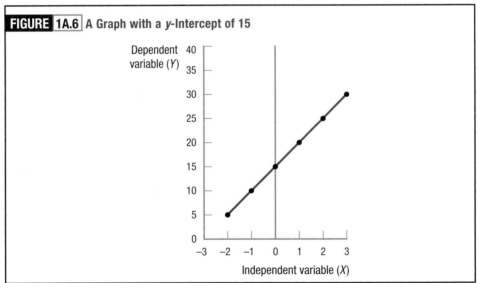

**FIGURE 1A.6** A Graph with a *y*-Intercept of 15

One way to find the *y*-intercept is to use the formula for a line $y = mx + b$, where:

$y$ = the value of $y$ at a given point
$x$ = the value of $x$ at a given point
$m$ = the slope of the line
$b$ = the *y*-intercept

To find the *y*-intercept, we need the slope of the line—which is 5—as well as a value for $x$ and $y$ on the line such as point (1, 20).

$m = 5$
$y = 20$
$x = 1$

After plugging our numbers into the equation,

$$y = mx + b$$
$$20 = 5(1) + b$$

we solve for $b$:

$$20 = 5 + b$$
$$20 - 5 = b$$
$$15 = b$$

After finding the slope and the $y$-intercept, we can write the general equation of the line:

$$y = 5x + 15$$

*Note:* If you are given just the equation of a line, you can simply plug in $x = 0$ to calculate the $y$-intercept.

Practice Problems
1. Graph the data in the following table.

| y | x |
|---|---|
| 10 | 1,800 |
| 15 | 1,600 |
| 20 | 1,400 |
| 25 | 1,200 |
| 30 | 1,000 |
| 35 | 800 |

2. Are $x$ and $y$ positively related or negatively (inversely) related?
3. Using the line you created for problem 1, what is the slope? What is the $y$-intercept? Write out the equation of the line in the form $y = mx + b$.
4. Suppose you have a second line represented by the data in the following table:

| y | x |
|---|---|
| 5 | 0 |
| 10 | 300 |
| 15 | 600 |
| 20 | 900 |
| 25 | 1,200 |
| 30 | 1,500 |

Graph this line on the same graph that you created for problem 1. What is the formula for this line in the form $y = mx + b$?
5. By examining the graph you created for problems 1 and 4, find the intersection of the two lines. Write this intersection as the ordered pair $(x, y)$.

## PERCENT CHANGE

In many cases, you will be asked to find the **percent change** or **growth rate** for different variables. For example, if the price of a good rises from $2.00 ($P_1$) to $2.50 ($P_2$) the $\Delta P = (P_2 - P_1) = \$2.50 - \$2.00 = \$0.50$. To calculate the %$\Delta P$, where %$\Delta P = {}^{\Delta P}\!/_{P_1}$, we have $\$0.50/\$2.00 = 0.25$. To convert this number to percent, multiply by 100, or $0.25 \times 100 = 25\%$. More generally, the formula for %$\Delta P$ is:

$$\%\Delta P = ({}^{\Delta P}\!/_{P_1}) \times 100$$

*Note:* Although $\Delta P$ carries the units of the original variable ($P$ in $'s in this example), %$\Delta P$ will be a pure number with no units because the numerator and denominator units cancel out (as seen in this example).

Practice Problems
1. Find the %$\Delta P$ when $P_1 = \$30$ and $P_2 = \$33$.
2. Find the %$\Delta Q$ when $Q_1 = 45$ and $Q_2 = 30$.
3. Compute the %$\Delta Q$/%$\Delta P$ for the above numbers.

## NONLINEAR CURVES

When finding the slope, we assumed that a graph was **linear**—that is, a straight line. Linear lines are the easiest to work with because they are completely described by their slope (constant) and *y*-intercept. However, many of the curves you will encounter in economics are not linear. Examining **Figure 1A.7**, we observe that between $x = 0$

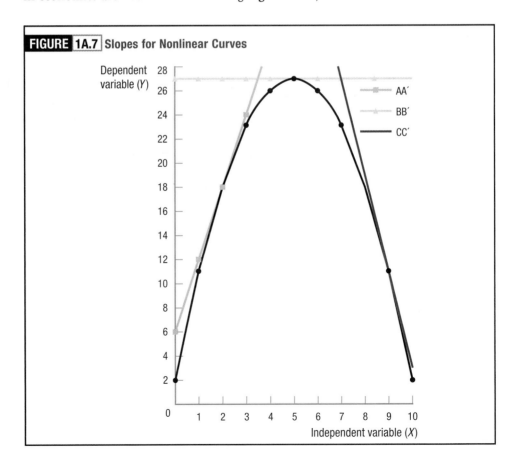

**FIGURE 1A.7** Slopes for Nonlinear Curves

and $x = 5$, $x$ and $y$ are positively related. However, for larger values of $x$, the slope is negative—that is, $x$ and $y$ are inversely related. It is clear from the graph that the slope of a nonlinear curve is not constant.

The slope of a **nonlinear** curve at any point is defined as the slope of a line tangent to the curve at that point. (This is the best approximation of the slope of a curve at a point without using more advanced math.) Let's look at Figure 1A.7 again, this time focusing on the tangent AA′ which just touches the curve at point (2,18). AA′ is the tangent to the curve where $x = 2$. Along the line AA′ if $x = 1$, $y = 12$. We know that at $x = 2$, $y = 18$. Using the formula discussed in part 2, $\Delta y/\Delta x =$ we get:

$$(18 - 12)/(2 - 1) = 6$$

Therefore, the slope of the curve at the point $x = 2$ is 6.

Practice Problems
1. Find the slope of the curve at $x = 5$ using the tangent BB′ (use the line to pick another point along that line).
2. Find the slope of the curve at $x = 9$ (point C) using the tangent CC′ (use the line to pick another point along that line).

## COMPUTING AN **AREA**

The formula for the area of a rectangle like the one in **Figure 1A.8** is:

Area = length × width

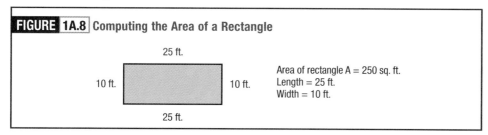

**FIGURE 1A.8** Computing the Area of a Rectangle

25 ft.

10 ft.  10 ft.

Area of rectangle A = 250 sq. ft.
Length = 25 ft.
Width = 10 ft.

25 ft.

In special situations such as in **Figure 1A.9**, the area of a rectangle on a graph can represent revenue received by sellers, or, equivalently, expenditures made by consumers. The following equation shows how the area is computed.

Area = revenue = price × quantity

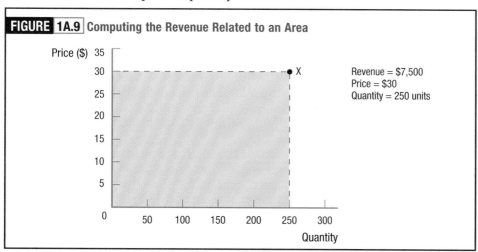

**FIGURE 1A.9** Computing the Revenue Related to an Area

Price ($)

Revenue = $7,500
Price = $30
Quantity = 250 units

Quantity

As shown in **Figure 1A.10**, the formula for the area of a triangle is:

Area = ½ base × height

Consider triangle A:

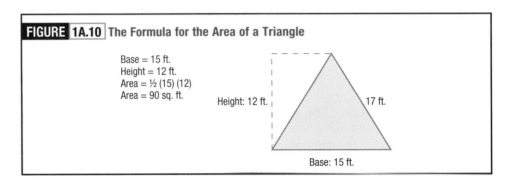

**FIGURE 1A.10**  The Formula for the Area of a Triangle

Base = 15 ft.
Height = 12 ft.
Area = ½ (15) (12)
Area = 90 sq. ft.

Height: 12 ft.

17 ft.

Base: 15 ft.

Practice Problems

1. Using a graph with *P* (price) on the vertical axis and *Q* (quantity) on the horizontal axis, represent the revenue that corresponds to each of the following sales conditions (use a different color pen to shade in each of these rectangles):

| P ($) | Q |
|-------|-----|
| 10 | 200 |
| 12 | 180 |
| 14 | 140 |

2. Show that if the government imposed a 50-percent tax on the producer in problem 1, you could calculate the seller's after-tax revenue by either (a) dividing your answers in 1 in half or (b) calculating the areas of the triangles in your graphs that reflect this after-tax revenue.

## VISUALLY DISPLAYING DATA

You often may be visually confronted by economic data. Economic data may, for example, appear in the form of a chart of stock prices, a table of figures showing the latest unemployment data, or some kind of graphic display of how much of a household's budget is spent on food, gasoline, and rent. We will display economic data using various forms of graphical tools throughout this text, so let's introduce you to a few and how to use them.

Some economic data are available over time. For example, each month the federal government announces what the level of consumer prices (actually, an index of those prices) was for the last month. What is important is how that month's price level compares with the level of prices in previous months. The level is often discussed as the percentage change in prices. You have already seen how to calculate a percentage change, so let's just recap it here. Suppose that last month the index of consumer prices was 133. In the previous month it was 125. Using our formula for calculating a

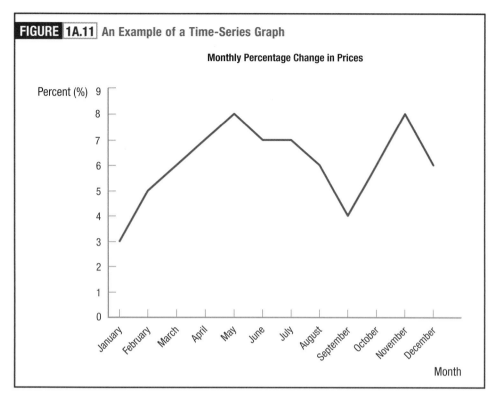

**FIGURE 1A.11** An Example of a Time-Series Graph

**Monthly Percentage Change in Prices**

percentage change, prices last month increased 6.4% = {[(133 − 125)/125] × 100}. But what if we would like to see how last month's price change compares to monthly changes over the past year?

**Figure 1A.11** shows one way to graphically present the monthly percentage change in prices. This is called a **time-series graph**, because the information is shown over time. As you can see, the vertical axis shows the percentage change in prices, and the horizontal axis shows the passage of time. You can easily see that from January through May, the percentage change in prices was increasing: prices were rising at a faster rate. You also can see that this changed in May when price increases subsided.

Such time-series graphs are quite useful when we want to see how an economic measure is changing over time, whether it is prices or the unemployment rate or average wages in the market for nurses. Because we can see the time-series behavior, this allows us to ask whether some change led to the observed shift in the pattern, such as occurred in Figure 1A.11 in May.

Instead of thinking about a variable's behavior over time, what if you wanted to display some economic measure across a number of firms at a point in time? For example, suppose you wanted to show the prices different companies charged for, say, a good cottage cheese, in the month of May. You could do this by using a chart like the one in **Figure 1A.12**, which is called a **bar chart**.

The bar chart allows you to quickly see the different prices charged by the different companies at a certain point in time (May). The price at which each producer sells can be easily compared with that of the competition. In Figure 1A.12, cottage cheese purchased from White Stuff is clearly more expensive than that bought from Cottage Cheese.

Bar charts can also be used to illustrate data over time. **Figure 1A.13** shows the changes in the level of prices from the previous time-series graph, only this time the percentage changes are plotted in a bar chart format. The bar chart is an alternate way of displaying the same data.

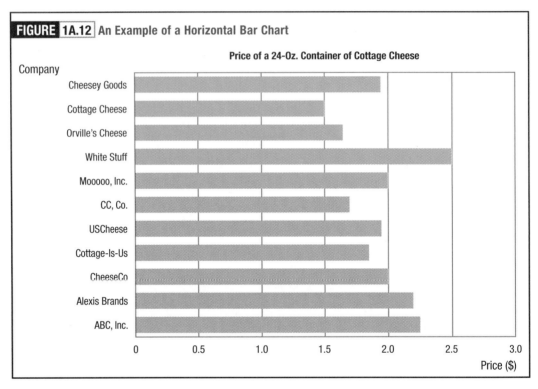

**FIGURE 1A.12** An Example of a Horizontal Bar Chart

**Price of a 24-Oz. Container of Cottage Cheese**

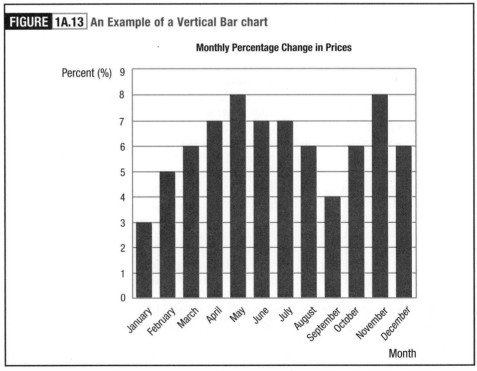

**FIGURE 1A.13** An Example of a Vertical Bar chart

**Monthly Percentage Change in Prices**

What if the data you want to show relates to how something is allocated? Suppose, for example, that you have information on college students' expenditures. You sometimes see survey results reported as: "A recent survey of college students revealed that 60 percent of their monthly income was spent on rent, 20 percent on food and

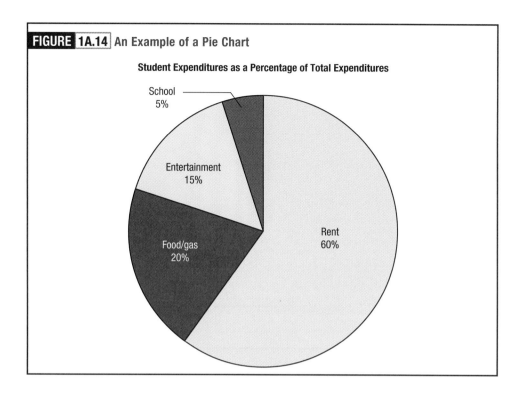

**FIGURE 1A.14** An Example of a Pie Chart

Student Expenditures as a Percentage of Total Expenditures

School
5%

Entertainment
15%

Food/gas
20%

Rent
60%

gasoline, 15 percent on entertainment, and 5 percent on school-related items." There is a much easier way to report the results, and **Figure 1A.14** is an example. It is called a **pie chart**. Pie charts are often used to plot percentages of a total. Because of this, the "pieces" of the pie must total 100 percent.

The pie chart shows the distribution of student expenditures across the various categories. Very quickly you can see that the lion's share of expenditures goes to rent compared with, say, school-related items.

Finally, to show the relation between two different measures, a **scatter plot** is sometimes used. A scatter plot can be used to "test" whether two variables are related, either positively or negatively. For example, suppose you would like to see whether an increase in study time is related to test performance. To do so, you would collect data from your classmates by asking them how many hours they studied for a midterm test and what their grades (in percentages) were. From your question-naire, you find that some students studied very little and some a lot. Some got good grades, and some did not. But are the two related in any meaningful way? Plotting the results in a scatter plot like that in **Figure 1A.15** will help you see the relation-ship between the two.

Each dot in the scatter plot represents a student's response to your question, "How many hours did you study, and what grade did you get?" What you can see from the scatter plot is that there is a positive relation between the hours studied and the grades students received. You know this because the scatter of points tends to rise: those students who studied more tended to get better grades. The line that we have inserted depicts the "average" relation. If there were no relation, the points would be scattered all over the graph, and we would not be able to draw a line that comes close to connecting them.

The use of graphs and charts is prevalent in economics. There is so much data that we analyze and use to test our theories. You will see most, if not all, of these graphical forms throughout the text.

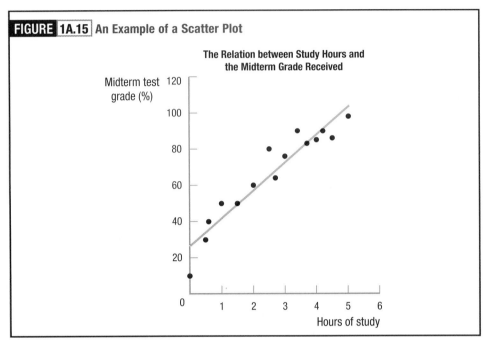

**FIGURE 1A.15** An Example of a Scatter Plot

The Relation between Study Hours and
the Midterm Grade Received

Practice Problems

1. The income and expenditure data shown at the beginning of this appendix was plotted using what kind of graph? From the plot used there, would you say that income and expenditures are positively or negatively related?

2. Suppose you take a survey in your class and ask these questions: what is your height, and what is your weight? The data you collect are shown in the following table.

| Name | Height (Inches) | Weight (Pounds) |
|------|------|------|
| Bill | 72 | 220 |
| Susan | 69 | 175 |
| Tom | 65 | 130 |
| Anne | 60 | 115 |
| Janet | 77 | 200 |
| John | 70 | 180 |
| Sarah | 63 | 180 |
| Mary | 68 | 190 |
| Gary | 69 | 160 |
| Molly | 74 | 195 |

a. Plot the weight data using a bar chart. Looking at the chart, identify the individual who is the heaviest and who is the lightest. If the average weight is about 175, how does the rest of the class compare to this number?

b. Can you tell if someone is overweight simply by knowing his or her weight? Plot the data in the table using a scatter diagram, with height on the horizontal axis and weight on the vertical axis. What kind of relationship exists between weight and height?

c. You hear on the news that the average weight of individuals has increased over the past 50 years and that this trend must be reversed. Based on your observation in your scatter plot, how might you react to the news story? What questions might you ask?

3. The following pie charts show two companies' expenditures in various areas. The size of the segment reflects the amount of money spent as a percent of total expenditures.

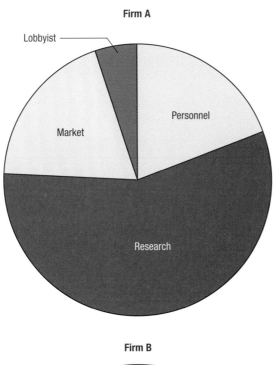

**Firm A**

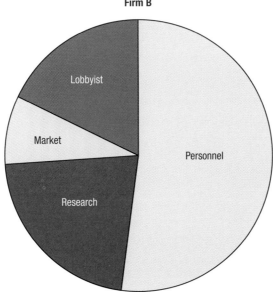

**Firm B**

a. Given the definitions, which firm is more heavily engaged in research? Which one is spending more money on lobbyists? If "personnel" reflects the salaries paid, which firm might you be more interested in working for?

## KEY TERMS

# The Benefits and Costs of an Activity: Specialization and Exchange

*"Idealism is fine, but as it approaches reality, the costs become prohibitive."*

*William F. Buckley, Jr., columnist*

**A**s you learned in Chapter 1, scarcity is everywhere. Your labor is scarce, cars are scarce, and clean air is scarce. Even the time you spend reading this chapter is scarce. How, then, do we prioritize our wants so that the scarce resources we do have are put to uses that provide us with the greatest happiness or satisfaction? In this chapter, we present a framework that will help us understand and even predict how each of us copes with scarcity when choosing among alternatives. Our economic model helps us approximate how people are likely to behave.

Even when something is offered to us for free, it often can come at a substantial economic cost. A free dog in need of a loving home requires food, veterinary care, and human play time. Spending free time at the park with one's family and friends means less time at work, a smaller paycheck, and consequently, fewer purchases that could have generated additional well-being.

Every time we make a choice, we weigh the costs of doing so. Because costs are such a key ingredient in making choices, this chapter explores what exactly these costs consist of. As you will discover, the monetary cost of a choice—the dollars you actually spend—is often a relatively small portion of a choice's total or economic cost. Knowing this makes choosing between alternatives more complex than just knowing how much money we take out of our wallets. Using the model we talked about, you also will see how we efficiently allocate our scarce resources across different choices. By the time you have finished this chapter, you will have a much better appreciation for how complex the process of making a choice really is.

## 2.1 Making Choices to Attain the Greatest Satisfaction Possible

How do you allocate the 24 hours that make up each day? You might choose to spend 16 hours sleeping, 4 hours at school, and the remaining 4 hours text messaging friends. Or, perhaps you choose to sleep 6 hours, spend 2 hours at the gym, 8 hours at work, 4 hours at school, and the rest of your day eating out with friends. However a person chooses to devote her scarce time is a personal choice that reflects her **preferences**.

> **PREFERENCES** Individual tastes based on how a person subjectively ranks alternative choices.
>
> **EXAMPLE** Most Americans prefer to eat dinner early, whereas some Europeans prefer to eat after 8 P.M.
>
> **EXAMPLE** Most residential college students prefer late morning classes, whereas commuter students prefer early morning or evening classes.

Our preferences reflect our individual tastes, likes, and dislikes and are often determined by our experiences, beliefs, education, and values. Economics doesn't judge people's preferences and the resulting choices they make. It simply assumes the choices are made because people *think* that doing so will maximize their well-being. As a result, using this approach, economists often assume that people's behavior is an outcome of rational decisions they make while acting in their own best interests. But do not think that rationality precludes errors in judgment. We all make bad decisions once in a while. In reality, it is rare that a person will have complete information about all the alternatives she faces. It is simply too costly and time consuming to acquire it. That is why she has to make decisions that she thinks will provide her with the greatest benefit.

When we allocate time to attend class, sleep, or work, we are making individual choices that we think will maximize the benefits we get from the limited amount of time we have. Each choice requires us to sacrifice other potential opportunities. Obviously, you can't be in two places at once. If you decide to stay home to take care of your children or paint the house, then you cannot be at work earning money. In other words, there is a cost associated with your choice to spend these hours at home versus at work. This cost is referred to as an **opportunity cost**. Had you gone to work instead of staying home, however, there would have been an opportunity cost to that decision as well—the benefit you would have enjoyed from staying home with your children or painting the house.

> **OPPORTUNITY COST** The opportunity cost of a decision is the satisfaction or well-being you forgo from not engaging in the next-highest-valued alternative.
>
> **EXAMPLE** By coming to class, you are forgoing the enjoyment of sleeping in, your next-highest-valued alternative.
>
> **EXAMPLE** By deciding to expend economic resources to send humans to the moon, the opportunity cost is not engaging in oceanic exploration.

**ECONOMIC FALLACY** If the price of something is zero, then its cost is zero.

**False.** Let's say that you receive a full scholarship to go to college. Going to college still has an opportunity cost such as the wages you forgo by attending classes rather than working. To get the free autograph of a sports or film star, you usually must wait in line for some time. This waiting is a cost. People who live in countries where the government provides "free" health care usually wait all day to be seen (in Australia, they often bring their lunches to their doctor's visits) and months or years more before their surgeries are performed. These are costs associated with free health care.

## 2.2 The Components of Opportunity Cost: Explicit and Implicit Costs

Ultimately, our decisions depend on what we expect to forgo. The opportunity cost of engaging in criminal behavior, for example, is much lower for an unemployed person with few promising job leads than for a person who is successfully climbing the corporate ladder. What is the opportunity cost of getting pregnant and dropping out of high school? Teen mothers have about a 60-percent chance of graduating from high school by age 25, compared to 90 percent of women who postpone having children until after graduation. What this tells us is that the true cost of having a baby as a teen is greater than simply the medical bills. The cost also includes any wages lost from dropping out of high school and not having a diploma. Women who wait to have children until they have a high school or college diploma don't bear this cost. However, they sometimes face another type of cost when they delay having children: an increased risk of infertility that can result in higher medical bills if they seek infertility treatment.

One component of opportunity cost—the most obvious one—is the monetary cost of a choice. This type of cost is referred to as the **explicit cost** of a decision.

**EXPLICIT COST** The monetary cost of a choice.

EXAMPLE The explicit cost of going on a date includes the cost of movie tickets, dinner, and transportation (and a babysitter if required).

EXAMPLE The explicit cost of attending college includes tuition and the cost of books and transportation.

EXAMPLE The explicit cost of using a toll bridge is the toll that is paid.

In addition to the explicit, or monetary, cost of making a choice, you also incur an **implicit cost** when you make a decision.

**IMPLICIT COST** The forgone opportunity cost of a choice.

EXAMPLE The implicit cost of using a toll-free road is the extra time you spend fighting more traffic during rush hour.

EXAMPLE The implicit cost of taking this course is not being able to take another one at the same time.

Every section of introductory economics is not equally attractive to all students. Even when the same instructor is teaching two sections, different time slots impose different implicit costs on each student. For example, the implicit cost of classes scheduled at midday is probably lower for nonworking, residential college students than for students who work off-campus. It is no surprise that colleges that cater predominantly to full-time students schedule the bulk of their classes between 9 A.M. and 5 P.M. In contrast, colleges that service working students offer many more classes early in the morning, later in the evening, and even on weekends.

Because implicit costs are nonmonetary, they are not always easy to quantify. Economists often use wage rates to approximate the value of time people spend in nonwork activities such as attending college, engaging in leisure activities, or volunteering. Using wage rates, the dollar value of an hour of volunteering in the United States in 2008 was estimated to be a little more than $20.[1] Likewise, when an attorney wins a wrongful-death lawsuit, she will calculate what the deceased person's lifetime earnings would have been before she asks the jury to award the plaintiff damages or money to compensate for the loss of the loved one.[2]

Even though implicit costs can be hard to quantify, people *do* factor them into their decision making. You might buy a car with side airbags or purchase sunscreen, even though you have never calculated the potential costs of having an accident or getting skin cancer. Why? Because the implicit costs that you place on *not* buying them are just too high.

Opportunity cost can be thought of as the sum of both explicit and implicit costs. This is why economists often disagree that the total cost of attending college is equal to tuition and room and board. How else can you explain the fact that so-called technogeeks such as Steve Jobs, Bill Gates, and Mark Zuckerberg dropped out of college to seek their fortunes in the development of hardware, software, and social network programs? As students they perceived that the *implicit* cost of staying in college for a couple more years was too high relative to the benefits they would get from the degree. They dropped out even though the *explicit* cost of staying in college had not changed. As you can see, even when the explicit cost of a choice remains unchanged, an increase in implicit cost can lead to a change in behavior.

## SOLVED PROBLEM

**Q** In March 2006, *Money* magazine featured a story about a pilot who couldn't afford to buy the antique planes he wanted to fly, so he built two of them from scratch. Fred Murrin, an engineer who earns approximately $72,800 per year, estimated that the cost of building both planes was around $39,000 and that they were then worth ten times this cost. He also estimated that he spent approximately 12,500 hours on the project over 18 years. Murrin emphasized that the value of the planes really wasn't what was most important to him—it was his passion for flying World War I planes. How much cost did Murrin incur to satisfy this passion?

**A** If we assume that Murrin works a 40-hour week, then the cost of his time is equal to $72,800/2,080 where 2,080 is (52 weeks × 40 hours per week). This comes out to $35 per hour, Murrin's hourly wage (ignoring taxes). Therefore, 12,500 hours would have an implicit cost, in terms of forgone wages of $35 × 12,500 = $437,500. If we add the $39,000 in explicit costs, we arrive at a total or true economic cost of $437,500 + $39,000 = $476,500. Murrin estimates that the two planes are now worth $39,000 × 10 = $390,000 if he were to sell them. Subtracting this revenue from the total cost of building the planes, we get $390,000 − $437,500 = −$47,500. In other words, the costs exceeded the monetary benefits by $47,500. If Murrin gets at least this amount of nonmonetary benefit from flying the planes, then he made an optimal decision to engage in his building project.

· · · · · · ·

[1]Based on the average hourly wage of nonmanagement, nonagricultural workers. Independent Sector. "Dollar Value of a Volunteer Hour: 1980–2007" (2009).

[2]Kip Viscusi, "The Value of Life in Legal Contexts: Survey and Critique." *American Law and Economics Review*, 2, no. 1 (2000): 195–210.

## Economic Costs versus Accounting Costs

Now that we better understand the nature of economic cost, we can compare it to other kinds of cost measures. In business, accounting costs usually refer to money outlays (what we've called explicit costs) paid by the business to purchase various supplies, or wages to employees. In effect, **accounting costs** are what most of us think are the outlays made in the course of doing business.

> **ACCOUNTING COSTS** Explicit costs, or monetary outlays, incurred in the course of doing business as well as costs considered expenses under the law.

> **EXAMPLE** An entrepreneur opens up a day-care center, investing $5,000 to fix up the space she has rented, and incurs such business expenses as utilities, insurance, renovation costs, and the wages she pays herself. These are the venture's accounting costs.

In the example, accounting costs ignore the implicit costs faced by our entrepreneur associated with opening the day-care center. For example, she could have invested the $5,000 in another way. The $5,000 could have earned interest in the bank or generated dividends from the purchase of a stock. From an economist's perspective, the opportunity cost of passing up these investment returns is as much a cost of the day-care venture as the rent payment. If the business does not generate sufficient revenue to cover all of her explicit *and* implicit costs, then she would be better off closing the center. Of course, if she gets satisfaction from the day-care center that is independent of the monetary profits she makes, then she might continue to keep the center open even when its economic costs exceed the money she takes in.

Generally speaking, because accounting costs and economic costs are usually not the same, they will lead to different predictions, depending on which ones we use to calculate profitability. This makes sense because **accounting profit** is usually defined as the difference between a company's revenue from the products it sells and the cost it incurs to produce and market these goods. In contrast, **economic profit** compares total revenue to the *economic* costs of doing business.

> **ACCOUNTING PROFIT** Total revenue less *accounting* costs.

> **EXAMPLE** Katie and Max collected $200 from selling cold cans of soda at a local art show. They spent six hours selling the soda, which cost them $128 at Sam's Club. They also paid $20 for a vendor's license to sell at the show. Because they agreed to take no salary, their accounting profit was $52 (= $200 − $148) which they split between them.

> **ECONOMIC PROFIT** Total revenue less *economic* costs.

> **EXAMPLE** Suppose that Katie gave up six hours of work time to help Max with his soda venture. Because she is an experienced ultrasound technician, the earnings she passed up were $28 per hour, or $168 in total. This means that the economic profit of the soda venture is at a minimum $168 lower than its accounting profits, or −$116 (= $200 − $148 − $168).

If economic costs are so difficult to quantify, do entrepreneurs and investors rely only on a company's accounting profit information rather than its economic profits to make decisions? For example, did investor perceptions about the profitability of companies change when companies began to take into account their future health coverage liabilities in the early 1990s? We know there were whopping write-downs as a result of this accounting change. General Motors, for example, took a $20.8 billion write-down, but on the very day this write-down was announced, GM's share price closed up by more than 2.5 percent. As then-GM Chief Executive Officer Rick Wagoner noted at the time, the financial community was already anticipating the impact of this change: investors had already "priced in" these liabilities when estimating the value of the company. This behavior is consistent with the notion that investors understand the difference between accounting and economic costs and that they have their eyes on economic profits, not accounting profits.

## Sunk Costs

Have you ever heard the expressions "Let bygones be bygones" and "Don't cry over spilled milk"? Both mean that we shouldn't spend more time or other scarce resources to undo something that can't be undone. Failing your first calculus test because you didn't study for it cannot be altered by studying harder. That may prevent you from failing the next test, but the F on the first test is a bygone: it is a sunk cost. Costs that can't be recouped are called **sunk costs**.

> **SUNK COST** Costs that cannot be recouped following a decision.

> **EXAMPLE** Sarah pays $2,500 for a laser-disc player she expects will be compatible with new industry standards. But laser discs do not catch on, and movie distributors quickly discontinue selling them. Sarah's purchase of the laser-disc player is a sunk cost. She has already borne the cost of this purchase. She can decide to keep the laser-disc player to play her very limited laser-disc collection (which is also a sunk cost), or she can choose to replace it with a Blu-ray player. Whatever she decides, the sunk cost of the player and laser-disc collection should not factor into the decision to buy the Blu-ray player.

A working mother enrolls her baby in a prestigious day-care center. The tuition is a nonrefundable, up-front payment of $9,500 a year. After a few months of this arrangement, the mother decides that she would rather stay home and take care of her child full-time. The nonrefundable tuition is a sunk cost, regardless of what she decides. Therefore, it should not factor into her current decision about whether or not to continue working.

As these examples suggest, sunk costs are just that: scarce resources that we have "sunk" into an activity as a result of a previous decision. We see that we are stuck with these costs whether we stand by our original decision or switch to another opportunity. After all, do we really want to continue to "throw good money after bad"? So, if your parents complain about all the money that was wasted when you tell them that you really want to fix cars instead of pursuing a career in accounting, just remind them that the cost of your college degree is a sunk cost.

**ECONOMIC FALLACY**   The fact that pharmaceutical companies earn profit margins in excess of 15 percent—as compared to 5 percent in the food and retailing sectors—is conclusive evidence that they are gouging consumers in terms of drug prices.

**False.** Profit margins reported in annual reports and by the media are accounting (explicit) profits. These profits do not include the implicit costs of production, which in the case of drug companies includes the risk that the billions of dollars they invest in the research and development of a new drug could be futile. Just as venture capitalists require a higher return on their investment in risky new ventures, investors in drug companies require a higher return to compensate for the risk that a new drug in the pipeline could be shown to be ineffective or for some other reason could be denied approval by the U.S. Food and Drug Administration.

## Transactions Costs

Suppose that you are in the market for a used car. You spend days searching for information on the reliability, fuel efficiency, safety records, and average repair costs for the dozen or so models you are considering. You also may check out industry sources such as the *Kelly Blue Book* to get some idea of how much the cars cost. Based on all of this information, you are able to identify the model you believe will provide you with the greatest overall satisfaction (comfort, safety, fuel efficiency, etc.).

The next step in the process is to find someone with the car you want who is willing to sell it to you at a price that is within the range you have in mind. The cost of identifying potential sellers has gone down considerably in the Internet age now that there are a number of Web sites that can locate specific cars for sale. Once you have located sellers of the car you want, you must assess their willingness to sell to you, which will depend on the price you offer. Bargaining often ensues. You may want the seller to show you a CARFAX report to see the car's maintenance records and to ensure it has not been in an accident.

When all is said and done, both you and the seller have incurred a whole host of costs to make the trade happen. They include the time costs of searching for information, negotiating costs, and costs to enforce the terms of the deal to make sure that each party holds up his or her end of the deal. Costs such as these are called **transactions costs**.

> **TRANSACTIONS COSTS** The costs people incur when exchanging goods and services. Transactions costs include search and information costs, bargaining costs, and payment and enforcement costs.

Sometimes the price of a good is mutually acceptable to both the seller and buyer, but the exchange doesn't occur because its transactions costs are too high. Suppose you live in San Francisco and find a car on the Internet that fits your needs at a price you are willing to pay. However, if the car is in Charleston, South Carolina, it might be too costly for you to transport it across the country. In other words, the transactions costs might be too high for you to make the deal.

As you can imagine, lowering transactions costs is likely to increase trading activity. Self-checkout stands at the grocery store allow you to purchase your two items faster than waiting in line behind someone buying a week's worth of groceries. The stands lower buyers' transactions costs—the cost of waiting in line—to buy groceries.

Similarly, allowing customers to use credit cards to buy their groceries also lowers transactions costs. Instead of carrying cash or making sure they have funds in their checking account, people have credit cards that allow them to buy goods today and pay for them in the future. By using your credit card, you can also buy groceries in Seattle or Miami, something you wouldn't be able to do with a personal check.

## Economic Habits

Most of us do not use MapQuest every morning to find the shortest route to school or work. We habitually take the same route every day unless there is an unexpected change that causes us to rethink our usual choice, either temporarily (there's an accident on the road ahead) or permanently (a new highway opens). In situations that are routine and repetitive, people rely on habits instead of active decision making.

Why do we rely on habits (rules of thumb) even if they do not always produce the best outcomes? A key element in making choices is information. As we have explained, information, just like any other economic good, is costly to acquire. Because gathering and evaluating information each and every time we face a routine choice (like choosing a route to school) requires us to use up scarce resources (time), we often adopt habits in order to economize on resources.

Brand names often facilitate the habit-based decisions consumers make. Some of us rely on McDonald's as a lunch spot rather than gathering information about other fast-food restaurants. We know that whether the McDonald's is in New York City or Seattle, it offers a predictable menu of predictable-tasting food (this may, however, not be the case in certain foreign locales). To get its customers to habitually choose its food, however, McDonald's attempts to ensure that its menu, cooking ingredients, and overall quality of service are uniform across locations. For this reason, McDonald's requires its franchisees to purchase key ingredients from a corporate supplier, offer a menu approved by the corporation, and train its employees a certain way. This helps McDonald's protect its brand name and the information-economizing signal that it gives to consumers.

What can cause us to change our habits? People change their habits when the circumstances they face change significantly—whether a change in road conditions, the availability of new alternatives, or the potential negative health effect of a habit. When Coca-Cola bottlers in the United States began to substitute corn syrup for cane sugar in 1985, they lost a large number of Coke drinkers who did not like the new taste. These people switched to other brands that were still using cane sugar. U.S. bottlers also lost market share to their Mexican counterparts, who continued to use only cane sugar for sweetness and began to ship Mexican Coke over the border.[3]

When we "break" an old habit, we are signaling that we believe that the opportunity cost of continuing to do it is too high. In other words, making a new choice outweighs our **switching costs**.

**SWITCHING COSTS** The explicit and implicit costs people incur when they change brands, providers, or products.

**EXAMPLE** You are considering changing your e-mail service from AOL to Comcast to save money. How long will it take to recoup your switching costs if you do? The costs include any termination fees and the time it takes to research the switch, get used to Comcast's e-mail screens, e-mail people about your address change, update your address on your Facebook page, and so forth.

Companies recognize that high switching costs can keep people locked into their existing behaviors. That's why your cell-phone company wants you to sign a contract with a fee if you break the contract. (Have you noticed that the fee

........

[3]Louise Chu, "Is Mexican Coke the Real Thing?" *San Diego Union Tribune*, November 9, 2004.

decreases over time?) Other companies attempt to earn your business by reducing your switching costs. They might offer to pay your termination fee or advertise that they have no long-term contracts. The federal government also intercedes periodically to reduce consumers' switching costs. In 2003, the Federal Communications Commission enacted a "local number portability" rule that required cell-phone carriers to let subscribers take their telephone numbers when they switched wireless carriers. It was estimated that more than 30 million subscribers would jump to a new company once the switching cost of having to give up a telephone number was eliminated.

Sometimes we are forced to break habits when we would prefer not to do so. Suppose your employer changes its health insurance plan and your family practitioner—whom you have gone to all your life—is no longer in your network of preferred providers. You feel bad about leaving your doctor. You also must spend time gathering information about the doctors that are in the new plan before you choose one. Whether you will switch to a new provider will depend on whether your switching costs outweigh the higher cost you will pay if you remain with your current doctor.

Habits are not of much use when we are making decisions that are neither repetitive nor routine. For example, the selection of a college is a once-in-a-lifetime choice for many of us. As a result, we make a substantial investment in gathering information about our options. We spend time on the Internet, make trips to various campuses, and discuss alternatives with teachers, family members, and friends. Because the choice is not a repetitive one, like choosing a route to work, a habit cannot lessen these information costs. Of course, if a student goes to his parent's alma mater without ever considering other opportunities, then we can think of this as a habitual choice. The higher we believe the cost of making a potentially poor decision is, the more we will be willing to invest to make a better, more-informed decision. So it makes sense for families to spend more of their scarce resources on their children's college selection process than they do on where they will go out to eat.

> **ECONOMIC FALLACY**    More choices will always improve a person's well-being.
>
> **False.** Because it can be costly to evaluate the costs and benefits of a new alternative, a person might simply continue to make the same choices as before and maintain his or her original level of well-being. Depending on the incremental benefit that can be derived from reconsidering a decision, sticking with an old choice might not be a "lazy" response. It may, indeed, lead to the greatest level of well-being possible. In fact, psychologists have documented that an increase in the number of choices people face can sometimes lead to indecision and "paralysis." Think about young children trying to decide which ice cream flavor to choose when confronted with many different flavors. Perhaps selecting a course to satisfy a cross-cultural or social science requirement for your undergraduate degree led to indecision on your part. On a more serious note, the choices people face when having to make end-of-life decisions for a loved one can also lead to indecision. As researchers have found, substantially increasing the number of people's choices can significantly decrease their satisfaction with the search process and lead to less-than-optimal decisions.[4]

· · · · · · ·

[4]Alina Tugend, "Too Many Choices: A Problem that Can Paralyze." *New York Times*, February 27, 2010.

## 2.3 Using Marginal Analysis to Compare Costs and Benefits

Each day people face competing opportunities when it comes to using scarce economic resources. Even leisure-activity choices require some thought. Perhaps you have asked yourself, "Should I rent a DVD or go to the movies?" "Should I go out to eat or fix dinner at home?" "If I go out, should I take the kids or find a babysitter?" For each and every one of these alternatives, there are corresponding economic benefits and opportunity costs. Of course, at the time a decision is made, we really are operating only on *what we think the benefits will be compared to what we think the economic costs are*. With that in mind, how can we model the process by which people make decisions?

Economists characterize the decision-making process as "thinking at the margin." Basically, this means asking yourself, "If I spend one more unit of a scarce resource (my time or money) on option 1, on option 2, or on option 3, which will give me the greatest satisfaction relative to the costs?" This thought process is called **marginal analysis**.

> **MARGINAL ANALYSIS** Comparing the net benefit resulting from allocating an additional unit of a scarce resource to one alternative versus another.

The idea behind marginal analysis is that we are not usually limited to "all-or-nothing" decisions. Marginal analysis suggests that when we make a decision, we are weighing the **marginal benefit** and the **marginal cost** of spending an additional unit of a scarce resource in a particular way.

> **MARGINAL BENEFIT (*MB*)** The incremental increase in an economic benefit that results when an additional unit of a scarce resource is allocated to a particular activity.

> **MARGINAL COST (*MC*)** The incremental increase in an economic cost that results when an additional unit of a scarce resource is allocated to a particular activity.

> **EXAMPLE** What is the net benefit of spending one more hour studying for an economics exam? The answer depends on the additional exam points you expect the hour to yield (this is your incremental, or marginal, benefit) compared to what the extra hour would yield if you were to spend it in the next best way, for example, by studying for a chemistry test (this is your incremental, or marginal, cost).

What is the net benefit of spending more money to upgrade to a faster 4G cell phone? It depends on the marginal benefit you get from saving time using the Internet on your phone compared to the marginal benefit you *could* have gotten from spending the money in another way—for example, buying more downloaded music or movies. If the marginal benefit of the upgrade is greater than the marginal cost, then spending the money on the 4G cell phone will increase your well-being.

Furthermore, it must be the case that at some point the marginal benefit of the last unit consumed will just equal its marginal cost. This last unit will generate zero net benefit because the difference between marginal benefit and marginal cost ($MB - MC$) is zero. When the net benefit is zero, we will not expend any more of our scarce resources to acquire any additional units.

## SOLVED PROBLEM

**Q** You are offered a free ride to go to Florida for your spring vacation. Alternatively, you can spend $299 to fly round-trip to Mexico. You would have been willing to spend up to $399 to fly to Mexico. What is the opportunity cost of going to Florida?

**A** The net benefit of flying to Mexico is equal to $399 − $299 = $100. If you go to Florida, the net benefit you pass up from flying to Mexico is $100. Therefore, the opportunity cost of accepting the ride to Florida is $100. This assumes that there are no additional costs or benefits of either trip that must be considered (and that everything else—hotel, food, etc.—is the same in both locations).

Do economists really believe that people consciously calculate their marginal benefits and costs before making each and every decision? Absolutely not. The best way to think about marginal decision making is that it is an approximation (a *model*) of people's behavior. For a model to be useful, it need not apply perfectly to every situation. What we really care about is whether it provides a reasonably good prediction of how people actually behave. Marginal analysis is a particularly powerful framework for understanding how our choices change when the world around us changes. For example, marginal analysis predicts that the amount of time a family spends preparing meals decreases when time-saving technologies such as microwave ovens cost less and become widely accessible. How? Because now the opportunity cost of spending additional time baking and cooking "the old-fashioned way" increases.

Time and time again, we find that people act in a manner consistent with marginal analysis. In most circumstances, individuals' choices can be predicted quite accurately by using our "marginalist" model of behavior. Economists have even applied laboratory experimental methods to animals and found that rats and pigeons conform to the elementary principles of economics: the animals act as if they are weighing the marginal costs and the marginal benefits of an activity.[5]

Although people weigh the marginal benefits and costs associated with different alternatives, they often choose to allocate their resources differently from one another, even if they have the same amount of resources available to them. This happens because they value the alternatives differently according to their personal preferences. What makes one person happy might not make another person happy. How often have you dined out with a friend, spent approximately the same amount of money, but ordered entirely different meals? While you are taking this economics course, how many other students are taking philosophy or accounting during the very same class time? The beauty of our economic model of decision making is that it provides a framework for predicting individual choices without imposing uniformity on the actual choices people make.

### Applying Marginal Analysis: How Many Children Should a Couple Have?

Suppose a couple is discussing the number of children they would like to have. They know that there is a monetary cost to having a child: money spent on medical care, food, a bigger house, child care, and education is money that cannot be spent on sports cars, vacations, and retirement savings. In fact, it is estimated that the average

· · · · · · ·

[5]John Kagel, Raymond C. Battalio, and Leonard Green, *Economic Choice Theory: An Experimental Analysis of Animal Behavior* (New York: Cambridge University Press, 1995), p. 3.

cost of raising a child born in 2005 through age 17 is upward of $250,000.[6] We also know there are significant nonmonetary costs associated with raising a child. The costs include the sacrifice of leisure, not to mention sleep. The costs parents experience differ from person to person, depending on their preferences and the alternatives they face. For example, a female college graduate faces a higher opportunity cost of having a child than a high-school dropout. Why? Because the college graduate would forgo higher wages if her pregnancy or child-rearing activities lead to a decline in the hours she worked.

How do couples weigh these costs and benefits to determine the number of children that will maximize their well-being? In the real world, couples almost certainly have imperfect information about the full range of costs and benefits associated with becoming parents. Extrapolating from others' experiences is, at best, an imperfect gauge. Oftentimes, it is only *after* someone has had a child that the costs and benefits of parenthood are fully appreciated. Thus, it is quite possible that the number of children the couple will want to have will change after they have had their first child. This point helps us reiterate the fact that the economic decisions people make are based on the information available to them at that time. After they make a choice, they often acquire information about it that they can use to make future decisions.

We can use marginal analysis to model a couple's decision to have a first child. If they believe the benefit outweighs the cost, they will choose to have the child. If the perceived benefit does not outweigh the perceived cost, they will defer having the child until their circumstances change and the net benefit of becoming parents becomes positive. For example, if the woman loses her job, the opportunity cost of her having a child might actually decrease. In that case, she might decide to go ahead and have the child. Or if the couple wins the lottery, the opportunity cost of having an additional child might decline if a nanny can be hired.

What about the decision to have a second or third or even tenth child? Marginal analysis tells us that the parents will again weigh the benefits and costs of having the additional child. Different criteria might be considered than the criteria used to decide to have the first child, though. For example, the parents might factor in the benefits and costs that they believe their existing child or children will experience as a result: will the firstborn be a spoiled brat if he is an only child? On the other hand, will the child or children suffer once there is an additional child vying for the family's limited resources?[7] We know, for example, that children from large families tend to earn less as adults than children who come from smaller families, because they generally have less education.[8] This suggests that adding children to the family can have a lifelong, negative economic effect on their older siblings.

As long as the perceived net benefit of having additional children is positive, the couple will continue to expand their family. This expansion will continue until the couple reaches a point where the marginal benefit of having an additional child will equal the marginal cost. At this point, the net benefit of having another child is zero. We say that the couple is "at the margin" when it comes to having this last child and will exhibit **indifference**—that is, they are indifferent to having the next child.

· · · · · · ·

[6]*Expenditures on Children By Families, 2005*. United States Department of Agriculture, Publication #1528–2005.

[7]Jeff Opdyke, "How Many Children?" *St. Louis Post-Dispatch*. October 20, 2002.

[8]J. Blake, "Family Size and the Quality of Children." *Demography*, 1981.

**INDIFFERENCE** A situation in which a person doesn't care whether an alternative is chosen or not because it yields zero net benefit.

EXAMPLE Your instructor doesn't care whether you read the textbook before or after class, as long as you read it. She is indifferent to your study routine if it results in good performance on exams.

EXAMPLE Most people in the United States don't care whether a newborn child is a boy or girl, as long as the baby is healthy. They are indifferent to the child's gender.

You might think that using marginal analysis to model a decision as personal as having a baby is unrealistic and even cold-hearted. In reality, demographers and policy makers *do* use behavioral models like this one to explain why people tend to have more children than others. To lower the opportunity costs of having children, countries with reproduction rates that are too low sometimes subsidize their citizens' child care or require employers to offer paid parental leaves. Germany and France actually give their citizens money to have children. In contrast, countries suffering from overpopulation sometimes offer their citizens free birth control or impose fines on families with more than a certain number of children.

Whether we are talking about having children, deciding how many hot dogs to eat at a baseball game, or selecting classes, economists presume that a useful starting point to analyze behavior is to assume that a person will maximize her satisfaction by engaging in an activity up to the point where the net benefit of additional consumption equals zero. Put another way, the person will stop consuming additional amounts of a particular good or engaging in more of an activity at the point where the marginal benefit derived from the last unit consumed just equals its marginal cost.

**ECONOMIC FALLACY**   Marginal analysis always works.

**False.** Marginal analysis can be problematic when we are dealing with addictive behaviors. This is because decisions for most addicts about how to use their scarce resources are all-or-none decisions. They get economic benefit from only one substance or activity—the one they are addicted to. The initial decision to smoke, drink, or gamble may actually be rational to the extent that people assess their perceived net benefit of engaging in the addictive behavior. However, once a person becomes addicted to some activity, he will likely spend a large part of his scarce resources on his addiction. At this point marginal benefits and costs are irrelevant. This is why it is easier to dissuade teenagers from starting to smoke by imposing huge taxes that raise the price per pack. Addicted smokers are far less responsive to increases in cigarette prices. So marginal analysis may not be well suited for predicting how an addict's behavior will change when his economic environment changes (for example, when the penalty for drunk driving increases to include mandatory jail time).

This is not to say that marginal analysis is totally irrelevant when it comes to some choices made by an addict. For example, smokers who are paid to quit smoking are more successful in breaking the habit than those who are not, and the amount they are paid matters.[9] Moreover, drug addicts seem to systematically choose the "optimal" type of crime to pay for their habits based on the particular

· · · · · · ·

[9]Associated Press, "Money Helps Smokers Quit, Study Says." *St. Louis Post-Dispatch,* February 12, 2009.

characteristics of their addiction. Users of methamphetamines favor identity theft because their drug addiction gives them long attention spans during which they can focus on the details that identity theft entails. In contrast, crack cocaine users are more likely to rely on muggings, carjackings, and robberies because crack cocaine gives them a sense of overwhelming strength and power, but only a short attention span.[10] These choices are consistent with marginal analysis. Addicts act as if they recognize that the marginal benefit and marginal cost of using their time to commit different types of crime will depend on the specific drug they are using.

## 2.4 Diminishing Marginal Benefits and the Principle of Increasing Marginal Costs

The average family in the United States has about two children, far fewer than just a century ago. Why are today's families relatively small when most couples are physically capable of producing more children? Why is it that you and your friends usually stop short of literally eating "all you can eat" at the local Chinese buffet? One reason is because the marginal benefit of a good—what you get from consuming one more egg roll—falls as more of it is consumed. The sense of well-being you gain from the first and second helpings of food might be positive, but the third, fourth, and fifth helpings don't deliver the same satisfaction as the first two because you will be getting fuller and fuller. This idea has general applicability. Whether it is extra helpings at the local buffet or more children, at some point the marginal benefit of an activity begins to decline. We refer to this phenomenon as the **diminishing marginal benefit**.

**DIMINISHING MARGINAL BENEFIT** A situation in which the economic benefit generated from an additional unit of a good or activity is less than the benefit derived from the preceding unit.

**EXAMPLE** The first cold lemonade on a hot summer's day will likely create a good deal more satisfaction than the fourth.

**EXAMPLE** Some television commercials are quite funny the first time they are viewed. By the 50th viewing, most of the extra enjoyment is gone.

Another reason the marginal benefit of consuming a good gradually declines is because people like variety. The more of one good we consume instead of another, the less variety we get. Imagine having the same dinner menu every day. Even your favorite dish will begin to lose its appeal after a while. Moreover, because people differ in their preferences, they are also likely to differ in terms of when a diminishing marginal benefit sets in. An insomniac might get a great deal of satisfaction from watching reruns of *Star Trek* well into the middle of the night. In contrast, this satisfaction will have already diminished considerably by 10 P.M. for people who are used to going to bed by then.

Like marginal analysis, the principle of diminishing marginal benefit helps us more accurately predict behavior. For example, if people pay a flat fee to connect to

· · · · · · ·

[10]John Leland, "Meth Users, Attuned to Detail, Add Another Habit: ID Theft." *New York Times,* July 11, 2006.

the Internet from their cell phones, then their marginal cost of accessing their favorite Web site for the 100th time is zero. Contrast this with what you predict would happen if people were charged instead by the minute or hour of connect time.

Returning to the decision about family size, we find that throughout history, the benefits from having additional children clearly diminished at some point. In many countries, including the United States, the trend over the past century has been toward smaller and smaller families. One explanation is that our economy has evolved from one focused on agricultural production to manufacturing to an information-technology economy. On the family farm of old, children were needed to work the fields and help with chores. Today's modern farm is technologically advanced, thereby reducing the benefit of having many children. Government programs such as Social Security have also reduced the need for people to have more children if the reason was to support and care for them in their old age. Changes such as these explain why the diminishing marginal benefits of having additional children may set in sooner today than in the past.

When we talk about the cost of an alternative, we really mean its opportunity cost. With that in mind, can we say anything about what happens to the marginal cost of using more and more of a good? In the case of expanding the size of one's family, is there some point at which the opportunity cost of having additional children begins to increase? There is indeed. The phenomenon is similar to the diminishing marginal benefits but in reverse: when it comes to having more children, because of the **principle of increasing marginal cost**, at some point the marginal cost of having an additional child is more than the marginal cost of the preceding child.

**PRINCIPLE OF INCREASING MARGINAL COST** A situation in which the opportunity cost of consuming additional units begins to rise.

EXAMPLE The cost of heating water in one's home using solar power is relatively low in sunny climates like the Middle East. However, the cost of shifting more and more of the home's energy supply to solar through the use of solar cells begins to rise dramatically because of the cells' limited capacity.

Think about the cost of housing as a family grows in size. Adding more children may mean that at some point the family must relocate to a community that offers larger homes at a lower price. This could mean the family has to relocate to the suburbs, resulting in a longer commute to work for the parents. Having additional children also increases the probability that one will be sick on any given day, forcing a parent to miss work.

We can depict the relationship between diminishing marginal benefit and increasing marginal cost using **marginal benefit** and **marginal cost curves**.

**MARGINAL BENEFIT CURVE** A graphic representation of the incremental economic benefit we receive from consuming an additional unit of an economic good.

**MARGINAL COST CURVE** A graphic representation of the incremental economic cost we incur to consume an additional unit of an economic good.

**Figure 2.1** puts both of the marginal benefit (*MB*) and marginal cost (*MC*) curves on the same graph. Notice that the marginal benefit curve at first increases and then begins to decline as we move out the horizontal (quantity) axis. In contrast, the marginal cost curve begins to rise.

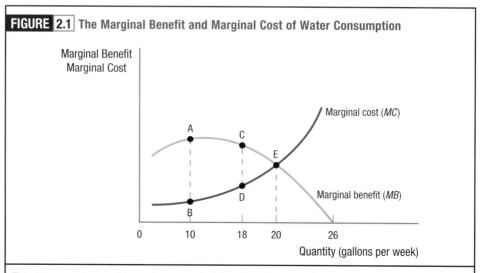

**FIGURE 2.1** The Marginal Benefit and Marginal Cost of Water Consumption

This figure can be used to analyze your decision about how much water to consume each week. The vertical distance between the marginal benefit (*MB*) and marginal cost (*MC*) curves represents the net benefit (*MB* minus *MC*) you receive from consuming more water. Notice how the net benefit of each incremental gallon decreases with the more water you consume (the distance CD becomes less than the distance AB). At the point where the marginal cost curve and the marginal benefit curve cross, the net benefit of consuming one more gallon of water is exactly equal to zero.

Let's use this graph to analyze your decision about how much water to consume each week. The vertical distance between the *MB* and *MC* curves represents the net benefit (*MB* minus *MC*) that you receive from consuming one more gallon of water. The net benefit of the 10th gallon per week is indicated by the line AB; the net benefit of the 18th gallon per week is represented by the line CD. As you can see, the net benefit of each incremental gallon is decreasing (the distance CD is less than the distance AB) the more we consume. At the 20th gallon, the net benefit is exactly equal to zero: at this point, the marginal cost curve and the marginal benefit curve intersect, which means that the marginal cost of the 20th gallon is just equal to the marginal benefit it generates. Beyond this level of water consumption, the net benefit from additional gallons is negative: the marginal cost of additional gallons exceeds any additional benefit that may be had. Note that until the 26th gallon, the marginal benefit received from consuming additional gallons of water is still positive. However, at the same time, the marginal cost of consuming additional gallons beyond the 20th gallon outweighs this marginal benefit, thereby resulting in a *negative* net benefit. So your *total* well-being from consuming water will decline if we consume more than 20 gallons per week.

Keep in mind that whether we are talking about water, education, music downloads, or children, the quantity at which the marginal cost and marginal benefit are equal will probably not be the same for everyone. People's perceptions of their marginal benefit and marginal costs differ, and so would our graphical representation of them. For example, the marginal benefit curve for water is likely to be very different for a suburban home owner than for an urban condominium owner without a yard.

**Figure 2.2** shows two marginal benefit curves—one for each type of home owner—along with a common marginal cost (*MC*) curve that assumes that the cost

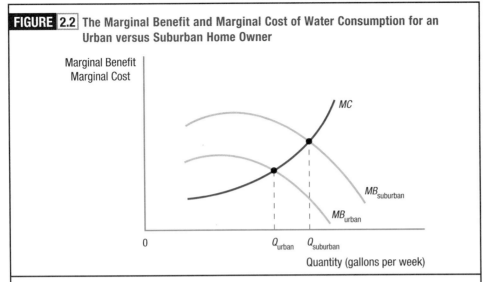

**FIGURE 2.2** **The Marginal Benefit and Marginal Cost of Water Consumption for an Urban versus Suburban Home Owner**

This figure shows two marginal benefit curves—one for a suburban home owner and one for a city dweller. It also shows a single marginal cost (*MC*) curve because we assume that the cost of water delivery is the same for each home owner. You can see that the suburban dweller consumes more water even though the marginal cost of the last gallon of water purchased is higher than the marginal cost of the last gallon purchased by the urban home owner. This makes sense because the suburbanite's marginal benefit curve is higher. Therefore, he justifies spending more to consume each additional gallon.

of water delivery is the same for each home owner. What you can see is that the level of water use where the net benefit equals zero differs for the two home owners. The suburban dweller (represented by the marginal benefit curve $MB_{suburban}$) will consume more water even though the marginal cost of the last gallon purchased is higher than the marginal cost of the last gallon purchased by the urban home owner (represented by $MB_{urban}$). This makes sense because the suburbanite's marginal benefit curve is higher, so he justifies spending more to consume additional gallons. If the water company in a drought-stricken community wants to reduce its overall water consumption, it should raise the water rates paid by suburban home owners before raising those on urban home owners.

What if the marginal benefit curves of two people are the same, but the marginal cost curves they face are different? Consider, for example, a couple that lives in a high-rent urban area like Manhattan versus one that lives in a sprawling suburban housing development in Topeka, Kansas. Suppose there is no other difference between the couples: they earn the same income, have the same set of preferences, and so on. **Figure 2.3** reveals a scenario in which the marginal cost curve for additional children is much higher for Manhattanites because of the cost of expanding their housing space. This application of marginal benefit and cost analysis predicts that they will tend to have smaller families (in this example, two children) compared with their suburban counterparts. And this prediction is borne out by the facts.[11] Likewise, applying this model to the question of who has more cars predicts that, because of the high cost they have to pay for garage space, Manhattanites tend to have fewer cars.

· · · · · · ·

[11]Jeff Opdyke, "Having Children: It's (Partly) About Money." *St. Louis Post-Dispatch*, September 29, 2002.

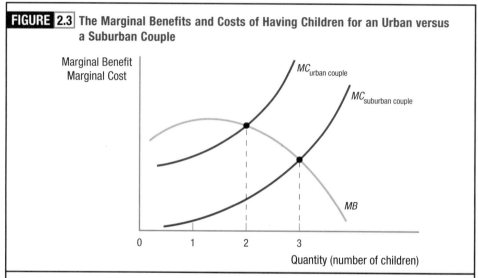

**FIGURE 2.3** The Marginal Benefits and Costs of Having Children for an Urban versus a Suburban Couple

This figure shows how marginal cost and marginal benefit curves can be used to explain the decision of how many children to have. The example compares a couple living in a high-rent urban area to a couple living in suburban housing. With a common marginal benefit curve for the two couples, the decision on how many children to have can be explained by their different marginal cost curves. The urban couple has a higher marginal cost because of the high rent the pair must pay. This analysis predicts that they will therefore tend to have smaller families than suburban couples.

We have already noted that we make economic decisions based on the imperfect information we currently have on hand, which can become more perfect with time, experience, and investment in additional information-gathering activities. When better information changes our assessment of the marginal benefit or marginal cost of consuming more of a particular economic good, then the corresponding curve(s) will adjust and so will our level of consumption.

Marketing gurus understand that it is costly for people to assess the benefits of new products and services. To reduce consumers' costs, they provide free samples or cost-saving coupons to encourage them to try their goods. Advertising campaigns are geared toward changing people's perceptions about the benefits gained from consuming a particular good. Likewise, public-service campaigns conducted by charities or government agencies are aimed at changing people's perceptions about the potential benefits of a wide range of activities, such as adopting rescue shelter dogs or naming a designated driver before partying begins. Advertising campaigns are also used to change people's perceptions about the costs of their decisions, such as driving drunk or speeding through a highway construction zone. As you would predict, when the campaigns are successful, more rescue dogs get adopted and less drunk driving occurs.

## SOLVED PROBLEM

**Q** Child labor laws in developed countries severely limit the amount of time a child under a certain age can spend working for a wage. Leaders of these countries insist that less-developed countries should adopt similar laws to protect their children from exploitation. Using MB and MC curves, show the impact of these new laws, if passed, on the optimal number of children that a typical family in such countries will have.

**A** As shown in the graph below, the marginal cost of having children is unchanged, but the marginal benefit of having children is reduced by this law. The prediction is that couples will have fewer children.

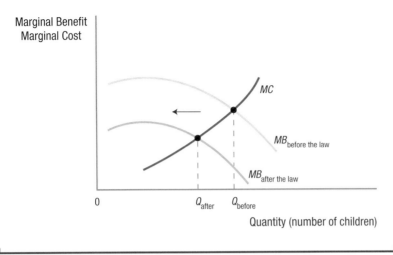

## 2.5 The Production Possibilities Frontier

When economists try to explain observed behavior, they think about individuals coming to terms with the marginal benefits and marginal costs of their decisions. But what happens when we move from looking at individual decision making to that of groups? Think of a household. Within each household, goods and services are produced that improve the well-being of everyone in the home. One or more members provide food services by shopping for groceries and doing the cooking. They nurture a family of children and pets by overseeing their safety, taking them to the doctor, and teaching, training, and socializing them. The household probably requires at least one member to work outside the home to earn income. Assuming there are two adult partners in a household—a husband and wife, mother and adult child, two sisters, and so on—can we predict how these tasks will be divided up? And will this division lead to the best outcome for all?

Let's start by examining the choices these partners face. The partners in our household are in a long-term relationship. We make this assumption because such commitment is central to the creation of trust, and it encourages them to use their scarce resources for the good of the household as a whole. Thus we assume the partners cooperate to maximize the well-being of the household rather than simply satisfy their own individual preferences. (Would behavior of the latter type help explain divorce rates?)

Here are the constraints the partners face. They can each produce two types of output: units of household services (H), such as laundry, cleaning, and mowing; and units of market-based consumption of goods and services (C), which is made possible by income earned in the labor market. The quantity of H produced is represented as $Q_H$, and the quantity of C produced as $Q_C$. Each partner can spend a maximum of 24 hours each day either producing $Q_H$ or $Q_C$, or sleeping. Time is therefore an important scarce resource. Although technically the partners can devote time to other activities such as leisure when they aren't working, it will simplify our analysis if we ignore all these other activities. The average number of hours a person sleeps each night is a given, dictated perhaps by his or her genetics. People who require less sleep have an advantage in terms of the amount of time available to produce $Q_H$ and $Q_C$.

Given these conditions, consider the following profiles of our two partners.

- Partner I, David, requires 8 hours of sleep per night. This leaves him 16 hours per day to produce $Q_H$ or $Q_C$. His take-home (after-tax) market wage is $10 per hour. He can produce 1 (standardized) unit of household services in 30 minutes.

- Partner II, Heidi, also requires 8 hours of sleep per night. That leaves her with 16 hours per day to produce $Q_H$ or $Q_C$. Her take-home market wage is $12 per hour. She can produce 1 (standardized) unit of household services in 40 minutes.

We can now illustrate the trade-offs each partner faces when deciding to produce household services (H) and market-based earnings for consumption goods (C). To be clear, we are imposing several constraints on the ability of the couple to produce household services and market-based earnings. These are the constraints: (1) only these two goods are produced; (2) the amount of productive resources, such as labor hours, machinery, and so on, are taken as given; (3) technology is fixed. The last assumption means our current production methods act as a constraint. In other words, the partners do not yet know or have at their disposal inventions that could increase their ability to produce more using fewer resources (as the computer dramatically did when it was introduced).

The graphical device economists use to illustrate these constraints, the **production possibilities frontier (PPF)**, holds only for a given point in time. The PPF for our couple shows the maximum combination of market-based earnings ($Q_C$) and household services ($Q_H$) each partner can produce in any given 24-hour period.

> **PRODUCTION POSSIBILITIES FRONTIER** A graph showing the maximum combination of outputs that can be produced from a given amount of scarce resources and technology over a specified period of time.

Figure 2.4a shows David's production possibilities frontier (PPF). If he spends all of his waking hours in the labor force, he will generate $160 of income per day ($10 per hour × 16 hours). This is represented by point A on the vertical axis of his PPF. Or David can spend all of his waking hours producing 32 units (2 units per hour × 16 hours) of household outputs. This is point B on the horizontal axis. Finally, he can spend a portion of time in the labor force and use the rest of his time producing household services. Such a combination would be point C. At point C, David spends 6 hours on household production. How many hours does this leave to earn wages, and how much $Q_C$ will he earn?

Keep in mind that David's PPF reflects all of the bundles of H and C that he can attain under the constraints we have imposed. This means that David cannot reach combinations of $Q_H$ and $Q_C$ that lie outside his PPF. For example, he cannot reach the combination of $Q_H$ and $Q_C$ represented by point D, because he is constrained in terms of his number of waking hours and earnings capacity. Moreover, because more household services ($Q_H$) and more market-based consumption ($Q_C$) increase the household's well-being, David will never want to choose a combination that lies inside the PPF, such as the combination represented by point E. Operating "inside" the PPF means that time is being wasted: a better allocation of time could be used

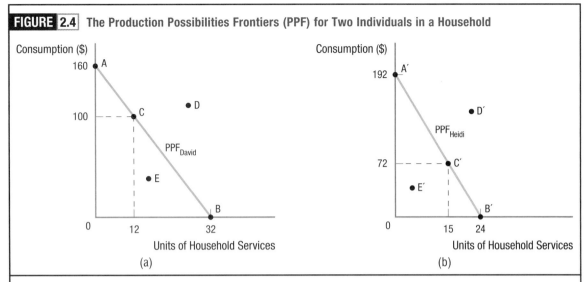

**FIGURE 2.4**   The Production Possibilities Frontiers (PPF) for Two Individuals in a Household

(a) If all of David's waking hours are spent in the labor force (point A), he will generate $160 of income per day. If all of his waking hours are spent doing household work (point B), he produces 32 units of household output. If he spends some time working and some time working around the house, he could produce some combination along the frontier, such as point C. However, David cannot at this time reach a combination that is outside of the frontier (point D). Nor will he want to allocate his time to generate an outcome that lies within his PPF (point E) because a better allocation of time will produce more $Q_H$ or $Q_C$, which would increase his household's well-being.

(b) If Heidi spends all of her available hours in the labor market, she will generate $192 per day in market consumption (point A'). If she spends all of her waking time producing household services (point B'), she will produce 24 units of output. If she dedicates some of her time to the labor market and some to producing household services, she can produce different combinations along her PPF, such as point C'. Like David, Heidi is unable to obtain a combination outside of the frontier (point D'), and it reduces the household's well-being for her to choose some combination inside the PPF (point E').

to produce more $Q_H$ or $Q_C$ that would place David on his PPF, thus increasing the household's well-being.

**Figure 2.4b** is Heidi's PPF. Her PPF indicates that if she spends all of her available hours in the labor market, she will generate $192 per day ($12 × 16 hours) in market purchases (point A'). If she spends all of her time producing household services (point B'), she will produce 24 units of output during her 16 waking hours each day. Like David, she can dedicate some of her time to the labor market and the rest to producing household services. Point C' is an example of this. At point C', Heidi spends 10 hours on household production. At this point, how many hours are left for her to earn money in the labor market to buy consumables? How much money will she earn?

The downward slope of David and Heidi's PPFs in Figure 2.4 reflects the trade-off between outputs. In fact, a PPF will always be downward sloping as long as acquiring more of one good requires a reduction in the other. We call this trade-off the **marginal rate of transformation (MRT)**. The MRT (which is the slope of the PPF) tells us how much of one output must be sacrificed in order to produce one more unit of the other output.

**MARGINAL RATE OF TRANSFORMATION (MRT)** The rate at which two outputs can be traded off for one another. The *opportunity cost* of producing one more unit of one good in terms of forgone units of the other good.

To better understand the MRT, let's take another look at our original example. David's MRT is dictated by his wage rate ($10 per hour) as well his efficiency in producing household services (30 minutes per unit). For David, gaining an additional unit of household services requires him to sacrifice one-half hour of wages. This means that his opportunity cost of 1 more unit of H in terms of forgone wages (and therefore C) is −$5. The negative sign reminds us that an increase in household services requires a reduction in work outside the home. Thus, David's MRT equals −$5. Following this same logic, we calculate that Heidi's MRT is −$8. She must sacrifice $8 worth of C (40 minutes worth of wages) for every additional unit of H she chooses to produce.

Because the PPFs in Figure 2.4 are drawn as straight lines, the slope doesn't change with different combinations of H and C. This also means that MRT is constant. This tells us that when David moves from point A to point C on his PPF, the opportunity cost of each additional unit of H in terms of forgone units of C doesn't change. In other words, each and every additional unit of household services will "cost" David $5 in forgone consumption. Conversely, each and every additional $5 of consumables will cost David 1 unit of forgone household services.

Even though the slope of the PPF is constant, it will change if the wage rate changes. An increase in Heidi's hourly wage will increase her opportunity cost of producing household services relative to producing consumables. If her wage rate doubles to $24 from the current $12 an hour, the opportunity cost of the 40 minutes she requires to perform 1 more unit of household services would increase to $16 per day ($24 × 0.66 hours).

What if wages fall? If a worker's wage is cut or his income tax rates rise, his net (take-home) wage falls. Consequently, his opportunity cost of producing one more unit of household services (H) in terms of forgone consumption (C) falls. This leads us to predict that a reduction in wage rates or higher income taxes can discourage labor-market activity, leading workers to favor household production.

Whenever a person's wage rate increases, his PPF becomes steeper, or more negatively sloped. In other words, the opportunity cost of household production increases compared with working outside the home. This explains why higher wages and more employment opportunities over the past fifty years have led to less in-home production. For women in the labor force, the time spent on household production fell from 18 to 12 hours a week between 1965 and 2003.[12]

The higher opportunity costs faced by women who work outside the home also helps explain the tremendous advance in substitutes for household production. The substitutes include market-based services, such as hired child care, take-out food, and laundry services. The higher opportunity costs women face also helps explain the increased demand for and purchase of labor-saving devices such as dishwashers, microwave ovens, dryers that steam out wrinkles in clothes, online banking services, and even automatic sprinkler systems. Innovations such as these reduce the amount of time that it takes to produce increasingly costly household services.

## When the MRT Is Not Constant

In our original example, both David and Heidi had constant marginal rates of transformation between working outside the home and producing household services. In other words, the trade-off between $Q_H$ and $Q_C$ didn't change as more of one was chosen. In contrast, if we are talking about a community's PPF—its production possibilities frontier with respect to food and drinking water—the slope of this PPF

· · · · · · ·

[12]Ibid.

might not be constant. Could the opportunity cost of producing one output—say, food—continue to increase as more and more of it is produced?

Recall that the principle of increasing marginal cost says that the opportunity cost of expanding a good's supply increases the more units of it we produce. The rationale is that we have to use more and more scarce resources to produce each additional unit of the good. We can illustrate this principle by contemplating the ways in which a community can supply water to its residents. The lowest cost source of water is rainwater captured by reservoirs. Groundwater is more costly to collect because of the need to locate and pump it to the surface. Seawater is probably the most expensive source of usable water because it is costly to desalinate. What the principle of increasing cost tells us is that expanding the supply of drinking water requires more and more resources— energy, capital equipment, labor, and "raw" water—that can no longer be used for the production of other outputs like food. Conversely, the more food we want to produce, the less water is available to the community to use as drinking water.

You may have seen news stories about the supply of drinking water for growing populations in the southwest United States: more and more food output has to be given up for the same incremental increase in supplies of drinking water. This scenario is currently being played out in California. Water diverted to farmers in the state's Central Valley is not available to people downstream for drinking water and other personal needs. For crop production to keep up with growing demand, more and more water is needed to irrigate less fertile and more arid land. Moreover, in recent years, many farmers have begun growing more water-intensive crops such as fruit. In terms of drinking water that can't be produced and consumed by the public, shifting production to these crops has increased the opportunity cost of growing food.[13]

When there are increasing costs of production, the PPF will be concave or bend outward from the juncture of the vertical and horizontal axes. The curved PPF in **Figure 2.5**

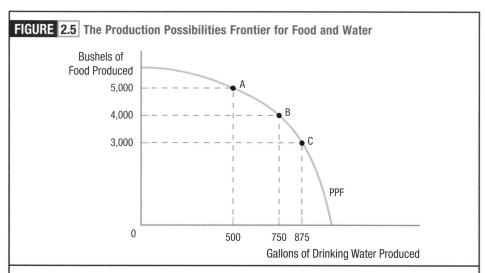

**FIGURE 2.5** The Production Possibilities Frontier for Food and Water

The curved PPF shows that the trade-off between using water to grow crops for food or as drinking water may not be constant. The same incremental reduction in food buys, or results in, less and less additional drinking water produced. In other words, producing water becomes more and more expensive in terms of forgone food production.

· · · · · · ·

[13]Felicity Barringer, "Rising Calls to Regulate California Ground Water." *New York Times*, May 13, 2009.

tells us that the trade-off between using water to grow crops for food and as drinking water is not constant. Specifically, the additional quantity of water we can produce every time we decrease our production of food by fixed amounts declines as we move from point A to point B to point C. This follows directly from the principle of increasing marginal cost. As we move down the food production (vertical) axis, the same incremental reduction in food production "buys us" less and less additional drinking water. In other words, the last unit of water produced becomes more and more expensive in terms of the forgone amount of food that can't be produced.

### Improving on One's PPF

Is there a way that individuals or communities can improve upon the trade-offs reflected by their PPFs? When a person like Heidi increases her education and gains marketable skills, she can increase her future wages. As shown in **Figure 2.6**, this will cause her future PPF to "rotate outward." Notice how increasing Heidi's knowledge can shift her future PPF to the line denoted as A′B. This means that she could potentially achieve a higher level of C for her household without having to give up any H.

Bundles such as C could not be attained in the future without making investments today that lead to the outward shift in Heidi's PPF. Similarly, investing in technological innovations today can improve future trade-offs. We have already seen this in the example of time-saving household innovations that permit people to produce the same level of H and increase their time in the labor market, thereby increasing C. When a community invests in technological innovations, such as a desalinization plant or water-conserving agricultural processes, it can improve on its future trade-offs and push its PPF outward. In fact, investment in new machinery and in ourselves

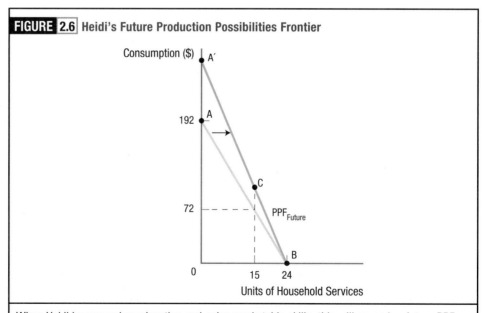

**FIGURE 2.6** Heidi's Future Production Possibilities Frontier

When Heidi increases her education and gains marketable skills, this will cause her future PPF to rotate outward. It will shift from AB to A′B. On the higher PPF, she could potentially achieve a higher level of consumption without having to give up any units of household services. In other words, previously unattainable combinations become possible. The same is true not only for Heidi but also for economies.

(through education) are important factors in explaining why some nations grow faster than others. Technology, advances in education, and the increased availability of machinery are all factors that appear to increase the economic growth of countries.

Is there any way a household, community, or economy can improve on its PPF *today* without making human and physical investments? There is if people specialize in producing goods and services that they create the most efficiently. Specializing will allow the group to reach a higher level of well-being than individual PPFs allow. Let's now look at how this works.

## 2.6 Absolute Advantage, Comparative Advantage, and Specialization

Look back at the PPFs of David and Heidi in Figure 2.4. David can produce household services at the rate of 1 unit per 30 minutes compared with the 40 minutes it takes Heidi. As a result, David can produce more household services during his waking hours than Heidi. David has what economists call an **absolute advantage** when it comes to household production. He is simply able to produce more of $Q_H$ than Heidi in any given day. If David and Heidi were to spend every one of their waking hours in the labor market, David would generate $160 in consumables, and Heidi would generate $192. This indicates that Heidi has an absolute advantage when it comes to producing consumables. She can produce more $Q_C$ than her partner.

> **ABSOLUTE ADVANTAGE** The ability to produce more output than others, using the same amount of resources.

> **EXAMPLE** Dr. Johnson not only can perform open heart surgery better but also can type faster than anyone else in the office.

Is it possible for one partner to have an absolute advantage in *both* production activities? To answer this, suppose that David tested the labor market and found out that he could actually make $13 per hour by switching jobs. As a result, David would have an absolute advantage in producing *both* household services and consumables. He can produce 32 units of $Q_H$ if he spends all of his time in the household, or he can produce $208 of $Q_C$ ($13 $\times$ 16 hours) if he spends all of his time working outside the household.

If David has an absolute advantage in producing both H and C, then you might ask why David would keep Heidi around. The fact of the matter is that even if David has the absolute advantage in both production activities, he cannot spend all of his time producing household services and simultaneously earning income in the labor force. This is where Heidi comes in. Despite her lack of absolute advantage in either activity, she still has a scarce resource that can contribute to the well-being of the household: her time. It is therefore in the interest of the household as a whole for David and Heidi to jointly determine how to best allocate their time.

Let's assume that each partner engages in just one of the two activities and that a unit of C is just as valuable to the household's well-being as a unit of H. In such a situation, the well-being of the household will be maximized if both members allocate their time according to their **comparative advantage**.

> **COMPARATIVE ADVANTAGE** The ability to produce a particular good or service at a lower opportunity cost than other producers.

> **EXAMPLE** Even though Dr. Johnson can type the fastest, the opportunity cost of him spending time typing and not performing open heart surgery is greater for him than it was for anyone else in his office.

By using their PPFs, David and Heidi can determine which one has the comparative advantage in which activity. First, what is David's opportunity cost of producing one more unit of household services (H) at his new wage rate of $13 per hour? Because he will lose $6.50 worth of C (30 minutes of wages at $13 per hour) to gain an additional unit of H, the opportunity cost of H in terms of forgone C is −$6.50. What is the household's opportunity cost of having Heidi produce one more unit of H? To produce an additional unit of H, she will have to sacrifice $8 worth of C (40 minutes of wages at $12 per hour). In other words, the opportunity cost of Heidi producing an additional unit of H is −$8.

David has a lower opportunity cost when it comes to household production. David will generate $6.50 more in consumables if he reduces his production of H by 1 unit, whereas Heidi will earn the household $8 in consumables if she reduces her production of H by 1 unit. Because David's opportunity cost of household production is lower than Heidi's, we say that he has a comparative advantage when it comes to producing household services. Heidi has a comparative advantage when it comes to earning wages. Even though David has an absolute advantage in producing C, he benefits the household more by staying home and producing 36 units of household services. Heidi benefits the household most by going to work each day and producing $192 in consumables.

## Specialization

To maximize the well-being of the household, at least in terms of procuring H and C, David should concentrate his time on that activity for which he has a comparative advantage—household production. Heidi should use her time solely to earn income. Via **specialization**, the household's overall well-being is maximized.

> **SPECIALIZATION** Allocating a person's scarce resources to a limited range of productive activities based on her comparative advantage.

> **EXAMPLE** Household members often specialize in the types of services they each produce. One may take care of the garden, while another takes care of meal preparation, and still another does laundry.

To verify that specialization will increase a household's well-being, consider what would happen if David took a job and Heidi stayed home and produced household services. Although the household could now earn $208 and buy more C, it would end up with 24 units of H. Of course, if David and Heidi place relatively little value on household services, David might also enter the labor force on a part-time basis. Suppose Heidi devotes all of her time to work, generating $192 in C. David, because of his comparative advantage in producing H, could work in the home for 12 hours (producing 24 units of H) and 6 hours outside the home, producing $78 (= $13 × 6) of C. When combined, the household now gets $270 (= $192 + $78) of C and still enjoys 24 units of H. However, as we have just seen, the opportunity cost in terms of forgone household production would be substantial.

Do all households specialize their activities in the way we just described? Not necessarily. It depends on what the partners want and value. David might want work outside the home, even though the household is harmed from an economic standpoint. This doesn't make it a bad choice. It just means we would need to bring back into the discussion the individuals' preferences and marginal benefit and marginal cost considerations.

---

**ECONOMIC FALLACY**   As women's wage rates have risen relative to men's in the last half century, the amount of time working wives spend with their children relative to the amount of time their husbands do has fallen significantly.

**False.** Although research studies indicate that both men and women who work spend less time with their children, the amount of time that a working mother spends with her children is, for the most part, unaffected by the number of hours she works.[14] This implies that she reduces her leisure or household work hours in order to maintain her time with her children. Moreover, even when fathers spend more time at home with their children, the time commitment mothers make to their children does not appear to decline. The two parents simply spend more time together with their children. Thus, the *relative* burden of at-home care between mothers and fathers has not changed much.

---

Why is this the case? Mothers might have such a large comparative advantage when it comes to taking care of their families' children that fathers will assume other household production tasks such as cooking, cleaning, or doing laundry. In fact, one study estimated that from 1965 to 1993, working women reduced their household production time—outside of child care—by more than 12 hours per week.[15] Some of this decline can be explained by technological advances that have reduced the time required to perform many household services. By contrast, during the same time period, working males increased their household work by about 4 hours per week, primarily in the areas of food preparation and indoor chores.

## Specialization Leads to Prosperity

The story of David and Heidi leads us to an important generalization: when workers specialize in those activities for which they have a comparative advantage, the amount of output produced by the workers *as a group* is maximized. Why is this so? When workers specialize, they don't have to shift back and forth between tasks that are often unrelated. In addition, by focusing on just one task, they are more likely to discover new ways to improve their productivity. This, in turn, increases each worker's output (productivity), and this pushes the production possibilities frontier outward. In other words, the total "economic pie" grows larger through specialization because we each do what we do comparatively best.

The extent to which members of a household can specialize depends on how many of them there are and the number of productive activities available. For example, when there is only one adult in a household, she must produce both household services and earn income to buy consumables (assuming for now that she cannot buy H in the market). She can't specialize in one activity or the other. Now consider a primitive economy in which there is no outside market where people can buy and sell

·······

[14]See, for example, Daniel Hallberg and Anders Klevmarken, "Time for Children: A Study of Parent's Time Allocation." *Journal of Population Economics*, 16, no. 2 (2003): 205–226.

[15]Mark Agiar and Erik Hurst, "Measuring Trends in Leisure: The Allocation of Time over Five Decades." Federal Reserve Bank of San Francisco, February, 2006.

consumables. Everything must be produced within the household. In this situation, everyone engages only in producing H, although we might expect specialization to eventually arise within the household itself.

### The Division of Labor

So far we have discussed specialization as it relates to people choosing different production activities based on their comparative advantage. The idea of specialization, based on comparative advantage, also helps explain why some of us become NBA players, whereas others of us become economists or pastry chefs. We can extend the concept of specialization to the way in which the production of a single good or service is organized. **Division of labor** occurs when workers are responsible for specific subtasks that must be done to produce the good or service.

> **DIVISION OF LABOR** The concentration of a worker's full work effort on a subtask that contributes to the production of a specific good or service.

> **EXAMPLE** Along an automobile assembly line, some employees are responsible for installing windshields, whereas others work on installing engine blocks.

> **EXAMPLE** In most restaurants, the chef does not also bus tables; busboys or servers are responsible for cleaning and setting tables.

Assigning workers to specific subtasks permits them to develop task-specific skills, find ways to improve their efficiency, and gain a comparative advantage in a particular subtask. The goal is to generate a greater amount of output than if each worker were responsible for producing a good from start to finish.

## 2.7 Specialization, the Division of Labor, and Exchange

Suppose David and Heidi each specialize in the production of H and C, respectively. As long as both partners value H and C, if each of them consumes only the good they produce, then their individual well-being will not be maximized. However, by exchanging H and C with one another, David and Heidi can increase the well-being of each individual and of the household. Think about what would happen if you were stranded alone on an island. You would have to produce each and every good that you ultimately consumed. By contrast, if you were one of a group of people stranded on the island, you could allocate tasks according to each person's comparative advantage. One person could gather firewood, another could make fishing nets, and a third person could use the nets to catch fish. This would result in a greater number and volume of goods to share among the entire group—as long as members of the group engage in trade.

The greater the differences in the comparative advantage of trading partners, the greater the gains from trading with one another. Think, for example, about a household member who does not drive, and her partner who cannot vacuum because he has a dust allergy. They would clearly increase each other's well-being by specializing and trading services. The same holds for a partner who is handy at home repairs but burns even the toast and her partner who is a gourmet cook.

Over time, the gains from trade can change because people's comparative advantages can change. For example, if Heidi is laid off from her job, her next best wage offer might lead her and David to switch roles. He might discontinue household production and go into the labor force. She might begin providing household services.

Or greater job opportunities might coax both partners to enter the labor force and purchase some household services.

It is straightforward to extend our analysis of comparative advantage and specialization in the household to the global economy. Suppose, for example, that the United States can produce both lumber and industrial lasers more cheaply than Canada. In other words, the United States has an absolute advantage in producing both goods. Nevertheless, there is an opportunity cost of using scarce labor, machinery, fuel, and so forth to harvest trees rather than produce lasers. Even a country as large and as well-endowed as the United States faces scarcity, which means that it (the people and firms that make up the economy) can't produce everything for which it holds an absolute advantage.

If the United States has the comparative advantage in producing industrial lasers, and Canada has the comparative advantage in producing lumber, then it would make sense for the United States to produce lasers and for Canada to produce lumber. Specializing will maximize the global output of lasers and lumber available for the two nations to trade. Assuming that there is no coercion, each is likely to end up with more of each good than if they tried to produce both goods independently. Whether we are talking about households or nations, significant specialization simply won't occur unless trading opportunities exist. Canada won't specialize in producing lumber if the United States won't trade at least some of its lasers with Canada.

**ECONOMIC FALLACY**   The fact that China has become the primary supplier of steel to the United States reflects its comparative advantage in steel production.

**Uncertain.** China's large and relatively uneducated population has made the country's opportunity cost of producing labor-intensive outputs such as steel low compared to the United States. However, other factors have also led to the emergence of China as a powerhouse in the global steel marketplace. For example, the Chinese government owns 100 percent of eight of its top-ten steel producers and holds a majority ownership share in many of the remaining Chinese steel producers. In this ownership role, the government has heavily subsidized its steel producers. This distorts the true opportunity cost of China's steel producers and the comparative advantage they have relative to U.S. steel producers.

## 2.8 Prices: Signals of Opportunity Cost in the Market

Economists pay a lot of attention (some say too much) to market-based prices. Why do they do this? Because prices are a good signal of what the opportunity cost of making trades are. The money you spend on a rare comic book is money that is no longer available to purchase what you perceive as your next best opportunity—say, five new video games. The price of the rare comic book and the fact that you are willing to spend your limited income on it says that the net benefit *you* get from it is greater than the net benefit you would get from the five video games. The price of a good and your willingness to actually pay it tells us a lot about the personal satisfaction you expect to get from making one purchase instead of another.

Prices also are related to specialization and exchange. Specialization leads to an increase in total output and lower prices: the more there is of some good, given the demand for it, the lower its price tends to be. This is common sense, although we will spend the next two chapters proving why it occurs. It also reflects an important economic principle: when people specialize (realize their comparative advantages), more goods and services will be produced more efficiently and traded. The prices at which those trades take place are the outward reflections of economic principles at work.

## WHAT YOU SHOULD HAVE LEARNED FROM CHAPTER 2

- That for each choice an individual makes, there is an opportunity cost in terms of forgone alternatives. The opportunity cost of a decision is the well-being forgone from the next highest-valued alternative.

- That economic costs and benefits include monetary and nonmonetary considerations, such as time given up, forgone leisure activities, and lost wages.

- That because information is itself scarce, individuals must make decisions in a world of imperfect information. They may make mistakes (choices that don't maximize their sense of well-being) and adjust their choices as they gain more information.

- That to maximize well-being in the face of scarcity, people must allocate their resources in a manner consistent with marginal analysis. As far as economists are concerned, however, they need only act as if they have examined the marginal trade-offs they face.

- That each additional unit of consumption yields a positive but declining amount of well-being (diminishing marginal benefit) and comes at an increasing opportunity cost (increasing marginal cost).

- That sunk costs are irrelevant to one's current decisions.

- That habits can be an information-economizing approach to making repetitive decisions.

- That the cost of switching brands, products, or providers can be enough to discourage breaking a habit.

- That trades may not take place because the transactions costs are greater than the net benefit received from the exchange.

- That the production possibility frontier (PPF) reflects the maximum combination of outputs that can be produced from a given amount of a scarce resource. The slope of the PPF measures the rate at which one output can be traded off for another and is called the marginal rate of transformation (MRT).

- That if a person's opportunity cost of producing an output is lower than the opportunity cost of her trading partners, then she has the comparative advantage.

- That specialization and trade allow each person's comparative advantage to be exploited to maximize the total amount of output that can be generated for a given amount of scarce resources.

## KEY TERMS

Preferences, p. 32

Opportunity cost, p. 32

Explicit cost, p. 33

Implicit cost, p. 33

Accounting costs, p. 35

Accounting profit, p. 35

Economic profit, p. 35

Sunk cost, p. 36

Transactions costs, p. 37

Switching costs, p. 38

Marginal analysis, p. 40

Marginal benefit, p. 40

Marginal cost, p. 40

Indifference, p. 42

Diminishing marginal benefit, p. 44

Principle of increasing marginal cost, p. 45

Marginal benefit curve, p. 45

Marginal cost curve, p. 45

Production possibilities frontier, p. 50

Marginal rate of transformation, p. 51

Absolute advantage, p. 55

Comparative advantage, p. 55

Specialization, p. 56

Division of labor, p. 58

## QUESTIONS AND PROBLEMS

1. Use marginal benefit and marginal cost curves to show the impact of the following conditions as they relate to the number of children parents decide to have:
   a) Children are required to go to school until age 16.
   b) Parents are required to pay for their children's college education.
   c) Children are required to support their elderly parents.
   d) Parents are promised job security if they take off for extended (unpaid) maternity leave.
   e) Parents are no longer required to pay Social Security taxes for household employees, including babysitters.

2. Opponents of disposable water bottles argue that these products are detrimental to the environment. Use marginal benefit and marginal cost curves to show the impact on the quantity of bottles consumed if the government:
   a) imposes a tax on disposable water bottles.
   b) provides a subsidy for using refillable bottles instead of disposable bottles.
   c) bans disposable bottles all together.

3. Blockbuster has a sales promotion in which for $24.99 per month you can have two DVDs in your possession at all times and can exchange them for other DVDs at any time during the month. Alternatively, you can rent each video for $3.99 for a two-day rental.
   a) Does the marginal cost of a DVD rental vary, depending on the rental plan?
   b) What is this marginal cost?
   c) Will people watch DVDs constantly if they opt for the monthly rental plan? Why or why not?

4. Cellular telephone companies often give away telephones to their subscribers. Does this mean that the *economic cost* of these telephones is zero? Why or why not?

5. Use marginal benefit and marginal cost curves to show that you can reduce population growth in less-developed countries by:
   a) educating women and giving them greater employment opportunities.
   b) prohibiting the employment of children under a certain age.
   c) Do you think that parents would prefer one of these policies to the other? Explain.

6. It is often said that higher education does better—in terms of enrollments—during bad economic times and worse during good economic times. Can you substantiate this prediction using marginal benefit and marginal cost curves? (Hint: Think about the opportunity cost of attending college.)

7. Water companies have a variety of ways to get consumers to reduce water use during droughts. One way is to increase the price of water. Another way is to prohibit consumers from watering their lawns. Which approach do you think is preferable from a consumer's perspective? Why? Explain.

8. Using separate marginal benefit and marginal cost curves for each group, explain why people tend to play less golf in their thirties and forties than when they are retired.

9. Some retailers offer a discount when people buy more of a particular product— for example, buy one medium pizza for $7.95 or three medium pizzas for $5 each.

    a) How would you reconcile this pricing practice with the principle of increasing cost?

    b) Why would anyone just buy one pizza? Explain.

10. Visit the Automobile Association of America (AAA) Web site to find out what a TripTik is. Then, using marginal benefit and marginal cost curves:

    a) predict how the number of TripTiks travel itineraries prepared by the AAA for its members changes as Internet mapping technologies such as MapQuest become increasingly accessible at low cost.

    b) What do you think happens to membership in AAA? Explain.

11. Using marginal benefit and marginal cost curves, show what happened to people's consumption of liquor when Prohibition—the federal government's ban on liquor production and distribution, which was intended to reduce consumption—was repealed.

12. Currently it is illegal for people to sell their kidneys to people who require a transplant. An argument in favor of legalizing trade in kidneys is that it would increase the supply and substantially reduce the amount of time someone has to wait for a transplant. Is there an *economic* (not moral) argument against making trade in kidneys legal? Explain your answer.

13. Using marginal benefit and marginal cost curves, show how a teenager's decision to have one or more children is affected when:

    a) she is paid $100 per month to remain in school and not become pregnant.

    b) she is paid $100 per month in food stamps for each child she has.

14. Suppose that people volunteer to staff a town's local fire department. Should the value of their time be included in calculating the cost of providing fire protection to the town? Explain your answer.

15. Identify three habits in your daily life that you think are information economizing. Is there any other reason why habits form and persist over time? Explain your answer.

16. Suppose that you are shopping for a new digital camera and can buy it online or in an electronics store such as Best Buy. Explain the benefits and costs that would contribute to your decision of where to buy the camera (assume that the price of the camera itself is the same for both online and box store vendors).

17. Mr. Teeples recently received a letter notifying him that his credit card company was changing from a fixed interest rate for unpaid balances to a variable interest rate. He calculates that he will pay an additional $580 per year under the new terms.

    a) What types of switching costs might he incur if he switched to another credit card provider?

    b) How much should Mr. Teeples be willing to spend in switching costs to find a credit card provider that offers the original terms he had?

    c) How do credit card companies reduce switching costs to attract new cardholders and their unpaid balances?

18. Your sister, who is currently a junior in college, has completed all but a few requirements to earn a degree in accounting. Suppose she calls you and tells you that she is taking her first economics course and is surprised to discover a passion and a talent for the subject. As a result, she is considering switching her major to economics.

    a) What costs would factor into her decision about whether or not to make the change?

    b) How would you advise her to respond when your parents tell her "Look at all the time and money you've already spent on your accounting courses"?

19. AJ and JJ have moved in together, and they must decide who will take care of their eight-month-old child (household services ($Q_H$) and who will go to work to increase the household's consumable goods ($Q_C$). Suppose their production possibilities frontiers (PPFs) are as follows. (Assume their nonsleeping hours are spent either working or taking care of the child.)

| AJ | | | | | |
|---|---|---|---|---|---|
| Net wages per day ($) | 140 | 100 | 50 | 20 | 0 |
| Child-care hours per day | 0 | 4 | 9 | 12 | 14 |
| JJ | | | | | |
| Net wages per day ($) | 204 | 156 | 96 | 60 | 0 |
| Child care hours per day | 0 | 4 | 9 | 12 | 17 |

a) Who has the absolute advantage in terms of producing $Q_C$?
b) Who has the absolute advantage in terms of providing child care?
c) Who has the comparative advantage in terms of providing child care?
d) Who will go to work and who will stay home?
e) What is AJ's hourly wage rate? How about JJ's hourly wage rate?
f) What is the maximum amount of consumables (in dollars) this family can achieve given AJ and JJ's PPFs?

20. Courts often have to estimate the value of nonmarket production. This occurs, for example, when a homemaker is severely disabled or killed by a negligent driver. We call this estimate the *imputed value* of the homemaker's future forgone services. Indicate whether you think this imputed value would increase, decrease, or remain unchanged depending on:

a) the number of minor children in the homemaker's home.
b) the age of the homemaker.
c) the educational level of the homemaker.
d) the age of the homemaker's youngest child.

21. Use a PPF like that in Figure 2.5 and illustrate how it will change if California:

a) invests some of its current resources in plant research and development.
b) discovers a low-cost way to extract salt from seawater.
c) decreases the number of immigrant workers it permits to work in farming.
d) wins a court case that gives the state a larger entitlement to water from the Rio Grande River.

22. Because the state of Georgia is suffering from an unprecedented drought, it is considering filing suit to challenge the location of its border with Tennessee. Relocating the border would give Georgia control over the water flow of the Tennessee River. If Georgia is successful in its challenge, what will the impact on its PPF be? What about Tennessee's PPF? (Both Georgia and Tennessee produce goods *X* and *Y*. Good *X* depends on the availability of water from the Tennessee River.)

23. Using the concept of comparative advantage, explain why the United States is:

a) an exporter of computer technology.
b) an importer of clothing.
c) an exporter of wheat.
d) an importer of oil.

24. George Stigler, a Nobel Laureate in economics, once wrote that the division of labor is limited by the size of a market. Explain the meaning of Stigler's assertion.

25. European companies have invested heavily in manufacturing technologies in order to create or preserve their comparative advantage in the production of such things as turbines (Nelson Schwartz, "In a Recession, Europe's Focus on Saving

Jobs Pays Off." *New York Times*, February 4, 2010, p. B1). In contrast, U.S. companies have exploited the comparative advantage of foreign production by closing older, uncompetitive manufacturing plants located in the United States in favor of newer plants located abroad and outsourcing jobs to countries with lower labor costs. Discuss the relative merits of the European versus United States approach to global competition in terms of maximizing the country's well-being:

a) in the short run.
b) in the long run.

# 3

# The Demand for and Supply of Economic Goods

*"Teach a parrot the terms 'supply and demand' and you've got an economist."*

Thomas Carlyle, historian

So far we have looked at how to apply our model of economic decision making to the types of everyday situations we all face. We have also gotten quite far in our ability to make predictions about people's choices using the marginal benefit and marginal cost framework. We have been focusing on factors that affect the willingness of people to pay for a particular good. Unfortunately, just because people are willing and able to pay for certain quantities of a good doesn't necessarily mean the goods will be available to them. For an exchange to take place, there must be suppliers who are willing and able to trade the goods they produce for prices equal to or less than what buyers are willing to pay. The bottom line is that suppliers behave just like anyone else: they attempt to maximize the net benefit they get from the scarce resources under their control.

In this chapter, we explore the choices suppliers face when they decide how to allocate their resources. We also explore how the prices of goods act as a signal between consumers and producers. On the consumer's side, prices are related to the marginal benefits that buyers believe they will realize. On the producer's side, prices are related to the underlying costs of producing the good, to the marginal costs of production. When you've finished this chapter, you will see that prices don't just happen. Prices in a market reflect the interplay between consumers and producers. Even in large, nationwide markets, such as the market for agricultural products or home mortgages, prices are determined through the interactions of these underlying market forces. The forces of demand and supply, the focus of this chapter, work together to find a price that in turn allocates products, whether the product is a pair of shoes, a heart transplant, or a college education.

## 3.1 The Willingness to Pay as the Basis of Demand

People often enjoy different levels of well-being from the same economic goods. This occurs because they have different preferences and face different alternatives. There is no reason to believe that you and your parents will get the same economic benefit from attending the symphony or the latest Black Eyed Peas concert. Because of these differences, even when two people have the same incomes, they may be unwilling to pay the same amount for a particular good. Put another way, their **willingness to pay** for the good may differ.

> **WILLINGNESS TO PAY** The maximum amount of money a person is willing to pay for a good.

> **EXAMPLE** A person who has a 3-acre yard is likely to be willing to pay more for a John Deere riding lawnmower than a person who lives in an apartment in New York City.

> **EXAMPLE** Meat eaters are willing to pay substantially more for McDonald's Quarter Pounders than vegetarians.

Economists sometimes call your willingness to pay for a good your *reservation price*. If the market price of a good is higher than your reservation price, then you will walk away without buying the good. What determines a person's willingness to pay for a good? If no other costs are related to the purchase of a good, then a person's reservation price would equal the monetary value she places on the benefits she receives from the good.

If, in fact, the market price exactly equals this reservation price, then the net benefit the consumer receives (value of benefits − market price) is equal to zero. She would be indifferent as to whether she buys the good or not. If the market price is greater than the consumer's reservation price, then the net benefit resulting from buying the good is negative and she would not purchase it.

A number of studies have measured people's willingness to pay for a variety of goods and services. Recently, researchers estimated the amount people would pay to protect their children and grandchildren from the effects of global warming. Researchers asked them how much more they would be willing to pay on their electricity bills each month to cover the costs of significantly reducing greenhouse gases, which have been linked to climate change. Although the answers varied widely, a majority of respondents became indifferent to addressing the problem of global warming when the cost to them exceeded $18.75 per month.[1]

Keep in mind that when economists talk about willingness to pay, they also mean that a person must not only be willing but also able to pay for the good or service desired. Although you might place a high value on the benefits of owning a Porsche Boxster, your willingness to pay from an economic standpoint equals the amount you can actually hand over for the car. The fact that our ability to pay often falls short of what we want explains why sellers frequently help buyers purchase big-ticket items such as homes and cars by offering financing plans.

· · · · · · ·

[1]"The Indifference Point on Global Warming." *St. Louis Post-Dispatch*, June 30, 2009.

## Diminishing Marginal Benefit and the Willingness to Pay

An interesting question to ask is whether a person's willingness to pay for the first unit of a good differs from his willingness to pay for the second unit of the same good. What about his willingness to pay for the third unit of the good? Recall that the principle of diminishing marginal benefit says that the marginal benefit a person gets from the first unit of a good is greater than from the second unit, which is greater than the benefit enjoyed from the third unit, and so on. Consequently, it would make sense that a person's willingness to pay declines as he acquires more and more of a good. Another way to put this is that a person's **marginal willingness to pay** declines with each additional unit he or she consumes.

> **MARGINAL WILLINGNESS TO PAY** The reservation price a consumer is willing to pay for each incremental unit of a good.

> **EXAMPLE** You might be willing to pay $9 to see a long-awaited movie at your local theater but only an additional $5 to sit through a second feature.

> **EXAMPLE** On a hot summer day, you might be willing to pay $4.25 for a 32-ounce soft drink at the ball game but only $1 for a refill.

In **Figure 3.1**, we graphically show an individual's willingness to pay street vendors for the first, second, fourth, or sixth hot dog purchased during a weekend visit to New York City. The vertical axis represents the person's willingness to pay—their reservation price—for each and every hot dog.

Notice that there is an inverse relationship between the reservation price for each hot dog and the total number of hot dogs sold; that is, what the tourist is willing to pay for an additional hot dog is less than what she is willing to pay for the previous

---

**FIGURE 3.1** An Individual's Willingness to Pay for Hot Dogs

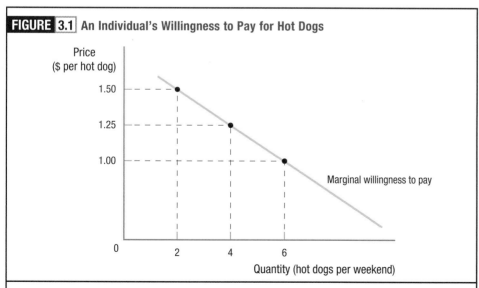

The vertical axis in this figure represents an individual's willingness to pay for hot dogs. Notice there is an inverse, or negative, relationship between the price the individual is willing to pay for each additional hot dog and the number of hot dogs. This is because the buyer's marginal benefit diminishes with each additional hot dog consumed.

one. This is why the graph shown in Figure 3.1 is downward sloping. The principle of diminishing marginal benefit guarantees this result.

Let's say the tourist can buy as many hot dogs as she wants at $1.25, which is the going price charged by street vendors. At this price, we see that she will buy a total of four hot dogs during her weekend visit. How do we know this? Because her reservation price for each of the first three hot dogs is higher than $1.25, the price that she must actually pay for them. For example, her reservation price for the second hot dog is $1.50, but that is not the price being charged by the vendor. When it comes to the fourth hot dog, however, her reservation price of $1.25 is just equal to the price that she must pay, which means that she will be *indifferent* as to whether she purchases the fourth hot dog or not. In other words, the fourth hot dog does not yield an additional *net* benefit: the value of the benefits enjoyed from the fourth hot dog just equals the economic cost of purchasing the fourth hot dog. Beyond the fourth hot dog, her reservation price for additional hot dogs is less than $1.25, so she is not willing to buy more.

We can generalize this result: as long as a person's willingness to pay for an additional unit of a good is higher than the market price, she will purchase this unit because the buyer receives a net benefit from purchasing the good. In contrast, if her reservation price is less than the market price of the additional unit, the net benefit she would receive is negative, and she will not make the purchase. To see this, consider what would happen if the price of hot dogs dropped from $1.25 to $1. We see in Figure 3.1 that the tourist will purchase two additional hot dogs over the weekend—for a total of six during her NYC visit—because her reservation price (what she is willing to pay) for the fifth hot dog is greater than $1 and just equal to $1 for the sixth hot dog. Now she is indifferent about the sixth hot dog.

So far we have assumed that the only cost a buyer incurs when making a purchase is the price. However, as you have learned, buyers often incur other costs during the purchasing process, such as the cost of looking for information about goods. A buyer will be *indifferent* to purchasing a good when his reservation price *plus* all of his other transactions costs just equals the total benefit he thinks he will get from owning the good. The buyer will be unwilling to offer a higher reservation price because his net benefit will then be negative. This suggests that there is a trade-off between a person's reservation price and the other costs incurred in making a trade.

In fact, you can see this trade-off reflected in people's everyday decisions. Think of how many people you know who purchase bottles of soda from on-campus machines at a far higher price than if they were purchased at the supermarket. Does this behavior make economic sense? Because on-campus machines are convenient and readily accessible between classes, they eliminate the driving and time costs incurred to shop off-campus. Your friends who make this choice reveal that they have a higher reservation price—which includes a "vending machine premium"—for "convenience." In other words, people will pay more for a good if they can reduce their other purchase costs (in this case, the time required to drive to the supermarket, park the car, stand in the checkout line, find a new parking spot on campus, and so on). For the same reason many people—especially those who place a high value on their time—are willing to pay higher fees to buy concert tickets online rather than stand in line at box-office windows or redialing Ticketmaster for hours on end. What we are saying is what most people already know—that convenience comes at a price.

## 3.2 Deriving an Individual's Demand Curve

Our hot dog example can be extended to other goods and services. But do we really expect that everyone gets out their calculators or fires a special app on their iPhones before buying lunch or a candy bar? Of course not. The idea is that using a sort of internal calculator, all of us act *as if* we are comparing our willingness to pay to the prices we face.

Based on the relationship between a person's willingness to pay and the price of a good, we can directly link that price to the quantity she will **demand** during any given time period (day, week, month).

**DEMAND** The quantity of a good a person is willing and able to purchase at any given price during a specified time period (day, week, month, and so forth), *all other factors held constant.*

**EXAMPLE** At a price of $1,200 per three-credit-hour course, Janet is willing and able to pay to enroll in two classes a semester. At a price of $900, she is willing and able to pay to enroll in three classes a semester.

We can represent a person's demand for a good by using a **demand schedule**.

**DEMAND SCHEDULE** A table that shows the price of a good and the number of units a buyer is willing to purchase at that price during a specific time period.

**Table 3.1** shows Janet's demand schedule for college courses in a semester. Notice that as the price of a course decreases, Janet is willing to pay for more classes. This follows from her marginal willingness to pay for each course, which is diminishing. The price of the courses must fall to entice Janet to purchase more of them. Conversely, if the price of a course rises, say from $600 to $900, Janet will reduce the number of courses she takes each semester from four to three because her marginal willingness to pay for the fourth course is less than $900.

**Figure 3.2** is a graph of the data in Table 3.1. By convention, the price ($P$) at which the good is sold is plotted on the vertical axis, and the number of units, or quantity demanded, is plotted on the horizontal axis. The points, or dots, shown are the four price–quantity demanded pairs taken from Table 3.1. However, instead of just showing Janet's demand relation as these distinct points, we can connect the

**Table 3.1   Janet's Demand Schedule for College Courses**

| Price per Course ($) | Quantity of Courses Demanded per Semester |
|---|---|
| 1,500 | 1 |
| 1,200 | 2 |
| 900 | 3 |
| 600 | 4 |

The demand schedule for college courses per semester in this table indicates that as the price of each course decreases, Janet is willing to buy more classes. Conversely, if the price of a course rises, the number of courses Janet purchases each semester decreases.

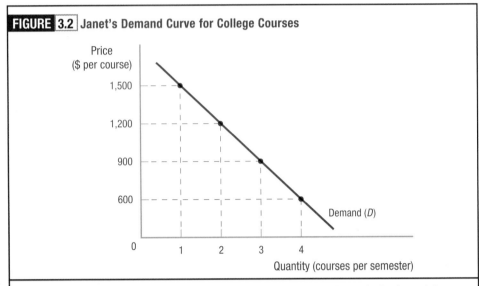

**FIGURE 3.2** Janet's Demand Curve for College Courses

By convention, the price (*P*) at which the good is sold is plotted on the vertical axis, and the number of units, or quantity demanded, is plotted on the horizontal axis. The points shown are the four representative price–quantity demanded pairs based on the data in Table 3.1. Instead of just showing the demand relation as these distinct points, we connect the points into a line that illustrates all possible price–quantity pairs. Even if drawn as a straight line, economists call this a demand curve.

points into a line. This is what economists call a **demand curve**. The demand curve (which from here on, we label simply as *D*) allows us to consider many more price–quantity combinations than those in a demand schedule like that in Table 3.1.

**DEMAND CURVE** A graphic representation of an individual's demand schedule. The demand curve plots all of the price–quantity combinations an individual is willing to accept.

Even though the graph is called a demand *curve*, it is often depicted as a straight line for convenience. The actual shape of a person's demand curve depends on how he responds to price changes in terms of the quantity he buys. Regardless of its actual shape, a demand curve generally slopes downward because your willingness to pay for additional units declines because of the principle of diminishing marginal benefit. This means that when the price of a good goes down, you will buy more of it; when the price goes up, you will buy less of it. This inverse relation between price and quantity demanded is sometimes referred to as the **law of demand**.

**LAW OF DEMAND** The observation that when the price of a good rises (falls), the quantity demanded of it falls (rises). Changes in price and quantity demanded are inversely related.

**EXAMPLE** The price of lunch at your favorite café has doubled. As a consequence, you eat there fewer times a week.

**EXAMPLE** The local oil change business runs a campaign of three oil changes for the price of two. In response, you get your car's oil changed more often than before.

Before we get too far along, let's deal with two important aspects of a demand schedule and a demand curve. First is the italicized portion of our definition of demand: *all other factors held constant*. What "other factors" do we mean, and why aren't they allowed to change? When you are deciding whether to buy some item—say, a car—more than just the price of the car influences your decision. Included in that list of other factors is likely to be your income, the price of other goods, your expectations of the future, and more.

We impose the restriction that these other influences are unchanged when drawing a demand curve because we want to focus on the effects that only a change in price has on your decision to buy. By holding constant other factors that influence your purchasing decision, we can better understand the role prices play in your decision-making process. If other factors are not confounding the analysis, we can better predict the outcome of a change in prices. If we do not assume the other factors are fixed, then observed increases or decreases in purchases when prices rise or fall could be because of a change in several other factors. We will deal with these other factors later in this chapter. As you will see, our more complete discussion allows us to include not only price changes but also changes in these other factors to understand demand.

The second aspect of our definition is that demand has a time element associated with it. In Table 3.1, we explicitly stated that this is Janet's demand schedule for total courses *per semester*. What if we instead wanted to know about her demand for courses each academic year, which is comprised of two semesters? As long as nothing else has changed, we would multiply the semester quantity demanded at each price by 2, giving us a different set of quantities demanded for each price. What this means is that whenever we are talking about quantity demanded, we must recognize that it depends on the time period we stipulate.

Looking back to Figure 3.2, we see that if we read *up* to the demand curve from any quantity level on the horizontal axis, we get Janet's reservation price for the very last unit. For example, if we read up from the third course per semester, we find that Janet's reservation price, or marginal willingness to pay, for a third course is $900. If, instead, we read *over* to the demand curve from the vertical price axis at $900, we see the total quantity (three courses) that Janet is willing and able to purchase at that price. In other words, Janet will enroll in courses up to the point where her willingness to pay for an additional course just equals its price.

You have learned that even when two people have the same income, there is no reason to believe that they will have the same willingness to pay for a particular good. As a result, the demand curve for a good usually differs across individuals. For example, when it comes to new cars, a person who does not have a driver's license and earns only a small income is unlikely to purchase a car no matter what the price is. As a result, his demand curve probably looks a lot different from someone like talk-show host Jay Leno, who loves cars and can afford to purchase nearly as many as he wants.

Suppose we compare demand curves for child care for a household in which both adults work versus one in which only one adult works. The household's willingness to pay for each hour of child care is likely to be higher when both adults work. We can illustrate this in **Figure 3.3**. The vertical axis shows the price per hour for child care, and the horizontal axis shows the hours of child care demanded per week. The household that has a higher willingness to pay for each hour of child care will have a higher demand curve. Consequently, more child care will be purchased at each and every price by this household. For instance, if the price of child care is $20 per hour, Figure 3.3 shows that the household with the higher willingness to pay will demand

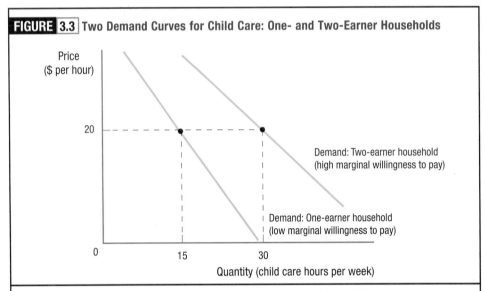

**FIGURE 3.3** Two Demand Curves for Child Care: One- and Two-Earner Households

Price
($ per hour)

20

Demand: Two-earner household
(high marginal willingness to pay)

Demand: One-earner household
(low marginal willingness to pay)

0       15        30

Quantity (child care hours per week)

We can compare the demand curves for child care for a household in which both adults work versus one in which only one adult works. The vertical axis shows the price per hour for child care. The horizontal axis shows the hours of child care demanded per week. The household with the higher willingness to pay for each hour of child care (the two-earner household) has the higher demand curve. Consequently, relatively more child care will be purchased by this household at each and every price.

30 hours of child care per week compared to 15 hours per week demanded by the household with the lower willingness to pay.

## 3.3 Distinguishing Shifts in the Demand Curve from Movements along the Curve

It is important for you to be able to distinguish *shifts* in a demand curve versus *movements along* it. (Here's a helpful hint: think of *shifts*—movements of the entire curve—and *slides*—moving along a given demand curve.) The demand curve for any good or service is drawn with price on the vertical axis and quantity demanded on the horizontal axis. This means that when we move from point-to-point *along* a demand curve, we are tracking how the quantity demanded changes as the good's price—*and only its price*—changes. **Figure 3.4** demonstrates this by showing how a person's quantity demanded for downloaded iTunes songs changes with the price of each download. When the price of each download changes—say, increasing from $1 to $1.50—we see that the quantity demanded decreases from 11 songs per week to 6. This is shown by moving from point A to point B on the demand curve: a change in price, all other factors held constant, leads to a change in the quantity demanded.

The effect of the price change, graphically speaking, is a move up or down the demand curve. Why doesn't the change in price lead to a shift in the demand curve? Because the buyer's marginal willingness to pay for each downloaded song has not changed—*only the price has changed*. In response to the price change, the buyer will purchase fewer downloads each week because his reservation price for each of the seventh through eleventh songs (which haven't changed) are less than the new price of $1.50 per downloaded song. The only change is the point on the demand curve

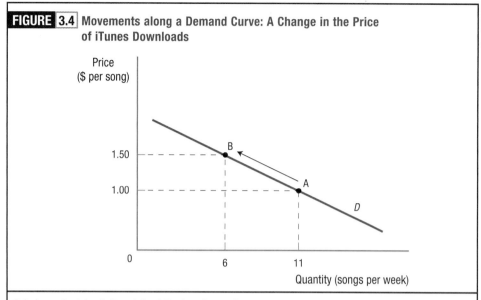

**FIGURE 3.4** Movements along a Demand Curve: A Change in the Price of iTunes Downloads

It is important to distinguish *shifts in* a demand curve versus *movements along* it. When we slide from point to point along a demand curve, this movement along the curve tracks how the quantity demanded changes as the good's price—and only its price—changes. This figure shows how the quantity demanded of downloaded iTunes songs changes with the price of each download. When the price of each download increases, the quantity demanded decreases. In other words, there is an inverse, or negative, relationship between the change in the price of downloads and the quantity demanded.

that a buyer has moved to; at this new point, the marginal willingness to pay for the last (sixth) song is just equal to the new price.

We say that movements along a demand curve show the effect of changes in a good's price on the quantity demanded of the good, assuming that nothing else changes. What will cause a demand curve to shift to a different position? If a change in the price causes movement along the curve, then something other than the good's price must change in order for the curve to shift. A shift in the demand curve reflects a change in the buyer's willingness to pay for each unit of the good compared to what he was willing to pay before.

Whether we are talking about movements along a demand curve or, as we will in a moment, shifts in the demand curve, realize that it often takes some time for people to change their purchasing habits. Consider what happens when the price of gasoline rises. In the short run, a person might not be able to reduce his gas consumption and move up his demand curve for gasoline (buy less of it) because he is limited by where he lives, works, and the type of car he owns. In the long run, however, he can relocate, change jobs, or trade in his car. These will cause him to change his gasoline-buying habits. Similarly, if one of the workers in a two-income household loses his job, it may take time for the household to reduce its demand for child care. For example, if the family has entered into a 12-month contract with its child-care provider, then the family's demand curve cannot actually shift during the contract period. Only over time, when the contract expires, is the household able to act on its new circumstances and purchase less child care at any given price, which is reflected in a shift (to the left) in its demand curve for child care.

## 3.4 What Factors Cause an Individual's Demand Curve to Shift?

Essentially, a demand curve is shifted by factors that are not included in the demand curve diagram—in other words, something other than a change in the price of the good. A number of variables can shift the demand curve for a product: changes in a person's income, changes in the price of related goods, and changes in the buyer's expectations and tastes. Although it is often ignored, changes in your ownership over your possessions—your property rights—also will affect your demand for those possessions. Next, we will look at each of these factors. We will assume that nothing else is changing, just the factor being considered. Although this might seem silly to you (aren't things changing all the time?), it will help us isolate the effect of one factor at a time.

### Change in Income

When someone's income changes, the person's willingness to pay for a good likely also changes. When your income increases, you are likely to spend some of it on goods that result in a smaller increase in your well-being ("splurges"). In contrast, if your income falls, you will tighten your belt and focus your scarce dollars on goods that generate the greatest amount of well-being.

How a change in income affects your demand for a good actually depends on the kind of good. Let's say that your income increases substantially. Instead of earning $15,000 a year working for a fast-food restaurant, you land a manager's job that pays $23,000 a year. If this happens, do you think you would continue to buy the very same things you did before? Would you continue to buy all of your clothes at a secondhand shop? Or would you start to shop at retail clothing stores and take in a few movies when they first open at the local movie theater? When people's incomes change—whether up or down—their buying habits also change. How these habits change depends on each individual's preferences for specific goods.

When increases in income raise the reservation price a person is willing to pay for a good, we say that it is a **normal good**.

> **NORMAL GOOD** A good that a person is willing to buy more of at each and every price as her income increases and less of as her income declines.
>
> **EXAMPLE** Eating out at a restaurant is a normal good.
>
> **EXAMPLE** Films shown at movie theaters are normal goods.

When a person's income increases, his demand for a normal good increases: his demand curve *shifts to the right*. This means that he is willing to purchase more of the good at every price. Demand decreases—the demand curve *shifts to the left*—when his income decreases. Let's illustrate this by looking at Dan's demand for tickets to Boston Red Sox baseball games as shown in **Figure 3.5**. At his initial level of income, say $10,000, his demand curve for Red Sox tickets is shown as $D_1$. At a price of $20 per ticket, Dan is willing to buy a ticket to 8 games. If Dan's income were to increase to $15,000, however, he would be willing to purchase more tickets, even though their price has not changed. We can show this by shifting his demand curve for Red Sox tickets to the right, assuming that Dan prefers seeing Red Sox games in person to watching them on TV. Red Sox tickets are a normal good for Dan. At a price of $20, Dan's demand for Red Sox tickets is $D_2$; at a price of $20, he is now

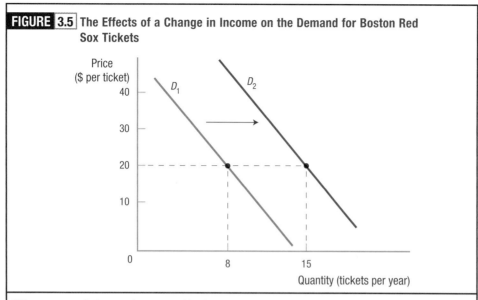

**FIGURE 3.5** The Effects of a Change in Income on the Demand for Boston Red Sox Tickets

When a person's income increases, his demand for a normal good increases. His demand curve shifts to the right. This is shown by the shift from $D_1$ to $D_2$. After the shift, he is willing to purchase more of the good at every price. In other words, at each price, the quantity of tickets he demands is greater, as shown by the increased number of tickets he purchases at $20.

willing to buy a ticket to 15 games. The shift in demand curve means that Dan's willingness to pay for the ninth ticket is now higher than the $20 price per ticket; the same now holds for the tenth through fourteenth tickets. At his initial level of income, Dan's willingness to pay for the eighth ticket just equals the ticket price; now this situation does not occur until the fifteenth ticket.

In some cases, when a person's income rises, the amount of a good she is willing to buy falls, even if its price doesn't change. In contrast, when the person's income falls, the amount of the good she is willing to buy rises, even if its price doesn't change. When this happens, we call the good an **inferior good**.

**INFERIOR GOOD** A good an individual is willing to buy less of at each and every price as her income increases and more of as her income declines.

**EXAMPLE** Secondhand clothing is an inferior good.

**EXAMPLE** Day-old bakery bread is an inferior good.

**EXAMPLE** "Staycations" (vacations spent at home) are inferior goods.

The relationship between a person's income and her demand for an inferior good is shown in **Figure 3.6**, which depicts Pam's demand for secondhand clothing. At her initial level of income, Pam's demand curve for secondhand clothes is represented by the curve $D_1$. If the price of a secondhand shirt is $5, Pam is willing to buy five shirts each month. Now suppose Pam's income increases. If Pam purchases fewer secondhand shirts after her income increased, then by her actions she considers them an inferior good. We can show this reaction in Figure 3.6 by the leftward shift in her demand curve (from $D_1$ to $D_2$) following her increase in income. What you see is that

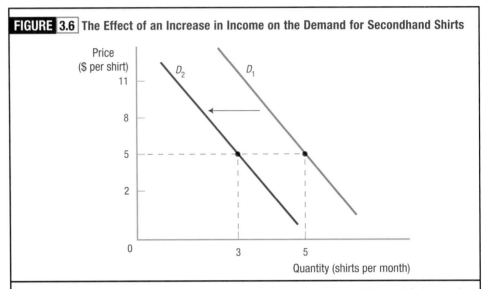

**FIGURE 3.6** The Effect of an Increase in Income on the Demand for Secondhand Shirts

This figure shows the relationship between a person's income and demand for an inferior good, in this case, secondhand clothing. At the person's initial level of income, her demand curve is represented by the curve $D_1$. If the individual's income increases, there is a leftward shift in the demand curve for this good, say to $D_2$. The leftward shift in demand means that at every price, the quantity she demands falls. As a rule, the demand curve for inferior goods shifts to the *left* when a person's income increases; it shifts to the *right* when the person's income falls.

at a price of $5, the number of secondhand shirts she is willing to buy each month drops to three. Again, it isn't necessary for Pam to state her beliefs about secondhand shirts being an inferior good: the change in her behavior reveals to the economist that secondhand shirts must be an inferior good in her mind. As a rule, the demand curve for an inferior good shifts to the *left* when a person's income increases. It shifts to the *right* when the person's income falls.

It is very important to understand that inferior goods are still economic "goods"— that is, they contribute positively to a person's sense of well-being. Moreover, the term *inferior* has nothing to do with the quality of a good. It is simply an economic term used to describe a person's preference for a good and how changes in his income will affect his demand for it.

People's perceptions about whether a good is inferior or not can also change over time. For many years, most people considered purebred puppies to be normal goods. Older and mixed-breed dogs were considered to be inferior. Over the past decade, however, these perceptions have changed. It has become an "in" thing to adopt animals rescued from the streets and puppy mills. The American Society for the Prevention of Cruelty to Animals, local media outlets, and programs on the cable station Animal Planet have all helped change people's perceptions about the benefits of adopting rescued dogs. The demand for mixed-breed dogs now increases with family income.

## The Prices of Related Goods

If the price of coffee falls, people are likely to buy more coffee (we are assuming it's a normal good). That's what the demand curve tells us: price changes and quantities purchased are inversely related. But the change in the price of one brand of coffee can affect the demand for another (that is, shift the demand curve). Suppose you consider coffee from the campus Coffee Bean to be just as good as coffee from the nearby Starbucks. Close substitutes are viewed as stand-ins for each other when it comes to the choices individuals make. If two goods are close substitutes, then small changes in the price of one can have a big impact on the demand for the other.

Two goods are substitutes if an increase in the price of one of them (say, Coffee Bean coffee) increases the demand for the other (Starbucks coffee). Conversely, a decrease in the price of one of the goods (Coffee Bean coffee) decreases the demand for the other (Starbucks coffee). This is how we will define **substitute goods**:

**SUBSTITUTE GOODS** Goods that are related in such a way that an increase in the price of one increases demand for the other; conversely, a decrease in the price of one decreases demand for the other.

**EXAMPLE** When tuition at a nearby private university rises, some students substitute classes there with classes at a local public university.

**EXAMPLE** When the price of Nike athletic shoes drops, some people substitute Nike shoes for Reeboks.

One way we can assess the degree of substitutability between two goods is by observing the amount by which one good's price must change before people begin to substitute the other good. For example, research shows that it takes a very dramatic increase in the price of gasoline before people will switch from driving their own cars to using mass transit. This would lead us to believe that cars and mass transit are "weak" substitutes for one another. However, when gas prices rise sharply, people are quite willing to substitute their gas-guzzling SUVs with fuel-efficient cars. This would lead us to believe that gas-guzzlers and fuel-efficient cars are "strong" substitutes for one another.[2]

To see the impact the price of a substitute can have on a good's demand curve, consider the following story. The price of adopting Russian-born babies fell with the demise of the Soviet Union in 1991. As the price of adopting foreign babies fell, U.S. couples moved *down* their existing demand curve for these children, as illustrated in **Figure 3.7a**. In other words, the decline in the price of adopting the children led to an increase in the quantity of Russian babies demanded. At the same time, the cost of adopting children born in the United States had not changed. Essentially, the price of adopting a child from the United States rose relative to the price of adopting a child from Russia. Many adopting parents viewed U.S.-born and Russian-born children as close substitutes, so the fall in the price for foreign-born babies resulted in a leftward shift in the demand curve for U.S.-born babies, as shown by the shift from $D_1$ to $D_2$ in **Figure 3.7b**. The quantity of U.S.-born babies demanded at each and every price declined because a close substitute had become relatively less expensive.

We can see the impact a change in a good's price has on the demand for a substitute by looking at government policies that affect international trade. You often hear people argue that cheap imported goods threaten jobs in U.S. industries. As a result, governments get pressured to introduce pricing policies that discourage their citizens from buying imported goods.

· · · · · · ·

[2]"One-Third of Consumers Looking at More Fuel-Efficient Cars." www.consumeraffairs.com, May 24, 2006. John Machacek, "Demand for Fuel-Efficient Cars Puts Pressure on Congress." *USA Today*, July 9, 2006.

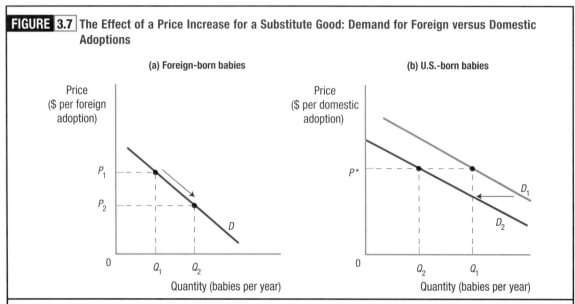

**FIGURE 3.7** The Effect of a Price Increase for a Substitute Good: Demand for Foreign versus Domestic Adoptions

When the price of substitutes changes, it affects the two markets differently. If the price to adopt a foreign-born baby falls, as shown in panel (a), more foreign-born babies will be adopted by U.S. parents. U.S. couples move *down* their existing demand curve for these children. If the price of adopting children born in the United States does not change, the price of adopting a child from the United States will rise relative to the price of adopting a child from Russia. If U.S.-born children and Russian-born children are considered as close substitutes, then the fall in the price of adopting foreign-born babies will result in a leftward shift (a decline) in the demand curve for U.S.-born babies, as shown in panel (b). In other words, the quantity of U.S.-born babies demanded by adopters at each and every price declines.

Suppose that you are willing to buy two pairs of jeans made in the United States each year at a price of $28. This is depicted in **Figure 3.8a**, which shows your demand curve for jeans manufactured in the United States. You are also willing and able to purchase four pairs of jeans made in China, which are selling for $22, as illustrated in **Figure 3.8b**.

If U.S.-made and foreign-made jeans are reasonably close substitutes, then a change in the price of foreign jeans will affect your demand for jeans manufactured in the United States, and vice versa. What if the U.S. government wants to stimulate purchases of U.S.-made clothing? One way to do this is to enact a policy that causes the price of foreign jeans to rise to $40. This price change decreases the quantity you demand of foreign-made jeans. As a result, you will move up your demand curve for foreign-made jeans, as Figure 3.8b shows. Meanwhile, because U.S.-made jeans are a close substitute, the price increase in the foreign jeans will cause the demand curve for U.S. jeans to shift from $D_1$ to $D_2$. Your willingness to pay for each pair of U.S. jeans increases because the opportunity to purchase foreign-made jeans has become more expensive.

Some goods are not viewed as substitutes for each other but as complements. By this we mean goods that go together. Examples include hot dog buns and hot dogs or shoelaces and shoes. **Complementary goods** are goods that are usually used in conjunction with one another.

**COMPLEMENTARY GOODS** Goods that are usually used in conjunction with one another.

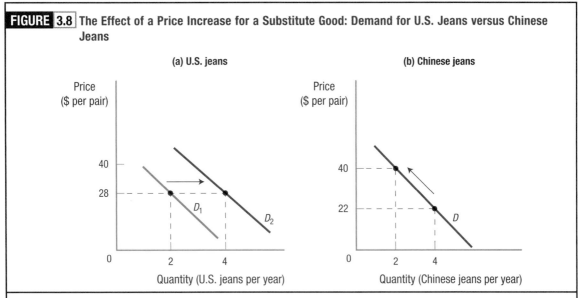

**FIGURE** **3.8** The Effect of a Price Increase for a Substitute Good: Demand for U.S. Jeans versus Chinese Jeans

If U.S.-made and Chinese-made jeans are considered close substitutes, a change in the price of jeans produced in China will affect the demand for jeans manufactured in the United States. If the price of Chinese jeans were made higher relative to U.S. jeans ($40 versus $28), then the quantity you demand per year of Chinese-made jeans will fall from four to two, as in panel (b). Because they are substitutes, the price increase in the foreign jeans will cause your demand curve for U.S. jeans to shift to the right from $D_1$ to $D_2$ in panel (a). At the price of $28, this increase in demand results in an increase in the quantity of jeans demanded. Your willingness to pay for each pair of U.S. jeans priced at $28 dollars increases because the opportunity to purchase foreign-made jeans has become more expensive.

**EXAMPLE** Cell phones and call-minute plans are complementary goods.

**EXAMPLE** iPods and iTunes are complementary goods.

**EXAMPLE** Hot dog buns and hot dogs are complementary goods.

You have probably noticed that some complementary goods are bundled together all the time. Others are bundled some of the time, and still others are never bundled together. Men's suits—which bundle jackets and trousers—are popular retail offerings. In contrast, separates tend to dominate women's clothing lines. Men's slacks rarely come with belts, although women's slacks often do.

What happens to the demand for a good when there is a change in the price of a complementary good? For example, how would a family's demand curve for calling minutes change if the price of cell phones dropped? **Figure 3.9** shows a family's demand curve for cell phones and for calling minutes. At an initial price of $89 per phone, the quantity of phones the family demands is two per year. When the price of phones drops—say, to $49—the quantity of cell phones demanded increases from two to four per year. In other words, the family moves down its demand curve for cell phones (**Figure 3.9a**). But what happens to the demand curve for calling minutes following the price change in phones? Because cell phones and calling minutes are complements, the decline in the price of cell phones causes the family's demand curve for calling minutes to shift to the right from $D_1$ to $D_2$ in **Figure 3.9b**. At the unchanged price of 10 cents per minute, the family is now willing and able to purchase 1,000 minutes per month instead of 500 minutes.

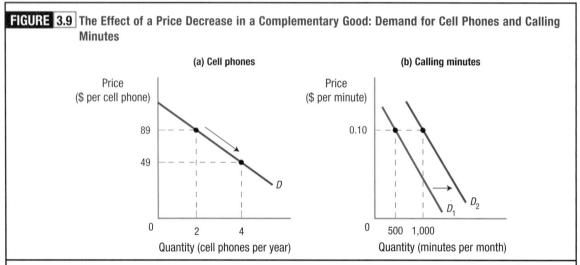

**FIGURE 3.9** The Effect of a Price Decrease in a Complementary Good: Demand for Cell Phones and Calling Minutes

When there is a change in the price of a complementary good, there are two effects. For example, when the price of cell phones drops as shown in panel (a), the quantity of cell phones demanded by a family increases. In other words, there is movement *down* the family's demand curve for cell phones. Cell phones and calling minutes are complements. The decline in the price of cell phones therefore causes the family's demand curve for calling minutes to shift to the right as shown in panel (b). This increase in the demand for calling minutes signals that buyers are willing to purchase more minutes per month at each and every price. (By contrast, if the price of cell phones increased, the quantity demanded of cell phones would fall, and the demand curve of calling minutes would shift to the left.)

Our example of cell phones and minutes suggests that goods that are strongly complementary are likely to be bundled and sold together. Many other complementary goods are bundled together as well, including cell phones and charger cords, and picture frames and glass. Because both goods are usually required if either is to be used, bundling them together serves as a convenience to buyers. More and more complementary goods are being bundled together all of the time. One possible explanation for the rise in the demand for bundled goods is that the opportunity cost of our time has increased. Rather than spend time doing our own bundling, we have welcomed the introduction of bundled goods.

Today's grocery shelves are full of complementary, or what are sometimes called bundled, goods. These include packages of crackers and cheese, premade sandwiches and salads, and the original bundled meal—frozen TV dinners. However, other bundled goods like laundry detergent that includes fabric softener and peanut butter and jelly blended in one jar have not fared as well. For bundled goods to succeed in the marketplace, consumers must get a net benefit from the bundling. Whether or not they do depends on whether the greater convenience outweighs the premium paid for the bundled good (that is, when compared to the prices of the unbundled goods).

## Changes in Expectations

On your way home from school, you hear on the radio that oil prices are expected to skyrocket because of a fire at a major refinery. In the newscast, the reporter mentions that when oil prices jump, gasoline prices are likely to follow. How do you react to the news?

You will be more likely to stop and buy gas at the current price because you expect the price to be higher tomorrow. Regardless of whether it actually happens, just the expectation of it happening will increase your demand. As a result, the demand curve for gas shifts to the right. Another example is how your buying behavior changes if you expect your income to rise in the future. If you anticipate an increase in your income, you might decide to buy more goods today—take out a home mortgage—on the expectation that your higher income tomorrow will enable you to pay for them later.

Changes in people's expectations can have big effects on demand. In the years prior to 2007, housing prices rose dramatically in many parts of the country. Many people bought homes simply because they expected that the price of them would continue to rapidly rise. "Flipping" homes—buying homes with the intent to sell them in a short time—became popular, especially in markets like California, Nevada, and Florida, where home prices were rising especially rapidly. Of course, when housing prices began to drop, such behavior looked foolish, especially to home buyers whose mortgages were now greater than the market value of their houses. Even if they wanted to flip them, they couldn't because the homes were worth less than they paid.

> **ECONOMIC FALLACY**   Although the price of gasoline declined after it hit $4 per gallon in 2008, sales of big SUVs haven't increased significantly, which means consumers' preferences have changed, and smaller cars are now considered preferable to larger gas-guzzlers.
>
> **False.** The fact that there has not been a significant movement back to large cars and SUVs with the fall in gasoline prices could indicate that people expect that gas prices will increase again in the future. In the 1970s when gas prices spiked, people did not return to buying large, low-gas-mileage cars for more than a decade after gas prices once again decreased. When they did, however, they did so in a big way: in the 1980s, sales of minivans rose dramatically. SUV sales jumped in the 1990s. In other words, although people's preferences for large vehicles probably haven't changed, their expectations of higher future gas prices have led to the decline in demand for gas-guzzlers.

## Changes in Tastes

There is an old saying: there is no accounting for taste. Put another way, what we like or dislike is an individual choice. Still, our tastes can be affected by external nudges, such as advertising, peer pressure, and so on. Changes in age also affect taste. Although your parents might have enjoyed loud and boisterous rock concerts when they were your age, today a quiet night in front of the television may be more to their liking.

Changes in people's taste will affect the demand for a good or service. In your parents' case, their demand for rock-concert tickets is probably lower than it was 25 years ago (their demand curves have shifted to the left). How do we know? Because they purchase fewer (if any) concert tickets at the same set of prices. Another example is fads. When the fad strikes, whether it is demand for Pet Rocks or Zhu Zhu Pets, we see shortages occur.

## Changes in Property Rights

What we own, whether our labor or our physical property, is determined partly by the rights that society's laws and institutions give us. We refer to these rights as **property rights**.

**PROPERTY RIGHT** The legal or social right to use a scarce resource in a particular way.

EXAMPLE You have property rights over your own labor, allowing you to sell it to whichever employer you wish.

EXAMPLE When you purchase your textbook, you have property rights over its use. Others in class may not take it from you.

EXAMPLE When entering a busy highway, you are supposed to yield the right of way because existing traffic has property rights over the lane.

Changes in property rights affect what a person is willing to pay. For example, in order to reduce automobile emissions and encourage people to purchase fuel-efficient cars, Virginia and California passed laws that allowed hybrid vehicles to use high-occupancy vehicle (HOV) lanes, no matter how many people were in the vehicles. In effect, this law altered "property rights" to the high-occupancy lanes. As a result of this change, drivers realized there was an additional benefit of driving a hybrid—the amount of time they would save commuting on congested highways. As a result, drivers were willing to pay more for hybrids.

We can illustrate how the change in property rights related to the use of HOV lanes affected the demand for hybrids versus regular cars. **Figure 3.10a** shows a California family's demand for hybrids before they were allowed in HOV lanes. Suppose that the family is willing to buy two hybrids every four years at a price of $26,000. **Figure 3.10b** also shows the family's demand for standard gas-powered cars during the same period. At the same price ($26,000), we show that the family is willing to purchase just three of these cars every four years.

---

**FIGURE 3.10** The Effect of a Change in Property Rights: HOV Lanes and the Demand for Hybrid versus Gas-Powered Cars

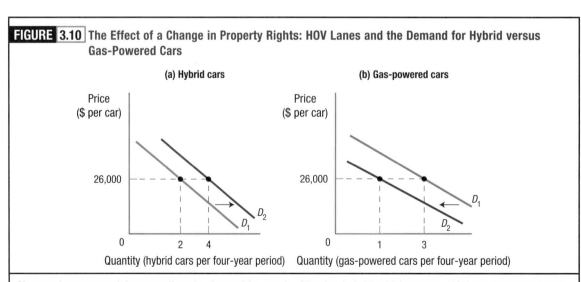

Changes in property rights can affect the demand for goods. Allowing hybrid vehicles to use HOV lanes even with only one person in the vehicle alters the property rights to the HOV lanes. The change increases the willingness of people to pay for hybrids while at the same time reducing their willingness to pay for standard gasoline-powered cars. A family's demand curve for hybrids, shown in panel (a), shifts outward from $D_1$ to $D_2$. Meanwhile, the family's demand curve for gasoline-powered cars shown in panel (b) shifts to the left from $D_1$ to $D_2$. At every price, the quantity of hybrid cars purchased increases, and the quantity of gasoline-powered cars purchased declines.

When hybrids are allowed in the HOV lanes, the willingness of people to pay for hybrids increases at the same time that the willingness to pay for standard gasoline-powered cars declines. This leads to a shift to the right in the demand curve for hybrids [panel (a)], and a shift to the left in the demand curve for gasoline-powered cars [panel (b)]. Now the number of hybrids the family buys at the $26,000 price increases to four, and the number of gasoline-powered cars purchased drops to one. This example illustrates that changes in property rights can change people's perceptions about the value, or net benefit, of acquiring a specific economic good. In the case of cars, the net benefit of buying a hybrid increased because laws changed that increased the benefit of driving this type of car. Meanwhile, the net benefit of driving gasoline-powered cars declined.

Ironically, Virginia's program to stimulate hybrid car purchases by giving them access to HOV lanes has resulted in traffic congestion in HOV lanes that is now just as great as in non-HOV lanes. The same thing is beginning to happen in California. As a result, both states are now grappling with ways to ration HOV permits for hybrid vehicles.

## 3.5 From an Individual's Demand Curve to Market Demand Curves

So far we have focused on an individual's demand curve and the factors that affect it. That makes sense because economics really is about how individuals weigh costs and benefits and make decisions. But economists aren't just interested in how individual buyers will react to changes. They want to know how groups of buyers will react to changes in the economic environment. Economists often ask questions such as the following: How have sales of SUVs fared in Minneapolis since gasoline prices rose to $4? How many houses were sold in Las Vegas since the beginning of the recession?

The most basic way to see what groups of people will demand is to add together their individual demand schedules to arrive at a group demand schedule. Do economists really add up individual demand curves? No. What is done, however, is the collection of sales data through market research, checkout scanners, and so on. This data shows the buying habits of many individuals at various prices. The resulting demand schedule shows the total quantity demanded, equal to the sum of individuals' quantity demanded, at each and every price. This is a basic example, but it shows you how economists gather information on a wider basis.

To illustrate this idea, suppose our market consists of only two college students, Gail and Jay. **Table 3.2** shows their individual demand schedules for college credits.

### Table 3.2 From Individual Demand Curves to the Market Demand Curve for College Credit Hours

| | Price per Credit Hour ($) | | | | |
|---|---|---|---|---|---|
| Credit hours demanded | 200 | 300 | 400 | 500 | 600 |
| Gail | 5 | 4 | 3 | 2 | 1 |
| Jay | 8 | 6 | 4 | 2 | 0 |
| Market (= Gail + Jay) | 13 | 10 | 7 | 4 | 1 |

The table shows Gail and Jay's individual demand schedules for college credits. If these two individuals are the only buyers in the market, then the total or market demand for college credits is found by adding together the quantity each of them is willing to purchase at various prices. At $200, the market demand for college credit hours is 13 hours. At $600, it is only 1 credit hour.

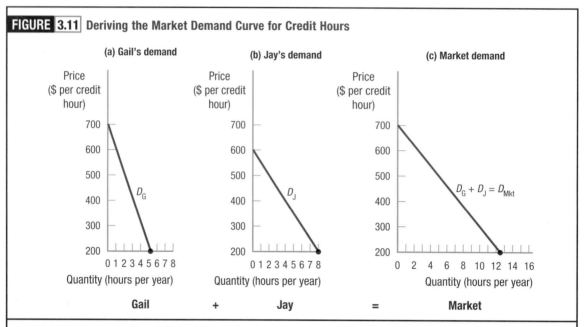

**FIGURE 3.11** Deriving the Market Demand Curve for Credit Hours

A market for a good consists of all the buyers who are willing and able to purchase it. In this market for college credit hours, the two college students have individual demand curves. The total, or market demand, that the two have for college credits is found by adding together the quantity that each buyer is willing to purchase at each price. The market demand curve represents the total quantity demanded by everyone willing to purchase college credits at each and every price.

To figure out the total or market demand the two have for college credits, we add together the quantity that each of them demands at various prices. At $200 per credit, Gail will demand five credit hours, and Jay will demand eight credit hours. Together they will demand $5 + 8 = 13$ credit hours. At $600 per credit hour, however, Gail will demand only one credit hour and Jay none. Graphically, this translates into the sum of the two demand curves, as **Figure 3.11** shows.

Obviously, there are many more students than just Gail and Jay demanding college credits in the real world. While adding more students to the example increases reality, it also increases complexity. Whether it is 2 or 2 million, the concept is the same. By adding up the quantity demanded students buy at each price, we can arrive at a market demand schedule and market demand curve that represent the total quantity demanded by everyone willing to purchase college credits at each and every price.

## Market Demand

Generally speaking, economists are interested in looking at the total demand exhibited by consumers purchasing the same good in the same **market**. By market, we mean a physical locale or virtual place like eBay where buyers and sellers interact to trade the good.

**MARKET** A location—physical or virtual—where buyers and sellers interact, directly or through representatives, to voluntarily exchange economic goods.

**EXAMPLE** The Farmer's Market in Charlotte, North Carolina, is physically located in downtown Charlotte. It is filled with buyers and sellers of produce and craft items such as soap and honey.

**EXAMPLE** eBay.com is a virtual market that brings together buyers and sellers from around the globe to trade a wide variety of goods, including books, music, shoes, and movies.

For any given good and any given market—from single-family houses in Las Vegas to honey at a local farmer's market—we can derive the **market demand** schedule by adding together the individual demand schedules of the buyers in the market.

**MARKET DEMAND** The total number of units of a good demanded at each and every price in a particular market. Market demand is the sum of the individual quantities demanded at each and every price.

Let's be clear: it isn't always easy to know which individual demand schedules should be added together to arrive at "the" market demand schedule. This may be because it's unclear whether or not the goods the individuals are willing to pay for are actually the same. For example, is there a single market demand for peanut butter? Or are there distinct market demand numbers for all-natural, chunky, and reduced-fat peanut butter? A second complication is that the market demand for a good can be geographically segregated. We know, for example, that people who work in New York City are much more likely to have demand schedules for houses in New York, New Jersey, and Connecticut than in Seattle. People living in Kansas City, Missouri, will have demand schedules for gasoline that can be purchased in Missouri (and possibly Kansas) but probably not in California. In other words, *where* a good is purchased can be an important dimension of how the market for it is defined.

One thing we do know is that adding up individual demand schedules guarantees that both the market demand schedule and demand curve will be affected by the number of individual demanders we add in. As the number of buyers increases, the market demand curve shifts to the right. This occurs because when there are additional consumers, there are additional units of the good demanded at each price. For a similar reason, when the number of buyers decreases, the market demand curve shifts to the left.

## Factors that Shift the Market Demand Curve

Market demand curves shift in the same direction as their underlying individual demand curves. In other words, market demand curves reflect what is going on at the individual level. If the demand of individuals is increasing, then so is the market demand. Recall that the factors that shift individual demand curves include changes in people's incomes, changes in the prices of substitutes and complements, changes in people's expectations and tastes, and changes in their property rights. If individuals increase their demand for a good, their demand curves shift to the right and so will the market demand curve. Even if only one person's demand curve shifts as a result of a change in circumstances, the market demand curve must also shift in the same direction. However, in most markets, such a shift is likely to be imperceptible because each individual demander is only one of many demanders who make up the market.

## 3.6 Summarizing the Factors that Affect Demand

We have identified several factors that lead to shifts in the individual and market demand curves for a good. To reiterate, a change in the price of the good is *not* one of these factors: a change in the price of a good moves you along the demand curve, changing the quantity demanded. **Table 3.3** summarizes the factors that lead to a shift in an individual's demand curve and the corresponding market demand curve.

---

**Table 3.3 | Factors that Cause a Shift in the Demand Curve**

→ An individual's demand curve shifts to the right when any one of the following occurs:

1. Her income increases, and it is a normal good.
2. Her income decreases, and it is an inferior good.
3. Her tastes change, and the good becomes more preferred.
4. Her expectations change, say, she believes prices of the good will increase, so she demands more of it today.
5. The price of a complementary good decreases.
6. The price of a substitute good increases.
7. The good is perceived to have become more valuable: an improvement in property rights.

← An individual's demand curve shifts to the left when any one of the following occurs:

1. His income decreases, and it is a normal good.
2. His income increases, and it is an inferior good.
3. His tastes change, and the good becomes less preferred.
4. His expectations change, say, he believes prices of the good will decrease, so he demands less of it today.
5. The price of a complementary good increases.
6. The price of a substitute good decreases.
7. The good is perceived to have become less valuable: a decrease in property rights.

The market demand curve responds to the same factors and shifts in the same direction as individual demand curves. In addition:

→ The market demand curve shifts to the right when the number of buyers increases.

← The market demand curve shifts to the left when the number of buyers decreases.

This table summarizes the factors that lead to a shift in an individual's demand curve and the corresponding market demand curve. The factors that lead to shifts in the individual demand curve and the market demand curve for a good include changes in people's incomes, tastes, and expectations, and changes in property rights and the prices of other goods. The market demand curve also shifts when the number of buyers changes. A change in the price of the good is *not* one of the factors that shifts demand curves: a change in the price of a good moves you along a demand curve but does not shift it.

## SOLVED PROBLEM

**Q** Using market demand curves, show the impact e-mail and instant messaging have had on (1) the postage-stamp market and (2) the high-speed cable market.

**A** E-mail and instant messaging are substitutes for other forms of communication. The success of electronic communication has resulted in a shift to the left in the demand for substitutes such as regular mail (and, hence, postage stamps) as shown in the market for postages stamps in the left-hand graph. Notice that if the price of stamps is $P$ before and after the shift in demand, then the new quantity demanded is lower. In contrast, e-mail and instant messaging have resulted in a shift right in the market demand for complementary goods—in this case, high-speed cable to the Internet, as illustrated in the right-hand figure. In this case, at a given price, the quantity demanded of minutes of high-speed cable is higher than before the shift.

**The Effect of the Introduction of E-Mail and Instant Messaging on the Markets for Postage Stamps and High-Speed Cable.**

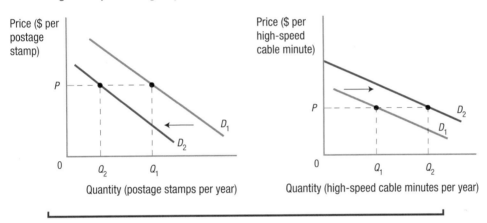

## 3.7 The Behavior of Individual Suppliers

We now turn to the other side of the market, the supply side. You should not think of suppliers as just stores or manufacturing companies that produce products for sale in the market. All of us are suppliers of economic goods at one time or another. Most of us supply our time in the form of work, and many of us supply money to lenders (banks, credit unions, and so on) when we open checking and savings accounts.

How do you decide how much of your time you should supply to your employer? Each and every potential supplier, in each and every market, must decide whether it makes economic sense to use scarce resources (like your time) to produce a particular good or service. A farmer has to decide whether to grow corn or soybeans. A worker has to decide whether to work in his mother's local business or take a job in another city.

A supplier considers the opportunity cost of supplying some good or service to the market. Recall that opportunity cost is the net benefit that you would have enjoyed by putting your scarce resources to their next best use. This means that a supplier has considered the net benefit he expects to receive from other supply opportunities and, based on this information, chooses which market to participate in. A salesperson, for example, must choose which line of products to sell—that is, which product market to participate in as a supplier. A restaurant owner must decide whether to be a supplier of fast-food meals, focus on the dine-in crowd, or serve both markets.

## The Opportunity Cost of Production: Increasing Marginal Cost

In Chapter 2, we introduced the principle of increasing marginal cost. The basic idea is that the cost of producing additional units of a good rises at some level of production. This can occur from the very first unit onward or occur at some higher level of production. The relationship between marginal cost and quantity supplied ($Q$) is shown in **Figure 3.12**. You can see that as additional units of the good are produced, the marginal cost of each of the units is higher than the unit before.

Why does the principle of increasing marginal cost make sense? Suppose you are a supplier of water. You can supply the first gallons of water at low cost simply by catching rainwater in a bucket. To increase your supply further, you could dig a well and pump water to the surface, which is a more expensive process than simply collecting rainwater. As more water is supplied, the cost of supplying additional gallons rises.

A person will maximize her net benefit if she engages in an economic activity to the point where her marginal benefit is equal to her marginal cost. There is no reason to believe that this would be any different for a firm. After all, each supplier is attempting to maximize the return to scarce resources that she owns. In the case of suppliers, the benefit they get when they sell a unit of a good is equal to the price ($P$) they receive. Therefore, to maximize the net benefit from supplying a good to the market, a producer will choose the output level where his marginal cost of the last unit he produces just equals the price he receives for the unit. If we assume that a supplier can sell all of his output at the same price per unit ($P$), then the optimal quantity supplied is where this price just covers the marginal cost of the very last unit produced.

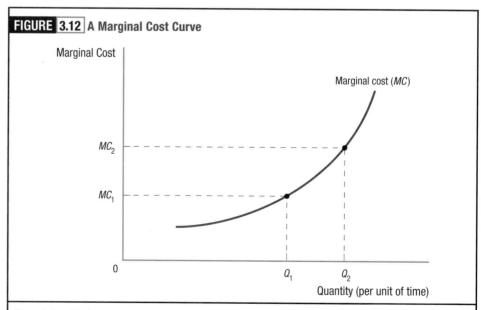

**FIGURE 3.12 A Marginal Cost Curve**

The relationship between marginal cost (*MC*) and quantity supplied (*Q*) is shown in the figure as an upward-sloping line. For a given set of inputs, at some point the marginal cost of the good must increase because the cost of producing additional units rises as more and more of units are produced.

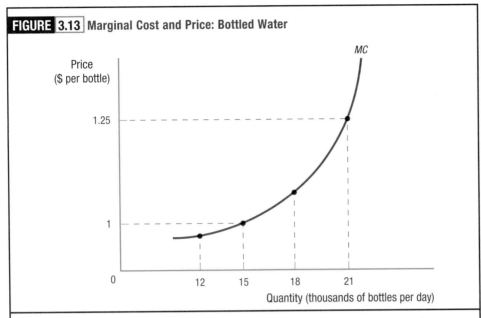

**FIGURE 3.13** Marginal Cost and Price: Bottled Water

The marginal cost for the production of bottled water rises with more output. If bottled water can be sold for $1, the producer will be willing to supply 15,000 bottles a day. At this level of output, the marginal cost of production is just equal to $1. If the supplier produces more than this, the cost of producing each extra bottle will be greater than $1, which means that the supplier will be losing money on each bottle of water produced. If the supplier produces less than 15,000 bottles a day, the cost of producing an additional bottle is less than the $1 received from selling it. The supplier will produce the number of bottles up to the point where the price is just equal to the marginal cost of producing the additional bottle.

**Figure 3.13** shows a typical marginal cost curve for the production of bottled water. Notice how the curve rises with more output because of the increasing marginal cost of production. If the price of bottled water is $1, then the producer will be willing to supply 15,000 bottles a day. At this level of output, the marginal cost of production is just equal to $1. Why is 15,000 bottles a day the optimal output level for the bottler? Suppose she chose instead to produce 18,000 bottles a day. At this level of output, the cost of producing the 18,000th bottle is greater than $1, meaning that she is losing money (incurring negative net benefit) on this bottle of water. In fact, for every bottle after the 15,000th bottle, she is losing money—the marginal cost of producing each of these bottles of water is greater than the $1 she receives. Thus, she will stop at the point where the marginal benefit is just equal to the marginal cost.

Suppose instead that the supplier decides to produce only 12,000 bottles of water a day. The marginal cost of producing the 12,001st bottle of water is less than $1, meaning that if she expanded her output, she could capture additional net benefits. This will be the case up to the 15,000th bottle of water. The supplier will not receive any net benefit from the last 15,000th bottle supplied because the price she receives ($1) is just equal to the marginal cost of producing the 15,000th bottle ($1). She will certainly not supply any more units unless her marginal costs of production go down, or the price goes up.

# 3.8 Deriving an Individual Producer's Supply Curve

Suppose the price that our bottler receives rises to $1.25. How will she respond to this change in her economic environment? The supplier will increase her production up to the point where the marginal cost of producing the last unit is now just equal to $1.25, the marginal benefit. Figure 3.13 shows that the supplier is willing to increase her output level to 21,000 bottles per day when the price is $1.25. This occurs because the higher price will cover the higher marginal cost of producing additional bottles. As price rises, the producer is "enticed" to move up her marginal cost curve and expand the quantity of bottled water supplied.

The fact is that higher prices tend to induce suppliers to supply more. A higher wage is an incentive to workers to put in overtime (supply more hours of labor). A higher interest rate on your bank deposits may entice you to save more (supply more funds to the bank). The bottom line is that when the price of a product increases, the marginal benefit the supplier gets from each unit of production also rises. Producers are enticed to expand their quantity supplied, even as they incur higher marginal costs. These observations gives us the definition of **supply**.

> **SUPPLY** The quantity of a good that a supplier is willing and able to provide at any given price during a specified time period (day, week, month, and so forth), with *all other factors held constant.*

> **EXAMPLE** At a price of $250 per bicycle, Miki's bike shop is willing and able to produce two bikes per day. At a price of $500, the shop is willing and able to produce three, all else being the same.

Earlier in this chapter, we discussed the relationship between the price of hot dogs in New York City and the number of hot dogs a tourist might buy during a weekend visit. Let's use that example here to see how many hot dogs our typical street vendor in New York City is willing to supply at different prices. **Table 3.4** shows the **supply schedule** for this vendor.

| Table 3.4 A Producer's Supply Schedule for Hot Dogs | |
|---|---|
| Price per Unit ($) | Units Supplied per Week (Dozens) |
| 1 | 5 |
| 1.25 | 10 |
| 1.50 | 15 |
| 1.75 | 20 |

The supply schedule in this table is consistent with the notion that as the price of hot dogs increases, so does the seller's willingness to supply more of them. At a price of $1 per hot dog, the seller is only willing to supply five dozen each week. As the price rises to $1.25, however, the seller is willing to increase production and supply an additional five dozen hot dogs for a total of ten dozen each week. There is a positive relationship between the price of hot dogs and the quantity that the seller is willing and able to supply.

> **SUPPLY SCHEDULE** A table that shows the price of a good and the number of units a producer is willing and able to supply at different prices during a specified period of time, *all other factors held constant.*

You can see that this supply schedule is consistent with the notion of supply: as the price of hot dogs increases, so does the street vendor's willingness to supply more hot dogs. At a price of $1 per hot dog, the vendor is only willing to supply five dozen each week. As the price rises to $1.25, however, he is willing to increase his production and supply five dozen additional hot dogs, for a total of ten dozen each week.

We can use the information in the supply schedule to construct a **supply curve**.

**SUPPLY CURVE** A graphic representation of a supplier's supply schedule. The supply curve plots various price–quantity combinations an individual producer is willing to accept.

A supply curve like the one shown in **Figure 3.14** plots the various price–quantity combinations a supplier is willing to accept. Similar to the demand curve, the convention is to put the price (*P*) of the good on the vertical axis and the number of units, or quantity (*Q*), of the good supplied on the horizontal axis. Remember, the principle of increasing marginal cost ensures that the supply curve is upward sloping.

In Figure 3.14, the height of the supply curve at any given output level reflects the opportunity cost of supplying the marginal unit. For example, the opportunity cost of supplying the tenth dozen of hot dogs equals $1.25 per hot dog. If we read over from the price axis instead, we can see the price the supplier must be paid to produce this much output. To get the vendor to supply the tenth dozen of hot dogs, the vendor

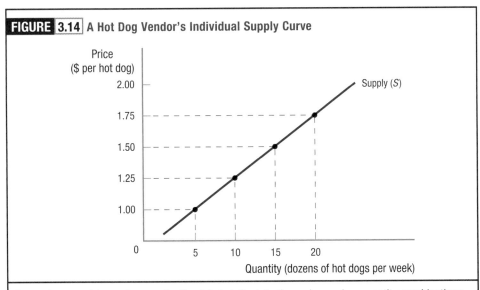

**FIGURE 3.14** **A Hot Dog Vendor's Individual Supply Curve**

A supply curve (shown here as the line labeled *S*) plots the various price–quantity combinations a supplier is willing to accept. The prices (*P*) of the good appear on the vertical axis, and the quantities (*Q*) of the good supplied are on the horizontal axis. Because of increasing marginal cost, the supply curve is upward sloping. The height of the supply curve at any given output level reflects the opportunity cost of supplying the marginal unit. In the figure, the opportunity cost of supplying the tenth dozen of hot dogs equals $1.25 per hot dog. Reading over from the price axis, the price the supplier must be paid to offer this much output is $1.25. This price just covers the marginal cost of producing each of the last dozen of hot dogs.

must receive $1.25 per hot dog, which just covers his marginal cost of producing each of the last dozen of hot dogs. At $1.25, the vendor is indifferent to whether or not he supplies the last (tenth dozen) unit of output because the marginal benefit is just equal to the marginal cost.

The observation that the quantity supplied is directly related to the price gives us the **law of supply**.

> **LAW OF SUPPLY** When the price of a good increases, suppliers are willing to produce more units of the good, all else being the same. Conversely, when the price falls, suppliers cut back on the number of units they are willing to produce.

> **EXAMPLE** You work an eight-hour shift as a waiter at a local restaurant, after which you are dead on your feet. Your boss offers you double time—twice your regular wage—to cover the next shift for a sick employee. You agree, but only because you will receive twice the money for the second shift.

Just as in our discussion about demand, notice that we couch our treatment of supply in terms of "willingness to supply." Suppliers may be willing to supply their product at lots of price levels but find no takers for their goods at some of these prices. Our street vendor might be willing to supply 60 dozen hot dogs a week if the price were $9 a hot dog, but at that price, the amount actually sold will likely be little or none. Similarly, you might be willing to supply 80 hours of work each week for $200 an hour. The trouble is you might have a hard time finding an employer who will hire you at that wage.

## 3.9 Movements along the Supply Curve versus Shifts in the Supply Curve

When a good's price changes, a supplier will respond by changing the quantity of the good she is willing to provide. As you saw in Figure 3.14, an increase in the price of hot dogs leads to an increase in the quantity of hot dogs a typical street vendor is willing to supply each day if he is able. A price increase, therefore, moves a supplier up (slides along) his supply curve. If the price of hot dogs falls, the vendor will reduce the number he supplies.

What leads to a shift in the supply curve? If you recall, a shift in the demand curve meant that there was a change in the quantity demanded at each and every price. Something other than a change in price caused the quantity demanded to increase or decrease. It turns out that it is a similar situation for the supply curve. **Figure 3.15** shows a producer's supply curve for cell phones. Suppose that if the price is $100, the quantity of cell phones supplied by phone-producer Qualcomm, is 1,000,000 units per year. This is found by reading off the supply curve labeled $S_1$. What if the price of cell phones increases to $120? At $120, you can see that Qualcomm will slide up its existing supply curve ($S_1$) and provide 1,250,000 phones for sale each year. A decrease in the price would have had the opposite effect.

For Qualcomm's supply curve to shift, there must be a change in the economic environment that affects the company's willingness to supply cell phones at each and every price. Suppose Qualcomm's supply curve shifts from $S_1$ to $S_2$. Supply curve $S_2$

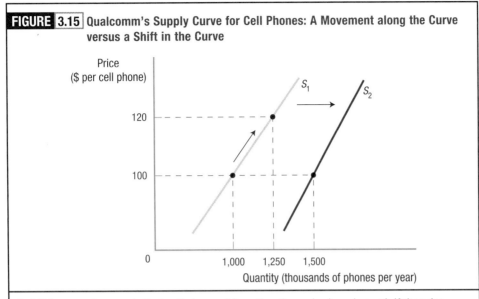

**FIGURE 3.15** Qualcomm's Supply Curve for Cell Phones: A Movement along the Curve versus a Shift in the Curve

A shift in a supply curve indicates that something other than price has changed. If the price of cell phones increases, the supplier is willing to provide more phones for sale each year: he moves up his supply curve, as shown by the increase in quantity supplied that accompanies the price increase along supply curve $S_1$. A decrease in the price has the opposite effect. A shift in the supply curve, shown by the shift from $S_1$ to $S_2$, changes the company's willingness to supply cell phones at each and every price. If the supply curve shifts from $S_1$ to $S_2$, Qualcomm is willing to supply more phones *at each and every* price. At $100, for example, the shift in supply means that the company is now willing and able to supply 1,500,000 phones instead of 1,000,000. The quantity supplied has increased even though the price of the cell phone has not.

indicates that Qualcomm is now willing to supply 1,500,000 phones per year priced at $100 each; that is, the quantity supplied has increased even though the price of the cell phone hasn't. This tells us that something has changed that affects Qualcomm's production decision, and it isn't the price of the cell phone.

A rightward shift in the supply curve increases the quantity supplied at each and every price. A leftward shift in the supply curve decreases the quantity supplied at each and every price. In this example, although we are allowing price changes to affect the quantity supplied, we are holding constant a number of other factors. Similar to our treatment of demand, it is these other factors that shift the supply curve. What can cause the supply curve to shift? We answer this question next.

## 3.10 Factors that Shift a Supply Curve

When it came to thinking about factors that shifted an individual's demand for a good, we considered changes in several variables, including the person's income, the price of alternatives, and even property rights—the things included under the *all other factors held constant* assumption. We must consider another set of factors when it comes to supply.

When it comes to the supply curve, it turns out that a change in the opportunity cost of production leads to a shift in the curve. In other words, anything that affects the marginal cost of supplying an additional unit of output will result in a shift in the supply curve. When that happens, the quantity supplied at each and every price changes. A number of things can change a supplier's costs of production. Perhaps the most obvious one is a change in the price of an input used in the production process, which we discuss next.

### Input Prices

If the marginal cost of production changes, it changes the net benefit that a supplier receives from selling a good or a service. For example, an increase in the cost of hiring workers will increase the marginal cost of production. This would be illustrated by an upward shift in the marginal cost curve. If the price of the good hasn't increased, then this is likely to have a negative impact on a supplier's decision about how much to produce.

Your labor, pieces of machinery, and barrels of oil are examples of inputs in the production process of various goods. Each input has a price, which is called an **input price**. An input price tells us the price of a unit of an input—the wage per hour, the monthly lease rate for a machine, the price per barrel of oil, and so forth.

**INPUT PRICE** The price paid for a unit of a resource used in the production of a good.

**EXAMPLE** Animators are employed to produce Disney films such as *The Lion King*. The wage they receive per hour, day, or week is an *input price* for Disney.

**EXAMPLE** Oil is used to produce rubber, steel, plastics, and other basic manufacturing materials. The price of oil per barrel is an *input price*.

How does a change in an input price affect the supply of some good? To answer this, let's look at the effect an increase in animators' wage rates has on Disney's supply of animated movies each year. **Figure 3.16** shows the supply curve, labeled $S_1$, of animated movies Disney is willing to supply each year based on its current costs of production. If film distributors are willing to pay $60 million per movie, then Disney will supply four films per year. What if the wage rate of animators increases from $45 an hour to $65 an hour? The cost of producing each animated movie will increase. As a result, the supply curve of animated movies shifts left to the supply curve $S_2$. Disney will make fewer films at each and every price. If Disney is now offered the same amount of money for each movie as before ($60 million), the number of movies it will supply will drop to two per year. To acquire the same number of animated films (four) per year as before the wage increase, the film distributors must now offer $85 million per movie. Why? Because the marginal cost of producing the third and fourth movie is now higher than the original price tag of $60 million per movie.

Virtually all goods use labor in either their production or distribution stages. Consequently, an increase in the cost of labor will translate directly into an increase in the cost of supplying most goods. As we have just shown, this will result in a leftward shift (a decrease) in the supply curve. Knowing this gives us an important insight about the potential effects of labor policies. Suppose, for example, that the government required all employers to provide workers with health-insurance coverage or a new paid holiday

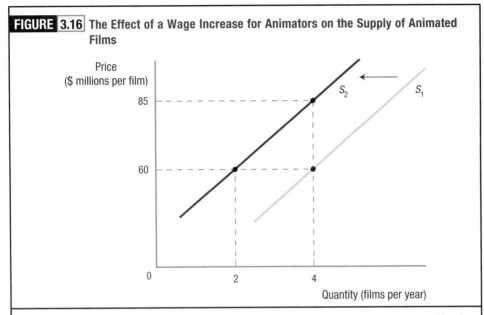

**FIGURE 3.16** The Effect of a Wage Increase for Animators on the Supply of Animated Films

If the wage of animators is $45 per hour, $S_1$ is the supply curve for animated film. At a price of $60 million per film, the movie studio is willing and able to supply (produce) four films per year. If the cost of producing films increases because animators demand higher wages, then the supply curve of animated movies shifts to $S_2$. After the wage increase, fewer films are supplied at each and every price. At $60 million, for example, two films will be produced instead of four after the shift in the supply curve.

(Super Bowl Monday?). The employer's cost of employing each worker would increase. The increased cost of employing each worker causes the firm to reduce its quantity of labor demanded: it will layoff or fire workers. With fewer employees, it is likely that the firm will not be willing to produce as much of the good as before at the going price. Because of the higher cost of employing workers, the firm's supply curve for the good it produces would shift to the left. Of course, if there is a supplier who is not subject to the new law—perhaps because he has only a small number of employees or is a foreign supplier—then his supply curve would not shift at all.

## Technology

Technological breakthroughs often lead to new cost-saving production processes. Examples abound: to reduce their labor costs, grocery stores have installed price scanners in their stores that allow customers to check themselves out; fast-food restaurants have installed self-serve, drink-filling machines; and banks now offer services through automatic teller machines (ATMs). These (and many more) cost-reducing technologies have increased the quantity of services supplied at each and every price.

By reducing the cost of production, technological innovations cause the supply curve for goods and services to shift to the right: more quantity is supplied at each and every price because the marginal cost of production has fallen. Computer-generated animation technologies have substantially reduced the cost of producing animated features. Because animators are no longer needed to draw each individual film frame by hand, the cost of producing such movies

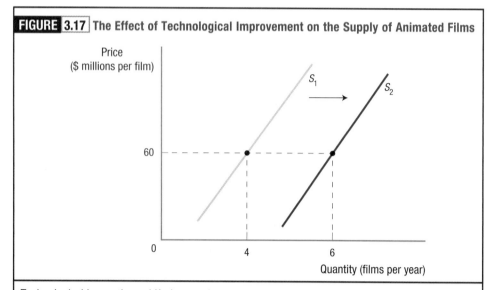

**FIGURE 3.17** The Effect of Technological Improvement on the Supply of Animated Films

Technological innovations shift the supply curve to the right because improved technology reduces the marginal cost of production. This example shows how improved computer animation translates into a rightward shift in the supply curve of animated films per year. At each and every price, more films are now being supplied each year.

has declined. Disney produced its first completely computer-animated movie, *Chicken Little*, in 2005.

**Figure 3.17** shows how computer animation has affected the supply of animated movies. The supply curve of animated movies before computerization is $S_1$. At a price of $60 million, four movies are produced each year. Computer-generated animation reduced the marginal cost of producing each movie, translating into a rightward shift in the supply curve to the new supply curve, $S_2$. At the original ($60 million) price, Disney is now willing to supply six movies instead of four per year. Now, the marginal cost of producing the fourth and fifth movies is less than $60 million, and the marginal cost of producing the sixth movie is just equal to $60 million. The vertical distance of the supply curve at each and every unit of output is lower than before.

### Expectations

In the case of demand, expectations played a role. If you expect gas prices to rise tomorrow, you might buy more today, for example. What if a gasoline producer expects gas prices to rise in the future? It may decide to produce less today and wait for prices to rise. Or think of home builders. A projection that the population will grow much more in the future may suggest an increase in future demand for housing. In such cases, expectations can shift the current supply curve. If home builders expect better conditions in the future, they may reduce their building activities today, shifting the supply curve of houses to the left.

### Property Rights

Just as for demanders, changes in property rights can have a big impact on the behavior of suppliers. Some of these changes reduce the costs of production, whereas others increase the costs. When court rulings established that the victims of drunk drivers had the right to sue bars that had served the drivers, this new property right increased the cost of operating a bar and selling drinks. This occurred because bar owners had to pay higher insurance premiums to cover this additional liability. As a result, there was a shift to the left in the supply curve for bar drinks. What were the outward signs of the shift? Bartenders began serving fewer drinks to individual patrons, last call came earlier in the night, and some bars paid for cabs to take inebriated customers home.

Some state legislatures have attempted to limit the liability of obstetricians—doctors who specialize in the care of pregnant women and child delivery—by placing caps on the size of medical malpractice awards. The intent was to reduce the malpractice insurance premiums doctors pay in order to reduce their marginal costs. **Figure 3.18** shows the supply curve for a doctor who provides obstetrical services. The good, or service, supplied is the number of deliveries she makes each month. At the price of $1,200 per delivery, the doctor is willing to supply 17 deliveries a month. Her cost of doing business includes her malpractice insurance premium, which typically increases with the number of deliveries she does each month—that is, it is part of her marginal cost curve. What happens if a cap is placed on medical malpractice awards and decreases her malpractice insurance premiums?

Because the opportunity cost of providing delivery services has declined, the supply curve in Figure 3.18 will shift to the right to the new supply curve labeled $S_2$. This means that the marginal cost of supplying each of the initial 17 deliveries has fallen. It also means that at the initial price of $1,200, the quantity of deliveries that the doctor is willing to supply increases to 29 per month. The eighteenth through

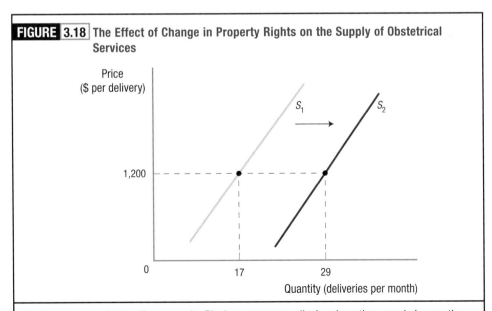

**FIGURE 3.18** The Effect of Change in Property Rights on the Supply of Obstetrical Services

Altering property rights affects supply. Placing caps on medical malpractice awards lowers the marginal cost of providing obstetrical care. Because the opportunity cost of providing delivery services is reduced, the supply curve shifts to the right. At each and every price, the quantity of deliveries that the doctor is willing to supply per month increases.

twenty-eighth deliveries now have a marginal cost that is less than $1,200, and the marginal cost of providing the twenty-ninth delivery is exactly equal to $1,200. As it turns out, after passage of these malpractice caps, the supply curves for obstetrics, neurosurgery, and other medical specialties subjected to frequent malpractice lawsuits did, in fact, shift to the right.[3] However, because only a subset of states has passed laws to cap malpractice awards, the shift in supply has not occurred everywhere.

## 3.11 The Market Supply Curve

Recall that the market demand curve was derived by summing up the quantity demanded by each buyer at each and every price. The **market supply** curve is derived in a similar way. To figure out what the market supply is for a good, we add up the quantity supplied by each producer at each and every price.

> **MARKET SUPPLY** The total number of units of a good supplied at each and every price in a particular market during a particular period of time. Market supply is the sum of the individual quantities supplied at each and every price.

Let's revisit our earlier example of the hot dog vendor. In the first panel of **Figure 3.19**, we show his supply curve. At a price of $1 per hot dog, the vendor is willing to provide 5 dozen hot dogs per week. The second panel shows the supply curve of the vendor on the next street corner. The vendors' supply curves are not identical, indicating that there are differences in the vendors' costs of production. Perhaps the second vendor has a lower cost of production because he doesn't have to pay for napkins—the

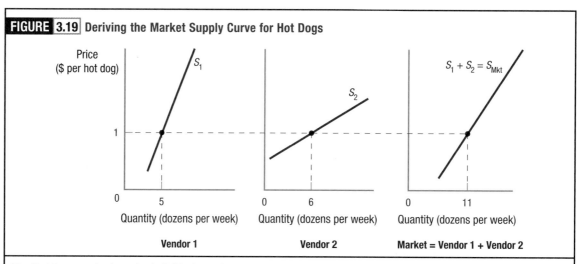

**FIGURE 3.19** Deriving the Market Supply Curve for Hot Dogs

Vendor 1

Vendor 2

Market = Vendor 1 + Vendor 2

The first two panels show the individual supply curves of two individual suppliers. The two supply curves are not identical, suggesting that the producers have different production costs. The market supply curve, the last panel on the right, is the total quantity supplied by all suppliers. Whether there are 2 vendors or 200 in the market, the market supply curve is the sum of quantities supplied by each vendor.

- - - - - - - -

[3]William E. Encinosa and Fred J. Hellinger, "Have State Caps on Malpractice Awards Increased the Supply of Physicians?" *Health Affairs*, May 2005.

theater down the street has given them to him to hand out to promote a new play. Because his marginal cost of production is lower, at a price of $1, the second vendor is willing to supply 6 dozen hot dogs per week. If these are the only vendors in the market, the market supply curve shown in the third panel of Figure 3.19 is the sum being supplied by both suppliers at each and every price. At a price of $1, the combined quantity supplied is equal to 11 dozen hot dogs per week. If there are more vendors, the market supply curve would be found by simply adding all of the quantities supplied at each price. Whether it is 2 vendors or 200, the process is the same.

All of the factors that shift individual supply curves will also shift the market supply curve, because the market supply curve is simply the sum of the individual curves. A change in the number of suppliers will also shift the supply curve. When the number of suppliers increases, there will be additional supply curves to add into the market supply curve, shifting the market supply curve to the right. Conversely, a decrease in the number of suppliers will shift the market supply curve to the left.

As markets become more global, the number of suppliers in many markets has increased dramatically. The Internet has promoted global e-commerce, expanding the number of retailers who are willing to supply consumers all over the world with DVDs, art, books, and electronics at a low cost. As markets expand, there are more suppliers and, therefore, the market supply curve for each of these products shifts to the right.

Let's illustrate this effect by looking at the impact technology has had on the supply of accounting services in the United States. The Internet and high-speed satellite telecommunication services have enabled skilled workers living in other countries to supply not only accounting but also software development and customer-support services to U.S. clients. In effect, technology has increased the number of suppliers in these markets. Outsourcing these types of jobs to workers located abroad shifts the supply curve of skilled labor available to U.S. employers to the right as **Figure 3.20** shows.

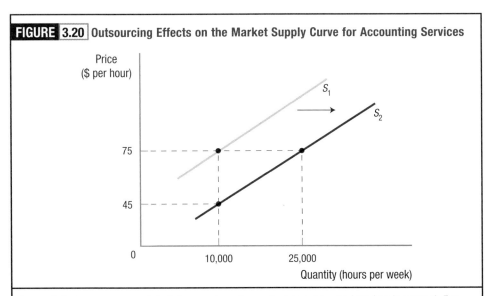

**FIGURE 3.20** **Outsourcing Effects on the Market Supply Curve for Accounting Services**

As markets become more global, the number of suppliers in many markets has increased. For example, an increase in the number of hours supplied by accounting firms domestically and abroad shifts the market supply curve to the right. An increase in supply means that there is an increase in the quantity of hours supplied at each and every price.

The supply curve labeled $S_1$ in Figure 3.20 is the supply of accounting services provided to U.S. companies before any outsourcing takes place. At a price of $75 per hour, accountants in the United States are willing to provide 10,000 hours per week. Now suppose accountants in India enter the market by providing accounting services to U.S. clients. The supply curve of accounting services now available to U.S. companies shifts to $S_2$, reflecting the increase in the number of suppliers of accounting services (we are horizontally summing more individual supply curves). At the initial price of $75, the number of hours of accounting services supplied increases sharply to 25,000 per week. The original number of accounting hours supplied at $75 (10,000 hours) will now be supplied at a price of $45 an hour. These hours will be supplied by the lowest-cost suppliers in the market—primarily by the foreign accountants. The vertical distance between the old supply curve ($S_1$) and the new supply curve ($S_2$) at 10,000 hours tells us that the marginal cost of supplying the 10,000th hour is now lower than before—$45 instead of $75. In this way, consumers of accounting services benefit from using lower-cost services provided through outsourcing.

As you might imagine, not everyone would look on this change in the market for accounting services favorably. The American Accounting Association, for example, might argue that allowing foreign-based accountants to offer their services to U.S. clients will severely reduce the income of its members. Accounting departments at U.S. universities might worry there will be a decline in the demand for accounting majors. We would expect the association and academics to lobby the government to intervene to protect U.S. accountants from any loss of income because of the outsourcing of accounting. At the same time, users of accounting services, from individuals at tax time to major corporations, would argue that outsourcing provides a valuable increase in available accounting services.

**ECONOMIC FALLACY**   The supply of digital cameras has increased at the same time as their prices have fallen. This is surely a violation of the "law" of supply.

**False.** There has been a shift in the supply curve that has been mistakenly interpreted as a movement along the supply curve. Technological improvements in the production of high-end optics and media storage have resulted in cost savings in the production of digital cameras. This has led to a rightward shift in the supply curve of cameras because the opportunity cost of supplying the cameras has declined. More cameras will now be supplied at all prices. As we will see in the next chapter, the rightward shift in supply will cause the market price to decline.

## 3.12 Summarizing the Factors that Affect Supply

To recap, a change in the price of a good leads to a change in the quantity of it supplied: the change moves each individual producer up or down his supply curve. Other nonprice factors shift the supply curve. **Table 3.5** summarizes the impact each of these factors has on individual supply curves and the market supply curve. It also reminds us that when the number of suppliers increases, the total quantity supplied at each and every price also increases, and the market supply curve shifts to the right. On the other hand, if the number of suppliers declines, the quantity of the good supplied at each and every price also declines, and the market supply curve shifts to the left.

Whereas demanders are willing to pay a certain amount for a specific good, suppliers are willing to supply a specific good if their opportunity costs are covered. If we assume that voluntary trade occurs without interference, under what conditions will

| Table **3.5** | **Factors that Cause a Shift in the Supply Curve** |
|---|---|

→ A producer's supply curve shifts to the right when any one of the following occurs:

1. The price of one or more of the producer's inputs falls.
2. Improved technology reduces the producer's marginal cost of production.
3. A change in property rights reduces the producer's marginal cost of production.
4. A government policy reduces the producer's marginal cost of production.

← A producer's supply curve shifts to the left when any one of the following occurs:

1. The price of one or more of the producer's inputs increases.
2. Outdated technology increases the producer's marginal cost of production.
3. A change in property rights increases the producer's marginal cost of production.
4. A government policy increases the producer's marginal cost of production.

The market supply curve responds to the same factors and shifts in the same direction as individual supply curves. In addition:

→ The market supply curve shifts to the right as the number of suppliers in the market increases.

← The market supply curve shifts to the left as the number of suppliers in the market decreases.

*This table summarizes the factors that lead to a shift in an individual producer's supply curve and the corresponding market supply curve. The factors that lead to shifts in these two curves for a good include changes in the price of inputs, advances in technology, changes in property rights, and changes in government regulations. The market supply curve also shifts when the number of suppliers in the market changes. A change in the price of the good is* not *one of the factors that shifts supply curves. A change in the price of a good slides you along a supply curve but does not shift the curve.*

demanders and suppliers actually buy and sell goods? To explore this key question, we need to put the two sides of the market together.

## 3.13 Bringing Demand and Supply Together

To identify under what conditions an actual trade takes place, we must first understand how demand and supply together determine the market price for a good. Suppose, for example, that the market demand and market supply schedules for a specific type of memory chip are as shown in **Table 3.6**. You can see that

| Table **3.6** | **The Market Demand and Supply Schedules for Memory Chips** | |
|---|---|---|
| $P$ ($) | $Q_D$ | $Q_S$ |
| 0 | 300,000 | 0 |
| 2 | 250,000 | 50,000 |
| 4 | 200,000 | 100,000 |
| **6** | **150,000** | **150,000** |
| 8 | 100,000 | 200,000 |
| 10 | 50,000 | 250,000 |
| 12 | 0 | 300,000 |

*The market demand and supply schedules for a specific type of memory chip are shown in this table. As the price of chips ($P$) increases, the quantity demanded ($Q_D$) declines, and the quantity supplied ($Q_S$) increases. Conversely, as the price of the chips declines, the quantity demanded increases, and the quantity supplied falls. As shown, there is one price ($6) at which the quantity supplied equals the quantity demanded (150,000). This price is called the market-clearing or equilibrium price.*

as the price increases, the quantity demanded declines, and the quantity supplied increases. For the sake of simplicity, the quantity demanded at a zero price is 300,000 in this example. But we know that in reality, the quantity demanded would approach infinity as the price gets closer and closer to zero, as long as "more is always better."

We can graph both the demand and supply schedules in Table 3.6 in the same diagram. When we do, we get **Figure 3.21**. You can see that the demand and supply curves have the same shapes as before: the demand curve is downward sloping, and the supply curve is upward sloping. What is new in Figure 3.21 is the fact that the demand and supply curves intersect at a unique price and quantity combination. This combination is unique because at $6—and only at $6—the quantity demanded (150,000) and the quantity supplied (150,000) are the same. This special price is called the market-clearing or **equilibrium price**. The special quantity demanded and supplied at this price is called the **equilibrium quantity**.

---

**EQUILIBRIUM PRICE** The price at which the quantity demanded in the market is exactly equal to the quantity supplied; the market-clearing price.

**EXAMPLE** At a price of $66 a barrel, the world's daily demand for barrels of oil just equals the world's daily supply of barrels of oil. The equilibrium price of a barrel of oil is $66.

---

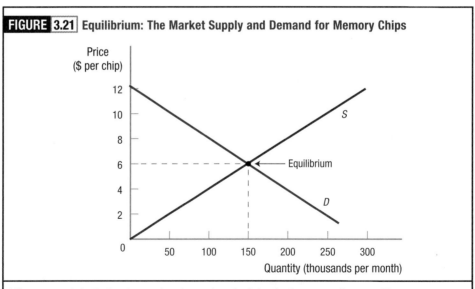

**FIGURE 3.21** **Equilibrium: The Market Supply and Demand for Memory Chips**

We can graph both the demand and supply schedules in the same diagram. You can see that the demand and supply curves have the same shapes as before: the demand curve is downward sloping, and the supply curve is upward sloping. The demand and supply curves intersect at a unique price and quantity combination. At this price, which is called the market-clearing or equilibrium price, the quantity demanded and the quantity supplied are the same. The quantity demanded and supplied at this price is called the equilibrium quantity.

**EQUILIBRIUM QUANTITY** The quantity bought and sold at the equilibrium price.

**EXAMPLE** At a price of $66 a barrel, the number of barrels of oil sold on the world market—85 million barrels a day—is just equal to the number of barrels purchased a day. Eighty-five million barrels per day is the equilibrium quantity of barrels of oil sold in the world market.

Equilibrium price and quantity are crucial economic concepts. In Figure 3.21, $6 is the only price at which the willingness of consumers to pay for the 150,000th chip purchased just equals the marginal cost of producers supplying the 150,000th chip. We will have much more to say about the usefulness of the supply-and-demand model in the next chapter. As it turns out, knowing how to apply this model—and recognizing its limitations—may be the most important lesson you learn in taking economics.

## WHAT YOU SHOULD HAVE LEARNED FROM CHAPTER 3

- That the principle of diminishing marginal benefits means that consumers will buy more of an item when its price falls and less when its price rises. The demand schedule and demand curve reflect a buyer's willingness to purchase different units of a good at different prices. An increase in price leads to a decrease in quantity demanded; a decrease in price leads to an increase in quantity demanded. This is the law of demand.

- That changes in price cause movements along a demand curve; that changes in underlying factors cause shifts in a demand curve.

- That the demand curve for normal and inferior goods will respond differently to changes in a person's income.

- That a substitute good is a close replacement for another, based on individual perceptions; changes in the price of a substitute will shift demand for the other good.

- That a complementary good is a good typically consumed with another good; that changes in the price of one of the complements will shift demand for the other good.

- That a market is a place where buyers and sellers directly or indirectly exchange products (grocery stores, eBay, the New York Stock Exchange, etc.).

- That a market demand curve will move in the same direction as its underlying individual demand curves in response to changes in economic circumstances.

- That a supplier is just like every other economic decision maker seeking to maximize the net benefit from allocating his scarce resources.

- That the principle of increasing marginal cost means that producers will provide more of an item when its price rises and less when its price falls. The supply schedule and supply curve reflect a supplier's willingness to provide different units of a good at different prices. An increase in price leads to an increase in quantity supplied; a decrease leads to a reduction in quantity supplied. This is the law of supply.

- That input prices, technology, and property rights affect the amount a supplier is willing to supply at each and every price; therefore, changes in any of these factors result in a shift in the individual supply curve.

- That the market supply curve is the summation of individual supply curves. That the same factors that shift individual supply curves will also shift the market supply curve.

- That the market supply curve will shift to the right when the number of suppliers increases and shift to the left when the number of suppliers decreases.

- That the interaction between demand and supply determines the equilibrium price and quantity.

## KEY TERMS

Willingness to pay, p. 66

Marginal willingness to pay, p. 67

Demand, p. 69

Demand schedule, p. 69

Demand curve, p. 70

Law of demand, p. 70

Normal good, p. 74

Inferior good, p. 75

Substitute goods, p. 77

Complementary goods, p. 78

Property rights, p. 81

Market, p. 84

Market demand, p. 85

Supply, p. 90

Supply schedule, p. 90

Supply curve, p. 91

Law of Supply, p. 92

Input prices, p. 94

Market supply, p. 98

Equilibrium price, p. 102

Equilibrium quantity, p. 102

## QUESTIONS AND PROBLEMS

1. The demand for dry-cleaning services has declined in the United States during the past few decades, even though per capita incomes have increased. Is this sufficient information to conclude that dry-cleaning services are an inferior good? Why or why not? Discuss your answer.

2. For the following markets, indicate whether there will be a movement along the demand curve or a shift right or left, in response to an increase in gasoline prices.
   a) The SUV market
   b) The mass-transit market
   c) The gasoline market
   d) The automobile tire market
   e) The telecommuting software market

3. Show what impact adoptions of babies from China by U.S. families have on the market demand curve for Chinese au pairs (young people who travel to the United States to take care of children).

4. Electronic forms of money—credit cards, PayPal, debit cards, and so on—have become popular forms of payment. Add to this the fact that the cost of making paper currency and coinage has risen dramatically. Do you think that paper and coins will be competed out of existence in the future? Explain your answer.

5. The Taxpayer Relief Act of 1997 exempted the first $500,000 of profits home owners receive when selling their homes. What type of effect has the act had on the market demand curve for owner-occupied housing?

6. Using one individual demand curve for gasoline and a second for recreational vehicle (RV) rentals, show the impact an increase in the price of gasoline has on the:
   a) quantity of gasoline demanded.
   b) quantity of RV rentals demanded.

7. When an individual demand curve shifts because of a change in income, will the new demand curve always be parallel to the old one? Why or why not? Would your answer change if we were talking about a shift in the demand curve

resulting from a change in the price of a substitute or a complement? Explain your answer.

8. Transplant surgeons have become ardent proponents of laws that would make organs more widely available. Why do you think this is the case?

9. Shena goes to school full-time and moonlights as a security guard nights and weekends. When her hourly wage increased from $10 per hour to $12 per hour, she requested a cut in her scheduled hours. How would you explain the downward slope of her supply curve for labor? Does this tell you anything about whether nonwork activities are inferior or normal goods for Shena?

10. Suppose accounting firms can either outsource accounting work to accountants in India via data-transmission technologies or import accountants from India to do the work. Explain carefully what factors might affect the decision to do one or the other.

11. Medical technology has advanced to the point where organs such as a liver can be split, with pieces transplanted into two patients rather than one. How has this technological change affected the market supply curve for transplantable livers?

12. A California court ruled that a dentist was liable for a car accident involving a patient who was given "laughing gas" (nitrous oxide) earlier in the day. Show how the market supply curve for dental treatments using gas as a pain reliever changed as a result of this ruling.

13. Several states are considering legislation giving the children of sperm donors the right to contact their fathers when they reach the age of 21. If the laws pass, what, if anything, do you think will happen to the market supply curve of sperm for infertility procedures?

14. The federal government has passed a number of medical-practice regulations: first, medical records must now be kept in special cabinets in locked rooms to protect the privacy of patients; second, electronic medical records systems must be used.

   a) Show how the market supply curve for knee surgery is affected by the new regulations.
   b) Suppose the amount that each orthopedic surgeon is reimbursed for knee procedures from insurance companies remains unchanged. Can you predict what will happen to the number of procedures each surgeon will perform under the new regulations?

15. Suppose you are a high-school student trying to decide whether or not to attend college. The government announces that it will provide interest-free loans to any students wanting to attend college, provided that they major in mathematics. What is the impact of this policy change on college tuition?

16. You've been asked to determine the equilibrium price and quantity in the market for after-dinner mints, the kind found in many restaurants as you leave. Your research reveals that the demand schedule can be represented by the equation $Q_D = 150 - 200\,P$. You also find that the supply equation can be represented by the equation $Q_S = 100 + 300\,P$. In each case, the quantity is measured in thousands of mints per day.

   a) Use these two equations to find the equilibrium price in this market. (Hint: Remember that in equilibrium, $Q_S = Q_D$.)
   b) Using the equilibrium price, solve for the equilibrium quantity demanded and supplied.
   c) What if the market price is 20 cents? How would you characterize this market?

17. The market supply and market demand schedules for veggie burgers are given in the following table. The quantities are expressed in thousands of burgers per day.

| Price ($) | Quantity Demanded | Quantity Supplied |
|-----------|-------------------|-------------------|
| 2 | 200 | 95 |
| 3 | 175 | 105 |
| 4 | 150 | 115 |
| 5 | 125 | 125 |
| 6 | 100 | 135 |

a) What is the equilibrium price and quantity in this market?
b) If the price was $6, what is true about the market? What would you expect to happen?
c) If the price was $3, what is true about this market? What would you expect to happen?
d) Draw the demand and supply curves for veggie burgers. What do you predict will happen in the short term to the equilibrium price and quantity if it is announced that new medical research finds that consumption of veggie burgers increases longevity?

# 4

# Applying the Supply-and-Demand Model

*"I am like any other man. All I do is supply a demand."*

*Al Capone, gangster*

Y ou learned in the last chapter that the equilibrium price and quantity occurs where a buyer's willingness to pay for a good just equals a producer's marginal cost of producing it. The buyer maximizes his net benefit when his marginal benefit is just equal to the marginal cost of the last unit he consumes of a good. The willingness to pay is simply the monetary value that demanders assign to the marginal benefit.

Another way to think about equilibrium price and quantity is to realize that no other combination of price and quantity makes sense. Figure 3.21 (in the previous chapter) shows the supply-and-demand graph for memory chips in which the equilibrium price per chip is $6, and the equilibrium quantity is 150,000 memory chips. At this price, buyers are willing to buy 150,000 chips, and suppliers are equally willing to make 150,000 chips available. But what if the price were higher than $6? Suppose it were $10? At this price, you can see that the quantity demanded would be less than the quantity supplied.

This is a very hands-on chapter. What we want to do is use the supply-and-demand model to analyze why prices might change and to try and predict in which direction they might go. We also will consider situations in which prices and quantities are not allowed to adjust to a change in demand or supply, and what the implications are for those markets and for related markets. We also will use supply and demand to show how taxes and government programs to restrict trade—tariffs and quotas—affect market prices and quantities. Before we get to those topics, let's take a minute to be clear about what the supply-and-demand model can be used for and its limitations.

## 4.1 The Usefulness of the Supply-and-Demand Model

Supply and demand are the foundation for virtually every predictive model economists develop, whether they are looking at international trade, a government's monetary policies, tax initiatives, population growth, or health-care reform. In this chapter, we will look at how you can use supply and demand to understand and actually explain price changes in the real world. We will also see why inhibiting the workings of supply and demand in a market can lead to undesirable outcomes from an economic standpoint.

We must caution you about a couple of things before we continue. When we draw supply-and-demand diagrams and argue that there is one equilibrium price, we really are making a prediction based on the model. In other words, given the current conditions in the market, we would *expect* the price per memory chip to gravitate more toward the equilibrium price than any other. The supply-and-demand framework allows us to predict that a market will find its equilibrium price and quantity. In other words, as individual suppliers and demanders make quantity adjustments in response to the prices they face, there will be a *convergence* toward equilibrium price and quantity.

Using supply and demand won't explain every wiggle in prices, though. It also tends to work better in stable markets than in volatile markets. The stock market is an example of the latter. News about government deficits or other world events can send stock prices soaring one day and crashing the next with little or no warning. The volatile nature of the stock market makes it harder for people to predict what prices in that market will be, even if the supply-and-demand model is used.

Finally, it is difficult to predict how long it will take for a price and quantity to reach equilibrium in every market. What we can say is that over time, quantities supplied and demanded will change, probably in a certain direction. We are less likely to know how rapidly the correction will occur. The adjustment will depend, in part, on how quickly information flows in the market, what barriers to adjusting prices firms and individuals face, and whether suppliers and demanders have some power to resist the change. What we *do* know is that the application of supply and demand is enormously useful because it predicts many outcomes so well. That is all that can be asked of any theory.

The equilibrium price and quantity won't change until there is a change in the economic environment that causes the supply or demand curves to shift. We will examine the effects of shifts in supply and demand on market equilibrium later in this chapter. First, let's explore a few additional intricacies of a market equilibrium.

## 4.2 Predicting Changes in a Market's Equilibrium

Recall from Chapter 3 that when a market is in equilibrium, its equilibrium price and quantity tend to remain stable unless there is a change in supply or demand. In other words, only when there is a change in the economic environment that causes the demand or supply curve to shift will the equilibrium price change. A new equilibrium price at which the quantity demanded just equals the quantity supplied must now be found by the market's participants because one of the curves has moved. In either case, the shift reflects a change in some factor other than the price of the good.

We identified factors that can cause a shift in either the demand or the supply curve. For example, a change in income or the price of a substitute or a complement will shift a good's demand curve but have no impact on its supply curve. Similarly, a change in the price of an input or production technology will shift the good's supply curve but leave its demand curve unaffected.

Now that you are able to identify how a change in the economic environment affects a market's supply and demand curves, you can make predictions about how its equilibrium price and quantity will change. To demonstrate, let's look at a market shock you are familiar with: an unexpected increase in the price of gasoline.

## A Market Disturbance: The Price of Gasoline Skyrockets

A significant increase in the price of gasoline will impact many markets. Let's speculate about just a few. An increase in gas prices increases the cost of commuting to work from the suburbs. Because the cost of commuting increases, over time the demand for suburban homes will fall. This will translate into a leftward shift in the demand curve for suburban homes. In contrast, the demand for fuel-efficient hybrid cars will increase following an increase in the price of gasoline. This will cause the demand curve for hybrid cars to shift to the right. When public transit is available, people will substitute toward this alternative and away from driving. As a result, the demand curve for public transportation will also shift to the right. In addition, because gasoline is an input in the production of overnight-delivery services—delivery trucks must fuel up—the supply curve for overnight-delivery services will shift to the left. The cost of delivering mail and packages at the same level as before now rises.

Given these varied responses to an increase in gas prices, let's use supply and demand to predict how each market's equilibrium might be affected. Because we want to know how equilibrium price and quantity are impacted by the gasoline price increase, we must compare the equilibrium in each market before and after the shock. This is done in **Figure 4.1**. In each market, we have assigned initial equilibrium prices and quantities.

Look first at the market for suburban homes. We predicted that the increase in gas prices would lead to a decline in the demand for these homes at all price levels. This is illustrated by the leftward shift in the demand curve to $D_2$ from $D_1$. The decline in demand, along with the unchanged supply curve, results in a lower market-clearing price and a smaller equilibrium quantity demanded. In the market for hybrid cars, the increase in demand is depicted by a rightward shift in the demand curve. This results in an equilibrium price and quantity that are higher than before the price of gas rose. A similar outcome occurs in the market for public transportation. The increase in demand for public transportation results in a higher price (fare) and a larger number of riders. Finally, the increase in production costs associated with higher gas prices leads to a leftward shift in the supply curve of overnight-delivery services. The market-clearing price for delivery services rises, and the equilibrium quantity demanded declines.

These results are striking in a number of ways. First, isn't it astonishing to realize that so many markets can be affected by just one price change? Although we have analyzed the impact of a change in gasoline prices on four markets, there are literally hundreds of others that also are affected. In just the labor market alone, an increase in the price of gasoline will impact the employment and wages of autoworkers, transit employees, airline pilots, suburban construction workers, and car salespeople, among others.

Second, our predictions about how equilibrium prices and quantities change will vary, depending on the market: sometimes the equilibrium price and quantity both increase (hybrid cars). At other times, the equilibrium price and quantity both decline (suburban homes). In still other instances, the equilibrium price increases, and the equilibrium quantity declines (overnight-delivery services). Now you know why it is difficult to make predictions about an economic shock until you have evaluated how it will affect the supply and demand curves in different markets.

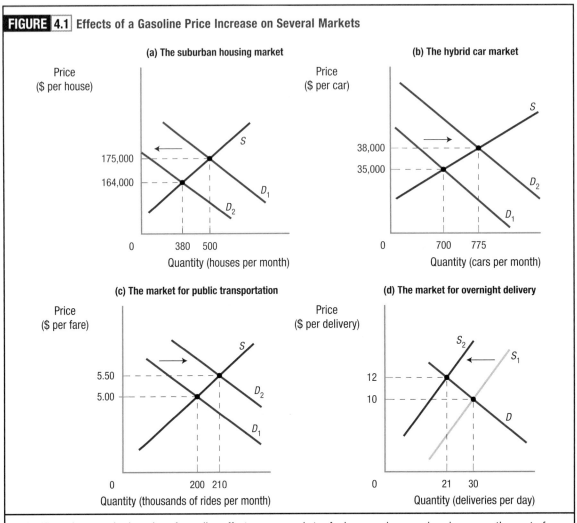

**FIGURE 4.1** Effects of a Gasoline Price Increase on Several Markets

A significant increase in the price of gasoline affects many markets. An increase in gas prices increases the cost of commuting to work from the suburbs. Increased commuting costs will lead to a decline in the demand for suburban homes as shown in panel (a). The demand for fuel-efficient hybrid cars will increase following an increase in the price of gasoline, causing the demand curve for hybrid cars to shift to the right as shown in panel (b). Facing higher gas prices, some people will substitute toward public transportation, shifting its demand curve to the right as shown in panel (c). Because gasoline is an input in the production of overnight-delivery services, the supply of overnight-delivery services will decline, as shown by the leftward shift in the supply curve in panel (d).

### Going from One Equilibrium to Another: Why Do Prices Change?

From your own personal experience, what usually happens when there is a lot more of a good for sale than there is demand for it? You're right if you predicted that the price must be reduced to clear the market. Let's use **Figure 4.2**, which shows the supply and demand curves for suburban houses, to dig deeper into what moves a market from its initial equilibrium. In this example, suppose there is a significant increase in the price of gasoline. Given the increase in gas prices, what happens in the market for suburban homes?

Given the decrease in demand (shown by the shift from $D_1$ to $D_2$), the first thing to ask is "why wouldn't the price just stay at $175,000?" At this price, builders are

CHAPTER 4 Applying the Supply-and-Demand Model 111

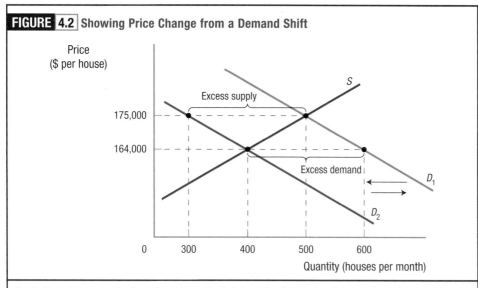

**FIGURE 4.2** Showing Price Change from a Demand Shift

A significant increase in the price of gas leads to a reduction in the demand for suburban homes, which is shown by the shift from $D_1$ to $D_2$. At the original equilibrium price of $175,000, builders supply and home buyers demand 500 houses per month. With the decline in demand, at the original equilibrium price, the quantity supplied is still 500 houses, but the quantity demanded is now only 300. With the decline in demand, and given the supply of homes, there is an excess supply of homes in the market at the original price. This excess supply puts downward pressure on prices until a new, lower equilibrium price is reached. At the new equilibrium price of $164,000, if demand for housing were to increase back to its original level ($D_1$), this would create excess demand for homes. When an excess demand occurs, there is upward pressure on prices. Prices will rise until a higher equilibrium price is reached.

still willing to supply 500 houses for sale per month. But at $175,000, the new quantity demanded from the buyers' side of the market has dropped to only 300. Another way of saying this is that after the increase in gas prices caused the demand for suburban homes to fall, the market for suburban houses was no longer in equilibrium at $175,000. When the demand curve shifted, at the original price and given the supply of homes, the market was in **disequilibrium**.

**DISEQUILIBRIUM** A situation in which the quantity demanded of a product does not equal the quantity of it supplied at the current price.

**EXAMPLE** At $95, there were ten times more people demanding tickets to Bruce Springsteen's last concert at the old Giants Stadium than the number of tickets available. The market for these tickets was in *disequilibrium* at the $95 ticket price.

**EXAMPLE** When American Airlines introduced the first nonstop flights from Los Angeles to New Zealand, it set the economy round-trip airfare at $1,895. At that price, the flights were only two-thirds full. The market for seats on these nonstop flights was in *disequilibrium*.

It is because the housing market is in disequilibrium that market prices and quantities eventually change. As Figure 4.2 shows, at $175,000, suppliers are willing to supply more houses than buyers are willing to purchase. A **surplus**, or **excess supply**, of houses is available.

**SURPLUS (EXCESS SUPPLY)** A situation in which the quantity supplied of a product exceeds the quantity of it demanded at the current price.

**EXAMPLE** At its cover price of $34.95, there were vast numbers of unsold, or *surplus*, copies of *A Dummy's Guide to Changing Lightbulbs*.

Because there is a surplus of houses, the price begins to drop as suppliers attempt to sell their inventories of homes. As the price drops, two things happen. First, the quantity demanded rises as individuals move down the new demand curve ($D_2$) in response to the falling price. Second, the quantity supplied decreases as suppliers move down the supply curve ($S$) in response to the falling price. This adjustment process pushes prices lower, toward the new equilibrium, or market-clearing price, of $164,000 and the new equilibrium quantity of houses traded (400 homes per month).

What if the price of gasoline remains high but incomes have also increased substantially? In other words, what if the demand for suburban homes increases, as illustrated by the demand curve shifting back to $D_1$ from $D_2$? After the gas hike, the market-clearing price is $164,000, and the quantity supplied is 400 homes per month. However, after the increase in demand, builders will see their homes being snapped up. At $164,000, the 400 homes supplied are less than the quantity demanded (600). This can be illustrated by extending a line from $164,000 over to the demand curve $D_1$. If the market is made up of the supply curve ($S$) and demand curve $D_1$ at a price of $164,000, the market is in disequilibrium. This time, however, the market suffers from a **shortage**, or **excess demand**, of homes at the going market price.

**SHORTAGE (EXCESS DEMAND)** A situation in which quantity demanded exceeds quantity supplied at the current price.

**EXAMPLE** For its fiftieth-anniversary celebration, McDonald's ran out of the hamburgers it was selling for 29 cents apiece. There was a *shortage* of hamburgers at that price.

You know what happens when something is in short supply: its price increases. In the presence of excess demand, buyers scramble to purchase the existing supply of the good. If suppliers are unable to meet the demand, they will ration its insufficient supply by increasing the price. As price rises, two things happen. First, the quantity demanded declines as individuals move up the new demand curve ($D_1$) in response to the higher price. Second, the quantity supplied increases as suppliers move up the supply curve ($S$) in response to the higher price. Eventually, these movements will lead to a market-clearing price where quantity demanded is just equal to quantity supplied.

The reason prices change in freely operating markets is because of an imbalance between quantities supplied and quantities demanded. How long does the adjustment process take? Prices and quantities usually do not instantly move to new equilibrium values. In our example, it may take some time for home builders to ramp up production (i.e., move up the market supply curve) in response to the increase in demand for suburban houses. The adjustment could take even longer if additional impediments, such as new regulations or zoning laws, prevent the adjustment from occurring.

The point is that through this type of adjustment process, prices in freely operating markets are always making their way toward equilibrium. The fact that the prices in some markets change quite often suggests that the underlying demand and supply conditions in these markets must also be changing frequently.

# 4.3 Consumer and Producer Surplus

A voluntary trade takes place only when it is mutually beneficial (at least at the time of the exchange) for both a buyer and a seller. The question is how much of the benefit from the exchange is captured by the buyer versus the seller? In our market for memory chips, for example, demanders were willing to pay at least $10 per chip for the first 50,000 memory chips produced by suppliers. But the buyers only needed to pay the equilibrium, or market-clearing, price of $6—not $10. The fact that the purchase price is less than what buyers were willing to pay means that they enjoyed a **consumer surplus (CS)**.

> **CONSUMER SURPLUS (CS)** The difference between a person's willingness to pay for a unit of a good and the amount that she actually pays.

> **EXAMPLE** You are willing to pay up to $15 for the newest book in the *Twilight* series. The book turns out to sell for $10.47, including tax. The difference between what you were willing to pay and what you actually paid—$4.53—is your consumer surplus.

The consumer surplus that memory-chip buyers enjoy amounts to the shaded area shown in **Figure 4.3**. Notice that the amount of consumer surplus declines with each additional unit purchased. In other words, the willingness of buyers to pay decreases as we move toward the last (150,000th) unit purchased. The 150,000th unit generates no consumer surplus.

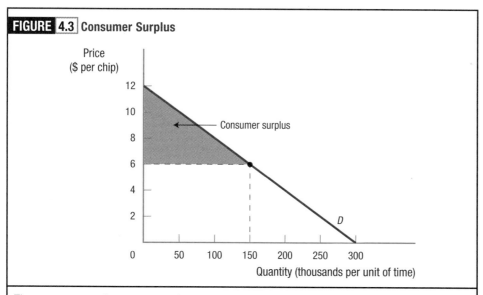

**FIGURE 4.3 Consumer Surplus**

The consumer surplus represents the gains from trade that buyers capture. At $6 per chip, buyers are willing and able to purchase 150,000 chips, more than the amount they are willing to buy at $10 (50,000 chips). At $10, some consumers are willing to buy memory chips. Even though buyers are willing to pay more for the first 50,000 chips, they don't have to. They get to keep some of what they were willing to pay, which is their consumer surplus. At a price of $6, the consumer surplus that memory-chip buyers enjoy equals the shaded area in the figure, which is the area above the price and below the demand curve. The amount of consumer surplus in the market declines with each additional unit purchased as we move toward the last (150,000th) unit purchased. The 150,000th unit generates no consumer surplus.

To better understand consumer surplus, think about what a demand curve actually represents: the demand curve shows the quantity of a good that consumers are willing and able to buy at different prices. At $6 per chip, buyers are willing and able to purchase 150,000 chips, which is more than the amount they are willing to buy at $10 (50,000 chips). However, even at $10, some consumers are willing to buy memory chips. This suggests that even though buyers are willing to pay more for the first 50,000 chips, they don't have to. They get to keep some of what they were willing to pay, which is their consumer surplus. Because of this consumer surplus, buyers are not indifferent to making a trade.

We can see from Figure 4.3 that if for some reason the price of memory chips rises, the amount of consumer surplus falls. This means that the gains from trade that buyers get also fall. Where does the loss in consumer surplus go? To answer this question, we must look at how suppliers fare in the market. **Figure 4.4** isolates the market supply curve for memory chips. The height of the supply curve at any output level tells us the marginal cost of the last unit produced. For example, the marginal cost of producing the 150,000th unit equals $6 per chip; the marginal cost of the 100,000th unit equals $4 per chip; and so on. At the equilibrium price ($6), the marginal cost of the very last chip sold just equals the price that the supplier receives. For all of the other units sold, the price received is greater than the marginal cost of production. The difference between equilibrium price and each unit's marginal cost is represented by the shaded area in Figure 4.4. We call this shaded area the **producer surplus (PS)**.

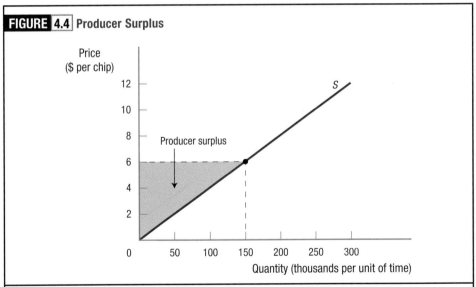

**FIGURE 4.4** Producer Surplus

The producer surplus represents the gains from trade that suppliers capture. At $6 per chip, producers are willing and able to sell 150,000 memory chips, which is more than the amount they are willing to supply at $4 per chip. At $4, producers are willing to supply 100,000 memory chips. Even though sellers are willing to take less than $6 apiece for the first 100,000 chips, they don't have to because some buyers are willing to pay that amount. As a result, the suppliers of the chips earn a producer surplus on 100,000 memory chips because all of the 150,000 chips are sold at one price ($6). The difference between the equilibrium price ($6) and each unit's marginal cost is the producer surplus.

**PRODUCER SURPLUS (PS)** The difference between the price a supplier receives for a unit of output and her marginal cost of producing that unit.

**EXAMPLE** Your opportunity cost of providing babysitting services to a neighbor on Saturday evenings is $7 an hour. However, because you are paid the going rate of $9 an hour, you enjoy $2 an hour of producer surplus every time you babysit.

To better understand producer surplus, think about what a supply curve represents: at various prices, the supply curve shows the quantity of a good that suppliers are willing and able to supply to the market. At $6 per chip, producers are willing and able to sell 150,000 memory chips, more than the amount they are willing to supply at $4 per chip. But even at $4, producers are willing to supply 100,000 memory chips. This suggests that even though sellers are willing to take less than $6 apiece for the first 100,000 chips, they don't have to. They earn a producer surplus on 100,000 memory chips because all of the 150,000 chips are sold at one price ($6). The existence of a producer surplus means that sellers are not just indifferent to a trade—they enjoy a net benefit. The producer surplus represents the gains from trade that suppliers capture.

By combining market demand and supply curves, we can compare the amount of surplus that each side of the market enjoys. This will help us answer the question we asked earlier: what happens to the lost consumer surplus when the market price increases? **Figure 4.5** shows two versions of the market supply and demand curves for

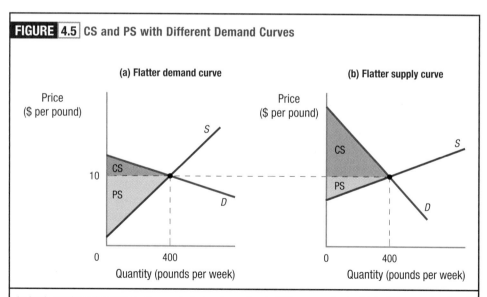

**FIGURE 4.5** CS and PS with Different Demand Curves

(a) Flatter demand curve

(b) Flatter supply curve

In both markets for coffee, the market-clearing price is $10 a pound, at which 400 pounds of coffee are purchased weekly. The consumer surplus (CS) is the highlighted area above the equilibrium price and below the demand curve. The producer surplus (PS) is the shaded area below the equilibrium price and above the supply curve. These two versions of the coffee market reveal that the amount of surplus each side enjoys depends on the slopes of the supply and demand curves. A market with a flatter demand curve like the one shown in panel (a) generates less consumer surplus and more producer surplus. A market with a flatter supply curve like the one shown in panel (b) generates more consumer surplus and less producer surplus.

some other good—let's say coffee. Suppose that in both instances the market-clearing price is $10 a pound. At that price, 400 pounds of coffee are purchased in the market each week. The consumer surplus is the area highlighted above the equilibrium price and below the demand curve. The producer surplus is shown by the shaded area under equilibrium price and above the supply curve.

What these two versions of the coffee market reveal is that the amount of surplus each side enjoys depends crucially on the slopes of the supply and demand curves. Even when the equilibrium price ($10) and quantity (400) are the same, a market with a flatter demand curve generates less consumer surplus and more producer surplus. In contrast, a market with a flatter supply curve generates more consumer surplus and less producer surplus. Why? A flatter demand curve means that the willingness of consumers to pay for the first and last units purchased are not very different. As a result, buyers will not realize much of an increase in consumer surplus even if the price falls. Similarly, a flatter supply curve means that the marginal cost of producing the first unit and the last are not very different. Therefore, suppliers will not reap as much producer surplus as when the supply curve is more steeply sloped.

Although we used coffee in our example, there are goods for which the demand and supply curves take on distinct slopes. For example, the demand for insulin is much less responsive to prices changes than, say, tennis shoes. In other words, if the price of insulin increases, the quantity demanded will not change much because users need it to survive. When it comes to tennis shoes, however, there are many substitutes in the market, so when the prices of one brand increase, consumers are much more willing to purchase another. This suggests that as the number of substitutes increases, the demand curve for the good tends to be more price-responsive or flatter. On the supply side, how much the quantity supplied changes when there is a change in price is affected by how easily the good's production can be changed. Think of something in very short supply: a mint-condition Ford Mustang Boss 302 built in 1970. Changes in the price of this car will not lead to an increase in the production of them. The supply curve would be very vertical. In contrast, the supply curve for a commodity such as soybeans (the ingredient in tofu) is much more responsive to a price change. It is much easier for corn farmers to switch to soybean production if the price of soybeans rises relative to corn.

We can use consumer and producer surplus to argue that the market-clearing, or equilibrium, price is the best price for the market. We mean *best* in the sense that it is the economically efficient price. The equilibrium price allocates goods between buyers and producers in a manner that equates marginal benefits to marginal costs. (You might argue that any lower price is best, but that ignores the impact on producers.) Consumer and producer surplus are important when governments consider the benefits of public-works projects such as roads and bridges.

Suppose the states of Illinois and Missouri are contemplating a new bridge spanning the Mississippi River between St. Louis and Illinois. The value that drivers place on the new bridge equals the consumer surplus they would receive from it—which would be the entire area under the demand curve if the bridge is toll-free. This amount would have to be quantified and incorporated into an assessment of the bridge's benefit, which then can be compared to the cost of building the new bridge. If this estimate is smaller than the projected cost of the bridge, then economics suggests that it shouldn't be built. Of course, whether it is or not depends on more than just economics: political will and public opinion often take precedence over cold calculations.

## SOLVED PROBLEM

**Q** Using supply and demand curves, show what happens in the residential mortgage loan market if the value of housing declines and thereby increases the risk of making these loans. How do consumer and producer surplus change?

**A** The increase in risk increases the opportunity cost of making residential loans, which results in a leftward shift in the supply curve of available money. The equilibrium interest rate increases, and the equilibrium number of loans made declines. The result is a reduction in consumer surplus and a decrease in producer surplus.

**The market for residential mortgage loans**

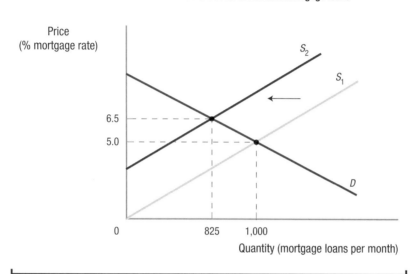

## 4.4 Putting the Supply-and-Demand Model to Work in Different Markets

As you have learned, you can use supply and demand to analyze any number of different markets and circumstances. The model can also help us see the impact certain government policies can have, such as what will happen if the minimum wage is raised or taxes are imposed. In this section, we will explore more applications of supply and demand like these. You might be surprised by the markets in which the model can be used and the outcomes it predicts.

### The Market for Human Organs

Do you think there should be a market in which transplantable human organs can be sold? Some blood banks pay people to donate blood. Why should organs be any different? The issue is a hotly debated one because of its ethical, legal, and economic aspects. Let's think about the economics of how such a market could work.

**Figure 4.6** presents hypothetical market demand and market supply curves for transplantable human kidneys. If a freely operating market existed, the market-clearing price would be $75,000. At that price, 100 kidneys per month would be made available for transplanting by living donors and the families of the deceased.

The market for transplantable kidneys *does* actually exist in the United States. However, it does not operate like other markets. Live kidney donors can legally be paid for supplying a kidney to someone else, but only an amount equal to the cost of their medical expenses. The families of deceased donors receive nothing. Wouldn't

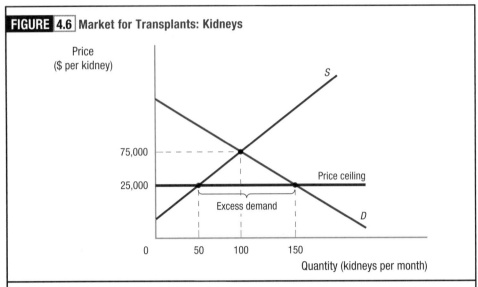

**FIGURE 4.6** **Market for Transplants: Kidneys**

This figure shows a hypothetical market for transplantable human kidneys. The demand and supply curves in this market establish an equilibrium, or market-clearing price, of $75,000, at which the equilibrium quantity of kidneys available is 100 per month. If a ceiling price on kidneys is set below the equilibrium price, then the market is in disequilibrium. At a ceiling price of $25,000, donors are willing to supply only 50 kidneys a month, far fewer than the 150 kidneys demanders are willing to buy. The price ceiling creates a shortage of kidneys available for transplant.

you think the opportunity cost of donating a kidney in either circumstance to be greater than the payment amount permitted by law? A live donor might suffer from lost wages, not to mention pain and potential long-term health problems. The families of the deceased might suffer mental anguish at the thought of having their loved one's kidneys removed and parceled out.

The reimbursement cap imposed on donors is, in effect, a **price ceiling**.

> **PRICE CEILING** The maximum price at which a good can be *legally* traded in a market.

> **EXAMPLE** Scalpers routinely get twice the face value sales price for St. Louis Cardinal baseball tickets they sell outside the stadium. If the city of St. Louis passed a law fixing the price scalpers could charge to be less than the ticket's face value, that would be a price ceiling.

Figure 4.6 depicts the effects of a price ceiling on kidneys. Suppose the ceiling price for reasonable medical costs is set at $25,000. At this below-equilibrium price, also shown in Figure 4.6, donors are willing to provide only 50 kidneys a month. But at this price, demanders would like to buy 150 kidneys a month. This artificial price ceiling creates a shortage of kidneys (in this case, 100 kidneys) available for transplant. It also reduces the number of kidneys that would be available if the market were allowed to function freely—that is, without the ceiling. At the market-clearing price of $75,000, there would be 100 kidneys available for transplant, a greater number than available with the price ceiling.

Do we know exactly what the ceiling price is? No, but we do know that the ceiling price must be below the market-determined equilibrium price because a long waiting list of needy kidney recipients exists. In 2008, more than 80,000 patients were registered on the official kidney waiting list of the United Network for Organ Sharing (UNOS) in the United States. With the price set too low, the model predicts a shortage, and a shortage actually exists.

The price ceiling also raises a number of other questions. First, who will get the kidneys that are supplied? Figuring out how to allocate kidneys in the United States has continued to vex economists, philosophers, transplant surgeons, and ethicists. A person's willingness to pay for a kidney has been ruled out because it is believed to be an unfair way to allocate the organs. Obviously, the richest people would get them first. Most people don't believe that is right. Consequently, some other way has to be used. Should the sickest among the potential recipients go to the head of the list (in which case, the number of lives actually saved by transplants would likely go down)? Should a patient's age matter?

The answer depends on the goals of the people who design the allocation rules. However, even transplant surgeons are at odds over how kidneys should be allocated. Some surgeons believe that organs should be used within the same geographic area in which they are collected. In other words, kidneys harvested in the Midwest would be transplanted into Midwest patients. Others argue for a national system of distribution. Because kidneys are essential to their livelihoods, transplant surgeons are particularly concerned about the allocation rule that is adopted. This may also explain their keen interest in new technologies that reduce the need for kidneys or increase the success of partial-kidney transplants.

The Canadian health system imposes stringent price ceilings on the prices Canadian surgeons can charge, which leads to long waits for elective surgical procedures. In response, some Canadians venture into U.S. border states where they pay the full tab but receive timelier hip-replacement or back surgeries. Some patients who are in need of a kidney transplant become "transplant tourists," traveling abroad to buy kidneys in countries where the illegal trade of them is not policed. Instead of waiting months or years in their home countries, these patients can find prepackaged deals abroad in which they receive both a kidney and transplant surgery.[1] As you can see, some of the excess demand created by the price ceiling leaks to other markets in which there are no price ceilings or they are not enforced.

We see a similar result in credit markets in which price ceilings are imposed. Most states have usury laws that set a maximum interest rate that can be charged a borrower. As a result, regulated lenders won't lend money to people or businesses with a high risk of default. The lenders can't charge them enough to make it worthwhile to assume such high risks. People who are a poor credit risk are then forced to borrow money from loan sharks or in the unregulated payday loan market. The annual interest rates in these markets can be as high as 2,400 percent (borrow $1, pay back $24), which is far greater than the 6- to 24-percent usury limits set by most states.

## SOLVED PROBLEM

**Q** Suppose the government is concerned that a rise in interest rates will adversely affect the adjustable mortgage rates of thousands of home owners and lead to numerous foreclosures. Show how imposing a price freeze on interest rates will impact the results in this chapter's first Solved Problem. Who wins and who loses when the price freeze is imposed?

· · · · · · ·

[1]Larry Rohter, "The Organ Trade: A Global Black Market; Tracking the Sale of a Kidney on a Path of Poverty and Hope." *New York Times*, May 23, 2004.

**A** Suppose the price freeze is set at the original equilibrium mortgage rate of 5 percent. Following the decrease in supply, which is shown by the shift from $S_1$ to $S_2$ in the following figure, there is an excess demand for loans. At a mortgage rate of 5 percent, the quantity of loans demanded equals 1,000, but the quantity supplied is only 600. The winners are those who already have adjustable loans with frozen rates. The losers are those who are willing to pay a higher interest rate for a home loan but are unable to get one because of the interest rate freeze.

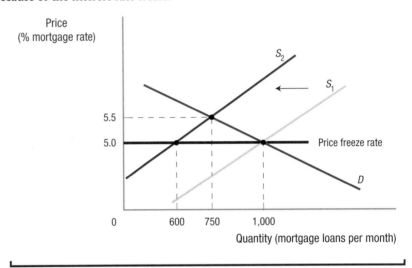

## The Market for Low-Skilled Labor

Many industries employ entry-level and low-skilled workers. Baggers at a grocery store, people who mow lawns, and dishwashers are just a few examples of workers who don't need advanced skills to be employed. **Figure 4.7** shows a segment of this market: dishwashers in the restaurant industry.

The price in Figure 4.7 is the hourly wage rate. The quantity is the number of jobs in this market. If employers are attempting to maximize their profits, they will demand more workers (create more jobs) as the price they pay for dishwashers—the wage rate—falls. If the wage rate rises, firms will demand fewer workers. The labor-supply curve takes the expected upward slope. As the wage rises, you are more likely to trade leisure for work because the opportunity cost of not working increases in terms of the income you forgo. The supply of labor, therefore, is based on the decisions made by individuals who determine how they wish to trade off hours working and not working at different wage rates. In this market, the market-clearing wage rate is $5.50 an hour. At this wage, firms are willing to provide 670,000 jobs workers are willing to do.

Suppose that this market experiences an influx of low-skilled workers because of an increase in immigration or the number of teenagers reaching working age. The increase in the supply of low-skilled workers shifts the supply curve leftward to $S_2$, as Figure 4.7 shows. If the demand is unchanged, the model predicts that the market-clearing wage will fall to $4.50, and the number of jobs will rise to 800,000.

Some people would argue that the $4.50 wage rate is too low for a person to live on. Some localities in fact have passed living-wage laws. Living-wage laws prohibit employers from paying workers anything less than the legal wage rate. In effect, laws such as these create a **price floor** below which the price cannot go.

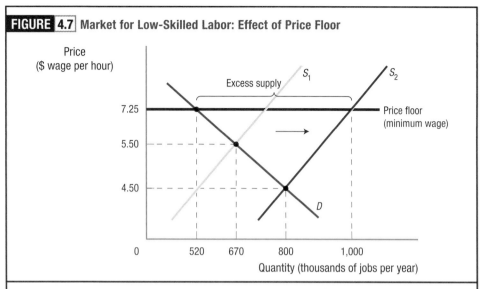

**FIGURE 4.7** Market for Low-Skilled Labor: Effect of Price Floor

The equilibrium "price" for dishwashers is an hourly wage rate of $5.50. At this wage rate, the equilibrium quantity of jobs is 670,000. The market experiences an influx of low-skilled workers, which is shown by the rightward shift in the supply curve. This causes the equilibrium wage to fall to $4.50, and the number of jobs to increase to 800,000. Suppose the government imposes a price floor (minimum wage) of $7.25. At this wage, 1 million individuals are willing to work as dishwashers, but employers are willing to hire only 520,000 people. The price floor creates a surplus of labor in the market.

**PRICE FLOOR** The minimum price at which a legal trade can occur in a market.

**EXAMPLE** Employers cannot hire employees at a wage below the minimum wage set by the federal government. The minimum wage is a price floor.

How does a price floor affect the allocation of labor in a market? Suppose the government imposes a minimum wage, or price floor, of $7.25 for all workers, including dishwashers. In Figure 4.7, you can see that at this wage—which is much higher than the equilibrium wage of $4.50—there is now a surplus of workers. At $7.25, 1 million individuals now would be willing to work. However, because the demand by employers hasn't changed, at a wage rate of $7.25, they are willing to hire only 520,000 people. If the market determined the wage, there would be more job opportunities (800,000 jobs) than occurs with the minimum wage (520,000 jobs). Like a price ceiling, a price floor in the market for low-skilled workers creates disequilibrium.

It is no surprise that the debate is ongoing over the federal government's minimum-wage laws. In 2010, the federal minimum wage was $7.25 per hour. However, other states and municipalities have established even higher wages in some markets. In 2007, the state of Maryland passed legislation mandating that state contractors working on jobs worth more than $100,000 must pay their workers $11.20 in some parts of the state and $8.30 in others. In Ottawa, Canada, the city council in early 2010 was set to impose an $11.30 minimum wage for city workers.

In markets in which there are price ceilings and price floors, there are gains from trade between buyers and sellers that go unexploited because fewer trades occur.

In our minimum-wage example, employees want to work up to the point where the opportunity cost of the last hour they worked just equals the wage they receive. At the same time, employers want to hire labor up to the point where their willingness to pay for an additional hour of labor just equals the wage rate. In other words, employers and employees, left alone to trade, will go to where the height of the supply curve just equals the height of the demand curve—that is, to the equilibrium wage of $5.50 an hour and 670,000 jobs. However, employers will be unable to hire employees at this wage rate because it falls below minimum wage. The shortfall in employment that results is sometimes referred to as the "underemployment" effect of the minimum wage.

When a minimum wage results in an excess supply of workers, who gets to work? Employers can decide who to hire based on factors other than the wage they will pay the worker. The factors might include the applicant's work history, education, hair length, number of facial piercings, or general attractiveness. Employers no longer have the option of hiring unskilled, high-risk applicants at a wage that's below the minimum wage. To some extent, this explains why many studies have found that minimum-wage laws have the worst impact on the employment rates of unskilled minority males, especially teenagers and young adults.[2]

Minimum-wage laws can also have a significant impact on markets in which labor is a major input into production. Recall that an increase in input costs leads to a leftward shift in the market supply curve. An increase in the minimum wage can result in a large leftward shift in the supply curve in markets that depend heavily on unskilled labor. Agricultural, food services, and clothing markets are examples. In these markets, a leftward shift in the supply curve leads to a higher equilibrium price and a lower equilibrium quantity of goods. This creates a dilemma for policy makers: raising the minimum wage improves the living standards of minimum-wage workers who have jobs. However, both the workers and the people unemployed as a result of the minimum wage have to pay higher prices for the goods produced with minimum-wage labor.

**ECONOMIC FALLACY**   When teachers' unions negotiate higher-than-equilibrium wages for their members, the total amount paid to all teachers rises.

**False.** Those teachers who continue to have jobs at the higher wage will earn more as long as there are rules that block any reduction in their hours. However, there will be teachers who will not be hired at the higher wage. The total amount spent on teachers may or may not increase, depending on each school district's ability to substitute other personnel for teachers or increase the student–teacher ratio. In any event, the union's most senior members will tend to be winners to the extent that seniority (time on the job) becomes the rule by which scarce teaching positions are allocated.

## Can Market Mechanisms Be Used to Enforce Price Controls?

Price floors and ceilings are difficult to sustain because the marketplace wants to move toward equilibrium prices and quantities. Short of arresting or fining violators, are there ways price controls can be sustained using natural market mechanisms? Suppose that the Indian government sets a price ceiling in the lentil market to make

· · · · · · ·

[2]David Neumark, *Minimum Wage Effects in the Post-Welfare Reform Era*. Employment Policies Institute, January 2007.

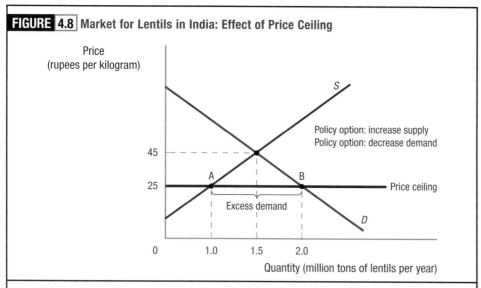

**FIGURE 4.8** **Market for Lentils in India: Effect of Price Ceiling**

Price ceilings are difficult to sustain because market forces drive prices and quantities toward equilibrium. The figure shows the hypothetical market for lentils in India. At the price ceiling of 25 rupees per kilogram, the quantity demanded is 2 million tons per year. However, the quantity supplied is only 1 million tons. To sustain the price ceiling, the Indian government could create a situation in which the price ceiling becomes the new equilibrium price. This can be done using a policy that shifts the supply curve for lentils to the right or by using a policy that shifts the demand curve for lentils to the left. Or the government could use some combination of the two policies to achieve its goal.

lentils more affordable for its population. **Figure 4.8** shows the hypothetical market for lentils in India. Suppose the price ceiling is set at 25 rupees per kilogram, which is lower than the market price of 45 rupees. At this lower, artificial price, the quantity demanded of lentils is 2 million tons per year; the quantity supplied is only 1 million tons. To sustain the price ceiling, the Indian government must either police each and every trade that takes place, or it can create a situation in which the price ceiling becomes the new equilibrium price. This can be done by enacting one of two policies: shift the market supply curve for lentils to the right, or shift the market demand curve for lentils to the left. The outcomes of these alternatives are represented as equilibrium A and equilibrium B.

What kinds of policies would have this effect? The supply curve would shift right if the government imported lentils to supply to the domestic market or banned the export of lentils produced in the country.[3] The demand curve for lentils would shift left if, for example, the government subsidized the price of products that could be substituted for lentils. If the Indian government can get these policies just right, there would no longer be a shortage of lentils, and the market-clearing price would now be at the price ceiling. Notice that the new equilibrium quantity would differ, depending on which policy is pursued: when the demand curve shifts to the left, the equilibrium quantity of lentils declines; when the supply curve shifts to the right, the equilibrium quantity of lentils increases.

· · · · · · ·

[3]Corey Kilgannon, "Trouble in Queens as Lentil Prices Rise." *New York Times,* September 29, 2006.

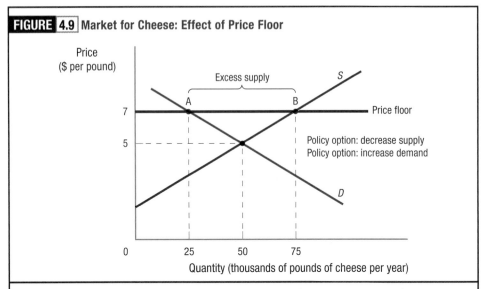

**FIGURE 4.9** **Market for Cheese: Effect of Price Floor**

A price floor for cheese is set above the equilibrium price of $5. The price floor of $7 creates a surplus in the market. To support this price, the government could enact policies that increase the demand for cheese, shifting the market demand for cheese to the right; or policies that decrease the supply of cheese, shifting the market supply of cheese to the left; or both. If the government achieves either goal in exactly the right measure, the price floor ($7) becomes the new market-clearing, equilibrium price. Regardless of the policy chosen, the price of cheese will be higher than it would have been at the market-clearing price of $5.

Suppose a price floor of $7 was imposed on cheese. As **Figure 4.9** shows, the price floor is above the equilibrium price of $5, which creates a surplus. At the price floor, too much cheese is being produced. Once again, the government could use the market's own internal tendencies to support this price. It could enact policies that shift the demand for cheese to the right. Or the government could enact policies that shift the supply of cheese to the left. If the government achieves either goal in exactly the right measure, the price floor becomes the new market-clearing, equilibrium price.

The U.S. government has, in fact, used both approaches in the domestic cheese market. In 2009, the Obama administration purchased surplus cheese from dairy farmers, thereby shifting the demand curve for cheese to the right and creating support for a price higher than the market's equilibrium price.[4] The surplus cheese was then distributed to food pantries in the United States and overseas. The government has also created programs to pay farmers to reduce their dairy herds in order to shift the supply curve for dairy products to the left. One failed policy—which actually led to spot shortages of milk—offered cash payments to dairy farmers who were willing to turn some of their dairy cows into hamburger.[5] Once again, if the government can get it just right, it can maintain its price floor by capitalizing on the market's own tendencies.

• • • • • • •

[4]Associated Press, "President Signs Emergency Aid for Dairy Farmers." *New York Times,* October 21, 2009.

[5]"Why Milk Consumers?" *New York Times,* April 4, 1989.

Of course, depending on the strategy adopted, the quantity of cheese produced will be less or more than the equilibrium quantity produced at the market's natural equilibrium price. In either case, however, the American consumer ends up paying more at the grocery store for cheese products. And both approaches can be costly to taxpayers. From a policy standpoint, you might ask whether paying dairy farmers to reduce their herd sizes or buying up surplus cheese is an efficient use of taxpayers' dollars. If the market prevailed, these expenditures would not be necessary. But at the same time, this could lead to severe hardship for dairy farmers and those whose incomes depend on the dairy business. As you can imagine, government policies involve a complicated mix of economics and politics.

## The Market for Houses

Over the past few years, the housing market has gotten a great deal of attention. One reason is because home prices across much of the country increased tremendously in the first half of the decade. Between 2001 and 2006, the average price of a house in the United States increased from about $140,000 to $250,000. In some markets, the increase was even greater. Then that changed. From 2006 through 2009, the average house in the United States lost about 30 percent of its value, falling to an average price of $173,000.

As of mid 2011, housing prices in many cities had not regained much, if any, of the lost value. The increase and decrease in housing prices may have affected you or your friends. Many owners had a great deal of wealth tied up in their house, so when home prices declined, they saw their wealth disappear. As a result, some home owners cut back on major expenses, such as the college tuition they were willing to pay for their children.

Because the developments in the housing market have had such widespread effects, let's use the supply-and-demand model to see if we can explain the observed surge in prices, both up and down. **Figure 4.10** illustrates the housing market in one

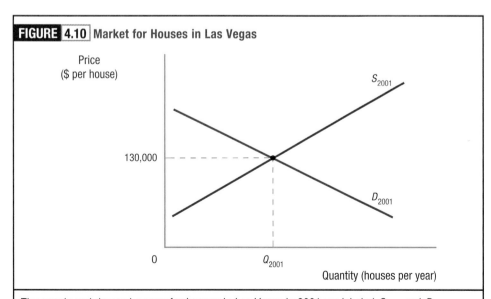

**FIGURE 4.10** Market for Houses in Las Vegas

The supply and demand curves for houses in Las Vegas in 2001 are labeled $S_{2001}$ and $D_{2001}$, respectively. Given these initial conditions, the market-clearing price for the average home is $130,000.

city, Las Vegas. We chose Las Vegas because it experienced one of the most startling increases and steepest falls in home prices. The average price of a house in Las Vegas soared from \$130,000 in 2001 to about \$310,000 in 2006. From 2006 to 2009, however, the price of an average house in Las Vegas declined by more than 50 percent. The supply and demand curves for Las Vegas housing in 2001 are labeled $S_{2001}$ and $D_{2001}$, respectively. Given these initial conditions, we've labeled the equilibrium price for the average home at \$130,000. Because we are mostly concerned with explaining the behavior of prices in this market, let's simplify things and let the quantity of houses sold be represented by the generic quantity of $Q_{2001}$.

Between 2001 and 2006, the demand for houses in Las Vegas and everywhere else was subject to a number of "shocks." Following the stock market crash of 2000, many people looked for ways to invest their savings instead of putting it in the stock market. Housing was one alternative, especially because it was commonly believed that house prices tend not to fall, but to rise over time. This investment effect caused the demand for housing to increase, shifting the demand curve to the right. A second effect occurred after the nation's central bank (the Federal Reserve) undertook a policy to significantly lower the costs of borrowing money. As a result, mortgage rates fell to historic lows. The low rates increased the demand for housing, further pushing the demand curve to the right.

At the time, there also was a push by the government to increase home ownership across many groups that had never been fully represented. This often led to a relaxation of lending criteria, the creation of zero-interest loans, and forbearance on loan delinquencies. (Many of these loans would later become the so-called toxic assets that helped fuel the financial crisis of 2007–2009.) Finally, when housing prices started to skyrocket, many buyers believed that prices in the future would only increase further. Buyers wanted to jump on the housing bandwagon before they were priced out of the market. This also increased demand for housing.

What about the supply side? The lowered borrowing costs made it cheaper for builders in Las Vegas to build houses on speculation; that is, houses for which there is no buyer when they are built. Contractors had a "build the houses, and buyers will come" mentality and borrowed funds to build more and more homes, which increased the supply of new homes. This shifted the supply curve to the right. Of course, seeing the prices of their houses skyrocket, more home owners put their houses up for sale. This also increases the supply of houses and pushed the supply curve to the right.

We can illustrate the interactive influences by shifting both the supply and demand curves in Figure 4.10. We do this in **Figure 4.11**. There we see that even though the supply of homes increased between 2001 and 2006, shown by the shift in supply from $S_{2001}$ to $S_{2006}$, the increase in demand was huge. We show this by shifting the demand curve from $D_{2001}$ to $D_{2006}$. The increase in demand was so much greater than the increase in supply that the market-clearing price for an average Las Vegas home increased from \$130,000 to more than \$300,000. Given that increasing the supply of homes takes more time than increasing demand, this slower reaction on the supply side helps explain the run-up in prices.

Was the increase in Las Vegas home prices an economic bubble that was about to pop? Many buyers truly expected that the double-digit percentage increase in home prices would continue indefinitely. Their expectations weren't based so much on economics as hope. Beginning in 2007, the economy and financial markets entered a very tumultuous period. Major financial institutions failed, loans that were once thought legitimate came under closer scrutiny, and by late 2007 the economy entered into a severe downturn. The demand for housing fell sharply in Las Vegas and elsewhere.

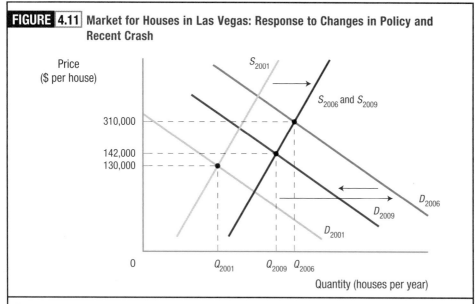

**FIGURE 4.11** Market for Houses in Las Vegas: Response to Changes in Policy and Recent Crash

Between 2001 and 2006, the demand for houses in Las Vegas increased, shifting the demand curve from $D_{2001}$ to $D_{2006}$. The supply of homes also increased, shifting the supply curve from $S_{2001}$ to $S_{2006}$. Because the increase in demand for houses exceeded the increase in supply, the average Las Vegas home price increased from \$130,000 in 2001 to more than \$300,000 in 2006. After 2006, the demand for housing in Las Vegas (and elsewhere) fell sharply, as shown by the leftward shift in the demand curve from $D_{2006}$ to $D_{2009}$. Given no change in the supply of homes, this decrease in demand resulted in the average home price in Las Vegas falling from \$310,000 in 2006 to \$142,000 in 2009.

We show this in Figure 4.11 as the leftward shift in the demand curve for housing, from $D_{2006}$ to $D_{2009}$. Assuming that the supply of houses has not yet adjusted—there remain many new homes on the market in addition to many foreclosed homes—the model predicts that the market-clearing price should adjust downward. This is just what happened: the average home price in Las Vegas fell from \$310,000 in 2006 to \$142,000 in 2009.

Before leaving this example, we should note that not all housing markets suffered the same fate as Las Vegas. In some markets, average home prices initially rose much more slowly. In other markets, average housing prices fell less dramatically. In Amarillo, Texas, home prices actually increased after 2007. So, although our example explains the changes in the Las Vegas housing market, clearly other factors have affected the supply and demand for houses in other areas of the nation.

**ECONOMIC FALLACY**   The price of housing has risen steadily over the last decade and so has the number of housing units purchased. This shows that demand curves can slope upward.

**False.** This situation violates the assumption we made in Chapter 3 that all other factors must be held constant to gauge the effect of prices in a market. In fact, other factors were at work. First, during this period interest rates were low and falling, meaning that more people had the ability to pay for housing because they could borrow against their future earnings at a lower cost. Their purchasing power for housing had increased, in other words. Second, there was an increase in the number of people willing and able to pay for more expensive housing because baby boomers were coming into their peak earning years, as well as an influx of wealthier immigrants. Both of these factors caused the market demand curve for housing to shift to the right. As a result, the marginal willingness of people to pay for each unit of housing was higher than it was before.

## The Economic Effects of a Tax

If faced with the question "Would you rather pay more in income taxes or less?" most of us would give that question little thought: less, of course. We want to retain more of our income to buy more goods or to put more into savings. We usually do not think about the fact that our taxes pay for the public university you might be attending or our elderly citizens' Social Security payments. Let's leave aside the personal aspects of the tax debate and focus on the basic economics of what an income tax does. We can do this with the supply-and-demand model.

Figure 4.12 illustrates the market for labor. The market-clearing wage rate is $8 an hour. At this wage, individuals are willing to supply an average of 40 hours of work per week. Now look what happens when an income tax is imposed. Because the tax reduces the after-tax income workers earn, workers will require a higher pretax wage to supply the same number of hours. This is illustrated in Figure 4.12 by the wage rate of $10. Because the firm's demand for labor has not changed, the higher wage rate they have to pay leads them to reduce the hours of labor they are willing to hire. In effect, the tax creates a wedge between supply and demand. The firm is forced to pay the higher pretax wage of $10, which reduces its hours demanded to 20. Because

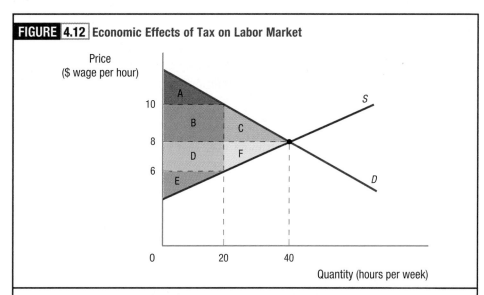

**FIGURE 4.12** Economic Effects of Tax on Labor Market

The market-clearing wage rate of $8 induces individuals to supply and firms to demand an average of 40 hours of work per week. An income tax reduces the after-tax income workers earn. Workers now require a higher pretax wage to supply the same number of hours. At this higher wage rate ($10), firms reduce the hours of labor they demand. The tax thus creates a wedge between supply and demand. The tax reduces both consumer and producer surplus. It also creates a deadweight loss to society equal to the area C + F.

workers respond only to their after-tax take-home wage, shown as $6 in the figure, 20 hours is all they are willing to supply.

The income tax thus leads to disequilibrium in the market, one it can't adjust from. The wage paid by firms is higher than in a nontax world, the after-tax wage received by workers is lower, and the number of hours worked is fewer. Taxes also generate significant economic losses to the economy. In its initial state, with the equilibrium wage and quantity of hours being determined by the demand and supply curves, the consumer surplus the firm gets is equal to the area A + B + C. The economic benefit to workers—their producer surplus—is equal to the area D + E + F. The market-based outcome maximizes consumer and producer surplus. However, the tax upsets this outcome. When the income tax is imposed, the government takes away some of the consumer and producer surplus in the form of tax revenues. The amount of tax revenues collected is equal to the area B + D. After taxes are imposed, the consumer surplus shrinks to the area A and the producer surplus shrinks to the area E.

After we account for the new consumer surplus, the new producer surplus, and the government's tax revenues, we find that some of the original consumer and producer surplus is unaccounted for. This unaccounted for surplus amounts to the area in the triangle C + F in Figure 4.12. This area is referred to as the **deadweight loss** from a tax. In a world with no income tax, the equilibrium wage and quantity of labor is established by individuals and firms making rational economic decisions. Imposing the tax moves the wage rate and quantity of labor to an inefficient solution. That inefficiency is captured by the deadweight loss.

> **DEADWEIGHT LOSS** The sum of consumer and producer surplus lost when an artificial price and quantity are imposed on a market.

So are income taxes bad? Without taxes, there would be no revenue to support local fire and police, no funds for infrastructure such as roads and bridges, and public education. But it still is true that a tax creates disequilibrium in the market, which can have real economic costs. For example, a number of studies have found that states with high tax rates have worse economic track records than states with lower tax rates. Taxes are not costless, in an economic sense.

## The Economic Effects of Tariffs and Quotas

Governments sometimes respond to foreign competition by increasing barriers to trade. Firms that produce goods abroad sometimes have an unfair advantage over firms that produce the same goods domestically. For example, some foreign governments subsidize the production of certain goods, especially agricultural goods. Should the U.S. government prevent these less-expensive goods from coming into the country so that they don't put domestic producers out of business? Many people say yes because the price of producing these products does not reflect the true costs of doing so. Other people argue that when foreign governments subsidize their domestic producers, they are essentially taxing their citizens, and we get the benefit in terms of cheaper goods.

**Figure 4.13** shows the demand and supply curves for steel. In this instance, however, the demand curve is the demand for imported steel by U.S. manufacturers. The supply curve is the supply of steel by foreign companies for export to the U.S. market. In other words, the United States is importing steel from abroad. The market-clearing or equilibrium price is $P_e$; the equilibrium quantity sold is $Q_e$.

Let's use this supply-and-demand model to predict the impact of raising barriers to trade. Suppose the U.S. government decides, usually because of political pressure

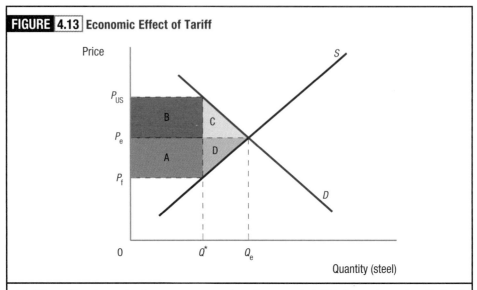

**FIGURE 4.13** Economic Effect of Tariff

A tariff acts like a tax and reduces consumer and producer surplus. This figure shows the effects of a tariff on imported goods, in this case, steel. The tariff, here equal to ($P_{US} - P_f$), raises the price paid by U.S. buyers ($P_{US}$) and lowers the price received by foreign exporters ($P_f$). It also lowers the quantity of steel available for purchase in the U.S. market. The U.S. government gains additional revenues equal to the area A + B, but the deadweight loss to society equals the area C + D.

from domestic steel producers, to limit steel imports. One way to do this is to impose a tariff on imported steel. Such an action was taken by the Bush administration in 2002.[6] A **tariff** is essentially a tax levied on an imported good. Like any tax, a tariff will distort the market's equilibrium price and quantity on the good on which it's been levied.

**TARIFF**   A tax levied on an imported good.

**EXAMPLE** In 1962, France and Germany levied a tariff on chickens imported from the United States. The goal was to reduce the consumption of U.S. chicken by French and German residents.

**EXAMPLE** In 1963, President Lyndon Johnson retaliated and imposed a tariff on various items imported from Europe, including light trucks. The goal was to reduce Americans' purchase of light trucks produced in Europe.

In Figure 4.13, the tariff imposed by U.S. officials on imported steel is measured as the vertical distance between the demand curve and the supply curve. The tariff amounts to the difference ($P_{US} - P_f$). The tariff, like an income tax, creates a wedge between the price that exporters receive (labeled $P_f$) and what U.S. buyers have to pay (labeled $P_{US}$). The tariff raises the price to U.S. buyers and lowers the price received by foreign exporters. It also lowers the quantity of steel available for purchase in the U.S. market.

· · · · · · ·

[6]"Bush Imposes Steel Tariffs." *USA Today*, March 5, 2002.

Who gains from the tariff? The U.S. government does. The area equal to A + B in Figure 4.13 measures the revenue received by the government from imposing the tariff. Notice, however, that the tariff results in a deadweight loss to society. The triangle equal to C + D represents the economic loss to everyone. Second, domestic producers of steel also gain from the tariff. Because Russian steel is now more expensive, U.S. producers are able to profitably continue producing steel.

Who loses because of the tariff? The losers are U.S. buyers of steel. Now they must pay a price that is higher than if there had been no government interference in the market. Foreign exporters (and those who work for them in the United States) also lose: they receive a lower price and are able to sell a smaller amount in the U.S. market. As you can imagine, if all nations imposed tariffs on others' goods, then international trade would be severely hampered, and many goods would probably cost much more.

Instead of imposing a tariff, another approach to limit the importation of foreign goods is to use a quota. You've probably experienced the effects of a quota: ever stand in line at a club or theater and about the time you get to the front, someone announces that no more people will be allowed in? In effect, there is a **quota**, or a limit, on the number of people allowed inside.

> **QUOTA** A quota sets limits on the amount of a good that can be imported.
>
> **EXAMPLE** The U.S. government restricts the number of watches and watch components that can be imported to the United States.
>
> **EXAMPLE** The U.S. Department of Agriculture oversees import quotas on a variety of items, including dried milk, dried cream, and several types of cheese.

How does a quota work? **Figure 4.14** shows the demand curve for imported sugar in the United States and the supply curve of sugar being shipped here. With no outside interference, the market-clearing price of sugar would be $P_e$, and the equilibrium quantity would be $Q_e$. Because the government wants to protect U.S. sugar producers, it limits the amount of sugar that foreign producers can export to the United States. The actual amount allowed in can vary with domestic production. In our example, let the quota on imported sugar be shown as the vertical line drawn left of the market-equilibrium quantity. As you can readily see, the quota has effects similar to those of a tariff: the price paid for sugar by U.S. consumers increases from $P_e$ to $P_{US}$, and the price received by foreign sugar exporters to the U.S. declines from $P_e$ to $P_f$. In 2010, in fact, the U.S. price paid for sugar was about $0.35 per pound, compared with a price of less than $0.20 per pound in the global market.[7]

The difference between a tariff and a quota, however, is that the revenue equal to the area A + B in Figure 4.14 does not go to the government. Instead, it goes to those foreign sugar producers who are allowed to sell within the U.S. quota system. They benefit at the expense of sugar exporters that didn't make the cutoff imposed by the quota. These producers are like the people who wait in line at a club but don't get in. Other winners include domestic sugar companies that also sell their sugar at the higher price. Workers for these companies also gain because they keep their jobs even though their employers are less efficient than foreign sugar producers. Who loses? Consumers who pay inflated prices for sugar. Because sugar is used in a wide variety of products—soft drinks, for example—you do not have to buy sugar to pay more.

· · · · · · ·

[7]Carolyn Cui, "Price Gap Puts Spice in Sugar-Quota Fight." *Wall Street Journal*, March 15, 2010.

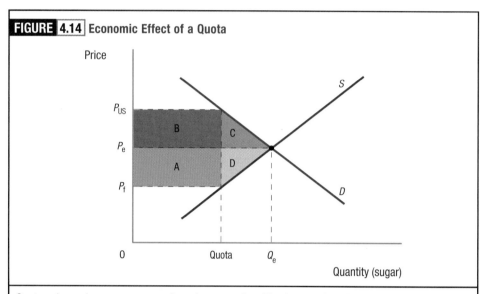

**FIGURE 4.14** Economic Effect of a Quota

Quotas also reduce consumer and producer surplus. The free market-clearing price of sugar is $P_e$, and the market-clearing quantity is $Q_e$. In the figure, the quota on imported sugar is shown as the vertical line at the quantity "Quota." The effect of the quota is to increase the price paid by U.S. consumers from $P_e$ to $P_{US}$. The price received by foreign producers selling in the U.S. market drops from $P_e$ to $P_f$. Revenues equal to the area A + B do not go to the government but to foreign sugar producers who are allowed to sell within the U.S. quota system. The quota imposes a deadweight loss on society equal to the area C + D.

What are the macroeconomic consequences of limiting trade through the use of tariffs and quotas? Let's look at an extreme example. What if the U.S. government abolished the importation (or set the tariff prohibitively high) of all foreign goods? The only way that shutting our borders to trade would improve our economic well-being is if the demand for American products by foreign consumers were offset by an increase in demand for those products by domestic consumers. Because there are some goods that we are not as efficient at producing or simply do not produce because of natural resource restraints (such as bananas), using tariffs and quotas to shut our borders to trade would reduce our economic well-being.

Could this ever occur? Surely the U.S. government would never impose trade barriers so severe Americans would be harmed. Or would it? In fact, one of the key factors that deepened the severity of the Great Depression was the passage of the Smoot-Hawley Act. Passed in 1930, the Smoot-Hawley Act raised tariffs on imported goods an average of nearly 60 percent. Enacted to protect U.S. jobs and stimulate domestic production, the act did neither. Because other nations retaliated quickly by raising their barriers to trade, Smoot-Hawley precipitated a global trade war that helped reduce trade worldwide: three years after it was passed, world trade had contracted by more than 70 percent.

### Predicting Interest-Rate Changes[8]

We also can use supply and demand to measure the prevailing rate of interest. You know from personal experience that there are many rates of interest out there: rates

........

[8]The Appendix provides a discussion of what an interest rate is and a discussion of present value.

on car loans, student loans, mortgages, savings rates, rates on bank CDs, and many more. Instead of trying to model each and every interest rate, we want to think about trying to explain what causes the *general* level of rates to change. We will simplify our discussion by finding "the" equilibrium interest rate that represents the rate for the entire financial market.

We can find the equilibrium, or prevailing, rate of interest by using the supply of and the demand for **loanable funds**.

**LOANABLE FUNDS** Funds that are available for borrowing. They are supplied by savers and demanded by borrowers.

**EXAMPLE** Liz decided to save part of her paycheck and deposited that amount into her bank account. This increased the supply of loanable funds in the economy.

**EXAMPLE** The recession ended, and the demand for homes and cars increased. To pay for these purchases, consumers increased their demand for loans. This increased the demand for loanable funds.

The *demand* for loanable funds comes from people, households, firms, and governments that want to borrow funds in order to make a purchase. Your use of a credit card makes up part of the demand for loanable funds: you get the clothes you want today by swiping your credit card. In doing so, you have in effect taken out a loan between you and the credit card company. Businesses also borrow funds for various reasons. Sometimes it's to cover their payroll expenses, pay for the shipment of goods, or purchase new or replace worn out machinery. Governments also borrow funds for all types of reasons, from funding Social Security payments to buying office supplies.

On the other side of the market, the *supply* of loanable funds comes from lenders who meet the need borrowers have for money. The lenders include banks, mortgage companies, credit card companies, and so forth. They acquire funds from people and organizations that are spending less than they earn: savers. When you deposit money in a savings account at your local bank, you are supplying loanable funds that the bank can lend.

Governments can be savers, too. When a government runs a budget surplus (its revenues exceed its expenditures), this form of saving increases the supply of loanable funds in the economy. Like people and organizations, the government wants to invest funds it is not using. The nation's central bank, the Federal Reserve, also can influence the amount of loanable funds through its monetary policy actions. During the 2007–2009 recession, the Federal Reserve acted to significantly increase the amount of loanable funds in the economy.[9] They did so to lower the interest rates on borrowed funds so the economy would start moving again. How did they expect to accomplish this? Let's use a supply-and-demand model for loanable funds to answer that question.

The supply of and demand for loanable funds is shown in **Figure 4.15**. When funds get loaned out, it is credit—like the credit you rack up when you use your credit card to buy clothing. The credit card company is essentially making you a loan so you can buy goods now instead of waiting until you have saved up the money. Like most loans, you must eventually pay the cost of borrowing those funds. And the price that you pay for borrowing the money is the interest rate. Consequently, in Figure 4.15,

· · · · · · ·

[9]We will provide more detail in Chapter 18.

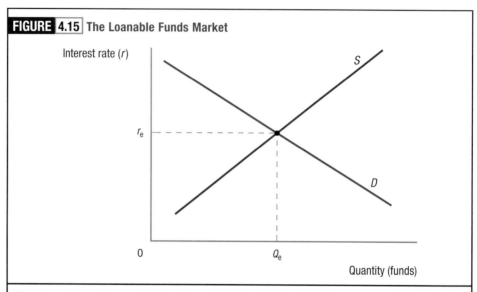

**FIGURE 4.15** The Loanable Funds Market

This figure shows the supply of and demand for loanable funds. The interest rate is on the vertical axis because it is the price you must pay to obtain loanable funds. The quantity of loanable funds is on the horizontal axis. An increase in the rate of interest leads to a reduction in the quantity of loanable funds demanded and an increase in the quantity supplied. A decrease in the interest rate has the opposite effect. The market-clearing or equilibrium interest rate ($r_e$) is the rate at which the quantity of loanable funds demanded is equal to the quantity supplied ($Q_e$).

we put the interest rate on the vertical axis because it is the price of borrowing or obtaining loanable funds: *the interest rate is the price of credit.* On the horizontal axis is the quantity of loanable funds.

You can see in Figure 4.15 that the demand curve for loanable funds is downward sloping. This shows that as the rate of interest increases, the quantity of loanable funds demanded falls: the more costly it is to borrow, the less borrowing there is. On the other side of the market, an increase in the interest rate induces more individuals to forgo more of their current consumption and increase their savings. Wouldn't you be more likely to save more if the bank paid you a 15 percent rate of interest on your deposits instead of 2 percent? As the interest rate rises the quantity supplied of loanable funds increases: the supply curve takes on the normal upward slope. Given these two relations, there is a market-clearing or equilibrium interest rate. At this interest rate, denoted as $r_e$ in Figure 4.15, the quantity of loanable funds demanded equals the quantity of them supplied ($Q_e$).

Just like all the other markets we have discussed, changes in the interest rate occur because of shifts in the demand and supply of loanable funds. What factors could lead to a change in the demand for loanable funds? If economic conditions improve, businesses wishing to expand their operations may need to increase their borrowing. Similarly, if household incomes increase, the demand for loans to purchase cars or houses might increase. Another player in the loanable funds market is, as we have stated, the government. During the last recession, government spending at many levels increased dramatically, whereas government revenues collected, mainly from taxes, fell. Without the revenue to support increased spending, the government increased its demand for loanable funds. Changes such as these increase the demand for loanable funds. This would be shown as a rightward shift in the demand curve in Figure 4.15.

What factors would cause the supply of loanable funds to change? You might be surprised to learn that households are the single largest net supplier of loanable funds. Consequently, the supply of funds can be affected by factors other than changes in the interest rate that alter the incentive to save. For example, an increase in the taxes savers must pay on the interest income they earn will reduce their incentive to save, which would result in a leftward shift in the supply curve in Figure 4.15. Another key player on the supply side of the loanable funds market is the Federal Reserve. Because the Federal Reserve's policies affect banks' lending decisions—they convert your savings deposits into loans—it also has an important impact on the supply of loanable funds.

Like most supply-and-demand models, the model of the loanable funds market is pretty general. It can't predict exactly what the rate of interest will be at every moment. Even so, it is extremely powerful when it comes to predicting the direction in which interest rates will change—that is, whether rates are going to increase or decrease. Let's use a couple of case studies to illustrate how the loanable funds model can be used to understand interest-rate changes.

**Credit Card Rates.** During the economic downturn of 2007–2009, consumers significantly reduced their use of credit cards. One reason for this change is that with unemployment rates rising and housing prices falling (see the discussion of housing markets earlier in this chapter), consumer incomes declined, and they felt less wealthy. In response, they reduced their consumer spending and credit card use. People also began to believe that the rates charged on credit cards were getting too high relative to other forms of credit such as using cash or taking out short-term bank loans.

How will the reduced use of credit cards affect interest rates? Can the loanable funds model tell us? The reduced use of credit cards should be associated with a leftward shift—a decline—in the demand for credit. In **Figure 4.16**, we illustrate

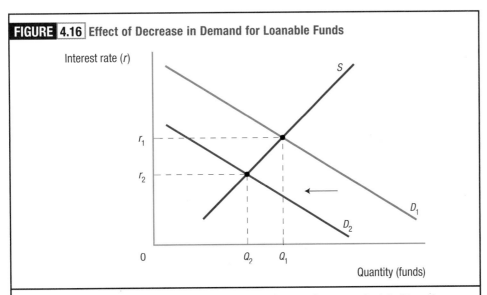

**FIGURE 4.16** Effect of Decrease in Demand for Loanable Funds

A reduction in the demand for loanable funds shifts the demand curve to the left. Given the supply of loanable funds, there is first an excess supply or a surplus of funds in the market at the original equilibrium interest rate, $r_1$. When such a surplus exists, the price—in this case, the interest rate—tends to fall. All other factors held constant, the reduction in consumers' use of credit cards (a reduction in the demand for credit) will lead to a reduction in the rate of interest.

this by shifting the demand curve from $D_1$ leftward to $D_2$. We do not shift the supply curve because we are focusing on the effects from the change in consumer behavior (demand). After the shift, there is a surplus of funds in the market at the original equilibrium interest rate, $r_1$. As you know, when a surplus exists, the price of the good—in this case, the interest rate—tends to fall. You can see in Figure 4.16, all else the same, the model predicts that the reduction in consumers' demand for credit should be accompanied by a reduction in the rate of interest.

How well does the model explain what actually occurred? Data reported by the Federal Reserve indicates that in the fall of 2007, the average rate on credit cards was about 13.6 percent. As economic activity declined, credit card use fell. By late 2008, the average rate declined to less than 12 percent. Although the credit card rates charged differed among groups of credit card users, all showed some reduction in the level of the interest rate charged.

**California State Bond Rates.** When governments spend more than they receive in taxes and fees, they run what's called a budget deficit. To get rid of the deficit, they must cut spending, raise taxes, or borrow money. Usually it is some combination of the three. The political debate over California's 2008 budget shortfall vacillated between cutting services—such as funds for universities—to raising taxes and borrowing money. Because Republican lawmakers vowed not to increase taxes, it became clear that the state would increase its demand for credit: it would borrow.[10] The loanable funds model shows that the increased borrowing should shift the demand curve for loanable funds to the right. Given the same supply curve, the shift should cause an increase in the equilibrium interest rate. Is this what actually happened? By late December 2008, California's budget crisis pushed the interest rate on the state's bonds to a four-year high.[11]

**Economic Recessions and Monetary Expansion.** Following the onset of the economic downturn in 2007, the Federal Reserve actively tried to reduce the severity of the recession and financial crisis by injecting funds into the financial market.[12] At the same time, the demand for loanable funds fell sharply as economic activity slowed and consumers (and businesses) reduced their borrowing. What does the loanable funds model suggest should have happened to interest rates?

By combining these two forces, the model predicts that interest rates should decline by an amount larger than would be predicted by either change alone. **Figure 4.17** shows what should happen to interest rates when an increase in the supply of loanable funds occurs with a decrease in the demand for loanable funds. (The effect on the quantity of funds is ambiguous, so we have shown it as no change.) Did the model accurately predict the direction of change in interest rates during this period? By early 2010, most short-term interest rates had declined sharply from their levels at the beginning of 2007, with some even approaching zero. For example, the rate on three-month securities of the U.S. Treasury, so-called three-month T-bills, dropped from about 5 percent at the beginning of 2007 to 0.06 percent at the beginning of 2010. Other interest rates also dramatically declined.

· · · · · · ·

[10]Juliet Williams, "California Gov Tries Again to Close $41.6B Deficit, but Still No Support from GOP Lawmakers." Chicagotribune.com, December 31, 2008.

[11]Michael B. Marois, "California Bond Yields Rise to Four-Year High on Budget Impasse." Bloomberg .com, December 26, 2008.

[12]We will have more to say about monetary policy during this time in Chapter 18.

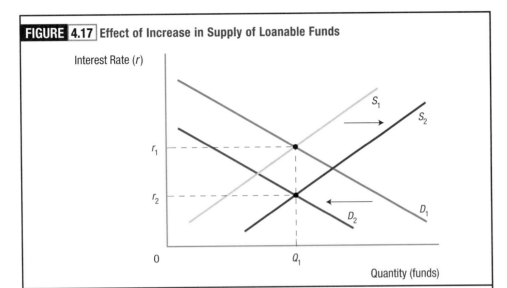

**FIGURE 4.17** Effect of Increase in Supply of Loanable Funds

The Federal Reserve increased the supply of loanable funds after 2007. This is shown by the increase in supply from $S_1$ to $S_2$. At the same time, the demand for loanable funds fell sharply as economic activity slowed and consumers (and businesses) reduced their borrowing. This is shown by the shift in demand from $D_1$ to $D_2$. Given these conditions, the loanable funds model predicted that interest rates would decline. In fact, many interest rates declined to all-time lows by 2010.

## WHAT YOU SHOULD HAVE LEARNED FROM CHAPTER 4

- That at equilibrium, the price of a good is equal to the marginal cost of producing the last unit of it sold and is also equal to the willingness to pay for the last unit purchased.

- That individual suppliers and demanders respond to price.

- That when there is a surplus in a market, the price begins to fall as suppliers attempt to sell off the excess supply. As this happens, consumers move down the market demand curve and suppliers move down the market supply curve until equilibrium is once again restored.

- That when there is a shortage in a market, price begins to rise as demanders bid up the price to obtain the scarce good. As this happens, consumers move up the market demand curve and suppliers move up the market supply curve until equilibrium is once again restored.

- That a price ceiling is the maximum price at which a good can be legally traded.

- That a price floor is the minimum price at which a good can be legally traded.

## KEY TERMS

Disequilibrium, p. 111

Surplus (excess supply), p. 111

Shortage (excess demand), p. 112

Consumer surplus, p. 113

Producer surplus, p. 114

Price ceiling, p. 118

Price floor, p. 120

Deadweight loss, p. 129

Tariff, p. 130

Quota, p. 131

Loanable funds, p. 133

## QUESTIONS AND PROBLEMS

1. Use a supply-and-demand graph to show what happens if the going price in a market is below the equilibrium price. Explain how pressures on price will lead the market to its equilibrium price and quantity.

2. The United States imposes restrictions that make Canadian prescription drugs relatively less expensive (after adjusting for exchange rates) than U.S. prescription drugs. U.S. residents have increasingly begun to travel across the border to buy these drugs. Using supply and demand graphs, show the impact of these activities on the equilibrium quantity and price of:

   a) prescription drugs in U.S. drugstores located near the Canadian–U.S. border.
   b) prescription drugs in Canadian drugstores located near the Canadian–U.S. border.
   c) Canadian drugstores near the U.S. border.
   d) bus tickets from major northern U.S. cities to Canadian cities.

3. Using supply and demand graphs, show the impact on equilibrium quantity and price of menu items when restaurants introduce:

   a) free delivery to homes and businesses.
   b) the acceptance of credit cards in lieu of cash only.
   c) self-serve soda machines.
   d) Show the impact on equilibrium quantity and price when restaurants eliminate reservations (i.e., seat people "first come, first served").

4. Using supply and demand graphs, show how cost-saving improvements in the production technology for plasma screens impact the equilibrium price and quantity in:

   a) the plasma TV market.
   b) the high-definition cable services market.
   c) the movie theater market.
   d) the LCD TV market.

5. Using supply and demand graphs, show the impact an economic downturn will have on the equilibrium price and quantity in:

   a) the jewelry market.
   b) the used car market.
   c) the new car market.
   d) the store-brand toilet paper market.

6. Using supply and demand graphs, show how reductions in the international supply of crude oil will affect the equilibrium price and quantity in:

   a) the U.S. gasoline market.
   b) the SUV market.
   c) the car tire market.
   d) the hybrid car market.
   e) the mass-transit market.

7. Suppose that U.S. lumber companies are successful in ending current limits on the amount of trees that can be harvested in our national forests. Using supply and demand graphs, show the impact on the equilibrium price and quantity in:

   a) the lumber market.
   b) the new housing market.
   c) the carpet market.
   d) the wood stain and varnish market.
   e) the lumberjack labor market.

8. As a result of the Iraq War and rebuilding effort, the worldwide demand for U.S. raw materials such as lumber and steel has skyrocketed. Using supply

and demand graphs, show the war's impact on the equilibrium price and quantity in:

a) the U.S. automobile market.
b) the U.S. carpet market.
c) the U.S. automotive worker labor market.

9. In response to numerous corporate financial scandals, the federal government enacted laws that make accountants personally liable for inaccuracies reported in audited financial statements they sign, regardless of the source of the error. Using supply and demand graphs, show the impact of the law on:

a) the equilibrium wage and quantity in the accountant market.
b) the equilibrium price and quantity in the corporate audits market.
c) the equilibrium price and quantity in the liability insurance policy market that provides malpractice insurance for accountants.

10. To generate voting support from dairy producers, congressional representatives from dairy-producing states have supported the use of price supports (floors) on milk and cheese. Using supply and demand graphs, show the impact of ending these policies on price and quantity in:

a) the milk market.
b) the pizza market.
c) the cereal market.

11. Using supply and demand graphs, show the effect that removing a price ceiling on natural gas will have on the quantity and price in:

a) the natural gas market.
b) the electric furnace market.
c) the natural gas oven market.
d) the heating oil market.

12. In response to the rapid rise in the price of gasoline, some have argued for a temporary or permanent suspension of the federal tax on gasoline (18.4 cents per gallon). Using supply and demand graphs, show the impact of removing this tax on equilibrium quantity and price on:

a) the gasoline market.
b) the automobile tire market.
c) on FedEx and other delivery companies.

13. Political leaders in Los Angeles and other big cities are campaigning to raise the minimum wage in the city (for all employment in the city) to a higher "living" wage of $15 an hour. Suppose that the market-clearing wage for skilled workers is $20, and for unskilled teenage workers, it is $8. Using supply and demand graphs, show the impact the higher minimum wage will have on:

a) the skilled labor market in the city.
b) the unskilled teenage worker market in the city.
c) the fast-food industry in the city.
d) Who wins and who loses if the minimum wage is raised?

14. Assume that the demand for cocaine is totally unresponsive to price, and assume further that users get the funds to pay for cocaine by stealing. Suppose the U.S. government is successful in intercepting shipments of the drug and, therefore, is able to reduce supply.

a) Using the supply-and-demand model, show the impact of the government's activity on the equilibrium price of cocaine.
b) What will happen to the amount of crime committed by cocaine users?
c) Does the government's activity have any effect on the amount of consumer and producer surplus enjoyed by buyers and sellers in the illegal drug market?

15. Explain the rationale for:
    a) the government keeping prices below equilibrium (e.g., rent control).
    b) private suppliers keeping quantity below equilibrium (e.g., concert tickets).

16. Suppose the federal government imposes a tax on the suppliers of soft drinks that contain sugar or corn syrup—soda, sports drinks, and so on—to discourage consumption and reduce obesity.
    a) Using supply and demand graphs, show the impact the tax will have on the equilibrium price and quantity in the regular soda market.
    b) Does consumer or producer surplus change as a result of this new tax? Explain your answer.

17. Using the supply-and-demand model of the loanable funds market, show what the effects are on interest rates if:
    a) the federal government runs a massive budget deficit.
    b) the monetary authority decides to reduce the amount of liquidity in the economy.
    c) households double the amount they save.
    d) banks decide it is getting too risky to make loans.

18. A *bubble* is the term often used to describe a situation where a rapid increase in the price for some good appears to have no good economic explanation. For example, the rapid run-up in housing prices that occurred in the United States and around the world between 2002 and 2007 is often called a "housing price bubble."
    a) Using your knowledge of supply and demand, can you explain the increase in housing prices?
    b) Would you agree that the increase in housing prices had no economic basis?

19. Oil prices over the past several years have trended upward in global markets. Some analysts argue that the increase is because of the growth in the economies of India and China.
    a) Use the supply-and-demand model to show and explain how improved economic conditions in these two countries could explain the rise in oil prices.
    b) Now use your answer in part (a) to analyze the impacts on the U.S. market for SUVs.

20. The Democratic governor of Illinois announced in 2010 that the way to solve the state's $13 billion budget shortfall was to raise income taxes on everyone. As an economic adviser to the Illinois Republican party, what points would you make about the effects of increasing income taxes?

21. A number of states have enacted tuition guarantees for entering freshmen. These guarantees fix tuition for four years. Suppose that the input costs to providing a college degree increase.
    a) Using the supply-and-demand model, show how the increase in input prices affect the market for college degrees.
    b) Given this change, predict what the outcome of the tuition-fixing policy will be.

22. In 2010, there was much talk of putting tariffs on imported goods from China.
    a) How would this affect your economic well-being?
    b) How would this policy affect the Chinese exporters who send their goods to the United States?
    c) Demonstrate how this policy leads to an inferior outcome compared to the nontariff world.
    d) Given your answers, explain why anyone would vote to impose a tariff.

23. When the U.S. dollar weakens against foreign currencies, foreigners enjoy an increase in their purchasing power for American goods. The exact opposite happens

for Americans purchasing foreign goods. How does a weaker dollar affect the market demand curve for:

a) vacations in the United States by foreign tourists?
b) vacations in the United States by U.S. tourists?

24. It is known that existing quotas on sugar imports to the United States have undesirable economic consequences for U.S. consumers. As mentioned in the text, the U.S. price paid in 2010 for sugar was about $35, compared with a price of less than $20 in the global market.

a) Using a supply-and-demand graph, show how removing the sugar quota would increase U.S. consumers' economic well-being.
b) Who is harmed by removing the quota?
c) Speculate why the sugar quota continues to exist.
d) What would happen in the market for corn syrup (a substitute for sugar) if the quota were removed?

25. Suppose the government imposes a quota on each fisherman to prevent overharvesting of fish.

a) Show what the fisherman's supply curve looks like after the quota is imposed.
b) What does the market supply curve look like?
c) What happens if there is an increase in the market demand for fish?

# Appendix 4A What Is an Interest Rate?

When you purchase a music CD or a pair of shoes, the price that you pay can be thought of as the "present price." This price signifies how many dollars you must relinquish for that Dave Matthews CD or those tennis shoes in the here and now. Could you be enticed to give up buying that Dave Matthews CD today for the promise of more CDs in the future? Suppose the deal is this: you do not buy the CD today in order to get two CDs a year from now at the same price. If you agree, then you have revealed your exchange rate between current consumption (buying and listening to the CD today) and future consumption (buying and listening to two CDs in the future).

Let's think of such a trade in monetary terms. You get a frantic call from your friend Amy. She needs some quick cash—say, $2,000—to help repair her dad's car, which she has wrecked. She promises that she will pay you back in a year, so you loan her the money. (She must be a *really* good friend!) Of course, during that year you lose the ability to purchase $2,000 in goods. How much will you require Amy to compensate you for your loss of consumption during the next year? One answer is nothing. You could loan the money to her free of charge.

Now suppose that Amy isn't *that* good of a friend. You decide that to forgo $2,000 worth of consumption over the next year, you will therefore require that she pay you $2,250 in a year's time. Another way to state this is that you are willing to trade off what $2,000 could buy now for what you expect $2,250 to buy you in a year. This also means that if she agrees to your terms, she prefers to have the car repaired and (if her father allows) consume more car services today for the trade-off of less money and what it can buy in the future.

Lending money to your friend Amy will help us calculate your rate of interest. The interest rate can be calculated using the two prices. The interest rate can be thought of as the ratio of the price next year to the present price; that is,

$$P_{\text{next year}}/P_{\text{today}} = 1 + r \tag{Eq. 1}$$

where $r$ stands for the rate of interest. Notice that the interest rate is written in a special form. This can be easily explained using Amy's request. You expect that the price of goods will increase over the coming year. By your estimate, what you can buy for $2,000 today will cost $2,250 in a year. Enter those values (prices) into equation (1), and the answer is

$$\$2,250/\$2,000 = 1.125$$

The additional $250 on top of the $2,000 you expect to get back is compensation to you for not consuming today. And $250 is 12.5 percent of $2,000. So in this example the interest rate ($r$) is 12.5 percent. This shows that the rate of interest is really the ratio of two prices: today's price and the price in the future.

To help clarify this, let's restate the scenario in terms of the opportunity cost of lending money to Amy. If you didn't make her the loan and instead put your money in the bank, how fast would your $2,000 have to grow to reach $2,250 in a year? To answer this, solve equation (1) for next year's price, or

$$P_{\text{next year}} = P_{\text{today}} (1 + r) \tag{Eq. 2}$$

Using the numbers given, $2,500 = $2,000 (1 + 0.125). If you could invest your $2,000 at 12.5 percent, in one year you would realize $2,250. The rate at which your money increased is 12.5 percent. Even though Amy is a dear friend, you understand opportunity cost. If the bank offers you an interest rate of 12.5 percent, you must get an equivalent return on your money invested in lending her the money as in your local bank. Of course, we are assuming that Amy and the bank will pay off in a year.

If it seems cold to think of making such calculations before lending a friend money, think of a bank's investment decision. You ask your local banker for a loan to buy a car. The banker can make you a loan or invest in government securities. You are risky—you may not pay the loan back. The government security guarantees the amount to be paid in the future. Aside from this risk factor, the bank must get an interest rate from you that is at least the same as it could get from investing in that government security. If you are unwilling to match the government's offer, the bank is not going to make you the loan.

These examples help illustrate the important concept of **present value**. Suppose you decide to go ahead and lend Amy $2,000 for her promise of paying you $2,250 in one year. That means that, given everything you know at this point in time, getting paid $2,250 one year from now must be equivalent to you having $2,000 now. If it weren't, you wouldn't make the loan, right? Again, using equation (1), we can solve for today's price—the present value—of getting $2,250 next year, or

$$P_{today} = P_{next\ year}/(1 + r) \qquad\qquad \text{(Eq. 3)}$$

**PRESENT VALUE** The price of some future payment stated in its current price equivalent.

In the jargon of economists, you *discount* next year's price by some amount. In this case, it is equivalent to the rate of interest. This is why sometimes market interest rates are used as the discount factor to make present value calculations. In the example, if you and Amy agree that she will pay you $2,250 in one year, and the interest rate is 12.5 percent, then you equate $2,000 today with $2,250 in the future.

Suppose the current rate of interest is 5 percent. Given this rate of interest, what is the current price of $1 promised to be paid in one year? Using equation (3) to find the answer, you get

$$P_{today} = P_{next\ year}/(1 + r)$$
$$= \$1/(1 + 0.05) = \$0.95$$

This result can be stated several ways, all of which are the same: if the rate of interest is 5 percent, you are indifferent between $0.95 today and $1 in one year. Alternatively, 95 cents invested today will be equal to $1 in one year if the interest rate is 5 percent.

What if the time delay for getting your money is longer than one year? Suppose the bank guarantees to pay you $1 but not for two years. What is the current price equivalent of $1 received in two years? To find the answer, let's ask the obverse question: if the interest rate is 5 percent, what is the value of $1 invested for two years? You know that $1 invested today at an interest rate of 5 percent will grow to $1.05 ($1 × 1.05) in one year. If you take that $1.05 and reinvest it for another year at

5 percent, you will get $1.1025 ($1.05 × 1.05). Instead of writing it out this way, you can simplify it to

$$\$1\,[(1.05)(1.05)] = \$1.1025$$

This also helps illustrate the fact that if the rate of interest is 5 percent, the present value of $1.1025 received in two years is $1; that is,

$$\$1 = \$1.1025/[(1.05)(1.05)]$$

In our example, we wanted to know what the present value is of $1 guaranteed in two years. You now can find this answer by using the general equation[13]

$$
\begin{aligned}
P_{\text{today}} &= P_{\text{two years hence}}/[(1 + r)(1 + r)] \\
&= \$1/[(1.05)(1.05)] \\
&= \$1/1.1025 \\
&= \$0.9070
\end{aligned}
$$

(Eq. 4)

This discussion illustrates an important property about present value (and of human nature). The further into the future a payment is delayed, all else the same, the less we value it today. Another way to say this is that the farther things are in the future, the more we discount it today. At an interest rate of 5 percent, you would be indifferent to $1 paid in two years or receiving $0.9070 today. If we delay the payment even farther into the future, the present value would be even less.

Present value and its underlying economic principles are very important in economics. We just noted that we tend to discount future events more highly than those about to happen. Does this help us understand why we worry about dieting and the health issues surrounding obesity only after we have gained that extra 50 pounds? Or why, given all of the medical evidence, some people take up smoking as teenagers? Present value also is a fundamental building block in fields like finance and accounting. Believe it or not, it is the underlying concept that explains how all financial assets are priced, whether it is bonds, stocks, or sophisticated financial derivatives.

· · · · · · ·

[13]You might see that this is equivalent to $P_{\text{today}} = P_{\text{two years hence}}/(1.05)^2$. This suggests a generalization: if the payment is to be made $n$ years hence, then the present value is $P_{n \text{ years hence}}/(1 + r)^n$. So, $1,000 to be paid in 6 years ($n = 6$) if the interest rate ($r$) is 5 percent has a present value of $1,000/(1.05)^6 = \$564.47$.

# PART 2

# An Introduction to Macroeconomics

**P**art 2 will show you how to use the concepts in Part 1 to understand the basics of macroeconomics. For example, our chapter on the labor market introduces the idea of unemployment of resources within the broad context of the production possibilities frontier before we focus on unemployment of labor. Our chapter on the global economy uses supply and demand to explain how exchange rates are determined. In that chapter, we also reinforce the idea of comparative advantage and specialization—ideas originally used to explain exchange between individuals—to analyze foreign trade. But first let's take a "big picture" look at the subject of macroeconomics.

# What Are the Big Issues: A Macroeconomic Overview

*"One of the greatest pieces of economic wisdom is to know what you do not know."*

—*John Kenneth Galbraith,*
*economist*

Beginning with this chapter, your economic horizons are going to expand. We want you to start thinking about exchange and trade on a much larger scale than between individuals or companies. In this chapter, your introduction to macroeconomics starts with you looking at economics through a wider lens. We will introduce you to some of the big picture issues that we will analyze in the rest of this book.

Among the questions we want you to start thinking about is why some economies grow richer than others. You probably know people who come from rich families. Why are their families rich and other families are not? Is it because they inherited the money or won the lottery? Or is it because someone in the family works harder, is better educated, or has special skills for which they are handsomely rewarded?

We also want to introduce you to ways of thinking about why economic downturns, usually associated with reductions in the output of goods and rising unemployment rates, occur in the economy. Why was the recession that began in late 2007 so much more severe than any recession in the past 80 years? Is there some common thread explaining why recessions occur? Are solutions to them always the same? We'll try to answer those questions in later chapters.

What causes the rate of inflation to be high or low? You have lived through a period of relatively low inflation, so this topic may not seem like an important concern to you. Even though the rate of inflation hovered in the 2 percent to 4 percent range during most of your lifetime, why did it reach double-digit rates in the 1970s? And could it skyrocket again?

It is important to understand the role of government policy in all of this. Some argue that government policies cause undesirable economic outcomes such as recessions and high inflation. Others argue that government policies explain good outcomes, such as the low inflation you have enjoyed over your life, or recoveries from economic downturns. We will examine the pros and cons of government policy in explaining macroeconomic events.

Macroeconomics is a continually evolving field of study within economics. Macroeconomists are still learning how economies, which are made up of thousands or millions of individuals, function. It may seem impossible to come up with economic models that explain why economies expand and contract, or why prices across many markets rise and fall. By the time you have finished this book, you will have all the tools you need to explain—and better understand—events that affect not only the U.S. economy but also economies around the world.

## 5.1  What Defines Macroeconomics?

As you have learned, microeconomics—which is the foundation for all economic analysis—explains the behavior of individuals, households, and firms. Macroeconomics does not focus on individual markets: it focuses on the behavior of the economy as a whole to understand trends in things such as inflation or unemployment. Here are some examples of how macroeconomics differs from microeconomics:

- In microeconomics, you learn about the demand behavior of individual people and households in particular markets, such as in the market for houses, babysitting services, and MP3 downloads. In macroeconomics you will lump together the spending by individuals and households in *all* of the markets of an economy into a category called *consumer spending*. Ever hear that consumer spending drives economic activity? By combining all consumers, macroeconomists can get a good picture of the total spending by individuals and households in the economy.

- In microeconomics, you learn why shoe prices change when the demand for them goes up. In macroeconomics we will explain why the price of shoes *along with* tuition, gas, and the multitude of other goods that exist in the economy increase or decrease over time. Sure, there are times when the price of one good–oil, for example—plays such an important role in the economy that it will get special attention. But for the most part, the focus for a macroeconomist is why prices *in general* rise and fall.

- Instead of trying to explain why autoworkers become unemployed, macroeconomics tries to explain why the unemployment rate of the entire work force rises and falls.

- Microeconomics predicts that your income rises compared to other workers because you are smarter or more productive. We will use that same logic in macroeconomics to explain why countries' incomes rise when their economies become more productive.

The bottom line is that in macroeconomics, we're looking at many of the same economic issues you have already considered in the preceding chapters, just on a larger scale. What this suggests is that macroeconomics deals with aggregates—such as combining or "aggregating" all household purchases and calling it *consumption*. We can also combine the production, or income, of all people and businesses in the economy in order to calculate the total output of the economy. Likewise, we can combine the prices across the economy to measure the price level and to understand what causes the change in the price level, or inflation. Or we can combine the number of people laid off across the nation to generate the unemployment rate. We can also combine all the sectors in the economy together to get some idea on how much they, as a group, buy foreign goods and how much they export to buyers in other countries. This allows us to look at a nation's international trade with other nations.

To get an introduction to the topics that lie ahead, let's take a quick look at the main areas of study. For now, we'll use some terms common to macroeconomics and briefly describe them. However, we will wait until later chapters for formal definitions.

## 5.2 Economic Growth

How tall are you? This may seem like a question that's unrelated to studying macroeconomics, but bear with us. If you are male and less than 5 foot 10 inches, you are shorter than today's average U.S. male. If you are female and taller than 5 foot 4 inches, you are taller than the average U.S. female. If you are a U.S. citizen of average height, you still are shorter than the average Dutch man or woman. Not only that, but the average Dutch person has been getting taller faster than the average person in the United States![1] What do trends in a population's height or height comparisons across countries have to do with economic growth? Actually, quite a lot.

Comparing people's height is a useful analogy to studying economic growth—a topic that's hugely important in the study and practice of macroeconomics. Similar to asking why one group of people—such as the Dutch—got to be taller than another, the study of economic growth asks why one country did or did not get to a higher economic standard of living than another.

The comparison also helps us understand how we can establish what causes each outcome. Auxology—the study of human growth—uses sophisticated models to explain the upward (or sometimes downward) trend in human height. The data indicate, for example, that the average U.S. male is taller today than his mid-1800s ancestor. The trend toward taller men can be explained by improvements in medicine, better nutrition, better sanitary systems, and so on. The "model" that explains why men are, on average, taller today than 150 years ago is based on sorting through the inputs to the human growth process.

Explaining economic growth uses a similar process. Economists believe that there are three key building blocks to explaining a country's economic growth: labor, capital, and technology, or, put differently, humans, machinery, and knowledge. *Capital* includes not only machinery, factories, and tools, but human capital as well. Recall that human capital is what people learn through education or on-the-job experience along with the natural talents they are endowed with. Human capital is the stuff that makes some workers more productive than others, given the same set of tools. As you can see, human capital and knowledge are closely linked. How they are combined, and the fact that some economies combine them more efficiently than others, is important in explaining why the average individual's economic standard of living in the United States is far higher than the average person in India or Argentina.

We will examine economic growth in two ways. First, we will consider the long-run growth of an economy. **Figure 5.1** shows one popular measure of output: real gross domestic product, or real GDP. We leave a formal definition of real GDP for Chapter 7. For now, just think of real GDP as a dollar measure of the goods and services produced in the economy adjusted for price increases. What you should notice is that the level of real GDP, often referred to simply as *output*, has a distinct upward trend. What you see in Figure 5.1 is that the level of output in the United States is

· · · · · · · ·

[1]Burkhard Bilger, "The Height Gap: Why Europeans Are Getting Taller and Taller—and Americans Aren't." *New Yorker*, April 5, 2004.

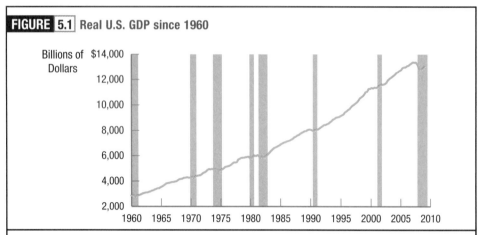

**FIGURE 5.1** Real U.S. GDP since 1960

Real GDP is a dollar measure of the goods and services produced in an economy adjusted for price increases. For the United States and many other thriving economies, the level of real GDP, which is often referred to simply as *output*, trends upward over time. The shaded bars in the figure are *recessions*—periods during which the level real GDP has a negative growth rate.

*Source:* Federal Reserve Bank of St. Louis

almost five times greater than it was as recently as 1960. This suggests that, at least in terms of goods and services available, the average person in the United States is probably much better off now than the average person 50 years ago.

What are the shaded bars in Figure 5.1? This is a convention that we will adopt for most of our charts. Those bars represent periods of *recession*. We will formally define what a recession is in a later chapter. For now, just think of a recession as a time when economic activity slows significantly. The most recent example is the economic downturn that occurred in 2007–2009. Notice that during a recession the level of real GDP dips a bit, and sometimes even takes a significant downturn. As you will see in the following sections, a recession is also a time when the unemployment rate rises. In the most recent recession, the unemployment rate reached nearly 10 percent, about double what it was when the recession started. Because much of what macroeconomics is about is to understand why real GDP rises over time, why real GDP fluctuates around this upward trend, and why the unemployment rate rises and falls, the recession bars will serve as useful reference guides.

Have those living in all other countries enjoyed the same increase in standards of living as we in the United States have? On the basis of this one measure, the answer is no. To show this, consider the fact that over the past 50 years real GDP *per person* in the United States has increased by a factor of almost three. The average person living in Bangladesh did not enjoy the same economic success. Over the same span of time, real GDP per person in Bangladesh didn't even double. More striking is the fact that even with this near doubling over this half century, real GDP per person in Bangladesh rose to less than $1,700. One objective in studying economic growth, therefore, is to explain why some economies move ahead faster than others.

A directly related question is to ask whether or not policy changes on the part of a country's government help explain why an economy is more or less successful. There is no question that the average person in the United States is better off now than 50 years ago. This is true not only in terms of Americans being able to afford more and better goods, like more powerful computers and safer cars and satellite television, but also in terms of having access to better services such as state-of-the-art medical care, higher education, and cultural events. (In other words, economic advancement is not always just about "goods.") This is definitely not true for every economy around the world. The question is, "Could different policies have generated better outcomes for, say, the average Bangladeshi than they realized?"

Another way of thinking about economic growth is to compare outcomes of past policies and experiences. Economists sometimes use such comparisons to identify those characteristics that seem to be associated with economically "successful" countries. Table 5.1 reports GDP per person in terms of purchasing power relative to the United States for a selected group of countries. In 2007, the average person in Luxembourg had a standard of living that was 74 percent higher than the average person in the United States. The average Canadian had a standard of living that was about 78 percent of someone in the United States. In contrast, in Bangladesh the average individual Bangladeshi had a standard of living that amounted to less than 3 percent of someone in the United States. Economists sometimes use such comparisons to try and identify the characteristics that seem to be associated with economically successful countries. They also are useful because the orderings change over time, and we'd like to know why. For example, it is likely that the comparison between the United States and China will change, perhaps even dramatically, in the future.

We could make many such comparisons, but you get the idea. For some reason, countries achieve different higher levels of output than others. A goal of studying economic growth is to try and explain why these outcomes occurred. In Chapter 10, we will attempt to do this by looking at how economies combine their labor, capital, and knowledge to produce goods and services. We also will look at how theoretical models used to explain the growth of economies stack up to the facts or end results.

| Table 5.1 | Living Standards in Select Countries as Measured by Purchasing Power in 2007 |
|---|---|
| **Country** | **GDP per Person (U.S. = 100)** |
| Luxembourg | 174.3 |
| United States | 100.0 |
| Canada | 78.5 |
| Russia | 32.2 |
| China | 11.8 |
| Nigeria | 4.3 |
| India | 6.0 |
| Bangladesh | 2.7 |
| Zimbabwe | 0.4 |

1. All figures are based on U.S. dollar equivalents.

The table reports GDP per person in terms of purchasing power relative to the United States for a selected group of countries. In 2007, the average person in Luxembourg had a standard of living that was 74 percent higher than the average person in the United States. The average Canadian had a standard of living about 78 percent of someone in the United States. In contrast, in Bangladesh, the average individual had a standard of living that amounted to less than 3 percent of someone in the United States. Economists sometimes use such comparisons to try and identify the characteristics that seem to be associated with economically "successful" countries.

**Source:** *The Economist: Pocket World in Figures* (2010)

In Chapter 9, we will extend this basic model of growth to see if there are other non-economic factors, such as extent of property rights, lack of government corruption, or the freedom to engage in international trade, that help explain economic success. Just looking at this list should remind you that these are the same types of microeconomic factors that affect the exchanges individuals make.

---

**ECONOMIC FALLACY**   Economies Always Grow.

**False.** Economists often use as a measure of economic growth changes over time in the amount of goods and services an economy produces relative to the size of its population. That is, real GDP per person. In the recessions you've lived through (most notably the one that began in December 2007), the economy has always bounced back and real GDP resumed its growth, increasing the level of output per person. This hasn't always been the case, however. Economist Angus Maddison estimated that by the year 1000 A.D., the output of goods and services relative to the number of people was about the same as it was in year 1 A.D. Even though output increased and decreased, over the millennium each person's share of it averaged out over time to be the same. Even in an economy as advanced as the United States, the pace of economic growth varies. In the United States, for example, output per person is about three times higher today than in 1950. Even so, during that time there have been several severe downturns in economic activity. During the most recent downturn, the level of output fell from $13.3 trillion in late 2007 to a low of $12.9 trillion in 2009. Even with the same population, this meant that real GDP per person also must have decreased during this period. As you will see from Figure 5.2, even though those living in the United States have enjoyed the fruits of sustained economic growth, it's been a bumpy ride.

---

## 5.3 Economic Fluctuations

The ups and downs in economic growth are what economists call economic *fluctuations*. By studying economic fluctuations, we are trying to understand how and why economic activity deviates from its long-term growth path. Think of these two areas of study—long-term growth and fluctuations—this way: a jet flying from San Francisco to New York has a cruising altitude of 40,000 feet. That is its desired flight path; its long-term economic growth path if you will. Anyone who has flown knows that even though the plane's desired cruising altitude is 40,000 feet, there are many bumps and bounces along the way. Some of them can be relatively large, such as when a plane hits turbulence and drops several hundred feet. After the disturbance passes, well-trained pilots (and automatic pilot controls) will return the plane to its cruising altitude.

The pilot can watch the plane's radar to see if there is potential air turbulence ahead. If radar detects a massive thunderstorm on the flight path, the pilot might alter the plane's course to steer the plane around the turbulence. Unforeseen air turbulence, however, will cause the plane to unexpectedly and abruptly deviate from its cruising altitude. Studying economic fluctuations is like trying to understand and even predict why bumps in the pace at which the economy is expanding occur so that policy makers can try and steer clear to avoid serious consequences.

Economists often discuss economic fluctuations using two measures. One is the *growth rate* of real GDP. Recall that real GDP is the economy's overall output of

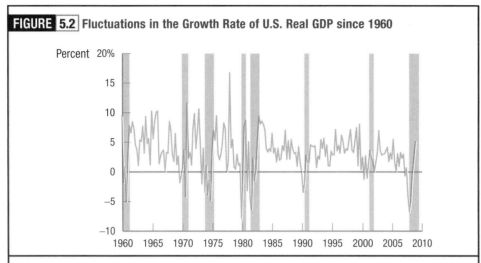

**FIGURE 5.2** Fluctuations in the Growth Rate of U.S. Real GDP since 1960

Although Figure 5.1 shows that the level of real GDP in the United States has been climbing steadily over the years, this figure shows that the *growth rate* of real GDP in the United States since 1960 has been anything but steady. Recessions (identified by the shaded bars) occur when real GDP has a negative growth rate. Because recessions and periods of positive real GDP growth do not occur regularly, the ups and downs of economic activity are commonly referred to as *business fluctuations*.

*Source:* Federal Reserve Bank of St. Louis

goods and services. **Figure 5.2** shows the growth rate of real GDP since 1960. Unlike the pattern in Figure 5.1, which showed the steady upward climb of the level of real GDP, you can see that although the growth rate from year to year is generally positive, it is anything but smooth. There are definitely ups and downs in the rate of growth of real GDP, and sometimes even fairly large dips into negative territory. Economists generally are most concerned about those times when the growth rate of real GDP is low, or negative: these are the really big disturbances on our economic plane ride—even if the plane's overall trajectory is upward. You can see that the times when real GDP has a negative growth rate (the level of real GDP is falling) are associated with the recessions (the shaded bars) mentioned earlier.

Notice that the recessions in Figure 5.2 do not occur on a regular schedule nor last for the same amount of time. For this reason, the term *business fluctuation* is really a more accurate description than the commonly used *business cycle*. Our discussion of economic growth will explore what causes long-term economic expansions. By contrast, our discussion of economic fluctuations will try to explain why the economy takes the shorter-term ups and downs that it does.

## 5.4 Unemployment

Another popular economic measure used in analyzing economic fluctuations is the unemployment rate. The unemployment rate is the percent of the labor force not working. (We'll get into exactly what the labor force is in Chapter 8.) With that in mind, it stands to reason that when the economy is producing fewer cars, sofas, and cups of coffee, it is likely that fewer workers will be needed. At the microlevel, the slowing economy in late 2007 caused reduced demand for goods and the labor needed to produce them—even Starbucks coffee and those making your morning

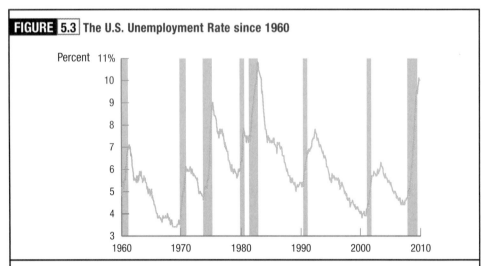

**FIGURE 5.3** The U.S. Unemployment Rate since 1960

The unemployment rate tends to rise during recessions (the shaded bars) and fall when economic activity picks up. The unemployment rate, even in times of significant economic expansion, never reaches zero because even when the economy is booming, there always are people leaving one job to search for a better one. When this occurs, they are counted as unemployed.

*Source:* Federal Reserve Bank of St. Louis

latte.[2] When we add together the effects of the reduction in demand and the related lay-off of workers across the entire economy, we should expect that the unemployment rate rises when economic activity slows significantly.

In **Figure 5.3**, we have plotted the unemployment rate since 1960 along with recessions (the shaded bars). As you can see, the unemployment rate rises during recessions when the pace of economic activity is falling, and it falls when business picks up. This figure helps to connect changes in the unemployment rate with changes in the overall pace of economic activity. As you can see, the unemployment rate relates a human experience—losing one's job—to an impersonal statistic—changes in the growth rate of real GDP.

Another interesting aspect about the unemployment rate is that even in non-recessionary times, it never gets to zero. During the past 50 years, the lowest unemployment rate is a little below 4 percent. Why doesn't it get any lower? We'll have more to say about this in Chapter 8, but a brief answer here is that even when the economy is booming, there are people unemployed. It may be by choice: people leave one job to search for a better one. Or it may be by someone else's choice: you get fired. Some people enter and leave the workforce, which also affects the unemployment rate. Perhaps the most important thing to keep in mind from Figure 5.3 is that the unemployment rate fluctuates with the level of economic activity but never reaches zero.

## 5.5 Inflation

You often hear about inflation. You probably already have some inkling that inflation has to do with rising prices. Sometimes people say that rising prices *cause* inflation, which is true by definition: inflation is defined as a rise in the general level of

· · · · · · ·

[2]Janet Adamy, "Starbucks to Shut 500 More Stores, Cut Jobs." *Wall Street Journal*, July 2, 2008, B1.

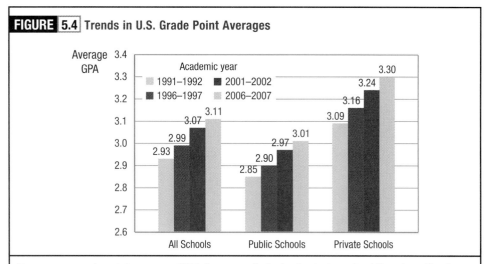

**FIGURE 5.4** Trends in U.S. Grade Point Averages

On average, grade point averages (GPAs) among students at private and public universities have increased in the United States since the early 1990s. The increase is evidence of grade inflation.

*Source:* gradeinflation.com, Copyright 2010

prices. Before we get to thinking about *price* inflation, let's use another measure of inflation—grade inflation—to understand what is happening.

**Figure 5.4** shows that grade point averages (GPAs) among college students have increased, on average, in the United States since the early 1990s. The results come from a sample of private and public universities. What you see is that there has been an overall increase in GPAs, with those at private schools increasing faster over time than those at public schools. Regardless of the type of school, average GPAs today are higher than they were in 1991. In other words, there has been grade inflation.

Research points to several causes of grade inflation. Beginning in the late 1960s, GPAs were inflated so that male students would not become classified 1-A, which meant the men could be drafted into the service and possibly sent to Vietnam. It wasn't a policy of universities, but many faculty members wanted to keep students from going to war, so they tended to give them higher grades. After the war ended, along with the draft, GPAs leveled off. So what explains the increase in GPA levels over the past 20 years?

Some people claim that competition among schools has led to increased GPAs. The idea is that to keep you in school, faculty members are encouraged to elevate grades: high GPAs lead to happy students who stay in school and pay tuition. It has even been suggested that, especially at some private schools with very high tuitions, students expect to receive nothing less than Bs—and usually they do. Whatever the explanation, the data indicate that GPAs have been increasing steadily over the past 20 years.

Your GPA is an average of grades received in various classes. The B in psych added to your A in music appreciation together with the C in accounting gives you a GPA of 3.0. So, on average, you are a B student. Economists employ a similar averaging of individual prices when they calculate a "general level of prices" so they can measure the rate of inflation. This is because in macroeconomics we want to explain *why* the average or general level of prices has increased or decreased over time. The best-known measure of average prices is the Consumer Price Index, or CPI. (We'll detail how the CPI is measured in the next chapter.)

**Figure 5.5a** shows the level of the CPI—the average of consumer prices in the economy—since 1960. Just like grade inflation, the CPI has increased over time from a value of about 30 in 1960 to more than 200 in recent years. Comparing these values is very informative. You can see that prices, on average, are significantly higher today than they were in 1960. In fact, they are about seven times higher.

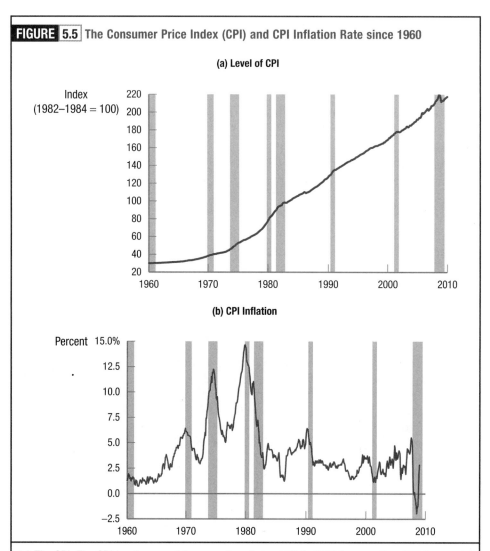

**FIGURE 5.5** The Consumer Price Index (CPI) and CPI Inflation Rate since 1960

**(a) Level of CPI**

**(b) CPI Inflation**

(a) The CPI. The CPI has increased from a value of about 30 in 1960 to more than 200 in recent years. Prices on average are now about seven times higher than they were in 1960. Shaded areas indicate recessions.

(b) The CPI Inflation Rate. This figure shows the rate of inflation in consumer prices, which is measured as the percentage change in the CPI. Notice that the CPI inflation rate rose significantly from 1960 through 1980. The rate spiked twice in the 1970s as a result of two major oil price increases. However, the upward *trend* in the inflation rate reversed in 1980 after the Federal Reserve changed its policies in an effort to combat inflation. Shaded areas indicate recessions.

*Source:* Federal Reserve Bank of St. Louis

Most people do not talk about the level of the CPI but about how the level changes—that is, they talk about what the rate of inflation is. The rate of inflation in consumer prices is measured as the percentage change in the CPI from one period to the next. We make the distinction that this is the inflation in *consumer prices* because we are using the CPI. As you will find in the next chapter, we also can measure the inflation rate of wholesale prices or of a broad array of prices. The CPI rate of inflation, which is shown in **Figure 5.5b**, tells an interesting story. One part of the story is that the rate of inflation rose significantly from 1960 through 1980. This general increase in the rate of inflation is punctuated by two spikes in the 1970s, both associated with significant increases in the price of oil.

If the spikes are associated with oil price increases, what explains the upward trend in inflation from 1960 to 1980? The upward trend in the U.S. inflation rate is a result of policy decisions made by the Federal Reserve, the nation's central bank. The fact that the rate of inflation trended downward after 1980 was, some people argue, because of a dramatic change in how the Federal Reserve conducts monetary policy. Some believe that the low inflation you have enjoyed over your lifetime occurred because, among other factors, the Federal Reserve has made it a priority to keep inflation low.

Why worry about inflation? Let's consider an economic explanation of what grade inflation really means: grade inflation—undeserving students now get As—lessens the market value of that grade. If everyone is getting As, how can prospective employers looking at university transcripts tell the difference between gifted, hardworking students and those who just got the grade? Price inflation has a similar effect, only it affects the purchasing power of your money. When there is price inflation, a dollar put in the cookie jar today will buy fewer goods in the future compared to now. If your annual wage raise does not increase at the same pace as inflation, your ability to maintain your current life style is diminished. Inflation reduces the purchasing power of the money you are earning by working and the money you have stashed away. In some countries—Zimbabwe is a good example—inflation has gotten so high that the national currency is practically worthless in exchange.[3]

Do prices only increase? It may seem that way, but the answer is no. Sometimes the general level of prices actually declines over time. This situation is referred to as *deflation*. Although there have been short periods in which prices fell in the United States, deflation is not a common occurrence in our economy. That is not true for all economies, however. Since the early 1990s, the Japanese economy has experienced persistent *deflation*. But don't make the mistake of thinking that deflation is good because it means that everything is becoming cheaper to buy. Deflation also means that some individuals' income isn't rising—it may be falling—which adversely affects their economic well-being. Deflation also can mean that the market value of your tangible assets, such as your home, is falling.

Another reason to be concerned about inflation is that there is a close link between inflation and interest rates. Interest is what you pay to borrow funds from someone else. An interest rate reflects the price at which a borrower is willing to exchange future buying for more current buying power. A borrower goes into debt—gets a loan—to own that new car now. To possess the car now means that she will pay the price of the car *plus* interest payments on the loan over the next several years. On the lender's side, an interest rate reflects just the opposite: a lender exchanges current buying power for

· · · · · · ·

[3]Marcus Walker and Andrew Higgins, "Zimbabwe Can't Paper Over Its Million-Percent Inflation Anymore." *Wall Street Journal*, July 2, 2008, A1.

more in the future. A higher interest rate may entice you to forgo buying a new car and lend your money to a bank; that is, deposit your money in a bank account.

The interest rate is the "price" at which borrowers and lenders agree to make loans. (Recall from the previous chapter that the interest rate is *not* the price of money. Although it may seem like splitting hairs, the price of money is what it can buy. If the money price of a soda is $1, the "soda price" of one dollar is one can of soda. By contrast, the interest rate is the price of borrowing money, or the price of credit.) A rising interest rate signals that lenders demand more money in return for letting borrowers use their funds. By contrast, when interest rates fall, lenders demand less money in return for letting borrowers use their funds, perhaps because the lenders have no better investing alternatives at that time.

If a bank makes a loan to you, it wants to make sure it gets back funds that have at least the same purchasing power as the funds loaned to you today. But you've just seen that price inflation reduces the purchasing power of money. An interest rate, therefore, incorporates the lender's guess of how fast prices are going to rise in the future.[4] If lenders expect higher rates of inflation in the future, interest rates will rise. This suggests that the rate of inflation and interest rates should move in tandem.

**Figure 5.6** shows the CPI inflation rate and a representative interest rate, the rate on three-month U.S. Treasury bills, over the past 50 years. The two series do not move in lockstep, but they do show a close tendency to rise and fall together. As you just learned, the rise and fall in interest rates stem directly from changes in the rate of inflation: if the rate of inflation increases or is expected to, then lenders are likely to charge higher interest rates for loans. This is just another reason why policy makers (and you) should be concerned about the rate of inflation getting out of control.

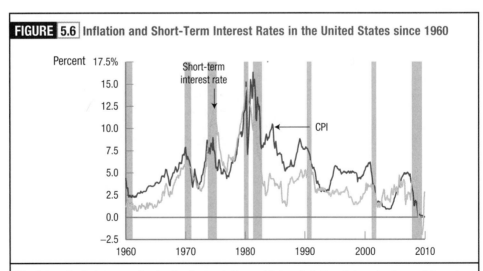

**FIGURE 5.6** | Inflation and Short-Term Interest Rates in the United States since 1960

The interest rate incorporates lenders' expectations of future inflation. Interest rates and the rate of inflation should be positively related. This figure shows the CPI inflation rate and a representative short-term interest rate, the rate on three-month U.S. Treasury bills, since 1960. The two have a distinct tendency to rise and fall together. Shaded areas indicate recessions.

*Source:* Federal Reserve Bank of St. Louis

· · · · · · ·

[4]The appendix to Chapter 4 describes how interest rates reflect the relationship between prices today and expected prices in the future.

# 5.6 Macroeconomic Policy Debates

Should the government do something about every increase in the unemployment rate? Can policy makers prevent recessions? Should policy be focused on keeping inflation low? If the trade-off of keeping the economy running close to its full employment level—keeping the economy on its long-run economic growth path—is higher inflation, would you be for it? What if doing so would increase the rate of inflation from 4 percent to 10 percent?

Believing that the world has learned much more about what affects economic activity, some economists actually predicted in the 1960s that government policy actions would prevent future recessions. That was several recessions ago. If you look at Figure 5.2, you can see that their rosy predictions weren't too accurate. That fact is that policy decisions are imperfect because they are made by human beings who lack perfect foresight.

Policy makers are just like you: you make decisions every day based on imperfect information. You time your drive to school or work based on the assumption that it will be free of traffic jams. But sometimes there are traffic jams, and you are late. Or you check the weather forecast on Thursday to plan your picnic for the weekend. Of course, Saturday arrives with storms. Policy decisions are made with similar uncertainties. Past experience helps guide current decisions, but what happened in the past is not always what will happen in the future. With such uncertainty, what are policy makers to do? Some economists argue that they should interfere in the workings of the economy as little as possible. This, of course, then brings up the question of just how much should be done and what we should reasonably expect policy actions to accomplish. That is still being debated. What the history of policy successes and failures does tell us is that policy decisions should at least be predictable.

Economists also have come to appreciate the longer-term consequences of policy decisions made today. Sometimes those effects (unintended consequences of policy action) are quite different from what we are attempting to accomplish. For example, we opened this section with a few questions that seemed to pose an either–or policy scenario: do you want lower unemployment if the cost is higher inflation? From past policies, we have learned that trying to keep the unemployment rate too low or the economy growing too fast can lead to undesirable increases in the rate of inflation. This means that, even if it appears that the economy is teetering on the brink of recession, we cannot fully ignore the longer-term inflationary effects of policy actions taken to lower unemployment in the short term.

As you can tell from this discussion, policy decisions, like your decision to sleep in or attend class, have opportunity costs. When economic activity looks like it is stalling, and the economy is going to sag into a period of slow growth, what is the opportunity cost of preventing this? Higher inflation? But what is the opportunity cost of keeping inflation low? Higher unemployment? Macroeconomic debates are made of such questions. The problem with such debates is that when bad economic policy decisions are made, the stakes are high because so many people are affected.

> **ECONOMIC FALLACY**   Economists Never Agree.
>
> **False.** Irish dramatist George Bernard Shaw once quipped that if you laid all economists end-to-end you'd never reach a conclusion. Economists are known for debating one another, but that doesn't mean we disagree on everything. For instance, there is widespread agreement that economic growth primarily results from advances in certain factors such as technology. Where disagreement usually arises is how to best increase the advancement of technology to improve the prospects for economic growth.

## 5.7 Summary

You have now been introduced to the major topics of macroeconomics: economic growth, business fluctuations, unemployment, and inflation. These are not listed in order of importance. Indeed, many of the debates between macroeconomists are on just how much importance to assign to each one. Regardless of what we argue about, each one of these topics holds an important place.

For the rest of this book, you will learn more about each. What we want to do is help you build a foundation on which you can understand and more effectively analyze the potential reasons for, say, differences in economic growth. With that knowledge you also will be better informed about possible policy responses. For example, even though having a rock concert to aid the poor of some nation is well intentioned, does it lead to any permanent improvement in the well-being of the citizens? Or should there be more public funding of education and improving sanitary conditions? Where money is spent and on what can have very large effects for future generations.

You also will be equipped with the knowledge that allows you to decide whether certain government policies should have been undertaken and what the potential consequences of those actions are. For instance, should the government have undertaken the policies it did during the economic and financial crisis of 2007 to 2009? Should the Federal Reserve have lowered interest rates as fast and as far as it did? What if the federal government had not initiated that huge stimulus spending package in 2009?

As you work through the rest of this book, you will come up with answers to these questions and more. Your answer may not match your fellow students' or the instructor's (or even ours), but the following chapters provide a foundation on which to base your claims and to rebuff those of others. After all, an informed viewpoint is necessary for a healthy debate.

### WHAT YOU SHOULD HAVE LEARNED FROM CHAPTER 5

- That real GDP in the United States has increased over time.
- That real GDP on a per person basis does not increase at the same rate across all countries or the same across time in one country.
- That the unemployment rate fluctuates with economic activity, rising during economic downturns and falling during periods of economic expansion.
- That even though prices in general have increased over the past 50 years, the rate at which they increase—the rate of inflation—has varied considerably.
- That interest rates and inflation are positively related.

### QUESTIONS AND PROBLEMS

1. What are the building blocks of economic growth?
2. Using Figure 5.1, estimate the level of real GDP in 1965, 1990, and 2008. Do you notice a trend in these numbers?
3. What do the vertical bars in Figure 5.1 mean? Based on your examination of the figure, has the U.S. economy been growing steadily over the past 50 years? Now look at Figure 5.2. Does your answer change?
4. Using Figure 5.5a, did the CPI increase more rapidly in the late 1970s than in the late 1990s? Does Figure 5.5b support your conclusion?

5. Describe a significant event in your life that caused you to change your plans. Was this event predictable or did it take you by surprise?

6. Using Figure 5.2, estimate the highest growth of real GDP since 1960. What is your guess for the lowest growth rate over this time? Before the most recent downturn, what do you notice about the volatility of real GDP growth before and after 1982?

7. Looking at Figures 5.2, 5.3, and 5.5b, do you see a pattern in the measures during periods before a recession occurs? Is there a pattern in the data as the economy comes out of a recession?

8. Macroeconomists focus on three major economic variables. What are they?

9. If you were in charge of policy making, which of the three macrovariables would you want to control the most? Why?

10. During the recession that began in 2007, do you think policy makers were more concerned about unemployment or inflation? Why? (Use Figures 5.3 and 5.6 in your answer.)

11. People often argue that higher rates of inflation bring about higher costs to borrowing money. Use Figure 5.6 to justify this claim.

12. A July 2, 2008, *Wall Street Journal* headline read, "Starbucks to Shut 500 More Stores, Cut Jobs." Looking at Figures 5.2 and 5.3, can you explain Starbucks' behavior? How did Starbucks' decision affect the overall economy?

13. Even in the best of economic times, the unemployment rate (Figure 5.3) never gets to zero. Why?

14. Some people argue that inflation is not a problem, whether it is 2 percent or 10 percent. Can you refute that claim?

15. China is one of the world's largest economies. If you measure size as real GDP per person, is that claim true? Why is it important to use GDP per person when comparing different economies?

# 6

# Measuring a Nation's Price Level

*"Price is what you pay. Value is what you get."*

*Warren Buffet,*
*investor*

I n the market for tennis shoes, you use your labor income to buy shoes. In the market for labor services, you trade your leisure time in exchange for a wage. Whatever it is you're exchanging, all of the trades you make take place in various markets: the market for labor, the market for shoes, the market for medical care, and so forth. And in each market there is a price associated with the trade: you get paid $15 an hour for your labor; the shoes you buy are priced at $65; replacing the brake pads on your car costs $100, and so on.

In this chapter, we will start thinking about how to measure not the prices of items in separate markets, but the prices of many goods and services traded throughout the entire economy. Instead of finding the market-clearing price for shoes or replacement brake pads, we are going to figure out how we can measure the economy's price level as a whole. To do this, we need a way that we can add up, or aggregate, prices across all of a nation's individual markets to arrive at a general price level.

Why go to all of this trouble? Finding a general or overall price level for an economy is useful, because we can then ask important policy questions. For example, are there policy actions taken by the government that cause the majority of prices and therefore the general level of prices to increase? Are there policies or economic events that cause prices in general to decline? Are people's salaries keeping up with the general increase in the cost of living?

We can answer such questions only after deriving some measure of overall prices. Once we have arrived at this general price measure, we will use it to see how and what causes the general price level to change over time—that is, the rate of inflation. You may not think inflation is a very important concern, but that is because you have lived through a period of comparatively low inflation. That doesn't mean it can't or won't reach double-digit rates—or even triple-digit rates as some countries have experienced. Knowing how the price level is measured gives you an important understanding of what causes inflation, a topic we leave for a more detailed examination in Chapter 12.

## 6.1 The General Level of Prices

You have learned that the purchasing power of your wages or salary depends on the prices of goods and services that you buy. If the price of apples increases but your wage does not, all else the same you lose the ability to buy the same number of apples as you were able to buy before. If the price of apples increases enough, and if you really like apples, you might request a higher wage rate. Only by increasing your wages as fast as apple prices rise can you continue to buy the same number of apples (and all other goods) over time.

How do you know if prices are rising? You might answer, "Just look at the price of apples!" Such a response is true, but it might be misleading. Even if apple prices are rising, what about other prices in the economy? After all, although some prices are higher than they were a few years ago, some are not. The laptop computer you bought last summer, which probably is much more powerful than a similar model available just five years ago, also probably costs less. We therefore would like a measure that tells us if prices *in general* are rising or falling. Knowing how such a measure might change would be most useful if you are negotiating with your boss for an increase in your wage rate.

### Price Indexes

When trying to measure changes in some economic measure such as prices, economists often employ something called an *index*. Think of an index as a weighted average. You could, for example, create a student weight index for your economics class. By having everyone record what they weigh on the first day of class and finding the average weight, you can make an index. This index could be used to see how the general weight level in your class changes over the semester. Suppose on the first day of class that the average student weighs 195.4 pounds. Let's use this value as the basis of comparison. To do this, set day one's average equal to 100. This is accomplished by dividing the first day's average weight by itself and multiplying it by 100 (to create an index): (195.4/195.4) × 100 = 100.

Now suppose that by midterm the ravages of dorm food have led to an increase in the class's average weight to 205.5 pounds. Instead of simply saying that the average student is now 10 pounds heavier, we'd like to know how much this increase is in percentage terms. To do this, we convert the midterm weight to an index form by dividing 205.5 by the initial weight—remember, that's our basis of comparison—and multiplying that value by 100. This gives us a midterm weight index value of 105.17 [= (205.5/195.4) × 100]. What this tells us is that by the middle of the semester, the average student weighs 105.17 percent of his or her initial weight. Put slightly differently, the average student is now 5.17 percent heavier than when the semester began.

When economists talk about a general measure of prices, they rely on a similar approach to try and measure the average of all prices out there in the economy. This measure is called a **price index**.

> **PRICE INDEX** An index allows one to measure changes in a numerical series. A price index shows how prices, in general, change from a reference year. If the index value is 110, this means that prices are 110 percent of the base-period level.

EXAMPLE A price index in 1995 equaled 100. By 2011, the price index had risen to 225. This increase means that prices in 2011 are 2.25 times higher than in 1995.

EXAMPLE Suppose the average height of economists in 1950 was 65 inches. In 2005, the average height was, say, 70 inches. If 1950 is the reference year (the height index equals 100), then the height index would be 107.7 in 2005. The average economist in 2005 was 7.7 percent taller than the average economist in 1950.

You probably are already familiar with a price index. The most often reported and discussed price index is called the **Consumer Price Index (CPI)**. The CPI is reported monthly by the U.S. government's Bureau of Labor Statistics (BLS) and reported widely in the media. While the number reported is the national figure, comparable CPI measures also are available from the BLS for many metropolitan areas in the United States. Other governments also generate CPI statistics for their countries. These statistics allow decision makers and economists to compare price changes in the United States and in other countries.

**CONSUMER PRICE INDEX** The CPI is a type of price index. It measures the change in prices for goods and services frequently bought by households. It is reported monthly by the U.S. government's Bureau of Labor Statistics.

EXAMPLE The CPI includes items purchased by consumers such as clothing, gasoline, and jewelry. It does not include items such as stocks and bonds.

The popularity of the CPI stems largely from the fact that it measures the change in prices for goods and services frequently bought by households. That's why it's called the *Consumer* Price Index. Because it is a general measure of prices paid by households, it's also used by many labor unions to calculate annual wage adjustments in their labor contracts. If the general price of consumer goods is increasing, labor unions want to know that so they can make sure that their members' wages keep pace. Annual cost-of-living adjustments such as those given to Social Security recipients also are based on changes in the CPI.

In addition to the CPI, the BLS calculates many different price indexes, each measuring the behavior of a different "basket" of goods and services. The differences come from the kinds of general prices they are trying to measure. You could, for example, find a CPI-type index for housing, food and beverages, and apparel, among other goods. Before we compare different measures of the price level, however, let's see how a price index like the CPI is measured. Our example admittedly is simplified, but the underlying approach is the same.

## 6.2 Calculating a Price Index

There are literally millions of goods and services in our economy selling at many different prices. How in the world does the BLS measure a general price level for all of those goods? A price index such as the CPI provides a good example.

For purposes of this illustration, we will make the world a lot simpler than it really is. To do this, we'll assume that there are only three goods in the economy: gasoline, music CDs, and laptop computers. These are the items in our basket of goods that we'll use to calculate the price index. The following table shows fictitious prices of these goods in 2009 and 2010: the market price of gasoline increased, and the price of laptop computers fell in 2010 relative to 2009. The price of CDs did not change. Given this information, do you think that the *general level* of prices rose, fell, or did not change?

| Item | 2009 ($) | 2010 ($) |
|------|----------|----------|
| Gallon of gas | 3.80 | 4.50 |
| CD | 15.00 | 15.00 |
| Laptop | 1,000 | 950.00 |

To figure out the answer, you need a price index. The basic formula for a price index is as follows:

Price index = (cost of basket today/cost of *same* basket in base year) × 100

To calculate a price index, you must first pick a **base year** from which to measure price changes. The base year becomes your point of reference. This is because the value of the price index is always equal to 100 in the base year.

**BASE YEAR** The base year is the reference point used to compare price changes over time. The value of the price index in the base year is 100.

**EXAMPLE** To estimate how much John grew during his teenage years, his parents measured his height at age 12 and used this base year height against which to measure his growth in later years.

To see this, let's make 2009 the base year in our economy. To find the cost of the basket of goods in the base year, multiply each good's 2009 price by its quantity sold that year as shown in the following table. Add up the total dollar amounts spent on each good and this is the total base-year expenditures for our basket of goods. Using our prices and quantities for 2009, total expenditures in 2009 amount to $2,170.

| | **2009** | | | |
|------|-----------|---|----------|---|
| | Price ($) | × | Quantity | = | Total Spent ($) |
| Gas | 3.80 | | 300 | | 1,140 |
| CDs | 15.00 | | 2 | | 30 |
| Laptops | 1,000 | | 1 | | 1,000 |
| | | | | | 2,170 |

Using the price index formula, divide the basket total in the base year (2009) by itself and multiply this by 100:

$$\text{Price index}_{\text{base year}} = (\$2,170/\$2,170) \times 100$$
$$= 1 \times 100$$
$$= 100$$

Because we've said that we want to make our base-year index value 100, you could interpret this equation to mean that the general price level in the base year (2009) is 100 percent of itself.

With 2009 as the base year, what we want to know is how much more expensive the same basket of goods bought in 2009 was in 2010: what happened to the cost of living? To find the answer, we are going to use base-year (2009) quantities to fix how much the consumer buys of each good. The amounts purchased—gas (in gallons), CDs, laptop computers—are called *expenditure weights*.

Does fixing the amount purchased (the expenditure weights) seem odd to you? Haven't you learned that price changes lead consumers to alter their buying patterns and substitute some goods for others? You should, indeed, be bothered by an approach that fixes expenditure weights when prices are changing. The Appendix at the end of this chapter provides a more realistic though more complicated approach that accounts for changes in buying patterns because of changes in prices. Though not perfect, using a fixed-weight basket of goods is still a reasonable approach.

Using base-year (2009) quantities allows us to focus on how prices—*not quantities purchased*—have changed over time. Remember, what we want the price index to reveal is how much the total cost of buying the 2009 basket of goods (300 gallons of gas, 2 CDs, and 1 laptop) changed when purchased at 2010 prices. To do this, we will compare the total expenditures in 2010 to 2009 for the same basket of goods. This is done using the information in the following table.

| Items | 2009 Price ($) | × Quantity | = Total ($) | 2010 Price ($) | × Quantity | = Total ($) |
|---|---|---|---|---|---|---|
| Gallons of gas | 3.80 | 300 | 1,140 | 4.50 | 300 | 1,350 |
| CDs | 15.00 | 2 | 30 | 15.00 | 2 | 30 |
| Laptops | 1,000 | 1 | 1,000 | 950 | 1 | 950 |
| | | | 2,170 | | | 2,330 |

$$\text{Price index}_{2010} = (\$2,330/\$2,170) \times 100$$
$$\text{Price index}_{2010} = 1.07 \times 100$$
$$\text{Price index}_{2010} = 107$$

These calculations indicate that if you spent $100 in 2009 to purchase this basket of goods in our economy, it would have cost you $107 in 2010 to purchase the identical basket of goods. Or think of it this way: because our basket of gas, CDs, and laptops is assumed to encompass the entire amount of goods available in the economy, the *general price level* in 2010 increased by 7 percent compared to the base year (2009).

The actual calculation of the CPI is much more complicated than the example.[1] For one, the CPI uses prices across many different categories. **Table 6.1** shows how extensive the product coverage of the CPI is. In total, there are more than 200 different categories of goods and services included in the monthly CPI. What we report in the table are just the major category headings. In reality, the coverage gets as specific as measuring price changes from "cakes and cupcakes (excluding frozen)" to "clocks, lamps, and decorator items." Overall, the BLS uses prices on about 80,000 items to calculate the CPI. As you can see, there are many major categories not to mention multitudes of subcategories.

· · · · · · ·

[1]For a complete description, visit the BLS Web site devoted to the CPI at www.bls.gov/cpi/home.htm.

| Table 6.1 Product Components of the CPI | | |
|---|---|---|
| **All Items** | | |
| Food and Beverages | Food | |
| | Food at home | |
| | Food away from home | |
| | Alcoholic beverages | |
| Housing | Shelter | |
| | Rent of primary residence | |
| | Owners' equivalent rent of primary residence | |
| | Fuels and utilities | |
| | Household energy | |
| | Gas (piped) and electricity | |
| | Electricity | |
| | Utility (piped) gas service | |
| | Household furnishings and operations | |
| Transportation | Private transportation | |
| | New and used motor vehicles | |
| | New vehicles | |
| | New cars and trucks | |
| | New cars | |
| | Used cars and trucks | |
| | Motor fuel | Gasoline (all types) |
| | | Gasoline, unleaded regular |
| | | Gasoline, unleaded midgrade |
| | | Gasoline, unleaded premium |
| Medical care | Medical care commodities | |
| | Medical care services | |
| | Professional services | |
| Recreation | | |
| Apparel | | |
| Education and communication | | |
| Other goods and services | | |

**Source:** Bureau of Labor Statistics

## 6.3 Measuring the Inflation Rate

In the previous chapter, you saw how the rate of inflation has increased and decreased over time. We'll have more to say about inflation in Chapter 12, but for now let's link together the price level that we just measured and the rate of inflation. The rate of inflation—the number that gets reported on the nightly news every month—is the *percentage change* in the price index. More correctly, let's define **inflation** as a sustained increase in the price level.

**INFLATION** A sustained increase in the general level of prices.

**EXAMPLE** The CPI increased in each of the past five years. This is inflation.

**EXAMPLE** The CPI increased in June because of an increase in the price of lettuce and strawberries. In July, it declined back to its May value. This is not inflation.

In our simplified example above, the rate of inflation between 2009 and 2010 is

$$\text{Inflation rate} = (\text{Price index}_{2010} - \text{Price index}_{2009})/\text{Price index}_{2009}$$
$$= (107 - 100)/100$$
$$= 7/100$$
$$= .07 \text{ or } 7\%$$

The price level in our example increased at a rate of 7 percent in 2010. To see how the price level and the rate of inflation are related, the two panels in **Figure 6.1** show the level of the CPI and the rate of inflation since 1960. Recall that you first saw these two figures in Chapter 5.

Again, notice that the increase in the level of the CPI, shown in panel (a), looks very smooth. Do not be deceived by this apparently steady increase, however. Between 1960 and 2010, the CPI increased from a value less than 50 to one of more than 200. The CPI uses a base year (or base period) of 1982–1984. So in the 1960s, a CPI of 30 meant that prices in general were 30 percent of those in the period 1982–1984. A more recent value of 210 means that prices are about seven times higher than in the 1960s and about double what they were in the early 1980s. In other words, the general level of prices has increased over time.

Notice that we keep couching this comparison in terms of prices "in general" because we are not measuring individual prices with the CPI but the behavior of the group, the assortment shown in Table 6.1. Consider the class weight index. Just because the *average* is higher at midterm than at the beginning of the semester doesn't mean that each and every student experienced weight gain. Some may even have lost weight. As we will cover momentarily, this is a well-known problem with indexes: they measure average behavior and can be influenced by large changes by a few students—or with a price index by a few prices.

Panel (b) of Figure 6.1 shows the rate at which the CPI increased over time. It is by no means constant. The fact that it is generally positive, however, means that the level of the price index is increasing but not at the same rate in each and every period. Notice also how it "jolts" up and down. What causes these temporary swings in the rate of inflation and how they can influence policy decisions are the subject of future chapters. For now, suffice it to say that the sharpest jumps in inflation, primarily in the 1970s, are associated with sharp increases in the price of oil.

You also might notice that the path of inflation has a very distinct pattern over the past 50 years. From 1960 through the early 1980s, the inflation rate was getting higher and higher. Since then, in contrast, the rate of inflation has come down. This pattern is often explained by changes in policy, especially monetary policy, over this time. We'll also have more to say about the pattern of inflation in later chapters.

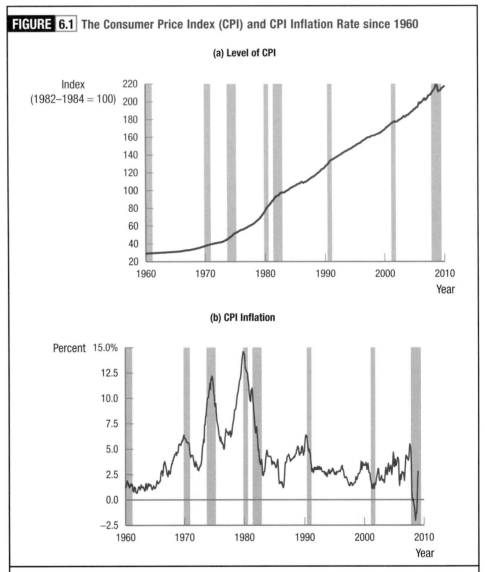

**FIGURE 6.1** The Consumer Price Index (CPI) and CPI Inflation Rate since 1960

a. Level of CPI. The CPI has increased from a value of about 30 in 1960 to more than 200 in recent years. Prices on average are now about seven times higher than they were in 1960. Shaded areas indicate U.S. recessions.

*Source:* Federal Reserve Bank of St. Louis

b. CPI Inflation. This figure shows the rate of inflation in consumer prices measured as the percentage change in the CPI. Notice that the CPI inflation rate rose significantly from 1960 through 1980. The rate spiked twice in the 1970s as a result of two major oil price increases. However, the upward *trend* in the inflation rate reversed in 1980 after the Federal Reserve changed its policies in an effort to combat inflation. Shaded areas indicate U.S. recessions.

*Source:* Federal Reserve Bank of St. Louis

Although there have been a few short-term outbreaks of relatively high rates of inflation over the past 30 years, inflation has remained relatively tame. Unless you are from another country, you have not experienced anything like the double-digit inflation of the 1970s. Why, then, does everyone make such a fuss over inflation even when it is only 3 or 4 percent? As you'll discover in Chapter 12, one reason to worry about high inflation is because there is no "normal" rate of inflation—that is, inflation does not tend to return to any average rate over time. Over the coming years, the rate of inflation could just as easily increase back to the double-digit rates of the 1970s as remain at its recent low levels. Moreover, the faster prices rise, the faster your money is losing purchasing power. We'll address this point momentarily.

## 6.4 Problems with Price Indexes

You should be aware of several issues related to using a price index. These "problems" do not mean that a price index such as the CPI isn't useful, just that you should be careful about how you (and others) use it.

### Weights

One problem that arises when calculating a price index relates to the way price changes are weighted. In our fictitious economy, the price of gasoline increased, the price of CDs remained unchanged, and the price of the laptop actually declined. Even though the price of gas was the only price that increased, the value of the price index was still higher in 2010. If the index is supposed to measure changes in the general level of prices, is it fair to say that prices *in general* increased when in reality only one did?

This example illustrates that some price changes can have a disproportionate effect on the index. This occurs because some goods have a greater weight or importance in the index. In our example, an increase in gas prices had a large impact—it swamped the decline in laptop prices—because gas represents an important share of total expenditures in the hypothetical basket of goods consumed. The actual behavior of the inflation rate in the mid- and late 1970s in Figure 6.1 shows how a sharp increase in the price of one key component of a basket of goods—in this case, gasoline—can lead to an overall increase in the price index and at least a temporary increase in the rate of inflation. The substantial run-up in oil and gas prices during the summer of 2008 helped push the CPI inflation rate higher, which was reminiscent of earlier effects.

The fact that the price index, simply because of how it is measured, can be affected by the price change of a few goods means that we must be careful in interpreting short-term movements in the CPI and the rate of inflation. In many years, late winter storms can ruin various crops such as lettuce and strawberries, making them temporarily in short supply and boosting their prices. When this occurs, all else the same, the CPI increases at a faster rate than it would otherwise. This causes the rate of inflation in the nearby months to jump from the anticipated rate. But such inflation spikes are temporary. Either additional produce enters the market from other areas of the globe, or replanted crops mature and are harvested. These inflation bumps do not last, and prices return to normal.

### Goods Substitution

If the price of gasoline rises, basic economic theory predicts that consumers will buy less of it (move up their demand curves for gasoline). They resort to alternative forms of transportation or simply drive less. Our treatment of consumer demand predicts that this will happen and it really does: when gas prices pushed above $4 in the summer of 2008, gasoline consumption declined relative to 2007. People traded in or stopped buying gas-guzzling SUVs and bought cars with higher gas mileage. Americans also drove fewer miles and relied more on public transportation systems.[2]

As we have indicated, the problem is that substitutions such as these are not captured in the CPI: even though consumers' preferences change, how gasoline is weighted in the CPI may not keep up. This problem is called *substitution bias*. It skews the accuracy of the CPI. To reduce this bias, the weights should be adjusted as consumers respond to price changes in the economy. If this is not done, then the inflation rate calculated using a *fixed-weight* approach will incorrectly measure inflation for households that substitute away from gasoline when its price increases relative to other goods. Indeed, over the past few years, the CPI inflation rate averages about a third of a percentage point higher than an alternative CPI that allows the weights to vary each month.

Beginning in the late 1990s, the BLS started updating the expenditure weights every two years. Although you might think that this still misses the effects of significant changes in some prices, you have to appreciate the fact that updating the weights is a massive undertaking and simply cannot be accomplished on an annual basis. (The alternative to the fixed-weight approach is known as the *chain-weighted approach* and is discussed in the Appendix at the end of the chapter.)

Economists and statisticians are well aware of price-index problems such as this. Indeed, using an incorrect measure of inflation can be costly. Consider the annual cost-of-living increases that Social Security recipients receive. If the adjustments are based on the CPI, the adjustments might actually be too generous (at least from the government's viewpoint). How significant is this problem? In 1995, Alan Greenspan, then the chairman of the U.S. Federal Reserve, suggested in congressional testimony that the CPI inflation rate was biased upward by as much as 1.5 percentage points over its "true" value. About that time, Congress established the Advisory Commission to Study the Consumer Price Index. This commission found that the CPI was higher than the true value by as much as 0.8 to 1.6 percentage points. This meant that the federal government was overpaying for cost-of-living adjustments, resulting in a larger federal budget deficit.

## Applicability

Another issue is the general usefulness of a price index or its resulting rate of inflation across individuals. How applicable is the CPI if you live in a city and rely on mass transit? If your household doesn't own a car, then you do not buy gasoline regularly. A price index that includes gasoline with a big expenditure weight may therefore overstate changes in the price of *your* basket of goods. Of course, you must be careful about thinking this way. Even if you do not buy gas, the bus you are riding on requires fuel, and higher fuel prices translate into higher bus fares.

It has been suggested that the CPI actually *underestimates* the inflation senior citizens in the United States experience because of the disproportionate share of medical and pharmaceutical expenses in their basket of goods and services consumed.[3] (You have perhaps noticed that your grandparents spend more on medical care than you do.) This is because the prices of these services and goods have been increasing faster

· · · · · · ·

[2]"U.S. Driving Miles Down 5.6% in Record Decline." *Wall Street Journal Online*, October 24, 2008. Clifford Krauss, "Gas Prices Send Surge of Riders to Mass Transit." *New York Times*, May 10, 2008.

[3]Humberto Cruz, "Government Statistics May Not Tell the Whole Story on How You're Affected by Inflation." *Boston Globe*, January 20, 2007.

than most other groups of goods and services in the CPI. At the same time, it has been suggested that the CPI *overstates* the inflation faced by this segment of the population because, as a group, seniors are more likely to take advantage of low-cost retailers (such as Walmart or Costco). Which is true clearly depends on the individual.

The point is that a price index such as the CPI simply cannot capture the price behavior of each and every household's buying experience. Nonetheless, the index includes so many items and covers such a large geographical area that it remains a useful gauge for the price changes faced by the *average* household.

### Quality Changes

Another potential problem with a price index such as the CPI is that it does not account for quality changes. In our example, we said nothing about changes in the quality of the laptop computer from 2009 to 2010. If the quality of the laptop improved from one year to the next—the computing speed of the computer doubled, for instance—*and* the price fell, then the laptop buyer in our economy was much better off in 2010 than in 2009. The laptop is not only cheaper but also a better product. Unfortunately, the CPI does not always account for such quality changes.

We do not want to leave you with the impression that the CPI is useless. It is important, however, that you are aware of the strengths and weaknesses of price indexes. Other than calculating inflation, what can you do with a price index? In the next section, you will find out.

## 6.5 Using a Price Index

Consider the following questions: is the price of a McDonald's cheeseburger higher today than it was in 1990? Does a gallon of gasoline cost more today than, say, when your parents were in high school? Is toothpaste more expensive today than it was when you were five years old? You might think that the questions are silly and the answers obvious: isn't the price of everything higher than it used to be? Actually, as we have explained, the prices of some products—think computers, plasma TVs, and digital cameras—are significantly lower than what they once were.

We want you to think about making price comparisons in a slightly different way, rather than just comparing sticker prices. We want you to think about *relative prices*—that is, the price of a particular good relative to all other goods. Just think of your wage rate as a price of your labor. Now think of your wage rate relative to what it can buy you. This is one (very important) measure of a relative price. Next, we will explain just what we mean and then show you how useful a relative price measure is when it comes to explaining observed behavior.

### Calculating a Relative Price

Fact: the price of gas is higher than it used to be. In late 2009, the national average for a gallon of unleaded gasoline was about $2.60. In 1988, a gallon of gas cost less than a dollar. These prices are **nominal prices**.

**NOMINAL PRICE** A nominal price is a price expressed in current dollars.

EXAMPLE The nominal price for a movie ticket is $15. In 1982, it was $5.

EXAMPLE When you pull into the gas station, the nominal price for a gallon of gas is the price on the pump.

In economics, an even more important price is the **relative price** of a good or service.

> **RELATIVE PRICE** The relative price of a good is its nominal price adjusted for changes in the general level of prices.

> **EXAMPLE** The nominal price for a gallon of gas is $3. Adjusted for the general increase in all other prices—inflation—gas is cheaper than it was in 1980.

What? How can gas be cheaper today than it was 30 years ago? Let's explain how the calculation of a relative price works and why it is such an important measure to understand.

The relative price of any good or service—sometimes referred to as its *real price*—is an important economic concept because it helps explain economic behavior. Because everyone likes to complain about it, let's use the price of gasoline to illustrate how nominal and relative prices are related. Given that nominal gas prices have just about doubled over the past 30 years, from $1.28 in 1982 to about $2.60 in late 2009, how can we explain the fact that, up until very recently, the sales of low-mileage vehicles—SUVs, trucks, and vans—actually increased? Or how can we explain the fact that drivers did not reduce their miles driven even as gas prices increased? To make sense of such behavior, you need to understand what happened to the *relative price* of gas over time.

You've just learned that the CPI at a point in time indicates how high prices are relative to the general level of prices in the base year. By comparing the nominal price of gas to the general level of prices, you can compute the relative price of gas at a point in time. Put differently, the relative price of gas in, say 2009, is the price of gas that is adjusted for the inflation effect between the base year and 2009. So, to measure a relative price of gas, you take its nominal price and divide it by the CPI at a point in time. To find the relative price of gas in June 1982, you divide its nominal price that month, which was $1.30, by the CPI for June 1982, which was 97:[4]

Relative price of gas (1982) = [($1.30/97) × 100] = $1.34

Now let's do the same calculation to find out the relative price of gas in late 2009. In December 2009, the nominal price for a gallon of gas in Omaha, Nebraska, was about $2.60. The CPI for that month was 216. Therefore, the relative price of gas in Omaha in December 2009 was

Relative price of gas (2009) = [($2.60/216) × 100] = $1.20

As you can see, the relative price of gasoline in 2009 ($1.20) was actually less than it was in 1982 ($1.34). In other words, gas in 2009 was less expensive *relative to* all other goods (as measured by the CPI) than it was in 1982. This means that someone living in Omaha in 1982 probably used more of his income to buy a gallon of gas than he did in 2009. But this comparison uses only one month and may be deceptive. After all, you might remember that nominal gas prices in the summer of 2008 and during 2011 reached $4 or more in many areas. Given the volatility of nominal gas prices, it is useful to compare the behavior of nominal and relative gas prices over time. After that we'll get to an explanation of why the sales of gas guzzling vehicles continued to rise for most of the past two decades even as nominal gas prices increased.

· · · · · · ·

[4]Monthly values of the CPI can be accessed at the Bureau of Labor Statistics (www.bls.gov).

## SOLVED PROBLEM

**Q** We have shown you how to measure a relative price: divide the observed or nominal price by the price index. That puts prices over time into comparable terms, because the price index has the same base period. But what if you want to look at past prices using today's price as the point of comparison?

**A** This can be done by rebasing the price index. Let's use the example of a good that cost $1.50 in 2008 and $1 in 2007. For those years, the CPI was 215 and 207, respectively. Using the CPI, the relative price for the good is $0.69 in 2008 [= ($1.50/215) × 100] and $0.48 in 2007. These values put the prices in comparable terms using the 1982–1984 base period.

Now let's ask what the item cost in 2007 using 2008 as the reference point. You can still use the CPI, but you need to rebase it to 2008. That is done by dividing the CPI values by the value for 2008, which is 215. Doing this gives you a rebased CPI equal to 100 in 2008 [= (215/215) × 100] and 96 in 2007 [= (207/215) × 100]. Now calculate the relative price of the good. For 2008, it is $1.50 because 2008 is also the new base year. The relative price for 2007 is $1.04 [= ($1/96) × 100]. You can see that the price of the good increased in real terms measured either way.

---

**Figure 6.2** plots the nominal and relative prices of gasoline in the United States since 1980. The relative price in Figure 6.2 is calculated just like we have done, using the base period 1982−1984 = 100. For this period, that means the nominal price and the relative price of gas are going to be very similar, if not the same.

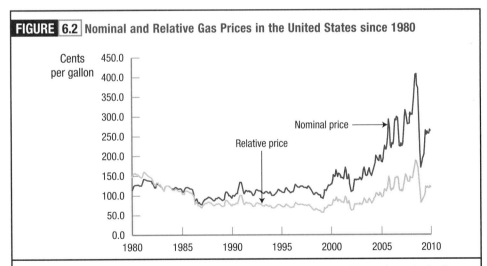

**FIGURE 6.2** Nominal and Relative Gas Prices in the United States since 1980

The nominal and relative prices of gasoline in the United States since 1980 are shown in the figure. The relative price is calculated using as the base period 1982−1984 = 100. After declining, the nominal price of gas remained fairly steady between 1985 and 2000: about $1 a gallon. The decline in the relative price of gasoline through 1999 shows that even though the nominal price of gas remained relatively constant, prices of other goods in the CPI were increasing. Beginning in 2002, both the nominal and the relative prices of gas increased, reaching a peak in 2008. The nominal gas price remained higher than in the past, but the relative price of gas by late 2009 had fallen back to its level in 1985 and in 2005.

*Source:* Energy Information Administration

The first thing to notice is that, after declining in the first half of the 1980s, the nominal price of gas didn't really change that much between 1985 and 2000. Roughly speaking, it hovered around $1 a gallon. The second thing to notice is that the relative price of gas declined over the same 20 years. Like the nominal price of gas, the relative price declined beginning in the early 1980s. Unlike nominal gas prices, however, the relative price continued to fall. This decline in the relative price of gasoline reflects the fact that even though the nominal price of gas remained relatively constant, other prices in the CPI were increasing. That is why the relative price of gas—the price of gas relative to all other consumer prices—fell. Beginning in the early part of this century, however, the nominal and the relative prices of gas both jumped noticeably. After reaching a peak in 2008, both retreated. Even though the nominal price of gas remains comparatively high, the relative price of gas in late 2009 is about where it was in 1985 and in 2005.

In the two decades between 1980 and 2000, the relative price of gas had been declining. In other words, compared to the price of other goods and services—including incomes—increases in the nominal price of gas did not keep pace. Gas, therefore, was getting relatively cheaper. A popular way of thinking about this is the following: if wages keep pace with inflation, a declining relative price means that it takes fewer hours worked to buy the good. With falling relative prices of gas, you could buy more gas per hour worked than before. Hence, gas was becoming less expensive in a relative sense.

Consumers responded accordingly by increasing their purchases of large SUVs, trucks, and minivans, all of which are not known for their gas mileage. Some automakers even brought back "muscle" cars that burned a lot of gas. As gas was, in an economic sense, becoming cheaper, our buying habits shifted from high-mileage vehicles to spacious though low-mileage ones. Not only did carmakers and buyers respond to the drop in the relative price of gas, but so did people who were deciding where to live. Relatively cheap gas meant that many families could afford to move out of inner cities to the far-flung suburbs because driving to work was becoming, in an economic sense, less and less expensive.

This recently changed. As shown in Figure 6.2 nominal and relative gas prices increased for most of the last decade. With the relative price of gas rising to new highs in the past few years, consumers reacted in a predictable manner: in April 2008 a car, not a truck, was the top-selling vehicle for the first time since 1992. The sharp increase in the relative price of gas led to a sharp decrease in the number of miles we drive.[5] Although some people may argue that these changes reflect greater interest in becoming "green," from an economist's point of view a more likely explanation is that the relative price of gas was getting much higher.

Measuring the relative price of gasoline and using it to explain observed behavior is just one example of how useful a relative price is. When the relative price of a good rises, all else the same, people are likely to buy less of it. When the relative price falls, however, people are more likely to buy more of it. In effect, this is the macroeconomic equivalent of our assumption when deriving the demand curve that "other prices remain the same." In macroeconomics, "other prices" are captured by a general price index, such as the CPI.[6]

· · · · · · ·

[5]David Leonhardt, "Big Vehicles Stagger Under Weight of $4 Gas." *New York Times*, June 4, 2008.

[6]To see how various relative prices have changed, the home page of the Federal Reserve Bank of Minneapolis allows you to compare the cost of goods bought today to any other year. Visit this site at www.minneapolisfed.org.

> **ECONOMIC FALLACY**   The price of everything goes up.
>
> **False.** A great example is the personal computer. In 1980, a desktop computer with the memory, speed, and the capability of current handheld calculators cost thousands of dollars. Today, a computer with several gigabytes of memory, accessories, and numerous preinstalled software packages costs less than $1,000. This drop in the nominal price and the even greater decline in the relative price of computers is an economic explanation of why everyone now seems to own one. Indeed, the same could be said of microwave ovens, cable and satellite-dish TV, digital cameras, and personal digital assistants.

## 6.6 Price Indexes Other than the CPI

Even though the CPI is the most quoted and widely used price index, there are other price indexes. For example, the BLS publishes several versions of the CPI. The version we've been using, the CPI-U, measures changes in the prices of goods purchased by *all urban* consumers (hence the *U*). The BLS also reports the CPI-W, a price index for a basket of goods purchased by urban wage earners and clerical workers. The BLS even publishes indexes that measure the price changes in different cities and, if you are interested, price indexes for water, sewer, and trash-collection services![7]

A frequently reported and discussed version of the CPI excludes price changes for goods included in the "food and fuel" category. This adjusted CPI is known as *core* CPI. Some believe that core CPI better measures the trend in the price level because it excludes these prices which, even though they represent a large portion of consumer spending, are particularly volatile. Just think of how many times you've read or heard about a freeze in Florida destroying the orange crop and how this will raise orange juice prices. That occurs, but it is short-lived. Still, the CPI can bump up for a month or two, only to fall back once orange juice prices return to normal levels as oranges from non-Florida producers come into the market. And if you watch gasoline prices, they jump around quite a bit—even from week to week.

**Figure 6.3** shows the CPI and core CPI inflation rates since 1960. Even though the two inflation measures have the same general pattern—they tend to trend upward and downward with each other—you can see that the inflation rate measured using the CPI, which is sometimes referred to as the *headline* CPI because it is the one often cited in newspapers, is more volatile than the core CPI inflation. To see this, look at the behavior of the two inflation rates since 2000. Core CPI inflation is much less volatile because it does not include the direct effects of oil and gas price changes. Even though headline inflation reached more than 5 percent in 2008, core inflation was only half that. And, during the economic crisis of 2007–2009, you can see that core inflation was much less volatile than headline inflation.

The interesting policy question is which inflation rate—headline or core—is the "correct" one on which to base decisions. Many economists believe that policy makers should focus more on the core inflation rate than the headline rate because core inflation may better reflect the effects of their policy decisions than headline inflation. There is some merit to this view: policy makers, after all, have little control over the price of oil and other commodities that can have big effects on the CPI. Although

· · · · · · · ·

[7]Visit the BLS Web site at www.bls.gov to see all of the different price indexes that are available.

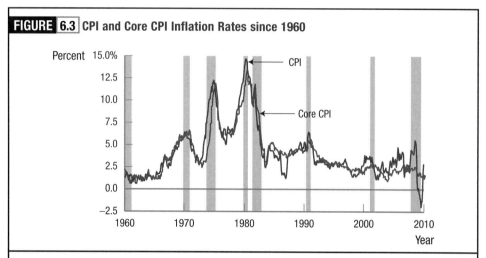

**FIGURE 6.3** CPI and Core CPI Inflation Rates since 1960

The CPI and core CPI inflation rates since 1960 are plotted in this graph (shaded areas indicate U.S. recessions). The two inflation rates have the same general pattern. However, notice that the inflation rate measured using the CPI is more volatile than the core CPI inflation rate. For example, even though CPI inflation reached more than 5 percent in 2008 when oil and gasoline prices spiked, core CPI inflation was only about 2.5 percent. And during the most recent recession, core CPI inflation rates never became negative as CPI inflation did.

*Source:* Federal Reserve Bank of St. Louis

some argue that core inflation is the one to watch, others counter with the fact that consumers do in fact pay for food and fuel and are, therefore, economically impacted when these prices rise. This issue remains debated among decision makers and among economists in general.[8]

In addition to the different versions of the CPI, the BLS also publishes the **Producer Price Index (PPI)**. The PPI measures the price changes of goods used in the production process of finished goods. Some analysts believe that the PPI is useful as a *leading* indicator of the price changes that will eventually occur at the consumer level.

**PRODUCER PRICE INDEX** The PPI measures changes in prices from the perspective of the seller. It measures the prices of raw materials, for example.

**EXAMPLE** The increase in the price of cotton directly affected the PPI and later showed up in the CPI through higher clothing prices.

**EXAMPLE** The price of crude oil increased in 1974. This directly affected the PPI and later showed up in the CPI when gasoline prices rose.

Another price index is the GDP (for gross domestic product) deflator. It covers the prices of many more goods and services than the CPI or the PPI. The **GDP deflator** measures prices of all new goods and services produced in our economy.

·······

[8]Daniel Gross, "If You Don't Eat or Drive, Inflation's No Problem." *New York Times*, October 23, 2005.

**GDP DEFLATOR** The GDP deflator measures prices of all new goods and services produced in the economy.

**EXAMPLE** The price of the 2010 Mustang sold by Ford is included in the GDP deflator for 2010. The price of the 1974 Mustang purchased in 2010 by your neighbor is not.

If the PPI is capturing prices faced by sellers, and the CPI is measuring final prices for goods and services, then how are the CPI and the GDP deflator different? One key difference is that the GDP deflator is based on the price of goods currently produced relative to some base year. In other words, in the GDP deflator, the price is "counted" only if the good was produced in the current period. (In the following chapter, we will be more specific about what the notion of the current period means in this context.) Another difference is that the CPI uses a fixed basket of goods to calculate the price level. In our earlier example, we measured the price index for 2009 and 2010 by using only three goods: gas, CDs, and laptop computers. In measuring the price index, we assumed that consumers would purchase the same quantity of these goods in each year. The GDP deflator, however, includes the prices of all goods and services produced within the country. As you can see, the GDP deflator is a much broader measure of prices than the CPI or the PPI.

Because the GDP deflator is often used in policy discussions, how do changes in that index compare with changes in the CPI? **Figure 6.4** compares inflation rates as measured by the headline CPI and the GDP deflator since 1960. You can immediately see that the rate of inflation using the CPI is often higher and more volatile than the rate of inflation using the GDP deflator. Look especially at the behavior in 1980,

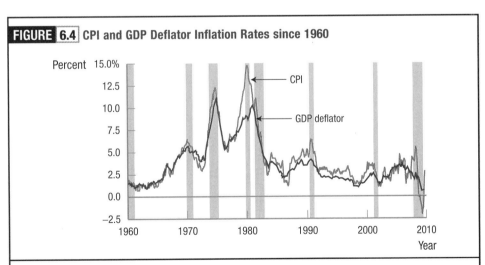

**FIGURE 6.4** CPI and GDP Deflator Inflation Rates since 1960

This figure plots inflation rates measured using the CPI and the GDP deflator (shaded areas indicate U.S. recessions). There was an upward trend in both rates of inflation between 1960 and 1980. Since then, both rates show a downward trend. Notice, however, that the CPI inflation rate is often higher and more volatile than the rate of inflation using the GDP deflator. The differences between the two rates often reflect times when changes in some CPI components, such as food and fuels, affect the CPI much more than the GDP deflator.

*Source:* Federal Reserve Bank of St. Louis

1990, and, most recently, 2008. These departures partly reflect the fact that changes in some CPI components, such as food and fuels, simply do not have the same proportional effect on the GDP deflator. Although the changes in these components are important, they don't affect the GDP deflator as much as they affect the CPI. Notice also that the general pattern of inflation using the two series is very similar: inflation rates in general rose in the 1960s and 1970s; beginning in the early 1980s, they fell back to levels comparable with the early 1960s.

Put yourself in the position of a government policy maker. Suppose your job is to make sure that inflation remains under control. Which inflation measure—CPI, core CPI, or GDP deflator—should you watch to see if your policies are working? Or suppose you are the head of a labor union. Which inflation series would you use to decide how much wages should increase for your members? What if you are representing management, sitting across from the union negotiator?

The answer to "Which price index is best?" depends on what you use it for. If you are negotiating a wage increase with your boss, you will want to use the CPI, because it most closely tracks the changes in the prices of the goods and services that you buy. Governments might use the GDP deflator or core CPI when they establish pension plans because they tend to be less volatile and often increase at a slower rate than the CPI. As you can see, understanding how a price index is constructed and what its limitations are is essential to making well-informed economic decisions.

## 6.7 Inflation in Other Countries

You have seen how different measures of inflation have a similar pattern over time, at least for U.S. price indexes. Is that true when comparing inflation across countries? **Figure 6.5** provides some answers.

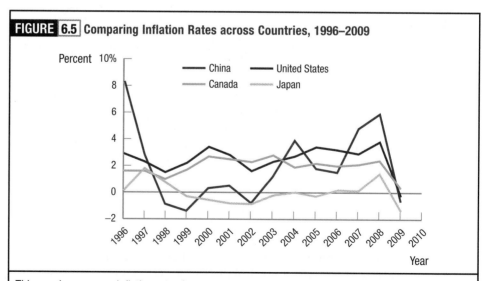

**FIGURE 6.5** Comparing Inflation Rates across Countries, 1996–2009

This graph compares inflation rates in consumer prices across several countries. Inflation rates in the United States and Canada were similar to one another during the time period. The inflation experiences of China and Japan are markedly different, however. Japan experienced deflation for many years, and China's inflation rate fluctuated widely.

*Source:* Federal Reserve Bank of St. Louis

First, you can see that the rate of inflation since 1996 followed a roughly similar pattern in some countries but not in others. Inflation in Canada and the United States closely mirror each other, hovering around 2 percent for most of the period. This might be expected because they are not only neighbors but also large trading partners. The inflation experiences of China and Japan are markedly different, however. Starting at more than 8 percent in 1996, inflation in China dropped significantly over the next few years, fluctuating around zero until 2003 when it began to increase. By 2008, inflation in China had increased back to 6 percent, high relative to the other countries.

Perhaps the most dramatic, at least from an economic perspective, is the experience of Japan. During the period covered in Figure 6.5, the rate of inflation in Japan was usually zero or even *negative*. That's right: during those years when the rate of inflation is negative, Japan's general level of prices was not increasing but actually falling. When the price level is falling, it is called **deflation**.

**DEFLATION** A sustained *decrease* in the general level of prices.

EXAMPLE Between 1999 and 2005, the rate of consumer price inflation in Japan was never positive. Japan's inflation rate using its GDP deflator was negative every year from 1999 through 2009.

EXAMPLE From the start to the end of the Great Depression in the United States (1929–1933) wholesale prices fell 33 percent.

Deflation is a fairly rare occurrence in modern economies. In the United States, only during the Great Depression did the CPI fall for an extended period of time. From 1929 through 1933, the inflation rate was negative, reaching a low of *minus* 10 percent. And even though the monthly rate of inflation was negative for many countries during the most recent downturn, there was not a sustained decrease in the general level of prices: already by mid-2010, prices were again increasing (except for Japan), though slowly, in the countries shown in Figure 6.5. Although rare, deflation has significant economic effects. If prices in general are falling, that means the income being derived from selling goods also is falling. When prices for shoes, eggs, and cars are dropping, the income earned by cobblers, farmers, and auto dealerships declines as well. As you can imagine, prolonged periods of deflation are as damaging to an economy as inflation.

After looking at Figure 6.5, you may be wondering, "Why does inflation differ among countries, even those that are closely linked by international trade?" Even for countries closely tied, like Canada and the United States, the price of a similar good may not be the same. Differences in prices may be explained by factors such as taxes. But if taxes are not changing often, why would prices change at different rates? The best answer is that transactions costs differ in each country. Such costs can include the actual cost to ship goods between locations. It also may be that the cost of bringing a good to market—costs to market and distribute the good—differs. Changes in any one of these components may give rise to different rates of change in the general level of prices. And, of course, different policies followed by the governments of the countries also may affect the rate at which the general level of prices is rising.

## WHAT YOU SHOULD HAVE LEARNED FROM CHAPTER 6

- That a price index such as the CPI can be used to measure the general level of prices in an economy.
- That the point of reference for a price index is called the *base year*.

■ That the percentage change in a price index is called *inflation* if the change is positive and *deflation* if the change is negative.

■ That price indexes are not perfect and can be affected by problems associated with how the different goods are weighted and whether there are close substitutes for goods in the index.

■ That quality changes are difficult to measure and that a price index may not be perfectly applicable to each and every situation.

■ That relative prices are found by adjusting nominal prices for changes in the overall price level.

■ That there are different price indexes that can be used for different purposes.

## KEY TERMS

Price index, p. 164

Consumer Price Index (CPI), p. 165

Base year, p. 166

Inflation, p. 168

Nominal price, p. 173

Relative price, p. 174

Producer Price Index (PPI), p. 178

GDP deflator, p. 178

Deflation, p. 181

## QUESTIONS AND PROBLEMS

1. In 2010, the CPI was 218. Was 2010 the base year for the CPI? Explain. Roughly speaking, how much have prices in general increased between the base year and 2010?

2. Use the following table to determine your answers.

| Year | Index | Inflation Rate |
|------|-------|----------------|
| 1 | 95 | _____ |
| 2 | 90 | _____ |
| 3 | 100 | _____ |
| 4 | 110 | _____ |

   a) What is the base year?
   b) What is the rate of inflation in year 2?
   c) What is the inflation rate in year 4?

3. Look at Figure 6.1. Have there been times over the past 50 years when the United States experienced a prolonged period of deflation? Were there periods when the rate of inflation was falling? Explain the difference.

4. Look at the items listed in Table 6.1. Are there any items listed that you do not purchase? Do you purchase some of the items listed more often than others? What does your spending behavior suggest about the applicability of the CPI to you personally?

5. Using the information in the following table, calculate the price index and the percentage change in the index, assuming that 2008 is the base year.

| Item | 2008 Quantity | 2008 Price ($) | 2009 Quantity | 2009 Price ($) | 2010 Quantity | 2010 Price ($) |
|------|---------------|----------------|---------------|----------------|---------------|----------------|
| Shoes | 2 | 10 | 5 | 5 | 4 | 5 |
| Tuition | 15 | 100 | 15 | 100 | 15 | 125 |
| Coffee | 100 | 4 | 100 | 4 | 150 | 3 |

| Year | Price Index | Percentage Change |
|------|-------------|-------------------|
| 2008 | _____ | _____ |
| 2009 | _____ | _____ |
| 2010 | _____ | _____ |

6. Statisticians define *range* as the difference between the largest value and the smallest value. Look at panel (b) of Figure 6.1. What is the approximate range of CPI inflation over the past 50 years? Now measure the range over the periods 1960–1985 and 1985–2009. Are they different? Has inflation become more or less variable over the most recent 25 years compared to the 25 years previous to that?

7. Sitting in the student lounge, your friends start arguing over which is the best movie. Because tastes vary, they decide to use opening weekend box-office receipts to settle the dispute. The following table shows the three candidates, their opening weekend grosses, and the months in which they were released.

| Movie | Release Date | Box Office ($) |
|-------|--------------|----------------|
| *Transformers* | July 2007 | 70,502,384 |
| *Quantum of Solace* | Nov 2008 | 67,582,882 |
| *Lord of the Rings: The Two Towers* | Dec 2002 | 62,007,528 |

    a) You are the only person taking economics in the group. What is wrong with making this comparison?

    b) On the Internet, you find the CPI for each of the films' opening months. Those numbers are 213.3 for November 2008, 207.3 for July 2007, and 181.8 for December 2002. With these data, calculate the inflation-adjusted opening weekend box-office take. How does your calculation affect the ordering in the preceding table?

8. Assume that the CPI overstates your grandparents' personal inflation by one percentage point. In other words, based on the goods they purchase, prices are rising at a 3-percent rate while the official CPI says the rate of inflation is 4 percent. If annual increases in their Social Security receipts are tied to the official inflation rate, what is happening to the purchasing power of their Social Security income over time?

9. Looking at Figure 6.4, which inflation rate—the CPI or the GDP deflator—seems to be more variable? Can you explain why that might be?

10. In the mid-1960s, NASA officials testified before Congress that the projected cost of the Apollo mission to put humans on the moon would cost about $23 billion for the 13-year program. If you adjusted that figure for inflation, would the program's cost rise or fall? Find the CPI for 1966, and calculate how much the Apollo mission would cost in real dollars. Were you correct?

11. The headline used in footnote 8 reads "If You Don't Eat or Drive, Inflation's No Problem." The author argues that because prices on food and gasoline were rising at the time, everyone was worse off. Given what you know about possible problems associated with measuring the CPI, is this assertion necessarily correct? Explain.

# Appendix 6A The Chained CPI

We mentioned that a price index like the CPI suffers from substitution bias. This means that individuals usually act like the rational beings economic theory predicts they are: when prices change, they substitute between similar goods. If the price of movie tickets rises, then maybe you rent or buy more DVDs. If the prices of houses rise, maybe you decide to rent. As we explained, the weights, or amounts of goods sold, in the CPI do not change with changes in their prices. As a result, the CPI will misstate the rate of inflation.

In an attempt to deal with the problem of substitution bias, the Bureau of Labor Statistics now publishes a supplemental CPI index called the *chained CPI*, or C-CPI-U. (The U again refers specifically to the *all urban consumers* version of the index.) This version, available since 1999, attempts to reduce the substitution bias by allowing the weights to change monthly. Thus, when relative prices diverge and people alter their spending habits, the C-CPI-U captures their substitution between goods.

To get a feel for how the inflation based on the chained CPI is calculated, let's simplify the economy by assuming it has only two goods: bottled water and a sports drink. Now assume that you have a fixed income and adjust your spending habits as prices change. Next we provide hypothetical prices and quantities for the goods that you will buy in two separate months. Notice that as the price of the sports drink increases in month 2 relative to month 1, you buy less of it. But because of your fixed income ($50), you also buy less bottled water in month 2 compared with the previous month. Based on this information, what is the rate of inflation between months 1 and 2?

| Consumer Good | Month 1 | | Month 2 | |
|---|---|---|---|---|
| | Price ($) | Quantity | Price ($) | Quantity |
| Sports drink | 5 | 6 | 8 | 4 |
| Bottled water | 2 | 10 | 2 | 9 |

Let's first calculate the rate of inflation using the standard CPI approach. For this illustration, we will make month 1 the base period. The price index for month 2 would be:

$$\text{Basket price in month 1: } (\$5 \times 6) + (\$2 \times 10) = \$50$$

$$\text{Basket price in month 2: } (\$8 \times 6) + (\$2 \times 10) = \$68$$

$$\text{CPI in month 2} = (\$68/\$50) \times 100$$

$$= 1.36 \times 100$$

$$= 136$$

In month 2, the CPI is 136. The fact that the index is 136 means that, using the CPI methodology, the rate of inflation is 36 percent. As you can see from the table, the inflation results entirely from the increase in the price of the sports drink because the price of bottled water did not change. However, because the price of the sports drink increased, you bought less of it. How can we capture the fact that you bought less of it in the price index?

As we have explained, the chained CPI approach allows the expenditure weights (quantities sold) to vary. One way to think of this is that the rate of inflation using the chained CPI is based on the average of two measures. One uses the weights of month 1 as the base period; the other uses the weights of month 2 as the base period. Because we already figured out that the CPI was 136 in month 1 when the weights of month 1 were used (the regular CPI formula), we're done with that part of the problem. We now need to find out instead what the CPI was for month 1 based on month 2 weights:

$$\text{Basket price in month 1: } (\$5 \times 4) + (\$2 \times 9) = \$38$$

$$\text{Basket price in month 2: } (\$8 \times 4) + (\$2 \times 9) = \$50$$

$$\text{CPI in month 1(based on month 2 weights)} = (\$38/\$50) \times 100$$

$$= 0.76 \times 100$$

$$= 76$$

Multiply this value by 100 and you get a CPI of 76. In other words, using month 2 weights, the CPI for month 1 is 76. What is the rate of inflation from month 1 to 2 when we use the month 2 weights? It is $(100 - 76)/76 = 31.58$ percent.

Now we can find the chained CPI rate of inflation simply by averaging the two values. In this case, the chained CPI rate of inflation is equal to 33.8 percent $[(36 + 31.58)/2]$. By allowing each month to serve as the base period, the chained CPI inflation rate accounted for the substitution away from the sports drink because of its price increase. As you can see from this example, allowing the expenditure weights to change as people's spending habits changes yields a different rate of inflation.

Just how big is the difference between inflation measured with the CPI and the C-CPI? **Figure 6A.1** compares the annual inflation rates using the two price indexes

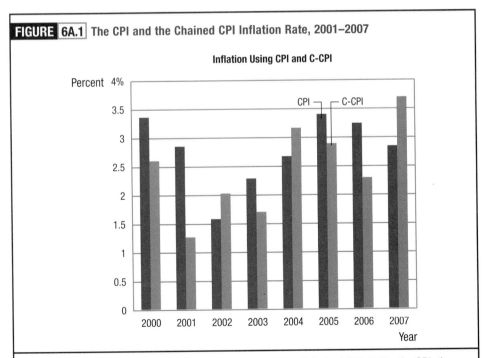

**FIGURE 6A.1** The CPI and the Chained CPI Inflation Rate, 2001–2007

**Inflation Using CPI and C-CPI**

This figure shows the annual rate of inflation using the CPI and chained CPI. Unlike the CPI, the chained CPI allows the expenditure weights (quantities sold) to vary. Over the time period, the average difference between the two inflation measures was about three-tenths of a percentage point.

*Source:* Bureau of Labor Statistics

from 2000 to 2007. The average difference between the two inflation measures—about three-tenths of a percentage point—may not seem huge, but it is enough to have important effects on economic decisions. For example, such a difference can significantly affect the state and local budgets of governments when they are deciding on cost-of-living increases for their employees and retirees. And in some years the difference is quite large: in 2001, the CPI-based rate of inflation was 2.8 percent compared to only 1.3 percent for the chained CPI. We've just scratched the surface of this topic, but if you are interested we suggest you visit the BLS Web site for more detail on the measurement of the chained CPI.[9]

. . . . . . .

[9]The figures in Table 6A.1 are taken from the Bureau of Labor Statistics Web site example. If you follow our example, you can see how this index is calculated and compare it to others discussed there.

# 7

# Output and Income

> *"A child of five would understand this. Send someone to fetch a child of five."*
>
> *Groucho Marx,*
> *comedian and actor*

**A**ccurately measuring a nation's income and output is difficult but not incomprehensible. If someone asked you how much income you earned last year, it wouldn't be too difficult to answer. You might be a salaried employee and know that your annual income is, say, $45,000. Or if you work for an hourly wage, you could multiply your wage rate by the number of hours you worked. In both cases, coming up with your total income wouldn't be too difficult. But what if that same person asks, how much output did you produce? If you produce handmade guitars, you could answer this question by the number of guitars you built. Trying to figure out the output of an accountant or the instructor of this course is more challenging. Even though trying to figure out what we produce and the income we get for our labor is sometimes difficult, economists have devised reasonable measures of the output and income of the entire economy. How that is done will be the focus of this chapter.

Why do we care how much an economy produces or what its *aggregate* level of income is? It isn't simply to see which economy has more goods or a greater income. Measuring output and income allows us to see if our overall economic well-being is advancing or falling. It also gives us an idea of how much better off (economically speaking) one economy is relative to another. Knowing whether your economy is expanding or contracting and what the level of income is per person are important facts to those making policy decisions aimed at improving our lives.

## 7.1 Aggregate Output and Income

Measures of national economic activity are relatively new. It wasn't until World War II that economists really began to systematically measure the amount of goods and services an economy produces or how much income it generates. At the time, it was important to see where resources were being used and for what purpose. Knowing this allowed the government to redirect some production to more urgent needs, such as tanks and bombers. Since then, national output and income statistics have become indispensable tools in shaping economic policy.

The basic principle behind measuring a nation's output and income boils down to the realization that a person's income is based on what she produces. Expanding this concept to the entire economy—that is, if we *aggregate* the output that all individuals and businesses in an economy produce—then we can estimate aggregate output and aggregate income for the entire economy.

## Gross Domestic Product

The most widely used measure of a nation's aggregate output—and income—is its gross domestic product (GDP). The fact that this one measure can be used to gauge both output and input is sometimes perplexing. How can one measure count for both? The answer is that GDP is a dollar measure. Not only does it measure income, but it also measures the dollar value of output: the money spent on goods and services produced in the economy. Think of the guitar maker mentioned earlier: If guitars are the only output of the economy, then the income earned by producing and selling guitars is just the same as the dollar value of guitar output. Obviously, the economy is more complex than one that just produces guitars, but the concept is very much the same. To try and make this all tractable, economists devised an accounting-like way of measuring the economy's income and output. We call these the *national income* accounts. Let's take a quick look at how these accounts are fashioned before we provide a detailed definition of GDP.

The U.S. economy is made up of millions of people and businesses, all interacting in a multitude of daily transactions. Instead of even trying to fathom how all of them work together to create output and generate income, let's simplify the problem. We'll assume that the economy consists of a wheat farmer in Kansas; the Old Time Mill Flour Company in Omaha, Nebraska; and the Mound City Doughnut Shoppe in suburban St. Louis, Missouri. The farmer grows wheat and sells it to the Old Time Mill Flour Company. The flour company mills the wheat into baking flour and sells it to the doughnut shop. The doughnut shop's baker subsequently turns the flour into doughnuts and sells them to you, the consumer. How can we account for the different products being produced and sold and the incomes being generated in this chain of production?

**Table 7.1** outlines the transactions in this hypothetical economy. The farmer sells his output, 10 bushels of wheat, to Old Time Mill for $4 a bushel. The $40 total he receives is money he uses to pay for the production of the wheat (seed, fertilizer, etc.) and to pay himself an income. In the second panel of the table, you see that the $40 for the 10 bushels of wheat is an expense for Old Time Mill. Like the farmer, the miller also incurs production costs. She must hire workers to run the milling machines and pay for rent, loans on the business's machinery, and so forth. For now, let's focus on the cost of the wheat and the wages paid to the workers. After the flour is milled, Old Time Mill sells the 50 bags of flour it produces for $2 each to the Mound City Doughnut Shoppe. The doughnut shop then transforms the flour into doughnuts and sells 100 of them for $2 apiece, earning a total of $200.

Isn't the link between wheat production and doughnut production more complicated than this? Sure, but our simple model economy actually delivers everything you need to know to understand the concept of national income accounting. Don't worry about real-world details right now, just stick with the example.

What is the dollar value of aggregate output for this economy? You might be tempted to answer $340. That would equal the sale of the wheat ($40), plus the sale

| Table **7.1** Tracking the Production of a Good | | |
|---|---|---|
| Farmer<br>Revenue: $40 | Old Time Mill<br>Revenue: $100 | Doughnut Shoppe<br>Revenue: $200 |
| | Expenses ($) | Expenses ($) |
| | Wages   50 | Wages   50 |
| | Wheat   40 | Flour   100 |
| |   90 |   150 |
| | Profit   $10 | Profit   $50 |

This table outlines transactions in a hypothetical economy that produces doughnuts as its final good. The farmer sells wheat to Old Time Mill and uses the proceeds to pay for the production of the wheat (seed, fertilizer, etc.) and to pay himself an income. The purchase of the wheat is an expense for Old Time Mill. The owner of the mill also incurs production costs: costs related to hiring workers to run the machines, rent payments, loan payments on the business's machinery, and so forth. After the flour is milled, Old Time Mill sells the flour to the Mound City Doughnut Shoppe. The doughnut shop then transforms the flour into doughnuts. At each stage of the production process, economic value is added to the product.

of the flour ($100), plus the sale of the doughnuts ($200). This answer is not the way economists measure aggregate output, however. The correct answer is $200, the final amount of revenue earned from doughnuts. Let's consider the reasoning behind this. When the bakery buys flour from the miller, the cost of flour—$100—includes the cost of all of the inputs that were required to produce the flour. This includes not only the wages paid to the mill workers ($50) and profits to the mill owner ($10) but also the cost of the raw material: the $40 spent on wheat. (Here we are referring to accounting profits, which is revenues less expenses. Profits go to the owners of the firm, which can be an individual or, in the case of publicly traded firms, to stockholders in the form of dividends.)

In the production of doughnuts, wheat is considered to be an **intermediate good**. An intermediate good is something that is used in the production of another good or produced for resale, in this case, doughnuts.

**INTERMEDIATE GOOD** Something that is used in the production of another good.

**EXAMPLE** Companies such as MEMC make and sell silicon wafers that are used in the production of integrated circuits. The silicon wafer is an intermediate good.

Now take this one step further. When the bakery sells doughnuts to you and your classmates, the $2 you pay for each doughnut includes all of the costs incurred up to the point of selling you the doughnut you buy. The costs include what the bakery paid for the flour in addition to its costs of producing doughnuts. Because it's reasonable to assume that the doughnuts are a final product people consume, we can simplify the process of measuring the economy's output and income by just looking at the revenue generated by the final goods—the doughnuts. Why? Their production includes all of the prices of the intermediate goods and payments made to the services (labor, rent, machinery, etc.) used to make them.

This is a simple example, but it actually works to illustrate the underlying concepts economists use to measure national output and income. First, it illustrates the idea that the value of final goods—100 doughnuts priced at $2 each, in this case—is equal to the sales revenue (income) earned from them. In our example, that revenue is distributed as income to the workers via the wages they earn and to the bakery owner as the profit he earns. In this sense, the value of output matches the income earned. This is true at each stage of the production process.

Another way of approaching this problem is to think of the income produced by the final sale of the doughnuts as being equal to the **value added** at each stage of the process. Think of the cost of the wheat seed and the farmer's labor as "adding value" to the final product he sells. The miller "adds" another $60 in value, which is the difference between the $40 of wheat she buys and the $100 she charges for the intermediate good she produces, flour. Finally, the baker adds another $100 in value to the flour, which is the difference between the revenue earned from doughnut sales and what the baker paid for the intermediate goods needed to produce those doughnuts.

> **VALUED ADDED** Value added is the increase in market value of an item as it progresses through stages of production. The sum of value added is reflected in the final price of the good.

> **EXAMPLE** Your uncle Waldo purchases a large tree stump for $50 and, with his chainsaw, creates a bear sculpture that he then sells for $500. His value added to the original stump can be measured as $450.

Sum together the value added at each stage, and you'll see that total value added ($40 + $60 + $100) equals the final sales revenue earned from the doughnuts ($200). Both methods result in the same dollar value for GDP. Even so, just counting the revenue from the sale of the final goods (doughnuts) is much simpler.

Using the prices of final goods to measure the value of production across the various stages makes measuring the value of national output and income more manageable. Figuring out how to do this was so important that two economists who were instrumental in establishing national income and product accounts, Simon Kuznets and Richard Stone, were awarded the Nobel Prize! It still isn't simple, by any means, but it is easier. It also leads us to a definition of **gross domestic product (GDP)**:

> **GROSS DOMESTIC PRODUCT (GDP)** The market value of all final goods and services produced in an economy during a given period.

In the case of our doughnut economy, GDP is the value of doughnut sales (the final good), in this example, $200. Let's decompose the definition of GDP to better understand what it measures and what it doesn't measure.

**The market value of all final goods and services . . .** We want to avoid counting the sale of intermediate goods because that would double count the value of production. Remember, the value of intermediate goods are included in the prices (revenues) of the final good being sold. Notice also that GDP is based on the market value of the final goods and services produced. This means that illegal drug trades or illicit Texas Hold 'em poker games are not counted in GDP. Even though these transactions occur in, strictly speaking, a market, there is no official record of any exchange taking place. That is why such transactions are generally referred to as nonmarket transactions.

This restriction also means that GDP excludes the unpaid services you provide around the house, such as doing the laundry or mowing the yard. It is widely agreed that unpaid activities generate economic benefits and that their market value can be approximated. After all, you can call a lawn service to figure out what your mowing job was worth. Nonetheless, trying to account for all of the unpaid lawn mowing, laundry washing, and so forth, would be so problematic and cumbersome that the benefit of deriving a more accurate measure of GDP would not be worth the extra cost. This part of the definition also means that the sale of used goods is not counted in GDP. Buy a new car in January 2011 and sell it to a friend in June, and your original purchase is in 2011 GDP. The resale—which is just a transfer of income from your friend to you for your car—is not. Otherwise, it would double-count the car.

**... produced in an economy ...** GDP statistics ignore nonearned income, income that is received but is not earned from current production. The easiest way to think about this is to imagine someone getting a Social Security check. The check is income to the recipient but not income for producing any good or service in the current period. Payments to welfare recipients or to farmers who receive payments for not putting land into production are other forms of income paid even though there is no good or service produced. Because GDP is based on goods and services produced in the economy, the income from payments such as these is not counted. However, when people spend this income on groceries or lawn-care services, it will be. GDP includes both the value of output produced and the income that this production generates.

We just noted that goods produced and sold in a country are counted as part of its GDP. Goods produced overseas are not included. Ford Motor Company, for instance, has plants in other countries that produce cars that are sold abroad. The market value of that production is not counted in U.S. (domestic) GDP. However, Fords produced here and sold here, as well as Fords produced here and sold overseas, are part of the GDP of the United States.

**... in a given period.** We want to measure the value of current production and income. For this reason, items that were produced in a previous period, say 1998, and sold in 2011, are not included in the GDP for 2011. A good example is a used car. The 1973 Mustang convertible that your neighbor drives on sunny weekends was produced in 1973 and was counted in 1973's GDP. If she sold it on eBay in June 2011, the money she makes does not count toward 2011 GDP. The market value of producing the Mustang already was counted in 1973, the year it was sold as a new good. Any good produced and purchased in a previous year, no matter how valuable it is, isn't counted in *current* GDP.

You now have the basics of measuring GDP. The actual measurement of GDP is more complicated. For our purposes, though, we don't need to go into such detail.

## 7.2 Should We Measure Production or Income?

We measured the GDP of our doughnut economy from the production, or output, side. Because we made such a big deal of noting that the value of the economy's output is the same as its income, couldn't we have measured it by looking at the income caused by the production of doughnuts? The income derived from the sale of the doughnuts created income not only for the workers but also for the doughnut shop owner, the mill owner and her workers, and the farmer. Let's look at how the value of an economy's output is directly related to the income the people within it earn.

### The Final Goods Approach

Figuring out a nation's GDP by adding up the dollar value of final goods and services sold in the economy is sometimes called, perhaps for obvious reasons, the **final goods approach**.

**FINAL GOODS APPROACH** The final goods approach to measuring GDP is based on adding up the dollar value of final goods and services sold in the economy in the current period.

**EXAMPLE** Josh owns an organic produce farm that produces only green beans. This season he produced 50 bushels of beans. To measure the market value of his bean output, he used the revenue from selling beans to restaurants and other customers.

The final goods approach (which, to be clear, includes services) also allows us to consider another wrinkle in understanding how the economy works. When economists try to explain why an economy expands or contracts, they divide it up into four sectors, or parts, so they can better examine each. The four sectors are (1) the household sector, which consists of individual consumers like you; (2) the business sector, which consists of individual for-profit and nonprofit businesses; (3) the government; (4) and the rest of the world. We can separate the expenditures made in the different sectors and see how each contributes to GDP. This allows us to think not only about how each sector contributes to GDP but also where goods go. This approach also will be useful when we build our model of the economy in Chapter 13.

A substantial portion of final goods consumed is by individuals—the household sector. This portion of GDP (around two-thirds) is simply called *consumption*. Consumption spending includes the purchase of goods and services, regardless of their origin. Businesses also purchase goods to be used in building factories or store-front shops, or to make machinery used to produce cars and bikes. This portion of GDP is called *gross private domestic investment*, or just investment for short. The various government entities in the economy—state, local, national—also purchase goods and services. These purchases—from pencils to labor and fighter jets—are included in *government purchases*. Finally, we must include international trade, or the "rest of the world" sector. When our guitar maker sells one of his creations to someone in Belgium, the market value of the guitar—which increases his income—is included in *exports* from the United States. In contrast, the items we buy from foreign producers, such as Canadian oil or Italian shoes, are included in *imports* from abroad. Because imports increase the income of foreigners, not our income, we subtract these expenditures from our calculation of GDP.[1]

This four-sector approach allows us to summarize the final goods approach to measuring GDP (which we will denote as $Y$) with the equation

$$Y = C + I + G + (X - M)$$

where $C$ stands for consumption spending, $I$ is investment, $G$ is government purchases, $X$ is exports, and $M$ is imports. Note that GDP ($Y$ in the equation) is the sum of all of the different domestic expenditures made in the economy. It includes the purchases of U.S.-produced goods by foreigners *minus* our purchases of foreign-produced goods. The difference between the values of the two in the equation ($X - M$) is referred to as *net exports*. If the value of a nation's exports is greater than the value of the goods it imports, then the value of its net exports is positive. When a nation's net exports are positive, it has a *trade surplus*. When a

........

[1]Each of these spending components of GDP will be defined in greater detail in Chapter 13.

| Table **7.2** | Measuring U.S. GDP for 2009 Using the Final Goods and Income Approaches (in trillions of dollars) | | |
|---|---|---|---|
| **Final Goods ($)** | | **Income ($)** | |
| Consumption | 10.1 | Employee compensation | 7.8 |
| Investment | 1.5 | Interest, profits, rent, etc. | 3.5 |
| Government purchases | 2.9 | Indirect taxes | 1.0 |
| Exports | 1.5 | Depreciation | 1.8 |
| Imports | 1.9 | | |
| GDP | 14.1 | GDP | 14.1 |

The final goods approach is one way of measuring GDP. Shown in the left-hand portion of the table, this approach is based on expenditures by segments of the economy. The right-hand portion of the table shows an alternative way to measure GDP, the income approach. As measured by the income approach, the value of goods and services produced in the economy—measured using the final goods approach—must be equal to the income received by individuals when they sell those goods.
**Source:** Bureau of Economic Analysis

nation's imports are greater than its exports, it has a *trade deficit*. For the United States, for many years the market value of the goods we imported exceeded the market value of the goods we exported. We'll have more to say about these trade numbers in Chapter 9.

The final goods approach to measuring GDP is the foundation for an economic model we'll use later in the book to explain fluctuations—periods of recession and periods of expansion—in economic activity. For now, let's look at how much each sector contributes to the GDP of the United States. **Table 7.2** shows the value of spending in each sector in 2009. As you can see, in 2009, the nation's GDP amounted to a little more than $14 trillion. Consumption spending is always by far the largest component. In 2009, it amounted to more than $10 trillion or a little over 70 percent of GDP. The second largest single spending component of GDP is government purchases, which were almost $3 trillion, or about 20 percent of GDP. This is followed by business investment at $1.5 trillion, or 10 percent of GDP. Finally, note that while exports increased GDP by $1.5 trillion, in 2009, we imported $1.9 trillion worth of goods and services from foreign producers. This means that, on net, international trade lowered GDP in 2009 by $0.4 trillion.

These numbers help illustrate why, especially during times of economic distress, many analysts and decision makers focus on the behavior of consumers. Consumers account for over two-thirds of total spending in the economy. So, if households decide to curtail their purchases, the overall economy might not expand as rapidly as desired, which has many undesirable effects. If the economy doesn't grow, new jobs are not created, and unemployment rates can rise. In fact, the specter of a slowing economy and lack of jobs is a major reason behind the government's massive stimulus spending programs during and after the Great Recession of 2007–2009.

## Income Approach

What you spend on a pair of shoes is income to the maker of the shoes. As we explained, we can measure GDP by adding up all of the incomes earned from people and businesses producing and selling goods and services. This is called the **income approach**.

**INCOME APPROACH** The income approach to measuring GDP adds up all of the incomes earned from people and businesses producing and selling goods and services.

**EXAMPLE** Remember Josh, the guy who owns the organic produce farm that produces only green beans? He wants to measure his income from producing beans. To do this, he uses the salary he pays himself. Because he is the only worker, his salary is equal to the income received from selling beans to restaurants and other customers. (Remember that this also is equal to the market value of his bean crop.)

This example is a little simplistic because we've ignored costs other than Josh's own salary. Even so, it is true that the market value of what is produced is equal to the income generated to produce it. In the case of the Mound City Doughnut Shoppe, for example, not only did the owner pay for flour (an input) but he also hired workers to make doughnuts. In the real world, firms must also pay other costs to remain in business. Often they have outstanding loans, on which they have to make interest payments. When you buy a doughnut, you likely pay a sales tax on the purchase. Although the tax is levied by your city or state (or both), the doughnut shop collects it for them. These are referred to as *indirect taxes*. Some of the shop's sales revenue also goes to replace worn-out machines, which is called *depreciation*. After all of these expenses are deducted, the leftover revenues make up the shop owner's profits.

The following formula shows where the revenue from the doughnut sales goes:

$$\text{Revenue} = \text{Wages} + \text{Interest Payments} + \text{Cost of Inputs}$$
$$+ \text{Indirect Business Taxes} + \text{Depreciation} + \text{Profits}$$

The formula tells us that the shop's sales revenue is used to pay various individuals. Each one of these payments represents income to someone. Individuals making loans get interest payments; the miller gets income from selling the flour; firms who make replacement machinery get income when the bakery shop replaces an oven; the workers get wages; and the bakery owner gets the profits.

Let's make use of the idea that started this discussion: as measured by the income approach, the value of final goods and services produced in the economy—measured using the final goods approach—must be equal to the income received by individuals when they sell those final goods and services. This observation suggests the equality (remember, $Y = GDP$)

$$C + I + G + X - M = Y = \text{Wages} + \text{Interest Payments} + \text{Cost of Inputs}$$
$$+ \text{Indirect Business Taxes} + \text{Depreciation}$$
$$+ \text{Profits}$$

In words, it must be true that *the dollar value of aggregate output equals the dollar value of aggregate income*. Or, GDP equals GDP. This is what we mean when we say that GDP not only measures the value of final goods and services produced and sold in a given period but also represents the aggregate income generated by that production. That is why GDP is often used to compare the relative level of success—from an economic standpoint—across countries.

To illustrate this important link, Table 7.2 shows how the final goods and income approaches deliver the same dollar value for GDP. The data for 2009 show this basic accounting identity to be true. Whether you use the final goods approach or the income approach, they both indicate that GDP in 2009 was slightly more than $14 trillion. Note also that while consumption expenditures by households account for the largest share of GDP, employee compensation (wages and salaries) is the biggest component on the income approach side of the ledger. In 2009, employee compensation was 55 percent of total income. Just remember that your expenditures create income for someone else. Aggregate that idea across the economy, and you've got the notion of national income accounting.

## 7.3  Is GDP a Good Measure of Well-Being?

We know that reported values of GDP, though the best we currently have, may miss some aspects of everyday life. GDP may not, in other words, be the best measure of economic well-being. Economists are constantly seeking to improve how we measure incomes and output of economies. In 2009, a commission appointed by French President Nicolas Sarkozy presented the results of its year-long study to improve measures of well-being.[2] One drawback of current GDP measurements is that it, as we noted earlier, values production using market prices. But what if there is no market price to use? For services such as education in the home or unpaid child care by relatives, imputed prices—guesses—are often far from the mark. Such mismeasurement probably means that official GDP understates the true economic value of all production in the economy.

It also has been suggested that GDP, especially when used to compare well-being across countries, does not adequately capture differences in quality of life. Based on modern measurements, there is a paradox: rising incomes, at least beyond a certain threshold, do not seem to make people happier. (See ECONOMIC FALLACY below.) Happiness is, however, positively related to such measures as health, marital status, and age (older people may not be happy as younger ones), and negatively related to crime and corruption. Although difficult to quantify, a number of studies are working to bring such richness to the GDP measurement process.

**ECONOMIC FALLACY**   A higher level of GDP guarantees a higher level of happiness.

**False.** It is often said that money cannot buy happiness. If we think of a nation's GDP as its level of income, does the same hold true for countries? Is a higher level of GDP always associated with a higher level of happiness? The following figure compares the 2003 level of GDP per person to a measure of happiness across many countries. You can see that there does seem to be a positive relation: higher GDP countries also tend to be located toward the upper end of the contentment scale, too. But a higher level of GDP does not guarantee more happiness. To see this, find the United States (denoted USA in the figure). In 2003, its GDP per person was about $35,000, and, according to the survey, its life satisfaction measure was about a 7. You can see in the plot that many countries with just as high a contentment measure have much lower levels of GDP per person: Venezuela, Costa Rica, and Spain all share the same level of contentment as the United States even though they have comparatively lower levels of income per person.

· · · · · · ·

[2]"Measuring What Matters." *The Economist*, September 17, 2009.

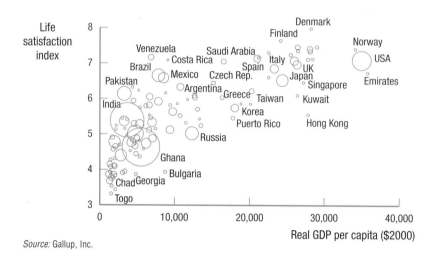

Source: Gallup, Inc.

GDP is not, as you can tell, a perfect measure of economic well-being. Still, the caveat is that it measures the standard of living based on economic measures, such as the number of goods and services available for consumers to purchase and enjoy. Most economists and noneconomists agree that having more goods and services is better than having fewer. Aren't you better off if there are more doctors doing open heart surgery, more clean water available for you to drink, more food for you to eat, and more clothing for you to wear? Don't get hung up in the knee-jerk response of "Yeah, but who can afford a heart operation? Those are only for the rich." Such procedures are expensive but also available to an increasingly large number of patients. It is likely that your income status does not affect your ability to get such a procedure if you need one.

That is what comparing GDP across time or across countries tells us. It doesn't tell us whether one country has a better standard of living in terms of happiness or in terms of less crime and pollution, for example. Senator Robert F. Kennedy said in a 1968 address at the University of Kansas that a measure such as GDP "does not include the beauty of our poetry or the strength of our marriages; the intelligence of our public debate or the integrity of our public officials...." There was more to his list, but he was correct: a statistical measure of economic output and income is limited in what it can include.

Nonetheless, GDP is still a useful measure to compare relative sizes of economies. Just like comparing income levels across individuals, we can look at a country's GDP relative to others to get a sense of how "big" the economy is. **Table 7.3** does this for the top five countries in terms of their GDP.

The table lists several of the economies that you tend to hear most about. The column labeled GDP reports each country's GDP in 2009, measured in billions of U.S. dollars. For example, GDP in the United States in 2009 was over $14 trillion (1 trillion is 1,000 billion). The second largest economy in the list is Japan with China close behind. (By the time you read this, China will have surpassed Japan as the second largest nation, based on GDP.) Notice, however, the distance between the United States and the rest of the economies. Using this measure, GDP in the United States is about three times the size of Japan's and China's GDP. From there, the size of the economies relative to the United States drops fairly quickly.

In Table 7.3, China's economy is larger, based on GDP, than is Germany's. So, is it fair to say that the average Chinese citizen is better off than someone in Germany? In making comparisons of GDP, you should consider how it is distributed across

| Table 7.3 | Comparing the World's Top Economies, 2009 | |
|---|---|---|
| Country | GDP ($Billion U.S.) | GDP per Capita ($U.S.) |
| United States | 14,256 | 46,436 |
| Japan | 5,067 | 39,726 |
| China | 4,985 | 3,744 |
| Germany | 3,347 | 40,873 |
| India | 1,310 | 1,134 |

The columns of the table provide the relative sizes of several economies in 2009. The left-hand columns report the countries by the size of their GDP in U.S. dollars. These are the countries that you most hear about. The numbers on the right-hand side are measures of GDP per person. When compared on a GDP per person basis, the relative sizes are much different.

**Source:** World Bank, *World Development Indicators*

the population. Although we can use many technical and controversial measures of income distribution, a basic approach is simply to adjust GDP by the size of the country's population. That is, divide GDP by population to arrive at GDP per person, or **GDP per capita**.

**GDP PER CAPITA** The value of GDP per person. This measures a nation's GDP proportional to the size of its population.

**EXAMPLE** Sylvania has a GDP of $21 billion, over twice that of Borscht, which has a GDP of $9 billion. The population of Sylvania is 70 million and that of Borscht is 30 million. Though GDP in Sylvania is much larger, GDP per capita (per person) in Sylvania and Borscht is the same: $300.

Using GDP or GDP per capita comparisons gives very different conclusions about economic well-being. Think about two households where each has a total income—income added up across all inhabitants—of $100,000. If one household is a couple without children, their economic well-being is likely to be higher compared to a household comprised of 2 parents and 10 children. The large household may in fact be happier, but from the vantage of a single objective measure—income—we can predict that economic well-being will be different.

To see how important this is, look at the right-hand column in Table 7.3. There we compare the relative size of each economy based on its GDP per person in 2009. In this group of countries, the United States still stands out with a GDP per person of more than $46,000. But notice that while China is one of the largest economies on a total GDP basis, it is nowhere near the top when viewed on a per person basis. Using this metric, China's economy is much smaller than either Japan or Germany. This suggests that to achieve a similar economic standard of living—at least based on GDP per person—China has quite a way to go before reaching the same level of other countries.

Do these limitations mean that using GDP as a basic measure of economic success is foolish? Hardly. You will see in the chapters on economic growth that there is a strong, positive correlation between countries with high levels of GDP per person and those noneconomic aspects of a better life, such as high literacy rates, better access to health care, longer life expectancies, and, believe it or not, cleaner air. Although economists debate the reason why, countries with higher GDP per person also tend to have more political and economic freedom. Thus, GDP is not a perfect measure, but it is a workable indicator of economic well-being.

## 7.4 Nominal versus Real GDP

Recall from the previous chapter that accounting for changes in the overall price level is important if you want to see how your purchasing power is changing over time. If prices are rising faster than your wages, your ability to buy the same basket of goods is diminishing. Your purchasing power is falling, in other words. In a related way, it is important for us to account for price-level changes when we measure GDP. That is, now we want to see if the economy is producing the same or a larger or smaller basket of goods over time. To do this, we need to account for price changes and changes in output separately.

In our doughnut economy, we figured out what GDP was by looking at the final sales of doughnuts: GDP was equal to $200 or the revenue from selling 100 doughnuts at $2 each. In a sense, if we let $P$ stand for the price of the doughnut ($2), and $Q$ equal the quantity produced and sold (100), GDP = $P \times Q$. Suppose we measure the GDP for our doughnut economy in a future year and determine that doughnut sales—and therefore GDP—amounted to $300. The crucial question to ask is, were you better off in the $200 economy or the $300 economy? To answer this question, you need to know the future levels of doughnut prices ($P$) and the quantity of doughnuts produced and sold ($Q$). In other words, the answer is "it depends."

In its most basic form, GDP is the aggregation of final goods and services sold at their market prices during a certain period of time. To see if you are better off in 2011 compared to 1990—based solely on the level of GDP—we must be able to distinguish whether the change in GDP stems from changes in prices, changes in the number of final goods and services produced and sold, or some combination of the two. If GDP in 2011 was greater than it was in 1990 only because of price increases, there were no more goods to buy in 2011; they just cost more. You were therefore not better off because there was no more $Q$ than before. The story is different if the GDP in 2011 was greater than it was in 1990 because there were more goods produced at the same price (more $Q$, same $P$). Think of it: this scenario means there were more flat-screen TVs, more medical care, and more hot dogs in 2011 than there were in 1990. The best part is that they did not cost more! Surely you'd agree that you would have been better off in such a world. (We'll discuss the potential complications with this line of thinking in a minute.)

To gauge how much better off you would be over time (in terms of material goods and services), you need to figure out how to adjust the nation's GDP for changes in the general level of prices. This adjustment will tell you what the economy's **real GDP** is.

> **REAL GDP** Real GDP is calculated by adjusting nominal GDP for changes in the price level.

Technically, GDP unadjusted for price changes is referred to as *nominal* GDP. Real GDP is nominal GDP adjusted for price-level changes. When commentators talk about GDP, they usually are referring to real GDP, not nominal GDP. Real and nominal GDP are directly related. That is,

Real GDP = (Nominal GDP/Price Index) × 100

You could use the CPI for the price index in this calculation, but it really isn't the appropriate measure. Because GDP includes many more goods and services than are included in the CPI, we should use an appropriately broader measure of prices.

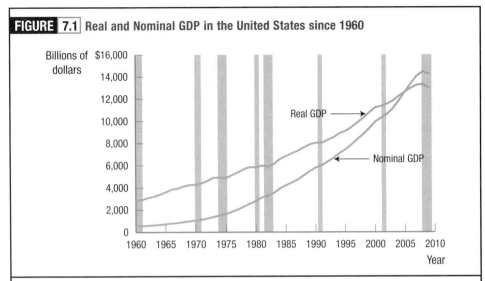

**FIGURE** 7.1 **Real and Nominal GDP in the United States since 1960**

Nominal and real GDP are plotted for the period since 1960. Real GDP was greater than nominal GDP until 2005, the base year for the price index used to deflate nominal GDP and calculate real GDP. Real GDP was above nominal GDP before the base year because prices were lower in this period relative to the base year. Nominal GDP was greater than real GDP after 2005 because prices continued to rise.

*Source:* Federal Reserve Bank of St. Louis

Economists therefore use the GDP deflator mentioned in the previous chapter to adjust the GDP for price-level changes over time.

**Figure 7.1** shows the *dollar values* of nominal and real GDP since 1960. (Even though the label reads "Billions of Dollars," to be precise, nominal GDP is billions of current dollars, and real GDP is billions of 2005 dollars.) Notice that real GDP was greater than nominal GDP until 2005, at which time they crossed. The crossover is the base year for the price index, when the GDP deflator is equal to 100. In the base year, nominal and real GDP are identical. The fact that real GDP was above nominal GDP before the base year shows that prices were lower in this period relative to the base year. After that, however, the continued increase in the price level (positive rates of inflation) deflated real GDP relative to nominal GDP. The fact that nominal GDP has been greater than real GDP in recent years indicates that prices have continued to rise over time. The economy continues to produce more goods and services, just not as fast as nominal GDP suggests.

To show why it's important to adjust the current GDP for price-level changes, **Figure 7.2** shows the *growth rates* of real and nominal GDP over a shorter period, since 1990. (Recall that the growth rate is calculated as the percentage change in a number from one period to the next.)

Why is the growth rate of nominal GDP always above that of real GDP? The answer is because the rate of inflation was positive during this period. If you were to only look at the growth of nominal GDP, you'd get a false impression of just how well the economy is doing. To bring this idea home, look at the most recent growth rates. During the recession that began in late 2007, the real output of the economy *declined* at rates approaching 3 percent per year. In other words, the level of real GDP in 2009 was less than the level in 2008. If policy makers were watching nominal GDP, they would have thought the downturn was much less severe, even though its growth rate also turned negative.

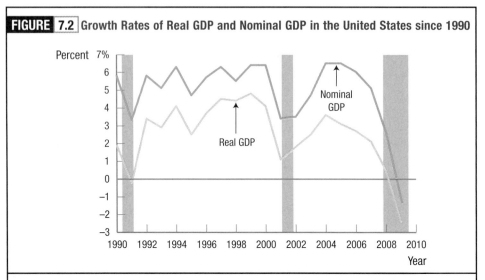

**FIGURE** 7.2 | **Growth Rates of Real GDP and Nominal GDP in the United States since 1990**

The growth rates of real and nominal GDP since 1990 are compared in this figure. The growth rate of nominal GDP was greater than real GDP because the rate of inflation was positive during this period. The growth of nominal GDP can create a false impression of economic conditions. During the recent 2007–2009 recession (denoted by the shaded bar), real GDP declined at rates approaching 3 percent. In other words, the level of real GDP in 2009 was less than the level in 2008. Nominal GDP growth would suggest a less-severe downturn, as this figure shows.

*Source:* Federal Reserve Bank of St. Louis

You can see in Figure 7.2 how inflation can affect comparisons of economic output over time. It also is an important consideration when comparing economic activity across countries. In countries plagued by high rates of inflation, their nominal GDP measure will overstate their citizens' economic well-being relative to using real GDP. The higher the rate of inflation, the higher the growth rate of nominal GDP will be relative to real GDP. So, a faster growing nominal GDP doesn't necessarily mean that more goods and services are being produced, just that their prices are rising.

## SOLVED PROBLEM

**Q** Should we watch nominal or real GDP?

**A** Given the choice of worrying about nominal or real GDP, which should get your attention? The answer is real GDP because it adjusts for changes in prices. Real GDP gives us a better—though not perfect—measure of how many more goods and services are available today compared with the past. In some instances, it is used to make relative comparisons of standards of living across countries. All else the same, you'd rather live in a country where real GDP per person is higher. The growth rate of real GDP also is the more important measure to watch. Suppose inflation averages about 5 percent year in and year out. Are you better off if nominal GDP is increasing at a 7 percent rate or with real GDP increasing at a 3 percent rate? The answer is real GDP at a 3 percent rate. Why? Because adjusting the 7 percent nominal GDP growth rate for inflation—subtracting the rate of inflation from nominal GDP growth gives you real GDP growth—gives you a real GDP growth rate of only 2 percent. So, unless you know what the rate of inflation is, when someone tells you that in their country GDP grows at a 10 percent rate year in and out, you might want to be skeptical of this claim and ask *which* GDP the person means.

## 7.5 Real GDP or Potential GDP?

We can measure the output of the economy in nominal or in real terms over time. But how do we know if some reported figure for real GDP, say $12 or $14 trillion, is actually close to the economy's potential? Think of how fast you can run 100 yards. If you go out and run 100 yards in, say, 20 seconds, that is comparable to your output right now. But is it as fast as you can run? What, in other words, is your potential? If your potential is 10 seconds, then running 100 yards in 20 seconds isn't very good. If your potential is 19 seconds, then running it in 20 seconds isn't too bad.

We have already considered a way to compare how much we actually produce to how much we could produce if operating at our peak performance level: the production possibilities frontier (PPF). In Chapter 2, we used the PPF to illustrate how a couple might determine the trade-off between producing household services (working in the home) or working outside the home to earn an income used to buy consumer goods. In that discussion, we imposed several constraints. These include the idea that only two goods are produced; productive resources, such as labor, machinery, and so on, are taken as given; and technology is fixed. This latter assumption basically means that the household, given labor, time, and knowledge constraints, could choose to produce different levels of household services or consumption goods.

Let's extend that example and look at a PPF for an economy as shown in **Figure 7.3**. In this example, two goods are produced: food and movies. By applying all the economy's resources to food production, the economy achieves point A on the vertical axis. If all resources are devoted to making movies, the economy will find itself at point B. How it chooses to allocate its resources will determine where it ends up on the PPF.

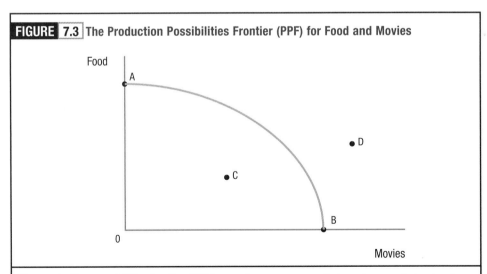

**FIGURE 7.3** The Production Possibilities Frontier (PPF) for Food and Movies

The production possibilities frontier (PPF) curve for an economy that produces only food and movies is shown in this graph. If all resources are applied to food production, the economy produces the output level designated by point A. If all resources are devoted to making movies, the economy produces the output level designated by point B. An economy operating at its full potential produces some combination of food and movies *on* the PPF. If the economy is producing at a point *inside* the PPF, a point like C, actual output is less than potential. If actual output is more than potential, this would be illustrated by a point *outside* the PPF, such as point D. Economies tend to move back toward their PPFs, making production at points like C and D temporary.

The concept of the PPF is useful for thinking about the actual output of the economy (real GDP) compared to what it could be. *If the economy is operating at full capacity, then it will produce some combination of food and movies that is* on *the PPF.* In Figure 7.3, this could be any point along the curve, including points A and B. It could be that actual output and this *potential* level of production are the same. But what if the economy is not producing at its potential? We can show this as a point inside the PPF, a point like C in Figure 7.3. At C, or any other point *inside* the PPF, actual output of both food and movies is less than it *could* be. If, at least temporarily, the economy is producing at more than potential, this would be illustrated by a point *outside* of the PPF, such as point D.

The measure for this potential level of output for an economy is called **potential GDP**. This measure is a calculated guess of what real GDP would be if the economy were operating at its peak performance, if the economy were operating at full production. In other words, all of the economy's resources would be put to their most highly valued uses and fully employed. In that case, the economy would be operating on its PPF.

**POTENTIAL GDP** Potential GDP is an estimate of what real GDP would be if the economy were operating at full production.

**EXAMPLE** Let's use an auto-assembly plant as an analogy for the economy. If the plant is operating all of its lines and running two eight-hour shifts seven days a week, its *potential* or full-production output is 6,720 cars a week.

**Figure 7.4** shows the levels of real GDP and potential GDP since 1960. Real GDP was above potential GDP when the economy was operating above its full employment

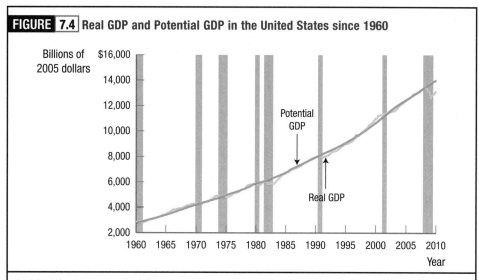

**FIGURE 7.4** Real GDP and Potential GDP in the United States since 1960

Real GDP is above potential GDP when the economy is operating, at least temporarily, outside of its PPF. When real GDP is below potential GDP, the economy is not producing as many goods and services as it could if it were operating on its PPF. An interesting aspect of the relation between real GDP and potential GDP is that real GDP fluctuates around potential GDP. This suggests that the economy tends to return to this potential output level after downturns and expansions.

*Source:* Federal Reserve Bank of St. Louis

level of production. When real GDP was below potential GDP, however, the economy was not producing as many goods and services as it could have been if it were operating at its full employment level, or on its PPF. For instance, the severity of the 2007–2009 economic downturn is evident in the relatively large deviation of real GDP from potential. An interesting aspect of the relation between real GDP and potential GDP is that real GDP fluctuates around potential GDP. This suggests that the economy tends to return to this potential output level after downturns and expansions alike.

Using the auto-assembly plant in the previous example as our economy, the plant could increase the number of cars it produces by adding a third shift, running the plant 24 hours a day. This, however, is not sustainable: the machinery would break down without the down-time needed for maintenance and repairs. The plant *could* produce outside of its PPF but only temporarily. The same holds true for the economy as a whole during those times when real GDP is greater than potential GDP.

Finally, how do the growth rates of real GDP and potential GDP compare? Economists often think in terms of how fast an economy is growing relative to how fast it could be growing if it were operating at its potential. **Figure 7.5** provides a look. Notice that the growth rate of potential GDP in the United States has been much smoother than actual real GDP. This is because potential GDP is an estimate of how fast the economy *could* grow if all of its productive resources were fully employed.

Against this benchmark, notice how real GDP growth has sometimes dipped far below potential GDP. In these instances, such as 1991, 2001, and 2008, the economy was producing goods and services at a much slower pace than it potentially could. When this occurs—if severe enough downturns such as these are designated

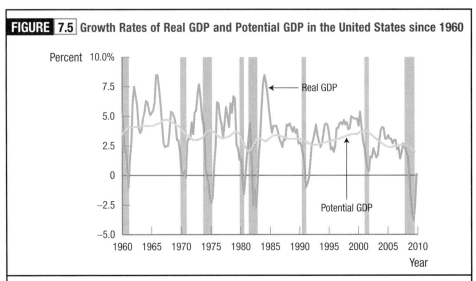

**FIGURE 7.5** Growth Rates of Real GDP and Potential GDP in the United States since 1960

Economists often worry about how fast the economy is growing relative to how fast it could be growing if it were operating at its potential. This figure plots the growth rates of real GDP and potential GDP. The growth rate of potential GDP is smoother than actual real GDP because potential GDP is an estimate of how fast the economy *could* grow if it were operating on its PPF. Actual real GDP growth fluctuates around potential GDP growth. When it dips far below potential, as it did during the recessions highlighted by the shaded bars, the economy is producing goods and services at a much slower pace than it potentially could.

*Source:* Federal Reserve Bank of St. Louis

as recessions—firms need fewer workers. Thus, if fewer doughnuts are demanded by customers, the bakery in our fictional economy is likely to lay off the workers producing the doughnuts and idle the machinery used. As a result, there is a general unemployment of resources—machinery and workers alike—when real GDP dips far below potential GDP. We will focus on the unemployment of labor and its link to movements in real GDP in the next chapter.

## 7.6  Does Real GDP Grow at the Same Rate Across Countries?

We asked in the previous chapter whether prices, more specifically inflation, behaved similarly across countries. Let's ask the same question here, but with reference to real GDP. And to make the comparison, let's use the same countries that we used in the previous chapter. **Figure 7.6** shows the growth rates of real GDP for our selection of countries.

Some countries have very similar patterns in the growth of real GDP. Though not identical, real GDP in Canada, the United Kingdom, and the United States seem to march in close order. From the mid-1990s through 2000, each country experienced a slight uptick in the growth rate of real GDP. There was a common downturn in 2001, followed by a slow recovery until 2008, the year the global financial crisis and ensuing recession really began to take hold. The figures for 2009 show that Canada, the United Kingdom, and the United States each experienced negative growth rates of real GDP.

Japan and China have followed very different paths, however. Japan experienced much slower growth during the period compared with any of the other countries. In a number of years, output in Japan fell (a negative real GDP growth rate) or increased only marginally. In contrast, real GDP growth in China has far surpassed that in

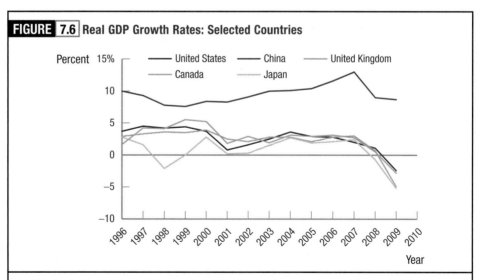

**FIGURE 7.6** Real GDP Growth Rates: Selected Countries

Is output growth similar across countries? Over the past decade, real GDP growth rates in Canada, the United Kingdom, and the United States have been fairly similar. By contrast, real GDP growth rates in Japan usually were lower during the period, and real GDP growth in China was always much faster.

*Source:* Federal Reserve Bank of St. Louis

the other countries. In fact, it remained positive even in 2009 when other countries experienced large negative growth rates.

Why was real GDP growth so much more robust in China than in Japan and the other countries in Figure 7.6? Why do some of the countries' real GDP growth seem to follow a similar pattern? Has this pattern continued for many years, or is it a more recent phenomenon? And, even if China's overall economic growth is greater than the other countries, is the average Chinese citizen doing better than someone living in, say, Canada?

These are all important questions that economists and policy makers seek to find answers to. We'll address some of them in Chapter 10 where we examine the factors that explain economic growth.

## WHAT YOU SHOULD HAVE LEARNED FROM CHAPTER 7

- That gross domestic product (GDP) is a widely accepted measure of an economy's output and income.
- That GDP measures the market value of final goods and services produced in an economy in a given period.
- That GDP can be measured using the final goods approach or the income approach.
- That GDP adjusted for price-level changes, called real GDP, is a better measure to assess changes in economic production over time.
- That potential GDP is a hypothetical measure of what real GDP would be if the economy were operating at its full capacity.

## KEY TERMS

Intermediate good, p. 189

Value added, p. 190

Gross domestic product (GDP), p. 190

Final goods approach, p. 191

Income approach, p. 193

GDP per capita (per person), p. 197

Real GDP, p. 198

Potential GDP, p. 202

## QUESTIONS AND PROBLEMS

1. When measuring gross domestic product (GDP) for a country, we subtract out imports. Why?

2. The income created in an economy can be measured by either adding up all expenditures or by adding up incomes. What is the rationale that economists use with each approach?

3. Which of the following items are or are not included in this year's GDP? Why?
   a) That 1966 vintage Mustang that your parents bought for you as a graduation present
   b) The iPhone you just purchased from the local electronics store
   c) The hops that arc sold to the local microbrewery
   d) The payment to the plumber who just fixed your leaky pipes
   e) Your professor's salary
   f) The Social Security check your grandparents receive
   g) The $1,000 you won in a recent poker game at a friend's house
   h) Increases in the sale of existing homes because mortgage rates are at historic lows

4. Real GDP per person in the United States is about $46,000. In Canada, it is, measured in U.S. dollars, about $40,000. Based on those numbers, can you say that the average person in Canada is worse off than the average person in the United Sates? Why might you not want to use real GDP as your only measure of well-being?

5. In Figure 7.1, nominal GDP and real GDP cross in 2005. Before then, nominal GDP is less than real GDP; since then, nominal GDP is greater than real GDP. Why do the two series cross in 2005? Does this mean that we are better off after 2000 than before? Explain your answer.

6. Some people argue that we'd all be better off if we just stopped trading with other countries. Using the final goods approach to measuring GDP, could this ever be true?

7. In 1975, the economy was in a deep recession. That year, real GDP growth was a negative 2 percent, but the growth of nominal GDP was actually positive. Explain how real GDP could be decreasing when nominal GDP was growing.

8. In Xanadu, the level of exports is $500 and the level of imports is $400. Does Xanadu have a trade surplus or a trade deficit? Does the United States have a trade surplus or a trade deficit?

9. David sells chocolate at Chocolate Confections. David buys the truffles from Sarah's Sugary, which produces a variety of chocolate candies for resale. The cost of the truffles is $220. David individually packages the truffles and then sells them in his shop. Sarah buys her chocolate from Jeannine's Imports for $100. The following table describes this small economy.

| Jeannine's Imports | | Sarah's Sugary | | Chocolate Confections | |
|---|---|---|---|---|---|
| Revenue | $100 | Revenue | $220 | Revenue | $550 |
| | | Expenses ($) | | Expenses ($) | |
| | | Utilities | 20 | Wages | 180 |
| | | Chocolate | 100 | Supplies | 100 |
| | | Supplies | 40 | Truffles | 220 |
| | | | 160 | | 500 |
| | | Profit ($) | 60 | Profit ($) | 50 |

a) Calculate the GDP for this economy using the final goods approach.
b) Is this a more meaningful measure than one using the income approach, which is based on wages, profits, and so on?

10. In each of the following instances, is the good an intermediate or final good?

a) Sugar purchased by a baker to make cupcakes
b) Sugar purchased by an individual to make cupcakes
c) Dresses purchased by Target
d) Dresses purchased by individuals from this class
e) Typing paper purchased by the local copy store for customers to use
f) Typing paper purchased by you

11. Use the information in Table 7.2 to answer the following questions.

a) Consumption spending is _____ percent of GDP.
b) Investment spending is _____ percent of GDP.
c) Net exports are _____ percent of GDP.
d) Why do economists focus on consumption spending when attempting to explain fluctuations in GDP?

12. For each of the following, determine if the item is included in 2011 GDP. Identify the component of GDP (*C*, *I*, *G*, *X*). If the item is not included in GDP, explain why.

   a) In May 2011, John purchased a flat of tomato plants from a nursery in his hometown.
   b) In July 2011, Alexandra visited Madrid, Spain.
   c) During 2011, Annabel took tennis lessons at the local YMCA.
   d) In August 2011, Eric purchased lumber for the deck that he is building onto the back of his house.
   e) In December 2011, Miki bought an antique table from her sister.
   f) Following a large lottery win, Wallie purchased 500 shares of Walmart stock.

# The Labor Market and Unemployment

*"More people out of work leads
to higher unemployment."*

Calvin Coolidge,
30th U.S. president

**W**e spend most of our lives at work. When something outside of our control disrupts or ends our employment, it has big consequences for us. When a wage earner is no longer working, families often are forced to reduce their spending. When the event that caused the unemployment is widespread, the economic consequences ripple throughout the economy. If many families no longer have the income to purchase the goods you sell, your income will fall, and you, too, may become unemployed. As you can see, unemployment not only damages the individual but it also takes a toll on the entire economy.

When people refer to unemployment, they usually mean the unemployment of workers. But the idea of unemployment is more general than just that of workers. In this chapter, we explore the idea of what we mean by unemployment and then get more specific by examining unemployment in the labor market. You've no doubt heard people talking about how high the unemployment rate can be. To measure unemployment, we commonly use the civilian unemployment rate. But what does this statistic really measure? And are there any problems with the measure? By the time you have finished this chapter, you will have a better understanding of what the unemployment rate is and what it measures. You also will understand why so many economists and people closely watch unemployment rates to gauge the health of the economy.

## 8.1  What Is Unemployment?

Unemployment in economics has a much broader meaning than whether someone has a job or not. Let's think of unemployment in this broader context by referring back to the production possibilities frontier (PPF). **Figure 8.1** shows a PPF for a hypothetical economy that produces two goods, jewelry and computers. Recall that when an economy is operating on its frontier, all of its productive resources are being

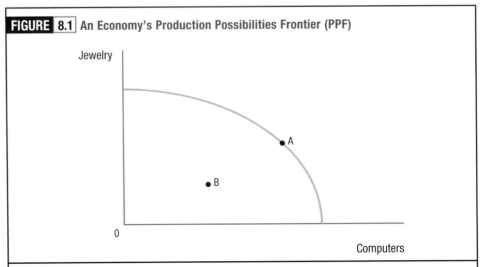

**FIGURE 8.1** An Economy's Production Possibilities Frontier (PPF)

This is a PPF for a hypothetical economy that produces jewelry and computers. When this economy is fully using all of its productive resources, it will produce some combination of jewelry and computers on the curve, such as point A. If the economy is operating inside of its PPF, say at point B, some resource, such as labor, is not being employed in its most productive way or is simply not being used. When an economy is operating at a point B, the economy is experiencing unemployment. At point B, the economy's real GDP is substantially less than its potential GDP.

fully used. This means that if the economy is producing the combination of jewelry and computers represented by point A in Figure 8.1, workers, machines, land, and knowledge are being fully used at their most productive jobs—brain surgeons are brain surgeons and not working as accountants, for example—and existing knowledge is being used. There simply is no unemployment of productive resources.

If an economy is operating inside of its PPF instead of on its frontier, some resource is not being employed in its most productive way. Or, it can mean that a resource simply is not being used. When an economy is operating at a point such as B in Figure 8.1, we say that the economy is experiencing unemployment. In this context, unemployment, whether it applies to workers or machinery, means that the economy is producing less than it *potentially* can. Another way of thinking about this is that at point B, the economy's real GDP is substantially less than its potential GDP, represented by point A.

Suppose that the resource not being fully utilized is labor. In other words, there is unemployment. If this is so, we should see a link between labor's underuse (the unemployment rate) and real GDP relative to potential GDP. Rising unemployment is, in fact, one signal that the pace of economic activity is slowing relative to its potential.

## Unemployment in the Labor Market

Let's look specifically at the market for labor to see how unemployment occurs. To do this, we will use a supply-and-demand model for labor, such as the one shown in **Figure 8.2**. The demand curve for labor (*D*), which represents labor demand by all of the firms, has the usual downward slope. By contrast, the supply curve (*S*) represents the amount of labor all workers are willing to supply. As usual, the supply curve is upward sloping. The "price" of labor shown on the *y*-axis in Figure 8.2 is the **real wage**. The real wage is the nominal wage adjusted for inflation.

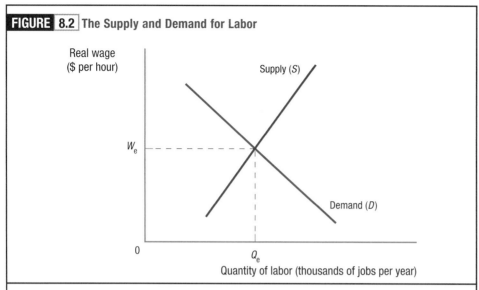

**FIGURE 8.2** The Supply and Demand for Labor

This supply-and-demand diagram represents the market for labor. The real wage rate is placed on the vertical, or price, axis. The quantity of labor, in this case, thousands of jobs per year, appears on the horizontal axis. The demand curve for labor ($D$) represents labor demand by all of the firms and has the usual downward slope. The upward-sloping supply curve ($S$) represents the amount of labor all workers are willing to supply. At the market-clearing or equilibrium real wage of $W_e$, the number of jobs that firms want to fill is equal to the number of workers willing to fill them.

**REAL WAGE** The nominal wage adjusted for changes in the price level.

**EXAMPLE** Betty earns $10 an hour working at a local bakery. The price level (CPI) is 150. This means that Betty's real wage is ($10/150) × 100 = $6.67. After ten years at the bakery, Betty's wage had risen to $20 an hour. The price level had increased to 175. Betty's real wage is ($20/175) × 100 = $11.43.

Betty's example shows you how to calculate the real wage. The example also explains why using the real wage is a better measure than the nominal wage. If you knew that Betty's wage had doubled, could you say with certainty that she was better off than before? No. The only way you could make such a statement is if you know how much her $20 wage is worth in terms of the goods it can buy. That is what the real wage tells you: the purchasing power of her wage in one year compared to the other. This also helps explain why the labor-supply curve is upward sloping. At higher levels of the real wage (more command over goods and services), people are willing to supply more labor.

Firms are more likely to consider the real wage when making hiring decisions. Firms pay wages with an eye toward the prices of the goods they sell. As the real wage increases, firms are, all else the same, less willing to increase the number of workers (or the hours of existing workers) they hire.

You already know that in this market, the equilibrium or market wage (shown as $W_e$) and the equilibrium quantity ($Q_e$) is where the demand and supply curves intersect. One way to think of this intersection is that it represents the amount of

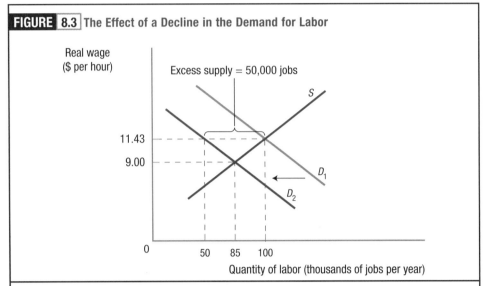

**FIGURE 8.3** The Effect of a Decline in the Demand for Labor

At the market-clearing wage of $11.43, there are 100,000 jobs in this hypothetical economy. Suppose firms reduce their demand for labor, shown by the leftward shift in the demand curve. At a wage of $11.43, firms are now willing to hire only 50,000 workers even though there are still 100,000 individuals willing to work. If the market-clearing wage does not adjust to the new, lower equilibrium, this decrease in labor demand leads to an excess supply of labor. This results in unemployment in the labor market.

labor used to put us on the PPF in Figure 8.1. How can we represent unemployment using Figure 8.2? Let's put some numbers to our example. Let's use Betty's real wage of $11.43 as the market-clearing wage. At this real wage, there are 100,000 jobs in this hypothetical economy. Using demand curve $D_1$ and the supply curve $S$, this is the initial equilibrium condition shown in **Figure 8.3**.

Now suppose an "event" causes firms to reduce their demand for labor. This could be from a decrease in the demand for their product, thus leading to a reduced need for workers. Or, the event could be a financial panic that raises their costs of borrowing funds to make payroll. This reduction in the demand for labor is shown as the leftward shift in the demand curve in Figure 8.3, from $D_1$ to $D_2$. Why would this decrease in labor demand lead to unemployment? It isn't unemployment if the real wage falls fast enough to its new, lower equilibrium shown as $9.00. But what if the real wage is slow to adjust? What if it stays at $11.43? Although firms now are willing to hire only 50,000 workers, there are still 100,000 individuals willing to work at the original wage. The gap between the quantity of jobs available and the number of individuals willing to work is an excess supply of workers. This is unemployment in the labor market.

You might be wondering how this can occur. After all, didn't we stress in Chapters 3 and 4 that markets always seek their equilibrium price and quantity? That's true, but we also warned that prices do not always react quickly to a change in market conditions. Sometimes they are "sticky" and slow to adjust to the new reality in the market. For example, how long would it take you to accept a job paying $9.00 after you lose one paying $11.43? How long would you look until you accept the fact that your labor isn't really worth $11.43 anymore?

Other factors can cause unemployment, too. In Chapter 4, we talked about the effect a minimum wage (a price floor) has on labor. A minimum wage can prevent the real wage from reaching its market-clearing level and cause excess labor supply and unemployment. The reverse situation can also affect unemployment. Some firms such as Google pay wages that are above the equilibrium level to attract the best talent, encourage higher worker productivity, reduce worker turnover, and improve morale. Wages such as these are called **efficiency wages**. If enough firms pay efficiency wages—a wage higher than the true market equilibrium—this will create an excess supply of labor.

> **EFFICIENCY WAGES** Wages paid above the market-equilibrium wage to attract the best workers, achieve higher worker productivity, reduce worker turnover, and improve morale.

> **EXAMPLE** Walter's Steel and Pipe Company pays its workers an average of $15 per hour. All other steel and pipe companies in the area pay only $12. Walter's not only has a waiting list of people who want to work for the company, but it also produces more steel pipe per hour of work than its competitors, even though the firms all have the same production technology.

With demand shifts, impediments to wages adjusting quickly, and some firms paying nonequilibrium wages, you can see that several forces can lead to unemployment.

## 8.2 Measuring the Unemployment Rate

There is a saying: "Times are bad when your neighbor loses her job. It's a recession when you lose yours." Even if you don't know how it is measured, an increase in the unemployment rate just sounds bad, doesn't it? When it increases, more people are unemployed, and surely that can't be good.

Each month the U.S. Census Bureau surveys approximately 60,000 households to determine the size of working age population—the number of people who are 16 and older. This Current Population Survey is conducted for the Bureau of Labor Statistics (BLS), the government agency that compiles the unemployment statistics. The **labor force** includes everyone in the working-age population who either has a paying job or is looking for one. The labor force does not include, for example, working-age individuals who are in school and not working, retired individuals who are not working, or individuals in jail. It also does not include individuals who are working in the home but not being paid for these services.

> **LABOR FORCE** Everyone in the working-age population who either has a paying job or is looking for one, excluding working-age individuals who are in school and not working, retired individuals who are not working, institutionalized individuals, and individuals working in the home but not being paid for these services.

> **EXAMPLE** Joe, the guy next to you in your econ class, is not working and not currently looking for a job. He is not included in the labor force.

> **EXAMPLE** Your uncle who got laid off from his job at GM has been looking for a job over the past month. He *is* included in the labor force.

What constitutes a paying job? Having a job usually means that you leave your home and go to work in a building downtown, at the corner grocery store, at a factory, or on campus. Some jobs, and this is becoming increasingly true with advances in computer and Internet technologies, can be done from home. People who are employed but do not leave their homes every day are counted as part of the labor force as long as they are being paid for their work. The person who edited this book, for example, has a paying job, but she is able to work from home. You also need not have a full-time job to get counted as part of the labor force. If you work part-time, considered to be between 1 and 34 hours a week, you are included in the labor force. Although the number fluctuates, about one-fifth of the labor force is employed in part-time jobs.

The fact that the labor force includes those people currently working and those people looking for a job suggests that the **unemployment rate** can be defined as:

Unemployment rate = (Unemployed/Labor Force) × 100

**UNEMPLOYMENT RATE** The unemployment rate measures the percent of the *labor force* that is not employed.

The unemployment rate that is reported on the nightly news is the percent of the labor force that is unemployed. (More precisely, the figure reported is the civilian, nonfarm unemployment rate.) In May 2008, the unemployment rate was 5.5 percent. This means that 5.5 percent of the people in the labor force (as defined previously) were not working but were looking for jobs. Just how many people are we talking about? In May 2008, the labor force was estimated to be about 154 million people, and the number unemployed was roughly 8.5 million. Divide the number unemployed by the labor force, and you get the 5.5 percent unemployment rate. Of course—although seldom presented this way—the May 2008 figure also means that 94.5 percent of the labor force *was* employed. By early 2010, however, the situation was much different. The unemployment rate was close to 10 percent.

**Figure 8.4** shows the unemployment rate in the United States since 1960. During this time period, the unemployment rate fluctuated between 3 percent and 11 percent.

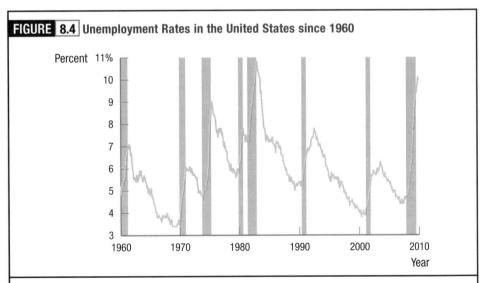

**FIGURE** **8.4** **Unemployment Rates in the United States since 1960**

During the period shown in the graph, unemployment rates fluctuated between 3 percent and 11 percent. The unemployment rate is cyclical: it tends to rise when the economy experiences an economic downturn (designated by the shaded bars) and fall during economic expansions.

*Source:* Federal Reserve Bank of St. Louis

You can see in the figure that the unemployment rate tends to rise when the economy experiences an economic downturn (designated by the shaded bars). If the real wage doesn't quickly adjust, excess supply is created in the labor market. The pattern of the unemployment rate shown in the figure suggests that, over time, a combination of changes in real wages and changes in the demand-and-supply conditions in the labor market can contribute to increases and decreases in the unemployment rate.

## Problems with the Measured Unemployment Rate

**The Discouraged Worker Effect.** The unemployment rate is a somewhat controversial statistic. One reason is that it does not include each and every individual in the labor force who is unemployed. Remember that individuals are counted as unemployed even if they are not working *but are looking for work*. But what if you decide that looking for a job is too much of a hassle and you begin watching daytime talk shows full time? If you choose to stop searching for a job, you are counted as a **discouraged worker**.

> **DISCOURAGED WORKER** The term applied to an unemployed individual who stops searching for employment. As a consequence, they are no longer counted as part of the labor force.

> EXAMPLE After being laid off by Walmart, Sam looked for another job for several months. Unsuccessful and discouraged, he stopped looking and decided to become a househusband.

Don't take it personally, but the statisticians at the BLS who compile the unemployment rate no longer consider you part of the labor force if you are a discouraged worker. The problem is that increased numbers of discouraged workers lower the number of officially unemployed individuals. It may seem backwards, but the more discouraged workers there are, the lower the unemployment rate is. (Mathematically, the numerator of the unemployment rate equation gets proportionally smaller than the denominator.) If every unemployed person becomes a discouraged worker, the unemployment rate will be zero. Although this is a problem with the unemployment rate, it is not one that usually persists. For example, during a recession, some people get tired of looking for jobs and decide to stop. Eventually, as the economy picks up, firms begin hiring again, and wages begin to rise, these people once again begin to look for work. The BLS also keeps track of the number of discouraged workers who reenter the labor force, thus accounting for people who, as job opportunities become more plentiful, restart their job searches.

**The Household Survey or the Establishment Survey?** Another issue with measuring the unemployment rate is how the data used to measure it are collected. The unemployment rate shown in Figure 8.4, because it is based on the monthly household survey, is cleverly referred to as the *household survey*. However, each month, the BLS, through its Current Employment Statistics program, also surveys about 140,000 nonfarm businesses and government agencies to gather information about employment, hours worked, and earnings. This survey is called the *establishment survey*. The BLS also calculates an unemployment rate based on this survey to get a more accurate gauge of the actual number of employees. Although the establishment survey is more accurate, it also covers a narrower swath of the workforce. The establishment survey, for instance, does not include the self-employed, agricultural workers, and private household workers. It also does not allow the BLS to track changes in employment among various demographic groups, such as teenagers, black males, or white females.

The two measures also can give different signals about employment changes. Suppose you work as a janitor at Nuts n' Bolts, a large manufacturing firm. Your company announces that it is outsourcing your job to a service company. You are still employed, but now by Janitorial, Inc., a service company. The household survey would show no change in the employment picture: you are still employed. The establishment survey, however, would indicate that there has been a loss of manufacturing jobs and an increase in service-industry jobs. Although both are correct, you need to know what each is telling you and how the numbers will be used for different purposes.

The two surveys also are used for political purposes. Over time, the difference between the two is not that large. There are times, however, when the difference is large. In 2004, officials in the Bush administration claimed, correctly, that there were 1.9 million more jobs than when he took office. That claim was based on the household survey. Others, also correctly, argued that the number of jobs actually had declined by 1.1 million. Their view was based on figures from the establishment survey. Although both measurements are correct, you have to keep in mind what each measures and its limitations.[1]

## 8.3 Economic Activity and Unemployment

President Coolidge had it right: when more people lose their jobs, there is more unemployment. The problem for policy makers and economists alike is to figure out what causes people to lose their jobs and try, when possible, to prevent it. We are not talking about losing your job if you are habitually late or if you just don't work very hard. What we're interested in, from a policy standpoint, is how changes in economic activity affect firms' hiring decisions. When economic times get tough, people usually start to become more frugal about their spending. If you go out to eat only twice a week instead of four times a week, that means your favorite restaurant's business is falling off. A decline in business translates into a decline in revenue, and that may mean the owner has to lay off some staff. If these people cannot find work, they become part of the unemployment rate. This microcosm is why many consider movements in the unemployment rate to be an indicator of the economy's health.

How closely related are the unemployment rate and the pace of economic activity? **Figure 8.5** shows the unemployment rate and the rate of change in real GDP in the United States since 1960. The shaded vertical bars in the figure again are times when the economy was in a recession. You can see that when the growth rate of real GDP falls close to or below zero, the unemployment rate tends to increase rather substantially. This suggests that increases in the unemployment rate go hand-in-hand with a sustained economic downturn. When the overall or aggregate level of business activity slows down—that is, when there is a significant decline in the growth of real GDP—restaurants, car dealerships, and even medical facilities cannot afford to keep as many employees on their payrolls. If business gets really bad, firms may close, thus leading to even more waiters and car salesmen being laid off.

One aspect about using the unemployment rate as an indicator of economic activity is worth mentioning. Notice in Figure 8.5 that the increase in the unemployment rate usually peaks *after* real GDP once again begins expanding at a positive rate. This explains why the unemployment rate is often thought of as a *lagging indicator*

· · · · · · ·

[1]Floyd Norris, "A Job Picture Painted with Different Brushes." *New York Times*, August 7, 2004.

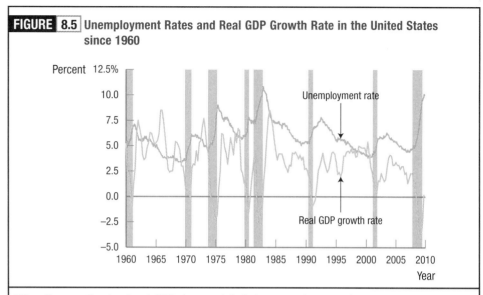

**FIGURE 8.5** | **Unemployment Rates and Real GDP Growth Rate in the United States since 1960**

When the growth rate of real GDP slows or falls below zero, the unemployment rate tends to rise. Note that the unemployment rate usually peaks *after* real GDP once again begins to grow at a positive rate. The unemployment rate also does not begin to rise until *after* the economy has already begun to slow down. This pattern is why the unemployment rate is often thought of as a *lagging indicator* of economic activity.

*Source:* Federal Reserve Bank of St. Louis

of economic activity. This also means that the unemployment rate usually does not begin to rise until after the economy has already begun to slow down.

Why does the unemployment rate behave this way? Think again about your favorite restaurant for a moment: until the owner knows for sure that the smaller nightly customer count at the restaurant is permanent, she will be reluctant to lay off staff. After all, what if after a couple of days business returns to normal? Firing a couple of waiters and then having a crush of customers is not likely to be good for long-term customer relations. Similarly, until the owner knows that business is returning to normal, she will not be willing to hire all of her staff back. Until that time, she might ask her existing staff of waiters to work extra hours, or maybe even the chef will venture into the restaurant to serve a few tables. This is why unemployment usually lags behind economic activity.

## SOLVED PROBLEM

**Q** You heard on the news that even though the economy is expanding, the unemployment rate increased. Can this be true?

**A** Let's begin with some figures to calculate the unemployment rate. Suppose that the working-age population is 200 million. This number is divided up between the employed, who total 125 million, and the unemployed, who total 10 million. The rest are working age but not in the labor force. The unemployment rate is the ratio of the unemployed to the labor force. Given these numbers, the unemployment rate is 10/135, or 7.4 percent. When the economy's outlook improves, suppose some of those individuals not in the labor force—those who retired early, some who went back to school, and others who simply stopped looking for work—decide to reenter the labor force and seek employment. For this exercise, let's assume that 5 million people come out of retirement and start looking for work. Because they are not yet employed, the number of unemployed people increases to 15 million. The total labor force (working and unemployed) also increases to 140. (Recall that the denominator of the equation used to calculate the unemployment rate is the entire labor force, which equals the sum of employed and unemployed people.) Using these new figures to calculate the unemployment rate, we get $15/140 = 10.7$ percent. So, even when times get better, the unemployment rate can, at least temporarily, rise.

## Why Worry about Unemployment?

We have already mentioned one important aspect about the unemployment rate: when it increases, the economy probably isn't performing as well as it could. A rising unemployment rate is associated with a reduction in the pace at which goods and services are being produced. In general, a rising unemployment rate signals that the incomes of some workers are falling.

A rising unemployment rate also signals that people's welfare is being harmed. Losing your job is likely to be financially and emotionally trying experience. Forty-six percent of the respondents to a *New York Times*/CBS News Poll conducted in December 2009 reported that their job loss was a major crisis in their lives.[2] Although some people chose to quit their jobs and search for different ones, other people become unemployed through no fault of their own. Rising oil and gas prices, for example, led to significant declines in the demand for SUVs in the mid-2000s.[3] This shift in consumer demand also led to a reduction in the number of workers needed to produce these vehicles. The fallout also affected dealerships: some dealerships simply closed their doors, putting even more people out of work.[4] For people who were laid off, maintaining their lifestyles became more difficult. Unemployment is generally not a pleasant experience, economically or personally.

### Unemployment in Other Countries

Does the relationship between the unemployment rate and economic activity in the United States hold for other countries as well? We can answer that by looking at **Figure 8.6**, which shows the unemployment rates of several European countries. Instead of including each country's real GDP growth, we show the unemployment rate in each country as it compares to economic downturns in the Euro area.[5]

One of the first things you see in Figure 8.6 is that the pattern of unemployment from country to country is fairly similar. The unemployment rates tend to rise when there is an economic downturn and fall as the pace of economic activity improves. You might be wondering why the unemployment rates were so low at the beginning of the most recent downturn in early 2008. Remember, unemployment is a lagging indicator and usually increases only after the economy has slowed. That

· · · · · · · ·

[2]"For Many, Uncertainty, Fear and Shame Often Follow Pink Slips." *New York Times*, December 15, 2009.

[3]Sholnn Freeman, "Truck and SUV Sales Plunge as Gas Prices Rise." *Washington Post*, October 4, 2005: D01.

[4]Chris Woodyard, "Car Dealers Close as Ford, GM, Chrysler Keep Cutting." *USA Today*, November 19, 2008.

[5]The Euro area consists of Austria, Belgium, Cyprus, Finland, France, Germany, Greece, Ireland, Italy, Luxembourg, Malta, Netherlands, Portugal, Slovakia, Slovenia, and Spain.

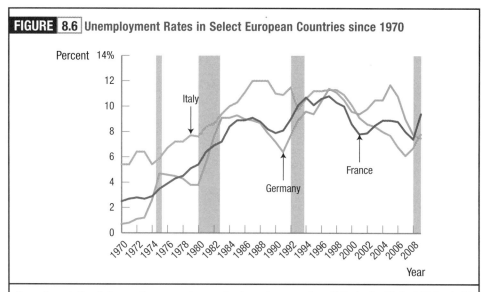

**FIGURE** **8.6** Unemployment Rates in Select European Countries since 1970

Does the relation between the unemployment rate and economic activity in the United States hold for other countries as well? This figure plots the unemployment rates of France, Germany, and Italy. The shaded bars represent recessions in the Euro area. The overall pattern of unemployment is fairly similar. The unemployment rates tend to rise during economic downturns and fall as economic activity improves. Because the unemployment rate is a lagging indicator, the rates beyond 2008—the beginning of the worldwide downturn—all increased.

*Source:* Organization for Economic Cooperation and Development

is what happened. For example, although the graph doesn't show it, in early 2010, the unemployment rate in Germany was closing in on 9 percent. In Italy, it stood at 7.5 percent in the fall of 2009 and was projected to increase to 8.5 percent in 2010.

## 8.4  Are There Different Types of Unemployment?

So far, we have only considered the behavior of the unemployment rate. We know that this measure can change over time, especially when the overall economic climate changes. When times are tough, economically speaking, we've seen that the unemployment rate is more likely to increase than not. Unemployment that occurs because of an economic downturn is known as **cyclical unemployment**. When the economy enters a recession, for example, the unemployment rate rises because firms are cutting back on production. In some sense, we'd expect cyclical unemployment to be close to zero when we are talking about an economy operating at its potential level of production.

**CYCLICAL UNEMPLOYMENT** The rise and fall of the unemployment rate that occurs due to changes in business activity.

EXAMPLE  With the economy in a deep recession, fewer people are going to the movies. Because of declining attendance, you lose your job at the CinePlex 24.

Another reason we observe a positive unemployment rate, even during boom times, is because the economy is dynamic. When you leave one job to search for another, you become unemployed. When you graduate from college and look for a job, you are considered unemployed. This type of unemployment is called **frictional unemployment**.

> **FRICTIONAL UNEMPLOYMENT** Unemployment that occurs because individuals are constantly moving between jobs.

> **EXAMPLE** Bill worked for the large aerospace company for four years and, after not getting promoted, decided to look for another job. He quit to devote more time to the job search.

Frictional unemployment is always occurring regardless of whether or not the economy is booming or in a recession. The idea is that moving from job to job may not occur as smoothly as expected. Your professor quits his position at the university, expecting to find another teaching job. But it may take him some time to find another suitable position. Even though the Internet and various job-related Web sites may accelerate the search process, while the professor is looking, he is considered frictionally unemployed.

Lastly, it may be the case that the skills you possess simply are not in demand. Even if you are the best blacksmith around, there may not be much demand for your ability to fashion a horseshoe. When workers lack the skills necessary to fill certain jobs, this is an example of **structural unemployment**.

> **STRUCTURAL UNEMPLOYMENT** The type of unemployment that occurs due to a mismatch between workers' skills and those demanded by employers.

> **EXAMPLE** With a degree in English literature, Sarah could not get a job as a macroeconomic forecaster.

> **EXAMPLE** Because he was illiterate, John was not able to find work at his desired wage of $20 an hour.

Structural unemployment can occur when new production technology is implemented, and workers are unable to operate the new machinery. Unless they alter their human capital—learn the new techniques—they could be unemployed for prolonged periods of time or employed in other jobs. Structural unemployment also may arise due to changes in social priorities. For example, the recent "green" movement has targeted coal-using technologies, such as coal-fired electricity generators. If the use of coal is limited, this would put coal miners out of work. However, coal miners in West Virginia who become unemployed due to a new mining technology or a switch by consumers to cleaner energy need not remain unemployed forever. People have the opportunity to improve their education, seek employment opportunities in other industries, and move to other areas of the country. Claiming that technology has *permanently* displaced workers and raised unemployment rates ignores the dynamics of labor markets. If the coal miners do not look for other opportunities, the unemployment rates in West Virginia might be higher than in other areas of the country.

There also can be other explanations for structural unemployment. In Chapter 4, we discussed the impact of minimum wages on the labor market. In theory, imposing a minimum wage that is higher than the market-clearing wage creates unemployment: at the higher wage, the quantity of labor supplied exceeds the quantity demanded, which creates structural unemployment.

## Is There a "Natural" Rate of Unemployment?

Because of conditions that lead to cyclical, frictional, and structural unemployment, the official unemployment rate never equals zero. At any point in time, some people in the economy are likely to be unemployed. But what if the economy was operating on its PPF, at its productive capacity? Is there an unemployment rate that is related to any economy operating at its potential? In our discussion of output, we discussed potential GDP—what GDP would be if the economy were operating at normal capacity. Is there a comparable "full-employment unemployment rate"? In other words, is there a "natural rate" of unemployment that exists even when it's operating at its potential GDP? Yes, there is. But like potential GDP, it is an estimate. **Figure 8.7** plots the actual unemployment rate along with one estimate of the **natural rate of unemployment**.

> **NATURAL RATE OF UNEMPLOYMENT** An estimate of what the unemployment rate would be if the economy were operating at its potential.

> EXAMPLE  The U.S. unemployment rate fell to 5.5 percent in the sixth year of the last economic boom. With the economy operating near its potential, many economists believed that this was close to the natural rate of unemployment.

This natural rate of unemployment fluctuates less than the actual unemployment rate because the actual unemployment rate varies with changes in the pace of economic activity. Because the natural rate is an estimate of what the rate of unemployment

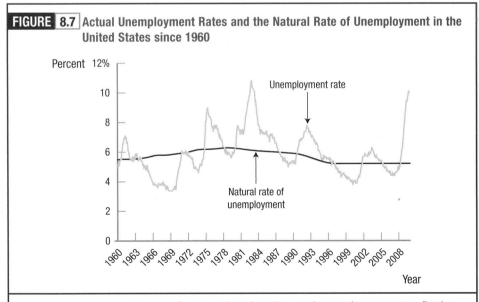

**FIGURE 8.7** | Actual Unemployment Rates and the Natural Rate of Unemployment in the United States since 1960

The natural rate of unemployment fluctuates less than the actual unemployment rate reflecting that the natural rate is an estimate of what the rate of unemployment would be *if* the economy were operating at its potential. The actual unemployment rate tends to fluctuate around the natural rate, a relation that is similar to that between real GDP and potential GDP.

*Sources:* Congressional Budget Office (Natural Rate) and Bureau of Labor Statistics (Unemployment Rate)

would be if the economy were operating at its potential and there is no cyclical unemployment, it is less volatile than the actual rate. One observation of the two series is that the actual unemployment rate tends to fluctuate around the natural rate. This type of behavior is similar to the relation between real GDP and potential GDP. Some economists believe that over time, the economy tends to revert to its full-employment level of activity. Whether this occurs naturally or because of a policy intervention by the government is a matter of debate that we'll explore in later chapters.

---

**ECONOMIC FALLACY**   The natural rate of unemployment is 5 percent.

**Maybe.** The natural rate of unemployment is related to the idea of being at full production, or on the PPF. Because the underlying conditions that shift the PPF outward change slowly, the natural rate also may change over time. It also may change because of underlying structural changes in the economy. For example, the increase in the number of women in the labor force after the 1950s was a cultural change that increased the natural rate of unemployment. Moreover, our precision in measuring the rate may mean that we sometimes incorrectly estimate it. For instance, in the early 1960s, the natural rate of unemployment was thought to be around 3 percent, even though later more objective measures pegged it closer to 6 percent. By the 1990s, it was estimated to be around 5 percent. As you can see in Figure 8.7, although it does appear that the natural rate hovers around 5 and 6 percent, picking one rate and calling it *the* natural rate is not wise.

---

## 8.5 Other Labor Market Indicators

As we have explained, the civilian unemployment rate is the most popular indicator of conditions in the labor market. However, other measures are used to track the labor market as well, especially long-term trends in employment. Two of these measures are the labor force participation rate and the employment-to-population ratio.

### Labor Force Participation Rate

The unemployment rate is the percentage of the labor force that is not employed. The **labor force participation rate** is the percent of the working-age population in the labor force.

> **LABOR FORCE PARTICIPATION RATE** The percent of the working-age population (16 years and older) in the labor force.

> **EXAMPLE** In Munchkin County, 10 million people are in the working-age population. Of those, 3 million decide to retire. The remaining 7 million, both employed and unemployed, make up the labor force. The labor force participation rate for Munchkin County is equal to 7/10, or 70 percent.
>
> Half of the Munchkin-County retirees grow weary of household chores and return to work. The labor force participation rate changes to 8.5/10, or 85 percent.

This statistic is important because it reveals the relative amount of labor available to produce goods and services. Think about your household. If there are four people in your home, and all four participate in providing household services—loading the dishwasher, taking out the trash, mowing the lawn, and so on—then the household

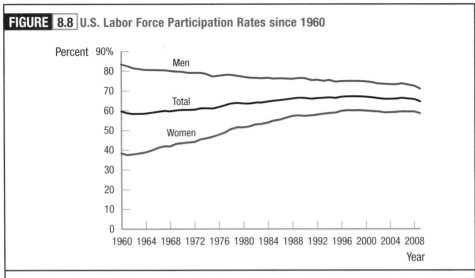

**FIGURE 8.8** U.S. Labor Force Participation Rates since 1960

After rising since 1960, the overall trend in the participation rate has been slightly down since 2000. Some attribute this change to the retirement of baby boomers. The increase in women's participation compared to the overall decline in male participation rates reflects a number of factors, including changing attitudes toward working women, smaller families, and an increase in the availability of household services, such as outside child care.

*Source:* Bureau of Labor Statistics

will produce more services than if only one or two people bear the burden. All else the same, reducing the number of productive people in your household will result in fewer household services getting done. The same is true of the economy. The fewer the number of people participating in the labor force, the fewer goods and services the economy will produce.

**Figure 8.8** shows the labor force participation rate over the past 50 years. The graph shows the total participation rate and the participation rates by gender. We have deliberately shown such a long time span in the graph because important trends have occurred during the period. Fifty years ago, the labor force participation rate was slightly less than 60 percent, and then it began a long upward march, reaching a peak of about 67 percent in the late 1990s. Since 2000, the overall trend in the participation rate has been down, exaggerated somewhat by the recent economic downturn. Why the decline since 2000? Some attribute it to the earlier retirement of baby boomers in the workforce.

Did the upward trend in the labor force participation rate beginning in the 1960s reflect the behavior of all workers? No. You can quickly see that the participation rates of men and women have been very different. The long-term reduction in the work activity of men stands in sharp contrast to the upward trend of women participating in the workforce. What explains these trends? One possible explanation for the decline in men's participation reflects the trend toward the earlier retirement of men.

The increase in women's participation, especially the sharp rise between 1960 and 1980, reflects a number of cultural and social changes. Social attitudes toward working women have changed dramatically over the past generation. The number of stay-at-home moms declined as women increased their educational training. Your college classes are probably split fairly evenly between men and women. In the 1960s, however, most classes were predominantly male. With increased education, women's opportunity cost of not working increased. Social changes also occurred that led to smaller families. Smaller families and more services such as outside child-care providers in the economy lowered the opportunity cost of women entering the workforce. The statistics reflect that change: women today account for a larger proportion of the workforce than they did 30 or 40 years ago.

Is the labor force participation rate of women in the United States representative? That is, have women in other countries reached the same level of labor market activity as those in the United States? **Table 8.1** lists labor force participation rates by women for various countries. The measures, all from 2006, indicate a fairly diverse level of activity. Note that participation by women is above 50 percent in most of the industrial countries listed. Surprisingly, the rate also is fairly high in some of the

| Table **8.1**   Women's Labor Force Participation Rates in 2006: Select Countries | |
| --- | --- |
| Country | Participation Rate (%) |
| Argentina | 54.3 |
| Australia | 56.3 |
| Austria | 50.4 |
| Bangladesh | 52.4 |
| Bolivia | 63.0 |
| Canada | 60.8 |
| China | 68.5 |
| Denmark | 59.0 |
| Egypt | 20.1 |
| France | 48.4 |
| Germany | 51.2 |
| India | 34.0 |
| Israel | 50.5 |
| Japan | 48.1 |
| Lebanon | 33.5 |
| Mexico | 40.3 |
| Nigeria | 45.5 |
| Philippines | 55.7 |
| Turkey | 27.7 |
| United Kingdom | 55.5 |
| United States | 59.7 |

This table lists the labor force participation rates by women for various countries. The list indicates a diverse level of activity. Although participation by women is above 50 percent in most of the industrial countries, it is also fairly high in some of the lesser-developed countries, such as Nigeria. In contrast, in some countries, women's participation rates are low. This may be explained by social or religious customs that discourage women from working outside of their homes.

**Source:** United Nations

lesser-developed countries, such as Nigeria. One possible explanation is that women are equals in the workforce of more agrarian economies. You also can see that in some countries, the participation rate of women is comparatively low. In some countries, social or religious customs discourage women from working outside the home. As you can imagine, trying to explain labor participation rates across countries and genders interests researchers from economics to sociology to political science.

## Employment-to-Population Ratio

Another indicator of labor market activity, the **employment-to-population ratio** is the ratio of those individuals employed to the working-age population.

**EMPLOYMENT-TO-POPULATION RATIO** The ratio of those individuals employed to the working-age population.

EXAMPLE Recall that in Munchkin County, 10 million people are in the working-age population. If 3 million decide to retire, the remaining 7 million make up the labor force. If 1.5 million people are unemployed, the employment-to-population ratio is equal to 5.5/10, or 55 percent.

**Figure 8.9** plots the total employment-to-population ratio and the ratios for men and women since 1960. Like the participation rate, you can see that there has been an upward trend in the number of people in the population at work over the past 50 years. In 1960, the ratio stood at about 55 percent. But by 2000, its peak, it had reached nearly 65 percent. In other words, nearly two-thirds of the working-age population was employed in 2000. This indicates that the economy has, over time,

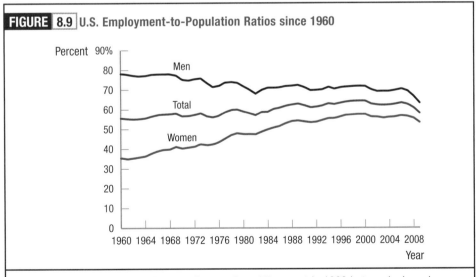

**FIGURE 8.9** U.S. Employment-to-Population Ratios since 1960

The total employment-to-population ratio was about 55 percent in 1960 but reached nearly 65 percent in 2000. Nearly two-thirds of the working-age population was employed in 2000, indicating the economy expanded fast enough to create many new jobs. The employment of working-age women has increased steadily over time while it has declined for men. The employment of working-age women increased from 35 percent in 1960 to almost 60 percent at its peak.

*Source:* Bureau of Labor Statistics

expanded fast enough to create many new jobs. You also can see in the figure that employment-to-population ratio is sensitive to changes in the economy. During the most recent economic downturn, the total ratio dropped sharply.

The employment of working-age women has increased steadily over time while it has declined for men. Figure 8.9 shows that the percentage of working-age women employed almost doubled since 1960, increasing from 35 percent in 1960 to almost 60 percent at its peak. As we mentioned in our discussion of the participation rate, the increase in the female employment-to-population ratio reflects the social and economic changes that have occurred over the past 50 years. The figure also shows that during the last economic downturn, women, as a group, fared better than men. Researchers have found that men were more heavily represented in those industries hardest hit by the downturn. Another part of the story is that more men rejoined the labor force but failed to find employment. Who were these reentrants? Most likely they were men who opted for early retirement but went back to work after their retirement nest eggs dried up following the decline in the stock market.[6]

## 8.6 Dissecting the Unemployment Rate

The unemployment rate, the labor force participation rate, and the employment-to-population ratio have now given you a broader picture of unemployment. Each of the measures provides useful clues about evolving trends in the labor market over time. However, digging into the unemployment rate at a single point in time also is insightful. This is because when the BLS assesses the condition of the labor market each month, it collects a vast array of data on the composition of the unemployment rate. From gender to age to race and all combinations, the BLS collects the information. We can use this information not only to see how different groups in the economy are faring but also to provide clues to develop policies that may help cushion the effects of unemployment on some groups in the future.

One drawback of the unemployment rate is that it obscures just how unemployment is distributed across different groups in the economy. That is, even though the headline rate may be 5 percent or 6.7 percent, the unemployment rates among various groups of workers in the economy may be much different. **Table 8.2** shows a breakdown of the unemployment rate for 2008. The overall rate reported on the nightly news was 5.8 percent, but you can see from the numbers in the table that unemployment rates by gender, age, and race are much different. Younger workers are more likely to be unemployed than older workers because younger workers tend to move from job to job more than older workers. They also, as a group, are likely to have acquired fewer job-related skills that employers find attractive.

You also can see that unemployment is not even across gender and race. Young black males tend to experience higher rates of unemployment than any other group in the table. Disparities such as these suggest that blanket policies aimed at lowering *the* unemployment rate can affect different groups of workers in the economy very differently. More specifically, policies intended to reduce unemployment must be considered carefully if there are target groups for whom lowering unemployment is the desired outcome.

Finally, we must point out that unemployment is also heavily influenced by education. The data in **Table 8.3** show that, holding other factors constant (i.e., race, gender, age), the more education a person has, the less likely he or she will become

· · · · · · ·

[6]Aysegul Sahin, Joseph Song, and Bart Hobijn, "The Unemployment Gender Gap during the 2007 Recession." Federal Reserve Bank of New York, *Current Issues* (February 2010).

## Table 8.2  U.S. Unemployment Rates for Select Groups, 2008

### Average: 5.8%

| Men/Age | All (%) | White (%) | Black (%) | Asian (%) |
|---|---|---|---|---|
| 16–19 | 21.2 | 19.1 | 35.9 | 16.6 |
| 20–24 | 11.4 | 10.2 | 19.3 | 6.5 |
| 25–34 | 5.0 | 4.5 | 9.1 | 3.5 |
| 55–64 | 3.8 | 3.4 | 7.1 | 4.3 |
| Women/Age | All (%) | White (%) | Black (%) | Asian (%) |
| 16–19 | 16.2 | 14.4 | 26.8 | 12.3 |
| 20–24 | 8.8 | 7.5 | 16.6 | 15.7 |
| 25–34 | 4.6 | 4.2 | 7.4 | 6.1 |
| 55–64 | 3.7 | 3.5 | 5.3 | 3.5 |

This table lists a breakdown of the unemployment rate for 2008. The overall rate reported was 5.8 percent. As indicated by the figures in the table, unemployment rates when measured across by gender, age, and race differ greatly. Younger workers are more likely to be unemployed than older workers. Nonwhite workers also are likely to have higher unemployment rates. Overall, women generally have higher rates of unemployment than men, although this generalization isn't true for nonwhite women. These figures indicate that unemployment is a very diverse measure.

**Source:** Bureau of Labor Statistics

## Table 8.3  Unemployment Rates and Education*

| Education | 2006 (%) | 2009 (%) |
|---|---|---|
| Less than a high-school diploma | 6.7 | 15.3 |
| High-school diploma, no college | 4.3 | 10.5 |
| Some college | 3.4 | 9.0 |
| College graduate | 1.8 | 5.0 |
| Overall unemployment rate | 4.4 | 10.0 |

*Individuals 25 years or older; data for December.

The first numeric column reports the 2006 unemployment rate associated with individuals in the labor force who attained the educational levels described to the left. At that time, the overall unemployment rate was quite low. In 2009, the overall civilian unemployment rate reached 10 percent. While all groups experienced higher rates of unemployment, people with less education experienced relatively higher rates than people with more education.

**Source:** Bureau of Labor Statistics

unemployed. The first column of numbers in Table 8.3 is the 2006 unemployment rate associated with individuals in the labor force who meet the educational levels described to the left. We chose 2006 because in that year, the overall unemployment rate reached its lowest level during the past decade, less than 5 percent by year's end. For college graduates, the unemployment rate in 2006 was less than 2 percent compared with an unemployment rate of nearly 7 percent for people without a high school diploma.

The second column shows a time when the overall unemployment rate was quite high. By the end of 2009, the civilian unemployment rate reached 10 percent, double what it was only a few years earlier. How did the different groups in Table 8.3 fare? You can see that while all groups experienced higher rates of unemployment, those with less education did relatively worse: the unemployment rate of workers without a high-school diploma rose to more than 15 percent. In contrast, the unemployment rate of workers with a college diploma rose to just 5 percent.

The ongoing debate is just how governments should respond when they observe that unemployment rates in their countries is on the rise. For example, government-sponsored unemployment benefits help cushion the decline in income experienced by people who lose their jobs. But just how far should those benefits go? Should they be available until people find work? What percentage of an unemployed worker's original compensation should be covered by the benefits? These questions are important because they all deal with incentives. If government benefits lower the opportunity cost of being unemployed, people will naturally have less of an incentive to find new jobs as quickly. Would it be better, then, not to have unemployment benefits? Most economists would answer no. Nonetheless, they continue to debate the level of unemployment benefits the government should provide.

**ECONOMIC FALLACY** More education guarantees employment.

**False.** The figures presented in Table 8.3 are overall averages for the various groups. Just because someone graduates from college does not mean the person will never experience unemployment. For example, when Boeing merged with the St. Louis aerospace firm McDonald-Douglas in 1997, many aeronautic engineers were laid off. These people, all with high levels of education, found themselves just as unemployed as those McDonald-Douglas workers with high-school diplomas. More recently, some faculty members at colleges and universities in California—including some with PhDs—lost their jobs and have not yet found full-time employment.

## 8.7 Policies to Combat Unemployment

Fighting unemployment often involves increasing the amount of unemployment benefits people who are out of work can receive or lengthening the amount of time they can receive the benefits. Both measures help alleviate some of the adverse effects of being unemployed. The question is whether they help prevent unemployment. Do they reduce the length of time someone is unemployed?

Perhaps not. Anything that reduces the cost of an action is likely to encourage more of it. If you are paid for not working, you must weigh the benefits of the income you are getting from the government against the cost of engaging in a serious job search or taking a job with less pay than your previous employment offered. If you have a spouse who is employed, and you have saved during your days of working, the presence of unemployment compensation may raise the opportunity cost of returning to work. Some evidence suggests that such an effect may exist. Based on U.S. data, one study found that extending unemployment compensation was a factor in extending the length of time individuals stayed out of work.

International comparisons also suggest that in countries with generous unemployment compensation, such as Western European countries, unemployment rates tend to be higher, and people are out of work longer. In fact, although we must be careful in making international comparisons of unemployment statistics—due to differences in how they are calculated—**Figure 8.10** shows that unemployment rates in the Euro area in general and in several specific European economies have been higher than in the United States.

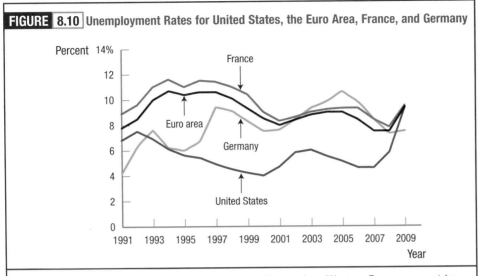

**FIGURE 8.10** Unemployment Rates for United States, the Euro Area, France, and Germany

In countries with generous unemployment compensation, such as Western European countries, unemployment rates tend to be higher and the time people are out of work is longer. Although care must be taken in making international comparisons of unemployment statistics, this figure shows that unemployment rates in the Euro area and two major European economies generally are higher than in the United States.

*Source:* Federal Reserve Bank of St. Louis

Why then do we find that unemployment compensation is often increased or extended during times of economic hardship? The answer is that no one wants people out of work to suffer economically more than they already are. As a society, we seem more willing to subsidize unemployment than we are to force people into employment situations that they may regret. It is a trade-off, but you should be aware of the potential costs when legislators make such decisions.

Minimum wage laws are also hotly debated by legislators and the public. Some argue that minimum wages are most harmful to the very group of workers they are supposedly trying to help: the undereducated and poorly trained. But, as you saw in Table 8.3, one possible explanation for those without a high-school diploma suffering the highest levels of unemployment, in good times and bad, is that, given the current wage structure, they are less or the least employable relative to people with more education.

Finally, one way to help reduce the occurrence of unemployment is to improve the education people get. Being able to recite the Gettysburg Address or knowing the dates of the major wars won't necessarily make you more employable, but education generally means that you become more adaptable and better able to move between jobs that are not identical. Think of a worker who has for years done the same job: riveting bolts into a car frame. If that person becomes unemployed, what are his options? How many jobs are there for bolt riveters? But for the person who runs the computer system that controls the auto-assembly line, finding another job may not be as difficult. Computer skills are transferable. In general, more education increases a worker's ability to adapt to changes in the work environment. As you will see later when we examine why some countries grow faster than others, one of the key explanations is that faster-growing countries, on average, tend to have better educated workers.

## WHAT YOU SHOULD HAVE LEARNED FROM CHAPTER 8

■ That unemployment can be thought of as underuse of resources, as being inside the production possibilities frontier (PPF), or as an excess supply of labor at the going wage rate.

■ That the official unemployment rate is the ratio of the number of unemployed to the labor force.

■ That the labor force doesn't include everyone, just those persons age 16 and older who are employed or looking for work.

■ That some people drop out of the labor force (discouraged workers) and reenter when economic conditions improve.

■ That two versions of the unemployment rate exist: one based on a survey of households and one based on a survey of businesses.

■ That the unemployment rate tends to lag behind economic activity.

■ That the measured rate of unemployment is never zero.

■ That the unemployment rate varies considerably across groups based on age, gender, race, and education.

■ That policies to offset the cost of unemployment may actually increase or prolong unemployment.

■ That alternative measures of the labor market indicate the growing importance of women in the workplace.

## KEY TERMS

Real wage, p. 210

Efficiency wages, p. 213

Labor force, p. 213

Unemployment rate, p. 214

Discouraged worker, p. 215

Cyclical unemployment, p. 219

Frictional unemployment, p. 220

Structural unemployment, p. 220

Natural rate of unemployment, p. 221

Labor force participation rate, p. 222

Employment-to-population
   ratio, p. 225

## QUESTIONS AND PROBLEMS

1. David Leonhardt, a journalist for the *New York Times*, wrote in March 2008 that "the average unemployment rate in this decade, just above 5 percent, has been lower than in any decade since the 1960s. Yet the percentage of prime-age men (those 25 to 54 years old) who are not working has been *higher* than in any decade since World War II." In other words, even though the *unemployment* rate was low, the *employment* rate is declining. Given how the BLS measures the unemployment rate, explain how this seemingly inconsistent observation could happen.

2. In March 2009, according to the BLS, 154,048,000 individuals were in the labor force. In that same month, 13,161,000 people were classified as unemployed. Using this information:

   a) What is the unemployment rate for March 2009?
   b) The job picture darkens. Suppose 161,000 of those people looking for work (counted as unemployed) stop doing so. Now what is the unemployment rate for March 2009?

c) The job picture brightens. Now, instead of 161,000 people stopping their job search, what if 400,000 people previously not looking for a job decide to start again. Now what is the unemployment rate for March 2009?

d) Based on your calculations, does the official unemployment rate always give the most accurate picture of trends in the labor market?

3. How is the unemployment rate calculated?

a) How many households are included in the survey?

b) Who conducts the survey?

c) If your household is in the survey for the first time this month, will you be in the survey next month? (You might want to visit www.bls.gov.)

d) How does the household survey differ from the establishment survey?

4. Think about a time when you started a new job.

a) Did the job have a training period? What happened to your output as you became more familiar with the job?

b) Why might it be costly for firms to hire individuals who are overqualified and who expect to leave the job as soon as they find something more appropriate for their skills?

5. When Steven receives unemployment benefits, he benefits directly. Is there any benefit to other members of the community?

6. Unemployment is thought of as a lagging indicator of economic activity. What does it mean to be a lagging indicator? Use a real-life example to explain why this happens.

7. For each of the following individuals, indicate if the person is cyclically, frictionally, or structurally unemployed or is not part of the labor force.

a) Katie has just completed nursing school and is searching for a job.

b) Christine has left her job to care for her children.

c) Peter lost his job at the brokerage firm following a downturn in the economy.

d) Geno lost his job at the university because students no longer want to take German.

8. The text described the natural rate of unemployment as the rate that would exist if the economy were producing at full capacity; on its PPF, in other words.

a) Why isn't the rate of unemployment zero when the economy is operating at its potential?

b) What would happen to the natural rate if people became less willing to relocate for a job?

c) What would happen to the natural rate if tools for communicating job openings nationwide improved?

d) What would happen to the natural rate if community colleges improved their ability to offer worker retraining?

9. Unemployment benefits are much higher in European countries than in the United States. For example, unemployed workers in France receive over 50 percent of their former earnings in unemployment compensation. In the United States, the amount is less than 30 percent.

a) How might this difference in unemployment benefits explain the divergence of unemployment rates shown in Figure 8.10?

b) Could higher unemployment benefits explain sticky wages?

c) How does the existence of unemployment benefits alter the opportunity cost of not working?

10. Mexico does not have a great record when it comes to economic growth. As a consequence, its economy does not produce new jobs at a very rapid rate. Even though many more Mexican children and young adults are gaining more education, they are not able to find full-time employment. Is this an example of cyclical unemployment or structural unemployment? Explain your answer.

11. In 2005, over 50 percent of individuals with a high-school education or above were out of work in Mexico. At the same time, the official unemployment rate in Mexico was quite low. How can you explain this contradiction?

12. The data indicate that labor force participation rates for men have declined, but for women, they have increased over the past few decades. Discuss how each of the following may explain these trends.

    a) Increased education of women
    b) Increased availability and knowledge of contraception
    c) Aging of the labor force
    d) Increased household incomes

13. Because of the severity of the recession of 2007–2009 Congress voted to extend the duration of unemployment benefits. The press reported that consumer confidence was low, due to the high unemployment numbers. How are these related?

14. In March 2010, the BLS announced that the civilian labor force was 153,910,000, that the number of employed was 138,905,000, and that the employment-to-population ratio was 58.6 percent. Using this information:

    a) Rounded to the nearest million, what was the working age population?
    b) What was the number of unemployed?
    c) What was the unemployment rate?

15. It is common that individuals with more education experience less unemployment than others. Explain why this is so.

16. If one goal of a labor union is to fight the reduction of its members' wages, how is this related to unemployment?

17. Sometimes, the household survey indicates that the number of employed persons increases while the establishment survey shows just the opposite. What is different about the two sources of employment data that can explain this? Which one is correct?

# The Global Economy

*"It says something about this new global economy that USA Today now reports every morning on the day's events in Asian markets."*

*Lawrence Summers,*
*economist and former*
*presidential adviser*

**Y**ou can't listen to the news or open a newspaper without hearing or seeing some mention of the "global economy." You probably have some idea about what this means: that many of the goods you purchase are produced in other countries. Conversely, many goods purchased by individuals and firms in foreign countries are produced in the United States and elsewhere. The upside is that the more products our country produces and sells in markets abroad, the better it is for our economy. In addition, we are better off if we can buy less-expensive foreign products. The downside of international trade is that sometimes local jobs migrate to other nations, sparking rally cries against foreign trade. Are they justified?

In Chapter 7, you learned that trade with other countries—exports and imports—is part of what determines an economy's total output (GDP). In this chapter, we take a deeper look into how economic activity in one country can impact another. After you have finished this chapter, you will have the tools to better understand the topics addressed in ongoing debates over trade, including who wins and who loses.

## 9.1 How Big Is International Trade?

In Chapter 7, you learned that the U.S. economy is the largest in the world, accounting for almost a quarter of the world's GDP. You might guess that due to its sheer size, the United States plays a major role in trade among countries. Recall from that chapter that the amount of a country's net exports is the value of the goods and services it exports less the value of the goods and services it imports. These "values" are expressed in terms of dollars, pounds, or whatever the country's currency unit is called. When a country's net exports are positive (exports exceed imports), the country has a trade surplus.

Many people think that a trade surplus is good because it increases a country's GDP. After all, when net exports are negative, this results in a trade deficit, which reduces a country's GDP. Actions taken by policy makers, both here and abroad, sometimes affect the trade between countries. As you can imagine, if these policies result in trade deficits or make the deficits worse, those policies quickly become the fuel for heated debates.

Sometimes the urge to limit imports and increase exports to achieve a trade surplus goes too far. The so-called mercantilists of England argued as far back as the 1700s that a country could achieve economic prosperity only by exporting more products to other countries than they receive—even if it meant severely limiting the inflow of imports. Adam Smith showed in *The Wealth of Nations*, published in 1776, that this approach is not conducive to maintaining the economic well-being of a nation. Arguments like those of the mercantilists—and you still hear them today under the label *protectionism*—suggest that international trade benefits only the exporting country.

One way to address this question is to compare the average level of real GDP per person across two sets of countries. Economists have classified a number of countries as "closed" and "open" based on the extent to which they engage in international trade. (We will have more to say on this in Chapter 11.) In those economies considered to be "closed," average real GDP per person in 2000 was $1,428. Contrast that figure with $24,316, the average real GDP per person in those economies classified as "open." These numbers suggest that increasing trade and openness does not lead to lower incomes per person, on average.

We also know that among the closed economies, one-third experienced a decline in real GDP per person between 1980 and 2000. For the open economies, that fate befell only one economy, Jordan. Could we find a contrary case? Sure. Between 1980 and 2000, Egypt, classified as a closed economy, averaged an annual growth in real GDP per capita of nearly 4 percent. But a special case is not a good test of a theory. Based on the relation across many economies, it appears that trade does not impoverish those who are actively engaged in it.

Even though it is tempting to think of the trade between the United States and, say, Canada as being something carried out by the two governments, do not fall into this trap. Keep in mind that *countries*, by and large, do not trade with one another. *Individuals* and *firms* within countries do. Although government policies play an important role in affecting how much trade takes place, international trade is really measuring the exchange of goods between consumers and producers who just happen to be located in different countries. In this way, international trade is really no different conceptually than trade between individuals in Connecticut and North Dakota. The only real difference is that in state-to-state cases, trade occurs using the same currency, a common set of laws, and so on. When international trade occurs, those commonalities are reduced. Let's now take a look at how large the global economy (trade around the world) is and how the trade between individual countries makes up the total amount of world trade.

## Imports, Exports, and the Trade Deficits and Surpluses of Nations

The United States is the single biggest economy in the world, as well as the biggest trading partner of many countries. In terms of the amount it imports, the United States also ranks number one. Almost 16 percent of exports from all the countries around the world end up in the United States. Americans have the biggest appetite for (and ability to purchase) goods and services.

Not only does the United States rank highly when it comes to how much we import, but the dollar value of our exports is greater than any other single country.

| Table | 9.1 | Top Exporting Countries in the World | | |
| --- | --- | --- | --- | --- |
| Country | Export % of World Total | Exports as % of GDP | Imports as % of GDP | Trade Surplus or Deficit? |
| United States | 11 | 12 | −17 | Deficit |
| China | 10 | 39 | −30 | Surplus |
| Germany | 9 | 47 | −40 | Surplus |
| United Kingdom | 6 | 26 | −30 | Deficit |
| Japan | 5 | 18 | −16 | Surplus |
| France | 4 | 27 | −28 | Deficit |
| Italy | 3 | 29 | −29 | Deficit* |
| Netherlands | 3 | 75 | −66 | Surplus |
| Canada | 3 | 35 | −33 | Surplus |

*Classified as deficit based on rounding of the numbers.

This table lists the top exporting countries, ranked on the basis of their exports as a percent of the world's total exports in 2007. The United States accounts for about 12 percent of the world's total exports. Negative signs appear in front of the import figures because they represent a reduction in a nation's domestic GDP. On the basis of this measuring of exports—as a percent of GDP, the United States ranks the lowest—our GDP depends less on exporting goods than other countries, such as Germany.

**Source:** *The Economist Pocket World in Figures* (2010). Data are for 2007.

**Table 9.1** provides a rundown of the top exporting countries, ranked on the basis of their exports as a percent of the world's total. Notice that the United States alone accounts for about 12 percent of the world's total exports.

Although it might not surprise you that the dollar value of U.S. exports is greater than that of any other country, the ordering of the biggest exporting countries in Table 9.1 might. You have probably heard that China and India are becoming economic powerhouses. As you can see, China's exports place it second behind the United States and only just ahead of Germany. India, on the other hand, does not make the list. In fact, India's exports amount to just slightly more than 1 percent of the world's total.

We can also use Table 9.1 to figure out how big a country's trade sector is relative to its economy. In other words, let's think about measuring the value of a country's exports and imports as a percent of its GDP. As you can see from Table 9.1, exports produced in the United States amount to about 12 percent of our GDP. By contrast, imports amount to 17 percent of GDP. These figures show that the dollar value of international trade, combining the exporting and importing of goods, is a bit over one-quarter of our GDP. This number is much larger than in the past, reflecting the fact that the United States is a much more "open" economy than many people think. That is, we increasingly depend on international trade to do business.

Note that in Table 9.1, we use a negative sign in front of imports because they represent a reduction in domestic GDP. As you learned in the previous chapter, when you import an item, the money you spend ultimately increases the income of a foreign producer, not a firm in your country. This combination is reflected in the final column of Table 9.1, which shows that the United States ran a trade deficit. In other words, the dollar value of the country's imports exceeded its exports.

What about other countries? Measuring exports as a percent of GDP, you can see that the United States ranks the lowest—our GDP depends less on exporting goods than other countries' GDPs do. Unlike the United States, some economies, such as the Netherlands, are much more heavily dependent on exporting. Three-fourths of the Netherlands' GDP is generated by its exports. Guess what they export and to whom? The answer might surprise you: the Netherlands' exports consist mostly of machinery, transportation equipment, and chemicals. Germany is the Netherlands' biggest customer, accounting for about one-quarter of Dutch exports.

What about China? From Table 9.1, you can see that China's exports comprise nearly 40 percent of that country's GDP, and its imports are about one-third of its GDP. This difference means that China ran a trade surplus: the value of China's exports exceeded that of its imports. This trade surplus amounted to $349 billion in 2007. Although running a trade surplus is not unique—four other countries in Table 9.1 also have trade surpluses—China's large trade surplus with the United States (we have a large trade deficit with China) has many people agitated.

---

**ECONOMIC FALLACY**  China is the United States' number-one trading partner.

**False.** Although China is the country with which we have the largest trade deficit, China is not our top trading partner. In late 2008, the United States imported more goods from China than we exported to China, to the tune of $19.9 billion. But this does not make China our largest trading partner. If you add together the dollar volume of exports and imports, Canada is our largest trading partner (at this time). As of late 2008, total trade with Canada amounted to $36.6 billion, while total trade with China was $30.3 billion. Of course, these numbers will change over time, and by the time you read this, China may be our largest trading partner.

Although we buy a lot of goods from China, the reverse is not true: people in that country do not buy a lot of goods from us. Japan, Taiwan, and South Korea all import a greater dollar value of U.S. goods than China does. Why is China's trade surplus so large? Why don't our policy makers do something about it? We'll explore questions such as these shortly. First, let's take another look at how we measure trade deficits and surpluses.

---

Most often trade statistics are reported in "nominal" terms, that is, in current dollars for the United States or pounds for the United Kingdom. Unfortunately, this is not the best measure to use. Smaller economies simply cannot produce and import enough to keep up with larger economies. It's like comparing the caloric intake of someone who weighs 100 pounds to that of someone who weighs 300 pounds. In most cases, the larger individual will consume more calories in a day. A more useful method is to compare trade statistics by holding constant the size of an economy, that is, to look at a country's trade relative to its GDP. **Table 9.2** shows the same countries as Table 9.1. However, in Table 9.2, we list the dollar value of their trade surpluses or deficits and the percentage of the GDPs that these figures represent.

By either measure, the U.S. trade deficit stands out compared with the other countries. The trade deficit is more than $700 billion and amounts to a little over 5 percent of America's GDP. Now look at the trade surplus for the Netherlands. In dollar terms, the Netherlands' trade surplus is only $66 billion, but it is a relatively larger percentage of its GDP (8.6 percent). Germany's trade surplus is much larger in dollar terms ($232 billion) but about the same when compared to its GDP (7 percent). Measured relative to their GDPs, the trade surpluses for Germany and

| Table 9.2 | The Trade Surpluses or Deficits of the World's Top Exporting Countries (Expressed in $U.S. and as Percentage of GDP) | |
|---|---|---|
| Country | Trade Surplus or Deficit ($U.S. Billion) | Percentage of GDP (%) |
| United States | −715 | −5.3 |
| Germany | 232 | 7.0 |
| United Kingdom | −94 | −3.4 |
| Japan | 74 | 1.7 |
| China | 349 | 8.9 |
| France | −49 | −1.9 |
| Italy | −4 | −0.2 |
| Netherlands | 66 | 8.6 |
| Canada | 27 | 2.0 |

A useful way to compare trade statistics is by looking at a country's trade statistics relative to its GDP. This table, which contains the same countries as in Table 9.1, lists the dollar value of the trade surpluses or deficits for these countries and the percentage of their GDPs that these figures represent. By either measure, the U.S. trade deficit is the largest at over $700 billion, which is a little over 5 percent of GDP. Although they differ in absolute size, the trade surpluses for Germany and the Netherlands are comparable when measured relative to their GDPs. As a percent of GDP, China's surplus is the largest of any other country listed.

**Source:** *The Economist Pocket World in Figures* (2010). Data are for 2007.

the Netherlands are comparable, even though their dollar figures are not. If you look at the surpluses and deficits in these terms, China's surplus is far and away the largest of any other country listed. But is it even the largest in the world? As a percent of its GDP, Singapore had a trade surplus that was 32 percent of its GDP. On the other end of the scale, Bulgaria's trade deficit amounted to over 22 percent of its GDP.

Before leaving this discussion, it is useful to note that the figures change over time. The figures reported in Tables 9.1 and 9.2 are for a specific year, in this case, 2007. If we had chosen a different year, we might get a different result. For example, in 2004, Japan's trade surplus was larger than China's. Why the change? Some have argued that China unfairly manipulates its currency to be undervalued in the world market (we'll touch on this later in the chapter), which makes Chinese goods less expensive to foreign buyers and makes foreign goods more expensive to Chinese consumers. Such actions artificially increase exports and decrease imports. More importantly, can such actions be sustained? Some argue that this policy harms residents of China by effectively increasing the price of goods they may want to purchase. Other governments, including the government of Japan, are engaged in ongoing negotiations to try to convince the Chinese government to alter the value of its currency.[1]

Trade deficits also are ready fuel for debates over other types of government policies. This is especially true during bad economic times. When workers are being laid off due to a slowing economy, political pundits and social commentators invariably bring up a nation's trade numbers. If there is a trade deficit, these people argue that the country's jobs are going overseas and something should be done to stop it. One

· · · · · · ·

[1]Paul Krugman, "China, Japan, America." *New York Times*, September 13, 2010. A20.

way to stem the tide of trade is for you to stop buying foreign-produced goods—that is, to buy American. Most of us do not want to buy only American goods, however. We enjoy buying relatively inexpensive electronics (how many people do you know who *do not* own a cell phone?), wearing the latest fashions, or driving a hybrid car, even if they aren't produced in the United States. Also, some products, such as certain raw materials, simply don't exist in abundance in the United States. There aren't many diamond mines in the United States, for example.

Many governments enact trade regulations in an effort to either limit or completely exclude foreign competition. This anticompetitive behavior creates seemingly continuous trade negotiations between countries. It's also why you read about complaints being brought before the World Trade Organization (WTO) and other international trade organizations. In these cases, the claim usually is made that one country is unfairly excluding foreign imports. A few years ago, the United States filed a complaint with the WTO that subsidies paid by European governments to the manufacturers of the Airbus led to unfair competition with rival airplane manufacturer, Boeing. Of course, the European Union immediately filed a counter-complaint, charging that the United States unfairly subsidized Boeing.[2]

Multinational bodies such as the WTO are, in fact, used by countries in an effort to level the playing field and create as free a flow of goods and services as possible. This is what economists have in mind when they extol the benefits of "free trade." However, even when trade flows freely between countries, not everyone benefits equally. *You* might be better off if you can buy a cheap cell phone from a Chinese-based company, but the employee at a U.S. cell-phone-making company such as Motorola might not be better off if she loses her job as a result.

From this brief introduction, you can see that international trade is big business. But why do some countries seem to specialize in producing some goods and not others? In some instances, the answer is simple: unless global warming severely shifts the world's climate, Canada will never become a major exporter of bananas. Figuring out why one country becomes "the" producer of a good is just like answering the question of why some individuals specialize in producing medical care and others specialize in accounting services. In both cases, the answer is that whoever has the comparative advantage becomes the producer.

## 9.2 Why Is There Trade between Countries? Comparative Advantage

You learned in the introductory chapters of this book that a voluntary exchange (meaning no coercion) benefits both parties of a trade. International trade really just amounts to voluntary exchanges between individuals made across international boundaries: the basic microeconomic concept of mutual gain still holds. Whether we are talking about international or household exchange, it is still necessary to first determine who will engage in which productive activity. Only after something is produced, whether it is steel or housekeeping, can it be traded.

Recall from Chapter 2 the basic idea of comparative advantage and how we used it to decide the distribution of work in a household. Now we can take that same idea and use it to understand why *nations* trade. The idea of comparative advantage applies

· · · · · · ·

[2]Michael Harrison, "WTO Complaints Bring Airbus Trade War a Step Nearer." *The (London) Independent*, October 7, 2007. Another example is China's complaint that the United States engaged in practices that imposed unfair measures on Chinese steel pipe, tires, and sacks.

to countries as well. Suppose we want to predict in which countries diamonds and coffee should be produced? To make the example tractable, we will focus on trade between two countries, which is called *bilateral* trade. We can do this using a production possibilities frontier (PPF) for each country. Recall that a PPF shows the amount of two products an economy can produce when it's efficiently using all of its resources—that is, its technology, labor, natural resources, and so on. We limit the PPF to two goods because we want to use a two-dimensional diagram. The PPF gives us a snapshot of how much of the two goods a country can produce right now given the amount of productive resources they have. With all of the preliminaries out of the way, let's see if we can explain why Brazil and Russia would trade coffee and diamonds.

Brazil is the world's leading producer of coffee. Russia is the world's leading producer of diamonds. **Figure 9.1** shows the PPFs for coffee production and diamond production for Brazil and for Russia, respectively. In Figure 9.1, we assigned fictitious production values for the sake of illustration.

Let point B represent the current level of production of diamonds and coffee by both countries. Total "world" production of coffee is 40 million units, equal to 20 million units of coffee being produced by both countries. At this point, there are 100 million units of diamonds being mined, the sum of diamond production in Brazil and Russia. Could overall world production of these two goods be improved? Could the two countries alter their current production levels to increase the global output of both coffee and diamonds? The answer is yes, and it all has to do with deciding which country has the comparative advantage in coffee production, and which has the comparative advantage in diamond production.

Looking at the Russian PPF, if Russia's coffee growers decrease their production by 10 million units (moving from 20 to 10 million) and move these resources to

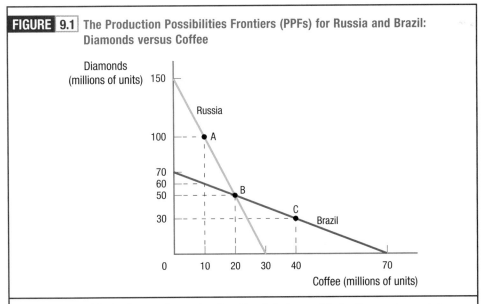

**FIGURE 9.1** The Production Possibilities Frontiers (PPFs) for Russia and Brazil: Diamonds versus Coffee

Brazil is the world's leading producer of coffee. Russia is the world's leading producer of diamonds. The countries' PPFs for coffee and diamonds are based on fictitious production values. It would be better for Russia to specialize in producing diamonds and for Brazil to specialize in producing coffee. If the two countries were to do so and engage in trade, the average Brazilian and Russian would be economically better off.

diamond production, this will increase Russia's diamond production by 50 million units (from 50 to 100 million). If Brazil reduces its coffee production by 10 million units (moving from 20 to 10 million) and shifts these freed-up resources to diamond production, diamond production in Brazil would increase by only 10 million units (from 50 to 60 million). This comparison suggests that it is more advantageous, in an opportunity-cost sense, for Russia to specialize in producing diamonds and for Brazil to specialize in producing coffee. As you know, reversing these changes yields the same conclusion. If Russia reduces its diamond production by 50 units, it gets only 10 more units of coffee. If Brazil reduces its diamond production by 10 units, it gets 10 more units of coffee production. That is, Brazil gets more coffee by giving up less diamond production. If productive resources in the countries are reallocated according to their comparative advantage, the total, combined production of both goods will increase.

The point of trade is that such a reallocation of resources within a country can make everyone—Brazilians and Russians—better off if they change production patterns and then trade. To see this, instead of each country producing at point B, Russia could devote more productive resources to mining diamonds so that it produces the amount that corresponds to point A. Sticking with its comparative advantage, Brazil should specialize in coffee production so that it produces the amount of coffee that corresponds to point C. If Brazil reduces its diamond production from 50 to 30 million units, its PPF shows that it now can increase coffee production from 20 to 40 million units of coffee. With Russia moving to point A on its PPF, this means that there is now a total production of 50 million units of coffee (40 million from Brazil and 10 million from Russia) and 130 million units of diamonds (100 million from Russia and 30 million from Brazil). By producing the good for which the country has the comparative advantage, the total output of coffee and diamonds produced by the two countries increases.

Specialization thus increases the total basket of goods—coffee and diamonds—that are available for consumers to buy. Think of it this way: specialization leads to an increase in world GDP, and by trading this larger amount of output, citizens in both countries can be made better off than before specialization and trade took place.

Would this outcome change if one country experienced an increase in productivity? For example, would the outcome change if productive resources in Brazil suddenly are able to produce more in the same amount of time? We can answer that question by looking at the production numbers for Russia and Brazil in **Table 9.3**. In the original state, Russia can produce 100 units of diamonds or 10 units of coffee; Brazil produces 40 units of diamonds or 30 units of coffee. The opportunity cost for each country's production decision also is reported. As you can see, because the opportunity cost of producing coffee (in terms of lost diamond production) is higher in Russia than in Brazil, Russia has the comparative advantage in diamond production. Brazil has the comparative advantage in coffee production.

Now suppose that Brazil becomes more productive. As shown in the table, Brazil can now produce twice as many diamonds and twice as much coffee as before. Does this change the comparative advantage? The answer is no. As you can see, after the change in productivity, the opportunity cost of producing diamonds or coffee in Brazil hasn't changed: even though Brazil can produce twice as much of each good as before, the *opportunity cost* of producing each one has not changed. Because opportunity cost determines comparative advantage, even if Brazil becomes more productive, both countries will specialize in producing that good for which their opportunity cost is lower. Russia still produces diamonds; Brazil still produces coffee. Now the question is, what are they going to do with these extra goods?

| Table **9.3** | Comparative Advantage and a Change in Productivity |

Before Brazil's productivity change:

| | Russia | | Brazil | |
|---|---|---|---|---|
| | Diamonds | Coffee | Diamonds | Coffee |
| Output (units) | 100 | 10 | 40 | 30 |
| Opportunity Cost | 1/10 coffee | 10 diamonds | .75 coffee | 1 1/3 diamonds |

After Brazil's productivity change:

| | Diamonds | Coffee | Diamonds | Coffee |
|---|---|---|---|---|
| Output | 100 | 10 | 80 | 60 |
| Opportunity Cost | 1/10 coffee | 10 diamonds | .75 coffee | 1 1/3 diamonds |

This table shows hypothetical production numbers for two countries: Russia and Brazil. Before any change in productivity, Russia can produce 100 units of diamonds or 10 units of coffee; Brazil can produce 40 units of diamonds or 30 units of coffee. The opportunity cost for each country's production decision indicates that because the opportunity cost of producing coffee (in terms of lost diamond production) is higher in Russia than in Brazil, Russia has the comparative advantage in diamond production. Brazil has the comparative advantage in coffee production.

## How Specialization Leads to Exports

When a country specializes in the production of one good, its production likely will exceed its domestic consumption. In other words, it produces more than its own residents want to consume. Otherwise, there may be no desire to alter production toward the country's comparative advantage. Specialization thus leads to exports. In 2003, for example, Brazil produced a total of 53.6 million bags of coffee beans. (Each bag weighs 60 kilograms, or about 132 pounds.) Of this, it exported 29.4 million bags to other markets. This implies that roughly 24.2 million bags of coffee were consumed in Brazil. In that same year, Russia produced 33 billion carats of diamonds, most of which were exported to Belgium, Great Britain, and Israel. Why Belgium, Great Britain, and Israel? As it turns out, they are the leading countries in which the raw diamonds are cut into the finished products available in jewelry stores throughout the world.[3] The rest are used for industrial purposes, such as making drill bits.

Knowing about comparative advantage helps you understand why it isn't always in a country's best economic interest to try and produce everything it needs. Even if one country *could* produce goods more effectively than another (the idea of absolute advantage), it still is in that country's best interest to find the good for which it has the comparative advantage and to specialize in producing that good. Increased production through specialization leads to exchange, whether it is between a couple in their household, or between producers and consumers living in different countries. The underlying economics are the same.

## Factors Affecting Comparative Advantage

A country's comparative advantage is affected by factors that affect its PPF. For example, a country with abundant natural resources might have a comparative

· · · · · · ·

[3]Following are the sources for these data: for Brazilian coffee production, USDA; for Russian diamond production, "Russia Conquers the Diamond Market with Striking Export Volumes." *Pravda*, December 23, 2004.

advantage over other countries when it comes to producing products that require those resources. Productivity differences across countries also affect their relative opportunity costs: how specialized a country's labor force is and the knowledge of its workers, as well as the machinery available for them to use, all can have an effect on a country's production.

Other factors affect a country's production as well. For example, when we looked at the production of Russia and Brazil, we assumed that producers in each country were willing to cut back their production in one area to increase their production in another. As you know, this won't always occur. Political lobbyists paid to protect the coffee producers in Russia or the diamond miners in Brazil may thwart an economically beneficial outcome.

Intervention by a country's government can also affect how firms allocate production. As we discussed in Chapter 4, in 2002, President George W. Bush imposed tariffs, essentially a tax on imported goods, on various types of imported steel. This action increased the price that U.S. companies had to pay for foreign steel. U.S. steel producers argued that tariffs were justified because the governments of foreign steel producers were unfairly subsidizing the production of steel in their countries. As a result, foreign steel producers were able to sell steel at lower prices than U.S. steel producers could. The tariff was supposed to level the playing field. The problem was that although the tariffs raised the prices at which U.S. steel producers could sell their products, it also increased the cost that U.S. firms that use steel had to pay.

In the end, we must ask ourselves whether the industry being protected by such intervention has a comparative advantage relative to other steel-producing companies around the world. In the president's 2003 message ending the tariffs, it seems that he recognized that the U.S. steel producers were less productive than their foreign competitors.[4] If the U.S. steel industry does not have the comparative advantage, politics aside, it is economically more efficient for foreign producers to specialize in the production of steel and for U.S. buyers to import it.

---

**ECONOMIC FALLACY**    "BUY AMERICAN" campaigns improve the economic well-being of everyone in the United States.

**False.** During the downturn of 2007–2009, many car dealerships ran advertisements that called for you to do your patriotic duty and buy American-made cars instead of imports. Of course, parts for many American cars are produced elsewhere, so even if you buy a Chevy or a Ford, it may not be wholly made in America. And that BMW could have been produced in South Carolina. What does economics tell you about this idea of buying locally? You know from comparative advantage that even though local jobs are on the line, the local industry might not be as efficient in producing that good compared with its competitor in another country. On a very personal level, would you continue to frequent a restaurant that has rude waiters and bad food just because it's local? Although the scale of the outcome is different, the underlying economics are the same when it comes to buying a car.

---

· · · · · · ·

[4]See "President's Statement on Steel," accessed at www.whitehouse.gov/news/releases, December 4, 2003.

## 9.3 World Trade and Foreign Exchange Rates

Specialization and trade generally lead to superior outcomes. Trade usually leads to more goods being produced, traded, and consumed, thereby making people better off. Of course, to facilitate exchanges around the world, buyers and sellers have to exchange different currencies.

You are more likely to have visited another country than your grandparents did at the same age. Perhaps you have taken a vacation to Mexico's beaches, studied abroad, or traveled overseas on a business trip. Regardless of where you went and why, to purchase items abroad, you had to exchange your dollars for the currency of the country you were visiting. The rate at which your money was exchanged for another currency is called the **foreign exchange rate**.

> **FOREIGN EXCHANGE RATE** The price of one currency in terms of another currency.

> **EXAMPLE** You cross the border into Canada and want to buy a sofa. The seller will not take U.S. dollars and demands Canadian dollars. You will need to exchange your U.S. dollars for Canadian dollars to buy the sofa. The exchange rate is how many Canadian dollars you get for each U.S. dollar.[5]

Because it gets so much attention, let's focus on the exchange rate between the U.S. dollar and the euro. In August 2008, it took about US$1.46 to "buy" €1. If you were used to paying a dollar for a candy bar, the same candy bar would cost you the equivalent of US$1.46 if you had purchased it in Europe. A few months later, in March 2009, it took US$1.27 to buy €1. These figures are the dollar–euro exchange rate. The fact that in August the euro was more expensive than in March means that the candy bar purchased in Europe cost less in March than in August. As you can imagine, changes in the dollar-equivalent prices will affect your decision to buy candy bars in Europe or purchase them someplace else.

### Fluctuations in Foreign Exchange Rates

Foreign exchange rates fluctuate over time, as **Figure 9.2** shows. As you can see, €1 didn't always exchange for US$1.46 or US$1.27. When the euro first became the currency of Europe, it took about US$1.20 to acquire €1. In the first few years of its existence, the rate fell to about US$0.80 dollars to the euro. Since then, however, the value of the euro relative to the dollar has increased. In that sense, the euro has **appreciated** in value relative to the dollar. This means that it took more dollars to buy euros. If the euro appreciated relative to the dollar, then it must be true that the dollar has **depreciated** in value relative to the euro. (Remember, when it comes to exchange rates, another rate is always the inverse.)

> **FOREIGN EXCHANGE RATE APPRECIATION** An increase in the foreign exchange value of a currency.

> **EXAMPLE** Yesterday it took US$1 to buy C$1 (Canada). Today, it takes US$2 to buy C$1. Overnight, the Canadian dollar appreciated relative to the U.S. dollar.

· · · · · · ·

[5]To circumvent this, why not just use your credit card? Credit card companies make the conversion from one currency to dollars and charge you the U.S. dollar equivalent price. You still have to make the exchange-rate conversion.

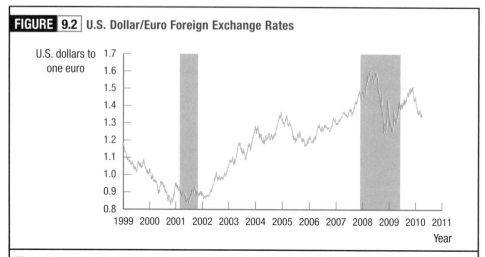

**FIGURE 9.2** U.S. Dollar/Euro Foreign Exchange Rates

The exchange rate between the dollar and the euro is shown in this graph. The exchange rate fluctuates over time. From 2002 through 2008, the euro generally appreciated relative to the dollar, although this trend was punctuated by both large and small reversals. After early 2008, the euro depreciated significantly against the dollar.

*Source:* Federal Reserve Bank of St. Louis

**FOREIGN EXCHANGE RATE DEPRECIATION** A decrease in the foreign exchange value of a currency.

**EXAMPLE** Yesterday it took US$1 to buy C$1. Today, it takes US$2 to buy C$1. Overnight, the U.S. dollar depreciated relative to the Canadian dollar.

Looking at Figure 9.2, you can see that the exchange rate between the dollar and the euro is by no means fixed at any one particular value over time. There are stretches of time, for example, 2002–2008, that the euro appreciated relative to the dollar. This trend was punctuated by both large and small reversals. Most recently, the euro depreciated significantly against the dollar as the worldwide recession took hold. Why exchange rates vary over time is a subject we will deal with shortly.

Do exchange rates differ across countries? There are as many exchange rates as there are countries with sovereign currencies. To give you a glimpse of how diverse they are, **Table 9.4** shows the exchange rates between the dollar and the currencies of some major economies as of early 2010. The exchange rates are reported two ways. The second column is how many U.S. dollars it takes to purchase one unit of the foreign currency. The third column shows how much of the foreign currency is needed to purchase one U.S. dollar. As you can see, in only a few instances does it take more than a dollar to purchase the other currency. Except for the British pound and the euro, at least in April 2010, the other currencies can be purchased for less than a dollar, sometimes much less, as is the case for the Japanese yen and the Mexican peso. In contrast—remember that there are always two rates at which two currencies exchange—the third column shows that, in most instances, it takes many units of the other currency to purchase a dollar. This conversion is calculated as the inverse of the dollar-per-currency value found in the second column. For example, if the dollar–euro exchange rate is $1.346, then the euro–dollar exchange rate is 0.743 (= 1/1.346).

| Table **9.4** Select Foreign Exchange Rates: April 10, 2010 | | |
|---|---|---|
| Foreign Currency | U.S. Dollars Needed to Purchase One Unit of Foreign Currency | Foreign Currency Needed to Purchase One U.S. Dollar |
| Euro | 1.346 | 0.743 |
| British Pound | 1.537 | 0.651 |
| Japanese Yen | 0.011 | 90.910 |
| Chinese Renminbi | 0.146 | 6.849 |
| Mexican Peso | 0.082 | 12.195 |
| Canadian Dollar | 0.995 | 1.005 |

The table shows the actual exchange rates between the U.S. dollar and the currencies of some major economies as of early April, 2010. The exchange rates are reported in two ways: (1) in terms of how many U.S. dollars it takes to purchase one unit of foreign currency, as the second column shows, and (2) in terms of how much of the foreign currency is needed to purchase one U.S. dollar, as the third column shows. There are always two rates at which two currencies exchange. For example, if the dollar–euro exchange rate is US$1.346, then the euro–dollar exchange rate is €0.743 (1/1.346). In April 2010, most of the currencies listed could be purchased for less than US$1. The exceptions are the euro and the British pound.

If this is confusing, try thinking of it this way: when you buy a can of soda from a street vendor, you pay $1. The can of soda-to-dollar "exchange rate" is one for one. The dollar price of one soda is 1, and the soda price of a dollar is, in terms of cans, also 1. What if next week, you can buy two sodas for $1? Now the dollar price for a can of soda is $0.50. In this case, the dollar appreciated relative to the soda, meaning that it takes fewer dollars to buy one can of soda. At the same time, the soda depreciated relative to the dollar, so the soda price of a dollar has increased to 2.

## The Foreign Exchange Market

You are visiting the Swatch store on Times Square in New York City and decide to buy yet another of the Swiss-made watches for your collection. When you buy the watch, you pay for it with U.S. dollars. So where does the need for foreign currency come into play? Even though you pay for your watch using dollars, Swatch AG, the manufacturer of the watches, must pay its employees back in Switzerland not in U.S. dollars, but in Swiss francs. This means that the demand for foreign-made goods—your desire to have another Swatch watch—creates a need for Swiss francs. And one way the company can acquire Swiss francs is by selling those dollars that you exchanged for the watch. This purchase and sale of foreign currencies takes place in the **foreign exchange market**.

**FOREIGN EXCHANGE MARKET** The international market in which foreign currencies are traded.

The foreign exchange market is bigger than the stock and bond markets. The need for foreign currencies is so vast that the trading volume in this market averages about $2 trillion *every day*. The foreign exchange market is a well-developed market where buyers and sellers of currencies (traders) come together, and the exchange rates we have been talking about get determined. But these traders do not meet at any one particular place: foreign exchange traders are located throughout the world and linked together electronically. The foreign exchange market, sometimes referred to as the *forex market*, is an example of an over-the-counter market. This means that the market is decentralized so traders can choose to place their orders with a number of dealers instead of one central dealer. This decentralization allows for much more price competition and increases the speed with which changes in exchange rates take place.

Why has the dollar–euro exchange rate fluctuated over time? Explaining movement in exchange rates, like any other price, can be done using demand and supply. This time, instead of trying to explain changes in the dollar price for iPods or Harley-Davidson motorcycles, we use demand and supply to explain changes in the market price—the exchange rate—of one currency in terms of another.

Let's illustrate the usefulness of the demand-and-supply model by focusing on the demand and supply for euros. **Figure 9.3** shows the demand and supply curves for euros. The equilibrium, or market-clearing exchange rate, labeled $FX_e$, is expressed in terms of dollars per euro. The vertical axis tells us how many dollars it takes to purchase one euro. The horizontal axis is the quantity of euros in the foreign exchange market. As you can see, the intersection of the demand for and supply of euros determines the equilibrium exchange rate and the equilibrium quantity in the market.

For illustration, suppose that only U.S. residents are buying goods produced in the euro area. Why does the demand curve (D) have the familiar downward slope? This reflects the fact that to purchase goods produced in the euro area, U.S. buyers (importers) must first acquire euros. If the exchange rate increases—it takes more dollars to buy a euro—it means that import prices are increasing, too. These higher import prices further imply that U.S. consumers will purchase fewer European goods, which, in turn, reduces the quantity of euros demanded by importers.

The upward slope of the supply curve has a similar explanation. The supply of euros reflects European importers' need for dollars to buy U.S. goods. The upward-sloping supply arises because if the exchange rate rises—it takes more dollars to buy a euro—then each euro buys more dollars. U.S. goods are thus relatively cheaper than

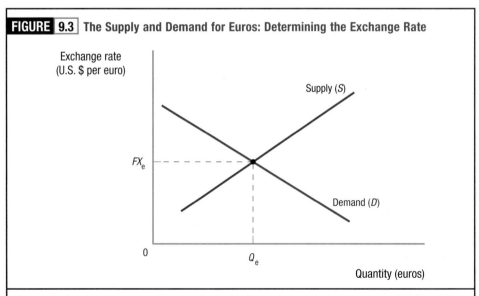

**FIGURE 9.3** The Supply and Demand for Euros: Determining the Exchange Rate

The demand and supply curves for euros in the foreign exchange market are shown in this graph. The price is expressed in dollars per euro; the quantity is expressed as euros. The intersection of demand and supply determines the equilibrium exchange rate ($FX_e$) and the equilibrium quantity ($Q_e$) in the market. The foreign exchange market matches up the demand for euros by Americans who want to purchase products produced in the euro area with the supply of euros in the world.

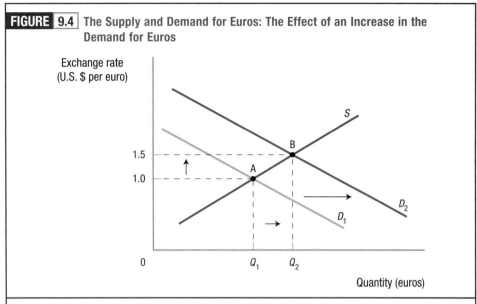

**FIGURE 9.4** The Supply and Demand for Euros: The Effect of an Increase in the Demand for Euros

An increase in the demand for euros is shown by a rightward shift in the demand curve. At the original market-clearing exchange rate (US$1.0), the quantity demanded of euros now exceeds the quantity supplied. This leads to an increase (an appreciation) in the exchange rate. The exchange rate of euros—in terms of dollars—increases from US$1 to US$1.50. The shift in the demand curve stems from an increase in demand for European goods by U.S. consumers.

European goods. European importers want to acquire dollars and can do so only by increasing the quantity of euros in the market.

Suppose the demand for euros increases as shown by a rightward shift in the demand curve in **Figure 9.4**. This increase in demand, from $D_1$ to $D_2$, eventually leads to a higher price for, or an appreciation of, the euro. After the increase in demand, there is an excess demand for euros at the initial exchange rate. The fact that the quantity demanded of euros exceeds the quantity supplied at the original exchange rate leads to an increase in the exchange rate. The exchange rate of euros—in terms of dollars—increases from US$1 to US$1.50 as we slide up the supply curve from point A to point B. It is important to note that whether we are talking about currencies, shoes, or concert tickets, an increase in the demand for an item—holding the supply constant—usually results in an increase in the equilibrium price.

Why would the demand curve shift outward from $D_1$ to $D_2$? As we just mentioned, the increase in demand for euros comes from an increase in the demand for European goods by U.S. consumers. Importers can meet this increased demand only by acquiring more euros to buy the European goods, and this causes the demand curve for euros to shift.

What causes the exchange rate to change from a given equilibrium? Any factor that causes the demand or the supply curve of the currency to shift will bring about a change in the equilibrium exchange rate. Suppose that the United States experiences an economic downturn: unemployment increases, and incomes fall. Economic downturns often are associated with reductions in the demand for imported goods. The decline in imports leads to a leftward shift in the demand for euros, which reverses the story we just told.

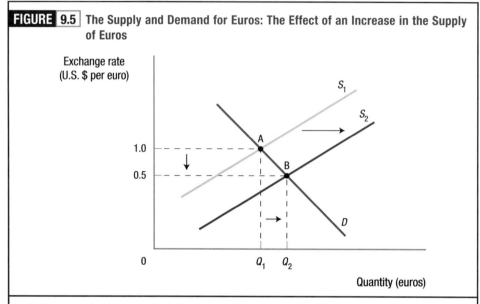

**FIGURE 9.5** The Supply and Demand for Euros: The Effect of an Increase in the Supply of Euros

If the European Central Bank (ECB) increases the number of euros in circulation, this results in a rightward shift in the supply curve of euros. At the original equilibrium exchange rate (US$1.0), the quantity supplied of euros is greater than the quantity demanded. This surplus puts downward pressure on the exchange rate. The decline in the market-clearing foreign exchange value of the euro from US$1.0 to US$0.5 indicates that the increase in the supply of euros, all else the same, leads to a depreciation in the euro relative to the dollar.

Let's think about effects coming from the supply side of the exchange market. What if the European Central Bank (ECB) decides to increase the number of euros in circulation? This is shown in **Figure 9.5** as a rightward shift in the supply curve of euros from $S_1$ to $S_2$. When the supply curve has shifted, the exchange market is first characterized by an excess supply of euros. That is, at the original equilibrium, the quantity supplied of euros is greater than the quantity demanded. As in most markets, an excess supply of something puts downward pressure on its price. In the exchange market, this means that the exchange rate will fall from 1.0 to 0.5 as we slide down the demand curve, from point A to point B. In this situation, the euro has depreciated relative to the dollar.

The foreign exchange market is made up of many different participants. As we have explained, corporations trade currencies in the foreign exchange market. For example, Caterpillar, whose home office is in Illinois, gets paid in dollars for the earth-moving equipment it sells to companies in other countries. Those foreign companies must acquire dollars to pay for the equipment. Similarly, U.S. importers of foreign goods must exchange their dollars for the foreign currency they need to pay for those foreign-made goods. Companies also trade currencies as a way to protect against future changes in exchange rates that can adversely affect the prices they pay for products and, therefore, their profits.

Similarly, investors who want to buy foreign financial assets need foreign currencies. For instance, suppose a U.S. investor can earn a better return on her investment if she buys British securities instead of U.S. securities. This might be the case, for example, if British interest rates are higher than those in the United States. In this instance, higher British interest rates are likely to increase the demand for pounds as investors want to convert their dollars into pounds.

Governments around the world also are active traders in the foreign exchange market. When a central bank trades in the market, it often does so to help regulate the exchange value of its country's currency—to keep it from drastically depreciating or appreciating. This can help the central bank maintain its country's money supply. While exchange rates do not play a major role in setting monetary policy in the United States, this is not true of many other countries. (We'll have more to say about the role of monetary policy and the effects on exchange rates in Chapter 17.) The bottom line in all of this is that each of these types of transactions requires the use of different currencies. This demand for and supply of foreign currency is what makes the foreign exchange market tick.

## Purchasing Power Parity and Foreign Exchange Rates

We have used demand and supply to find the equilibrium exchange rate, at least in theory. Is there any way to actually measure what that rate might be? That is, can we tell if the exchange rate is out of line with the equilibrium that we might expect based on the underlying fundamentals that determine the demand for and supply of a currency? Although it is not scientific, one approach, developed by the magazine *The Economist*, is the Big Mac index.

The idea behind the Big Mac index is that under some very strict conditions, the exchange rate should adjust to equalize the price of an identical good—in this case, McDonald's Big Mac sandwich—across countries. Why use the Big Mac? Mainly because of its commonality across markets. It turns out that the ingredients in making the sandwich are very uniform, regardless of whether it is bought in Orlando, Florida, or London, England.

The principle being illustrated using the Big Mac index is known as **purchasing power parity (PPP)**.

> **PURCHASING POWER PARITY (PPP)** A way to compare the relative purchasing power of currencies by comparing the amount of each needed to buy a common bundle of goods and services.

> **EXAMPLE** A wool topcoat costs US$300. The same topcoat costs C$200 (Canadian). All else the same, if PPP holds, the exchange rate should be US$1.50 per C$1. If the current exchange rate is US$1.50 per C$1, then a topcoat selling for US$300 in the United States should be selling for C$200.

The PPP principle basically says that a good will trade for the same price when that price is expressed in a common currency. Setting aside complicating (though important) real-world factors such as transportation costs, taxes, and so on, if the PPP principle holds, then the price of a Big Mac in the United States should equal the price of a Big Mac in Japan after we've adjusted for the exchange rate. Consequently, if $P_j$ is the Japanese price of a Big Mac, and $P_{US}$ is the U.S. price of a Big Mac, then $P_j/P_{US}$ should equal the foreign exchange rate in terms of yen per dollar. If the actual exchange rate is higher, this suggests that the dollar is overvalued against the yen. If it is lower, then the dollar is undervalued against the yen.

Let's use some real numbers to see if PPP actually works. In July 2008, the average price of a Big Mac in the United States was around US$3.57. This U.S. price is measured as the average price of a Big Mac in New York, Chicago, Atlanta, and San Francisco. In that same month, the comparable price of a Big Mac in Japan was ¥280. To equalize the two prices, according to PPP, the exchange rate should have been ¥78.4 per US$1. That exchange rate is found by dividing the yen price of the Big Mac (¥280) by the U.S.

price ($3.57). The actual exchange rate at the time, however, was ¥106.8 per US$1. Because the actual exchange rate was higher than that suggested by the Big Mac index, the economic principles underlying PPP suggest that the dollar was overvalued against the yen. According to PPP, the dollar should have depreciated against the yen. Did it? Although you should not place too much weight on the predictions of the Big Mac index, the yen–dollar exchange rate did in fact fall to about 100 by November 2008.

**Table 9.5** gives you another way of thinking about how to use the Big Mac index. Listed in the table are a number of countries and what a Big Mac costs in dollar terms. You can see that in the United States, in October 2010, the average price of a Big Mac was US$3.71. In Switzerland, local consumers paid the equivalent of US$6.81 for their Big Mac. In other words, the Swiss franc was overvalued relative to the dollar. If not, then the two prices would be equal when measured in dollars. At the other end of the valuation spectrum, you can see that a Big Mac sandwich in China costs only the equivalent of US$2.18. This reflects the fact that the Chinese currency was undervalued relative to the dollar.

Just how big were the overvaluations and undervaluations based on the Big Mac index? **Figure 9.6** shows in percentage terms just how big the overvaluations

| Table 9.5 | Big Mac Prices in Selected Countries Stated in U.S. Dollars |
|---|---|
| **Country** | **Big Mac Price ($)** |
| Switzerland | 6.81 |
| Brazil | 5.26 |
| Euro Area | 4.79[1] |
| Canada | 4.18 |
| Japan | 3.91 |
| United States | 3.71[2] |
| Britain | 3.68 |
| Singapore | 3.46 |
| South Korea | 3.03 |
| South Africa | 2.79 |
| Mexico | 2.58 |
| Thailand | 2.44 |
| Russia | 2.39 |
| Malaysia | 2.25 |
| China | 2.18[3] |

[1]Weighted average of member countries
[2]Average of four cities
[3]Average of two cities

This table lists the price of a Big Mac sandwich, stated in equivalent dollar terms, for a sample of countries. The price is found by multiplying the local price of a Big Mac by the country's exchange rate with the dollar. Prices above the U.S. price ($3.71) indicate that the country's currency is overvalued relative to the dollar. According to the PPP theory, this means that the currency should depreciate in the future. Prices below the U.S. price indicate that the country's currency is undervalued relative to the dollar and should appreciate in the future if PPP holds.

**Source:** *The Economist* (October 16, 2010)

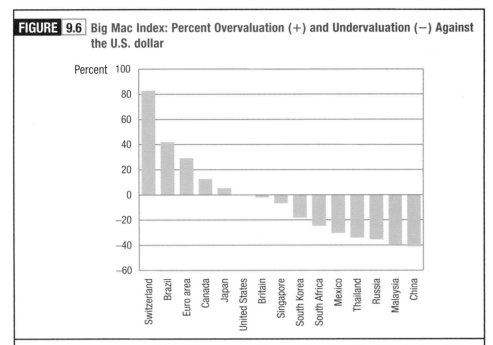

**FIGURE 9.6** Big Mac Index: Percent Overvaluation (+) and Undervaluation (−) Against the U.S. dollar

This figure uses the prices in Table 9.5 to measure the overvaluation and undervaluation of the different currencies. The index is calculated by dividing each country's dollar-equivalent Big Mac price by US$3.71 (the price in the United States), subtracting 1.0, and multiplying the resulting number by 100. This shows that the Swiss franc is overvalued relative to the dollar by about 80 percent. The Chinese renminbi, on the other hand, is undervalued by about 40 percent. According to PPP theory, the exchange rate of the overvalued currencies should decline, and the exchange rate of the undervalued currencies should rise.

*Source: The Economist* (October 16, 2010)

and undervaluations were in October 2010. The percent deviation from parity is calculated by dividing each country's dollar-equivalent Big Mac price by $3.71 (the price in the United States), subtracting 1.0, and multiplying the resulting number by 100. Measured in this fashion, the Swiss franc was about 80 percent overvalued relative to the dollar, and the Chinese renminbi was about 40 percent undervalued. Although we seldom find that dollar-equivalent prices hold at points in time, application of PPP does suggest whether exchange values of currencies should depreciate or appreciate over time.

You might think that the Big Mac index is too simple to take seriously. Nonetheless, researchers have undertaken studies to see if it really works as a predictor of future exchange-rate movements. One such study measured the average deviation of the dollar exchange rate, based on the Big Mac, to a broad set of other currencies. It then compared this average deviation with the behavior of the dollar's value in the foreign exchange market over time. The study found that actual exchange rates, in general, really do move over time in accordance with the predictions of the Big Mac index.[6] Something to chew on?

· · · · · · ·

[6]Michael Pakko and Patricia Pollard, "Burgernomics: A Big Mac Guide to Purchasing Power Parity." Federal Reserve Bank of St. Louis *Review* (November/December 2003).

## 9.4 Globalization

During the past few decades, there seems to have been a growing unease about the rapid pace at which international trade and the interconnectedness of financial markets has proceeded. However, as you will see in Chapter 11, the economic growth of nations often is associated with their openness, or willingness, to trade with other countries. Arguably, trading with individuals in other countries benefits everyone if it is based on the underlying principles of comparative advantage. Right?

Not quite. Although economies benefit as a whole from free trade, it isn't costless to some groups in the economy. For example, after new trade routes opened from Europe to the East as the Middle Ages came to a close, merchants in Europe faced new competition from foreign suppliers. Think of the spice merchants in Venice who had to contend with new products such as nutmeg and cinnamon drawing away their customers. Although consumers were made better off—they had access to a greater number of spices and cheaper spices—some vendors, those who were not able to acquire the new spices, were made worse off.

Globalization also occurs because of the advance of knowledge. New trade routes in the 1300s were made possible by technological advances in navigation and ship construction. Today, tech help once provided by your local computer store is now a mouse click that just as easily links you to a technician in India or in Indiana. The popular term **outsourcing** describes this shift in responsibility for certain jobs. For example, manufacturing firms or your university may outsource the provision of cafeteria services to a company that specializes in this work. Sometimes outsourcing can send jobs abroad. When this occurs, it is called **offshoring**. Offshoring occurs when jobs once done here are being done elsewhere. They are outsourced to a different country. But is offshoring, other than the description, any different if your job in Idaho is being sent to Florida? Other than the fact that it stays in the United States, you still lose your job unless you are willing to move. The economic effects on the local economy of outsourcing your job to another state are the same as outsourcing your job to another country.

> **OUTSOURCING/OFFSHORING** The act of shifting employment to another provider or to another location; the terms are usually used to refer to sending jobs to another country.

> **EXAMPLE** Many companies now hire catering services to manage cafeterias for their employees. This is *outsourcing*. U.S. software companies have located their online service centers in India. This is *offshoring* by a U.S. firm. BASF, the German-based chemical company, employs a number of workers in Missouri and other U.S. states. This is *offshoring* to the United States by a German firm.

Outsourcing and offshoring aren't one-way streets, as they are so often portrayed. Many foreign companies have subsidiaries located throughout the United States. Why? Because they seek to lower their costs of production, reduce transportation costs for their products, and realize the gains from comparative advantage in the production of various goods. In fact, in the state of Missouri, foreign-based companies employ more than 85,000 workers. At the national level, subsidiaries of foreign companies account for over 4 percent of private-sector employment.

The bottom line is that international exchange, whether it is in auto parts, financial assets such as bonds, or knowledge, has expanded and will continue to grow as the costs of doing business over long distances fall. Seeking the low-cost supplier is now a global endeavor, not merely looking in your city or state. As technology improves, our ability to expand trade to even more nations will grow. And that expansion in trade will affect how we finance our transactions, thereby making exchange rates and their changes more important.

## WHAT YOU SHOULD HAVE LEARNED FROM CHAPTER 9

■ That even though the United States is the world's largest economy, its exports and imports are a smaller fraction of GDP than in many other countries where exports and imports usually account for a much larger share of GDP.

■ That a useful tool to explain the opportunity cost of production is the production possibilities frontier (PPF).

■ That comparative advantage, which is based on relative opportunity cost, helps explain why some countries specialize in the production of and export of certain goods and services.

■ That other factors besides comparative advantage can help explain observed production and trade. Government intervention and differences in worker productivity are two such factors.

■ That exchange rates measure the cost of one currency in terms of another.

■ That exchange rates are determined by demand and supply for currencies, where the demand and supply for currencies are based on underlying demands for other countries' goods and services.

■ That one method to compare one currency's purchasing power to another is called purchasing power parity.

■ That globalization results in a more dynamic marketplace, not only for goods and services, but also for labor and ideas.

## KEY TERMS

Foreign exchange rate, p. 243

Foreign exchange rate appreciation, p. 243

Foreign exchange rate depreciation, p. 243

Foreign exchange market, p. 245

Purchasing power parity, p. 249

Outsourcing/offshoring, p. 252

## QUESTIONS AND PROBLEMS

1. Do you consume imports?
   a) Look at the labels in your clothing. Where were these items produced?
   b) What fresh fruit is available at the grocery store today? Where were these items produced?
   c) What items would you have to give up if you only purchased goods and services produced in your local community?

2. Suppose that Cait and Emily, roommates, are planning a salsa party. They need to complete two tasks: clean the apartment and prepare the food. In 1 hour, Cait can vacuum and dust 1 room or prepare 2 cups of guacamole. In 1 hour, Emily can vacuum and dust 2 rooms or prepare 1 cup of guacamole. Given this information, answer the following questions.
   a) For Cait, what is the opportunity cost of spending an hour vacuuming?
   b) For Emily, what is the opportunity cost of spending an hour vacuuming?

c) Who has a comparative advantage in vacuuming?

d) For Cait, what is the opportunity cost of spending an hour preparing guacamole?

e) For Emily, what is the opportunity cost of spending an hour preparing guacamole?

f) Who has a comparative advantage in guacamole production?

g) Could you have answered part (f) after completing part (c)? Explain.

3. Suppose that Cait and Emily, the same two roommates, are now planning a costume party. They need to complete the same two tasks: clean the apartment and prepare the food. In 1 hour, Cait can vacuum and dust 2 rooms or prepare 4 cups of spinach dip. In 1 hour, Emily can vacuum and dust 2 rooms or prepare 1 cup of spinach dip. Given this information, answer the following questions.

a) For Cait, what is the opportunity cost of spending an hour cleaning?

b) For Emily, what is the opportunity cost of spending an hour cleaning?

c) Who has a comparative advantage in cleaning?

d) For Cait, what is the opportunity cost of spending an hour preparing spinach dip?

e) For Emily, what is the opportunity cost of spending an hour preparing spinach dip?

f) Who has a comparative advantage in spinach dip production?

g) Could you have answered (f) after completing (c)? Explain.

4. Assume that the roommates in question 3 have 3 hours to work.

a) Draw a PPF for Cait.

b) Draw a PPF for Emily.

c) Describe the shape of the curves. What does the shape represent?

d) What is the slope of Cait's PPF? How is this related to her comparative advantage?

5. Rick's parents send him a vacuum cleaner to replace the ailing model that he bought at a yard sale. With the new vacuum cleaner, Rick can double the number of rooms vacuumed per hour. Draw Rick's original and new PPF.

6. Assume that the roommates in question 3 specialize based on their comparative advantage and trade. (This means that one roommate specializes in vacuuming, while the other specializes in the production of dip.) Under this arrangement, they are able to produce more dip and clean more rooms than without trade. Even so, Emily is very unhappy with this arrangement. What might be the source of Emily's discontentment?

7. You are planning a trip to South Africa where the local currency is called the rand. You have budgeted US$100 for a hotel room in Johannesburg for when you arrive. The exchange rate is rand9.31 per US$1.

a) If the hotel prices are quoted in rand, what is the most expensive room that you can afford?

b) The exchange rate rises to rand12 per US$1. Has the dollar appreciated or depreciated relative to the rand? (Hint: How much does it cost to purchase rand1?)

8. Tadessa, who lives in Ireland, is planning a trip to the United States. He has budgeted €200 for a hotel room in New York City on the day of his arrival. The hotel prices are quoted in dollars.

a) On the day of his arrival the exchange rate is US$1.35 per €1. What is the most expensive room that he can afford?

b) The exchange rate changes to €0.95 per US$1. Has the euro appreciated or depreciated relative to the dollar? (Hint: recalculate the most expensive room that he can afford.)

9. If you are a U.S. resident, are you helped or harmed by an appreciation in the value of the dollar relative to other currencies? Explain. (Hint: think about both purchasing imports and selling exports.)

10. Look at the graph in Figure 9.2. In what years did one U.S. dollar exchange for one euro?

11. With decreases in the price of housing in Florida, many Europeans have decided to purchase vacation homes along the Gulf Coast.

    a)  What will happen to the demand for U.S. dollars?
    b)  What will happen to the exchange rate between the euro and the U.S. dollar?
    c)  Does the U.S. dollar appreciate or depreciate relative to the euro?

12. For each of the following, would the dollar appreciate or depreciate relative to the euro?

    a)  The demand for euros increases.
    b)  The demand for U.S. dollars increases.
    c)  The supply of euros decreases.
    d)  The supply of U.S. dollars increases.

13. In November 2010, the Federal Reserve, the central bank of the United States, announced that it was going to increase the amount of money in the economy by buying $600 billion of U.S. Treasury securities. At the time, many observers warned that such an action would lead to a depreciation of the dollar in foreign exchange markets.

    a)  Using the supply-and-demand model of the foreign exchange market, show why such a depreciation might occur.
    b)  Do an Internet search to see if in fact the dollar did depreciate following this announced policy change. If it did not, what factors might have caused the dollar not to depreciate?

# PART 3

## The Economics of the Long Run

**P**art 3 will explain why some economies grow and some do not. After we introduce a basic model of economic growth, we'll use it to see how factors such as labor, capital, knowledge, health, education, and population growth explain why some countries' economic standards of living have increased faster than others. Part 3 also will explain why some economies experience very high rates of inflation while others do not. To understand the rate of inflation, we look to the long-run rate of growth of the money supply, and the relationship between the two. You will learn that while the actions of monetary policy makers influence the rate of inflation over time, they cannot control short-run "wiggles" in the inflation rate.

# 10

# The Basics of Growth Economics

*"The potential for improving the lives of people by finding different ways of redistributing current production is nothing compared to the apparently limitless potential of increasing production."*

*Robert Lucas,*
*Nobel Prize Laureate (2003)*

The topic of *economic growth* deals with how and why economies grow over long periods of time, such as decades or even longer. With such a long horizon, why should you be concerned about economic growth? Shouldn't you be learning macroeconomics so you can explain what's going on in the economy over the next year or two? A key reason to study economic growth—and why we place it before your study of short-term economic fluctuations—is because it in large part determines how economically well-off people are or can become. The United States has experienced significant economic growth in the past 100 years. As a result, you are economically far better off than the average American was 100 years ago. In fact, even relatively poor Americans today are much better off than those in the middle class were in 1900.

Just look around you to understand the benefits of economic growth. Instead of having to haul wood into your house to cook dinner on a wood burning stove, you use a microwave oven. Even though you could read a book (in paper format or on your iPad), you might have several hundred cable TV channels to watch. You can also choose to have your vision surgically corrected instead of wearing thick glasses. Once considered exotic, operations such as open-heart surgery or knee-replacement surgery are now common. And, people are living much longer than they used to.

How is the lifestyle of the average American or Canadian different from someone who lives in an African, Latin American, or Asian country that has not experienced such prolonged economic growth? In the poorest of countries, many people live on less than $1 a day. For many more people in these countries, the amenities that we take for granted, such as indoor plumbing, are luxuries. And there's a dark side to some of these poor economies: infant mortality rates are high, outbreaks of disease occur often, and minorities and women tend to be more oppressed.

The noted growth economist William Easterly links the study of economic growth to the human factor this way: "The improvement in hunger, mortality, and poverty as GDP per capita [per person] rises over time motivates us on our quest for growth. Poverty is not just low GDP: it is dying babies, starving children, and oppression of women and the downtrodden."[1] For this reason alone, economic growth is one of the most important areas in economics to study and a goal for policy makers to pursue.

## 10.1 A Perspective on Economic Growth

In a couple of the preceding chapters, we compared the size of economies around the world. Our common yardstick was real GDP, the total output of an economy. When we compared real GDPs to see what the largest economies in the world are, the United States came in first. But has that always been true? **Table 10.1** ranks the world's largest economies in terms of their GDP beginning with the year 1820. We know that the data from 1820 is not nearly as reliable as the more recent figures. Even so, the table helps you see which economies grew over nearly two centuries.

There have been some notable shifts in rankings. In 1820, China and India claimed the top two spots. The United States was a comparatively small economy in 1820 and ranked next to last in the top ten. Now fast-forward to 2005—what a difference there is in the rankings! Today's top-five countries are those you would expect to see. But notice how the United States and Japan leapfrogged many countries to the top. And while China and India slipped down the list, China's recent growth is helping to push it back toward the top. Other countries, in contrast, completely fell out of the top ten.

| Table 10.1 | Top Ten Economies in 1820 and 2005 as a Percentage of World GDP | | |
|---|---|---|---|
| **1820** | **GDP (%)** | **2005** | **GDP (%)** |
| China | 28.7 | United States | 28.1 |
| India | 16.0 | Japan | 10.3 |
| France | 5.4 | Germany | 6.3 |
| United Kingdom | 5.2 | China | 5.0 |
| Prussia | 4.9 | United Kingdom | 5.0 |
| Japan | 3.1 | France | 4.7 |
| Austria-Hungary | 1.9 | Italy | 4.0 |
| Spain | 1.9 | Spain | 2.5 |
| United States | 1.8 | Canada | 2.5 |
| Russia | 1.7 | South Korea | 1.8 |

This table helps identify which economies grew significantly over the past couple of centuries and which did not. The United States, a comparatively small economy in 1820, now is the largest. Although some countries have grown (the United States and Japan leapfrogged many countries to the top), others such as China and India slipped down the list. Other top-ten countries in 1820 have disappeared from the list.

**Source:** *The Milken Institute Review* (3rd Quarter, 2007)

- - - - - - -

[1]William Easterly, *The Elusive Quest for Growth: Economists' Adventures and Misadventures in the Tropics* (MIT Press: Cambridge, 2001), p. 14.

In this and the next chapter, our goal is to give you the tools and insights to help you understand why countries in Table 10.1 have traded places over time. Remember that just because the United States is the number one economy today does not guarantee it will be in the future. For that reason, understanding the forces that explain why some economies grow and others do not is a fundamental aspect of macroeconomics.

## 10.2 Economic Growth and Production

One way to think about economic growth is within the context of a production possibilities frontier (PPF). We have used the PPF in several chapters already. You recall that a PPF shows the maximum output of two goods given full employment of existing resources at a point in time. Suppose a country produces two goods: breakfast burritos and iPhones. The PPF for this economy tells us the *maximum amount* of burritos and iPhones that the economy can produce using all of its available resources, such as machinery and labor. In addition, a PPF reflects the country's current production-process knowledge, or "know-how." **Figure 10.1** shows such a PPF for our fictional burrito/iPhone economy.

The economy depicted in Figure 10.1 "can" produce at any point along the production possibilities frontier labeled $PPF_1$. For example, if the economy is producing at point A on the curve, then it is producing 1 million burritos and 200,000 iPhones. At point B, the economy is producing half a million burritos and 400,000 iPhones. The resources used to produce burritos and iPhones are limited and not perfectly substituted between the production of the two goods. This is why the PPF is drawn as a curved line. As the resources specialized to iPhone production (think of specialized electronics and math whizzes) are pushed toward the making of breakfast burritos,

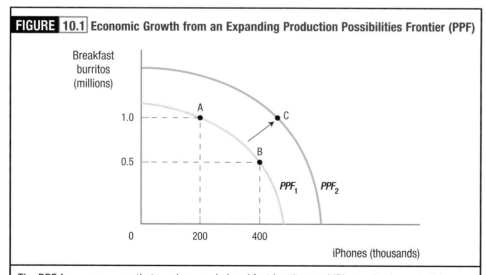

**FIGURE 10.1** Economic Growth from an Expanding Production Possibilities Frontier (PPF)

The PPF for an economy that produces only breakfast burritos and iPhones is shown in this graph. The PPF represents the maximum amount of burritos and iPhones that the economy can produce using all of its available resources, including state-of-the-art production. Increases in available resources or an improvement in production know-how (knowledge) will shift the PPF outward to the right. On the frontier labeled $PPF_2$, a whole new set of production levels—more burritos and more iPhones—becomes possible. This expanded set of possible output levels, if sustained, is economic growth.

they are likely to be less productive because there is a mismatch of skills and employment. In other words, the extra burrito output from using more iPhone resources is declining. An alternative way of stating this is that the opportunity cost of producing more of one good (burritos) is the increased number of forgone iPhones. This reflects the fact that as more burritos get produced, the opportunity cost is an increasing loss of iPhones.

Even with diminishing returns present, any point along the frontier, such as A or B, is a level of production that "can" be achieved. Choosing which combination of the two goods to produce—A, B, or any other point on the frontier—is determined by the people, markets, and government in the economy. In a market economy, consumers generally decide how much of and which good is produced.

Even if an economy is using its resources efficiently, the PPF shows output combinations at a fixed point in time: there is only so much machinery and so many workers in, say, 1912 or 2012. In addition, the PPF assumes that people's knowledge of production processes is given. What these constraints boil down to is that it's not possible to produce any combination of products *outside of the frontier*. In other words, producing a combination of burritos and iPhones represented by point C in Figure 10.1 is just not possible, at least, not for an extended amount of time.

But what if the amount of resources available for producing iPhones and burritos increases? Suppose there are more machines or an influx of workers to the economy. Or suppose people figure out a way to produce these goods more efficiently using available resources. When such changes occur, combinations outside the frontier, like those at point C, become attainable because these additional resources, or an improvement in production technology, will shift the PPF outward to the right. As the PPF shifts to the right, to the curve labeled PPF$_2$ in Figure 10.1, a whole new set of production levels—more burritos and more iPhones—becomes possible.

A basic way of thinking about economic growth is the rightward, or outward, shift in the PPF. When the frontier shifts to the right, there are more goods—burritos and iPhones, in this case—for everyone in the economy to consume. But does this represent economic *growth*? We must be very careful about what defines economic growth, however. If the PPF shifts outward once, more goods can be produced. But for economic *growth* to occur, the PPF must be constantly shifting out and shifting out faster than the population is growing. As we'll see later in this chapter, changes in resources available for production may generate temporary increases in output—reaching point C in Figure 10.1—but may not create the kind of sustained increase in output that defines economic growth.

## 10.3 Income, Output, and Economic Growth

Thinking about economic growth in terms of shifting the PPF outward is a useful start, but it is limiting. After all, economies usually produce more than just two goods. Also, the kinds of goods they produce over time change. When cars replaced horses for transportation purposes, did this make the average person better or worse off? By how much? The number of black-and-white televisions produced is much, much lower today than it was 50 years ago, but has your economic well-being suffered as a result?

As you can probably tell, trying to measure economic growth by looking at just the number and types of goods an economy produces, as the PPF does, limits our ability to assess changes in people's economic well-being over time. We need a different measure. The measure used most often is some measure of income or output, such as real GDP. GDP allows us to track how our income, and therefore our "command" over goods, has changed over time. We really don't care *which* goods were bought. After all, some people still buy horses for transportation, and some buy black-and-white TVs. What we care about is whether people *are able to* buy more of these and other goods. This means that economic growth is best measured as the growth of real income (income adjusted for changes in prices) over time. More specifically, **economic growth** is defined as a *sustained* increase in real income *per person* over time.

---

**ECONOMIC GROWTH** A *sustained* increase in real income *per person* over time.

**EXAMPLE** Examples of economic growth include: the rising trend in the average person's ability to consume more and better goods and services; producing goods and creating income faster than the increase in population over time; and the rising trend in real GDP per person in the United States over the past century.

---

Notice that our definition revolves around sustained increases in real income (real GDP) per person. *Sustained* refers to the idea that economic growth occurs over time. A one-time increase in real GDP is not growth: an increase in real GDP per person that spans decades is economic growth. Real income can and does fluctuate over time. This is as true for individuals as it is for economies. If you lose your job, your income (real and nominal) falls. But for most of us, this decline is transitory (temporary) and doesn't affect our long-term standard of living. For an economy, when a recession occurs, aggregate (total) real income falls. If the size of the population doesn't change during a recession, does this mean that economic growth declined? According to our definition of economic growth, the answer is no. It just means that the economy is facing a temporary setback.

The real income part of the definition reflects the fact that we want to account for changes in the prices of goods over time to track true increases in purchasing power. As you have learned, real GDP is often used as a measure for this purpose. Lastly, the fact that we measure growth as increases in real income *per person* recognizes that what we care about is the income an economy creates relative to the size of its population. If an economy is not producing goods and creating income faster than its population is growing, the average person isn't better off over time, economically speaking. Does this ever occur? This is exactly what happened during the 1980s in Mexico. The country's total real income increased, but its real income per person actually fell. Even though Mexico's economy was expanding, the population was increasing so much faster that, using real GDP per person as the measure of economic growth, the average Mexican citizen's command over goods (share of the economic pie) was lower in 1990 compared to 1980.

The decline in real income per person is not unique to Mexico. In Peru, for instance, real income per person in 2000 was lower than it was in 1970. The same is true for Bolivia, Cambodia, Liberia, Madagascar, and Nicaragua. Do you notice a pattern here? What you'll not find in this group is any one of the so-called advanced industrial countries, such as the United States, Canada, or France. In these countries, real income per capita has tended to increase over time. In the United States, it has increased a little over three-fold in the past 50 years.

To study economic growth and discover why some economies are richer than others, we look at long periods of time—at trends that last for decades—not just years. Focusing on longer time horizons allows us to disregard the effects of transitory events, even though they may be very interesting and important. The Black Plague, an epidemic that struck Europe in the fourteenth century, is an example of an important but transitory event, in terms of analyzing economic growth. The Plague killed about one-third of Europe's population in just five years. As a result, real income per person in Europe actually increased because the size of the population declined faster than production levels did. But this condition didn't last long. Populations once again began to increase, and real income per person returned to pre-Plague levels. Aside from the Black Plague period, no sustained increase in real income per person occurred in the Middle Ages. In fact, for about ten centuries, there was no economic growth: most people born in the 1400s were no better off (economically) than those born in the 400s.

As mentioned, the most commonly used measure of economic growth is growth in real GDP per person. Recall from Chapter 7 that real GDP measures an economy's output of goods and services adjusted for changes in the price level. Although real GDP combines the production of oranges, shoes, and surgeries performed in one aggregate measure, it also measures total income in an economy. Remember that what is produced and purchased must generate income. Still, you already know that GDP is not a trouble-free measure. And comparing one country's real GDP per person to another country's may not fully reflect how the output is distributed across the population. Even with such problems, real GDP per person over time is a pretty good indicator of whether an economy is expanding or contracting. That is the basis for our discussion of economic growth.

## 10.4  Does Everyone Benefit from Economic Growth?

Does everyone benefit from economic growth? How you answer this question depends on your perspective. Economists generally believe that people are economically better off when their ability to purchase more goods and services improves. If real GDP per person is increasing, isn't that a good thing? Rising real incomes mean that the typical person's ability to buy more goods increases. In very poor countries, this alleviates poverty. In rich countries, it means people have more income and can, for example, send their children to a prestigious college. They can also take more vacations instead of working constantly. Isn't that a good thing?

The fact is that economic growth is not good for *everyone* in the short term. Advances in production and technology seem to make life better for everybody. But some people are actually made worse off by these advancements. As the car replaced the horse-drawn carriage, the need for blacksmiths declined along with the need for carriage makers. Displaced carriage makers who switched to making cars perhaps saw their fortunes rise. Carriage makers who were unwilling or unable to make this change sought employment in other parts of the economy. Still others probably became unemployed, perhaps structurally so. Economic growth, measured using real GDP per person, does not mean that everyone's real income rises at the same pace as everyone else's over time—just that the *average* person's does. How well people do individually depends on their personal ingenuity; for example, they may find something other people want to buy, produce it, and sell it.

But such adjustments are not only due to economic growth. These changes would occur even if an economy were not growing. Shifts in demand give rise to new industries and products that replace others. Decisions made in the marketplace always lead to reallocations of scarce resources and, as a consequence, income. For example, the declining demand for landline telephones has resulted in declining incomes for the producers of those products, motivating them to seek out new market opportunities. Dynamic economies always are characterized by advancing and declining industries. Economic growth, in and of itself, cannot always be blamed for why some industries decline while others expand.

Economic growth can also produce some undesirable externalities. For example, the tremendous growth of the economies of China and India in the past decade has substantially increased the average citizen's share of real GDP. However, the rapid growth has also increased pollution levels in urban areas.[2] This side effect of growth, in addition to increased traffic congestion, is not accounted for in the countries' real GDP numbers. Even so, it is important to recognize that the average individual living in both countries today is experiencing more economic opportunities than that person would have 20 years ago. In fact, such an increase in economic well-being, some argue, will create increased demand by the public for *less* pollution (cleaner air) over time, a demand that politicians in developing countries are beginning to recognize.[3]

## 10.5 Do More Labor and Capital Always Lead to Economic Growth?

We've already suggested that one way to think of economic growth is an outward shift in the PPF. Thinking of economic growth as occurring when we increase the availability of inputs into production—labor, machinery, and our knowledge about production processes—is a solid foundation to build on. With this idea in mind, let's explore how changes in the use of labor and capital—along with advances in knowledge—affect the amount of output an economy can produce.

### The Production Function

Producing a good or service, whether it is making a cup of coffee or mowing a lawn, happens when human labor, machinery, and knowledge are combined. For example, when you stop by your neighborhood coffee shop in the morning, your piping hot latte is produced by combining labor, capital, and knowledge. The person who takes your order and makes your coffee is the labor input. The coffee machine represents capital. The knowledge required to make the cup of coffee is multifaceted. Some of the knowledge is embedded in the coffee machine: it represents the latest innovation in an otherwise age-old process. Knowledge also is embodied in the worker filling the order: her human capital is reflected in her ability to operate the machine, read directions, count change, and so forth. Recall from Chapter 1 that human capital is a broad-based concept of what we know, our ideas and talents, our physical endowments, and maybe even our tolerance for entrepreneurial risk taking.

We can represent the process by which these inputs are combined to produce a latte by way of the production function. A **production function** shows the amount of output that can be produced using various combinations of inputs.

· · · · · · ·

[2]Keith Bradsher, "Clean Air or TV: Paying in Pollution for Energy Hunger: India and China Explore Alternatives, But Too Often the Diesel Generator Rules." *New York Times*, January 9, 2007, C1.

[3]Jim Yardley, "Chinese Premier Focuses on Pollution and the Poor." *New York Times*, March 5, 2007, A8.

**PRODUCTION FUNCTION** A relationship that shows the amount of output that can be produced using various combinations of labor, capital, and knowledge.

**EXAMPLE** A worker trained on the use of a jack hammer can break up to 400 square feet of concrete in an hour.

**EXAMPLE** With the use of modern machinery and farming techniques, some Illinois farmers can produce more than 180 bushels of corn per acre.

**EXAMPLE** Your university, given the number of buildings on campus and the number of faculty, will grant 1,500 undergraduate degrees this year.

Table 10.2 shows how, using the production function, various combinations of labor and capital—workers and machines—are combined to yield various amounts of latte output at your local coffeehouse. Each cell in the table represents the number of lattes produced. We'll assume, for now, that the current level of knowledge needed to make lattes is taken as a given.

The first thing you should notice about the production function is that varying the quantity of labor and/or capital used changes the number of lattes the coffee shop can produce in an hour. For instance, suppose the owner of the business wants to know what happens to the number of lattes produced with the shop's two coffeemakers if she increases the number of the shop's baristas from three to six. Table 10.2 indicates that this increase in labor increases the maximum number of lattes produced from 10 to 18. What if the owner decides to add another three workers? Going from six to nine workers and keeping the number of coffeemakers the same increases latte production to 22. Apparently, increasing the number of workers (i.e., labor) leads to more output.

There is another important aspect of the table you need to notice. Do you see how the additional number of lattes produced per additional barista gets smaller and smaller as more and more workers are added? For instance, three workers using two machines produce 10 lattes per hour. Add another three workers and the shop produces 18 lattes. This means that the addition of three more workers raised output not by 10—like the first three workers did—but only by 8 lattes. And the next three workers increase total latte output by only 4 additional cups. This reflects what is called **diminishing marginal returns** to labor.

**Table 10.2** The Production Function in Action: Your Neighborhood Latte Shop

| No. of Machines | No. of Workers | | |
| --- | --- | --- | --- |
| | 3 | 6 | 9 |
| 2 | 10 | 18 | 22 |
| 4 | 17 | 25 | 29 |
| 6 | 23 | 31 | 35 |

Each cell represents the number of lattes produced using that combination of machines and workers. Knowledge is taken as a given. Using this "production function," you can find the combinations of labor and capital—workers and machines—that yield different latte output. Increasing the quantity of labor or capital used increases the number of lattes produced in an hour but at a decreasing rate.

**DIMINISHING MARGINAL RETURNS** The condition where the adding of one more unit of some input such as labor, holding capital and knowledge constant, leads to a smaller increase in output compared with the last unit of labor added.

**EXAMPLE** Todd, the tenth person hired by Shazam Shoes, increased shoe production by ten pair per day. Evelyn, the eleventh person hired, increased shoe production by eight pair per day.

**EXAMPLE** When the thirtieth person crammed their way into the kitchen to help bake cookies, production of cookies per hour actually declined.

Using more and more workers without increasing the machines available creates a situation in which each additional worker contributes a smaller amount to total output than each previous worker. It's not because the first few workers are inherently more productive than the last few. It does make sense, however, for a firm to hire the best and the brightest first. All else the same, wouldn't you pick the brightest student to be the first to join your study group? Rather, it's because there is not enough capital (machines) to keep up with the additional workers. As a result, their incremental productivity falls.

Table 10.2 also shows what happens when the number of latte machines (capital) increases, but the number of workers does not. Adding more machines means more lattes can be produced. By increasing the number of machines from two to four, while holding the number of workers at three, latte output increases by seven, from 10 to 17. Adding another two machines increases output, but only by 6 cups. Just like when more workers were added, adding more machines without changing the number of workers yields more lattes. But, as before, the incremental increase in output due to each additional machine diminishes. Like labor, capital (machines) also is subject to diminishing returns. Whether we change the amount of labor or the amount of capital, the result is the same: increasing one but not the other increases total output—but at a decreasing rate.

Of course, most economies produce more than just lattes. We can generalize from our two-good production function to show the total output of goods and services an economy can produce. In **Figure 10.2**, the curved lines represent the production function, only this time for an entire economy.

The top panel of Figure 10.2 shows that as the number of workers in an economy increases, given a certain amount of capital and knowledge, total output increases. For instance, going from zero to 20 million workers increases output (real GDP) from zero to $1 trillion. Adding another 20 million workers, going from 20 million workers to 40 million workers, increases real GDP from $1 trillion to only $1.5 trillion. The shape of the production function indicates that adding more workers while keeping the amount of capital and knowledge constant will increase total output, but each incremental increase in real GDP will be smaller per extra worker.

The lower panel in Figure 10.2 shows that the same happens with capital. (Notice that we measure capital not by the number of machines but by their dollar value. This enables us to add together capital such as tractors, printing presses, and surgical lasers.) The initial $50 billion in capital generates $1.3 trillion in real GDP. Increasing the amount of capital from $50 billion to $75 billion, while keeping the number of workers and knowledge constant, increases real GDP from $1.3 trillion to $1.5 trillion. The additional $25 billion in capital did not yield as big an increase in real GDP as before. The shape of the production function again indicates that

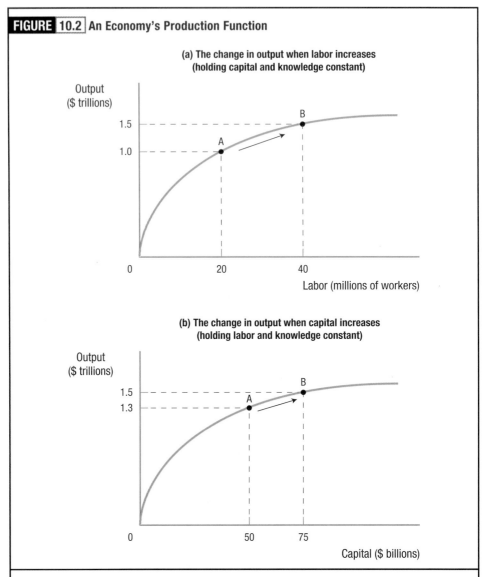

**FIGURE 10.2** An Economy's Production Function

**(a) The change in output when labor increases (holding capital and knowledge constant)**

Output ($ trillions)

**(b) The change in output when capital increases (holding labor and knowledge constant)**

Output ($ trillions)

The top panel shows that as the number of workers in an economy increases, given existing amounts of capital and knowledge, total output increases but at a decreasing rate. The lower panel shows that increasing the amount of capital while keeping the number of workers constant increases output but at a decreasing rate.

additional increases in real GDP will be smaller for each incremental increase in the stock of capital.

Instead of trying to determine the separate effects from changes in the number of machines or the number of workers, economists and policy makers usually focus on productivity. **Productivity** is often measured as output produced per hour of work. If a factory employs ten workers, and its production of shoes increases from 100 pairs per hour to 150 pairs per hour, productivity increases by 50 percent.

> **PRODUCTIVITY** Production of goods and services per hour of work, or per worker.

**EXAMPLE** By using the tablet PC, the doctor was able to see 1.5 more patients an hour because he reduced time writing up patient notes.

**EXAMPLE** Henry Ford decides to use assembly-line production. The same number of workers now produces three times as many cars per hour as before.

**EXAMPLE** Using a computer, Professor Jones can produce twice as many homework assignments per hour compared to using a typewriter.

Productivity is a topic that, for good and bad, captures newspaper headlines and the attention of policy makers. The reason is that an increase in worker productivity means that more goods are being produced by the same amount of labor resources employed. If the cost of using those resources hasn't changed, then increased productivity not only means more goods but also more goods at a lower price. As you can imagine, productivity is an important concept on several different levels.

Due to new computer technology, many people believe that productivity of U.S. workers increased substantially during the 1990s. However, at times prior to 1990, it was common to see newspaper headlines like "U.S. workers less productive than German workers." The writers of such newspaper articles often reported the economy's latest "productivity" numbers and used them to predict whether economic conditions in the country would improve or deteriorate. Productivity increases are sometimes viewed as an indication of better economic times ahead. And when productivity decreases occur, it often sends up alarms of future declines in standards of living.

## Productivity and Economic Growth

Why is productivity so important to explaining economic growth? Before we see how productivity is related to economic growth, we first need to explain how productivity changes. To do this, let's relate output per worker—productivity—to the amount of capital per worker. For now, we will assume that the amount of knowledge is a given—that workers know what they know. These assumptions allow us to convert the production function in Figure 10.2 into a **productivity curve**.

> **PRODUCTIVITY CURVE** A relation showing the amount of output produced for a given amount of capital per worker, holding knowledge constant.

**EXAMPLE** Adding two new microkeratomes (a knife used to cut a flap in the cornea) allowed a doctor to perform 50 percent more corrective eye surgeries each month.

**EXAMPLE** Adding another coffee machine allowed a local coffee shop to serve more customers without hiring more workers.

The productivity curve shown in **Figure 10.3** looks very similar to the production function. Even so, there is one important difference: the productivity curve shows how increasing the amount of capital per worker—sometimes called the *capital-labor ratio*—leads to an increase in productivity, measured by output per worker. Let's use the following mnemonics: $K$ stands for capital, $L$ represents labor, and $Y$ is output. The productivity curve shows that when the capital-labor ratio increases from $(K/L)_1$ to $(K/L)_2$, output per worker—our definition of productivity—increases from $(Y/L)_1$

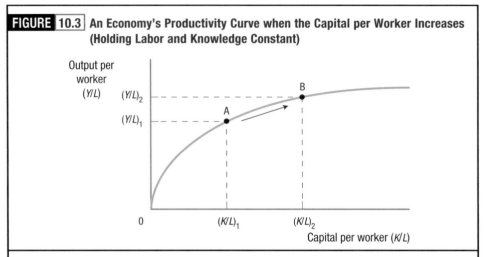

**FIGURE 10.3** An Economy's Productivity Curve when the Capital per Worker Increases (Holding Labor and Knowledge Constant)

The productivity curve shows how increasing the amount of capital per worker—sometimes called the capital-labor ratio or ($K/L$)—leads to an increase in productivity, measured by output per worker or ($Y/L$). This is shown by the economy sliding up to the right along the productivity curve in Figure 10.3 from point A to point B. Even though increasing the capital per worker increases worker productivity, there are diminishing returns: as more and more capital is added to the existing number of workers, the output per worker increases but at a decreasing rate. The productivity curve illustrates how diminishing returns limit the ability of increases in capital to explain economic growth.

to $(Y/L)_2$. This is shown by the economy moving up to the right along the productivity curve in Figure 10.3 from point A to point B.

Notice that even though increasing the capital per worker (e.g., coffeemakers per employee) increases worker productivity, there are diminishing returns to additional increases in capital. As more and more machines are added to the existing number of workers, the output per worker increases but at a decreasing rate. (Think of workers scrambling between increasing numbers of machines to maintain a certain level of output.) In other words, the productivity curve doesn't continue to climb steeply; it flattens out over time.

The productivity curve illustrates how diminishing returns, this time affecting capital, limit its ability to explain economic growth. To see this, let's assume that the number of workers is fixed. Increasing capital per worker ($K/L$) moves the economy up along the productivity curve in Figure 10.3. As the economy moves out along the curve, the increase in output per worker ($Y/L$) is getting smaller and smaller. In other words, the rate of growth in output per worker is diminishing as more and more capital is added. This means that after some point, further increases in capital simply do not generate bigger increases in real output per person.

The implication of this observation is that countries with similar rates of investment in capital—increases in the number of machines per worker—may experience very different rates of increase in output per person. It depends on where the country is on their productivity curve. In developing countries, ones that are on the steep side of the productivity curve, increasing capital per worker may produce a bigger "bang" in terms of increased productivity, and therefore income. A good example is Taiwan. Over the past 40 years, Taiwan's investment in capital, relative to the size of its economy, is about the same as the United States. This shows up in the fact that the *growth* of real GDP per person in Taiwan is more than three times faster than it is in the United

States. Even so, the *level* of real GDP per person in the United States is much higher. As economies move further up along their productivity curve, increases in capital may not produce higher rates of economic growth. Countries such as the United States may be "richer," but they also are not growing as fast as countries such as Taiwan.

This observation suggests that an increase in capital per worker does not by itself generate sustained increases in output or income per person. Doubling the number of machines does not permanently double the growth rate in goods being produced by existing workers. If expanding the capital stock isn't the explanation for economic growth, then what is?

## 10.6  It's Knowledge, Stupid

During the 1992 presidential campaign, Bill Clinton's campaign frequently used the phrase "It's the economy, stupid" to draw voters' attention to the economic policies of President George H. W. Bush, whom he ultimately defeated. Similarly, ask a witty economist what is perhaps the single most important driving force of economic growth, and she is likely to respond, "It's knowledge, stupid."

Many economists refer to advances in knowledge as improved technology. Advances in technology can improve the productivity of workers. However, in addition to technological and productivity improvements, advancing knowledge includes the accumulation of facts and people's improved understanding of how the world works. Not only is knowledge embodied in the physical objects used in production (such as coffee machines), but it's also embodied in you. Going to college expands your base of knowledge. It builds up your human capital.

After you first learned how to use a computer, it was a smaller step to learn various software packages and how to access information via the Internet. Instead of spending hours in the library looking up economic statistics, it's much more efficient for you to find those numbers online. Technology and knowing how to use it increases the productivity of workers doing everything from scholarly research, to building houses, to performing dental exams. Therefore, we will use the term "knowledge" more broadly than some economists do.

What happens to the productivity curve when advances in knowledge improve production technology? The productivity curve based on some initial amount of knowledge and technology ($T_1$) in **Figure 10.4** duplicates the initial condition shown in Figure 10.3. Now, instead of increasing the amount of capital used per hour worked, suppose knowledge increases. And look at how we represent the effect of this increase in knowledge: it does not move us along the productivity curve but shifts it upward, from the productivity curve designated with $T_1$ to the higher curve labeled $T_2$.

The fact that increased knowledge shifts the productivity curve upward, from the curve labeled $T_1$ to $T_2$, is very important when thinking about economic growth. Advances in knowledge—better production techniques, advances in technology, workers with better training, and so on—make workers more productive even though there has been no change in the amount of capital or labor used. That is, given a fixed amount of capital and no change in the size of the labor force, an increase in knowledge raises output per worker from $(Y/L)_1$ to $(Y/L)_2$. If the size of the population is unchanged, the increase in productivity due to advancement in knowledge generates an increase in real output per person. An economy that promotes continual advances in knowledge is, therefore, one that is likely to experience sustained increases in productivity and real output per person. For this reason, many economists believe that knowledge is *the* engine of economic growth.

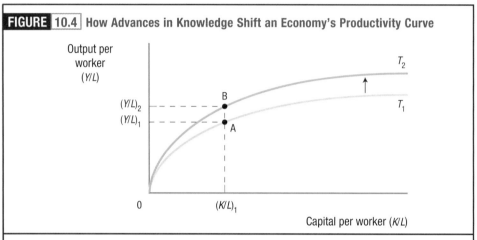

**FIGURE 10.4** How Advances in Knowledge Shift an Economy's Productivity Curve

In the figure, $T_1$ is a productivity curve based on some initial amount of knowledge and technology, labor, and capital in an economy. Suppose knowledge advances, resulting in more efficient production techniques. This improvement does not move the economy along the productivity curve: it shifts the entire productivity curve upward, from $T_1$ to $T_2$. This shift in the productivity curve means that advances in knowledge—better production techniques, advances in technology, workers with better training, and so on—make workers more productive even if there has been no change in the amount of capital or labor used. Continual advances in knowledge are likely to result in sustained increases in productivity and economic growth for a country.

## SOLVED PROBLEM

**Q** Is knowledge really that important?

**A** To illustrate the importance of advances in knowledge, let's address the question using an algebraic version of the productivity curve. A common version of the productivity equation sets productivity ($Y/L$) equal to knowledge plus the square root of the ratio of capital to labor ($K/L$):

$$Y/L = T + \sqrt{(K/L)}$$

What happens when we apply some numbers to this relation? First, let's let knowledge be equal to 100 and see what happens to productivity when we vary the ratio of capital to labor ($K/L$). When knowledge ($T$) and ($K/L$) are equal to 100, productivity is

$$Y/L = 100 + \sqrt{(100)}$$
$$= 110$$

If we double the capital-labor ratio, say, because of an increase in machinery, what happens to productivity? It increases to

$$Y/L = 100 + \sqrt{(200)}$$
$$= 114.14$$

If we double the ratio ($K/L$) yet again, setting it equal to 400, productivity increases to 120. As you can see, the doubling of the capital-labor ratio does not give you a doubling in productivity. Why? In the real world this occurs because of diminishing returns.

Now let's see what happens if we double knowledge but hold the capital-labor ratio constant at 100. Increasing knowledge from 100 to 200 gives us

$$Y/L = 200 + \sqrt{(100)}$$
$$= 210$$

If we double knowledge again, making it 400, productivity increases to 410. As you can see, increases in knowledge have a direct, one-to-one effect on productivity. Many economists believe that there are no diminishing returns to knowledge like there are with increasing the amount of capital or labor used in production. The problem, as you can probably guess, is how to measure knowledge. We'll turn to that question later in this chapter.

---

Could advances in knowledge explain much of the sustained increases in real income per person that we have seen? Most economists would answer this with a resounding yes! Unlike labor and capital, acquiring and applying new knowledge is not subject to diminishing marginal returns. Put another way, there doesn't seem to be an upper limit on what we can learn or the various ways in which new ideas are used. Could anyone in the 1950s have foreseen the widespread development and use of the Internet when the first computers were being assembled? One of the best misstatements regarding the computer is attributed to Thomas Watson, chairman of IBM. In 1954, Watson quipped, "I think there is a world market for maybe five computers." In contrast, Intel co-founder Gordon Moore made the brash claim in 1965 that microprocessors' computing power would double every 18 months! It turns out that he was not very far off: by 2002, Intel was producing a microprocessor with a capacity that was more than 95,000 times that of the original 1971 version. This turns out to be a doubling every 22 or so months. In the field of medicine, open-heart surgeries now are almost routine, with more than 600,000 operations performed a year. Safe and reliable laser eye surgery wasn't possible until a decade ago. Twenty years ago, who knew there would be text messaging?

Some economists believe that advancing knowledge is *the* explanation for economic growth. Not only do workers become more productive as knowledge increases, but the very production of knowledge appears self-perpetuating. In other words, the more you know, the easier it is to learn even more. This is what economist Paul Romer suggested back in the 1980s. Romer proposed the idea that economic growth explains advances in knowledge, and that advances in knowledge explain economic growth. If this sounds circular, in a sense it is. The thrust of Romer's theory, which is often referred to as the **endogenous growth model**, is that after the production of new knowledge and technology occurs, it "feeds" on itself.[4]

**ENDOGENOUS GROWTH MODEL** A model of economic growth in which the development and spread of knowledge (technology) plays a central role.

EXAMPLE The discovery of antibiotics reduced absence rates from schools, leading to better educated children, one of whom invented the microprocessor.

EXAMPLE The discovery of preserving food through canning allowed individuals to travel many miles, even making space travel possible.

EXAMPLE Advances in computer technology have improved productivity in a wide variety of fields, from the production of cars and textbooks to advances in medical diagnostics and pharmaceuticals to computers themselves.

According to the endogenous growth model, economic advancements don't result from outside shocks but from spillovers of knowledge across different sectors in the

· · · · · · ·

[4]The best statement of this is, though highly technical, in Paul Romer, "Endogenous Technical Change." *Journal of Political Economy*, Vol. 98, Pt. 2 (1990): S71–S102.

economy and from increases in human capital. Think about inventions such as the internal combustion engine, the integrated circuit, the microprocessor, or endoscopic surgery. The return to society from each of these inventions has been much greater than their inventors probably ever expected. The existence of new procedures and technologies leads exponentially to yet more advances. Romer and others believe that this self-perpetuating nature of knowledge is the best explanation of economic growth.

## 10.7  Does the Theory Fit Reality?

So far, we've suggested that increases in labor, capital, and knowledge all play a role in explaining why some economies have gotten richer than others. What separates the effect of each is that increases in labor and capital are subject to diminishing marginal returns. Advances in knowledge are not. You might think that even advancing knowledge requires a certain increase in the number of "knowledge producing" employees—labor—to succeed. Not necessarily. Think of all the inventions that came about when just a couple of people built a better mousetrap. Hewlett-Packard started out in a garage. Microsoft and Apple Computer began in an equally modest manner. Thomas Alva Edison worked mostly by himself but produced many important inventions.

Likewise, wouldn't it be possible for knowledge to be subject to diminishing returns if the amount of capital used to produce it declined drastically? Certainly some projects succeed only because large-scale investments in equipment have been made. After all, splitting atoms requires an accelerator, which is usually not found in someone's basement. Still, it is not stretching reality to think of knowledge as *not* being subject to diminishing returns.

Does this mean that a country shouldn't bother to invest in more capital or promote policies encouraging people to join the workforce? No. If the country is poor, and its economy is not expanding very rapidly, increases in labor and capital can exert a big, although temporary, impact on the growth of average real income per person. The recent growth of China's economy is evidence of that. But as the Chinese economy transitions to a higher level of income per person, the growth of real GDP per person is likely to slow. In other words, the growth of the Chinese economy will slow over time, even though the average Chinese citizen will be getting richer.

The same kind of growth spurt has occurred for other economies in the past, notably, Japan. In fact, just like Japan in the 1980s, the recent claims that China will economically overtake the United States is usually, and incorrectly, based on simply projecting into the future its current rate of economic growth.[5] Such projections are about as accurate as projecting your current height by using your "growth rate" between the ages of three and four. You did not grow to be 8 foot 7 inches, and Japan did not economically overtake the United States for a number of reasons.[6] It's not likely that China will do so, either. (See the following Economic Fallacy section.) Like the advanced economies of the United States, France, and Germany, China can maintain sustained increases in real GDP per person only if the productivity of China's workers continues to advance. The most likely source of such productivity increases is through advances in knowledge.

· · · · · · ·

[5]Charles Hutzler, "China on Path to Overtake U.S. Economy." *Wall Street Journal*, January 24, 2005.

[6]Richard Katz, *Japan: The System that Soured: The Rise and Fall of the Japanese Economic Miracle* (Armonk: M.E. Sharpe, 1998).

ECONOMIC FALLACY China's economic standard of living will soon surpass that of the United States.

**False.** Economic growth is measured over a period of many years. A positive growth in real GDP per person, year after year, has a *compounding* effect. Compound growth takes place because you are applying a growth rate, say 2 percent, to a larger and larger level of real GDP each year. For example, if real GDP per person is $1,000 in the first year, it is $1,020 (= $1000 × 1.02) in year two, a 2-percent, or $20, increase. In year three, real GDP per person increases to $1,040.40, and in year four, it is $1,061.20. Notice that in each successive year, the value is increasing by more than just (in this case) $20. This is because the 2-percent increase is being applied not only to the original base amount but also to the annual additions to the base.

Compound growth is a very important tool when it comes to thinking about future economic standards of living. Because of its sheer size, China's real GDP is quite large. On a per person basis, however, you have seen that the numbers tell a much different story. According to Table 10.3, in 2004, real GDP per person was $5,771 in China, and $39,535 in the United States. Given these values, how fast would the Chinese economy need to grow for the average individual in China to enjoy the same level of real GDP as someone in the United States?

Using the 2004 figures, if real GDP per person in China increased at an 8 percent rate year in and year out, it would reach a level of about $27,000 in 20 years. And even then, it would still be far below the current level of real GDP per capita in the United States. Because U.S. economic growth will continue as well, it is highly unlikely that the level of real GDP per person in China will surpass that of the United States anytime soon.

Just how much does each factor—capital, labor, and knowledge—contribute to the actual growth of real income per person? We'll answer that question by looking at the U.S. experience and whether the facts fit the theory across many different countries.

## Sources of Economic Growth in the United States

How much each factor—capital, labor, and knowledge—contributes to the actual growth of real GDP or income per person is a question that economists continue to research. Edward F. Denison's classic 1985 study of the United States was one of the first to provide some specific answers.[7] Denison figured out how much of the growth in real income per person can be attributed to increases in labor and capital versus that portion of growth that can be attributed to advances in knowledge. Using data from 1929–1982, Denison estimates that increases in capital and labor together account for about half of the growth in income per person. Denison claims that the rest of the increase is explained by advances in technology alone. Denison, as do others, referred to this nonresource component as *total factor productivity*. In essence, total factor productivity, an idea that we'll expand on later, is that part of growth in real income not explained by changes in capital and labor. In our terminology, that amounts to changes in "knowledge." Think of it this way: if production technology had remained at its 1929 level, the growth in real income per person in the United States would have reached only half of its actual rate. Let's state that

. . . . . . .

[7]Edward F. Denison, *Trends in American Economic Growth, 1929–1982* (Washington: Brookings Institution, 1985).

differently: without advances in knowledge, your standard of living would be significantly lower today than it is.[8]

More recent investigations support Denison's general findings. For example, one study found that over 50 percent of the growth in real output per capita from 1948 to 1996 was due to advances in knowledge. Another, conducted by the Bureau of Labor Statistics (BLS), estimates that during the past 50 years, about one-half of the annual increase in U.S. productivity is due to advances in knowledge alone. Although the studies differ slightly in terms of what they measured and the time period analyzed, they tell a consistent story. At least in the United States, advances in knowledge explain the lion's share of sustained increases in real GDP per person. In other words, the results of these studies fit our theory—that advances in knowledge are the key determinants to long-term economic growth.

## Sources of Economic Growth around the World

How are changes in capital, labor, and knowledge related to economic growth in countries other than the United States? Let's first look at changes in capital.

**Economic Growth and Capital Investment**. **Figure 10.5** shows the relation between the growth of GDP per person and investment in capital (as a percent of GDP) for a large number of countries.[9] Each point in the figure is for a specific country and is found by plotting the values of the two variables. For instance, from 1980 to 2002, the United States had an average yearly growth rate in real GDP of about 2.7 percent. Its average investment-to-GDP ratio during this time was about 20 percent. Those two numbers correspond to the "point" labeled United States in Figure 10.5. Doing the same for the other countries—Ireland, Singapore, and so on—creates the scatter of points in the figure. To help make sense of this scatter of points, we've included a line that represents the average relation between real GDP growth and capital investment across all the countries shown.

This reference line is a useful and informative tool. What it suggests is that countries that experienced higher investment rates in their capital stock tended to experience higher growth rates of real GDP per person. That is what the upward sloping line in Figure 10.5 tells us: all else the same, building up the capital stock in an economy—increasing machines per worker, for example—increases the rate at which real GDP per person increases. But wait a minute! Didn't we say earlier that increases in capital were subject to diminishing returns and couldn't explain all of economic growth? That's true, and Figure 10.5 helps make that point.

We've identified some of the countries in Figure 10.5. The countries located farthest to the left in the graph tend to be developing countries, in which increases in capital could have had a big effect on the growth of real GDP per person. Look at where the United States and Germany are located. Even though the United States and Germany also had relatively high levels of capital, they did not experience the fastest growth in incomes. As economies mature, similar increases in capital simply do not increase economic-growth rates as much as in the developing countries. As an analogy, think of your diet: all else the same, having a 3,000 calorie diet when you are 15 has a different effect on your weight gain (and growth) than when you are 60. When young, those calories go to building your skeleton and muscle, and fueling growth.

· · · · · · ·

[8]This relation is sometimes referred to as the *growth accounting formula*. We provide more detail of this relation in the Appendix to this chapter.

[9]Investment represents the replacement of old and purchase of new capital.

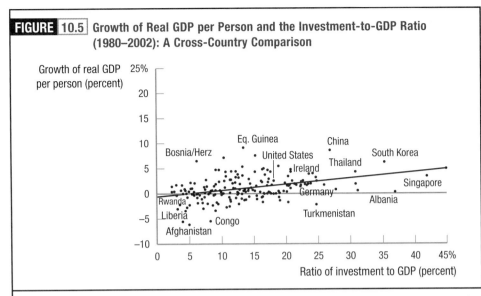

**FIGURE 10.5** Growth of Real GDP per Person and the Investment-to-GDP Ratio (1980–2002): A Cross-Country Comparison

Each point in this figure is the combination of a country's growth in real GDP per person and the average amount of investment as a percent of GDP, both over the period from 1980 to 2002. The line drawn through this scatter of points represents the "average" relation between the two economic measures. Countries located farthest to the left in the figure are ones in which increases in capital *could* have had a big effect on the growth of output per person. Countries clustered in the lower left-hand corner of the figure are those that did not increase their capital stock during these two decades. By contrast, China and South Korea have both increased their capital, and their per person GDP growth rates have increased, as their location toward the right of the graph shows. Even though some countries, like the United States and Germany, have relatively high levels of capital invested, they do not experience faster economic growth. This reflects, in part, diminishing returns from further increases in the capital-labor ratio.

*Source: Penn World Tables*

By the time you hit 60, the calories more likely go to an expanding midsection, which is the kind of growth you are not looking for.

**Economic Growth and Population.** Figure 10.5 also points out a disturbing fact: countries that are mired in poverty and sometimes considered "growth disasters" generally are those countries that have not increased their capital stock over time. Clustered in the lower left-hand corner of the figure are countries such as Rwanda and Liberia. In many such countries, average citizens actually experienced a reduction in their incomes over the past several decades, measured as declines in real GDP per person. You might be wondering how this can happen. Among other possible explanations (we'll explore some of these in the next chapter) is that the populations of these countries increased dramatically faster than the growth in output.

An increase in a country's population reduces the slice of the economic "pie" available for each person. This is why real income per person can and does fall. Second, if the stock of capital doesn't change or increases at a slower pace than the country's labor supply—the number of workers is increasing much faster than the machines available for them to use—the nation's capital-labor ratio also will fall. This

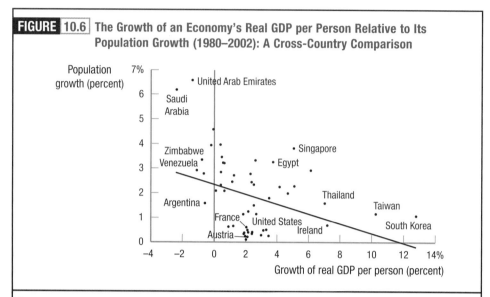

**FIGURE 10.6** The Growth of an Economy's Real GDP per Person Relative to Its Population Growth (1980–2002): A Cross-Country Comparison

This figure suggests that a sustained period of rapid growth in a country's population, in general, is not likely to be associated with a faster rate in its economic growth or with higher future levels of real GDP per person. The policy implication is that if a country's population growth outpaces its productivity, it is not likely to experience a sustained increase in real GDP per person.

*Source: Penn World Tables*

reduces the productivity of each worker. As a result, even if the country's workforce increases due to population growth, it won't lead to increases in real income per person. In other words, if a country's capital investment doesn't keep pace with its population growth, the country is likely to experience slower economic growth. This is why poor countries often try to control their population growth so they don't spiral into worse poverty. It is also why China has followed a "one-child" policy to reduce the growth of its population.[10]

The scatter of points in **Figure 10.6** shows the relevant growth rates for real GDP per person and population for a large number of countries. Using data from the past couple of decades, there is a noticeable *negative* relation between population growth and the growth in real GDP per person. This can be interpreted to mean that, all else the same, faster population growth is associated with slower rates of economic growth. The positions of Saudi Arabia and the United Arab Emirates on the graph, for example, show this is the case. A sustained period of rapid growth in the population, in general, is not likely to be associated with faster rates of economic growth or with higher future levels of GDP per person. If your country's population growth outpaces the productivity of your workers, you are not likely to experience a sustained increase in real GDP per person.

⋯⋯⋯

[10]Howard French, "China: One-Child Policy Spurred Gender Gap." *New York Times*, January 24, 2007; Joseph Kahn, "Harsh Birth Control Steps Fuel Violence in China." *New York Times*, May 22, 2007.

## SOLVED PROBLEM

**Q** The 1973 cult-classic movie *Soylent Green* is a tale of the planet earth in 2022. The movie paints a pretty nasty picture: the earth is overcrowded, only a few natural foods are left (due to global warming), and buying something we take for granted—strawberries—costs exorbitant sums of money. The 40 million citizens of New York City, the movie's setting, survive on water and a mysterious food produced by the Soylent Corporation, called Soylent Green. Although believed to be a plankton-based food, the movie's star, Charlton Heston, spoils it for everybody when he closes the movie by shouting the immortal line "It's people! Soylent Green is made out of people." Does Soylent Green present a real doomsday scenario? If so, shouldn't we minimize population growth?

**A** You have seen in this chapter that some population growth is necessary. Presently, some advanced countries are experiencing population declines. Lower output of goods and services and lower government revenues from workers' incomes needed to pay for strained entitlement programs such as Social Security and Medicare, are just two of the adverse effects of zero population growth.

---

So what is the optimal population growth rate? It may sound a bit "soylent," but if you knew what rate of economic growth was desired, using the production function, you could actually calculate the optimal rate, although doing so would be beyond what's required of you in this course. For a related discussion, see the Appendix to this chapter, which discusses the growth accounting equation.

**Economic Growth and Knowledge.** Let's now turn to the remaining source of increases in productivity and incomes: advances in knowledge. The theory predicts that we should see a positive relation between advances in knowledge and output growth rates. Unfortunately, measuring advances in knowledge across many countries is not as easy as measuring how much is spent on new machines over time or changes in the size of the population.

So how do we measure changes in knowledge? One approach is to first measure how much of the growth in output is explained by increases in a country's stock of capital or labor force. Because the production function tells us that output comes from combining labor, capital, and knowledge, whatever growth in real GDP is unexplained after accounting for labor and capital must be due to advances in knowledge. The residual that is left is called **total factor productivity**.

**TOTAL FACTOR PRODUCTIVITY** The growth in output not explained by growth in capital and labor.

**EXAMPLE** Attending the seminar on using the Internet made Ms. Barker a more efficient and productive teacher.

**EXAMPLE** Instead of having everyone produce loaves of bread, the owner of Bob's Bakery split the work up according to each employee's comparative advantage. One worker now mixes the dough, two specialize in making certain kinds of bread, and another oversees the baking process. This division of labor increased bread production threefold.

As you saw with our discussion of Denison's work, economists use this approach to estimate how much advances in knowledge account for increases in output per person. (In the next chapter, we'll see how specific measures that may influence the advancement of knowledge, such as level of education, are related to economic growth.)

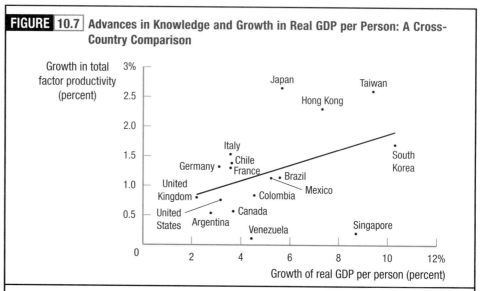

**FIGURE 10.7** | **Advances in Knowledge and Growth in Real GDP per Person: A Cross-Country Comparison**

All else equal, advances in knowledge lead to increased output growth in an economy. In other words, there is a positive relationship between the two, which is exhibited by the fact that the countries are clustered around the positively sloped line in the figure. If knowledge is not subject to the same diminishing returns faced by labor and capital, improvements in knowledge and advances in technology may be key factors explaining economic growth.

**Note:** Growth rates are 1960–1995 for OECD countries; 1940–1990 for Latin American countries; and 1966–1990 for East Asian countries.

*Source:* Robert Barro and Xavier Sala-I-Martin, *Economic Growth* (Cambridge: MIT Press, 2004)

To see how total factor productivity—our stand-in for advances in knowledge—relates to economic growth, we use a measure of total factor productivity compiled from a number of studies. This collection of total factor productivity estimates for several different countries provides a useful barometer to see if, as our theory predicts, advances in knowledge contribute to increased growth in real GDP.

**Figure 10.7** shows growth in output plotted against the growth in total factor productivity, our measure of advances in knowledge. The line in Figure 10.7 shows that, on average, advances in knowledge and economic growth are positively correlated. This suggests that advances in knowledge lead to higher growth rates in real GDP per person and to higher levels of real income per person. That's why the countries on the graph are (loosely) clustered around the upward-sloping line. All else the same, the outcome in Figure 10.7 suggests that improvements in knowledge shift an economy's productivity curve upward, as shown earlier in Figure 10.4.

The general relation shown in Figure 10.7 agrees with the findings of the U.S. studies mentioned earlier. It also supports the belief among economists that advances in knowledge are, in general, associated with increases in the growth of worker productivity. Because we believe that increasing knowledge is not subject to the diminishing returns faced by labor and capital, the positive relation shown in Figure 10.7 suggests that improvements in knowledge may indeed be the key factor that explains sustained economic growth.

The figures we've used to compare the theory of economic growth to the real world show that not every country's track record exactly fits our predictions. The points in each figure—each representing a different country's experience—are not always neatly bunched together, nor do they lie atop one another along the average line. But this result should not lead you to believe that our theory is not a valuable tool to explain economic growth. Arguing that the looseness of the relation signifies a faulty theory is like arguing that the generally positive relation between caloric intake and weight is faulty because everyone who takes in the same calories doesn't weigh the same. Just like individuals, countries have different economic-growth experiences even with similar inputs of labor, capital, and knowledge.

Besides trying to better understand how capital, labor, and knowledge can be combined to yield better economic results, economists also are searching for other factors that help explain why some countries grow faster than others and why some are richer than others. In the next chapter, we will identify and explore the role some of these other factors play.

## 10.8 Is Economic Growth the *Best* Measure of Well-Being?

You might be wondering if economic growth is the *best* measure of people's well-being. Are sustained advances in real GDP per person the economic tide that raises all boats? (If you recall, we asked a similar question back in Chapter 7.) The results so far in this chapter seem to indicate as much. We have said that economic growth leads to higher and higher levels of real income per person. The common way to state this is that economic growth leads to a higher **economic standard of living**.

> **ECONOMIC STANDARD OF LIVING** The average person's command over goods and services produced in an economy measured as real GDP or income per person.
>
> EXAMPLE The average person in some African countries lives on an income of less than $500 a year. In contrast, the average person in the United States lives on an income closer to $40,000 a year.
>
> EXAMPLE Today, average incomes in Australia are more than four times higher than they were 100 years ago.
>
> EXAMPLE The average person today can buy more airplane travel per hour of work than the average person could 40 years ago.

A higher standard of living does not mean that each and every individual experiences the same level of economic well-being. There always has been and always will be inequality in incomes. The critical issue is whether economic growth, over time, translates into improved economic opportunities to a broader group of people. When the average person in a country has access to a wider set of economic opportunities, this means that they can acquire more TVs, cars, or better clothes. Economic growth also means, however, that they are more likely to have access to more (and better) education and health care.

Our economic definition of standard of living is not perfect, but it is a useful yardstick or benchmark from which a more extensive discussion can begin. It says nothing about a specific country's crime rate, level of pollution, or life expectancy. It also says nothing about how the nation's income is distributed. Even with these caveats, real GDP per person and its growth rate remain useful yardsticks to compare economic success. Higher levels of real GDP per person are associated with an increased probability that a country's citizens will live longer, healthier, and more productive lives.

Let's put an international perspective on standards of living. Table 10.1 showed a ranking based on sheer size of economy. **Table 10.3** lists a number of countries

| Table 10.3 Comparing Standards of Living across the Globe | |
|---|---|
| **Country** | **Real GDP per Person* ($)** |
| **Most Industrialized Countries** | |
| Canada | 31,600 |
| France | 28,759 |
| Germany | 28,073 |
| Japan | 26,657 |
| Russia* | 12,217 |
| United Kingdom | 29,461 |
| United States | 39,535 |
| **Asia** | |
| China | 5,771 |
| Cambodia* | 616 |
| India* | 3,212 |
| Korea | 19,353 |
| Philippines | 4,343 |
| Singapore | 31,709 |
| Thailand* | 7,668 |
| Vietnam* | 2,647 |
| **Latin America** | |
| Argentina | 12,315 |
| Brazil* | 7,800 |
| Colombia* | 6,485 |
| Costa Rica | 5,870 |
| Mexico | 8,882 |
| Panama* | 8,991 |
| Peru* | 4,641 |
| **Africa** | |
| Egypt* | 5,099 |
| Ethiopia* | 703 |
| Kenya* | 1,294 |
| Mozambique* | 1,700 |
| Nigeria | 1,312 |
| South Africa | 10,078 |
| Uganda* | 1,183 |
| Zimbabwe* | 2,543 |

*All figures are for 2004, except those with an asterisk (*), which are for 2003.

How do standards of living compare across countries? In France, Germany, and Japan, real GDP per person is about 30 percent lower than in the United States. African countries are incredibly poor. Latin America countries are somewhat better off than African countries but not much. Some Asian nations, such as Singapore, have high levels of income per person while other Asian countries do not. And although the economies of China and India are large, on a per person basis their standards of living are more comparable to Costa Rica and Egypt than to the United States or Germany.

**Source:** *Penn World Tables*

and their respective real GDP per person. All figures are converted to U.S. dollar equivalents to allow comparison of incomes with the "average" individual in the United States. In 2004, real GDP per person in the United States amounted to a bit over $39,000.

How does the standard of living compare across countries around the world? You might be surprised to find that the comparable figures for other industrialized countries like the United States—countries such as France, Germany, and Japan— are each about 30 percent lower than the United States. When compared to these nations, many African countries are incredibly poor. Although South Africa stands out as a "success story" with a per capita GDP level of more than $10,000, countries such as Kenya and Zimbabwe have incomes that are a mere fraction of their Western counterparts. The average individual's daily share of Ethiopia's output, for example, is less than what you pay for a gallon of gasoline. People in Latin America appear to fare somewhat better, but not much. Annual real GDP per person was $5,870 in Costa Rica, and it was $8,882 in Mexico. While far higher than some African countries, these data indicate that the average individual in Latin American countries is much poorer than their counterparts in the United States and European countries.

Would you have guessed that the standard of living in Singapore is actually higher than it is in Japan? Or that Koreans enjoy a higher standard of living compared with the Chinese? There has been much hoopla and concern over the rapid economic expansion that the Chinese economy has experienced in the past few years. We mentioned earlier that this fact has led many to speculate that China is poised to overtake the United States as the global economic powerhouse. Although each economy is large in absolute size, the figures in Table 10.3 show that *on a per person basis*, China (and India for that matter) has a standard of living in 2004 more comparable to those of Costa Rica and Egypt than to the United States.

## WHAT YOU SHOULD HAVE LEARNED FROM CHAPTER 10

- That countries experience temporary increases in their output when their stock of capital increases faster than their populations grow.

- That increasing populations can boost a country's output temporarily, but only if labor is very scarce.

- That for labor and capital, diminishing returns set in, preventing a sustained increase in economic growth.

- That over long periods of time, advances in knowledge are key to sustained increases in real income per person.

- That all countries do not experience the same economic growth even with similar increases in labor, capital, and knowledge.

- That researchers are investigating why an increase in capital or knowledge results in different growth paths across different countries. They believe it is due to the different social, cultural, and institutional factors of countries.

## KEY TERMS

Economic growth, p. 263

Production function, p. 265

Diminishing marginal returns, p. 266

Productivity, p. 268

Productivity curve, p. 269

Endogenous growth model, p. 273

Total factor productivity, p. 279

Economic standard of living, p. 281

## QUESTIONS AND PROBLEMS

1. Look at the table of possible outputs for the Kirkwood Deli. Brian operates the Deli alone.

| Sandwiches | Salads |
|:----------:|:------:|
| 10 | 0 |
| 9 | 1 |
| 7 | 2 |
| 4 | 3 |
| 0 | 4 |

   a) If Brian is currently making 10 sandwiches and no salads, how many sandwiches does he give up to make 1 salad?
   b) If Brian is currently making 9 sandwiches and 1 salad, how many sandwiches does he give up to make 1 more salad?
   c) If Brian is currently making 4 sandwiches and 3 salads, how many sandwiches does he give up to make 1 more salad?
   d) What do you know about the shape of the deli's PPF? Explain.

2. If Brian hires a student to take orders and work the cash register during busy hours, what will happen to the deli's PPF? Explain. Does this represent economic growth?

3. Look at each of the following graphs. Which graph (or graphs) best illustrates economic growth? Explain your choice.

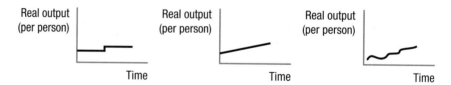

4. Using the information in this table, answer the following questions.

| Economic Measure | 1960 ($) | 2010 ($) |
|:-----------------|:--------:|:--------:|
| Nominal GDP (billions) | 1,350 | 2,855 |
| GDP deflator | 100 | 250 |
| Population (millions) | 250 | 380 |

   a) Real GDP in 1960 is _____.
   b) Real GDP in 2010 is _____. Has the economy demonstrated economic growth?
   c) Real GDP per person in 1960 is _____.
   d) Real GDP per person in 2010 is _____. Has the economy demonstrated economic growth? Is the average person better off or worse off in 2010 compared with 1960?

5. Thinking about the factors that explain economic growth, what might limit the ability of some individuals to share equally in economic growth? (Hint: Consider educational opportunities, and racial and gender discrimination.)

6. Can you see the Milky Way galaxy at night? If you live in an urban area, is not being able to see it an externality associated with economic growth? If you live in a rural area, does being able to see the Milky Way outweigh the opportunity cost of not seeing it?

7. The following table illustrates the hourly production function for statistics problems by a study group. Use the table to answer the following questions.

| | Number of Students | |
|---|---|---|
| Number of Calculators | 2 | 4 |
| 1 | 5 problems | 9 problems |
| 2 | 7 problems | 10 problems |

   a) What happens to the number of problems produced when the 2 students increase the number of calculators from 1 to 2?
   b) What happens to the number of problems produced when the number of students increases from 2 to 4?
   c) Use the table to illustrate diminishing marginal returns to labor.
   d) What factors do you believe are held constant in this example?
   e) Holding the number of calculators constant at 2, draw a production function for statistics problems.

8. How does the graph in panel b of Figure 10.2 differ from the graph in Figure 10.3?

9. In Question 7, adding an additional calculator increased the level of output.

   a) Assuming that 4 students are working, what do you predict will happen to output if the number of calculators increases to 3?
   b) Why don't increases in the number of calculators continue to improve the group's production of statistics problems after the addition of the "nth" calculator?

10. In Figure 10.3, the economy moved from point A to point B. Using the study group example in Questions 7 and 9, explain why the group moved along its productivity curve.

11. In Figure 10.4, the economy moved from point A to point B. Using the study group example, explain why one group might move from point A on curve $T_1$ to point B on curve $T_2$. What might have caused the group to move from point B on $T_2$ to point A on $T_1$?

12. How might the growth rate of real GDP in the United States have differed if only males had been allowed to receive education beyond grade school?

13. In this chapter, we suggested that, based on research results, advancement in knowledge is important for explaining differences in countries' economic growth.

   a) Thinking about your own education, how would you measure the change in your knowledge?
   b) How might we measure improvements in a country's stock of knowledge?

# Appendix 10A The Growth Accounting Formula

An increase in the amount of capital, holding the number of hours worked, leads to an increase in productivity. This means more goods and services are being produced, hence increasing real GDP per person. The theory also predicts that improvements in or widespread use of technology also leads to an increase in productivity. Just how important are these two factors in explaining how countries became so rich? In other words, how do they help us understand economic growth?

To answer that question, MIT economist and Nobel Laureate Robert Solow derived a straightforward formula in the 1950s that allows us to measure the relative contribution of capital and technology to increases in productivity. Though simple looking, Solow's contribution has been the basis for studying economic growth since it was first published. His idea is captured in the following formula:

$$\text{Growth in } Y/L = A(\text{Growth in } K/L) + \text{Growth in Technology}$$

The *growth accounting formula* states that growth in productivity ($Y/L$) is directly related to the growth of two factors: the ratio of capital to labor ($K/L$) and technology. The logic is that an increase in the amount of machinery available per hour of work or per worker should increase worker productivity. Thus, an increase in $K/L$ should result in an increase in productivity. Similarly, Solow's insight suggests that an increase in the hours worked or the number of workers ($L$) without an equal or larger increase in capital (a reduction in $K/L$) would lead to slower growth in productivity. As we've already suggested, an increase in technology is thought to also have a positive impact on productivity growth.

The formula makes a clear distinction as to what the effects of an increase in capital and technology have on productivity. The formula indicates that an increase in the capital-labor ratio ($K/L$) affects productivity by the coefficient "$A$". Statistical estimates of how big this coefficient is vary, but it often takes a value of about 1/3. This means that a 10-percent increase in the capital-labor ratio ($K/L$) increases an economy's productivity growth by about 3 percent. This could reflect the idea that increases in capital are subject to diminishing returns, as discussed earlier. In contrast, note that the "coefficient" for the growth in technology is 1. Unlike increases in the growth of capital, research has found that a 10-percent increase in technology growth leads to a 10-percent increase in productivity growth. This kind of one-for-one effect stems from the idea that increases in technology are not subject to diminishing marginal returns, as is capital.

# Other Aspects of Economic Growth: Why Isn't Everyone Rich?

*"All societies used to be poor. Most are now lifting out of it; why are others stuck?"*

Paul Collier,
*The Bottom Billion (2007)*

The message from the previous chapter is that economic growth and the higher standards of living that result from it are greatly influenced by a few key factors: how much a country invests in capital, how fast its population and labor force grows, and its accumulation of knowledge. You have learned that economists think the most important of these factors in explaining sustained economic growth is the extent to which a country expands its knowledge. Countries where the population has acquired a high level of skills by advancing their knowledge and technology generally realize economic growth and, as a result, benefit from higher levels of real income per person.

If everyone knows this, why don't all countries experience the same rates of economic growth and achieve higher standards of living? As growth economist William Easterly asks, "How did some people (about 900 million of them) in Western Europe, North America, and parts of the Pacific Rim find prosperity, while 5 billion people live in poor nations? Why do 1.2 billion people live in extreme poverty on less than one dollar per day?"[1] In other words, why isn't everyone rich?

In this chapter, we expand our look into what may cause, or hold back, economic growth. With the basics established, we now look into the role of "other" factors that may help explain why some countries have become economically successful while others still struggle in poverty. To keep the discussion manageable, we will focus on only a few of the conditions that economists believe help explain observed differences in living standards. Given the importance of knowledge demonstrated in the previous chapter, we will start by looking at whether differences in education explain differences in economic success across countries. We will then see if an economy's

· · · · · · ·

[1]William Easterly, *The Elusive Quest for Growth: Economists' Adventures and Misadventures in the Tropics* (Cambridge: MIT Press, 2002), p. 289.

social institutions, such as property rights and corruption, are related to a country's economic well-being. Could it be that the health and nutrition of a country's citizens affect their standards of living? We'll consider that connection also. We also will look into how the level of "openness"—the amount of trade—explains differences in standards of living across countries. This is currently a hot topic here and around the globe. No doubt you have heard someone argue about the pros and cons of free trade and globalization? Finally, we'll consider the question "Is economic growth good for everyone?"

These other potential factors explaining growth are not just a laundry list of possibilities. Economists have found that given labor, capital, and knowledge, the fundamental building blocks of growth, the additional factors explored here (and economists have considered many more) are thought to be critical areas that at the margin help us answer the question posed by Collier.

As you will see, these "socio-economic" factors have important policy implications for any country that is trying to raise its population out of the depths of poverty, or to keep it from falling back into that trap. In the end, there may be no single "one-size-fits-all" remedy for anemic economic growth and poverty. Perhaps, as Easterly has suggested, the best approach is one tailored to each country's culture, history, and problems. As you can probably tell, improving a country's economic growth is a topic of continued interest not only for economists but also for policy makers trying to improve their citizens' economic well-being.

## 11.1 Educational Differences

The fact that you are reading this book means that at some point in your life someone impressed upon you the importance of getting a college degree. Perhaps you were told that furthering your education would make you a better citizen. More than likely, you were told that getting a college education was necessary if you wanted to get a good job and earn more money.

Ample evidence shows that college graduates, on average, suffer less unemployment and earn more money over their lifetimes than nongraduates. Sometimes people like to point out that Bill Gates and Mick Jagger don't have college degrees, and they still have been successful. What undermines this argument is that both Gates and Jagger have rare sets of talents that give them a competitive edge in their respective professions. When we talk about the *average* relationship between educational attainment and economic success, we understand that there will always be exceptions to the rule. Still the question remains: If becoming better educated tends to improve individuals' economic well-being, does this generality hold for countries as well?

Education builds human capital. People with more human capital generally are more productive. Education provides specific skills and enhances your ability to adapt to new situations and new technologies. To the extent that education expands the existing state of knowledge in an economy, a more educated population should, therefore, be associated with a higher level of productivity. As you saw in the previous chapter, knowledge raises the level of output for an existing amount of capital and labor, which generates higher incomes per worker.

### Years of Schooling

If more education is positively related to the earnings potential of individuals, do countries with higher levels of educational attainment on average also achieve higher standards of living? **Figure 11.1** shows the relationship between levels of real income

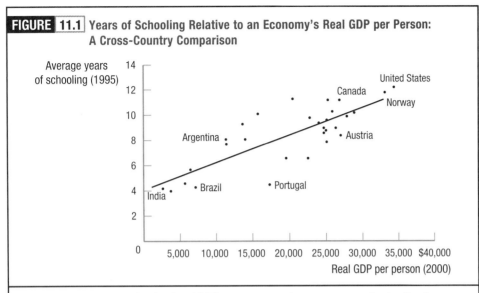

**FIGURE 11.1** Years of Schooling Relative to an Economy's Real GDP per Person: A Cross-Country Comparison

The relationship between levels of real GDP per person and average years of schooling for a number of countries is shown. The scatter of points and the line that represents the average relation between the two measures support the idea that higher standards of living are associated with higher levels of educational attainment. The upward slope to the scatter of points suggests that, on average, the more education a country's population receives, the more likely that the country will achieve a higher standard of living.

*Sources:* Robert J. and Jong-Wha Lee, "International Data on Educational Attainment, Updates and Implications." *Oxford Economic Papers*, 53 (July 2001): 541–63; *Penn World Tables.*

(measured as real GDP) per person and average years of schooling for a number of countries.

As in the previous chapter, the line drawn in the figure represents the average relation between the two measures. The scatter of points in Figure 11.1 fits with the idea that higher standards of living are associated with higher levels of educational attainment. When you compare current standards of living with the level of educational attainment 50 years ago, the same relation as that shown in Figure 11.1 emerges. This suggests that countries with higher levels of education in the past achieved higher standards of living, rather than the reverse. The upward slope to the scatter of points suggests that the more schooling the average country's population receives, the more likely that country will achieve a higher standard of living. This also means that the converse is true: the less educated a country's population is, the more likely it is to have a lower level of real income per person.

## Quality of Education

Economists have come to believe that measuring education merely by years in school may be misleading. Think about the link between education and economic success in a slightly different way. You attend a small, liberal-arts college several states from home, and your best friend stays at home to attend a large state university. You both major in economics (of course), and after four or so years, you both graduate with honors. Looking forward 20 years, why is it that one of you is still in that entry-level position with the local utility company while the other is the CEO of a global corporation?

The relative success of you and your friend, aside from innate skills, tenacity, willingness to take risk, and so on, could stem from the fact that years in school are not a good measure to compare your education, that is, the improvement in human capital or knowledge. If *what* you learn is not the same across colleges, states, or school districts, wouldn't it be important to account for differences in the *quality* of education instead of just years in school? In our global comparison of education and economic success, does it make sense to assume that 12 years' worth of education in Mozambique, where many teachers have only a few more years of schooling, is comparable to 12 years of education in, say, Germany, where teachers have at least a college degree? Not only do teachers in different countries have different skills and training, but the resources available to students vary considerably across countries. Unfortunately, out-of-date textbooks and dilapidated facilities are the norm in many poor countries (and in some poor areas of rich countries).

To see if quality of education helps explain differences in economic success, let's compare the results from standardized math tests of students in the seventh grade to real GDP per person across countries. If quality of education matters, we expect to find a positive relation between quality of education and the level of real income per person across countries.

**Figure 11.2** shows the relation between one measure of education quality and real GDP per person across a number of countries. Notice that the countries in which the average student scores higher on the standardized tests generally are the same countries that have higher levels of real GDP per person. This does not mean simply raising test scores will automatically increase real GDP per person. It does suggest,

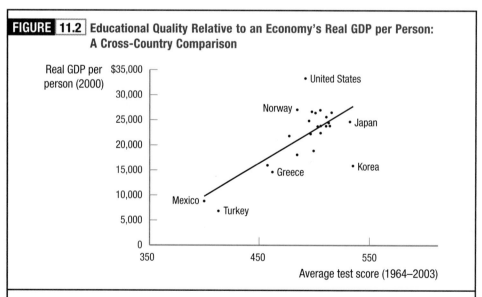

**FIGURE 11.2** | **Educational Quality Relative to an Economy's Real GDP per Person: A Cross-Country Comparison**

If the quality of education matters, we would expect to see a positive relation between the quality of education and real GDP per person across countries. This figure shows exactly that. The countries in which the average student scored higher on standardized tests—one measure of education quality and cognitive skills—generally have higher levels of real GDP per person. This is more evidence that improving human capital is positively related to economic well-being.

*Sources:* Eric A. Hanushek and Ludger Woessmann, "How Much Do Educational Outcomes Matter in OECD Countries?" National Bureau of Economic Research Working Paper 16515 (November 2010); *Penn World Tables*

however, that improving the population's human capital by improving the *quality* of the education, not just years in school, may improve future economic growth. Even though some of the countries with the highest levels of real GDP per person, such as the United States, do not necessarily have the highest test scores, the average relation (indicated by the line) in Figure 11.2 suggests that, all else the same, improving the quality of education pays off in higher standards of living.

## Education Policies and Economic Growth

Finding that education and economic success are positively related has important policy implications. Put yourself in the role of adviser to a leader of a country who is looking for a way to promote economic growth. Given the positive correlation between education and economic success, you might lobby for increased public investment in education: a better trained workforce is more productive, and higher productivity is associated with improved economic growth.

If you believe that increased education is a key to economic growth, would you suggest that your country's education policy focus on improving the *quality* of the nation's educational system or just keeping kids in school longer? Getting more people to attend school is a good thing, but spending that time in a quality learning environment may be better. Even if both seem to improve economic conditions, which provides more economic bang for the policy buck spent? And if you are thinking that this trade-off sounds familiar, the same debate occurs over schooling in the suburbs versus the inner cities and in cities versus rural school districts.

## SOLVED PROBLEM

**Q** Should we educate everyone for more growth? As a policy maker, would it be economically beneficial to educate more women?

**A** Education contributes to economic growth, but who receives it could be equally important. In many cultures, it is common for only men to receive a formal education beyond elementary school. In the United States, the idea that women should pursue college degrees is a relatively recent phenomenon. Fifty years ago, many women chose or were expected to stay home, engage in household-based production activities, and raise the family's children. Look around your classroom, and you'll see that it is probably evenly split between men and women.

Researchers are finding that increased education of females—especially girls and young women—leads to reduced fertility rates (births per woman). You saw in the previous chapter that countries with higher population growth also tend to be the poorest countries. Reducing fertility rates—and therefore population growth rates—could be one way to foster improved economic conditions. Advancing the education of women is, therefore, an important policy initiative to stem the population growth in poor countries.

## 11.2 Differences in Social Infrastructure

A country's **social infrastructure** can be thought of as its collection of institutions and cultural norms. For example, the political system and legal system are important components in this infrastructure. These two institutions help define property rights, which, as we've seen in an earlier chapter, are the basis for exchange. To refresh your memory, we define property rights as the legal or social right to use a scarce resource in a particular way. The question is how such institutions that define the social infrastructure are related to a country's economic well-being.

**SOCIAL INFRASTRUCTURE** The rules, regulations, and institutions that affect decisions to invest in capital, both human and physical.

**EXAMPLE** A drug company is spending billions to develop the new drug because its formula will be protected legally by a patent. The return the firm will realize will be enough to cover the cost of the product's research and development as well as result in a profit for the company.

**EXAMPLE** Countries are passing new laws and stiffening the penalties for pirating online music.

**EXAMPLE** Your city has a property owner's code requiring you to maintain your house and yard. Your house is in shambles, and your yard looks like a forest of weeds. Not wanting to see their property values decline, your neighbors contact the local government, which forces you to clean the place up or pay a hefty penalty.

Countries without a legal system that protects individuals' property rights could weaken incentives to succeed economically. Suppose you live in a country where, by law, all wages are equal, regardless of a worker's skill or education. If you graduate from college but cannot realize the economic benefits of your improved human capital, why bother? What if college graduates with degrees in education are unable to teach in any state they want to? What if they are forced to find work only in the state where they have obtained the necessary certification? Such impediments to the free flow of productive resources often lead to less than desirable economic outcomes. We see it in states across the United States; we also see it across countries.

A country's social infrastructure can affect the ability of its citizens to improve their economic well-being. Countries have different judicial and legislative structures, have different systems of property rights, and use different forms of market and nonmarket processes to achieve some distribution of incomes. Let's see if there are discernible relations between such social structures and economic standards of living.

## Differences in the Legal Environments of Countries

We often take our well-established and enforced laws for granted. Laws establish the rules of the game when it comes to social and economic interaction. Laws create conditions in which contracts are enforced. This greatly affects how we interact in our daily economic lives and how we trade with one another.

When you buy jeans at the mall, you pay for them with money that you've earned. This money usually comes from your (or your parents') ability to voluntarily exchange hours of work for an agreed-upon wage. A legal system such as ours gives you the property rights to sell your labor and reap most of the rewards (but not *all* of the rewards because the government gets a share in the form of taxes). The law also prevents you from owning someone else's labor: there is no slavery. Because we own the rights to the fruits of our labor, we have an incentive to invest in our own human capital, whether by going to college or by exercising to stay healthy.

Property rights also create an important incentive for individuals and firms to invent new products and production technologies. Intel, the giant computer-chip maker, announced in early 2007 that it had developed a new microchip that runs faster on less power.[2] Intel incurred great expense to develop the new chip. But if Intel

· · · · · · ·

[2]John Markoff, "Intel Says Chips Will Run Faster, Using Less Power." *New York Times*, January 27, 2007, A1.

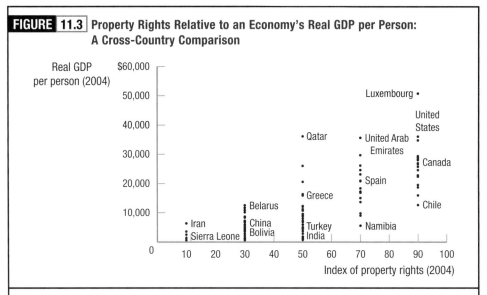

**FIGURE 11.3** **Property Rights Relative to an Economy's Real GDP per Person: A Cross-Country Comparison**

To see if property rights and economic success are linked, this figure compares a nation's real GDP per person to the strength of its property rights. On average, countries with the lowest property right measure (10) also tend to have the lowest levels of real GDP per person. Countries at the other end of the property rights spectrum tend to have higher levels of real GDP per person. Research indicates that not only are economic standards of living positively related to an improvement in property rights but so are rates of economic growth.

*Sources:* Heritage Foundation; *Penn World Tables*

couldn't expect to realize the potential economic rewards from developing and selling the chip, the firm wouldn't have bothered. The prospect of owning the patent for the chip and profiting from it gave Intel a powerful economic incentive to both design and market it. As you can see, people (and firms) respond to incentives.

Given the importance of property rights as a basis for exchange, do countries with better property rights enjoy higher economic standards of living? To see if property rights and economic success are linked, **Figure 11.3** compares standards of living to the strength of property rights for a large sample of countries. Because the property rights measure assigns values only at 10, 30, 50, and so on, this leads to the "stacks" you see along the horizontal axis. The higher the value for the property rights index the stronger is that country's system of property rights.

Figure 11.3 reveals that, on average, countries with the lowest property right measure (10) also tend to have the lowest levels of real GDP per person. Countries at the other end of the property rights spectrum, including the United States and Canada, tend to have higher levels of real GDP per person. This positive relationship between a country's property rights and economic standard of living has been found in a number of studies. The more sophisticated studies also find that developing a system of adequate property rights—creating laws and enforcing them—generally precedes economic advancement. Thus, economic standards of living are positively related to an improvement in and enforcement of property rights.

This relation between property rights and economic success is not lost on the political leaders in many countries that recently abandoned the communist economic model. For instance, China adopted a law in 2007 that strengthened the property rights of individuals.[3] This change is a significant step away from its traditional state-controlled approach to business and the private sector. Rearranging property rights can result in conflict among different groups in society, however. As you might expect, the change in China sparked controversy and debate, largely because it was viewed as a way for the rising middle class to maintain its recent economic success. The fact that property rights are being improved in China and in other previously nonmarket-oriented countries means that those governments are beginning to recognize how important property rights are in terms of promoting economic growth and raising standards of living.

## Government Corruption

Government corruption takes many forms. In some countries, government officials skim off aid intended for public-investment programs, such as education or the building of sewer systems. Sometimes government officials use the government's taxing power as their own personal income, taking "loans" from government coffers that enable them to enhance their lifestyles. You have probably read or watched news stories about how firms often resort to paying bribes simply to stay in business in some countries. In its 2006 edition of the *Bribe Payers Index*, Transparency International ranked China, India, and Russia as the worst offenders out of 30 countries examined. That is, companies are more likely to pay bribes to government officials and other businesses in these countries than, say, in Switzerland or Sweden.

Corrupt governments or governments that allow corruption to run unchecked foul up people's incentive to produce. If you aren't entitled to keep most of what you earn because some corrupt government official is pocketing the profits, often through bribes, would you bother to work very hard? People need incentives to engage in activities that bring about economic growth: to work, to open new businesses, and/or to get more education. In effect, corruption renders laws ineffective, impedes property rights, and thus hinders economic growth.[4]

Is the conventional wisdom that corruption seems to occur more often in poor and developing countries supported by the facts? **Figure 11.4** shows the relation between government corruption and real income per person for a large number of countries. The corruption measure comes from worldwide surveys of government officials and businesses executives as well as an examination of each country's laws. Corruption in the figure runs from "high corruption" at the bottom to "low corruption" at the top of the vertical axis. Countries that have a high level of corruption, for example, are Bangladesh with a score of 12 and Kazakhstan with a score of 23. Countries characterized by relatively low levels of corruption include the United States and Finland, with corruption index numbers of 77 and 97, respectively.

The scatter of points in Figure 11.4 reveals a distinctly positive relation between low corruption and income per person: lower levels of corruption, on average, are associated with higher levels of real income per person. This suggests that countries being run by "bad" governments, especially if they already are poor, are less likely to achieve

· · · · · · · ·

[3]"New Law Backing Individuals' Property Rights Highlights Divisions about Economic Change." *The Wall Street Journal*, March 10, 2007, A5.

[4]Jason Higbee and Frank A. Schmid, "Rule of Law and Economic Growth." Federal Reserve Bank of St. Louis, *International Economic Trends* (August 2004).

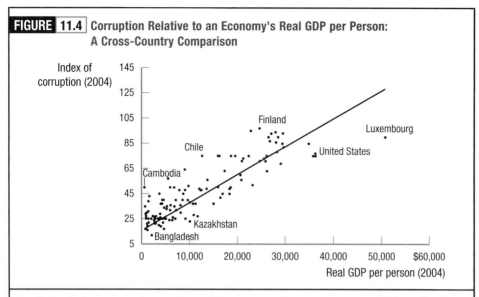

**FIGURE 11.4** | Corruption Relative to an Economy's Real GDP per Person: A Cross-Country Comparison

Are the level of government corruption and the average citizen's economic well-being related? The corruption measured in this figure is based on surveys of government officials and businesses executives as well as an examination of each country's laws. Corruption in the figure runs from "high corruption" at the bottom to "low corruption" at the top of the vertical axis. When plotted against real GDP per person for a large number of countries, the scatter of points reveals a distinctly negative relation between the two measures: higher levels of corruption, on average, are associated with lower levels of real GDP per person.

*Sources:* Heritage Foundation; *Penn World Tables*

economic growth. For example, the eight-year reign of Idi Amin over Uganda during the 1970s led not only to mass murder and terror but also to economic collapse.[5]

Many people believe that establishing legal constraints on government actions and government leaders may significantly improve poor countries' chances for economic growth. Have you noticed so far that some of the poorest nations in the world also have the weakest property rights and the most intrusive and corrupt governments?

## 11.3  Health and Economic Success

Healthier people are more productive than the sick. Sick people miss work; healthy people don't. Healthy people generally work more years during their lifetimes than the chronically ill. A recent study published in the *New York Times* even showed that sick people do not get as much education as healthy people do.[6] You already have seen that economic success is positively related to more education. So, could there be a link between missing out on education due to illness and the lack of economic success?

If good health improves worker productivity, whether by allowing people to attend school and improving their human capital or by keeping workers on the job, a positive link between measures of health and standards of living would indicate

· · · · · · ·

[5]Michael T. Kaufman, "Idi Amin, Brutal Ruler of Uganda in the 70s, Dies." *New York Times International,* August 16, 2003. The 2006 movie *The Last King of Scotland* is based on Amin's rule.

[6]Gina Kolata, "A Surprising Secret to a Long Life: Stay in School." *New York Times,* January 3, 2007, A1.

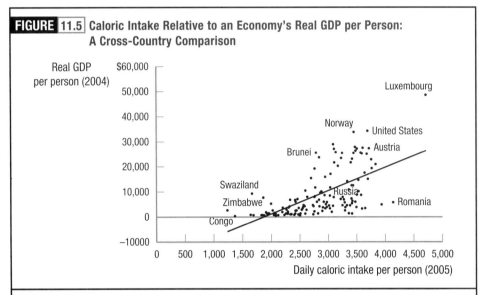

**FIGURE 11.5** Caloric Intake Relative to an Economy's Real GDP per Person: A Cross-Country Comparison

Comparing the average daily intake of calories per person and real GDP per person in a number of countries shows that there is a definite positive relation between the two. This suggests that countries whose populations are better fed also are more likely to have higher standards of living.

*Sources:* United Nations; *Penn World Tables*

that a policy of improving health conditions in a country might promote economic growth. To test the validity of this proposition, let's look at the relation between economic success and "health" using two measures of the latter. One is basic nutrition. Economists have found that improvements in basic nutrition often precede economic growth. One study has shown that advances in nutrition were a contributing factor to economic growth in the United Kingdom during the nineteenth century. The other health measure is a country's average life expectancy. Arguably, a lower life expectancy is one indicator of an unhealthy living environment.

What's the relation between nutrition and standards of living? **Figure 11.5** compares the average daily intake of calories per person and income per person in a number of countries. You can see that there is a positive relation between nutrition and income per person across countries. Even though the link between health and economic growth is probably more complicated than our attempt to capture it, a positive relation between the two measures clearly exists across countries. This suggests that countries whose populations are better fed—and presumably healthier—are also more likely to have higher levels of real income per person. To state the obvious, malnourishment is not conducive to increased worker productivity and economic growth.

**ECONOMIC FALLACY**    The more calories you consume, the more productive you become.

**False.** You are named to be the diet czar by the president. Looking at the positive relation between caloric intake and real GDP per person in Figure 11.5, you decide to embark on a plan to increase the calories consumed by everyone in the economy—not to improve their diets but to simply increase their caloric intake. Why would this policy fail to achieve the goal of raising real GDP per person?

More calories do not mean healthier diets. In the United States, we are seeing that the population is, on average, becoming heavier. This trend is showing up as increases in certain diseases, such as diabetes and heart disease. When increased caloric intake simply means fattier diets and fatter people, it does not translate into healthier and more productive workers. That said, a policy that ensures some minimum caloric intake—and therefore a diet that meets some minimum consumption of healthy food—should improve the health of the population. If improved health in turn means better chances at improved education and fewer days missing work, then increased calories may indeed make the average person more productive.

The life expectancy of people in the United States and other economically advanced countries is about 70 years. By contrast, life expectancy in Zimbabwe is less than 40 years. But be careful how you use such statistics: life expectancy is measured from the time of birth. If the infant mortality rate is high, this drastically reduces the life-expectancy number. Even with this caveat, life expectancy is a useful barometer because it reflects a number of different factors related to overall health. So, what is the relation between life expectancy and economic success?

**Figure 11.6** shows that there is a definite positive relationship between life expectancy and real GDP per person across countries. (The life-expectancy figures are for males.) Countries with low life expectancies tend to be very poor countries. Once again, determining the direction of causation is difficult, but the following scenario seems reasonable: as people become more economically successful, they demand

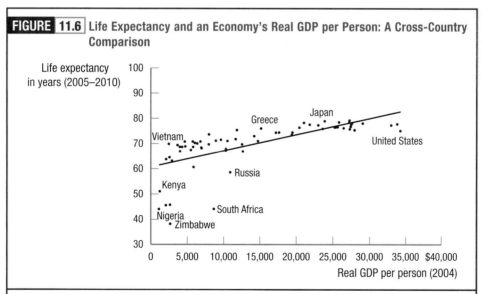

**FIGURE 11.6** Life Expectancy and an Economy's Real GDP per Person: A Cross-Country Comparison

As this figure shows, countries with low life expectancies also tend to be countries with low per person real GDPs. However, the figure also shows that the positive relationship between life expectancy and real GDP per person largely disappears after a country achieves a life expectancy of about 75 years. This implies that, regardless of how wealthy a country and its citizens are, there is a limit to how much medical technology can extend the average human life span.

*Sources: The Economist; Penn World Tables*

more and better medical services and recognize the benefits of better nutrition. These actions lead to a greater life expectancy for the newly born, who become productive workers.

Notice anything odd about the shape of the scatter of points? Figure 11.6 shows us that the positive relationship between life expectancy and level of GDP per person largely disappears after a country achieves a life expectancy of about 75 years. This implies that, regardless of how wealthy a country is, there is a limit to which economic success—and medical technology—can extend the average human life.

Many individuals living in poor countries simply do not have access to the level of medical care people in richer countries do. Some do not have access to the basic hygiene afforded by indoor plumbing and clean water. Without proper sanitation, disease spreads, and life expectancy is low. One step to improving the economic outlook of some countries, such as those in the lower-left portion of Figure 11.6, may be simply providing greater access to modern sanitation. After all, it worked in the past for New York City and London.

## Policy Issues

Figures 11.5 and 11.6 raise important policy issues. Countries with pervasive malnutrition often get caught in a vicious cycle of illness and poverty. Malnourished people are unable to work and, as a result, remain mired in poverty. If malnourishment increases throughout the population, overall productivity falls, and the economy is unable to prosper economically. This scenario is why many relief funds try to get food and medicine to the poorest nations. As we saw earlier, however, such funds or material are sometimes diverted by corrupt government officials, thus creating the link between corruption, poor health, and weak economic growth.

A healthier population also has a lower childhood mortality rate, which actually creates an economic incentive that we often do not think about. If a parent believes that her child will live to adulthood, she is more likely to invest in the child's future—build their human capital. Parents facing the prospect that most of their children will die at an early age are not as likely to make that investment, or they may focus the investment on one infant. Improved health care, especially for children, also reduces the incentive for couples to have many children, thus reducing population growth. In this way, improving health may provide incentives that indirectly but very importantly lead to economic growth.

Improving people's health is not always a complicated process. Something as simple as using mosquito nets can reduce the incidence of malaria and significantly reduce child mortality in some of the poorest nations.[7] Access to things that most of us take for granted, such as working sanitation systems, also reduces the spread of disease and promotes better health. A United Nations study showed that increasing the use of toilets could reduce disease rates in many areas.[8]

Often, however, preventing diseases is difficult. The seemingly unchecked spread of the virus that causes HIV in several sub-Saharan African countries apparently

- - - - - - -

[7]See Celia W. Dugger, "Report on Child Deaths Finds Some Hope in Poorest Nations." *New York Times*, May 8, 2007, A6.

[8]Celia W. Dugger, "Toilets Underused to Fight Disease, U.N. Study Finds." *New York Times*, November 10, 2006.

knows no geographical boundaries. The incidence of HIV in India has even raised concerns about that country's future economic growth.[9]

The conclusion we can draw is that chances for economic growth can be enhanced by improving the health of many people currently living in some of the poorest and unhealthiest economies. Policies to undertake public-health programs that improve overall health conditions and increase life expectancy could promote economic growth and help countries improve their economic standard of living.

## 11.4  Differences in Openness

**Openness** refers to the freedom with which a country's citizens trade goods and services with the citizens of other countries. You might be wondering why we use the term *openness* rather than *free trade*. One reason is because *free trade* often connotes only the exchange of goods, such as televisions or trucks. Although that is part of openness, the term also refers to the flow of ideas, labor, and financial capital across national boundaries. The greater the degree of openness, the easier it is for ideas, capital, and labor, as well as goods and services, to flow between economies. Openness ranges from countries that are relatively open to those that are relatively closed. We use the term "relative" because it would be difficult to find a country that generates all of its income from exporting, just as it would be difficult to find a country that engages in absolutely no external trade.

> **OPENNESS** The extent to which goods, services, capital, labor, and ideas flow into and out of a country.

> **EXAMPLE** The North American Free Trade Agreement (NAFTA) lowered trade barriers among the United States, Canada, and Mexico, which led to a large increase in U.S. agricultural exports.

> **EXAMPLE** Between 1870 and 1925, an estimated 10 percent of the world's population moved to other countries, resulting in a relocation of labor that has not been matched since.

> **EXAMPLE** The computer you are working on contains parts from several Asian countries, was assembled in Mexico, and was delivered to your door by a U.S.-based company.

Countries that ban foreign firms from investing in their domestic industries may retard economic growth. When Volkswagen builds a manufacturing facility in Mexico, it "exports" its current production technology—from assembly line automation to management techniques—to Mexico. This "transplanted" knowledge can lead to substantial improvements in the living standards of the importing country. It is estimated that 73 percent of Japan's technological progress following World War II came from ideas produced in other countries. The comparable numbers for Canada and the United States are 97 percent and 18 percent, respectively.[10]

· · · · · · ·

[9]Peter Wonacott, "India's Economy Risks Slowdown if HIV Spreads." *The Wall Street Journal*, July 24, 2006.

[10]Jonathan Eaton and Samuel Kortum, "Trade in Ideas: Patenting and Productivity in the OECD." *Journal of International Economics* (May 1996): 251–278.

Is there a relationship between a country's degree of openness and its growth in income per person? We use the scheme created by Jeffrey Sachs and Andrew Warner to decide if a country is, to use their terms, "open" or "closed."[11] Their approach tries to gauge a country's openness based on information about trade policies, the extent of regulations that block trade, and so on. Although countries differ in terms of their relative openness, we will simply classify a country as open or closed. We want to see if those economies that Sachs and Warner define as open are also economies that tend to grow faster than those economies that are closed.

**Figure 11.7** compares the average annual growth rate of real GDP per person from 1980 to 2000 with the initial level of real GDP per person in 1980. We use 1980 as a basis of comparison to account for the fact that a country's initial level of income can affect its subsequent growth rate. Low-income countries do not have to experience much of an increase in income per person to generate a large percentage increase. This figure allows us to ask the following question: After we've accounted for their initial level of income, do countries that are more open tend to grow faster than countries that are less open?

You will notice that the figure has two panels. Panel (a) includes open economies while panel (b) consists of countries having the characteristics of being closed. How do the growth rates of the closed economies compare to those of the open economies? First, there is no discernible relationship between the original level of income per person and its subsequent growth for the countries in the closed group. In other words, the economy in this group that started out relatively poor probably did not experience much economic growth over the past couple of decades. In fact, for the closed economies, growth in real GDP per person over the 20-year period averaged *less than* 1 percent per year. A number of countries in this group even experienced *negative* average growth rates in real income. This is not a ringing endorsement for keeping or even raising barriers to trade, both in terms of goods and ideas.

In contrast, the majority of "open" economies experienced much faster average rates of growth since 1980. The average annual growth in real income per person for the open economies is about 4.5 percent, more than four times that of the closed economies. Whereas a number of closed countries experienced zero or even negative growth rates, only one open economy experienced slightly negative average growth over the 1980–2000 period.

### Economic Convergence?

Figure 11.7 also reveals that some open countries, such as South Korea and Taiwan, started out relatively poor but experienced much *faster* rates of growth in income than their high-income counterparts such as the United States or Switzerland. Economists find that when closed economies become more open, their economic-growth rates often jump significantly. For instance, embracing a liberalized trading system at the end of the 1800s led some Scandinavian countries and Ireland to experience faster rates of economic growth compared with countries that remained closed. As mentioned, Taiwan and South Korea are modern-day examples of countries that have adopted more open trade policies and have experienced rapid economic growth.

Outcomes such as these have led some people to suggest that openness is one explanation for **convergence**, the idea that poorer countries experience faster growth rates than rich ones.

· · · · · · ·

[11]Jeffrey Sachs and Andrew Warner, "Economic Reform and the Process of Global Integration." *Brookings Papers on Economic Activity*, 1 (1995): 1–118.

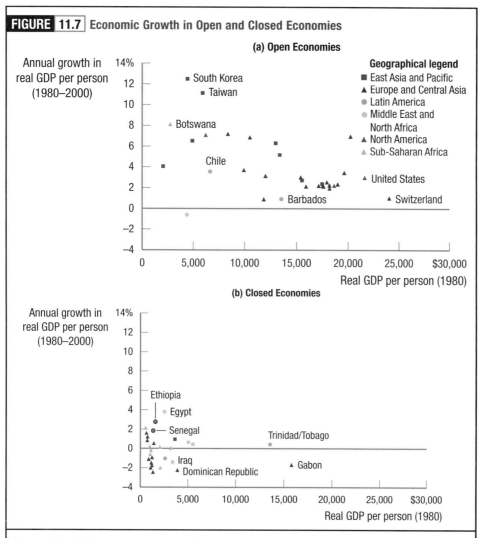

**FIGURE 11.7** | Economic Growth in Open and Closed Economies

**(a) Open Economies**

Annual growth in real GDP per person (1980–2000)

**Geographical legend**
- East Asia and Pacific
- Europe and Central Asia
- Latin America
- Middle East and North Africa
- North America
- Sub-Saharan Africa
- United States

South Korea, Taiwan, Botswana, Chile, Barbados, Switzerland

Real GDP per person (1980)

**(b) Closed Economies**

Annual growth in real GDP per person (1980–2000)

Ethiopia, Egypt, Senegal, Trinidad/Tobago, Iraq, Dominican Republic, Gabon

Real GDP per person (1980)

Do countries that are more open grow faster, on average, than economies that are less open? The open economies, which are shown in panel (a) of the figure, experienced an average annual growth rate in real GDP per person of about 4.5 percent. This is more than four times that of the closed economies, which are shown in panel (b). The closed economies show no discernible relationship between the original level of GDP per person (shown on the horizontal axis) and subsequent economic growth. The cluster of points near the origin suggests that the average closed economy that started out relatively poor did not experience much economic growth over the following 20 years.

*Sources:* Jeffrey D. Sachs and Andrew Warner, "Economic Reform and the Process of Global Integration." *Brookings Papers on Economic Activity* (1995): 1–118; *Penn World Tables*

**CONVERGENCE** The observation that real income per person in a poor country grows at a faster rate than in a rich one. If it continues, the level of real income per person in the poor country will converge—or catch up to—that of the rich country.

EXAMPLE The traffic ahead of you is moving at 60 miles per hour. You are traveling at 75 miles per hour. If you do not slow down, and the cars in front of you do not speed up, you will eventually pass them by.

**EXAMPLE** The average baby quickly increases its weight by about two times its birth weight. For a 6-pound baby, if this rate of weight gain continued, the child would weigh as much as his 200-pound father by the time he reaches kindergarten. As we mature—as we converge to our adult height and weight—our growth rate slows down and eventually stops.

The idea of convergence is that the levels of real income per person in some countries are converging, or catching up, with the richer countries. This is why their growth rates are higher compared to more "mature" countries such as the United States or Germany. Think of children growing taller and catching up to their parents' height. As in human growth, economic convergence does not mean that faster growing countries will always pass by currently rich countries. For countries, at some point, diminishing returns to inputs—capital and labor—set in, and economic growth slows. Such observations suggest that China's income per person probably will not surpass that of the United States any more than Japan, which was similarly predicted to surpass the United States in the 1980s. (Refer to the Economic Fallacy, "China's economic standard of living will soon surpass that of the United States," in Chapter 10 for details.)

Unlike humans, countries can continue to grow after they've "matured"; they just do not grow as fast. But are countries' economic-growth rates actually converging? Is what the model predicts happening? As we have seen, not all countries experience equal economic growth. Some have prospered while others remain bogged down in poverty. This remains an area of continued study, one that you will some day perhaps provide the answer.

## 11.5 Economic Growth and Improved Income Distributions

People who believe that economic growth stems directly from foreign trade argue for putting fewer restrictions on trade with other countries. Others see international trade as exploitive: they believe "rich" nations are extracting natural resources and cheap labor from poorer, developing nations without adequately compensating them.[12] Still other critics argue that we are simply sending jobs overseas when the government allows domestic businesses to relocate abroad in search of lower costs, or when foreign firms enter local markets to compete with "our" industries.

Trade does lead to some individuals losing their jobs to overseas competition. Sending jobs to other parts of the world in search of less-expensive production benefits those of us buying the goods produced elsewhere. It is argued that globalization is one important factor that has held down price increases over the past decade. We live in a global economy, which means that jobs are just as likely to move to another country as to another state. (See the discussion of globalization in Chapter 9.) It also means that jobs will move here from foreign countries.

When you consider who wins and who loses from increased openness, you also have to look at factors other than just job loss or job gain. Would you be willing to

[12]David Wessel, "As Globalization's Benefits Grow, So Do Its Skeptics." *The Wall Street Journal,* March 29, 2007, A6.

pay several thousand dollars a year more to buy clothing if doing so prevented jobs at U.S. clothing manufacturers from going overseas? What if the costs to U.S. consumers were far greater than the total income these workers earned? It has been estimated that for every dollar related to offshoring, the United States gets back about $1.12.[13] It might seem cold and calculating, but those who debate the pros and cons of allowing trade to occur freely among nations routinely ask these questions—and so should you.

Even though trade creates winners and losers, we have seen that trade—openness, that is—and faster economic growth are related. Have increased openness and related growth positively affected the distribution of income across countries? Stated differently, are there fewer desperately poor people today than there were 30 or 40 years ago? To address this important question, one of the foremost authorities on economic growth, economist Xavier Sala-i-Martin, looked at how the distribution of income across countries has evolved over the past 40 years. The curves in **Figure 11.8** show Sala-i-Martin's estimated income distributions for the 1970s, 1980s, 1990s, and into the 2000s. Each curve shows the number of people in the world who experienced very low to very high levels of income per person in that decade.

---

**FIGURE 11.8** World Income Distribution by Decade

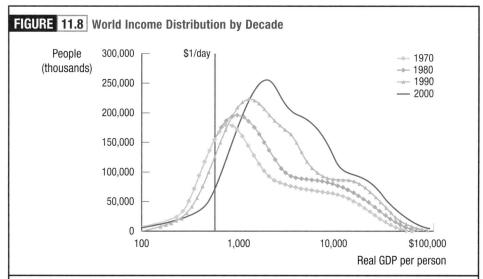

Are there fewer desperately poor people today in the world than there were 30 or 40 years ago? Each curve in the figure shows the number of people in the world who experienced very low to very high levels of income per person in one of four decades. The graph shows that since the 1970s, more and more people around the world have begun to experience higher income levels, as evidenced by the fact that today more of the population lies to the right of the $1/day mark (i.e., $1 of income per day per person, which is a commonly used benchmark of poverty). Not only is the world's income distribution shifting further and further to the right (fewer people are living in extreme poverty), but the peak of the distribution also has moved to higher income levels over time. The highest curve is the 2000s curve.

*Source:* Xavier Sala-i-Martin, "The World Distribution of Income: Falling Poverty and ... Convergence, Period." *Quarterly Journal of Economics,* 121 (May 2006): 351–67.

---

· · · · · · ·

[13]McKinsey Global Institute 2004 as reported in http://gregmankiw.blogspot.com (2004).

The important story from Figure 11.8 is that the distribution of income over time has marched steadily rightward and is becoming more peaked. Compared to the 1970s, more and more people around the world have higher real incomes. This conclusion comes from the fact that today more of the population lies to the right of the $1/day mark (i.e., $1 of income per day per person, which is a commonly used benchmark of poverty). That benchmark is shown as the vertical line in the figure. You can see that over time, less and less of the distribution lies to the left of the $1/day reference line.

Not only is the world's income distribution shifting further and further to the right—fewer people are living under such extreme poverty—but the peak of the distribution also has moved to higher income levels over time. Notice that the highest peak of all occurred in this decade. This means that the average individual's income has been increasing over the 40-year period.

Opponents of globalization often argue that it leads to increased earnings differences between upper- and lower-income groups. That is, they argue that the rich are getting richer, and the poor are getting poorer. That claim is not evident from Figure 11.8, however. This does not mean that significant discrepancies in income do not exist in some countries. But even if the income gap is widening, the evidence suggests that those at the lower end have benefited substantially from economic growth. If incomes in some of the poorest yet most populated countries—China and India, for example—are growing faster than ever before, the unequal distribution of income is becoming less dramatic than it was in the past. To paraphrase the old saying, the rising tide of economic growth raises all incomes.

The income of more and more of the world's population is moving toward that of the relatively rich countries. Whether this is economic convergence remains a debated and extensively studied area in economics. This important outcome should not lead us to ignore the fact that some societies remain mired in poverty. In this chapter, we have touched upon some of the more "institutional" aspects that help explain why poverty and the lack of economic improvement persist. As you have seen, lack of openness, the poorly protected property rights, the bad behavior of governments, and the ill health of the population are factors that help explain this.

## 11.6 Declining Populations

In the early 1800s, a British economist and demographer named Thomas Malthus made the dire prediction that the human population would increase at a rate that would outstrip food production. In most countries, such a catastrophe has been avoided. New technology has helped farmers around the world increase their food production at a pace fast enough that the bulk of the world's population hasn't starved.

Even though Malthus was wrong, the concern over expanding populations received greater attention beginning in the 1960s. Some modern Malthusians warned that people would strain the world's food resources in the twenty-first century.[14] Unless the world's population growth was slowed to the point of zero population growth, it was predicted that there would be widespread famine and, as a result, political unrest.

Modern demographers expect the world population to peak at about 10 billion sometime in the next 50 years or so. Although this is still a big increase compared to

· · · · · · ·

[14]Perhaps the best known is the ecologist Paul Ehrlich, author of the 1968 best-seller *The Population Bomb*. The editorial "Zero Population Growth: It Cannot Come Too Soon," *New York Times*, November 17, 1982, makes it all too clear that such ideas persist.

the world's current population (which is about 6.5 billion), the trend has economists worried. The reason is that populations in three areas of the globe are actually beginning to decline: central and eastern Europe, countries in the northern Mediterranean, and some countries in east Asia, especially Japan.

What are the economic implications of a decrease in population? Let's use the tools we've developed to address this question on two fronts. First we will examine the implications of a slowdown in population growth on the economy's ability to produce goods and services. Then we'll see how a change in the population, more specifically the aging of the population, could affect the funding of government programs aimed at providing income assistance to retired people, such as Social Security.

## Declining Population and Economic Growth

To begin with, let's provide a perspective on what today's population trends look like across three groups of countries. **Table 11.1** shows the average population growth rates over the past 50 years and projections for the next 50 years. The "more-developed" countries include countries of North America, Europe, Japan, Australia, and New Zealand. The "least-developed" countries include the 48 poorest countries. Finally, the "less-developed" are countries between these two extremes. As you can see, the population growth in the more-developed countries is expected to stop. In the less-developed group of countries, population growth is expected to slow dramatically. In contrast, population growth will continue at about the same pace in the least-developed country group.[15]

Let's first consider the potential long-run effects of a reduction in population growth. You know from the previous chapter on economic growth (Chapter 10) that output per person can be linked to the amount of capital available to each worker

---

**Table 11.1** **Average Annual Population Growth Rates (Historical and Projected) by Country Group**

| Country Group | Time Period | |
|---|---|---|
| | 1950–2000 | 2000–2050 |
| More developed | 0.8% | 0.0% |
| Less developed | 2.1 | 0.8 |
| Least developed | 2.4 | 2.1 |

This table reports the average population growth rates over the past 50 years and the projected rates for the next 50 years. The group designated as "more-developed countries" includes those in North America and Europe as well as the countries of Japan, Australia, and New Zealand. Countries in the group "least-developed countries" include the 48 poorest countries. Countries in the group "less developed" fall between these two extremes. From the projections shown, population growth in the more-developed and less-developed countries is expected to slow or even stop over the next 50 years. In contrast, populations in the least-developed countries are expected to continue expanding at a rate only slightly slower than in the past 50 years.

**Source:** David N. Weil, *Economic Growth* (Boston: Pearson, 2005), p. 139.

---

· · · · · · ·

[15]Population growth can also be thought of as the reorganization of where people live. For example, there can be population decline if everyone moves out of your town. This has the same effect as a decline in population growth. See, for example, "The Great Plains Drain: How the Interior Is Learning to Live with a Shrinking Population," *The Economist*, January 19, 2008.

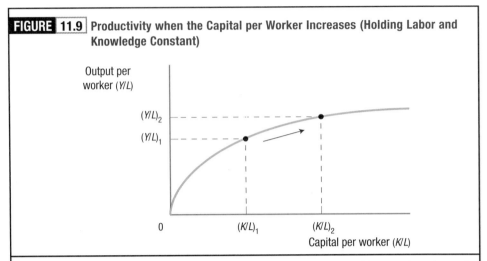

**FIGURE 11.9** | Productivity when the Capital per Worker Increases (Holding Labor and Knowledge Constant)

Recall that output per person can be linked to the amount of capital available to each worker and to an economy's technology (or knowledge). An increase in capital per worker ($K/L$), shown as a movement up along the productivity curve, increases a nation's level of output per worker ($Y/L$). More capital per worker increases productivity, which translates into more output. What happens if the population—and the size of an economy's labor force ($L$)—shrinks? If this happens, all else the same, the ratio of capital to labor ($K/L$) will rise, and we will get the same outcome as when we increased the nation's capital. Consequently, a decline in the population growth of a country *could* actually increase its per worker output.

and to an economy's technology (or knowledge). **Figure 11.9** shows this relation. It shows how an increase in capital per worker (K/L) affects a nation's level of output per worker (Y/L). More capital per worker increases productivity, which translates into more output.

Instead of thinking of the movement from $(K/L)_1$ to $(K/L)_2$ as being caused by an increase in capital, what happens if the population—and the size of an economy's labor force (*L*)—shrinks? In other words, we want to think about the effects on productivity when capital and knowledge are held constant, and only the labor force shrinks. If the amount of capital is unchanged, having fewer workers increases the ratio of capital to labor (increases the *K/L* ratio), and we get the same outcome as when we increased capital only: the capital-labor ratio rises from $(K/L)_1$ to $(K/L)_2$, and the output per worker increases. So, as you can see, a decline in the population growth of a country *could* actually increase its per worker output.

But this prediction has a catch. Along with lower population growth, many countries are also seeing a shift in the age distribution of their populations. People are getting, on average, older. The United Nations predicts that by 2050, the average age of people living in developed nations will rise to over 46 years from its current level of about 37 years. Let's use another example to make this point: about 50 years ago in Japan, people over 65 accounted for about 5 percent of the population. Today, people over 65 make up nearly 20 percent of the Japanese population.[16]

"So what if the population is getting older? How does that affect me?" you might be wondering. One problem is that when the population ages, there are fewer people

- - - - - - -

[16]"Cloud, or Silver Linings?" *The Economist*, July 28, 2007.

of working age. Even though the remaining workers might be more productive than those who have retired, the increase in the nonworking portion of the population will have a negative impact on output. To see this, the link between the growth of real output and the growth of the labor force and population can be written as:

> Growth rate of real output per person = the growth rate of real output per worker + the growth rate of (workers/population)

The growth rate of real output per worker is a measure of productivity. The growth rate of the workers-to-population ratio captures the change in the working-age population caused by aging. If worker productivity remains the same, an aging population will reduce output growth. This is because the second component of growth in real GDP per person is becoming smaller: the number of workers is falling relative to the total size of the population. For instance, in the United States, the worker-to-population ratio is projected by some to fall from .60 to .54 over the next 20 years.[17] This might not sound like much, but it implies that there will be about a .5 percent *reduction* in the annual growth rate of real output per person. In a $10-trillion economy, this drop in the growth rate translates into a $50-billion reduction in the amount of goods and services produced over the next few decades, which translates into your future standard of living being lower than where it would be otherwise.

Will this always be the outcome of an aging population? No. For countries that have historically had very high fertility rates and, therefore, very young populations, an aging population can have just the opposite effect. If fewer children are born, the percentage of a country's population that is working age might increase over time. This will lead to just the opposite effect we described for the United States. In these countries, an increase in the growth of the working-age population will increase the growth of output per person, at least until that population also begins to age. Immigration might also increase the population to an extent that offsets declining birth rates. If true, it puts the ongoing immigration debate in a different light, doesn't it?

## An Aging Population and Social Insurance Programs

Recent population trends—shrinking and aging populations—are expected to affect economic growth in the coming decades, but what about current changes in demographics? Most developed economies have established social programs to assist the elderly. For example, Social Security in the United States was originally created as an old-age insurance program. The goal of other federal programs, such as Medicare, Medicaid, and the health care reform bill enacted in 2010, is to help people receive better health care. But will an aging population—and the associated increase in demand for such services—strain the budgets of these programs? If the workforce fails to expand, or if technology does not increase worker productivity, will the economy expand fast enough (and tax revenues rise enough) to fund these programs?[18] What if substantially higher taxes are necessary to build up the Social Security fund so we can meet those future commitments? Will a younger and reduced workforce be able (or willing) to foot the bill for the programs enjoyed and expected by the elderly? Time (and politics) will tell.

· · · · · · ·

[17]These figures are taken from David N. Weil, *Economic Growth*, (Boston: Pearson, 2005).

[18]Sheryl WuDunn, "Economic Threat of Aging Populace." *New York Times*, September 2, 1997.

## WHAT YOU SHOULD HAVE LEARNED FROM CHAPTER 11

■ That differences in education, whether measured by years of schooling or quality of education, can help explain differences in economic standards of living.

■ That countries with higher levels of real income per person also are characterized by better systems to protect property rights and by less corruption.

■ That healthier economies also tend to be those that have higher economic standards of living.

■ That relatively more open economies tend to experience faster economic growth than relatively closed economies.

■ That the distribution of income across the world is improving, meaning that fewer people are living in dire poverty than at any time in the past 40 years.

■ That changes in the population of a country, both in its size (populations do not always grow) and in its demographics, can have important effects on economic growth.

## KEY TERMS

Social infrastructure, p. 291                    Convergence, p. 300

Openness, p. 299

## QUESTIONS AND PROBLEMS

1. In this chapter we have focused on real GDP per person as the yardstick of economic success. What are possible problems with using only this measure for that purpose?

2. The authors of this book each spent an additional four (or more) years in school to earn an advanced degree in economics. Other economists of approximately the same age spent just as much time in graduate school, but have already won the Nobel Prize.

   a) If they all went to school the same number of years, why haven't they all won a Nobel Prize?

   b) How does this relate to what you have learned about education and economic growth?

3. In early 2008, the Chinese government announced that it would maintain its one-child policy for another decade. This policy calls on families to limit the number of children.

   a) Based on the growth model developed in the previous chapter, explain what the potential long-term impact of such a policy is on China's economic growth. Is it positive or negative?

   b) Critics of this policy allege that it has created a gender imbalance: the proportion of males is greater than females in the population. Could such an imbalance affect economic growth? Explain.

   c) According to the evidence presented in this chapter, what kind of educational policy would you develop in light of the one-child policy?

4. In 2007, Nigeria was Africa's most populous country and the world's eighth-largest oil exporter. Yet it ranked only 159 out of 177 countries on the United Nations' Human Development Index. In other words, much of Nigeria's population lived in wretched poverty.

   a) Do an Internet search on Nigeria to see what you can find about its government.

   b) Is the evidence you uncovered consistent with the results in Figure 11.4?

5. If you own your home, you have the right to sell it at whatever price you deem correct. But sometimes individual property rights are at odds with the economic well-being of the public. Suppose you are the individual presiding over the following conflicts. What is your decision? Explain what you based your decision on.

    a) Bill's property is directly in the middle of a planned highway extension. The state is willing to pay him fair market value for his property, $125,000, but he wants $500,000 instead.

    b) Valerie's property, along with her neighbors', is where a private developer wants to build a new shopping mall. Representatives of the developer have offered each of them $150,000 for their homes, a price 20 percent above fair market values. Valerie is the only holdout. It isn't the price; she just doesn't want to move.

6. In some cultures, there is pressure for children to excel in their education, especially in math and science. Knowing this:

    a) Is it necessarily true that these countries will also be the most economically successful?

    b) What other factors might hinder the economic success of the country?

7. Transparency International collects data on corruption across countries. One of the measures they publish is the *Bribe Payers Index*, or BPI. The higher the BPI, the more bribes are being paid to achieve business objectives. According to the 2008 survey, Belgium and Canada share the prize as being the least corrupt. At the other extreme, Russia is the most corrupt, followed closely by China, Mexico, and India.

    a) If Russia is the most corrupt, can you explain how it also can have one of the fastest-growing economies in the world?

    b) If you were put in charge and outlawed bribery in Russia, what do you think would happen to economic output? Does your answer depend on whether it is short term or long term?

    c) If your U.S. company makes shoes, and you are trying to enter the Russian market, would you pay the bribes needed to get the contract?

8. Mr. Spock of *Star Trek* fame (as opposed to the famous baby doctor) often uttered the phrase "Live long and prosper." Based on what you have seen in this chapter, can this friendly advice be pushed to its logical limit of "the longer you live, the more prosperous you will be"? Explain why or why not.

9. In the early 1990s when the North American Free Trade Agreement (NAFTA) was passed, a rural Illinois straw broom manufacturer feared it would go out of business because Mexican broom makers would be able to undercut their prices by employing cheaper labor. This fear was not unique to this company or this industry.

    a) Based on the possibility that importing brooms from Mexico would cause this company and others like it to close down, would you have allowed the opening of the straw broom trade with Mexico? Justify your answer.

    b) If you were told that the straw used to make brooms in Illinois was imported from Mexico, and that the imported straw brooms from Mexico prior to NAFTA were subject to import tariffs aimed at raising their prices, would that affect your answer in (a)?

    c) If, after all of this, you found out that import restrictions on some items, such as brooms, arose after NAFTA was passed, how would you explain this?

10. "There is no such thing as *free* trade." Considering both short-run and long-run perspectives:

    a) What are the potential costs of increased openness?

    b) What are the potential benefits of increased openness?

11. Is faster economic growth the only criterion that should be used to assess the costs and benefits of various economic policies? If not, what other criteria should be considered?

12. Ever hear the comment "the rich are getting richer faster than the poor"? This comment has been applied to groups in the United States and to countries.

    a) How does this comment square with the notion of economic convergence?
    b) Does this comment mean that the poor are becoming less well off?
    c) Does the evidence about income distributions around the world support this view?

13. It often is argued that increases in productivity will solve any future problems stemming from population declines.

    a) Use the productivity curve in Figure 11.9 to explain this idea.
    b) Does such an increase in productivity lead to a permanent increase in the growth rate of potential GDP?
    c) What if the population shrinks and those who are left are less skilled?

14. Look at the data in Table 11.1. From this information, can you form an educated guess as to whether children are an inferior or a normal good? Explain.

15. If, as some believe, raising taxes to fund future entitlement programs (Social Security, Medicare, etc.) reduces worker productivity, what are the economic implications for the projected decline in the working-age population?

# 12

# Inflation: What It Is, and Why It's Bad

*"Inflation is always and everywhere a monetary phenomenon."*

Milton Friedman,
Nobel Laureate (1963)

Over the past 40 years, inflation has led a double life: during the early 1980s, the inflation rate in the United States reached a high of about 15 percent. By contrast, during your lifetime, it probably has not exceeded 5 percent in any given year. If inflation hasn't been any worse than 5 percent for most of the past couple of decades, why should you be concerned?

Inflation, even at relatively low rates, still means that prices are increasing. As long as the rate of inflation is greater than zero, the purchasing power of money is steadily, sometimes imperceptibly, being reduced. If your income increases faster than inflation, then you're ahead of the game: your purchasing power will increase because your income is growing faster than your loss of purchasing power. If your income doesn't increase as fast as inflation, you will be unable to buy as many cars, movie tickets, or college credit hours as in the past. Inflation imposes a direct cost on nearly everyone.

Another cost of inflation stems from the fact that when it gets high enough, people use resources to try to avoid its cost. When inflation was in double-digit territory in the 1970s, many people tried to "beat" inflation by buying goods whose market value they thought would keep pace with rising prices. Some of the more popular items purchased were things such as baseball cards (yes, baseball cards), apartment buildings, gold, platinum, and rare artwork. The idea was to buy goods that were either relatively scarce—there is only one Van Gogh *Starry Night* painting—or whose market value was expected to rise along with inflation, such as real estate.

When you spend time simply trying to protect your purchasing power, you are not spending that time producing new goods or creating new ideas. Time is scarce, after all. A great example of this is how people behave when inflation is extremely high. When inflation is extremely high, most people sensibly spend a lot of time trying to buy real goods before their prices get higher. If you and many other people spend all of your time trying to buy things instead of working, even fewer goods and services are produced. This is one reason why hyperinflation, a situation when inflation reaches triple digits or more, often leads to a breakdown in the workings of economic markets.

You've been fortunate enough to live in an era of low rates of inflation. This is not by mere chance: policy makers today place a higher priority on keeping the lid on inflation than they did in the past. Could the super-high rates of inflation seen in other countries happen here in the United States? The answer is yes. History has shown that high inflation can plague even the world's strongest economies, given the right conditions. That's why it is important for you to fully understand the causes and consequences of inflation.

## 12.1 Some Perspective on Measuring Inflation

In macroeconomics, we focus on changes in the overall level of prices, not the prices of particular goods. The prices of some goods change fairly regularly. Gasoline prices certainly do. Agricultural products are subject to seasonal price changes and to price swings resulting from bad weather. For example, the price of fresh asparagus is highest in the winter and lowest in the spring when it is harvested. Similarly, a severe freeze in California can send the prices for many agricultural products, from lemons to broccoli, shooting upward.[1] That said, such events often do not lead to permanently higher prices: most farmers are able to replant and harvest another crop. Sometimes produce from other countries substitute for California crops in your local grocery store. The bottom line is that such price changes reflect fluctuations in supplies and demands in specific markets. This microeconomic phenomenon usually has only a temporary effect on a macroeconomic measure like this.

In Chapter 6, we defined inflation as a sustained increase in the general level of prices. Inflation thought of in this manner is a macroeconomic phenomenon. That's why when we think about inflation, we don't want to focus on how the price of a *single* good or service behaves but on how prices across the *entire economy* behave. That is why in Chapter 6 we introduced the idea of a *price index*. Although there are several price indexes, probably the best known is the Consumer Price Index (CPI).

In Chapter 6, we discussed several aspects of price indexes and how you can measure inflation using them. We did not at that time talk about the importance of distinguishing short-term movements in prices and inflation from the longer-term trends. Let's consider that issue now.

The monthly CPI numbers often are reported with great importance placed upon them, which is a problem because they can be quite volatile due to temporary events. A severe, early spring freeze in California or Florida, two major agricultural states, can ruin crops and send food prices soaring, at least temporarily. Depending on how widespread the damage is, such a freeze could significantly affect the change in the CPI during March and April. Even so, it is unlikely to have any effect on the change in the CPI between August and September. To "even out" the impact of temporary events such as these, it is best to measure inflation using averages of the CPI over several months. Another approach is to measure inflation in a "year-over-year" manner; that is, from this month last year to the current month (e.g., April to April).

Getting away from placing too much weight on the volatile monthly numbers is important, especially if you want to use the resulting inflation rate to determine

---

[1]Kim Severson, "California Freeze Limits Citrus Supply, Sending Prices Up." *New York Times,* February 14, 2007: F8.

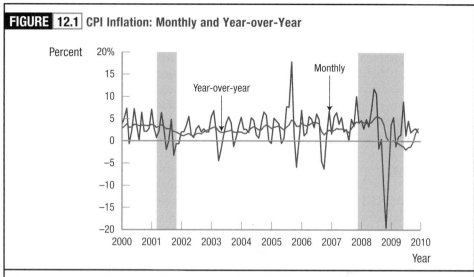

**FIGURE 12.1** **CPI Inflation: Monthly and Year-over-Year**

How we measure inflation can affect our perception of it. Shown here is the rate of CPI inflation since 2000 calculated as the monthly percentage change and as the percentage change on a year-over-year basis. You can see that the year-over-year approach provides a better picture of the drift of inflation over time. It puts less emphasis on the temporary effects of those events that may cause short-term fluctuations in the inflation rate. The smoothed approach also helps make the point about policy responses. Instead of reacting to every wiggle in the monthly numbers, policy makers are well-advised to focus on the year-over-year values so that they are not misled by transitory price changes. (Shaded areas indicate recessions.)

*Source:* Federal Reserve Bank of St. Louis

policy actions. The reason is because policy makers can do little to offset the effects of a bad freeze or a sudden increase in the demand for gasoline. Markets for lettuce and gasoline will work out the proper change in prices in response to changes in their markets' demand or supply. If policy decisions were based on every monthly wiggle in inflation, there would be very little predictability in how to respond over time. And poor or ill-conceived policy decisions adversely affect the economy.

Let's see how averaging the rate of inflation over time can affect our perception of it. **Figure 12.1** plots the rate of CPI inflation since 2000 calculated two different ways. One inflation series, the jagged one, is the monthly percentage change in the CPI. The other, smoother series uses the same CPI numbers, but measures the percentage change on a year-over-year basis. So, instead of measuring the percentage change from August to September, the smoother series measures inflation from August of last year to August of this year.

Why bother to think about inflation calculated the "smoothed" way? The answer to this question is that we get a better picture of the drift or trend of inflation over time. The year-over-year approach puts less emphasis on the temporary effects of, say, a bad harvest, a storm that increased the price of plywood, or the shutdown of an oil refinery that increased gas prices in a particular month. Looking at the smoothed inflation numbers helps reinforce the point about policy responses. Suppose it is summer 2005, and the latest CPI number is announced. You can see in Figure 12.1 that this new value is associated with a *monthly* inflation rate of over 15 percent. What to do? Before running off to initiate some policy to fight inflation, you'd be wise to look at the year-over-year inflation rate. Because the year-over-year rate didn't even reach 5 percent, your policy response is much different.

More recently, the monthly inflation values indicated just the opposite of rapid inflation. During late 2008, the decline in certain components of the CPI led to a large *negative* rate of inflation measured on a monthly basis. Should policy makers have reacted immediately to this rare decline in prices? Again, the year-over-year inflation shows that the reduction in the rate of inflation, while impressive, was nowhere near the drop seen in the volatile monthly numbers.

As you can see, much more is often made of monthly inflation numbers than there should be. They are highly volatile because of changes in certain components of the CPI. Measuring the rate of inflation over some longer time span allows us to not to be distracted by temporary events. It also leads us to ask a very important policy question: What explains the tendency of the rate of inflation to rise and fall over longer periods at a time? For example, the rate of inflation drifted steadily upward between 1960 and 1980 and then reversed course and drifted downward ever since. Don't confuse the falling rate of inflation since 1980 as a falling price level. The lower inflation rates after 1980 mean that prices in general were increasing but not as fast as they were over the previous 20 years or so. As long as the rate of inflation is positive, the general level of prices is increasing. What explains these *sustained* changes in the general level of prices? Answering this question, and not why the CPI rose or fell in any one month, is the focus for the rest of this chapter.

**ECONOMIC FALLACY**    An increase in oil prices causes a sustained increase in the price level.

**False.** First, recall that we define inflation as "a sustained increase in the general level of prices." Inflation defined this way, not the month-to-month percentage change in the price level, is something policy makers have some impact over. When the prices of oil and its derivative products such as gasoline increase, this causes the prices of goods to rise for which oil and gas are inputs to the production process. From plastic cups to tennis balls to ice cream, a significant increase in the price of oil can cause other prices to increase as well. Such a response brings about relative price changes: the prices of oil-dependent goods rise relative to others. For example, transportation prices might increase, whereas the prices for haircuts remain unchanged. As you have learned, when relative prices change, people substitute away from higher-priced goods to lower-priced ones. So, if driving becomes more costly due to a gas price increase, people will try to substitute cheaper mass transit or walk. You also might reallocate your budget, reducing your spending on movie tickets so you can continue your driving habits.

All this means that, given an increase in the price of oil, *some* prices will rise, which will cause a price index such as the CPI to increase. The percentage change in the CPI—what is commonly referred to as inflation—will also increase. But two crucial points are worth noting: the increase in the CPI isn't due to an increase in all prices. The other point is that an increase in the percentage change in the CPI due to a temporary price increase in one or several goods in the price index does not fit our definition of inflation. Some prices adjust to the new norm of higher oil prices. When that adjustment is complete, the rate of inflation returns to what it was before the oil-price shock rate. It may seem semantic, but an oil-price increase is not inflationary because it does not produce a *sustained increase in the general level of prices.*

The behavior of inflation in Figure 12.2, shown later, makes this point. There were pronounced jumps in the rate of inflation in 1974 and again in 1979. Both jumps were related to significant increases in the price of oil. (The 1974 spike is also due to the relaxation of price controls, which the Nixon administration instituted.) The uptick in the rate of inflation in 1990, which was associated with the Gulf War, and the uptick that occurred more recently in 2008 are partly explained by rising oil and gas prices. In every instance, soon after the price of oil increased, the rate of inflation subsided. Based on our working definition of inflation, the facts simply do not support the notion that "an increase in oil prices causes inflation."

## 12.2  What Causes Inflation?

From 1960 through 1980, the rate of inflation in the United States seemed only to increase. Some people argue that politics is to blame: the Johnson administration and Congress expanded government programs for the needy and the elderly in the 1960s while fighting a war in Vietnam. Some believe that the combination of these two endeavors helped push prices and, therefore, inflation, higher. How? Because the government was buying a lot of goods and services to take care of the needy and elderly as well as buying war-related materials, it was increasing the overall demand for goods and services relative to their supply in the United States. Although this may have contributed to an increase in some prices, it was not the real source of inflation.

Another reason often given for the rise in inflation is related to increases in oil prices. In 1960, several oil-producing countries around the world met in Baghdad, Iraq, and formed the Organization of the Petroleum Exporting Countries (OPEC) in an effort to influence the supply of oil and its price among member countries.[2] In 1973, OPEC members collectively embargoed, or cut their oil exports to all countries that had supported Israel in their conflict with Syria and Egypt. In these countries (the United States, Japan, Portugal, and South Africa, among others), the price of gasoline shot up dramatically. The outbreak of the Iranian Revolution in 1979 again led OPEC to increase oil prices, and gas prices once again rose dramatically.

But neither of these explanations—increased government spending and oil-price spikes—explains the *upward trend* in the rate of inflation between 1960 and 1980. As shown in **Figure 12.2**, if the cost of the Vietnam War explains inflation—a sustained increase in the general level of prices—then why didn't inflation fall once the war ended? Why didn't inflation remain at its lofty levels following the 1974 and 1979 oil-induced spikes? Such events simply *do not* explain the sustained increase in the *trend* of inflation from 1960 to 1980.

You can also see by looking at Figure 12.2 that the upward drift in the rate of inflation reversed course in the early 1980s. In contrast to the previous two decades, oil prices fell during the mid-1980s because OPEC members couldn't agree on how to price the oil their countries were producing. These "negative" oil-price shocks appear as downward spikes in the quarterly rate of inflation in the first half of the 1980s. Even with short-lived bumps in inflation, up and down, the rate of inflation trended downward since 1980.

This decline in the rate of inflation is called **disinflation**. Let's be clear on this point: *dis*inflation occurs when the rate of inflation is getting smaller. Prices are still increasing; they are just rising at a slower pace. This is not the same as *de*flation. **Deflation** occurs when the rate of inflation is negative. If the rate of inflation is negative, this means that prices in general are actually falling. Although it is fairly

· · · · · · ·

[2]The founding OPEC members were Iran, Iraq, Kuwait, Saudi Arabia, and Venezuela. The OPEC membership later expanded to include Qatar, Indonesia, Libya, United Arab Emirates, Algeria, Nigeria, Ecuador, Gabon, and Angola.

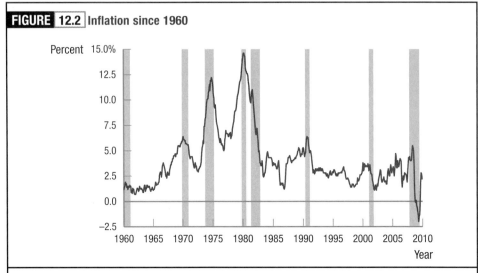

**FIGURE** 12.2 Inflation since 1960

What causes sustained inflation rather than transitory spikes in inflation? Between 1960 and 1980, two popular explanations for the upward trend in inflation were increased government spending due to the Vietnam War and oil-price spikes. If the cost of the Vietnam War explains inflation, then why didn't inflation fall after the war ended? If oil-price increases explain inflation, why didn't inflation remain high following the 1974 and 1979 oil-induced spikes? Events such as these do not explain the sustained increase in inflation. (Shaded areas indicate U.S. recessions.)

*Source:* Federal Reserve Bank of St. Louis

rare, deflation has occurred in recent times, most notably in Japan. Whereas disinflation is good, deflation can have very negative effects on the economy.[3]

**DISINFLATION** A reduction in the rate of inflation. Prices are rising at a slower rate.

**EXAMPLE** The rate of inflation in 2008 reached 5 percent, and by 2011 the rate of inflation had fallen to half of that. This reduction in the rate of inflation is disinflation.

**DEFLATION** A rate of inflation that is negative. A sustained decrease in the general level of prices.

**EXAMPLE** Over the past decade Japan experienced prolonged periods in which prices were falling. The rate of inflation was negative.

You can see in Figure 12.2 that the rate of inflation today is back to where it was 50 years ago. It is just as important to understand why the rate of inflation rose from 1960 to 1980 as it is to understand why it fell since 1980. If the pricing shenanigans of oil-producing countries, of government programs, or the effects of bad harvests do not explain changes in the rising or falling trends in inflation, what does? The best explanation for why inflation behaves the way it does over time is based on decisions made by policy makers, and specifically those in charge of a country's monetary policy.

• • • • • • •

[3]"Japan's Deflation Disaster: Plunging Prices Are Clobbering the Country's Economy." *Businessweek,* March 18, 2002.

## Inflation and Money: What's the Link?

By now you've probably gotten the impression that inflation—a sustained increase in the general level of prices—is not caused by events such as oil-price increases or bad harvests. This may be why dictionaries often define inflation as "too much money chasing too few goods." As we'll show, inflation is related directly to increases in the amount of money in circulation in a country. To explain why the general level of prices rose in the United States during the 1960s and 1970s and then declined after 1980, we need only look to the growth in the supply of money.

We used supply-and-demand analysis in earlier chapters to find the price and quantity that would clear the market for any good or service. Whether we are talking about the price of a computer, a manicure, or an open-heart surgery, supply and demand interact to determine the market price for each good or service. Applying supply and demand to the "market" for money is a good way to explain why the rate of inflation changes over time.

## The Supply of Money[4]

Let's first be clear about what we mean by money. Money can be measured in several different ways. For our purposes, think of money as the sum of the currency in the economy—the one-, five-, and ten-dollar bills we carry around—and the balances in our checking and savings accounts. Even though putting money in a bank and then having to take it out again to pay for things is slightly more complicated than simply reaching into your pocket and pulling out cash, the benefits of keeping your money at a bank largely outweigh the costs related to retrieving the money from your account on short notice. When we use the term *money*, what we really mean is the dollar value of currency and readily accessible deposits at financial institutions such as banks or credit unions.

With this working definition of money in hand, what causes the amount of it—the supply of money—to change? Historically, changes in the supply of money were greatly affected by changes in the quantity of gold and silver from mining operations or the discovery of new sources. This is no longer true because precious metals no longer "back" our money. Today, the monetary authority of a country, its **central bank**, ultimately controls the quantity of money in their economies. In the United States, our central bank is the Federal Reserve. More than 150 central banks exist around the world, including the Bank of Japan, the Bank of Canada, and the European Central Bank (ECB).

**CENTRAL BANK** The monetary authority of a country; the part of a country's government that determines and carries out monetary policy.

**EXAMPLES** The Federal Reserve is the central bank of the United States. The European Central Bank (ECB) sets monetary policy for the countries that are members of the European Union.

The Federal Reserve does *not* control the money supply by controlling the printing of that stuff you carry around in your pocket. Printing currency is the job of the U.S. Treasury Department. In that regard, the Federal Reserve dispenses currency to banks for the Treasury. How the Federal Reserve actually influences the supply of money is

· · · · · · ·

[4]A more detailed description of money and how it is affected by banks and monetary policy is provided in Chapters 17 and 18. For purposes of the present discussion, such detail is not needed.

by altering the economic incentives of banks, government bond dealers, and eventually you to hold or not to hold money instead of other types of financial assets. That is, the Federal Reserve really controls the growth of that part of money comprised of checking and savings accounts. The Federal Reserve mainly accomplishes changes in the money supply by enticing the public to buy or sell government securities.

Let's consider a hypothetical example where the Federal Reserve, for whatever reason, wants to increase the amount of money in the U.S. economy. The Federal Reserve could accomplish this by offering you $100 for that $25 savings bond you received as a high-school graduation gift. Even if you had planned to hold on to the bond until it matured, the opportunity cost of holding the bond is now much higher than before the Fed's offer. You agree to sell, so you send the Fed the bond, and it wires your bank to put $100 into your checking account. You get more money in your checking account than you had before, and the Federal Reserve gets your bond. This transaction increases the money supply (remember: money equals the sum of currency and bank deposits) in the economy by $100.

If the Fed wants to reduce the supply of money, it does just the opposite. To lower the supply of money, the Fed now wants to sell to the public some of the government bonds it holds. At the right price, you (and other people) will be willing to exchange your money for the bond. Now you send the Fed a check for, say, $100, and it sends you the bond. This action reduces the supply of money in the economy because you've reduced your checking deposits by $100.

These examples are overly simplified, of course. In reality, the Federal Reserve buys and sells government bonds through a select network of government bond dealers. Still, the examples capture the underlying basics of how the Federal Reserve (or any other central bank) can affect the supply of money in the economy.[5] The point here is not to discuss how it is accomplished but to illustrate that central banks are ultimately responsible for increases and decreases in the money supply over time.

## The Demand for Money

The Federal Reserve manages the supply of money in the United States primarily through the sale and purchase of government bonds. The Fed (and any other central bank) ultimately controls the *supply* of money, but it is the public that decides the *demand* for money. Think of why you would demand money. You hold money because you want to buy lunch, an MP3 player, and pay rent. Businesses hold money—cash in the drawer, deposits in the local bank—because they must make change for customers, pay suppliers, and meet payrolls. If the price of lunch, MP3 players, and your rent increases, you will need more money to buy the same amount of goods that you currently consume. In this sense, the amount of money that you demand—the amount of cash you carry and the amount you hold in your bank accounts—can be thought of as a demand for purchasing power, a demand for the ability to buy things. We use the term **purchasing power** because if prices double, it takes twice as much money (a $10 bill instead of $5 bill) just to buy the same items.

**PURCHASING POWER** The amount of goods and services a unit of money can buy. Purchasing power moves in the opposite direction to changes in the price level.

· · · · · · ·

[5]We will get deeper into this subject in Chapter 18. This process is similar to that used by many other central banks. An excellent comparison of the process can be found in Patricia S. Pollard, "A Look Inside Two Central Banks: The European Central Bank and the Federal Reserve." Federal Reserve Bank of St. Louis *Review* (January/February 2003).

**EXAMPLE** Tuition at the state university increased from $150 a credit hour to $200 a credit hour. If you have $1,000 to spend on education, this increase means you can now afford fewer credit hours than before.

**EXAMPLE** You earned $100 in 1983. You earn $100 now. Because the CPI has more than doubled over that time, you now can buy half as many goods as you could in 1983. (Self-test: Is this true for *all* goods?)

To better understand purchasing power, consider the following. You know that prices have risen over time—that's inflation. But how bad has it been? Suppose you had $100 in 1960 to buy food, clothes, gas, records, or whatever. By 2011, it would take almost $750 to buy the same basket of goods. The fact that the price level—the CPI—has risen so much over the past 50 years means that the purchasing power of money has fallen by quite a lot.[6] As the prices of goods and services rise, so does your quantity of money demanded.

What else affects your demand for money? A key factor is your income. Your parents likely have more money in their checking account than you do. One explanation is because their income is larger. Usually, a larger income increases the desire (and ability) to buy more goods, pay for college tuition, get a weekly massage, and so on. This suggests that as your income rises, so will the quantity of money you want to hold. More specifically, an increase in your income is likely to increase your demand for money, evidenced by larger bank accounts or maybe more cash in your pocket. A decrease in income is likely to reduce your demand for money.

Another important factor that affects your demand for money is the opportunity cost of holding it. As applied to money, the opportunity cost is what your money could be doing if you did not have it either in currency or in a checking account. Many consider a useful way to measure the opportunity cost of holding money is the interest rate on financial assets. To see this, suppose you can choose between putting your income into a noninterest-paying checking account at your bank and buying a government savings bond. The government bond pays you interest; the checking account doesn't. All else the same, which should you pick? The answer depends on how much you believe the convenience of the checking account is worth relative to the interest you get from owning the bond. As the interest rate on the bond rises, so does the opportunity cost of having money in a non-interest checking account or in cash.

Economists agree that the interest rate is an important measure of the opportunity cost of holding money. If interest rates rise, people are likely to reduce their money holdings as they try to find ways to shift out of money and into interest-earning assets. In this way, an increase in interest rates reduces the demand for money. Conversely, when interest rates fall, people are more likely to increase their money holdings.

## How Money Supply and Money Demand Determine the Price Level

We've laid out the foundation for applying the supply-and-demand model to money. Let's now use the supply and demand for money to explain changes in the price level. **Figure 12.3** is just like any supply-and-demand graph you used in previous

. . . . . . .

[6]The Web site http://measuringworth.com allows you to compare the purchasing power of a dollar over time.

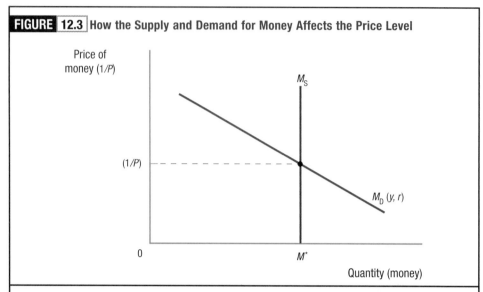

**FIGURE 12.3** How the Supply and Demand for Money Affects the Price Level

Changes in the price level are linked to the supply and demand for money. In the figure, the demand for money is labeled $M_D$ and is shown as the usual downward-sloping line. Shown in parentheses are the factors we hold constant for this demand curve: income ($y$) and the opportunity cost of holding money, measured by the interest rate ($r$). The supply of money is labeled $M_S$ and is drawn as a vertical line to reflect our assumption that a country's central bank controls the quantity of money in the economy. As with any other supply-and-demand model, the intersection of money demand and money supply determines the equilibrium price. The equilibrium price of money ($1/P$) is the inverse of the general level of prices, measured by some price index such as the CPI. This equilibrium occurs at a quantity of money equal to $M^*$.

chapters. This time, instead of the market for oranges or MP3 players, it is the market for money. Figure 12.3 shows how the relation between the supply and demand for money determines the price level and changes in it.

The demand for money is labeled $M_D$ and is shown as the usual downward-sloping line. In parentheses, we've listed the factors we're holding constant for this demand curve: income ($y$) and the opportunity cost of holding money, measured by the interest rate ($r$). Recall from earlier discussions of demand that we want to hold constant those factors that shift the demand curve. The supply of money is labeled $M_S$ and is drawn as a vertical line at a specific quantity of money, labeled $M^*$. The supply of money is drawn as a vertical line to reflect our assumption that the Federal Reserve ultimately controls the quantity of money in the economy.

As with any other supply-and-demand analysis, where the quantity of money demanded equals the quantity of money supplied, we find the equilibrium price. Graphically this occurs at the intersection of the money demand and money supply lines. As you can see in the figure, the intersection of money demand and money supply means that the equilibrium quantity is $M^*$, and the equilibrium price is labeled as ($1/P$). But what kind of equilibrium price is that?

The price of money in Figure 12.3 is measured on the vertical axis as $1/P$, where $P$ stands for the general level of prices in the economy. Think of $1/P$ as the inverse of the CPI, which is the same as saying that the "price" of money is the inverse of the price level. If this seems odd, an example will help.

Suppose there is only one good in the economy: soda. Suppose that the price of a single can of soda is $0.50. Another way of saying this is that the *money price* of soda is 50 cents. A dollar will get you two cans of soda. This is how you are used to thinking about prices for goods. But what about the *price* of money? In this example, the price of a dollar is two cans of soda. If we can measure the price of goods in terms of money, we can just as easily measure the price of money in terms of the number of goods it can buy. In this case, the price of money can be stated in terms of cans of soda. The *goods price* of money, therefore, is measured by what it will buy, which, in this case, is cans of soda.

Now suppose that the money price of a soda doubles to $1. One dollar now buys you only one can of soda. What happened to the goods price of money? As the money price of soda increases, the goods price of money—how many sodas a dollar buys—falls. When the price of a soda increased to $1 from 50 cents, the price of money *in terms of soda* fell to 1 can from 2 cans. When the money price of goods rises, it is the same as your dollar losing purchasing power. In this case, your purchasing power was cut in half.

Now extend the example to the entire economy. Obviously, there are many more goods in the economy than just cans of soda. Nonetheless, the goods price of money can be measured by the inverse of a measure of the general level of prices. When the price level—for example, the CPI—rises, the price of money—what a dollar can buy—falls. The price of money—what we use on the vertical axis of the supply-and-demand diagram—is, therefore, the inverse of the price level.

> **ECONOMIC FALLACY**   The price of money is the rate of interest.
>
> **False.** Although this is a common perception, it is wrong. The interest rate is the *opportunity cost* of holding money. That is, if you hold cash, it is not earning any interest as it would if you owned a bond or even put it into a savings account. The interest rate is the opportunity cost of holding money, but this is not the same thing as the price of money. Correctly speaking, the interest rate is the price of *credit*—that is, the price to *borrow* money. Although it is a common mistake to think the interest rate is the price of money, it is just not correct. The price of money is related to what money can buy.

## Changes in the Supply of Money and Changes in the Price Level

We can make use of the money-demand and money-supply model in Figure 12.3 to explain changes in the price level (and hence the rate of inflation). Let's first show the relationship between changes in the supply of money and changes in the price level. Suppose the Federal Reserve undertakes a policy to increase the supply of money in the economy. As shown in **Figure 12.4**, this results in a rightward shift in the supply of money from $M_{S1}$ to $M_{S2}$.

Why does the Fed's action lead to an increase in the price level? At the original price level $(1/P_1)$, the Fed's action results in an excess supply of money. At the original equilibrium price of money $(1/P_1)$ the quantity of money demanded $(M^*)$ is less than the quantity of money supplied $(M^{**})$. You might find this hard to believe, but given the level of income, interest rates, and prices in the economy, the increase in the money supply creates a situation in which people want to reduce the amount of money they are holding. One way for them to do this is to buy more goods. As the increased demand for goods puts upward pressure on prices, the overall price level

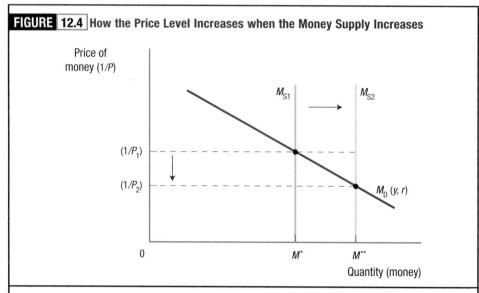

**FIGURE 12.4** **How the Price Level Increases when the Money Supply Increases**

The money demand-and-supply model can be used to explain changes in the price level and, therefore, the rate of inflation. The demand for money ($M_D$) and the supply of money ($M_{S1}$) determine the equilibrium price of money ($1/P_1$) and the quantity, $M^*$. Now suppose the Federal Reserve undertakes a policy to increase the supply of money in the economy, which is shown by the rightward shift in the supply of money from $M_{S1}$ to $M_{S2}$. At the original equilibrium price of money ($1/P_1$), the quantity of money demanded ($M^*$) is less than the quantity of money supplied ($M^{**}$). The increase in the money supply induces people to reduce the amount of money they are holding. One response is to buy more goods, which increases the demand for goods and puts upward pressure on prices. If the demand for money is unchanged, increasing the money supply increases the overall price level. The price of money falls (the price level rises) until equilibrium between the demand for money and the new supply of money is restored. This occurs at the price ($1/P_2$) and quantity $M^{**}$.

begins to rise. In Figure 12.4, an increase in the price level ($P$) results in a decline in the price of money ($1/P$). If the demand for money is unchanged, increasing the money supply increases the price level. The price of money falls (the price level rises) until equilibrium between the demand for money and the new supply of money is restored. In Figure 12.4, this occurs at the price ($1/P_2$) and quantity $M^{**}$.

Let's recap: if there is no change in the demand for money, an increase in the supply of money results in an increase in the general price level. Why all prices? When the money supply increases, we assume that there is an overall increase in the demand for and purchases of goods of all types. Conversely, if there is no change in the demand for money, a decrease in the supply of money results in a decrease in the price level. Put bluntly, if the Federal Reserve or any other central bank ultimately controls the growth of the supply of money with its policies, all else the same, it ultimately controls the rate at which prices in the economy change, that is, the rate of inflation. This may seem extreme, but it is why one governor of the Federal Reserve acknowledged that "... central bankers ultimately determine the inflation rate."[7]

· · · · · · ·

[7]Laurence H. Meyer, "Does Money Matter?" Federal Reserve Bank of St. Louis *Review* (September/ October 2001): 3.

## Changes in the Demand for Money and Changes in the Price Level

Changes in the demand for money, resulting from changes in income or interest rates, also can affect the price level. To see this, suppose there is an increase in the demand for money. The increase occurs because income has increased, from $y$ to $y'$. Graphically this is captured by a rightward shift in the money demand curve, as shown in **Figure 12.5**. (This shift also could occur if interest rates had fallen.) When the demand curve for money shifts to the right, and the supply of money is unchanged, disequilibrium exists at the initial price $(1/P_1)$. At the original price level, the quantity of money people want to hold is $M^{**}$, but the quantity supplied is only $M^*$. This means that the increase in the demand for money created a shortage.

If people are not holding as much money as they would like, one avenue to increase their money holdings is to reduce their spending. They may even attempt to increase their money holdings by selling some of their goods or financial assets. The outcome of such actions is a fall in the price of goods. As the prices of goods fall during this adjustment of money holdings relative to the supply, the price of money $(1/P)$ adjusts upward to its new equilibrium level, from $(1/P_1)$ to $(1/P_2)$ in Figure 12.5. Of course, you already know that an increase in the price of money must mean that the prices for goods are declining. That is, as $(1/P)$ rises, the general level of prices $(P)$ must be falling. Given the supply of money, then, an increase in money

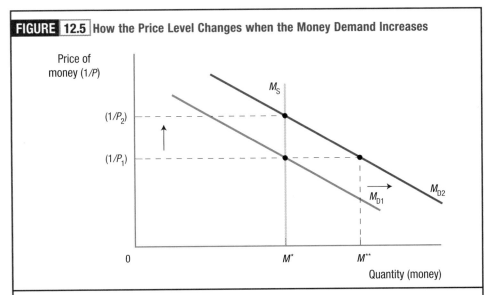

**FIGURE 12.5** How the Price Level Changes when the Money Demand Increases

Changes in the demand for money, resulting from changes in income or interest rates, also affect the price level. Suppose there is an increase in the demand for money, shown here as a rightward shift in the money demand line. (This shift can occur because of an increase in income or if interest rates fall.) If the supply of money is unchanged, at the original price level, the quantity of money people want to hold is $M^{**}$, but the quantity supplied is only $M^*$. People are not holding as much money as they would like, so they try to increase their money holdings by reducing their spending. This results in a decline in the demand for goods and a fall in the price level. As the general price level falls, the price of money $(1/P)$ adjusts upward until it reaches its new equilibrium level $(1/P_2)$. Given the supply of money, then, an increase in money demand is associated with a decline in the general price level.

demand must be associated with a decline in the general price level. Conversely, if the demand for money falls—the money demand curve shifts to the left—then the price of money $(1/P)$ falls, and the general level of prices rises.

### Does It Work? A Case Study[8]

A real-world example may help illustrate how changes in the supply of money can affect the price level, the value of money (purchasing power), and ultimately the rate of inflation. Following the 2003 capture of Iraq's leader, Saddam Hussein, the U.S. Treasury Department worked to help Iraq establish a viable banking system. One among many difficulties the people working for the Treasury encountered was that two currencies were circulating in Iraq: the "Saddam dinar," festooned with Saddam's picture, circulated in the south. In the northern parts of the country, the "Swiss dinar" was used to make purchases. The northern currency apparently got the name "Swiss dinar" either because it was considered as safe as a Swiss franc, or because the engraving plates to make it came from Switzerland. Unlike the Saddam dinar of the south, the Swiss dinar featured images from Iraq's past.

Following the first Gulf War, production of the Swiss dinar was severely limited by the Hussein government. By contrast, the Saddam dinar was printed at the whim of Saddam, who simply authorized the printing of more money to finance increased spending, often on personal items, palaces, and so on. Want to guess the outcome of these actions in terms of changes in prices?

In the north (more specifically in the Kurdish provinces) where the supply of Swiss dinars increased very little, prices for goods did not rise very rapidly: there was very little inflation. In the southern provinces, where more and more Saddam dinars were being printed and circulated, prices rose rapidly, and inflation was high. Ultimately, due to the unchecked increase in the supply of Saddam dinars and the subsequent inflation in the south, the purchasing power of the Saddam dinar plummeted over time. At the time of the 2003 overthrow, the Swiss dinar survived as the acceptable, trusted currency to be used in exchange. The Saddam dinar did not.

This story illustrates how the money supply and the general level of prices are linked. In the next section, we'll focus on whether changes in the money supply explain inflation. This allows us to focus on the following policy question: Because they control the supply of money, are central banks ultimately responsible for inflation?

## 12.3  The Quantity Theory of Money

You've just seen how changes in the supply and demand for money can affect prices in an economy. Now we want to extend that idea a bit by considering one of the oldest theories in economics: the **Quantity Theory of Money**.

> **QUANTITY THEORY OF MONEY** A theory that links changes in the price level directly to changes in the supply of money.

The Quantity Theory is a relatively simple model, but it has very important implications. To see this, let's start with the equation

$$MV = Py$$

where $M$ is the supply of money, and $P$ is the price level. The term $y$ here represents real output, such as real GDP. The new term $V$ is called velocity, and it measures

........

[8]John B. Taylor, *Global Financial Warriors: The Untold Story of International Finance in the Post-9/11 World* (New York: W.W. Norton & Company, 2007).

how fast a dollar "turns over" in the economy as it passes from person to person in exchange for goods and services. It measures how often a dollar is used in payments for final goods and services over some specified time period.

It turns out that velocity actually is directly related to how much money people want to hold for every dollar of their income: their money demand. If velocity rises, then money is turning over more rapidly (being passed from one person to another via exchange) and is not being held long; that is, the demand for money is falling. When velocity falls, just the opposite occurs: people are holding on to their money longer, not buying goods and services.

Consider what this equation is saying. What is it that we really demand when it comes to money? More pieces of paper in our pockets and larger balances in our checking accounts? No. What we demand is purchasing power, which means that our demand for money is equal to the demand for purchasing power of money, which can be represented by $M/P$. If money demand equals money supply, there is no change in the price level. But what if the money supply ($M$) keeps increasing even though the demand for money does not? The demand-and-supply model predicts that the price level will continue to rise over time. That is, a sustained increase in the money supply relative to the demand for money leads to a sustained increase in the price level, what we've defined as inflation.

How can we operationalize that idea using the Quantity Theory? First, let's re-write the Quantity Theory equation in a rate-of-change or growth-rate form. That is, instead of levels, we want to focus on the growth rates of the variables. Using *bolded italics* to represent the rate of change for each measure, the rate-of-change version of the Quantity Theory can be written as[9]

$$\boldsymbol{M} + \boldsymbol{V} = \boldsymbol{P} + \boldsymbol{y}$$

Now let's make one more change to focus attention on the predictive power of the Quantity Theory. Let's manipulate this equation to isolate the rate of inflation ($\boldsymbol{P}$) on one side of the equation. A little algebra gets us to

$$\boldsymbol{P} = \boldsymbol{M} + \boldsymbol{V} - \boldsymbol{y}$$

This version of the Quantity Theory gives rise to Milton Friedman's assertion that opened this chapter. To see this, let's first assume for the sake of argument that the growth of velocity ($\boldsymbol{V}$) is, over time, relatively constant. That is, the growth in the demand for real money balances—the demand for purchasing power—is a fixed proportion of the real income in an economy. Second, based on our discussion about economic growth in the previous two chapters, it isn't unreasonable to assume that, over time, the growth of real income ($\boldsymbol{y}$) is determined largely by economic forces unrelated to money supply or money demand—you know, labor, capital, and knowledge. So, for this discussion, the growth in real output ($\boldsymbol{y}$) also is relatively constant.

These assumptions make the Quantity Theory a valuable tool to test whether inflation is really a monetary phenomenon. How? If we assume that both $\boldsymbol{V}$ and $\boldsymbol{y}$ are relatively constant, why not go all the way and, for sake of argument, just place a value of zero on them? Zero is a constant, after all. When we do this, the only thing left to explain the rate of inflation ($\boldsymbol{P}$) is the growth of the money supply ($\boldsymbol{M}$). If a central bank's policies are largely the cause of changes in the growth rate of the supply of money, the Quantity Theory tells us that we should observe a direct, positive relation

· · · · · · · ·

[9]This equation is arrived at by first taking the logarithm of both sides of the levels equation and then taking the first-difference of the resulting equation. The variables in the equation are, therefore, log differences.

between the growth rate of the money supply (**M**) and the rate of inflation (**P**). That is, given velocity growth (**V**) and the growth in real output (**y**), an increase in the rate of inflation is directly associated with an increase in the growth rate of the supply of money. Or, as Friedman said, inflation is a monetary phenomenon.

## SOLVED PROBLEM

**Q** The relation between money growth and inflation described by the Quantity Theory is useful for thinking about the long-term outcome of letting money growth get too high. Suppose, for example, that velocity growth over the past decade was 3 percent, output growth averaged 3 percent over the same time, *and these were expected to continue into the future.* Given these conditions, the Quantity Theory predicts that a money growth rate of 2 percent should produce an inflation rate of 2 percent. That is,

$$M + V - y = P$$
$$M + 3\% - 3\% = P$$

or

$$M = P = 2\%$$

But, what if our assumption about velocity growth continuing into the future is wrong?

**A** Let's assume that based on our discussion of economic growth in the previous chapters, the **y** in the Quantity Theory is the growth in output associated with full employment: potential output. So, over time, it shouldn't vary. That means that changes in velocity can really mess up the relation between money growth and inflation. What if, say, velocity growth doesn't turn out to be 3 percent but is zero. If money growth is set to 2% as determined previously, inflation is more likely to be negative instead of positive:

$$M + V - y = 2\% + 0\% - 3\% = -1\%$$

The fact that velocity can change, especially in the short run, cautions us about using the Quantity Theory to make short-range predictions of inflation based on recent money growth. We'll have more to say about this in several of the problems found at the end of the chapter.

Friedman's statement is powerful coming from such a simple equation, isn't it? But it is a statement that must be considered with some caution. It does not mean that every increase in money growth will lead to an increase in the rate of inflation. Remember, that prediction holds only if the strong assumptions about velocity and output growth also are met. It also is a statement that most economists believe is a relation that holds over time, that is, perhaps not over six months or even a year, but over several years. Even with these caveats in mind, this simple relation explains why, when the Fed or any other central bank begins to follow a policy of rapidly increasing the supply of money, many in the economy begin to raise concerns about higher rates of inflation in the future. This connection caused many to worry about the potential increase in inflation following the Fed's policy actions taken during the Great Recession of 2007 to 2009.[10] We'll have more to say about that in Chapter 18.

Just how accurate is Friedman's assertion? In other words, were the events in Iraq described earlier an isolated incident, or are they consistent with the predictions of the Quantity Theory? One way to see how well money and inflation are connected is to look at how their movements are related over time.

[10]Irwin Stelzer, "Recovery Today, Inflation Tomorrow." *The Weekly Standard,* March 20, 2009.

## 12.4 Money Growth and Inflation across Countries

One approach to testing Friedman's conviction and the prediction of the Quantity Theory is to look at the money-inflation experience of a wide variety of countries over the same time period. This is typically done by averaging money growth rates and inflation rates over time periods long enough to reduce short-term fluctuations in money demand and output. The use of multiyear averages also allows any lag between changes in money growth and inflation to be completed. **Figure 12.6** does this by comparing the average money growth and average inflation rate for many countries.

**FIGURE** 12.6 Money Growth Rates and Inflation Rates across Countries

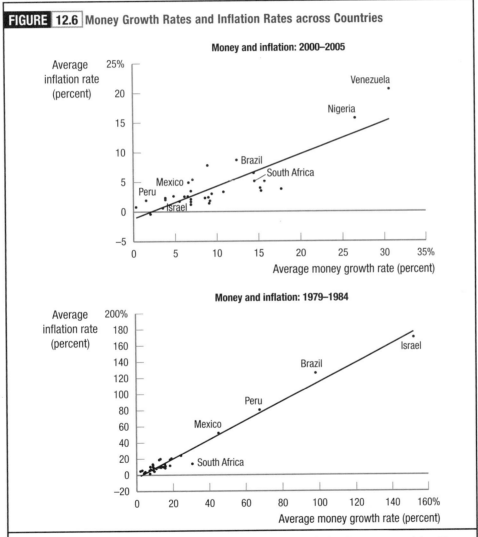

These figures show five-year averages for money growth and inflation for many countries. The top panel uses data from 2000 to 2005; the bottom panel uses data from 1979 to 1984. In both figures, money growth and inflation, on average, are positively related: higher rates of inflation are associated with higher rates of money growth. This is true even though inflation was much different in the two periods—inflation was much higher, on average, in the 1979–1984 period.

*Sources:* Gerald P. Dwyer, Jr. and R. W. Hafer, "Is Money Irrelevant?" Federal Reserve Bank of St. Louis *Review* (May/June, 1988): 3–17; *The Economist* (2010); and authors' calculations.

Each dot in Figure 12.6 represents a specific country's average money growth rate and average inflation rate. In the top panel of the figure, we use data from 2000 to 2005. This is, worldwide, a relatively low inflation period. What you see is that money growth and inflation, on average, have a positive relationship across countries. This result is what the money supply–money demand discussion predicts should happen. The Quantity Theory model also predicts this outcome: the upward-sloping line, which represents the "best" relation, indicates that, on average, higher rates of inflation are associated with higher rates of money growth.

The bottom panel shows the money-inflation link using data from 1979 to 1984. We include this plot because, as previously discussed, this is a period of generally much higher rates of inflation, some of which are blamed on higher oil prices. One thing to notice is that the positive relation between money growth and inflation continues to hold using the 1979–1984 data compared with the more recent observations. Even though inflationary experiences were much more varied between those two periods, a clear, positive relation exists between money growth and inflation.

Finally, it is instructive to locate the high-inflation countries noted in the lower panel. Israel, Brazil, Mexico, and Peru were all countries that had very high growth rates in their money supplies and, as a result, high rates of inflation in the 1979–1984 period. In contrast, during the five-year period ending in 2005, each country had much lower money growth rates. Did this reduction in money growth lead to a reduction in their rates of inflation? As predicted by the Quantity Theory, these countries also enjoyed much lower rates of inflation. Countries with high money growth rates and high inflation became low-inflation countries when their central banks got money growth under control.

Although the averages are affected by some of the "big inflation" countries, consider this: for the countries used in Figure 12.6, the average rate of money growth in the 1979–1984 period was about 21 percent. The average rate of inflation also was about 21 percent. In the more recent 2000–2005 period, the average rate of money growth was about 9 percent, which is quite a drop from earlier. As you might have guessed, the average rate of inflation also fell: the average rate of inflation for the 2000–2005 period was only 4 percent. From a policy perspective, this evidence suggests that, all else the same, increasing the growth rate of the money supply is likely to put upward pressure on a country's rate of inflation. Conversely, lower rates of money growth are associated with lower rates of inflation.

## 12.5 Inflation Gone Wild

The double-digit inflation rate the United States suffered in the late 1970s might sound scary if you've become accustomed to inflation of 3 or 4 percent. But, even that rate of inflation pales in comparison to the triple-digit or *higher* inflation rates some countries have experienced. Economists refer to these incredible inflation episodes as **hyperinflation**.

**HYPERINFLATION** A condition when the general price level is increasing at a rate of at least 50 percent *per month*.

**EXAMPLE** You received $500 on June 1 for helping clean up the house. Deciding to wait to buy that iPod was a bad idea: by July 1, it and everything else cost 50 percent more.

**EXAMPLE** At its peak, inflation in the first year (1992) of post-Soviet economic reform was over 2,500 percent.

Hyperinflation occurs when inflation rates reach stratospheric levels. The rule of thumb is that hyperinflation occurs when prices are rising at a rate of at least 50 percent *per month*. Think about it: the highest rates of inflation endured by the U.S. public during the 1960–1980 period—as high as 15 percent *per year*—pale in comparison to an episode of even mild hyperinflation. Can you imagine the price of a McDonald's hamburger increasing from $4 to $16 in one month, then to $64 in the next, and so on? That's the sort of thing that can happen during a hyperinflation. Hyperinflations damage economies badly because prices lose their purpose of relating supplies and demands. Many hyperinflations are accompanied by a breakdown in the economic system. For this reason, it's vital to understand what causes them.

## Hyperinflation in Germany

One of the most studied hyperinflations occurred in Germany in the early 1920s.[11] Following World War I, the German government could not raise enough revenue from taxes to pay the war reparations (money to cover damages and injury) demanded by the victors of World War I. One of the best discussions of this episode is John Maynard Keynes's *The Economic Consequences of the Peace* (1920). Keynes, the famous economist and a member of the British delegation to the negotiations, resigned when it became clear that the reparations being demanded of Germany would lead to the country's economic ruin. Instead of raising taxes on a nation that was struggling economically, the German government's response was simply to rapidly increase the printing of money, which it used to pay for goods and services. This policy led to a tremendous increase in the growth rate of the German money supply and, as you might expect, soon produced higher rates of inflation.

The German money supply exploded in 1923 and with it prices. For example, during the first six months of 1923, notes in circulation—paper money—increased by a factor of over 8,700 and went from 1.28 billion notes in circulation to 17,291 billion. But that pales in comparison to what happened next. By the end of 1923, the notes in circulation had increased to 496,507,424,772 *million* (or 497 quintillion). Needless to say, the increase in the amount of money in circulation quickly spilled over into price increases. In January of 1923, the German price index stood at 278,500. By June, the price index had risen to 1,938,500, and, by December, it had reached 126,160,000,000,000. At its peak, the *monthly* rate of inflation in Germany was over 3.2 million percent.

A consequence of the government's policies and the resulting hyperinflation was that German residents tried desperately to avoid holding German money (called reichsmarks). One outcome of people and businesses unloading their marks is the decline in the foreign-exchange value of the mark. Measured in U.S. cents per mark, the exchange rate fell from .007 cents per mark in January 1923 to .000,000,000,022,7 in December 1923. Because it was rapidly becoming worthless, many people also were trying to convert their paper money into real goods as quickly as possible. There are stories of wives waiting outside factory fences for their husbands to toss over their wages so they could rush to the store and buy bread and other staples. At the peak of the hyperinflation, this scenario played out several times a day with wives gathering wheelbarrows full of money—equivalent to a half day's pay—to buy a loaf of bread before the bakery ran out.

. . . . . . .

[11]The following draws on Thomas Sargent, "The Ends of Four Big Inflations," in R. Hall, ed., *Inflation: Causes and Cures* (Chicago: University of Chicago Press, 1982). The classic discussion of the German hyperinflation is Frank D. Graham, *Exchange, Prices and Production in Hyperinflation German, 1920-25* (Princeton, N.J.: Princeton University Press, 1930).

As German residents rid themselves of marks they drove prices higher and at a faster rate than the government could introduce new bills into circulation.

### Hyperinflations Elsewhere

There are other noteworthy hyperinflations. Hungary, for example, suffered one of the worst incidences of hyperinflation. Between August 1945 and July 1946, prices in Hungary increased at a rate of 19,000 percent *per month*. At its peak, the rate of inflation in Hungary was 19 percent *per day*! In the 1990s, Yugoslavia experienced hyperinflation severe enough to give it a high ranking in the "hyperinflation hall of fame."[12] At its peak in January 1994, the month's inflation rate was 313,000,000 percent. In other words, at its worst, prices in Yugoslavia were doubling in less than a day's time. Imagine if what you paid for your lunch today cost twice as much as what you paid yesterday.

More recently, in May 2007, the annual rate of inflation in Zimbabwe had reached about 4,500 percent. This inflation not only made it impossible for people to keep up with changing prices but also led the government to impose price controls. Believe it or not, part of the government's crackdown was the threat of death to any business owner who raised prices. Needless to say, such policies led to riots and mass confusion.[13] Sadly, Zimbabwe's response to hyperinflation is not, as history proves, unique.

Although the specific circumstances vary across countries, there is a common denominator to all hyperinflations: each is accompanied by similarly astounding increases in the supply of money. No hyperinflation has ever occurred without a correspondingly high rate of money growth. This is more, and extreme, evidence that high rates of money growth cause high rates of inflation.

## 12.6 The Costs of Inflation

Whether it is the seemingly tame 2 or 3 percent inflation of the United States or the 4,000-plus percent rate of Zimbabwe, inflation always imposes an economic cost on the citizens of any economy. Hyperinflations devastate economies because they reduce the information contained in prices, they lead to nonproductive uses of scarce resources, and they more often than not foster political instability. Even milder inflations impose economic costs on people.

### Inflation Tax

You might hear some people suggest that a "little" inflation is good. It surely isn't if your income doesn't keep pace with rising prices. One cost of inflation we have mentioned is money's loss of purchasing power. If prices are rising, but your income isn't, then your ability to buy goods and services—to maintain your standard of living—is threatened. This is why people on fixed incomes get very upset when prices rise.

Inflation imposes a cost on anyone holding currency. The cost is imposed on those who have their money in noninterest-bearing checking accounts. At some rate of inflation, the convenience of using a checking account is outweighed by the loss of purchasing power of keeping your money there. Inflation, especially if high enough, interferes with the use of money in exchange. If inflation raises the cost of holding money, people

· · · · · · ·

[12]Steve H. Hanke, "Inflation Nation." *Wall Street Journal*, May 24, 2006: A14.

[13]Michael Wines, "Anti-Inflation Curbs on Prices Create Havoc for Zimbabwe." *New York Times*, July 4, 2007. Recall from our discussion of economic growth that Zimbabwe also is one of the poorest and most corrupt nations in the world.

rationally will substitute out of money into something that others will take in trade. In the cases of hyperinflation, this other "good" often becomes some other country's currency.

The costs of inflation do not fall evenly on everyone in the economy. Not everyone has an interest-bearing checking account. Not everyone can manipulate his financial portfolio to find the best returns to avoid loss of purchasing power. In these instances, inflation imposes a higher cost on some people relative to those who can move their funds around to higher-paying deposits. Economists call this distorting effect an **inflation tax**.

**INFLATION TAX** The economic cost imposed on holders of money caused by inflation.

**EXAMPLE** You store your savings in a tin can above the kitchen sink. As inflation continues, the purchasing power of your savings declines. Inflation acts as a tax on your savings.

**EXAMPLE** You buy a bond that pays a 6-percent return each year for the next ten years. During that time, the rate of inflation increases each year. The purchasing power you get from the bond is progressively worth less and less.

## Inflation and Interest Rates

As you have learned, inflation has an important impact on financial transactions. In fact, we know that interest rates, especially short-term rates, tend to move with inflation. The inflation–interest rate link can best be described by an example.

Your friend Tom asks to borrow $100 from you to buy books. He agrees to pay you back in one year. How much do you charge him for the use of your money over the year? Suppose Tom is a really good friend, and you don't want to financially gouge him for the loan. Nonetheless, you want to get back your $100 plus any lost purchasing power. That means you want to get back $100 plus the increase in the price level over the year. In other words, you want to get back your $100 plus the rate of inflation. If prices increase 5 percent over the year, then you want to get $105 from Tom. In essence, this extra amount to cover lost purchasing power is the interest you are charging Tom for the loan.

Suppose that you guess incorrectly, and over the coming year, the rate of inflation turns out to be 10 percent. Even though Tom pays the loan back with the agreed 5 percent added on, what you get back is money that has lost its purchasing power. What cost $100 a year ago now cost $110, but you only get $105 from your lending. Of course, if inflation turned out to be 2 percent, you gain. You get $105 from Tom, and what cost $100 a year ago now costs $102.

This difference between what you charge for borrowing the money (extending credit to someone) and what you realize in terms of purchasing power helps us refine our picture of what an interest rate is. The rate that is charged for a loan with no adjustment for inflation is known as the **nominal rate of interest**. This is the interest rate you see advertised in the newspaper on bank deposits or auto loans. The **real rate of interest** is the nominal rate less the rate of inflation people expect.

**NOMINAL RATE OF INTEREST** The stated interest rate, unadjusted for inflation.

**EXAMPLE** The Bank of St. Louis is advertising one-year certificates of deposit (CDs) paying 5 percent.

**EXAMPLE** You are having a tough time covering the cost of your education, so you take out a student loan. The interest rate on the loan is 4 percent.

**REAL RATE OF INTEREST** The nominal interest rate minus the rate of inflation people expect.

**EXAMPLE** A consumer has extra money and buys a $100, one-year CD paying 5 percent from the Bank of Omaha. At the end of a year, she cashes it in and gets her 5-percent return, or $105. But inflation during the year was 8 percent. In real terms, therefore, her return was a negative 3 percent. She lost purchasing power: What cost $100 last year now costs $108, and she only received $105 on her investment.

**EXAMPLE** You graduate from college and start repaying your 5 percent loan to the Bank of Laramie. However, inflation is running at 10 percent. In real terms, the bank is getting money that is worth less. The real return to the bank is minus 5 percent. The bank is losing purchasing power.

Not wanting to lose purchasing power when lending or borrowing suggests that nominal interest rates and inflation should be related. (You might recall that we made this point in Chapter 5.) **Figure 12.7** plots the link between the nominal interest rate as measured by a three-month Treasury bill rate and inflation, as measured by the CPI. The figure reveals that the two series tend to move together over time. This positive correlation suggests that when inflation increases, the nominal rate of interest rises along with it. If the rate of inflation were perfectly anticipated, the two series would move even more closely over time. They do not because, even though there is a link between the two, the future inflation rate can't be anticipated with absolute certainty.

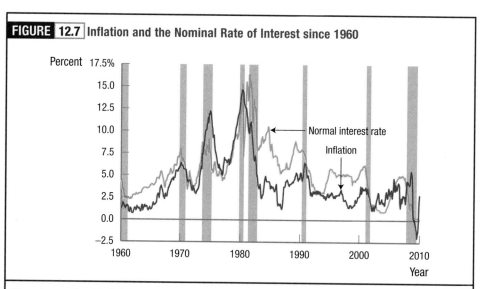

**FIGURE 12.7** Inflation and the Nominal Rate of Interest since 1960

There is a noticeable link between movements in the nominal interest rate (measured by a three-month Treasury bill rate in the graph) and the rate of inflation. Over the past 50 years, the rate of inflation and the nominal interest rate have moved together. If the rate of inflation were perfectly anticipated, the two series would move in more perfect harmony over time. They do not because, even though they are related, the future inflation rate can't be anticipated with absolute certainty. (Shaded areas indicate U.S. recessions.)

*Source:* Federal Reserve Bank of St. Louis

Lenders often suffer from the distorting effects of inflation, especially when inflation increases unexpectedly. Most loans banks make do not contain provisions that fully protect the banks against unexpected increases in the future rate of inflation. When deciding what interest rate to charge on a loan, part of this decision-making process includes what the banker thinks inflation will be over the life of the loan. If bankers underestimate how high inflation will rise, they will charge interest rates that are too low. That's what happened when many banks and lending institutions loaned out money on 30-year mortgages in the 1960s. The bankers didn't anticipate the high inflation rates the United States would experience during the following two decades. Consequently, the money they received each month as payment for those loans had ever-declining purchasing power. Some banks were able to cope by increasing their interest rates on new loans. Others, especially those who had made very long-term loans at low interest rates—loans such as mortgages—went bankrupt.

How does inflation affect borrowers? Borrowers often gain from inflation. Suppose you get a 30-year, fixed-rate loan to buy a home. Your loan rate is 5 percent, and, at the time, the rate of inflation is 5 percent. Several years later, the rate of inflation increases far above your loan rate, say to 8 percent. If this happens, you will benefit because you will be paying the bank back with money that has less purchasing power, and you will have a house that is increasing in market price. If your income also is keeping pace with inflation, as would occur even if you received only a cost-of-living allowance in terms of your pay raises, this will make it easier for you to pay off your loan than it was when you originally borrowed the money. Inflation can therefore lead to a redistribution of wealth from lenders to borrowers. In fact, this is one of the reasons why lenders developed flexible-rate mortgages. Flexible-rate mortgages allow the interest rate charged to vary over time with changes in inflation. As a result, borrowers absorb some of the effects of changing inflation. Flexible-rate mortgages lessen the redistribution of wealth from lenders to borrowers when there are unexpected increases in inflation.

## Inflation and the Price System

Inflation can also create serious informational distortions in the economy. Prices signal the interaction of supply and demand in a market as they help efficiently allocate goods and services in the economy. This is why hyperinflations result in a breakdown of the price system. Think of the potential effects: What if producers face tremendous uncertainty about the price they will pay for raw materials in two months? What if consumers think, but aren't certain, that price of beef tomorrow will be three times higher than today, but the price of chicken will only be twice as high? Such uncertainty causes economic resources to get distributed in inefficient ways.

Inflation uncertainty increases with higher rates of inflation. With increased uncertainty, deciding where to put your savings to maintain your purchasing power in the future becomes more difficult and more expensive. Increased uncertainty means you have to hire an information specialist—a broker, banker, or economist—to help you make the decision. Higher inflation imposes a significant economic cost, even more on those who guessed wrong, which is just another reason why keeping inflation low has become a key policy objective of the Federal Reserve and other central banks around the world.

Finally, unpredictable inflation raises the uncertainty of financial planning. How much of each paycheck do you decide to put into savings? As you get older, this becomes an increasingly important financial decision. Suppose you decide to put one-third of your current income into a retirement plan that guarantees some fixed return, say 3 percent. What if the promised return on that asset—your interest income—doesn't keep pace with inflation? If inflation turns out to be higher than you expected your savings may not be enough to cover expenses when you retire.

## WHAT YOU SHOULD HAVE LEARNED FROM CHAPTER 12

- That inflation means sustained price increases over time.

- That inflation erodes the purchasing power of money. If your wages aren't growing as fast as inflation, you are losing purchasing power.

- That sustained increases in the growth of money can lead to inflation. "Inflation *is* always and everywhere a monetary phenomenon."

- That central banks control the growth of their country's supply of money, which means that, in the final analysis, inflation is largely the result of central bank policy.

- That inflation imposes a tax on those people who rely on cash and cannot move their funds around to protect their purchasing power.

- That inflation, especially when it is very high, causes uncertainty about the future value of incomes, investments, and prices.

- That if inflation gets bad enough, as in a hyperinflation, it not only erodes purchasing power but can lead to a collapse of the price system and a breakdown of the economy.

- That interest rates and inflation tend to move in unison, although not perfectly. This gives rise to changes in the real rate of interest, measured as the nominal rate of interest adjusted for expected inflation.

## KEY TERMS

Disinflation, p. 315

Deflation, p. 315

Central bank, p. 317

Purchasing power, p. 318

Quantity Theory of Money, p. 324

Hyperinflation, p. 328

Inflation tax, p. 331

Nominal rate of interest, p. 331

Real rate of interest, p. 331

## QUESTIONS AND PROBLEMS

1. This chapter makes a clear distinction between inflation as a sustained increase in the price level and inflation as a short-term increase in prices.
   a) Why is it important, especially from a policy perspective, to make that distinction?
   b) Given the way the CPI is constructed, explain how a 5-percent increase in the CPI for April may not be considered as "inflation."

2. During the last recession there was much talk of the United States entering a period of deflation.
   a) What makes deflation different from inflation?
   b) Is deflation the same as disinflation?
   c) Looking at Figure 12.1, what evidence can you provide to support you answer in (a)?

3. Look at Figure 12.2. The rate of inflation has two distinct spikes during the time before 1980. Can you explain what caused these jumps in the rate of inflation? Can you explain why the rate of inflation did not remain at the peak rates in each instance?

4. During a recession, you often hear people say something like "The Fed is printing money to get the economy going."
   a) Why is this statement incorrect?
   b) How does the Federal Reserve actually affect the supply of money in the economy?

5. Suppose someone asks you "Would you rather have $1,000 today or $5,000 in ten years?" While the answer may seem obvious, why is the correct answer "it depends"?
   a) On what does your answer depend?
   b) If you know that the CPI is 100 today, what would the level of the CPI have to be in ten years to make you prefer getting the money today?

6. In August 1971, President Richard Nixon imposed wage and price controls to try and contain inflation. These controls put lids on how fast wages and some prices could increase. The program lasted for approximately three years.
   a) Looking at Figure 12.2, about what was the rate of inflation in 1971?
   b) What happened to the rate of inflation over the next couple of years?
   c) Based on your visual assessment, can you say that Nixon's program was successful?
   d) Based on the behavior of inflation after 1973, would you say it was successful?
   e) Given what you know about supply and demand, and about how a price index is constructed, was Nixon's program bound to succeed or fail? Explain your answer using a supply and demand diagram for some representative good, called "schmoo."

7. In 2007, the Zimbabwe government enacted a policy that forced merchants to lower prices. This policy was taken to fight the country's hyperinflation. In 2008, the Zimbabwe government further attempted to stop its hyperinflation by removing ten zeros off of its currency, effectively turning 10 billion Zimbabwe dollars into 1 dollar.
   a) Based on you answer for question 6, predict the success of the Zimbabwe government's actions.
   b) To see if your prediction is correct, visit the CIA's Web site (www.cia.gov), and look up Zimbabwe's inflation rate for 2008 in *The World Factbook*.

8. During economic downturns, you often see headlines like "Fed lowers interest rates; price of money falls." Why is this commonly held perception incorrect? Explain.

9. Let's think about Question 8 in a different context. Using a money supply–money demand diagram like that in Figure 12.4, show how the lowering of interest rates could lead to an *increase* in the price of money. Be sure to explain your reasoning.

10. During the Civil War, the Confederacy substantially increased its printing of currency to pay its bills. Using a money supply–money demand diagram, predict what happened to the price level—and the rate of inflation—in the South. Be sure to specify any assumptions made in your analysis.

11. In February 2007, the government of Argentina announced that inflation for January was 1.1 percent, significantly below the 1.5 percent to 2 percent rate most economists expected. The lower number was, many believe, achieved by simply fudging the numbers. That is, by falsely reporting the actual increase in the cost of some foods and the increase in health insurance, among others.
    a) Explain why such misreporting of inflation could be viewed as good or bad. To do this, put yourself in the place of a union negotiating for a new wage contract. Then put yourself on the other side of the table and think about it as the negotiator for management.

b) How might such actions affect the public's reliance on these inflation numbers in the future?

c) How might such actions affect perceptions by the public and potential investors in bonds issued by the Argentine government?

12. The *Oxford English Dictionary* defines inflation as an "increase in the quantity of money circulating, in relation to the goods available for purchase."

a) Use the Quantity Theory equation to explain this definition.

b) What assumptions do you make to get your answer in part (a)?

13. You have been asked by a spokesperson for the European Union, made up of 27 European countries, to help establish monetary policy. Their mutually agreed-upon policy objective is to keep the rate of inflation as close to 3 percent as possible.

a) Using the Quantity Theory equation, what information do you need to know before making your policy proposal?

b) Can you guarantee that after following your proposal, the rate of inflation will be 3 percent?

14. Look at Figure 12.6. Can you explain why the relation between money growth and the rate of inflation is much closer for the 1979–1984 period compared with the relation in the 2000–2005 period?

15. It is 2011, and the interest rate on a 30-year mortgage loan is fixed at 4.5 percent. You have just graduated from college, and you landed a good job with a guarantee that your real salary will increase as long as you stay with the firm. Given this information, would you be in favor of or would you oppose a plan to raise the rate of inflation? Be sure to include any assumptions made in arriving at your answer.

# PART 4

## Explaining Business Fluctuations

In Part 3 we focused on the longer-term relations in economics, explaining the long-run trend in real GDP—potential GDP—and inflation. Now, in Part 4, we will switch gears a bit and provide you with the basic tools to answer such questions as: Why does the real output of an economy fluctuate around its long-term trend? Or, more basically: Why do economies experience booms and busts?

To answer important questions like these we will make use of the expenditure categories suggested in Chapter 7 where we first introduced how we measure an economy's output, or GDP. Recall that we divided the economy into four sectors: households, businesses, government, and foreign trade. In Chapter 13 we'll make use of that framework to link changes in spending by these sectors to changes in the output of an economy. In Chapter 14 we look into the process by which inflation expectations are generated and how changes in these expectations can lead to differences in real GDP and potential GDP. Building up from your individual experience, you will see how changes in expectations of inflation can have significant effects on the economy. Once you have completed these two chapters, you will have the workings of a modern, dynamic macro model. This model not only helps us understand why there are recessions, but also why inflation changes. But it isn't just useless theorizing. To demonstrate how useful the model can be to explain economic fluctuations, both in the United States and in other countries, Chapter 15 puts the model to work. As you will find, it actually performs quite well.

# 13

# Aggregate Expenditures and Real Output

*"You got to be careful if you don't know where you're going, because you might not get there."*

Yogi Berra, Member, Baseball
Hall of Fame

The previous couple of chapters focused on long-run aspects of the macro economy: economic growth and inflation. Two important goals of macroeconomic policy are to keep the economy growing and to keep inflation low. This chapter begins our study of short-run fluctuations in economic activity. One objective of macroeconomic policy is to keep the economy on an even keel—staying near its production possibilities frontier (PPF)—means trying to prevent economic activity from dipping too far below or above its potential. If this is not possible, then another objective of policy is to cushion the economic effects that come from a recession. What is debated is just how far a country should go to achieve these policy goals. For example, should policy try to fully offset the effects of a downturn, such as rising unemployment, if that means significantly increasing the rate of inflation?

Before you can choose one policy option over another, or understand why policy makers did what they did, you must have some model of how the economy works. Such a tool is useful when trying to predict where the economy might be headed if government policies change. Our goal in this chapter is to begin developing such a model that you can use to explain why a nation's real income and output fluctuates around potential output. You've already seen that real GDP in most countries tends to increase over time. Now we will investigate why it fluctuates—sometimes a lot—over shorter time spans.

When you've finished with this and the next couple of chapters, you will have a good understanding of why recessions occur and how governments try to deal with them. And you will be fully equipped to understand the role that macroeconomic policy plays in affecting short-term changes in your economic well-being.

## 13.1 Total Expenditures

Economists generally agree that fluctuations in economic activity are often caused by changes coming from the so-called demand side of the economy. Any time you hear someone predict a recession or a tepid economic recovery because "consumers aren't spending enough," they are referring to the demand side of the economy. When the dot.com bubble burst in 2000 and businesses stopped investing in new plant and equipment, that reduction in spending—again the demand side of the economy—led to an overall reduction in real GDP. In each instance, the concern really is about what is causing total or "aggregate" expenditures to change.

To find total, or aggregate, expenditures, we add together the spending by various groups in the economy. The terms *aggregate* and *total* reflect the idea that we want to think about expenditures for the economy as a whole. Think of it this way: we can measure your income over time and watch how you spend it. To measure *family* household income and spending, we need to add up, or aggregate, the income and expenditures for each member of the family.

Economists are deeply concerned about how to measure total expenditures and to understand why they change over time because changes in total expenditures can have huge effects on the economy. To analyze such expenditures, economists long ago recognized the usefulness of dividing the economy into different sectors. The four major sectors of the economy are households, businesses, government, and the foreign trade sector. Explaining fluctuations in economic activity—measured by changes in real GDP—is grounded in understanding why households increase or decrease their purchases and why businesses cut back on investment. If this sounds familiar, it should: you were introduced to these concepts in Chapter 7 as the final goods or expenditure approach to measuring GDP.

By dividing the economy up into these groups, you can more easily calculate what each group contributes to total spending on goods and services produced in the economy. Based on the idea underlying our measurement of GDP, changes in total expenditures—reflected in changes in spending in the different sectors of the economy—are directly linked to changes in total income and to total output. Thus, the approach we are developing creates a direct link between changes in total, or aggregate, expenditures in an economy and changes in the economy's output.

## Consumption

The term *consumption* is a catchall term for the final goods and services purchased by all households in the economy. Anything bought by households, from cars to a visit to the dentist to food from grocery stores, is included under the heading of consumption. Note that it is not the good sold that qualifies it for being included in consumption. Consumption spending does not, for example, include purchases of computers or pencils by governments and businesses—only purchases made by consumers.

Consumption spending is, to many people, the engine that drives the demand side of economy. In most years, real consumption spending in the United States amounts to about 70 percent of real GDP. As you can imagine, when consumption spending falls, as it did in 2008, it has serious implications for the pace of overall economic activity. We'll focus on two factors that help explain consumption spending; one is changes in income, the other is changes in interest rates.

**Consumption and Income.** It might seem obvious to say that your consumption—how much you spend on final goods and services—depends on your income. It seems logical that if your income doubles, you are likely to spend more on eating out, better clothes, or health care.[1] You intuitively know that income and consumption spending are positively related. This also suggests that there is a positive relation between *changes*

· · · · · · ·

[1]"Personal Income Rise Lifts Consumer Spending," *New York Times*, March 20, 1987.

in income and consumption. What is important here is not just that they are positively correlated—that they both tend to rise and fall together—but that changes in one results in changes in the other. For example, changes in people's incomes cause changes in their consumption spending, which has an effect on the economy's income. Remember, if you stop buying dental care, then your dentist's income falls, and she cuts back on eating at restaurants.

Economists have observed, however, that increases or decreases in people's income are not matched exactly by dollar-for-dollar changes in their consumption spending. That is, when the average person receives an additional dollar of income, the incremental increase in their consumption spending is less than a dollar. We can describe how your consumption spending will change with a change in your income by using the **consumption function**. The consumption function is an equation or a graph that shows how consumption spending and income are related.

> **CONSUMPTION FUNCTION** The consumption function shows a positive relation between consumer spending and the level of income.

> **EXAMPLE** Joe earns about $1,000 a week and spends $800 of it. Sheila's weekly income is $3,500, and she spends $2,000.

> **EXAMPLE** When you graduate and get a full-time job, your income will increase and so will your spending.

The influential British economist John Maynard Keynes decided nearly 80 years ago that the relation between consumption and income was so important that he made it the cornerstone of his macroeconomic model, one that many economists still use. Keynes used the idea that individuals would spend part of any increase in income they received and not spend (save) the rest. As you'll see in a moment, this seemingly obvious point has important implications for explaining changes in an economy's level of income.

**Figure 13.1** shows a hypothetical consumption-income relation for an economy. The two axes are consumption spending by the household sector and the aggregate income of the economy. The consumption function is drawn with a positive slope to illustrate that as the level of income increases, so does the level of consumption spending. In addition to this positive relationship, there are a couple of other important aspects about the consumption function that you should note.

First, the consumption function intersects the axis labeled "consumption spending" at a positive level of consumption. The implication in the figure is that consumption spending is $6 trillion even though the level of income (GDP) is zero. This level of consumption spending is called **autonomous consumption**. (Another word for autonomous is *independent*.) The idea behind autonomous consumption is that no matter what income is, this amount of consumption spending is independent of it.

> **AUTONOMOUS CONSUMPTION** The level of consumption spending that is independent of your level of income.

> **EXAMPLE** John's income doubled, yet he continued to spend the same amount on toiletries.

> **EXAMPLE** Your household budget for rent is $600 per month. If you lose your job, you still need to pay the $600 in rent.

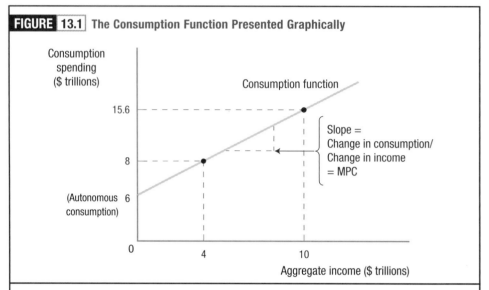

**FIGURE 13.1** The Consumption Function Presented Graphically

This is a hypothetical consumption–income relation for an economy. The consumption function intersects the *y*-axis at a positive level of consumption, called *autonomous consumption*. This level of consumption occurs no matter what the level of income is. The slope of the consumption function is measured as the change in consumption spending divided by the change in income. It is called the marginal propensity to consume (MPC). The MPC is positive because as people's incomes rise, they tend to spend some of it to buy more goods and services.

Why is this spending called autonomous consumption? Think about what happens if you lose your job and your income drops to zero. You still need to buy food and pay rent, both of which are included in consumption spending. You can only accomplish this by using the savings you accumulated while working, by borrowing from a financial institution, or by receiving some sort of government assistance. Regardless of how it is financed, you are still buying goods and services even though your income is zero. That is what the figure shows: a certain amount of consumption spending—autonomous consumption—happens even at zero income.

The other aspect of the consumption function to notice is its slope. What's the rubric that most of us learned to define the slope of a line? *The slope is the rise over the run.* Apply that definition to the consumption function and you get the following economic interpretation: the slope of the consumption function is measured as the change in consumption spending (the rise) divided by the change in income (the run). This connection between changes in consumption spending and changes in income is called the **marginal propensity to consume (MPC)**.

**MARGINAL PROPENSITY TO CONSUME (MPC)** The marginal propensity to consume (MPC) measures how much consumption spending changes for a given change in income.

**EXAMPLE** You get a $100 per week raise. Out of that extra $100, you plan to increase your spending by $80. Your MPC is 80 percent, or .80.

**EXAMPLE** Your brother gets a $100 per week raise. Out of that extra $100, he plans to increase his spending by $50. His MPC is 50 percent, or .50.

The marginal propensity to consume (MPC) captures the idea that as your income rises, you have a greater inclination or tendency to buy more goods and services. If you spent *every* extra dollar of income you received, your personal MPC would equal one, and your personal consumption function would have a slope of one: it would be a 45-degree line starting from some level of autonomous consumption. The aggregate consumption function drawn in Figure 13.1 has a slope that is less than one—it's flatter than a 45-degree line. This reflects the finding that for the U.S. economy the MPC is about 0.8. In other words, for every additional trillion dollars of national income, consumption spending increases about $800 billion. So, if GDP rises to $14 trillion from $12 trillion, we would expect consumption spending to increase from $9 trillion to $10.6 trillion.

If you work you might be saying to yourself "Hey, wait a minute!If I get a $1 raise, I don't get all of it because I have to pay taxes. Shouldn't this affect the consumption–income link?" Okay, we need to be a bit more careful in how we use these terms. The income that households really use to buy things is **disposable income**. Disposable income is not income you can throw away. It is the income you derive from various sources (from working, dividend payments from financial assets, interest payments from bank accounts, payments made to you by the government, etc.) *minus* federal, state, and local taxes paid.

**DISPOSABLE INCOME** Income available for spending after taxes are subtracted.

**EXAMPLE** Remember that $100 a week raise you got? Because you must pay an extra $25 in taxes, the disposable part of your raise—the part you can actually spend—is not $100 but $75.

Your consumption spending changes based on changes in your disposable income, not your pretax income, in other words. As you will see later, changes in the taxes you pay affect the economy through changes in consumption spending. An increase in taxes reduces disposable income, which lowers consumption spending. A reduction in taxes, however, should increase consumption spending because it increases disposable income.

Let's take a minute to write down the algebraic version of the consumption function drawn in Figure 13.1. Because the consumption function is a line, we can write it as

$$C = a + b\,(Y - T)$$

where $C$ represents real consumption spending, $Y$ is real income, and taxes are represented by the letter $T$. In this version, we show the relation between consumption spending and disposable income when taxes are not proportional to your income. That is, you just pay some lump sum tax ($T$) out of your income regardless of what it is. This means that the term in parentheses—$(Y - T)$—is your disposable (after-tax) income available for spending. Autonomous consumption is represented by the intercept term in the equation, the term $a$. The economic interpretation of the slope of the line, here shown as $b$, is the MPC. Even though we will not make extensive use of this equation, it is in fact useful for solving specific issues regarding changes in income, taxes, and consumption. (To see this, look at the upcoming Solved Problem and, after you've finished the chapter, look at Appendix B.)

Our objective is to explain the relation between aggregate expenditures and aggregate income, so we do no real harm by assuming that taxes are zero. If taxes are positive but unchanged, disposable income and an aggregate income measure such as GDP still tend to move together anyway. So, for the sake of convenience, unless otherwise noted, we will let aggregate income, or real GDP, represent the measure of income.

## SOLVED PROBLEM

**Q** What if autonomous consumption spending falls?

**A** When the security of workers' jobs becomes uncertain, many of them begin to reduce their spending even though their incomes have not changed. The reduced spending can be thought of as a decrease in autonomous consumption. What is the impact on consumption spending in the economy? To answer this question, let's use the algebraic version of the consumption function you just learned about in this chapter. The consumption function (with taxes not equal to zero) can be written as

$$C = a + b(Y - T)$$

where $C$ represents consumption spending by households, $Y$ is income, $T$ is taxes, $(Y - T)$ is disposable income, $b$ is the MPC, and $a$ is autonomous consumption. Let's put some numbers on these variables to see what happens when there is a change in autonomous consumption. Suppose, for this example, that the income of each household is $1,000, its taxes are $200, its MPC is 0.8, and its autonomous consumption is $200. Given these figures, the dollar value of a household's consumption spending is

$$C = \$200 + 0.8(\$1,000 - \$200)$$
$$= \$840$$

Now suppose a number of households reduce their spending out of their disposable income. That is, let their autonomous consumption $(a)$ fall to $100. Solving for the new level of consumption spending, you get

$$C = \$100 + 0.8(\$1,000 - \$200)$$
$$= \$740$$

The decline in autonomous consumption has a direct effect on the level of household spending. In terms of the graphical analysis, this example would be represented by a downward, parallel shift in the consumption function.

**Consumption and the Real Rate of Interest.** Changes in the level of income—moving back and forth on the horizontal axis in Figure 13.1—slides us *along* the consumption function. What then causes the entire function to shift up and down? One is the change in autonomous consumption just analyzed in the Solved Problem. Among several other possible factors, we will focus on one: changes in real interest rates. As you learned in the previous chapter, real interest rates are nominal interest rates—the ones you see banks advertise, the rates on U.S. Treasury debt reported in the financial pages, and so on—adjusted for inflation. Suppose, for example, a bank advertises that you can get a 4-percent rate of return on deposits. If inflation is 3 percent, the inflation-adjusted rate of interest—the real rate—is 1 percent. It is how much you actually receive in terms of purchasing power, not just in terms of dollars. In other words, if the nominal interest rate is close to the rate of inflation, you will not gain very much purchasing power by putting money in the bank. If the nominal rate is less than the rate of inflation, you would actually lose purchasing power by doing so.

An increase in the real rate of interest is associated with a decline in consumption spending, given that the level of real income and the rate of inflation are unchanged. Why assume that inflation is unchanged? Nominal interest rates could increase simply because the rate of inflation is rising. In this case, rising interest rates are not an incentive to put more money into savings. For example, suppose the rate of inflation and the rate of interest on a bank savings account are both 5 percent. If the rate of inflation doubles to 10 percent, and the interest rate on the savings account increases to 8 percent, putting more money into savings would be foolish: your return on savings is less than the loss of purchasing power. What affects consumption are not changes in the *nominal* rate of interest, but changes in the *real* rate of interest.

Why would an increase in real interest rates reduce your spending? Think about it: the higher interest rates go, the less likely you are, for example, to buy a car and finance it. Not only that, but you will have more of an incentive to save money if you can invest it at a high real interest rate. Put another way, an increase in the real rate of interest raises the opportunity cost of current spending. For the economy as a whole, this means that an increase in the real rate of interest lowers consumption spending at every level of income.

As shown in **Figure 13.2**, an increase in the real rate of interest leads to a downward shift in the consumption function. When the real rate of interest (shown in parentheses) increases from 3 percent to 5 percent, the level of consumption spending decreases at every level of income. Another way of thinking

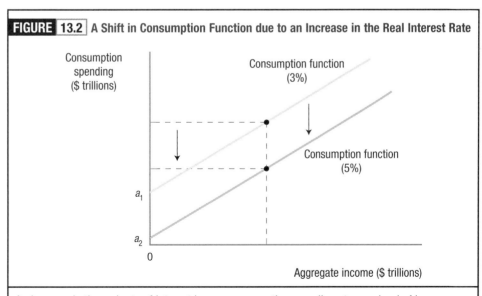

**FIGURE 13.2** A Shift in Consumption Function due to an Increase in the Real Interest Rate

An increase in the real rate of interest lowers consumption spending at every level of income, shifting the consumption function downward. Another way to state this reaction is that the intercept of the consumption function—autonomous consumption—declines, here from $a_1$ to $a_2$. The slope (the MPC) does not change, just the level of consumption at every level of income. Conversely, when the real interest rate falls, the opportunity cost of current spending falls, and the consumption function shifts upward.

about this downward shift in the consumption function is that the intercept of the consumption function declines. In Figure 13.2, this is shown as a decline in autonomous consumption from $a_1$ to $a_2$. The slope (the MPC) does not change, just the level of consumption at every level of income. What happens to the consumption function when real interest rates fall? When real interest rates fall, the opportunity cost of current spending falls, and the consumption function shifts upward.

## Investment

The term **investment**, as it is used here, does *not* mean buying stocks and bonds. Rather, investment refers to the purchases of final goods by businesses that are used in the production of other goods. When an automaker buys a new machine to stamp out door panels, for instance, that purchase is counted in investment expenditures. Thus, investment measures how much firms spend on new plants and equipment. The value of inventories carried by businesses is also included in this measure, as are the purchase of newly constructed residences by households. (We'll explain why this is so shortly.)

> **INVESTMENT** The purchase of final goods by businesses that are used in the production of other goods plus the purchase of new homes by individuals.

> **EXAMPLE** With the expectation that business would grow, Bagels 'n' More decided to purchase two new ovens.

> **EXAMPLE** With falling mortgage rates, more and more people moved out of the city and purchased newly built homes in the suburbs.

Investment is comprised of several components. *Business fixed investment* refers to expenditures on plant and equipment that firms buy to produce goods. Business fixed investment is largely what we mean when we talk about changes in the nation's *capital stock*. Yes, this is the dollar value of the capital stock used in our growth model in Chapters 10 and 11.

Another component of investment is *inventory investment*. Inventories are those items that a business has purchased from suppliers but hasn't sold. Every electronics store carries a stock—an inventory—of computers, flat-screen TVs, and so on. If the store is unable to sell those items, they just sit in a backroom collecting dust and are counted as inventory investment. Have you ever seen an advertisement for an "inventory liquidation sale"? The firm is reducing the goods that it can't sell by lowering the price. When inventories rise, the inventory investment number is getting bigger.

Inventory investment is an important number. When we measure an economy's total output, we really want to know how many goods are being produced. If electronics stores buy 5 million 52-inch flat-screen TVs and sell 3 million of them, 2 million TVs remain in inventory. If we just used the number of TVs purchased by consumers (3 million), this wouldn't completely measure the output of flat-screen TVs. As the TVs are sold off one by one, the dollar value of the nation's consumption spending increases by the market value of one TV. At the same time, the dollar value of the nation's inventory investment declines by one TV. When the entire inventory is sold, consumption spending on TVs is equal to the dollar value of the TVs produced. Before that time, however, the dollar values of consumption spending and output do not match. This is why rising inventories are an indicator that some economists use to predict the pace of economic activity. If flat-screen TVs are starting to pile up at electronics stores, this could signal that consumers are reining in their spending. It also means that fewer new TVs are needed, which could lead to a reduction in their production and a decline in GDP.

The last component of investment is *residential investment*. It may not seem proper to include your new home with some piece of factory machinery, but there is a good economic reason to do so. When you buy a house or a condominium, you really are buying a flow of services: shelter from the elements, a place to raise your family, and a place to watch your 52-inch flat-screen TV. Although a computer also provides a flow of services, big-ticket items such as a house are different. For one, generally they last longer than a computer or a car. This makes buying a house more like a firms' purchase of a new machine—capital—than like buying a bunch of bananas.

How much does each component contribute to investment spending? In 2007, total real-investment spending in the United States amounted to $1.8 trillion.[2] This is a little over 15 percent of GDP, a much smaller percentage than consumption spending. Of this $1.8 trillion, fixed-investment spending by businesses was by far the largest part of investment, followed by residential investment. That explains why when people talk about "investment," they usually are referring to the fixed-investment spending made by businesses.

We are going to make two simplifying assumptions. The first assumption is that investment *is not* related to total real income. It is independent of current real income, in other words. Is this realistic? The answer depends on your time frame. Over short periods of time, investment spending by businesses is not affected very much by changes in aggregate income. Why? Because investment requires businesses to look into the future and decide if building new factories or buying new machines will be worth it. For this reason, *in the short run*, changes in income levels often don't result in changes in investment spending by businesses because they don't know if the changes in income will continue in the future. Maybe the new factories and machines will not be needed. This does *not* mean, however, that changes in investment spending have *no* effect on GDP. Recall that earlier we said some people believe that the bursting of the dot.com bubble in early 2000 led to a severe reduction in business investment and this, in turn, depressed GDP.

The assumption that investment is not related to income is shown in the left-hand panel of **Figure 13.3**. Unlike consumption, when income rises, we'll assume that investment remains at some given level. In the figure, this assumption is shown by investment remaining at $1,000 billion (or $1 trillion) no matter what the level of income is. If investment is unrelated to the level of income, what would cause investment to change from, say, $1,000 billion to $875 billion? This question allows us to introduce our second assumption: investment spending *is* related to the level of the real interest rate.

The relation between investment and the real rate of interest is shown in the right-hand panel of Figure 13.3. This relation looks a lot like a demand curve, and in some sense it is. A key factor in any business's decision to buy a new piece of

· · · · · · ·

[2]Why use 2007? It was the last year before the severe recession that began in late 2007 and ran through the end of 2009. Even though the economy has recovered somewhat from this episode, the 2007 numbers are more representative of the percentages that consumption spending, investment, and the other components are of GDP.

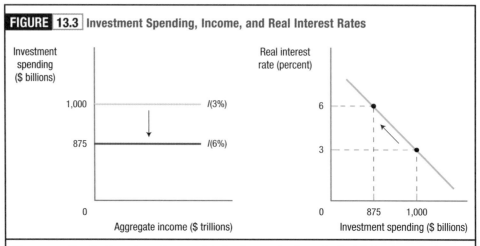

**FIGURE 13.3** Investment Spending, Income, and Real Interest Rates

The assumption that investment is not related to income is shown in the left-hand panel. This is shown by the level of investment remaining at $1,000 billion (the horizontal line) no matter what the level of income is. The rate of interest affects the level of investment spending. The right-hand panel shows how investment spending is related to the level of the real interest rate. An increase in real rates of interest—a rise in borrowing costs—is associated with a reduction in investment spending by firms. A rise in the interest rate from 3 percent to 6 percent reduces investment from $1,000 billion to $875 billion. This fall in investment shifts down the investment spending line, as shown in the left-hand panel. Conversely, a fall in real interest rates—a fall in borrowing costs—is associated with an increase in investment spending.

equipment is how much it will cost to borrow the money needed to buy the machine. When your neighborhood latte shop borrows money to purchase more latte machines, it's making a prediction about the revenue it will earn from the additional lattes it can sell using the additional machines. If the expected revenues are enough to cover the expense incurred from borrowing the money, the latte shop borrows the money and buys the machines.

As the cost of borrowing money rises—measured by an increase in the real interest rate—the number of profitable projects declines. The more it costs to borrow money, the less likely a firm will go ahead with its investment plan. Higher real rates of interest, therefore, are associated with a reduction in investment spending by firms. Conversely, a fall in real interest rates—a fall in borrowing costs—makes more projects economically viable, and investment spending increases.

Changes in the real interest rate also affect a more personal component of investment: home purchases. Have you ever heard a radio ad by the local mortgage company saying something like "Rates can't get any lower! Borrow now and buy the dream home you've always wanted." They do this because people, like the owners of the latte shop, are more likely to buy new homes when mortgage rates fall than when mortgage rates rise. This is because people compare the cost of the home investment—the cost of borrowing the mortgage—to the services they get from a new home. Like a business, higher mortgage rates, all else the same, reduce individuals' home purchases. This is another avenue through which higher rates reduce investment spending.

In the right-hand panel of Figure 13.3, you will see two interest rates and their related levels of investment spending. At a real interest rate of, say, 3 percent, investment spending is $1,000 billion. If the interest rate increases to 6 percent, the level of investment spending falls from $1,000 billion to $875 billion. An increase in the real rate of interest leads to a fall in the level of investment spending.

This relation also explains the two investment spending lines in the left-hand panel of Figure 13.3. The investment line labeled $I(3\%)$ shows the level of investment ($1,000 billion) when the interest rate is 3 percent. You've just seen that an increase in the real rate of interest reduces the amount of investment spending. When the real rate of interest rises to 6 percent, we can show this in the left-hand panel of Figure 13.3 as the investment spending line shifting downward to $I(6\%)$. Because the rate of interest and investment are inversely related, as real rate of interest changes, the investment spending line shifts up or down at every level of income.

## Government Purchases

Spending by federal, state, and local governments on newly produced goods and services defines **government purchases**.

**GOVERNMENT PURCHASES** New goods and services purchased by federal, state, and local governments.

EXAMPLE The Bureau of Labor Statistics (BLS) purchases boxes and boxes of paper each month for its employees to use.

EXAMPLE Many city governments purchase cell phones for their key employees.

The U.S. government's purchases amounted to a little over $2 trillion, or 17 percent of real GDP in 2007. We are going to be very specific about how the government-purchases component of aggregate expenditures is defined. Notice that we use the term "purchases" and not government "outlays." Unlike government purchases, government outlays add in payments to individuals that are *not* made directly to buy currently produced goods and services. For instance, Social Security payments to your grandparents are a government outlay, but they are not payments made for the current production of some good, such as a fighter jet or a bridge. Government purchases go directly toward current production and are a part of GDP. Instead, Social Security payments are **transfer payments**—payments that simply transfer income from current taxpayers to Social Security recipients. Transfer payments, which include unemployment compensation, welfare payments, and subsidies to farmers not to grow crops, do not represent direct payments for goods and services currently being produced.

**TRANSFER PAYMENTS** Payments made to individuals by governments that are not related to the current production of goods and services.

EXAMPLE When she reached retirement age, Sally started getting monthly Social Security checks from the federal government.

EXAMPLE Uncle Morris decided to take half of his 500 acres of farmland out of corn production and enter it into the state's prairie-restoration program. He now receives an annual check from the state government for $10,000.

Similar to investment spending, we will consider government purchases to be independent of the economy's level of income. When governments decide to purchase more or fewer goods and services, they can do so with little regard to what the level of real GDP is. Of course, this isn't the case when the government increases spending to halt an economic downturn. Some government spending, such as unemployment insurance (benefits), actually changes with the rise and fall of income. For now, however, we will assume that although the government can decide to increase or decrease its spending, such spending is not a function of the economy's income level. (We will look at government spending in more detail in Chapter 16.)

Graphically, the relation between government purchases and income is similar to the investment line shown in Figure 13.3. If we assume that government purchases are, say, $2,000 billion, this means that the level of government purchases will not change with changes in the level of aggregate income. Government purchases are determined by the politicians who make budgetary decisions. Later in the chapter, however, you will see that changes in government purchases can change the level of a country's aggregate income.

## Net Exports

When someone talks about "net income," they mean income "net of" or less taxes. **Net exports** can be defined similarly as the dollar value of goods and services exported to other countries minus the dollar value of goods and services imported from other countries. Suppose Boeing sells its fighter jets not only to the U.S. government but also to other governments. If the Canadian government buys a Boeing jet, the dollar value of that trade is included in the exports column. On the other side of the ledger, we buy many goods from producers located in Canada. The dollar value of these purchases is counted as an import. The difference between the two—exports minus imports—is net exports. What's on the list of imports? Many brands of cars are built elsewhere and imported to the United States, as are wines (Australia), CD players (Korea), lumber (Canada), and much of the clothing we wear (China).

**NET EXPORTS** The value of exports minus the value of imports.

**EXAMPLE** In 2008, Russia exported about $472 billion worth of goods and imported about $292 billion worth of goods. In 2008 Russia's net exports were $180 billion.

**EXAMPLE** In the same year, Australia exported about $190 billion in goods and imported about $194 billion in goods. Net exports in Australia were –$4 billion.

In our model of the economy, net exports make up the difference between what a country exports and what it imports. If net exports are positive—the value of exports exceeds the value of the country's imports—there is a **trade surplus**. If net exports are negative—the value of exports is less than the value of imports—there is a **trade deficit**. For the United States, net exports have been negative for many years. In fact, we've run a trade deficit for most of the past 20 years. In 2007, the nation's real net exports were −$546 billion, or about 5 percent of real GDP. Other countries, in contrast, often run large trade surpluses. As we mentioned in Chapter 9, the trade relationship between the United States and China recently has received much attention. China has a huge trade surplus, whereas the United States has a huge trade deficit.[3]

· · · · · · ·

[3]"China's Trade Surplus Near High," *New York Times*, June 12, 2007.

**TRADE SURPLUS** A situation in which a country's exports exceed its imports.

**TRADE DEFICIT** A situation in which a country's exports are less than its imports.

**ECONOMIC FALLACY**   Imports should be restricted to lower the trade deficit and increase real GDP.

**False.** Some people believe that citizens of the United States would be better off if its trade deficit were zero. Some suggest that getting there means restricting imports. Restricting international trade to reduce our trade deficit does mean that fewer dollars would be spent on goods produced in other countries. But would this make people in the United States better off? Hardly. For one, everyone engaged in the importing business would lose their jobs. We would also need to replace many of the goods produced in other countries with ones produced in the United States. Could farmers in the United States somehow grow bananas? What about the inexpensive but high-quality electronic goods we import? If we close our borders to foreign-produced goods, goods such as these will be less available to us, although we might be able to buy them on the black market by paying a premium for them. Reducing the trade deficit by restricting imports might sound good to some, but closing the country to imports is not good for consumers or economies. Not only does the idea reject the principles of comparative advantage, but it also ignores the evidence presented in Chapter 11 that more open economies tend to be those with faster rates of economic growth.

We will treat net exports much the same way we treated investment spending and government purchases. That is, we are assuming that net exports are independent of income, which is clearly not true: if incomes in the United States are rising relative to other countries, we tend to import more from them than they do from us. At this point, however, we make this assumption simply to make the analysis less complicated.

With this assumption, the relation between net exports and total income looks just like investment spending and government purchases. We show the relation between net exports and income in the left-hand panel of **Figure 13.4** as a horizontal line drawn at some level of net exports. (We made net exports a positive number to make it more straightforward to show the relation between net exports and real GDP.) This implies that no matter what the level of income is in the economy, net exports are equal to, say, $150 billion.

Like investment, net exports are sensitive to changes in real interest rates. In this case, however, net exports can change because of changes in real interest rates in the United States *relative to* changes in real interest rates in other countries. Changes in real interest rates affect the relative attractiveness of U.S. investments, which, in turn, affects the exchange rate of the dollar. (Refresh your memory by referring to Chapter 9.) This, in turn, affects how expensive U.S. goods are relative to foreign goods.

To see this, suppose real interest rates in the United States increase, but rates in Canada do not. With this change, U.S. financial assets become more attractive to foreigners. All else the same, Canadian residents will be enticed to buy more U.S. financial assets because they now pay a higher rate of return than Canadian financial assets. To do this, however, the Canadians must acquire U.S. dollars. So, higher U.S. real interest rates increase the demand for U.S. dollars, which in turn bids up the price of U.S. dollars relative to Canadian dollars. The exchange rate rises: the

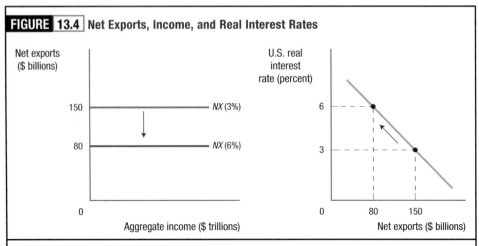

**FIGURE 13.4** Net Exports, Income, and Real Interest Rates

To show the effect real interest rates have on net exports, in the left-hand panel, net exports are treated as independent of income, as shown by the horizontal lines. The location of these net-export lines is determined by changes in the real rate of interest. In the right-hand panel of the figure, the negatively sloped net-export line reflects the idea that as U.S. interest rates increase relative to those in other countries, U.S. net exports decline. In the left-hand panel, the effect of such an increase in U.S. interest rates is shown by a downward shift in the net-export line at every level of income. A decrease in U.S. interest rates has just the opposite effect on net exports.

U.S. dollar appreciates relative to the Canadian dollar, and U.S. exports to Canadians become relatively more expensive for Canadian citizens to purchase. On the flip side, Canadian goods now become less expensive to U.S. buyers.

This rather complicated sequence of events can be summarized: all else the same, U.S. net exports fall when U.S. real interest rates rise relative to those in other countries. The reverse is just as true: U.S. net exports rise when U.S. real interest rates fall relative to those in other countries. A decrease in U.S. real interest rates makes U.S. exports more attractive to foreign buyers and imports from other countries less attractive to U.S. buyers, so net exports increase.

We can illustrate the relation between net exports and interest rates by using a diagram similar to that used for investment. In the right-hand panel of Figure 13.4, you will find a graphical version of the story we just told. The negatively sloped net-export line reflects the idea that as U.S. real interest rates increase relative to those in other countries, U.S. net exports decline. As the figure shows, when the U.S. real interest rate increases from, say, 3 percent to 6 percent, net exports fall from $150 billion to $80 billion. The left-hand panel of the figure shows that the increase in the real U.S. interest rate leads to a decrease in net exports at all levels of income. We show this effect by shifting the net-export line down at every level of income. At the higher real interest rate, net exports decline from $150 billion to $80 billion. In short, changes in net exports are negatively related to changes in a country's relative real interest rate and not the country's level of income.

## 13.2 An International Perspective

Thus far, we've focused on the United States. If we look at other countries, is it still true that consumption is the major component of GDP? The top line of **Table 13.1** shows an estimate of world GDP. The world result shows that global consumption

**Table 13.1  Expenditure Components: An International Comparison**

Component as a Percent of GDP

| Country | Consumption (%) | Investment (%) | Government (%) | Net Exports (%) |
|---|---|---|---|---|
| World | 62 | 21 | 17 | 0 |
| United States | 70 | 15 | 19 | −4 |
| Australia | 61 | 25 | 18 | −4 |
| Canada | 56 | 19 | 19 | 6 |
| Germany | 59 | 17 | 19 | 5 |
| United Kingdom | 65 | 17 | 21 | −3 |
| Argentina | 63 | 19 | 11 | 7 |
| Brazil | 57 | 20 | 20 | 3 |
| Mexico | 68 | 22 | 12 | −2 |
| China | 41 | 44 | 12 | 3 |
| Japan | 56 | 24 | 18 | 2 |
| Singapore | 42 | 18 | 11 | 29 |
| South Korea | 53 | 31 | 12 | 4 |
| Vietnam | 63 | 38 | 6 | −7 |
| Egypt | 71 | 16 | 12 | 1 |
| Kenya | 75 | 17 | 17 | −9 |
| Nigeria | 85 | 20 | 2 | −7 |
| South Africa | 63 | 19 | 20 | −2 |

World consumption (see the top line of table) is about two-thirds of total global GDP, investment is about 20 percent, and spending by governments is 17 percent. Net exports are zero because in the aggregate, someone's exports must be equal to someone else's imports. The percentage of GDP for each component varies across countries. Consumption as a percent of GDP ranges from a low of 41 percent in China to a high of 85 percent in Nigeria. Investment relative to GDP in China is 44 percent but only 15 percent in the United States. Government purchases as a percent of GDP range from 2 to 21 percent, and net exports as a percent of GDP are fairly small, although in Singapore they amount to nearly one-third of GDP.

**Note:** U.S. figures for 2007; all others for 2006.

**Source:** *The Economist* (2010)

is about two-thirds of global GDP, investment is about 20 percent, spending by governments is 17 percent, and net exports are zero. You might be wondering how net exports can be zero. The fact is that someone's exports are equal to someone else's imports wherever in the world they may be. Thus, across the world, exports must equal imports, so *net* exports must be zero.

The percentages for each component is revealing and, for the most part, consistent with our claims about the percentages that consumption, investment, government spending, and net exports are for the United States. For instance, consumption ranges from a low of 41 percent in China to a high of 85 percent in Nigeria. Also in sharp contrast, in China, investment amounts to 44 percent of GDP, whereas it is only 15 percent in the United States. For the most part, government as a percent of the economy ranges from 10 to 20 percent, with Nigeria and Vietnam being notable exceptions. Finally, net exports as a percent of GDP is fairly small for most countries listed, generally less than 10 percent. The country that stands out in that category is Singapore: net exports in Singapore amount to almost one-third of GDP.

## 13.3 The Total Expenditures Line

By now, you might be wondering how all the different components of total expenditures come together to represent the demand side of the economy. A good first step is to realize that when we add together all of the components—consumption spending (C), investment spending (I), government purchases (G), and net exports (NX)— we are really measuring total spending in the economy. You saw in Chapter 7 that total spending, or total expenditures, is directly related to the total output of the economy. In equilibrium, what is spent must equal what is earned. In equilibrium, total income equals total output.

Economists show this relation using

$$Y = C + I + G + NX$$

where Y stands for real GDP, and C, I, G, and NX are defined as before. Recall that finding real GDP is done by dividing nominal GDP by the price level (P). That is, real GDP = (nominal GDP/P). If we simply let P = 1, dividing both sides of the equation by 1(= P) leaves the relation between the different components unchanged. In other words, the sum of *real* expenditures (C + I + G + NX) is equal to *real* GDP. We will use this definition to see how changes on the demand side of the economy—captured by changes in total spending—impact the level of real output.

**Figure 13.5** graphically brings together all of the spending components and relates their sum to total income or output. First notice how the axes of the diagram

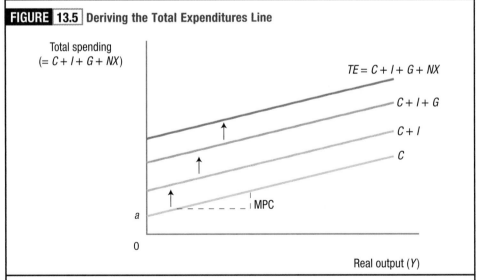

**FIGURE 13.5** Deriving the Total Expenditures Line

This figure brings together all of the spending components—consumption spending (C), investment spending (I), government purchases (G), and net exports (NX)—and relates their sum to total income or output. This slope of the consumption line (C) is the slope of the economy's consumption function (the MPC). The y-intercept of the consumption line represents the autonomous consumption in the economy. The total expenditures line (TE) is the vertical summation of all of the spending components (C + I + G + NX) at each level of output. The slope of the total expenditures line (TE) is the same as the consumption line: the MPC.

are labeled. The vertical axis measures total spending, or $C + I + G + NX$. The horizontal axis measures total real output, or real GDP. The consumption function provides the slope of the total expenditures line. To see this, imagine a world with no business investment, no government purchases, and net exports are equal to zero. In this world, total expenditures are just consumption spending ($C$). The intercept of the total expenditures line is simply consumption when income is zero (autonomous consumption), and the slope of the line is the slope of the consumption function, or the MPC.

Of course, in the real world, there are governments, businesses do invest, and nations trade. To get the total expenditures for the economy, we add to consumption spending at every level of income the amount of investment spending, government purchases, and net exports. This is done graphically by shifting the total expenditures line upward and parallel to the consumption function. The line increases parallel to the consumption function because each additional spending component is assumed to be a fixed number. For instance, by adding investment spending to consumption spending in Figure 13.5, we get the new total expenditures line $C + I$, which is greater than consumption by the amount of investment. Adding government purchases gives us the line $C + I + G$, and adding net exports produces the line $C + I + G + NX$. This final line is the **total expenditures line**, labeled $TE$.

> **TOTAL EXPENDITURES LINE** The relation between the four spending components and total income or output.

The total expenditures line, by itself, actually isn't very useful. We really want to know what level of spending occurs when the economy is near its potential. That way, if we see expenditures drop in one area, then we have some idea that the economy may be slipping inside its PPF. Figure 13.5 won't tell us this, though. To make the graph useful in this regard, let's make a slight alteration. **Figure 13.6** reproduces the total expenditures line from Figure 13.5 but adds another line, one with a 45-degree angle. This 45-degree line has nothing to do with economics. It really is just a useful geometric tool because every point along this 45-degree line is the same distance from both axes.

Because the axes are total expenditures and real output, it must be true (geometry doesn't lie) that every point along the 45-degree line is where total real spending ($C + I + G + NX$) equals total real output ($Y$). At the point where the total expenditures line ($TE$) and the 45-degree line cross, it must be true that total real spending in the economy equals the dollar value of the economy's total real output. At that point, aggregate or total real expenditure ($C + I + G + NX$) is equal to total real output ($Y$). (If you are thinking that this is just restating the relation used when we discussed the spending approach to measuring GDP, you are correct. Appendix B provides a mathematical way to solve for equilibrium income and output.) This equality of spending and output exists for no other levels of spending and output. At any other expenditure–output pair—off of the 45-degree line—the two measures simply are not equal. If such a condition exists, adjustments in spending and output must take place to achieve the spending–output equality. Trying to understand this dynamic adjustment of spending and output is one reason why economists followed Keynes's insights and further developed this approach. And it is why we will use it to explain economic fluctuations.

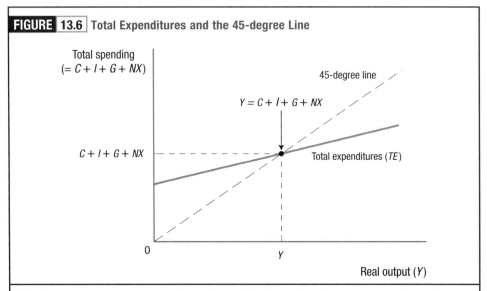

**FIGURE 13.6** Total Expenditures and the 45-degree Line

This figure shows the total expenditures line and 45-degree line drawn from the origin of the graph. Because the 45-degree line is the same distance from both axes, at every point along it, total expenditures equal total output ($Y$). Where the total expenditures line crosses the 45-degree line, it must be true that total real spending in the economy ($TE = C + I + G + NX$) at this level equals the dollar value of the economy's total real output ($Y$). At any other spending and output combination—total expenditures off the 45-degree line—adjustments in spending and output must take place to achieve the spending–output equality.

## 13.4 Interest Rates, Total Expenditures, and Aggregate Demand

You've been exposed to a lot of information so far. You have seen how we can add together the spending by different sectors in the economy to arrive at a total expenditures measure for the economy. You've also seen that changes in the real rate of interest affect consumption spending, business investment, and net exports. In this section, we'll use the connection between changes in the real rate of interest and spending to make one more important connection: the link between inflation and real output.

The main reason for developing this model is to explain why economies experience periods of economic expansion and periods of economic slumps. Economists for years have been trying to figure out why recessions occur, why some are worse than others, and whether economic policies can prevent them from happening. Some economists even believe that if we fully understood the factors that relate expenditures and output, governments could fine-tune economic activity by altering total spending enough to keep the economy close to full employment.

You've seen that changes in the level of total expenditures are related to changes in the output of the economy, *at least in the short run*. We make this caveat because, as you learned in Chapter 10, in the long run, economic growth is based on how an economy combines labor, capital, and knowledge. In equilibrium, the dollar amount of spending in a country equals the nation's dollar amount of output produced. Even though we can link spending and output separately, eventually we will tie together inflation and output because these are two of the most important policy objectives in macroeconomics.

So far we have discussed total expenditures by stating everything in terms of real expenditures and matching real expenditures to real output. Prices have been fixed. If changes in prices played no role in that discussion, how can we get inflation into the mix? The link between the two comes through the real rate of interest.

## Changes in the Real Rate of Interest and Total Expenditures

Changes in the real rate of interest affect consumption spending, investment, and net exports. In every instance, we suggested that an increase in the real rate of interest leads to a reduction in that component of total spending. Conversely, a decrease in the real rate of interest is associated with an increase in spending. Although the mechanism by which a change in the real rate of interest affects each of the three expenditure types is different, the final result on total expenditures is the same. If the real rate of interest plays such an important role, it is vital to understand why the real rate of interest increases or decreases.

A growing body of evidence indicates that central banks, such as the Federal Reserve, manipulate the real rate of interest to try to achieve their policy objectives, which usually are economic growth and low inflation. In the United States, for instance, many people believe that the Fed responds to increases in the rate of inflation by increasing *nominal* interest rates. Specifically, the Fed increases nominal interest rates when it perceives that the rate of inflation is getting too high.[4] By increasing the interest rate when it thinks inflation is getting out of hand, the Fed is trying to reduce total expenditures in the economy. Remember, an increase in the real rate of interest has a dampening effect on consumer spending, investment spending, and net exports.

How does the Fed bring about these desired changes? The scenario goes like this: the policy makers at the Fed perceive that the rate of inflation is rising above some "desired" rate. To reduce this threat, they raise nominal interest rates to reduce aggregate spending in the economy. But isn't it the real rate that they should be increasing? Yes. To increase the real rate of interest (the nominal rate of interest adjusted for inflation) and therefore reduce spending, the Fed raises nominal interest rates by *more than* what they expect the increase in the rate of inflation will be.

Some numbers will help. Suppose policy makers expect the rate of inflation to increase from 2 to 5 percent (+3 percentage points), which they believe is too large of an increase and will harm our economic well-being. So, if nominal interest rates currently are 4 percent, the Fed might adjust its policies so that nominal interest rates increase to 9 percent (+5 percentage points). This action will increase the real rate of interest (which is equal to the nominal rate minus inflation) from 2 percent to 4 percent. By increasing the real rate of interest, the policy makers hope to reduce total expenditures and, as a result, dampen the upward pressures on prices in the economy.

This reaction by policy makers to expected increases in inflation represents what economists call a *policy rule*. (We will have more to say about policy rules in Chapter 18.) In essence, this rule is to increase the nominal interest rate by more than the expected increase in the rate of inflation to restrict increases in total expenditures. In other words, the Fed tries to lower expenditures (shift down the total expenditures line in Figure 13.6) by increasing the real rate of interest. Let's use this policy rule to tie together changes in the rate of inflation and real output and to derive the aggregate demand curve.

· · · · · · ·

[4]The interest rate that the Fed focuses on is called the federal funds rate. It is the interest rate that banks charge each other for short-term, usually overnight, loans. We will have much more to say about how the Fed uses it for policy purposes in Chapter 18.

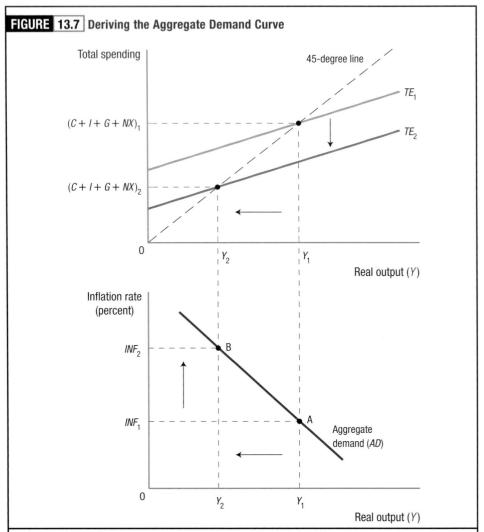

**FIGURE 13.7** | Deriving the Aggregate Demand Curve

The aggregate demand curve is made up of different inflation–output combinations. In the lower panel, $INF_1$ is the rate of inflation associated with the level of output $Y_1$ (point A). The upper panel shows that at this rate of inflation, the level of the economy's output is equal to the economy's total expenditures, $TE_1 = (C+I+G+NX)_1$. Now let the rate of inflation rise to $INF_2$. If the Fed reacts by raising the real rate of interest enough, the total expenditures line shifts downward to $TE_2$. At the higher rate of inflation and the lower level of total expenditures, equal to $TE_2 = (C+I+G+NX)_2$, a new, lower level of output ($Y_2$) is now determined. In the bottom panel, the higher rate of inflation is associated with a lower level of output, $Y_2$ (point B). Connecting points A and B and all points in between gives us the aggregate demand curve (AD).

## Deriving the Aggregate Demand Curve

**Figure 13.7** gives you everything you need to derive an economy's aggregate demand curve. Look first at the lower panel of the figure. To derive the aggregate demand curve, let's start with a rate of inflation, $INF_1$, which is the rate of inflation associated with some level of output, say $Y_1$. In the upper panel, you will see that at this rate of inflation, the level of the economy's output is equal to the economy's total expenditures. It happens to be the rate of inflation where the total expenditures line ($TE_1$) and the 45-degree line cross. Now let's put into motion the preceding scenario: the rate of inflation rises from $INF_1$ to $INF_2$. The Fed reacts by raising the real rate of interest. As you have learned, an increase in the real rate of interest reduces total expenditures. Graphically this is shown by the total expenditures line shifting downward, to $TE_2$. At the higher rate of inflation and the lower level of total expenditures, a new, lower level of output is now determined. The intersection of the new, lower total expenditures line ($TE_2$) and the 45-degree line occurs at output level ($Y_2$), which is lower than the original level ($Y_1$). In the bottom panel of Figure 13.7, the higher rate of inflation is associated with a lower level of output. Connecting this point with the original one, and all points in between, gives us the **aggregate demand curve (AD)**.

> **AGGREGATE DEMAND CURVE (AD)** A line showing the negative relation between the rate of inflation and the level of real output.

The aggregate demand curve is a relation between the rate of inflation and real output. The fact that it is downward sloping does not mean, however, that as inflation increases, the quantity demanded for all goods in an economy declines. Although they look similar, *the aggregate demand curve is not the same as the demand curve for a good*. A demand curve for some good, such as apples, slopes downward because of the relation between the price of the good and its substitutes. Raise the price of apples, and people will substitute into relatively lower-priced pears: at a higher apple price, the quantity demanded of apples falls. This is not what the aggregate demand curve illustrates. The aggregate demand curve tells us that at higher rates of inflation, given the change in the real rate of interest, the equality between total spending and total output—that is, the points of intersection between the total expenditures line and the 45-degree line—can only occur at a lower level of real output.

The aggregate demand curve is made up of different inflation–output combinations that lead to equality between total real expenditures and real output. That is, it is made up of different inflation–output combinations where $TE = Y = C + I + G + NX$. This means that changes in aggregate demand—shifts of the aggregate demand curve—are very important when it comes to determining the rate of inflation and the level of output at which the economy is operating. This is important because it will help us predict how policies that change the real rate of interest, or change the level of government purchases (and taxes), will affect total expenditures and, therefore, output (and even inflation) in the economy.

## 13.5 What Affects Aggregate Demand? What Shifts the Aggregate Demand Curve?

For the sake of convenience, let's imagine we are trying to devise a policy that keeps the economy expanding at a steady pace. For instance, we are trying to keep the economy as close to its PPF as we can. For the time being, let's assume that the rate of inflation is given. You might be thinking that this is absurd: Don't inflation rates change monthly? But recall that inflation is defined as the persistent increase in the general level of prices. We are assuming that the trend of inflation doesn't change in the short run, which allows us to focus on what causes the aggregate demand curve to shift and how changes in aggregate demand affect the level of output, at least in the immediate future.

We will consider three possible causes for aggregate demand to change. Two are policy related: changes in the real rate of interest and changes in government expenditures. Then we will look at nonpolicy causes, stemming from changes in consumption spending, investment spending, and net exports.

## Changes in the Real Rate of Interest

People often believe that central banks such as the Federal Reserve can determine the pace of economic growth by setting interest rates to this or that level. You learned earlier that by increasing nominal interest rates by more than inflation is expected to increase, the Fed is attempting to raise the real rate of interest and lower total expenditures. Conversely, by lowering nominal interest rates more than inflation is expected to fall, the Fed can reduce the real interest rate to try and spur total spending and economic activity. All else the same, lowering interest rates reduces the borrowing costs to people and businesses, induces greater consumption spending and investment spending, and increases net exports. Consequently, it's no wonder that the press, when covering meetings by Federal Reserve officials, usually focus on their interest-rate decisions.

Why should you care whether the Fed raises or lowers interest rates? The answer to this question is shown in **Figure 13.8**. A policy decision to change the level of the real rate of interest shifts the aggregate demand curve. In Figure 13.8, we depict a situation in which the Fed lowers the real rate of interest. Recall that for now, we are assuming that the rate of inflation is given, here set equal to 4 percent. When such a policy action is taken, all else the same, the Fed is trying to increase total expenditures and shift the aggregate demand curve to the right, shown as the shift from $AD_1$ to $AD_2$. The aggregate demand curve shifts to the right because lowering the real rate of interest decreases borrowing costs and induces households and businesses to spend

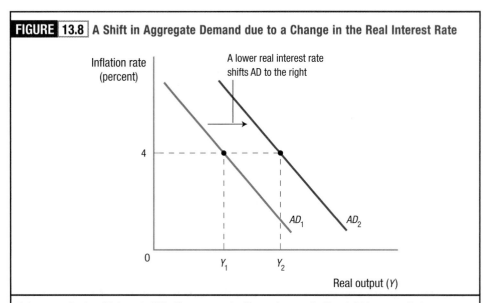

**FIGURE 13.8** A Shift in Aggregate Demand due to a Change in the Real Interest Rate

A lower real rate of interest shifts the aggregate demand curve to the right because it decreases borrowing costs and induces households and businesses to spend more. Because the rate of inflation is unchanged, the new intersection between aggregate demand and the inflation line will occur at a higher level of output ($Y_2$). Conversely, raising the real rate of interest shifts the aggregate demand curve to the left.

more. With the rate of inflation unchanged, the new intersection between aggregate demand and the given rate of inflation (4%) must occur at a higher level of output. Lowering the real rate of interest increases total expenditures and, given the rate of inflation, shifts the aggregate demand curve to the right. The desired effect is to increase output from $Y_1$ to $Y_2$.

A policy that lowers the real rate of interest (given inflation) is designed to increase economic output. By contrast, a policy that raises the real rate of interest is designed to produce the exact opposite effect: raising the real rate of interest, which should shift the aggregate demand curve to the left, is aimed at decreasing the economy's level of output. We will look at more monetary policy issues in Chapter 18.

## Changes in Government Purchases

Suppose lawmakers in Washington, D.C. (or London, Beijing, or Paris) decide to expand several government programs. What if they decide to make college education free to everyone, extend health care benefits to all people, and fix all roadways? Of course, this situation can only occur if the government purchases more goods and services. Increases in government expenditures (the $G$ in the $Y = C + I + G + NX$ equation) mean that total expenditures in the economy will increase as well. If the rate of inflation is unchanged, a policy that increases the government's purchases will shift the economy's aggregate demand curve to the right and, given the rate of inflation, increase the nation's real output.

An example of such a policy is the multibillion dollar stimulus package proposed by the Obama administration and passed by Congress in 2009. The goal of the increase in government spending was to increase total expenditures in an economy mired in a deep recession: the goal was to increase (or, at a minimum, check the decline in) aggregate demand. The idea was that funding road-repair projects, expanding mass-transit systems, and increasing the number of police in many cities would create jobs for people who then use the money they earn to buy goods and services. This, in turn, boosts aggregate demand and ultimately should lead to an increase in the nation's economic output. Other countries around the world experiencing the global recession, including Germany, China, France, and the United Kingdom, also took similar policy actions to boost government spending.[5]

**Figure 13.9** shows how an increase in government purchases affects aggregate demand. Similar to the outcome of monetary policy actions taken to lower the real rate of interest, an increase in government purchases shifts the aggregate demand curve, in this example, from $AD_1$ to $AD_2$. At the given inflation rate of 4 percent, this action leads to an increase in real output, from $Y_1$ to $Y_2$. What about when government purchases decline? You probably can guess what happens: total expenditures ($C + I + G + NX$) decline, which in turn shifts the aggregate demand curve in Figure 13.9 to the left. At the given rate of inflation, a reduction in government purchases results in a decline in aggregate demand and a fall in the level of output.

We haven't talked much about how tax changes affect aggregate demand and total real output. We did note earlier that consumption spending is based on disposable income or income after taxes have been taken out. So let's suppose the government raises taxes on your income. Because your disposable income will fall as a

- - - - - - -

[5]"Germany Seals 50 Billion Euro Stimulus Plan," *Spiegel Online*, January 13, 2009; Michael Wines, "China Outlines Ambitious Plan for Stimulus," *New York Times*, March 4, 2009.

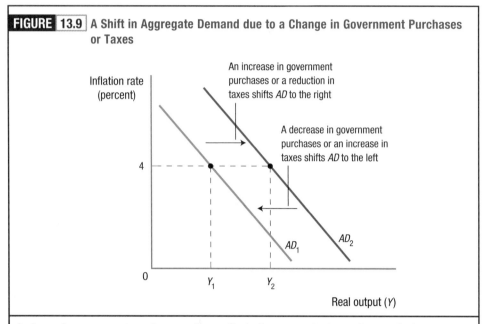

**FIGURE 13.9** A Shift in Aggregate Demand due to a Change in Government Purchases or Taxes

A change in government purchases or taxes affects the aggregate demand curve. An increase in government purchases—an increase in total expenditures—shifts the aggregate demand curve to the right. At a given inflation rate, this action leads to an increase in real output. The same effect—an increase in aggregate demand and output—occurs when taxes are lowered. Conversely, when government purchases decline, total expenditures decline, and the aggregate demand curve shifts to the left; that is, output falls. The same effect—a decrease in aggregate demand and output—occurs when taxes are raised.

result, your consumption spending will fall as well. An increase in taxes that lowers consumption spending will also lower total expenditures which, all else the same, will shift the aggregate demand curve to the left. All else the same, an *increase* in taxes has the same effect on aggregate demand and total output as a *reduction* in government purchases. A reduction in taxes has just the opposite impact: lowering taxes shifts the aggregate demand curve to the right and, given inflation, raises real output. Even though changes in taxes have similar effects as changes in spending, the debate over their use often revolves around whose taxes will be cut (or increased).

## SOLVED PROBLEM

**Q** What if taxes are raised?

**A** For much of this discussion, we have assumed that taxes are zero. But, because you often hear people argue that raising taxes is just a bad idea, it may be useful to see how taxes affect consumption and, therefore, income. Although this argument is sometimes based largely on an individual's attitude toward government, there is an economic foundation to reconsider raising taxes because raising taxes reduces consumer spending. How does this happen? What is the magnitude of the effect? Let's address these questions using the example in the previous Solved Problem. There we said that the consumption function looked like

$$C = a + b (Y - T)$$

where all of the terms are defined as before. Using the values in our previous example, we can write this as

$$C = \$200 + 0.8(\$1{,}000 - \$200)$$
$$= \$840$$

Now let's raise taxes from $200 to $300. What happens to consumption spending? Rewrite the consumption function using the new figures, and you'll find that

$$C = \$200 + 0.8(\$1{,}000 - \$300)$$
$$= \$760$$

Or, the $100 increase in taxes reduced consumption spending from $840 to $760, an $80 decline. Why wasn't the drop in spending equal to $100? The answer is because consumption spending isn't directly affected by taxes but indirectly through changes in disposable income. Because consumption spending is related to changes in disposable income times the MPC, which is less than one, the change in taxes has less than a one-to-one effect on consumption spending. Still, raising taxes lowers consumption spending and, all else the same, reduces aggregate demand and real output.

## Other Factors

If you are thinking that surely something other than changes in the real rate of interest or government purchases or taxes must affect aggregate demand, you are correct. We've chosen to call attention to these factors because governments (really, the people who make those decisions) policy actions have significant effects on your economic well-being. There are other factors that can impact aggregate demand and, therefore, output of the economy. For instance, a sharp decline in consumer and business confidence about the future can lead to sharp changes in aggregate demand. Such a change occurred following the stock market crash of 2000 and the attacks on New York City and Washington, D.C. that occurred on September 11, 2001. Significant declines in consumer and business confidence also occurred during the 2008 financial crisis and lingered for several years. When a drop in confidence occurs, we can predict that total expenditures will fall, and the aggregate demand curve will shift to the left. Beginning in 2007, aggregate demand fell sharply around the world, leading to the worst economic downturn since the Great Depression of the 1930s. It took until late 2009 for aggregate demand in most countries to recover somewhat.

Generally, any *autonomous* change in expenditures—that is, a change in any of the expenditure components that are not a function of income—shifts the aggregate demand curve. An autonomous *increase* in spending, caused by an increase in autonomous consumption, investment spending, government purchases, or net exports, will increase aggregate demand and shift the aggregate demand curve to the right. If inflation is unchanged, any of these increases in expenditures will lead to an increase in real output. Conversely, an autonomous *decrease* in expenditures will shift the aggregate demand curve to the left and, given the rate of inflation, be associated with a lower level of real output.

Finally, monetary policy actions can also take the form of increasing and decreasing the growth rate of the money supply. Although monetary policy actions

| Table **13.2** A Summary of the Factors that Change Aggregate Demand | |
| --- | --- |
| Factors that *Increase* Aggregate Demand | Factors that *Decrease* Aggregate Demand |
| **Policy Sources:** | **Policy Sources:** |
| A decrease in the real rate of interest | An increase in the real rate of interest |
| A decrease in taxes | An increase in taxes |
| An increase in government purchases | A decrease in government purchases |
| An increase in money growth | A decrease in money growth |
| **Nonpolicy Sources:** | **Nonpolicy Sources:** |
| An increase in autonomous consumption spending | A decrease in autonomous consumption spending |
| An increase in investment spending | A decrease in investment spending |
| An increase in net exports | A decrease in net exports |

This table summarizes possible causes of a change in aggregate demand. Some of these changes are the result of policy decisions, such as increasing or decreasing government spending. Others stem from actions taken by individuals (via consumption) and firms (via investment) throughout the economy. Some changes, those listed as "nonpolicy sources" include changes in spending following unexpected events, such as natural disasters or financial market crises.

usually are related to movements in the real rate of interest, changes in the growth rate of the money supply also will affect aggregate demand. An increase in the growth rate of the money supply shifts the aggregate demand curve to the right. On the other hand, a decrease in the growth rate of the money supply decreases aggregate demand, shifting the aggregate demand curve to the left.

We have uncovered a number of reasons why aggregate demand might change. **Table 13.2** summarizes this discussion by listing the causes of changes in aggregate demand and how each will shift the aggregate demand curve. As you can see, a change in aggregate demand can originate from a variety of sources. Some of these shifts are the result of policy decisions. Others are the outcome of actions taken by individuals and firms throughout the economy, independent of some policy action. Because it is so encompassing, the aggregate demand curve is an incredibly useful tool that we will use to help explain fluctuations of real output. As you will see in the next chapter, we can also use it to better understand why the rate of inflation increases and decreases over time.

## WHAT YOU SHOULD HAVE LEARNED FROM CHAPTER 13

- That total expenditures can be measured as the sum of consumption spending, business investment, government purchases, and net exports.

- That changes in the level of consumption spending are related to changes in the level of income, where for each additional dollar in income, you increase your consumption spending by some fraction called the marginal propensity to consume (MPC).

- That business investment is negatively related to changes in the real interest rate.

- That government purchases do not include transfer payments, such as Social Security payments.

- That net exports, the difference between exports and imports, are negatively related to changes in the real rate of interest.

- That changes in total expenditures, given the rate of inflation, directly affect the level of real output.

■ That the aggregate demand curve shows the negative relation between the rate of inflation and the level of real output in an economy.

■ That the aggregate demand curve is not a summation of individual market demands but represents equality between spending and income at different levels of inflation and real output.

■ That any increase in aggregate demand, given inflation, is associated with an increase in the level of real output.

■ That changes in aggregate demand stem from changes in autonomous spending (in C, I, G, or NX) and from changes in the real rate of interest.

■ That policies that change government spending, taxes, real interest rates, and the money supply all affect aggregate demand and therefore may be used to influence the level of real output in an economy.

## KEY TERMS

Consumption function, p. 341

Autonomous consumption, p. 341

Marginal propensity to consume (MPC), p. 342

Disposable income, p. 343

Investment, p. 346

Government purchases, p. 349

Transfer payments, p. 349

Net exports, p. 350

Trade surplus, p. 350

Trade deficit, p. 350

Total expenditures line, p. 355

Aggregate demand curve (AD), p. 359

## QUESTIONS AND PROBLEMS

1. Marty's income doubles from $25,000 per year to $50,000 per year. Is it likely that his consumption spending will also double? Why or why not?

2. Explain why consumption spending can be determined by income and yet helps determine the level of income in the economy.

3. Look at Figure 13.1. Suppose that the consumption function drawn there intersected the y-axis at $8 trillion instead of $6 trillion. Without any other change than that:
   a) What would the new level of autonomous consumption be?
   b) Using the information in Figure 13.1, what would the new MPC be?

4. Autonomous consumption is the level of consumption spending at zero income. If you have no income, where is the money you are spending coming from? Does this suggest a role for credit markets? (Hint: The mirror image of autonomous consumption is autonomous saving.)

5. You know that autonomous consumption is $250 billion, that disposable income is $500 billion (assume taxes are equal to zero), and that the MPC is 0.8. Using these figures:
   a) Calculate the level of consumption spending.
   b) Given only the information provided, what is the equilibrium level of income?
   c) Suppose the general mood is that the economy will expand and that economic prospects are rosy. On the basis of this optimism, autonomous consumption increases from $250 billion to $400 billion. Now what is the equilibrium level of income?
   d) Does this change in income in part (c) also change the MPC? Why or why not?

6. At a recent family gathering, you overheard Walter exclaim "Investment is investment. Stocks, bonds, or tractors, it's all the same!" Is he correct? Explain.

7. You know that the consumption function can be written as $C = \$300 + 0.8\,(Y - T)$. Using that information:

a) If $Y = \$600$, and $T = \$100$, what is consumption spending?

b) Suppose you find out that business fixed investment ($I$) is equal to $250. Given the value for consumption you just determined, what is the equilibrium level of income for this economy?

c) If investment spending declined to $150, what is the change in the equilibrium level of income?

8. A financial analyst on one of the business-news programs your father watches proclaims that the economy is about to head into a slump. She bases her prediction on the observation that inventory investment is increasing rapidly. Explain how that observation can lead to her forecast.

9. A common belief is that when a country's central bank, such as the Bank of Canada or the Bank of Japan, wants to reduce or slow the increase in overall spending, it raises the real rate of interest.

a) Explain how raising the real rate of interest affects consumption spending.

b) Explain how raising the real rate of interest affects investment spending.

c) Explain how raising the real rate of interest affects government spending.

d) Explain how raising the real rate of interest affects net exports.

e) Given what you know about how GDP is constructed, how will this policy affect the overall level of income in the economy?

10. Some people use the terms government "outlays" and government "purchases" interchangeably. Is this a wise thing to do? Explain.

11. Which of the following is considered a transfer payment?

a) A Social Security payment

b) Retirement payment to an ex-government employee

c) Government payments to an economic consulting firm

d) Payments to farmers not to produce certain crops

e) Payments by your state to faculty at your school

12. In early 2009, President Obama signed legislation to enact a massive federal government-spending program. The stimulus spending program was aimed at limiting the downturn in the economy caused by the collapse in the housing market and by the financial crisis.

a) Using a diagram like Figure 13.6, illustrate the effect of the increase in government spending.

b) In your diagram, does the total expenditures line shift up or down after the stimulus money is spent?

c) Does the total expenditures line in your diagram rotate (become steeper or flatter) after the stimulus spending occurs? Why or why not?

13. Sometimes you hear your cousin Zach say "If we just cut off all trade with other countries, no jobs would be exported, and we would be better off." Use a diagram like Figure 13.6 to analyze his statement. Is he right or wrong?

14. Suppose the United States vigorously lowers the real rate of interest while the European Central Bank increases its real rate of interest. If the only two trading partners were the United States and Europe:

a) Predict what would happen to U.S. net exports.

b) Predict what would happen to European total expenditures.

15. Betty, a member of your economics study group, announces to all who will listen that the aggregate demand curve has a negative slope because as the price of goods rise, the quantity demanded falls. Is Betty correct? Why or why not?

16. In this chapter, the equilibrium condition between expenditures and output is written as $TE = Y = C + I + G + NX$. Where have you seen this before? What does this suggest about income in the economy?

17. Assume that the rate of inflation is fixed at, say, 4 percent. Using a diagram like Figure 13.8, show what happens to real GDP (output) when:
    a)  The government increases its purchases of airplanes from Boeing.
    b)  The Italian government decreases taxes.
    c)  The business community increases investment spending.
    d)  The Federal Reserve drastically lowers the real interest rate.
    e)  Households collectively decide to reduce spending out of current income.
    f)  Other governments block the importation of U.S. goods.
    g)  The housing bubble in Spain bursts, and residential investment plummets.
    h)  A financial crisis occurs, retirement savings are halved, and people become increasingly fearful that they will lose their jobs.
    i)  The Bank of China doubles the growth rate of the money supply.

## Appendix 13A    The Money Supply, Aggregate Demand, and Real Output

We used the Quantity Theory of Money in Chapter 12 to relate changes in inflation to changes in the growth of the money supply. We argued that an increase in the supply of money relative to the amount of goods and services being produced would lead to an increase in the price level, all else the same. We can use this theory also to show how changes in the supply of money can affect the aggregate demand curve.

Recall that the rate-of-change from of the Quantity Theory equation can be written as

$$\boldsymbol{M} + \boldsymbol{V} = \boldsymbol{P} + \boldsymbol{y}$$

where $\boldsymbol{M}$ is the growth rate of the money supply, $\boldsymbol{P}$ is the rate of inflation, $\boldsymbol{V}$ is the growth in the velocity or turnover of money, and $\boldsymbol{y}$ is the growth in real output. (To be consistent with that earlier discussion, we are letting $\boldsymbol{y}$ represent real output.) If the central bank's policies largely determine the growth rate of the supply of money ($\boldsymbol{M}$), and $\boldsymbol{V}$ is unchanged, this equation tells us that there is an inverse relation between the rate of inflation ($\boldsymbol{P}$) and the growth of real income ($\boldsymbol{y}$). That is, given $\boldsymbol{M}$ and $\boldsymbol{V}$—given the growth rates of the supply of money and the demand for it—an increase in the rate of inflation must be associated with a decline in the growth rate of real output.

You learned in this chapter that graphing the negative relation between inflation and real output based on total expenditures and the policy rule gives you an aggregate demand curve. With the preceding assumptions, the aggregate demand curve also reflects a relation between money supply and money demand. To see this, notice that if $\boldsymbol{M}$ and $\boldsymbol{V}$ are fixed values in the preceding equation, an increase in the rate of inflation *must* lead to a decline in the growth rate of real output. This mathematical explanation is not too interesting, but the economic explanation is.

Suppose you have $50 in cash and $200 in your checking account. Relative to your income and current prices, let's suppose that $250 is exactly the amount of money that you want to hold. Now suppose that the rate of inflation increases. If velocity ($\boldsymbol{V}$) and the money supply ($\boldsymbol{M}$) are unchanged, the reduced purchasing power of your cash holdings results in a reduction in total real expenditures. Because a reduction in purchases translates into a reduction in the production of goods and services, output falls with the decline in real money balances. This is just another way of illustrating the negative relation between inflation and real output. That is, another approach to showing that the aggregate demand curve is downward sloping.

This also allows us to illustrate the link between changes in the growth rate of the supply of money ($\boldsymbol{M}$) and aggregate demand. If, for example, the central bank decides to double the growth rate of the money supply, it will increase aggregate demand. Why? If the proportion of the income held as money doesn't change (i.e., $\boldsymbol{V}$ remains constant), an increase in the growth rate of the money supply means people are holding more money than they want to hold at the current rate of inflation. To get back to their desired ratio of money to income, people will spend these extra money balances. They may buy more cars or have liposuction; they may even buy more savings bonds and stocks. Until prices begin to adjust, this increased spending raises total expenditures and, therefore, is associated with an increase in real output. This means that for any given rate of inflation, an increase in the growth rate of the money supply initially increases total expenditures. As shown in

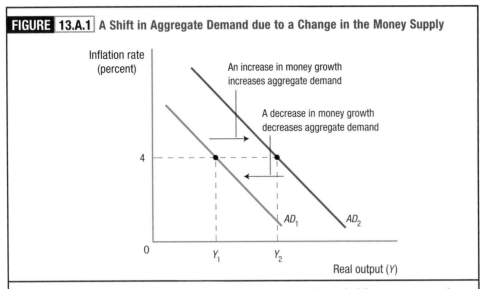

**FIGURE 13.A.1** A Shift in Aggregate Demand due to a Change in the Money Supply

An increase in the growth rate of the money supply means people are holding more money than they want to at the current rate of inflation, so they will spend these extra money balances. For any given rate of inflation, an increase in the growth rate of the money supply increases total expenditures and aggregate demand. This shifts the aggregate demand curve to the right. If the growth rate of the money supply falls, all else the same, aggregate demand falls, and the aggregate demand curve shifts to the left.

Figure 13.A.1, an increase in the growth rate of the money supply, all else the same, shifts the aggregate demand curve to the right from $AD_1$ to $AD_2$.

What happens if the growth rate of the money supply is decreased? A reduction in the growth rate of the money supply, holding the rate of inflation constant, shifts the aggregate demand curve to the left, from $AD_2$ to $AD_1$. Actions taken by a country's central bank to increase or decrease the growth of the money supply can, therefore, significantly affect the level of economic activity, at least in the short run.

## Appendix 13B The Mathematics of Equilibrium Income

In the chapter, we illustrated the link between expenditures and income (and output) using graphical analysis. We also can show this relation, albeit with more precision, using the formulas that actually underlie the graphs. This appendix provides that alternative approach.

Let's begin by stating the equilibrium condition. That is, income equals expenditures. Or,

$$Y = C + I + G + NX$$

where $Y$ represents total income (or output), $C$ is consumption expenditures, $I$ is investment spending, $G$ is government purchases, and $NX$ is net exports. As in the text, let's write the consumption function as

$$C = a + b\,(Y - T)$$

Recall that the intercept of the equation ($a$) is autonomous consumption spending—the amount of consumption spending not related to the level of income. The slope of the consumption function ($b$) measures the response of consumption spending to a marginal change in income (the MPC). Finally, $T$ represents lump-sum taxes, which are taxes that are not proportional to your income.

If this equation defines consumption, how should we define the other components of spending? In the chapter, we assumed that each was independent, or autonomous, of the level of income. They may be affected by changes in other variables, such as the real rate of interest, but not by income. So, let each of these measures be some fixed amount, and let's represent these fixed amounts as $I'$, $G'$, and $NX'$.

Using the equation for equilibrium and the definitions of the expenditures, we can solve for equilibrium income ($Y$). This is done by substituting our definitions of $C$, $I$, $G$, and $NX$ into the equilibrium formula above. Doing so gives us

$$Y = a + b\,(Y - T) + I' + G' + NX'$$

This equation says that total income ($Y$) is equal to total expenditures. The problem, however, is that income ($Y$) appears on both sides of the equation. To correct this, we first multiply $b$ through the parenthesis ($Y - T$) (which is the MPC) and collect like terms on the left-hand side of the equation. This produces the formula

$$Y - bY = a - bT + I' + G' + NX'$$

Factoring out $Y$ on the left-hand side gives

$$Y(1 - b) = a - bT + I' + G' + NX'$$

Now solve for income by dividing both sides by $(1 - b)$ to get the solution

$$Y = [a - bT + I' + G' + NX']/(1 - b)$$

This equation is the mathematical version of Figure 13.6. In equilibrium, total income equals total expenditures. This approach is useful because we can now assign values to each term to arrive at some quantitative measure of income. For example, suppose each term in the equation takes on the following values:

$a$ = $100
$T$ = $30
$I$ = $50
$G$ = $40
$NX$ = $10
$b(=\text{MPC})$ = 0.8

What is the equilibrium value of income based on these numerical values? Substitute them into the equilibrium equation, and you will find the answer to be:

$Y = [\$100 - 0.8(\$30) + \$50 + \$40 + \$10]/(1 - 0.8)$
$Y = \$176/0.2$
or $Y = \$880$

The formula is useful not only for determining the actual value of equilibrium income but also for determining how much it might change given a change in one of the spending measures. For example, in the chapter, we illustrated the effect on an increase in government purchases ($G$). We showed that an increase in government purchases led to an increase in income. By how much? To answer this, suppose that government purchases increase from the $40 used to derive the preceding relation to, say, $75. Now what is the equilibrium income? Substitute $75 for $40 in the preceding equation, and you will find that the new level of equilibrium income is $1,055. Just as the graphical approach shows, an increase in government purchases leads to an increase in equilibrium income. In fact, you can now see that an increase in any of the autonomous spending components—except taxes—in the equilibrium equation must be associated with an increase in the equilibrium level of income.

Because taxes are different from spending measures, let's take a moment to show the effect of a change in taxes. Suppose taxes, in our example set equal to $30, are increased to $50. You already know that such an increase will reduce equilibrium income—it reduces total expenditures—but how much? Substituting $50 for $30 and solving the equation reveals that the new equilibrium level of income is reduced from $880 to $800.

Question
1. The equation that describes equilibrium income (and output) in the economy is given by

$Y = [a - bT + I' + G' + NX']/(1 - b)$

Suppose autonomous consumption is $300, taxes are $50, investment is $200, government purchases are $300, exports are $200, imports are $250, and the MPC is 0.8. Based on these values:

a. What is the value for net exports?
b. What is equilibrium income?

c. The government decides that it must balance its budget (i.e., equate taxes and spending), so it raises taxes from $50 to $300. Calculate what the impact of this decision is on income.

d. Suppose that instead of raising taxes as in part (c), the government decides to reduce government spending, from $300 to $50, and leave taxes the same at $50. Now calculate what the impact of this decision is on income.

e. Explain why your answers in (c) and (d) are different.

# 14

# Inflation Expectations and Their Effect on the Economy

*"Climate is what we expect, weather is what we get."*

*Mark Twain*

Every day you make decisions based on expectations. When you plan to have lunch at your favorite café, you *expect* that it is still in business; you *expect* that your favorite sandwich is still on the menu; and you *expect* that prices haven't changed from yesterday. If any one of these expectations isn't met, you might decide to try a different café. Your decision, in turn, affects the café owner's revenues, which affects how many workers she hires, and how much food she orders from suppliers. As you can see, when reality does not match your expectations, your change in behavior can have real economic consequences to many people.

Helping you understand the process by which your expectations about inflation change and how those changes affect—and are affected by—economic activity is the goal of this chapter. In the previous chapter, we focused on how a change in aggregate demand affects the level of real economic activity. We did this by assuming that the rate of inflation was fixed. If the actual rate of inflation doesn't change, then it is reasonable to assume that the expected rate of inflation also is unchanging. In this chapter, we relax that assumption. By doing so, you will see how changes in people's inflation expectations can affect the economy.

Relaxing our assumption that inflation and inflation expectations are fixed throws a monkey wrench into the workings of the previous chapter. There we said that an increase in aggregate demand leads to an increase in real output. If expectations about inflation—expectations held by workers and employers alike—vary with increases or decreases in aggregate demand, however, policy makers might not always be able to increase a nation's real economic activity by cutting interest rates or by increasing the amount of government purchases. This is the very problem that policy makers faced in 2011 when, following the government's massive stimulus program and the Federal Reserve's lowering of short-term interest rates to essentially zero, the economy stubbornly remained in a state of low growth and high unemployment. It is therefore important to understand just how inflation expectations are formed and how those expectations interact with economic changes.

## 14.1 How People Form Expectations about Inflation

*USA Today* asked the following question in July 2008: What will happen to the price of a gallon of regular gas in the year ahead? The national average (nominal) price for a gallon of regular unleaded gas was about $3.80 at the time, although it had peaked at over $4 just before the survey was taken. The majority of those surveyed (85 percent) believed that gas prices would be above $4. Some (11 percent) of the respondents even thought it would exceed $6. Between the time of the survey and now, gas prices have fallen below $3 and have increased to over $4. As you can imagine, recent events have a way of coloring our expectations of the future.

How are your expectations formed? Most people's expectations are based on what they have observed in the past. Answer this question: What do you expect the price of gasoline to be tomorrow or a year from now? Like respondents to the *USA Today* survey, the price you are thinking of probably is based on the price you most recently observed. Now think of how upset you will be if you go to a gas station and find that the price of gas is $2 more per gallon than you expected. Or, on the positive side, think of how happy (and surprised) you will be if you go there and find out that gas costs $2 *less* than you expected. The fact that gas prices are volatile means that just expecting (hoping?) gas prices to remain the same over the next few weeks probably is no longer a good way to accurately predict future gas prices. If your past observations alone don't reliably predict the future price of gasoline, what is your alternative?

One approach is just to hope for the best—that is, hope that gas prices will be the same or lower today than they were yesterday. A better approach is to acquire additional information. For example, you could visit Internet sites that post prices from stations located throughout your town. You could ask your friends what they paid recently. Or you could even create a sophisticated mathematical model that predicts gas prices based on the price for a barrel of crude oil, the time of year, and the level of gasoline inventories.

Most of us take some time to acquire information because making an uninformed decision is costly. If you expect that gas costs $3 a gallon, and you discover—when your car is running on fumes, and you are late for an exam—that it costs $4.50 a gallon, you might not be able to buy as much gas as you expected. With less gas, you might not be able to make it to campus for that exam. And that incorrect expectation could have real consequences on your GPA.

Because incorrect expectations can impose significant economic costs on us (i.e., failing the exam), economists assume that people behave in a rational manner when it comes to forming expectations. That is, you try to collect enough relevant information to make an informed guess. Economists call such informed guesses **rational expectations**.

**RATIONAL EXPECTATIONS** Expectations that are based on available and relevant information.

**EXAMPLE** Joanne expected the price of gasoline to increase because she read in the paper that the price of oil had doubled in price.

**EXAMPLE** Steven expected to do well on the calculus test because he used the professor's study guide and completed the practice test.

The idea behind rational expectations is, well, rational. It is based on the economic principle that people usually act in their own best interest. In our example using gasoline prices, rational expectations take for granted that you will use scarce resources (time, the Internet, your friends' knowledge, etc.) to gather information about gas prices before you search out a gas station. As a good economist, you gather information up to the point where the cost of gathering additional information no longer pays off. You will not gather more information after the marginal cost of doing so (to you) is greater than your expected marginal benefit.[1] Most of us are not going to pay someone $100 each week for a daily forecast of gasoline prices, for example. But what if you own a trucking firm that every week spends thousands of dollars on fuel? Then it might make a great deal of sense—it would be rational, in other words— to purchase this forecast if it saves you $100 or more in fuel costs.

The idea of rational expectations is straightforward: because it is costly to be wrong, you are willing to use up some of your resources not to be wrong. Often the information you collect is based on past observations. For example, if you want an idea of what tomorrow's weather will be like, a pretty good forecast of tomorrow's average temperature is today's average temperature.

Rational expectations do not mean, however, that people's forecasts of events, including inflation, are never wrong. It does suggest that you will not knowingly make the same mistake over and over. That wouldn't be rational, would it? In addition, studies (both in economics and psychology) have shown people adapt their forecasts when they *are* wrong. In other words, people tend to learn what is causing an event such as inflation and adjust their predictions accordingly.

## 14.2 Inflation Expectations, the Economy's Output, and Changes in Aggregate Demand

The belief that expectations are formed rationally has important implications. One such implication is that as you gather information, your behavior adjusts accordingly. If the evidence is mounting that inflation rates are going to increase significantly over the coming year, you might, for example, go to your boss and request a higher wage. Even though you are not working any harder or producing more goods, you want to at least maintain the purchasing power of your wage. Recall that by *purchasing power*, we mean the amount of goods and services you can buy with a given dollar. If prices rise and your wage doesn't, the purchasing power of the dollars you are paid falls.

But what if your employer isn't as adept as you—and other employers—at predicting price increases, so he denies your request? If you do not get the raise, and prices increase as *you* expected, you might quit and search for a higher-paying job. After all, you really do not like to work hard while you lose purchasing power. Other people who work for your employer, if they have the same expectations, might also seek better-paying jobs. And those jobs will exist because other employers recognize the increase in inflation: they will raise wages to maintain their employees' purchasing power and to keep employees from leaving. You might think that your employer's response is "Okay, fine, go to other jobs, and I will just hire replacements." But this will not occur if markets are competitive: no one with your skills will work for a wage that, in terms of purchasing power, is less than it was for the same amount of work. As you can see, changes in expectations—that inflation is going to increase—can have important real effects.

• • • • • • •

[1]If you need a refresher on the idea of marginal analysis, take a quick look back at Chapter 2.

But suppose that *everyone*, even your penny-pinching boss, knows just how much inflation is going to increase. If he does not want to lose employees, presumably your boss would raise the wages he pays everyone. If he correctly adjusts the wages he pays, including yours, the purchasing power of your earnings will not change even if inflation increases as expected. If you are able to still buy the things you want—your purchasing power has not fallen—you will be less likely to look for another job. If this scenario plays out with workers and bosses across the economy, an increase in the rate of inflation will not lead to workers moving between jobs (we called this *frictional unemployment* in Chapter 8) or a change in the production of goods and services. As a result, even though the rate of inflation increases the rate of growth in output (real GDP) will not change.

Does this scenario of knowing future price changes seem far-fetched? Surely everyone cannot know future price changes with such pinpoint accuracy. Okay, that universal level of accuracy is a stretch, but we do know, for example, that in the short run, say, over a month or maybe even a year, many prices in the economy are relatively slow to change. Some prices, such as gasoline prices, seem to change daily. But many other prices, such as the price of the daily newspaper, tuition, a fast-food hamburger, or an office visit to your dentist, do not.

Economists refer to this phenomenon—that in the short run, many prices do not change much—as "sticky" prices. One way economists have studied the phenomena of sticky prices is to observe the frequency with which catalog prices change. In a study of selected goods from companies such as REI, Orvis, and L.L.Bean, economist Anil Kashyap found that prices quoted in their catalogs tended to be fixed for as long as a year or more.[2] Why don't prices change very much?

The observation that prices and wages are sticky could arise from the fact that people (and businesses) do not get the same information at the same time. This means that informational delays can explain why not all prices change at the same time or that different people have different expectations about what inflation is going to be in the future. Sticky prices also can occur simply because of contracts. When you sign a labor contract, for example, your salary most likely will not adjust monthly with the ups and downs in inflation. Or, prices may be slow to adjust simply because adjusting them costs the company money and changing them too often alienates customers.

We assumed in the previous chapter that if the actual rate of inflation and individuals' expectations about it don't change very rapidly (or, in the extreme, are fixed), government policies to increase aggregate demand (shift the aggregate demand curve to the right) will lead to more output being produced. But what if workers and employers learn that the long-term effect of such expansionary policies—such as a doubling the rate of money growth—historically is higher inflation? Isn't that the message of the Quantity Theory of Money? If workers and employers understand that higher inflation is a likely outcome of these policies, and they rationally demand higher wages based on an expected increase in inflation, how does it affect the increase in output caused by the increase in aggregate demand? As you will find, the answer depends on the time horizon used.

Such expansionary fiscal and monetary policies can increase real output because expectations, and actual prices themselves, are relatively slow to adjust. Consider this: if there were no impediments (such as contracts) to price changes and if everyone

[2]Anil Kashyap, "Sticky Prices: New Evidence from Retail Catalogs," *Quarterly Journal of Economics*, 110, no. 1 (1995): 245–274.

knew the long-term effects of policy actions, would any increase in output occur for an increase in aggregate demand?

In the previous chapter, we did not allow inflation or inflation expectations to vary. Now we relax that constraint to see how policy actions that change aggregate demand affect not only the pace of economic activity but also the rate of inflation and inflation expectations. As you will see, the outcome of this deeper dive into the workings of the economy is to realize that depending on the time horizon of analysis, a given policy action can produce very different effects.

## 14.3 Changes in Inflation Expectations, Labor Markets, and Economic Activity

We know that expectations, even those formed rationally, often are based on old or imperfect information. When new information becomes available—your neighbor tells you she bought gas for $1—sometimes we are not sure that it is accurate or relevant. Take, for example, the effect of Super Bowl Sunday on TV sales. On an average Saturday, the manager of an electronics store expects to sell, say, 10 big-screen TVs. On the Saturday before the Super Bowl, however, there are more customers, and 20 big-screen TVs are sold. If you were the manager of such a store, how many big-screen TVs would you expect to sell the Monday *after* Super Bowl Sunday? And how do you respond to the increased volume before the Super Bowl? Let's see.

You know from your economics class that the increase in TV sales before the Super Bowl could signal an increase in demand, a rightward shift of the demand curve for big-screen TVs. Because you are closed on Sunday, on the Monday after the Super Bowl, you should raise your prices. Right? You could certainly do that, but what if the doubling of sales on Saturday was just a temporary increase? What if Monday's TV sales returns to normal (the increase in demand was temporary), but you have already increased your prices? If other stores did not increase their prices, customers will go elsewhere, and your sales will fall. Real-world decisions, it turns out, are a lot like this. Making pricing decisions are more complicated than simply shifting demand and supply curves around to locate equilibrium prices and quantities. That is why economists often talk about the market constantly "searching" for the equilibrium price.

In fact, when facing unexpected, or temporary, increases in demand, many managers often respond not by raising prices but by increasing the amount of merchandise they have for sale. In terms of our Super Bowl example, the manager of the electronics store would probably first reduce the inventory of TVs in his store's backroom when facing an unexpected increase in sales. He might also call in more salespeople to handle the increased number of customers. This is where the link between the goods side of the economy—the sale of big-screen TVs—and the labor market occurs. It also is where the changes in demand work to effect changes in output and, eventually, changes in prices.

Let's continue with our story about the electronics store. Now, however, let's assume that instead of the manager of the store, you are a regular employee. More customers than expected start coming into the store on Saturday before the Super Bowl to buy big-screen TVs. To handle the unexpected crush of customers, the manager asks you to work extra hours. In response to this request, why don't you take this opportunity to negotiate a higher wage rate? After all, isn't this a textbook example of an increase in demand for your labor services? Isn't the correct response to raise the price of your labor?

If you're reluctant to negotiate a higher wage rate every time your boss asks you to work some extra hours, you're not alone. In economic terms, your wage is sticky. This also suggests that in the short run, our labor supply curves are pretty flat: a given change in demand affects the quantity of hours worked, not the wage. Most of us do not want to anger our bosses or develop a reputation as not being a team player. When there is an increase in demand for our labor, we agree to work a couple extra hours at the same wage. We believe that establishing a good longer-term employment relationship is often more valuable than squeezing out a couple of bucks for a few extra hours of work.[3]

You can take comfort in the fact that the labor relation is two-sided. When business is slow, managers usually do not lower your wage, do they? While they continue to pay you the agreed-upon wage, they may reduce the hours you work. Businesses also value the long-term employment relationship they have with their employees. Just like you, they do not want to expend the resources to constantly renegotiate wages or hire new workers. (The employer-employee relationship is very similar to a marriage relationship: most couples do not divorce every time they have an argument because the value of the long-term marriage relationship outweighs the cost of divorcing one another and having to find new spouses.) As we suggested, like the prices of many other goods, wages are sticky.

**Figure 14.1** shows the market demand, labeled LD, and supply curve, labeled LS, for labor. We could do the analysis using an individual firm and an individual worker,

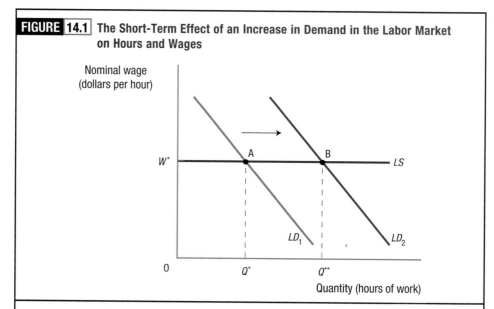

**FIGURE 14.1**   **The Short-Term Effect of an Increase in Demand in the Labor Market on Hours and Wages**

The labor market is shown with the market demand for labor labeled $LD$, and the market supply of labor labeled $LS$. The labor supply curve is drawn as a horizontal line at $W^*$ to reflect the idea that in the short run, workers are more likely to adjust the quantity of hours they will work than renegotiate their wages. The demand and supply curves for labor determine the market-clearing wage rate, shown as $W^*$. At wage rate $W^*$, the market-clearing amount of labor supplied (in hours) is $Q^*$. An increase in the demand for labor shifts the labor demand curve to the right, from $LD_1$ to $LD_2$. In the short run, because workers do not immediately demand a higher wage to work the extra hours, they increase the hours of labor they supply, moving the new quantity to $Q^{**}$.

· · · · · · · ·

[3]This is the theme underlying the work done by Truman Bewley in his "Work Motivation," Federal Reserve Bank of St. Louis *Review* (May/June 1999): 35–49.

but the same story holds if we aggregate all firms and all workers into one "labor market." The demand and supply curves for labor, $LD_1$ and $LS$, determine the market-clearing nominal wage rate, shown as $W^*$. At wage rate $W^*$, the market-clearing amount of labor supplied occurs at $Q^*$. In keeping with our earlier example, let the quantity of labor here be measured in hours of work.

Notice that the labor supply curve is drawn as a horizontal line at $W^*$. This reflects the idea that, at least in the short run, workers are more likely to adjust the quantity of hours they will work than renegotiate their wages. You can see this when there is an increase in the demand for labor. (Remember, this increase in the demand for labor occurs because there is an increase in the demand for the product that these workers are producing or selling.) An increase in the demand for labor shifts the labor demand curve to the right. In Figure 14.1, this is shown by the demand curve shifting from $LD_1$ to $LD_2$. Because workers do not immediately demand a higher wage to work the extra hours, they adjust the quantity of hours they are willing to supply: the increase in the demand for labor slides us along the labor supply curve. The result is a higher equilibrium quantity of hours worked, shown as $Q^{**}$, with no change in the wage rate.

Let's now connect this reaction in the labor market to production in the economy. Suppose the electronics store sees its inventory of TVs fall as sales continue to increase. It doubles its order of TVs. Initially, firms producing the TVs will try to meet the increased demand for their product not by raising their price but by producing and selling more. This means that suppliers will also ask drivers to work more hours to deliver them, assembly workers to put in overtime to assemble them, and so forth.

But what if big-screen TV sales continue to surpass normal sales expectations during the weeks following the Super Bowl? Will firms be able to meet this increased demand by asking their employees to simply work a few extra hours? Would you continue to work "a few extra hours" for the same wage? Could TV manufacturers simply run their production facilities at a higher-than-normal level indefinitely? The answer is no, on both counts.

As we have explained, *if* the manager of the electronics store believes that the increase in TV demand is permanent, he will start raising the price of the TVs. He might even repeatedly ask you to work a few extra hours. You, in turn, might suggest to him that you need a raise. Now consider what happens if up and down the production chain for TVs, the firms raise their prices, and workers all request wage increases. That is, as the prices of big-screen TVs start to increase so do workers' demands for higher wages. In **Figure 14.2**, we show how this plays out in the labor market. Let point A represent the initial equilibrium between labor supply ($LS_1$) and labor demand ($LD_1$).

When the increased TV demand seemed temporary, you were willing to work more hours for the same nominal wage rate (remember that your nominal wage hasn't changed). But because firms are beginning to raises their prices on their goods—think of the TV phenomenon as more general—your *real* wage rate is actually falling. Think of it this way: your nominal wage increase is not keeping pace with the price of big-screen TVs. You are working more hours but cannot buy as many TVs as before. The purchasing power of your nominal wage is declining because your real wage is falling, too. (If you need a refresher on the real wage, revisit Chapter 8.)

When you realize that your real wage is falling, you have three options:

- Continue working even though your purchasing power is declining.
- Negotiate a higher wage.
- Quit your job and search for a higher-paying one.

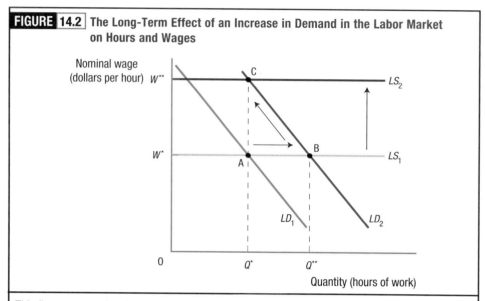

**FIGURE 14.2** The Long-Term Effect of an Increase in Demand in the Labor Market on Hours and Wages

This figure summarizes how the labor market reacts to an increase in the demand for labor. The demand for labor increases, shifting the labor demand curve $LD_1$ to $LD_2$. Initially, workers are willing to supply more hours of work ($Q^{**}$) at the original nominal wage rate, $W^*$. If firms are raising prices, workers face higher prices for the goods and services they buy. At the nominal wage $W^*$, they begin to recognize that their real wages are decreasing. Workers undertake various ways to reduce their hours worked at the original nominal wage $W^*$, reducing their supply of labor. The decline in the real wage causes the labor supply curve to shift upward until a new, higher *nominal* wage rate is established. This higher equilibrium nominal wage rate ($W^{**}$) settles in where the nominal wage rate relative to the new higher level of prices for goods and services is equal to the ratio between the original nominal wage rate and the original price level. The quantity of hours supplied returns to the original level $Q^*$.

A reaction that combines options two and three is, if you are a member of a union, to strike. In that case, work stops while negotiations for higher wages take place.

If we assume that the first option is not in your long-term best interest, options two and three are more likely. The impact of options two and three are illustrated by the upward shift in the labor supply curve in Figure 14.2. Suppose you were willing to sacrifice an hour of your leisure for an hourly real wage of $10. If you still put this value on your leisure time, after prices start rising, and your real wage begins to fall, you are less likely to supply the hours at the level of $Q^{**}$. This means that point B in Figure 14.2—a condition of excess demand at the original wage $W^*$—is unlikely to exist for very long. If your personal valuation of leisure time doesn't change, there will be a reduction in the supply of labor (your labor supply curve will shift upward) until your real wage is once again equal to $10. Under the conditions used for this example, that will occur at the quantity of hours equal to the original equilibrium of $Q^*$.

Let's summarize the effect of this scenario on the labor market. The demand for labor increases, shown in Figure 14.2 as the labor demand curve $LD_1$ shifting outward to $LD_2$. At first, workers are willing to supply more hours of work at the original nominal wage rate, $W^*$. If the higher demand for products is sustained, however, firms will begin to raise their prices and workers must pay higher prices for the goods and services they buy. Workers begin to recognize that their real wages are decreasing:

their previous expectations of how much things cost are being readjusted to the new higher-price reality.

Facing this decline in real wages, some workers simply quit and look for other jobs. Think of someone working a second job or someone who is a second-income earner in the household. With another income, it may be easier to quit and search for a new job than to work for less purchasing power. Other workers will stay on the job but bargain for higher wages. If they do not get a wage increase, they reduce their supply of labor by quitting.

Does this really happen? Think of the times you've heard someone say "Yeah, I quit that job. The pay wasn't that bad, but it just wasn't worth my time." In effect, the real wage just wasn't enough to compensate that person for the time taken from leisure. Unless nominal wage rates are rising as fast as prices, the decline in the real wage causes workers to reduce their supply of labor. In Figure 14.2, this is shown as an upward shift in the labor supply curve. (Because the labor supply curve is horizontal, this upward shift corresponds to the leftward shift that you are familiar with: in both cases, the intercept of the supply curve is higher.) After all, no one wants to work just as hard for the ability to buy fewer goods and services.

This process continues until a new, higher *nominal* wage rate is established. Think of the dynamics as the economy moving from point A toward B and eventually settling in at point C in Figure 14.2. But how high will this nominal wage go? This higher equilibrium nominal wage rate ($W^{**}$ in Figure 14.2) settles in where the nominal wage rate relative to the new higher level of prices for goods and services is equal to the ratio between the original nominal wage rate and original price level. That is, even though the *nominal* wage rate is higher, the new and the original *real* wage actually are the same. It isn't in the firm's long-term interest to pay you more in real terms. Your wage rate may have doubled, but so did prices. In the end, you are not better off, but you also are no worse off.

We've left out an important aspect of this story. Until you (and other workers) catch on to the fact that prices are rising faster than your wages, you contentedly supply more hours to your employer. (At the least, you are not arguing for higher wages.) Consequently, employers are able to produce more goods and services. This increase in the quantity of labor has, at least temporarily, increased the output of the economy. In the period of time before wages in the labor market readjust to higher prices, the increase in demand for products results in increased employment, and production.

As we noted earlier, wages are sticky and may not adjust immediately to changes in labor-market conditions. Consider the effect of a contract. Your professors have a contract with your university to work for a specified annual salary, which is usually determined in late summer. If the prices of goods and services increase dramatically during the school year, faculty cannot simply renegotiate a higher wage in December. That is what a labor contract is all about. It locks in nominal wages. Contracts are one reason some prices and wages (wages are just a price) adjust slower than others.

This condition is unsustainable, however: the economy cannot permanently operate at a level that puts it outside of its production possibilities frontier (PPF). As prices move higher, nominal wages are renegotiated and eventually follow along. After the adjustment to the increase in demand is complete, the equilibrium quantity of labor will have returned to its original level, and, even though the *nominal* wage is higher, the *real wage* also is back to its original level. Equally important, the rate at which goods are being produced has returned to potential: with other factors of production unchanged, the same amount of labor means that the economy is back on its PPF.

This story has important implications not just for wage adjustment and output but also for changes in the rate of inflation. If the quantity of labor (hours worked) returns to its original amount, then production of goods and services also must return to its original level of activity (assuming no change in worker productivity). What persists after this adjustment on the "real" side of the economy is a higher price level. If this dynamic continues, higher rates of inflation occur. You work the same number of hours, and, even though your nominal wage is higher, you just don't get ahead—and neither does the economy. Higher inflation rates do not generate more goods and services. Higher rates of inflation do not create more shoes, more computers, or more dorm rooms. Higher rates of inflation just mean that goods and services, in general, cost more than they used to.

## SOLVED PROBLEM

**Q** How do you measure inflation expectations?

**A** You can get expectations of inflation in a number of ways. The most direct is to ask people what they think. Two popular surveys of inflation expectations are conducted by the University of Michigan and by the Federal Reserve of Philadelphia. The Michigan survey asks individuals what they think inflation will be over the coming year. The Philadelphia Fed surveys professional forecasters and asks the same question. You could assume that the Philadelphia Fed survey results are based more heavily on sophisticated statistical models than the University of Michigan survey.

How do the results compare? The following figure indicates that, over the past 15 years at least, both inflation expectations series come fairly close to predicting the general movement in inflation one year out. You might notice that neither measure does a good job at predicting short-term swings in inflation, however. This suggests that inflation expectations are slow to adjust and do so only after evidence indicates to people that the underlying trend in inflation is changing.

*Source:* Federal Reserve Bank of St. Louis

# 14.4 Putting Together Changes in Aggregate Demand, Inflation, and Output

Our story about the market for big-screen TVs is really a microcosm of how changes in aggregate demand bring about changes in output and in inflation. What happens when some shift in monetary or fiscal policy leads to an increase in aggregate demand? In the previous chapter, we showed that a decrease in the real rate of interest or an increase in government spending increases aggregate demand. Holding inflation constant, this leads to a higher level of production, at least temporarily. The adjustment process we described in the labor market is the guide for thinking about how the economywide labor market adjusts, and how prices and expectations adjust, too.

Let's now connect the aggregate demand discussion from the previous chapter to our story about labor-market dynamics to predict the short-run *and* long-run effects on the economy from an increase in aggregate demand. To do this, we will use the aggregate-demand figure from Chapter 13, with a couple of modifications. To start the analysis, we let the initial rate of inflation and the expected rate of inflation be equal. If the rate of inflation has been, say, 4 percent for a long time, then a workers and firms will expect it to be 4 percent in the future as well. The term often used is that these expectations are "anchored." Because we assume that actual inflation and expected inflation are the same, an **inflation expectations line**, or IE, can be added to the aggregate-demand diagram and drawn horizontally at the initial rate of inflation, 4 percent.

**INFLATION EXPECTATIONS LINE** A horizontal line showing the expected rate of inflation in the economy.

**EXAMPLE** The rate of inflation has been 3 percent for the past several years. Looking forward, almost everyone agrees that it is not likely to change. Inflation expectations are not likely to change, holding other factors constant.

A second modification to the aggregate demand discussion is that we want you to start thinking about where the economy's level of production is *relative to potential output*. This modification gives us a basis from which to analyze the effects on the economy from a change in aggregate demand, or in the rate of inflation. Let's use an analogy to make the point. In the wake of the 2008 financial crisis, suppose you are asked by the Restaurateurs Association of Greater New York to predict the price effect of a decrease in income on the demand for dinners at high-end restaurants.[4] To do the analysis, you start from an initial equilibrium where quantity supplied equals quantity demanded. Now, given the decrease in income due to layoffs and smaller year-end bonuses for hedge-fund managers, you would shift the demand curve to the left and find the new equilibrium price for luxury dinners. In this instance, all else the same, the equilibrium price for dining out at expensive restaurants is predicted to fall.

For our current purpose, we need to introduce a new term: the **GDP gap**.

**GDP GAP** The percentage deviation of actual real GDP from potential GDP.

**EXAMPLE** The GDP gap is the deviation of an economy from its PPF.

**EXAMPLE** You are capable of producing 10 pizzas an hour at your job. In hour 2 of your shift, you make only 8. You are working below your potential. Your "output gap" is a negative 20 percent. In hour 5 of your shift, you produce 11 pizzas: your output gap is a positive 10 percent.

· · · · · · ·

[4]Ianthe Jeanne-Dugan, "Wall Street's Insecurity: Cuts in Jobs, Bonuses Add to Ripple Effect; More Home-Cooking." *Wall Street Journal*, April 12, 2008: B1.

The GDP gap is a way of determining how far the economy is from operating at its full potential. When the gap is positive, the economy is operating above its long-run potential. Think of it as being outside its PPF. When the gap is negative, the economy is operating below its long-run potential, or inside the PPF. Recall from earlier discussions that being on the PPF means that the economy is operating at full employment. Being inside the PPF translates into unemployed resources, for instance, underutilized machinery or workers without jobs. Being outside the PPF means that somehow the economy is operating at more than full employment, which is not sustainable. In both instances, the conditions are assumed to be temporary as the economy is expected to return to the PPF. Thus, the GDP gap is a useful gauge to help us see how the economy is doing relative to its long-run potential.

**Figure 14.3** is drawn to show an economy that is in equilibrium: it is operating at its long-run potential (GDP gap = 0) and with some initial level of inflation and inflation expectations. In this graph, that state of the world occurs where the aggregate demand curve (*AD*) intersects the inflation expectations line (*IE*) with inflation equal to 4 percent. Figure 14.3 provides you with all of the tools you need to predict what the effects stemming from a change in aggregate demand will be. Figure 14.3 not only illustrates the short-run effects from a change in aggregate demand but also the long-term effects. This model thus allows you to link policy actions to short-term and long-term economic changes, such as recessions, booms, and changes in the rate of inflation.

## An Increase in Aggregate Demand

Let's put the model to work. In **Figure 14.4**, we start with the economy operating at its potential level of output (GDP gap = 0), and the rates of inflation, both actual and expected, are 4 percent. We let this be represented by the point A. Now suppose

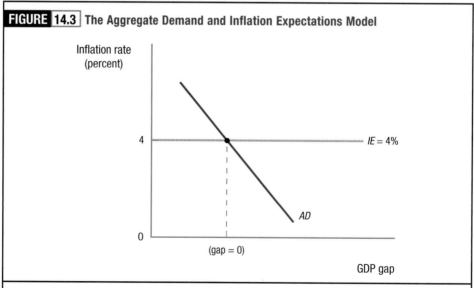

**FIGURE 14.3** | **The Aggregate Demand and Inflation Expectations Model**

This figure portrays an economy that is in equilibrium: it is operating at its long-run potential (GDP gap = 0) and with some initial level of inflation expectations. In this figure, we assume it's 4 percent. This state of the world occurs where the aggregate demand curve (*AD*) intersects the inflation expectations line (*IE*). This model provides the tools with which we can predict the short-term and long-term effects of a change in aggregate demand and inflation expectations.

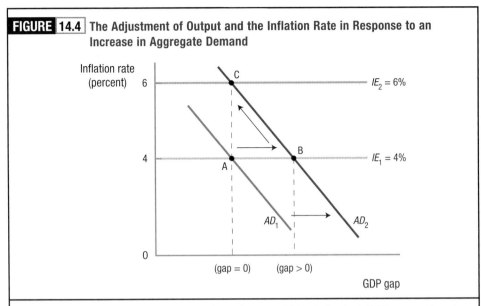

**FIGURE 14.4**  **The Adjustment of Output and the Inflation Rate in Response to an Increase in Aggregate Demand**

We start at point A. The economy is operating at its potential level of output (GDP gap = 0), and the rates of inflation, both actual and expected, are 4 percent. Following an increase in aggregate demand, which is shown in the figure as a rightward shift in the aggregate demand curve, from $AD_1$ to $AD_2$, the economy begins operating at point B. Without an immediate change in inflation, firms and workers respond to the increased expenditures by increasing production and supplying more labor, respectively, so the GDP gap becomes positive. The positive GDP gap in turn puts upward pressure on prices, sending actual and expected inflation to 6 percent and the economy to point C, in the long run. As you can see, the long-term response to an increase in aggregate demand is that the GDP gap returns to zero, but actual and expected rates of inflation will be higher.

an increase in aggregate demand occurs due to some expansionary policy. We show this in Figure 14.4 as a rightward shift in the aggregate demand curve, from $AD_1$ to $AD_2$. What happens in the economy? The increased expenditures *initially* put pressure on firms to supply more goods and services. As long as workers are willing to put in the extra hours without demanding higher wages, and as long as firms increase production without charging higher prices, the increase in aggregate demand raises economic activity to a level above its long-run potential. Think of this increase in aggregate demand as pushing economic output to a level outside of the economy's PPF. Another way of saying this is that the GDP gap becomes positive. As we've shown it, the economy slides toward point B because inflation expectations ($IE = 4\%$) have yet to adjust.

We have suggested many different times that an economy cannot operate outside its PPF indefinitely. Now we can explain why we use the model depicted in Figure 14.4. When the GDP gap is positive, there is upward pressure on prices and wages. If the increase in aggregate demand is permanent, increased expenditures by households, businesses, and the government signal to firms that the higher demand for their goods is not temporary. They respond accordingly by raising their prices. As workers' expectations of inflation adjust, they also begin to demand higher wages, and nominal wages begin to increase. These reactions set into motion a dynamic process that slows the pace of economic output: higher prices lead to higher real wages, which reduce the use of labor. As inflation adjusts upward, and real wages return to their original levels, the amount of labor employed also returns to the level before the aggregate demand increased. Because we have not altered workers' productivity, the return of labor to its initial level means that the output of the economy must also be returning to its initial level. In the end, as inflation and expectations of inflation adjust upward, the pace of economic output returns to its long-run potential (the GDP gap once again is zero).

As Figure 14.4 shows, an increase in aggregate demand drives the economy from its initial inflation-GDP gap combination (point A) to a condition in which the level of output is greater than before (the GDP gap is positive), but inflation and expectations of it haven't yet adjusted (point B). This is essentially the scenario used in the preceding chapter to discuss the effects of an increase in aggregate demand. The difference now is that we relax the assumption that inflation doesn't change. What you've learned in this chapter is that it may take time, but inflation and expectations of inflation do adjust to increases in demand.

Figure 14.4 illustrates the idea that expected inflation shifts upward—shown by the upward shift in the $IE$ line—until it settles in at a new level where there is no continued upward pressure on prices (point C). Don't think of the shift in the inflation expectations line as an instantaneous jump from $IE_1$ to $IE_2$, or that the economy moves in precision from point A to B to C. Rather, the adjustment takes place in a series of steps, perhaps very uneven steps, as the economy adjusts to the new conditions. For purposes of illustration, however, we show the shift in inflation expectations as a one-time move. After the adjustment has been completed, the economy settles in at a higher expected and actual rate of inflation where the GDP gap is once again zero.

Figure 14.4 shows that for an economy starting out at its full-employment equilibrium (point A), the *long-term* effect of the increase in aggregate demand is that the GDP gap returns to zero, but the rate of inflation (actual and expected) will be higher. This prediction has important policy implications. Think for a minute what it implies about the ability of government policies that try to *permanently* affect the level of real economic activity. The process depicted in Figure 14.4 indicates that such policies are doomed to fail if, that is, they were designed to permanently increase the economy's rate of economic growth. Although such policies that increase aggregate demand yield short-run increases in output above potential, they only increase the rate of inflation in the long run. Clearly those who make policies affecting aggregate demand must fully consider both the short-run and long-run impact of their actions.

## A Decrease in Aggregate Demand

What if aggregate demand decreases? Suppose consumers, as they did in late 2008 and early 2009, become concerned that unemployment associated with the imminent recession is going to be severe. In this situation, many people pull back on their consumption spending out of fear that they may lose their jobs and not have enough income to meet essential purchases. In such an environment, consumers decide to reduce their spending at every level of income. In addition, with the curtailment of lending in financial markets, many firms faced credit shortages that led to a decline in investment activity. The effect of these declines in autonomous expenditures is illustrated in **Figure 14.5** by the leftward shift in the aggregate demand curve.

Again we start the analysis from an initial equilibrium (point A). At point A, the GDP gap is zero (potential output = actual output), and inflation expectations are equal to the actual inflation rate (here set at 4 percent). The reduction in spending shifts the aggregate demand curve to the left, from $AD_1$ to $AD_2$. This sets the economy on a path from point A to point B in Figure 14.5. You can see that the effects of a decrease in aggregate demand are just the opposite of an increase in aggregate demand.

---

**FIGURE 14.5** The Dynamic (Long-Term) Adjustment to Output and the Inflation Rate after a Decrease in Aggregate Demand

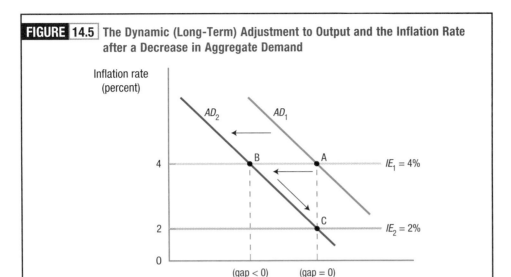

We start at point A. At point A, the GDP gap is zero (potential output = actual output), and inflation expectations are equal to the actual inflation rate, 4 percent. A reduction in spending shifts the aggregate demand curve from $AD_1$ to $AD_2$. The effects of a decrease in aggregate demand are just the opposite of an increase in aggregate demand. Initially, the economy's output of goods and services exceeds the demand for them, so firms reduce production, and the GDP gap becomes negative. In response to reduced demands, firms curtail price increases, leading to a reduction in the actual and expected rate of inflation. This is illustrated by the inflation expectations line declining from $IE_1$ to $IE_2$. In response to a decline in aggregate demand and the drop in inflation, the economy reaches its new equilibrium (point C) at a lower rate of inflation with the economy once again at a zero GDP gap.

---

The initial effect is to reduce the economy's output of goods and services to some level of production that is below its potential: the GDP gap becomes negative.

With the economy operating below its potential (inside its PPF), there are downward pressures on prices. Firms begin to reduce the rate of their price increases, perhaps even lowering their prices. This reduces the actual and expected rate of inflation, which we show by the inflation expectations line dropping from $IE_1$ to $IE_2$. As the rate of inflation and expectations of inflation decline, the adjustment process is the reverse of what occurs when there is an increase in aggregate demand. Now the economy moves from point B to point C. In Figure 14.5, the culmination of the adjustment process—the economy reaching its new equilibrium—occurs when the expected rate of inflation settles in at some lower rate of inflation, here 2 percent, and the economy is once again producing at potential GDP. That is what the model predicts. Just how well does this model capture the real events of recent years? We'll answer that question in the next chapter.

## What Are the Policy Implications?

We cannot leave this discussion without stressing the importance of what you have just learned. Think about how the predictions of this model relate to what you have learned so far about economic growth and inflation. You learned that economic growth is explained basically by how labor, capital, and knowledge are combined.

We use this recipe to predict potential GDP. The model we have just derived gives us one explanation for why real GDP fluctuates around this long-term trend. Changes in aggregate demand are one source of deviations in real GDP from its potential.

Equally important, however, is the fact that the model also predicts that such deviations will not be permanent. This means policies that try to permanently increase real GDP growth beyond the growth of potential GDP by increasing aggregate demand will fail: an increase in aggregate demand does not translate into an increase in economic growth. It also means that recessions, periods when real GDP is below potential (the GDP gap is negative), also will not be permanent. Our model predicts that the economy will rebound, and output will return to its potential.

On the inflation side, you learned earlier (Chapter 12) that a sustained increase in the general level of prices occurs when the supply of money grows faster than the output of the economy. How can we relate that discussion to the model just developed? Think of a sustained increase in the money supply as causing a sustained increase in aggregate demand. That is, a policy of trying to constantly keep the level of real GDP in the economy above its long-term potential. When the GDP gap is positive, you now know that this leads not to permanently higher real GDP growth but to an increase in inflation and inflation expectations. Thus, the model explains why we sometimes see inflation rates trending upward over time. For example, inflation in the United States started out around 2 percent in 1960 and ended up around 15 percent in 1980. The general upward trend in the rate of inflation during the period is directly related to policies that, as our model predicts, tried to keep real GDP growing faster than the economy's potential.

Don't get the idea that only economists try to predict inflation in the future. You know that changes in inflation rates affect your real wage. Consequently, you, too, would like to accurately predict future inflation to know how much of a salary increase to ask for. In the past, when inflation was high and volatile, many groups, including unions, pension plans, and the Internal Revenue Service, automatically adjusted wages, government transfers, and people's income taxes based on inflation increases. Adjustments such as these are often called COLAs, or cost-of-living adjustments. The idea is to prevent inflation from eroding real purchasing power.[5]

## 14.5 A Different View: The Effect of Price Shocks on Inflation Expectations, Output, and Inflation

In the recent history of the U.S. economy, generally the negative real GDP gaps are associated with declines in the rate of inflation (disinflation). That is what the theoretical model predicts *should be* the relationship. But is it theoretically possible to have a negative GDP gap associated with an *increase* in the rate of inflation? Such an "inappropriate" episode occurred during the 1970s and is more fully discussed in the next chapter. It puzzled economists and policy makers at the time. Using the model we have developed, we can solve their dilemma and show how a negative GDP gap and an increase in the rate of inflation can occur together.

Generally, a negative real GDP gap and increase in inflation happens when there is a **price shock**. A price shock is an unexpected price change for a particular good or service, usually some important commodity such as oil or food. In the terminology of

· · · · · · ·

[5]Robert Pear, "Social Security Benefits not Expected to Rise in '10." *New York Times*, May 3, 2009.

Chapter 6, this is a large change in the relative or real price of the good. When this happens, people's expectations about inflation in the economy increase *independent* of a change in aggregate demand.

**PRICE SHOCK** A significant change in the price level, usually caused by the change in the price of an important commodity.

**EXAMPLE** The local police department's annual operating budget included $5,600 for fuel expenses, based on the expectation that gasoline prices would be $2. When gas prices jumped to $4, the police chief was forced to cut back services and lay off nonessential personnel.

Why does the price change of just one commodity have such an impact? Recall from Chapter 6 that our measures of inflation use a price index, which is made up of many items. Some of these items, however, represent a significant portion of consumer expenditures. When the price of one of these key components increases, the overall price index—and the measured rate of inflation—increases. That is, it isn't an increase in aggregate demand that causes an increase in inflation and your expectations of higher rates of inflation—it is some other event.

The events of the 1970s provide a good example of what can cause price shocks and why they are sometimes referred to as *supply shocks*. In 1972, the old Soviet Union experienced an incredibly bad grain harvest. This reduced stocks of grain (think of a leftward shift in the supply curve of grain), which, given demand, significantly increased the price of grain and related products. In the United States, the retail price of food soared, increasing at about a 20-percent rate in 1973 alone. In addition to that negative event, in October 1973, the Organization of the Petroleum Exporting Countries (OPEC) announced that they would embargo oil shipments to the United States and other countries that had backed Israel in their conflict with Syria and Egypt.[6] This reduction in the supply of oil, given demand for it, raised the price of oil from $3 to $12 a barrel. Although $12 per barrel oil may seem cheap compared with today's prices, at the time, the increase to $12 was economically significant. Together, these events led to severe shortages in key goods—food and fuel—which significantly raised the measured rate of inflation and, perhaps more importantly, peoples' expectation of higher rates of inflation in the future.

**ECONOMIC FALLACY**    All price shocks have the same effect.

**False.** In 1973, the members of OPEC, a group of the world's leading oil-producing nations, increased the worldwide price of oil by a factor of 4. They were able to increase the price of oil by putting an embargo on shipments of oil to many countries. The increase is thought to have set into motion a recession, both here and abroad. Since then, there have been other episodes of significant oil-price increases. But why haven't there been similarly severe economic downturns in their wake?

Believe it or not, much of the developed, high oil-consuming nations of the world have become much more efficient users of energy. Today's cars get much

· · · · · · ·

[6]This conflict is referred to as the Yom Kippur War because the initial attack began on Yom Kippur, the Jewish Day of Atonement. The conflict lasted 20 days, from October 6 to October 26, 1973, when a cease-fire was agreed to.

better gas mileage than cars did 40 years ago. Our use of energy in homes is more efficient, too. Modern insulation, improvements in electronics and in heating systems all have contributed to our improved use of energy. Consequently, when an energy-based price shock occurs, the economic effect is relatively smaller than it was in the past.[7]

Let's use **Figure 14.6** to show how a price shock works. We start with the economy at point A, where the economy is producing at its potential (GDP gap = 0), and the actual and expected rates of inflation are 4 percent. Now the price shocks hit. Oil is in short supply, food grains have become scarce, and prices of these commodities rise sharply. Prices of related goods, especially goods that use these raw materials, also increase. As the effects of these shortage-induced price increases unfold, people's expectation of future inflation begins to adjust upward. Output and inflation expectations begin to adjust, moving the economy toward point B. For our example, let's suppose that instead of everyone expecting inflation to remain at 4 percent, the new, widely held expectation is that it will jump to 7 percent. Graphically, this is shown by inflation expectations line $IE_1$ shifting upward to $IE_2$.

If the inflation expectation line shifts upward in response to the price shocks, and there has been no change in aggregate demand, the new equilibrium between aggregate demand and inflation can only occur at some higher rate of inflation (here,

**FIGURE 14.6** The Long-Term Adjustment of Output and the Inflation Rate to a Price Shock

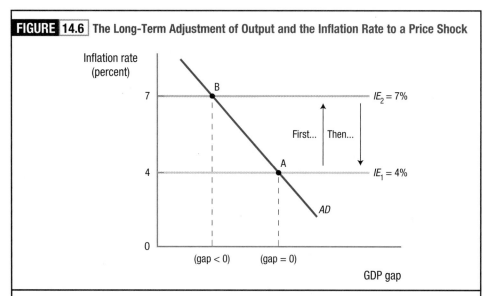

To show how a price shock works, suppose the economy is in equilibrium at point A, and then a price shock hits. People's expectations of future inflation increase as shown by the $IE_1$ line shifting upward to $IE_2$. If the inflation expectation line shifts upward in response to the price shock, but aggregate demand remains unchanged, the new equilibrium between aggregate demand and inflation occurs at a higher rate of inflation (7 percent) and a negative GDP gap (point B). Over time, if there is no change in aggregate demand, the effect of a price shock is transitory. In the long run, the economy once again returns to operating at potential (the GDP gap becomes zero), and the rate of expected inflation falls back to its original value (point A).

· · · · · · · ·

[7]For more information on how our energy affects the economy, see Richard Andersen, "Energy and the Economy." *National Economic Trends*, Federal Reserve Bank of St. Louis (April 2008).

7 percent) and at some level of real GDP that is below potential. In other words, *a price shock is associated with an increase in the rate of inflation and a reduction in the level of economic activity.* This combination of rising actual and expected rates of inflation and slow or negative output growth is called **stagflation**. In other words, economic growth is stagnating (the GDP gap is negative), even though the rate of inflation continues unabated or even increases.[8]

> **STAGFLATION** A situation of high or increasing inflation and low or negative real GDP growth.

> EXAMPLE During the price shocks of the mid-1970s, the rate of inflation sky-rocketed, and the rate growth of real GDP was negative.

> EXAMPLE During the early 2000s, the annual rate of inflation in Zimbabwe averaged over 1,000 percent while the annual growth rate of real GDP averaged negative 5 percent.

If a price shock is associated with output growth falling below potential and increases the rate of inflation, what is the long-run effect? If there is no change in aggregate demand, the effect of a price shock is transitory. As economic activity falls below potential, market forces put downward pressure on prices that dampen inflation. When the GDP gap is negative, firms are less likely to raise prices at the same rate as before. This response reduces the rate of inflation and inflation expectations: they will recede back to their original values. In Figure 14.6, this is illustrated by the $IE_2$ line falling back to $IE_1$, which results in an adjustment from point B back to point A. In the long run, the economy once again returns to operating at potential (the GDP gap becomes zero), and the rate of inflation falls back to its original value.

But what happens if the government decides to do something about stagflation in an effort to stimulate aggregate demand and avoid the economic downturn? We leave that question and answer for the following Solved Problem. We'll also explore that idea in the next chapter where we look at the 1970s oil price shock, and the recession it helped cause, in more detail.

## SOLVED PROBLEM

**Q** Can the government fight stagflation?

**A** You have learned that stagflation occurs when the rate of inflation increases and the growth of real GDP falls. In the most severe case, inflation rates are rising while the economy is in recession; that is, when the GDP gap is negative. Let's assume that most policy makers are more concerned about recessions and increases in unemployment than about rising inflation. Those are the problems they want to tackle. How should policy makers respond?

In the following figure, you can see that the inflation expectations line has shifted upward, from $IE_1$ to $IE_2$, reflecting the price shock. With aggregate demand ($AD_1$) unchanged, the rate of inflation rises from 4 percent to 7 percent, and the GDP gap goes negative. If policy makers decide to fight the downturn in economic activity, what should they do? If you said increase aggregate demand, that would shift $AD_1$ to, say, $AD_2$. That solves the problem of the gap because it takes you back to

· · · · · · ·

[8]Stagflation is not a relic of the past, either. See, for example, Edmund Conway, "Oil Price Shock Fuels Fear of UK Stagflation." Telegraph.com.uk (February 27, 2009).

full employment: aggregate demand ($AD_2$) and inflation expectations ($IE_2$) again intersect at a zero GDP gap. But look at inflation. It is now at the new, higher level (7 percent). A cost of trying to offset the negative output effects of a price shock is a higher rate of expected and actual inflation.

What if you decide to fight the higher inflation? What if you do nothing? We'll ask you to answer these questions at the end of the chapter.

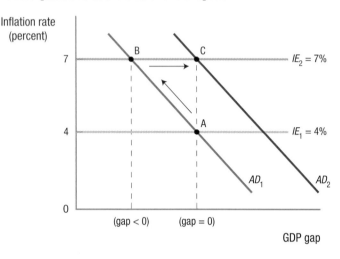

An increase in aggregate demand, whether it stems from a policy action or from an autonomous increase in total expenditures, causes an increase in the expected rate of inflation. For a price shock, increasing aggregate demand to soften the downturn in economic activity means that inflation will not return to its original rate. Instead, the combination of a price shock and an expansion in aggregate demand leads to a permanent increase in the expected rate of inflation. Accommodating a price shock by increasing aggregate demand only cements the higher rate of inflation without any long-term benefit to output.

## WHAT YOU SHOULD HAVE LEARNED IN CHAPTER 14

■ That expectations of prices and inflation are formed using available information, gathered to the point where the marginal cost of gathering more information is equal to the marginal benefit of doing so. Such expectations are said to be rational.

■ That prices for many goods tend not to change significantly in the short run and are thus sometimes referred to as sticky.

■ That if expectations of inflation are formed rationally and do not change much in the short run, real-wage demands are similarly slow to adjust over time.

■ That changes in real wages affect the amount of labor used in the production of goods and services.

■ That an increase in aggregate demand has the temporary effect of creating a positive GDP gap—an increase in output above the economy's long-run potential.

■ That a positive GDP gap is associated with an increase in inflation expectations and an increase in real-wage demands.

■ That the upward adjustment in inflation expectations and wage demands leads to a reduction in labor used and the level of production.

■ That over time, the level of output adjusts back to potential, but inflation and inflation expectations remain permanently higher.

■ That a decrease in aggregate demand has the opposite effect on the economy, bringing about a temporary decrease in output relative to potential (a negative GDP gap) until inflation expectations adjust downward, returning output to potential at a permanently lower rate of inflation.

■ That a price shock can lead to a temporary reduction in production—a negative real GDP gap—and a temporary increase in the rate of inflation.

## KEY TERMS

Rational expectations, p. 374

Inflation expectations line, p. 383

GDP gap, p. 383

Price shock, p. 388

Stagflation, p. 391

## QUESTIONS AND PROBLEMS

1. Yesterday's average temperature is a pretty good predictor of today's average temperature. If this is true, why do many people spend so much time watching the nightly weather report on the local TV station?

2. Rational expectations are often based on observed patterns. For example, because Professor Jones is always five minutes late to class, it is rational for me to be five minutes late also. How is your behavior different in Professor Smith's class, where she is sometimes early and sometimes late?

3. In one year, your boss announces a 5-percent pay raise, and everyone is happy. In another, your boss announces a 5-percent pay decrease, and everyone is incensed and threatens to quit. What might explain the difference in behavior? What relevant economic information should you gather before looking for another job?

4. Some prices, such as for gasoline, milk, and bread, change fairly often. Other prices, such as for movie tickets, newspapers, and catalog items, tend to be rather stable and do not often change.
   a) Why might this occur? (Hint: think substitutes.)
   b) How do such price changes or lack thereof affect the way you establish your inflation expectations?
   c) Do you adjust your expectations with every change in prices, or do you have some base or average price that you use when considering price changes?

5. Forty years ago, economist and Nobel Laureate Robert Lucas, Jr., likened the economy to a set of islands, where information about changes in demand flowed but not evenly nor immediately. His analogy reflected the fact that businesses do not know if a surge in demand is unique to them or widespread.
   a) Explain how this informational uncertainty can affect a firm's demand for labor.
   b) If you could measure the speed with which such information flows, what changes in the past 40 years would affect this flow of information?
   c) Given the changes noted in (b), would you expect prices and price changes to be more or less uniform across the economy?

6. In Chapter 12, we talked about hyperinflation, a condition where prices are increasing at astronomical rates. If prices are rising day by day and increasing at unpredictable rates, what do you suppose happens to the wage agreements between workers and employers? How would this affect your decision to work or enjoy more leisure? Predict the effect of hyperinflation on output.

7. As a 2010 college graduate, you get two job offers to start work in September of that year. One is to work in Salem, Oregon, for an economic-consulting firm.

The other is to work for an economic-consulting firm in Kansas City, Missouri. Both jobs pay $45,000 per year. Which job should you take? Explain the economics of how you arrived at your answer.

8. Our discussion of labor-market adjustment suggests that an increase in the demand for labor, brought about by an increase in the demand for products, leads to an increase in nominal wages but not to an increase in the quantity of hours worked. If worker productivity hasn't changed, and the economy is operating on its PPF, will this increase in demand for goods increase potential output?

9. Explain the concept of the GDP gap using the PPF.

10. Economists sometimes worry about whether inflation expectations are anchored or not. By anchored, they mean that expectations are not likely to change. Using a diagram like Figure 14.3, explain and show how changes in inflation expectations can upset policy makers' predictions of how an increase in government spending will affect the GDP gap.

11. In March 2002, *Businessweek* ran a story titled "Japan's Deflation Disaster." In the article, it was suggested that Japan's condition of deflation seemed permanent. Could this be? Analyze this belief by drawing Figure 14.3 and, instead of expected inflation being 4 percent, make it 0. Then shift the aggregate demand curve to the left, and describe the adjustment process. Does this outcome help explain why so many U.S. policy makers in 2010 worried more about deflation than inflation?

12. In 2008, the economy was in a deep recession (the GDP gap was negative), and the rate of inflation was 2.5 percent. Given these economic conditions, the Federal Reserve lowered the real rate of interest. Using a diagram like Figure 14.3:

a) Show and explain the desired outcome of this policy.

b) Show and explain why some economists worried that this policy would lead to higher inflation in the future.

13. It is the summer of 2020, and oil prices are $150 a barrel, where they have been for many years. Due to new discoveries, by spring 2021, oil was selling for about $50 a barrel. Assume that in the summer of 2020, expected inflation was 3 percent.

a) Use a diagram like Figure 14.3 to explain the potential effect on inflation and the GDP gap of this reduction in oil prices. Be sure to consider both the short-term and long-term effects.

b) Some commentators at the time equated the oil-price decline to a cut in taxes. Explain their reasoning.

14. In the Solved Problem in the text, we described the outcome of policies to fight the economic downturn that arises with a price shock. With expected inflation at 4 percent and the economy operating at a zero GDP gap, use a diagram like Figure 14.3 to:

a) Show and explain the effects on output and inflation of using policies to fight the higher inflation. Be sure to consider the short-term and long-term results.

b) Show and explain the effects on output and inflation of doing nothing. Be sure to consider the short-term and long-term results.

c) Of the two possible responses—fight inflation or do nothing—which policy response would you favor? Justify your answer.

15. In the early 1980s, the chairman of the Federal Reserve, Paul Volcker, announced that inflation was too high and that monetary policy makers would attempt to lower it. Part of the plan to lower inflation was to raise real interest rates. Using a diagram like Figure 14.3, show the short-term and long-term outcome of this policy. Start your analysis at a condition of zero GDP gap and an inflation rate (actual and expected) of 10 percent. After you have complete your analysis, look back at Figure 12.2 in Chapter 12 to see if your predicted outcome matches up with what actually happened.

# 15

## Can Economic Fluctuations Be Predicted? Using the Aggregate Demand and Inflation Expectations Model

*"The long run is a misleading guide to current affairs. In the long run we are all dead. Economists set themselves too easy, too useless a task if in tempestuous seasons they can only tell us that when the storm is past the ocean is flat again."*

John Maynard Keynes, A Tract on Monetary Reform *(1923)*

The model developed in the previous two chapters gives you the basics to analyze and explain economic fluctuations in any economy. But the model is only as good as its ability to predict actual outcomes. A model that bases winter forecasts on the bushiness of caterpillars is an alternative to the sophisticated mathematical models used by the U.S. Weather Service. The fact that airline companies and NASA do not observe "wooly worms" (caterpillars) before setting winter flight schedules indicates that such a "model" is not too trustworthy.

Our objective in this chapter is to show just how applicable the aggregate demand-inflation expectations (AD-IE) model is. The model condenses the varied economic forces that bring about short-term fluctuations in economic activity and fluctuations of real GDP around its long-run or potential growth. It also will help you to further understand the causes of increases and decreases in the rate of inflation. When stacked up against real examples from around the world, just how well does the model predict fluctuations in economic activity?

To answer this question, we pit the model's theoretical predictions against real world outcomes. To see whether the model is useful—does it tell a plausible story—we look at several case studies. These case studies include several past and more recent recessions in the United States; others look at recessions in the neighboring countries of Mexico and Canada. Before we get to these applications, though, let's first establish exactly what economic fluctuations are and recap the broad predictions of the model.

## 15.1 What Are Economic Fluctuations?

We have used the phrase "economic fluctuations" to describe the ups and downs of economic activity in the economy. Sometimes you will hear someone refer to these changes as "business cycles." We prefer to use economic fluctuation rather than business cycle because the term "cycle" usually indicates some regular occurrence. For

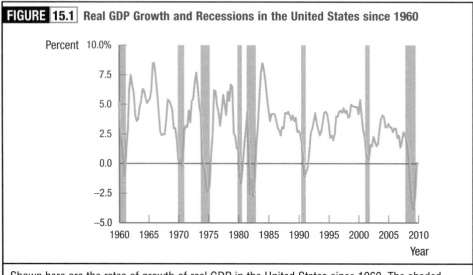

**FIGURE 15.1** Real GDP Growth and Recessions in the United States since 1960

Shown here are the rates of growth of real GDP in the United States since 1960. The shaded vertical bars denote recessions.

*Source:* Federal Reserve Bank of St. Louis

example, you can determine the dates of the moon's phases—the moon-phase cycle, so to speak—from as long ago as the mid-1800s and as far into the future as the mid-2000s because the cycles are *regular*. Similarly, ovulation cycles for different mammals are fairly predictable because they occur regularly. In contrast, the ups and downs of economic activity are anything but regular, which makes them more difficult to predict.

Irregular variations in the pace of economic activity are why we prefer to use the term economic fluctuations. To justify our choice, look at **Figure 15.1**. You've seen this figure several times already in this book. Figure 15.1 shows the rates of growth of real GDP in the United States since 1960. As before, the shaded vertical bars are used to denote recessions. We have used the term recession in previous chapters, and you are probably familiar with it from everyday use. But let's now assign a definition to the term **recession**:

**RECESSION** A significant downturn in economic activity, usually measured by negative real GDP growth and rising unemployment.

**EXAMPLE** The recession that began in July 1990 was relatively mild, with only a slight downturn in the level of real GDP.

**EXAMPLE** The recession that began in December 2007 resulted in a steep drop in the level of real GDP (a negative growth rate in output) and a sharp rise in the unemployment rate. The unemployment rate reached nearly 10 percent by late 2008.

You should be aware of a couple of aspects about recessions. First, they do not last the same length of time. Some are very short, whereas others, like the one that began in December 2007, last much longer. Second, periods between recessions, called **expansions**, also vary in length. Notice in Figure 15.1 how much time lapses between the recessions in the early 1980s and 1990, and again from 1991 through 2000. The period from the mid-1980s through 2000 is characterized by relatively strong economic growth interrupted by two rather mild recessions. Because of this record of fairly sustained expansion, this nearly two decade period is often referred to as the Long Boom or the Great Moderation.

> **EXPANSION** The period of positive economic growth between the end of one recession and the beginning of the next.

> EXAMPLE The recession which began in 1990 ended in March 1991. From March 1991 until March 2001, the start of the next recession, the economy experienced sustained positive economic growth.

After looking at Figure 15.1, we think you'll agree that the more accurate phrase to describe the short-run behavior of the economy is economic fluctuations, not business cycles.

## 15.2 Dating Recessions in the United States

The "official" designator of when recessions begin and end, at least in the United States, is the National Bureau of Economic Research (NBER). The NBER is not a government agency but a private organization devoted to economic research. According to the NBER's Web site, "A recession is a significant decline in economic activity spread across the economy, lasting more than a few months, normally visible in production, employment, real income, and other indicators." Based on NBER's analysis of these factors, the Business Cycle Dating Committee, a group of economists within the NBER who are experts in macroeconomics and economic forecasting, establishes the dates of recessions (and therefore expansions) in the United States. Even though we may feel the effects of being in a recession—reduced output growth, fewer jobs being created, higher unemployment, and so forth—it's not an official recession until the NBER says it is.

**Table 15.1** lists the recessions that have occurred in the United States since World War II, as designated by the NBER. You can see that the length of recessions—measured from the *peak* of business activity to the bottom or *trough* of the recession—varies considerably. One thing to notice is that recessions are occurring less often than in the past. For instance, since 1985, there have been three recessions. Between 1960 and 1985, in contrast, there were five recessions. This is a relative statement: in the past decade, we have had two recessions, the most recent one being quite severe. In fact, the recession which lasted 18 months, from December 2007 to June 2009, was the longest recession since the Great Depression, which lasted 43 months, from August 1929 until March 1933. Even with this recent downturn, some believe that fewer recessions in the past several decades signal the success of policy makers at managing economic activity. We will have more to say about this conjecture later in the chapter.

Although the NBER is the official dater of recessions, one problem is that the NBER's announcement that a recession has begun or ended always occurs after the fact. The dates shown in Table 15.1 are not, therefore, useful for making real-time policy decisions. To pick one example, the December 2007 start of the Great Recession wasn't announced until December 2008. And even though by late 2009 the economy was already expanding, and there were signs that the recession had ended, it wasn't until September 2010 that the NBER officially announced that the recession had ended a year earlier in June 2009. Luckily, policy makers rely on their own interpretation of the data when deciding how to act. Waiting for the NBER's dating decision would put policy way behind the curve.

| Table 15.1 Recessions in the United States since 1945 | | |
| --- | --- | --- |
| **Reference Dates** | | |
| Peak | Trough | Duration in Months |
| February 1945 | October 1945 | 8 |
| November 1948 | October 1949 | 11 |
| July 1953 | May 1954 | 10 |
| August 1957 | April 1958 | 8 |
| April 1960 | February 1961 | 10 |
| December 1969 | November 1970 | 11 |
| November 1973 | March 1975 | 16 |
| January 1980 | July 1980 | 6 |
| July 1981 | November 1982 | 16 |
| July 1990 | March 1991 | 8 |
| March 2001 | November 2001 | 8 |
| December 2007 | June 2009 | 18 |

This table lists the recessions that have occurred in the United States since World War II, as designated by the National Bureau of Economic Research (NBER). The length of recessions varies considerably. The dating also suggests that recessions are occurring less often than in the past. Between 1960 and 1985 there were five recessions; since 1985, there have been only three recessions. However, two of them occurred in the past decade, and the most recent downturn was the longest recession since the Great Depression of the 1930s.

**Source:** National Bureau of Economic Research

## Recessions Are Not the Same

Table 15.1 also reveals that recessions vary in intensity. To illustrate such differences, **Figure 15.2** compares the level of real GDP before and after the onset of three recessions: the recession that began in April 1960, the recession that began in July of 1990, and the recession that began in December 2007. By indexing the value of real GDP equal to 100 in the quarter that each recession began, each line illustrates the relative strength or weakness of real GDP before and after the recession began. The idea is that before the recession hits, real GDP should be rising toward 100. This would be the peak quarter of economic activity. The onset of the recession leads to a decline in real GDP until the next expansion begins.

You can see in Figure 15.2 that the behavior of real GDP is not uniform, especially after a recession has begun. Both the 1960 and 1990 recessions were fairly short-lived. This is why real GDP begins to increase only a few quarters after those recessions began. And although the recovery was fairly slow in 1990, real GDP expanded comparatively fast following the 1960 downturn, quickly surpassing its pre-recession level within a few quarters.

The behavior of real GDP following the 2007–2009 recession is much different, however. Not only did real GDP fall far below its value at the onset of the recession—a sign of the severity of the downturn—but it did not bounce back as in 1960 and 1990. As you are probably aware, the hangover effects of this recession lasted for many months, continuing into 2011. Not only did real GDP remain below its prerecession level for many months into the recovery, but unemployment rates remained stubbornly high for several years after the recession had "officially" ended.

**FIGURE 15.2** **Tracking Recessions**

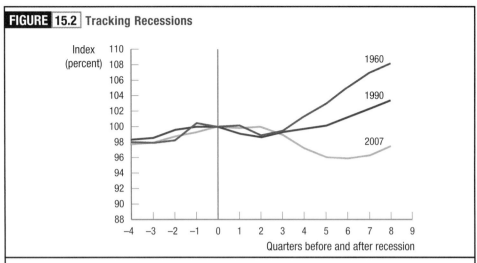

The figure compares the level of real GDP before and after the onset of three recessions. The behavior of real GDP following a recession is not uniform. Real GDP began to increase much more rapidly following the 1960 recession compared with the 1990 and the 2007 recessions. In contrast to both 1960 and 1990, two years after the 2007 recession started, real GDP was still far below its peak.

*Source:* Federal Reserve Bank of St. Louis

## Dating Recessions Abroad

Economic fluctuations are by no means unique to the United States. **Table 15.2** lists the beginning dates for recessions in several large countries since 1980. We also included the dates for the United States as points of reference. The first thing to notice is that the beginnings of a recession are not coordinated across countries. The United States

**Table 15.2** **Comparing Starts of Recessions across Countries since 1980**

(Month/Year)

| United States | Australia | Canada | France | Germany | Japan | United Kingdom |
|---|---|---|---|---|---|---|
| 1/1980 | 3/1982 | 8/1984 | 2/1984 | 1/1980 | 11/1984 | 11/1983 |
| 7/1981 | 7/1985 | 4/1988 | 3/1980 | 10/1985 | 2/1991 | 11/1988 |
| 7/1990 | 12/1988 | 1/1995 | 2/1985 | 2/1991 | 6/1997 | 10/1994 |
| 3/2001 | 2/1996 | 8/2000 | 4/1988 | 12/1994 | 10/2000 | 11/2000 |
| 12/2007 | 7/2000 | 7/2007 | 12/2000 | 4/1998 | 3/2008 | 4/2004 |
| | 5/2008 | | 2/2008 | 12/2000 | | 2/2008 |
| | | | | 3/2008 | | |

Economic fluctuations are not unique to the United States. Listed here are the start dates for recessions in several countries since 1980. It is clear that recessions do not begin in any coordinated way across countries. The United States experienced a severe recession beginning in mid-1981, but this date is not shared by any other country in the table. The most recent recession was different. The U.S. recession began in late 2007 and coincides fairly closely with the start of recessions in every other country listed.

**Source:** Organization for Economic Co-Operation and Development (OECD) and NBER

experienced a severe recession beginning in mid-1981, but this date is not common to any other country in the table. For most of the countries listed, a recession did occur in the mid-1980s but not in 1981. This is not true, however, for the most recent downturn. The recession that started in December 2007 in the United States coincides fairly closely with the start of recessions in every other country listed. The information in Table 15.2 reflects the fact that economies often experience recessions (fluctuations) independently of each other. In Chapter 10, you saw that countries often experience different histories of economic growth. For a variety of reasons, not the least of which is different economic policies, they also have different episodes of recessions and expansions.

## 15.3  An Overview of the AD-IE Model's Predictions

If the AD-IE model we have constructed is to be useful, it should be able to explain why there are changes in the GDP gap and inflation. Being able to predict if the GDP gap is positive or negative is valuable to assess the likelihood that the economy is moving into a recession or an expansion. It also will help us understand if higher rates of inflation are likely to occur in the future. And don't think that policy makers in Washington, D.C., London, or Beijing are the only ones using this kind of model: many businesses employ economists and hire economic-consulting firms to predict economic activity and inflation to forecast future sales, resource needs, and the like.

The previous chapter ended with the prediction that increases and decreases in aggregate demand lead to short-run changes in the GDP gap. We also observed that whether the GDP gap is positive or negative is associated with movements in the expected and actual rate of inflation over time. More precisely, if an increase in aggregated demand causes the GDP gap to become positive—output growth exceeds its potential—the economy is likely to experience an uptick in the rate of expected and actual inflation. Similarly, when economic output falls below its potential (a negative GDP gap), the model predicts that the expected rate of inflation will decline.

**Table 15.3** lists sources of aggregate demand changes, and summarizes how those changes affect the GDP gap, which over time will affect the expected rate of inflation. You will notice that we list only those factors that cause aggregate demand to decline. This is not to suggest that the model cannot help us understand expansions and increases in inflation, but we usually place more weight on trying to avoid recessions and so place more weight on trying to understand why they occur. Moreover, the effects of aggregate demand changes are symmetric: increases in aggregate demand will have the opposite effect on the GDP gap as decreases in aggregate demand.

In each "experiment," we start with the economy operating at its potential GDP, given some actual and expected rate of inflation. Now suppose there is a decrease in any one of the expenditure components that comprise aggregate demand, or there is an increase in the real rate of interest. All else the same, a decline in autonomous consumption spending, for example, lowers aggregate demand and reduces the pace of economic activity below its potential, creating a negative GDP gap. (Graphically this is a leftward shift in the aggregate demand curve.) A similar decline in aggregate demand takes place if there is a decline in investment spending, a reduction in government spending, or a decrease in net exports. As you learned in the previous chapter, a negative GDP gap puts downward pressure on expected inflation. An *increase* in real interest rates brought about by monetary policy makers also reduces aggregate demand and economic activity. If the drop in aggregate demand caused by any of these factors is sufficiently large and/or prolonged, the outcome is a negative GDP gap: a recession occurs and there is, over time, a reduction in the expected and actual rates of inflation.

| Table **15.3** Factors that Decrease Aggregate Demand and Affect Output in the Short Run and Long Run | | |
|---|---|---|
| A Decrease in... | Causes Aggregate Demand to... | And This Leads to... |
| **Short-Run Output Effects** | | |
| Consumption* | decrease | real GDP below its potential |
| Business investment* | decrease | real GDP below its potential |
| Government spending | decrease | real GDP below its potential |
| Net exports* | decrease | real GDP below its potential |
| **Long-Run Output Effects** | | |
| Consumption* | decrease | real GDP back to its potential |
| Business investment* | decrease | real GDP back to its potential |
| Government spending | decrease | real GDP back to its potential |
| Net exports* | decrease | real GDP back to its potential |
| An Increase in... | Causes Aggregate Demand to... | And This Leads to... |
| **Short-Run Output Effects** | | |
| Interest rates | decrease | real GDP below its potential |
| **Long-Run Output Effects** | | |
| Interest rates | decrease | real GDP back to its potential |

*Refers to a decrease that is not related to a change in income or interest rates.

This table summarizes the factors that change aggregate demand and how they affect the GDP gap and, over time, the rate of inflation. To conserve space, only those changes that cause aggregate demand to decline are listed. Increases in aggregate demand will have the opposite effect on the GDP gap and, in turn, the rate of inflation, as those listed in the table.

Our purpose in this chapter is to focus on using the AD-IE model to explain short-term economic fluctuations. Still, keep in mind what you learned in the previous chapter about the long-term effects of a shift in aggregate demand. Increases and decreases in aggregate demand do not *permanently* alter economic growth. As you saw in Chapter 10, the economy invariably returns to producing goods and services at its long-run potential. What a shift in aggregate demand *does* change in the long run is the expected and actual rates of inflation. Over time, changes in aggregate demand often lead to lasting effects on the prevailing rate of inflation and, therefore, people's expectation of future inflation.

To see if the model's predictions match up with reality—to see if the story we tell with it is a plausible approximation of reality—we should see the following patterns in the data. If the economy is operating at full employment—the gap is near zero—then a reduction in aggregate demand should be evidenced first by a negative GDP gap, and then, if there are no offsetting changes to aggregate demand, the rate of inflation should fall as the gap once again approaches zero. If aggregate demand increases, we should see just the opposite dynamics: a positive real GDP gap means faster output growth, but only temporarily, as expected inflation rates rise and the economy once again returns to its potential.

Let's now address an important question that often is the basis for much debate: If it is only a matter of time until the economy returns back to expanding at its potential, why are policy-makers compelled to increase aggregate demand and try to push real GDP back to its potential? John Maynard Keynes's famous quote at the beginning of the chapter was his way of alerting us to the fact that even though an economy in recession returns to its long-term potential growth, the time it takes to do so comes at a price. Economic downturns not only mean that fewer goods are being produced but also that people suffer significant economic and personal hardships. Losing your job in a recession can have substantial and long-term effects on your life and on others' lives as well. What if you or your parents become unemployed, and there is no money to pay for your college education? Think about how this could affect your future. Without a degree, you are likely to earn less. As you can imagine, the public's discourse over the correct policy response to an impending downturn is usually emotional.[1]

## 15.4 Explaining Economic Fluctuations: Case Studies from the United States

Although there have been a number of recessions and expansions in the United States, we will examine just a few to "test" the AD-IE model. A word of caution is in order: even though we draw the model with the precision of geometry, most economists believe that, due to measurement difficulties, when the GDP gap is between minus and positive 1 percent, that is close enough to consider the economy to be operating at its potential.

We have chosen several recessions to illustrate how reductions in aggregate demand lead to economic slowdowns. These are the recessions of 1990 and 2001, which were relatively mild, and the 2007–2009 recession, which was the most severe in 80 years. (In later chapters, we will discuss in more detail the fiscal and monetary policy responses surrounding the recession.) We also look at the 1973–1975 recession because it was associated with a very large price shock along with a reduction in aggregate demand.

### The 1990–1991 Recession

The U.S. economy expanded for most of the 1980s. From November of 1982 until July of 1990, the U.S. economy grew, on average, at about a 3.3-percent annual rate. This was one of the longest expansions in U.S. economic history. What brought it to an end?

The recession that occurred in the early 1980s was long and severe. Most economists argue that the 1981–1982 recession was the price paid to rid the economy of the excessive rates of inflation and to lower people's inflation expectations. This is sometimes called the Volcker recession, so named because Paul Volcker was the chairman of the Federal Reserve who oversaw the change in monetary policy that largely brought about the reduction of inflation from double-digit territory. The cost was one of the deepest postwar recessions, an outcome not appreciated by the Reagan White House.[2]

During the economic expansion that began in November 1982, the economy returned to its long-run growth trend, and, after a few years, real GDP was increasing faster than potential GDP. Although the stock market crash of 1987 temporarily halted the upward climb, beginning in 1988 the economy once again was operating above potential. The economy was outside of its PPF, in other words. The expected rate of inflation also began to increase in the second half of the decade, and this had policy makers, especially those at the Federal Reserve, worried. Their concern led them to raise short-term real interest rates in the latter half of the decade to try and slow

· · · · · · ·

[1]Matthew Saltmarsh, "Safety Net Not Enough to Allay Fears in Europe." *New York Times*, April 2, 2009.

[2]Jonathan Huerbringer, "The Fed vs. the White House: A Collision Is Brewing over the Course of the Recovery." *New York Times*, January 10, 1982.

aggregate demand. By late 1989, for example, the Federal Reserve had raised short-term nominal interest rates by more than the increase in expected inflation.

Let's use **Figure 15.3** to set up the economic conditions of the late 1980s. In the upper panel of the figure, we use the AD-IE model to show where the economy was in

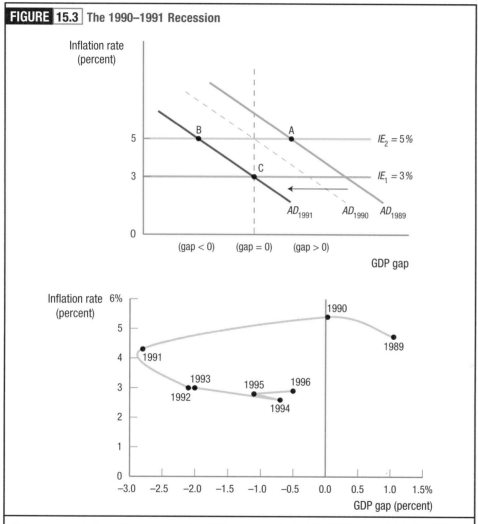

**FIGURE 15.3** The 1990–1991 Recession

The upper panel shows the model version of the economy in the late 1980s. At point A, the GDP gap was positive, and the inflation rate (actual and expected) was about 5 percent. The Federal Reserve raised interest rates to reduce aggregate demand and keep inflation in check. This policy was designed to shift the $AD_{1989}$ curve leftward to $AD_{1990}$ and was somewhat successful. As shown in the lower panel, by 1990, the GDP gap was zero. However, economic activity continued to fall because of negative effects stemming from several events, such as the first war in Iraq. By 1991, reductions in consumer and business spending combined with the Fed's higher interest-rate policy created a large negative GDP gap. The economy was pushed to a point such as B in the upper panel. The model predicts that the economy should have returned to its potential (a zero GDP gap) at a lower rate of inflation (point C). In fact, after 1991, economic activity began to increase (the negative GDP gap shrank), and the rate of inflation edged lower, as the lower panel shows.

*Source:* Federal Reserve Bank of St. Louis; author calculations

the late 1980s. As we have depicted it, the economy was initially operating above potential in 1989 (the GDP gap was positive), and the inflation rate (actual and expected) was almost 5 percent. These facts are represented by the intersection of aggregate demand, $AD_{1989}$, and inflation expectations, $IE_1(5\%)$, at point A. The policy action taken by the Federal Reserve (raising interest rates) was aimed at reducing aggregate demand to keep inflation in check. The policy makers could only do this by shrinking the size of the positive GDP gap. In other words, the Fed wanted to shift the aggregate demand curve labeled $AD_{1989}$ in Figure 15.3 to the left. Optimally, the goal was to shift the $AD$ curve leftward to $AD_{1990}$, to the point where it intersected the expected rate of inflation $(IE_2)$ with an expected inflation rate of 5 percent. This would have contained inflation, and inflation expectations, and returned the economy to operating with a zero GDP gap.

The policy successfully reduced aggregate demand. The lower panel of Figure 15.3 shows the actual values for the GDP gap and the rate of inflation for a few years before and after the 1990 recession. In the lower panel, you can see that the GDP gap was zero in 1990. Consistent with the theoretical model, a continued leftward shift in the aggregate demand curve resulted in no immediate reaction to the rate of inflation, though a continued slowing in real GDP would reduce expected inflation. As shown in the lower panel, economic activity continued to fall relative to potential, and the GDP gap became negative by 1991. Indeed, the NBER dated the start of the recession as July 1990.

There were some events in 1990 that the policy makers could not have foreseen when they undertook the policy of reducing the GDP gap. The first war in Iraq negatively affected spending by households and businesses. By the end of 1990, consumer spending and private investment by businesses were both declining. Even though net exports actually improved, it was not enough to offset these significant declines. In the upper panel of Figure 15.3, these combined effects are shown by the further leftward shift in aggregate demand to $AD_{1991}$. Notice that these influences, on top of the policy-driven push to lower aggregate demand, match up with the large negative GDP gap shown in the bottom panel. This combination of demand-reducing events reduced real GDP further below potential, to a point such as B in the upper panel.

The model predicts that over time, the economy would return to a zero GDP gap at a lower rate of inflation, depicted as point C in Figure 15.3. Did the economy actually behave this way? As you can see in Figure 15.3, what occurred is pretty close to what the model predicts. After 1991, the level of economic activity began to increase (the negative GDP gap shrank), and the rate of inflation edged lower.

The 1990 recession came about due to a combination of factors. The Fed had increased interest rates in the late 1980s to dampen an expanding aggregate demand. To be fair, by itself, this was not the only factor that led to the recession. Add to this policy action the decline in consumer and investment spending caused by the war, and aggregate demand fell enough to push the economy into recession.

### The 2001 Recession

According to Table 15.1, the NBER dated the 2001 recession as beginning in March and ending in November that year. What makes this relatively minor recession worth studying? You might think the answer is the attacks on the United States by terrorists on September 11, 2001. Although the economic effects caused by the unprecedented attacks were significant, they actually occurred *after* the recession had begun. Even though the 9/11 attacks did not *cause* the recession, they surely contributed to it and help explain the unusually slow rate of economic growth that lasted for the next several years (see Figure 15.2). The 2001 recession is, therefore, different enough from the 1990 recession to be worth analyzing.

The U.S. economy had come out of the 1990 recession and expanded for the rest of the decade. Productivity was increasing, it seemed, year in and year out. Unemployment rates had dropped to levels not seen in 20 years. Even the federal budget, which had rarely been in surplus since World War II, turned from a large deficit to a surplus by 1998. The stock market boomed, reaching new highs almost every year. In addition to this glowing economic report card, inflation remained surprisingly subdued. As the economic good times rolled along, some started referring to the 1990s as the "Golden Age" of the U.S. economy. In fact, by the end of the decade, many people, including many prominent economists, politicians, and pundits believed the good economic times would last far into the foreseeable future.[3]

One explanation for this growth-without-inflation scenario comes from the major gains in productivity that occurred. You learned in our discussion of economic growth (Chapter 10) that increased productivity allows more goods to be produced with the same amount of inputs. Many people believed that the long-awaited technology revolution spurred by computer technology was finally here. Surely the widespread use of computers and advances in information technology had finally passed some threshold from which economic growth and prosperity were assured indefinitely. At least that is what many believed.

By the close of 2000, the policy makers at the Federal Reserve had become increasingly concerned that the rate of economic growth was excessive and feared that its continuation would trigger higher rates of inflation. They expressed this concern throughout the latter half of the 1990s.[4] After all, that is what the AD-IE model predicts, isn't it? To minimize this inflation threat, the Fed began increasing short-term nominal interest rates in early 1999. It continued to do so until the middle of 2000, when short-term (nominal) interest rates had reached 6.5 percent. As you know, by increasing nominal interest rates by more than the increase in expected inflation, the Fed sought to increase the real cost of borrowing and reduce investment and consumer spending. In fact, investment spending by businesses to purchase plants and equipment peaked in mid-2000 and began to fall.

The Federal Reserve's actions were not the only factors that caused investment spending to fall, however. We can't ignore the decline in the stock market and especially the widespread failure of the dot.coms in all of this. The tech-heavy NASDAQ stock exchange, which peaked in March 2000, dropped by a staggering 50 percent by the end of the year. The Dow Jones stock index had peaked in January 2000, and soon started to fall, a drop that continued until 2003. This collapse in stock prices also had a negative effect on investment spending by businesses. And it significantly impacted individuals: investors lost about $3 trillion in paper wealth from the NASDAQ drop alone. This loss of wealth caused consumer spending to decline sharply.

Let's use the AD-IE model to analyze the 2001 recession. First, we know that the economy was operating above its full-employment potential in the late 1990s. Inflation was expected to be around 3 percent. The upper panel of **Figure 15.4** illustrates this with the aggregate demand curve in 2000 intersecting the inflation expectation line at a point to the right of a zero GDP gap. This is point A in the figure.

· · · · · · · ·

[3]E. Drumond Ayres, Jr. "How Good Is It? As Good as It Gets, Governors Say." *New York Times*, February 2, 1998.

[4]Peter Passell, "Erring on the Side of Fighting Inflation at the Expense of Jobs." *New York Times*, April 10, 1997.

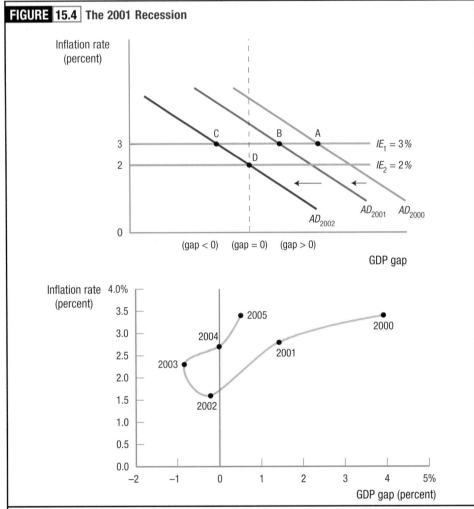

**FIGURE 15.4** | **The 2001 Recession**

The economy was operating above its full-employment potential in the late 1990s, represented by point A in the upper panel. The model predicts that the rate of inflation (actual and expected) should increase. Concerned about rising inflation, the Fed raised interest rates. Together with the crash in the stock market, this sharply reduced consumer spending and business investment. Aggregate demand fell, as illustrated by the curve shifting from $AD_{2000}$ to $AD_{2001}$. Aggregate demand continued to fall, putting the economy in a recession, illustrated by point C. The bottom panel shows what actually occurred. The positive GDP gap shrank and became slightly negative as aggregate demand declined. Though the rate of inflation declined between 2000 and 2003, the rate of inflation bounced back as the economy expanded due to expansionary policy actions—most notably the Fed's lowering of interest rates—that increased aggregate demand.

*Source:* Federal Reserve Bank of St. Louis; author calculations

Even though inflation was only a little over 3 percent, the model predicts that the rate of inflation (actual and expected) would increase over time. Concern about possible increases in inflation is why the Fed began raising nominal and real interest rates even higher. What happened next? Partly in response to the Fed's actions, business investment declined. The crash in the stock market also led to a significant cutback in households' consumer spending. These factors would cause aggregate demand to fall, shown in Figure 15.4 as the aggregate demand curve shifting from $AD_{2000}$ to $AD_{2001}$. With the economy going from point A to point B, the predicted outcome is a reduction in economic activity—a shrinking GDP gap. But aggregate demand continued to fall to $AD_{2002}$, producing the recession as illustrated by point C. From this point, we'd expect that if there were no other interventions, the economy would end up at point D: a lower expected rate of inflation (say, 2%) and back at a zero GDP gap.

Now look at the bottom panel in Figure 15.4 to see if the model predicts what actually occurred. The pattern is similar to the 1990 recession: the positive GDP gap shrank and became slightly negative as increasing interest rates and the collapse in business investment and the stock market pushed the aggregate demand curve to the left. As predicted, there was a reduction, though slight, in the rate of inflation. Between 2000 and 2003, the rate of inflation declined from about 3.5 percent to 2.5 percent. Note, however, that the rate of inflation rebounded as the economy began to grow in 2004 and 2005. Again, this is consistent with the model's prediction: a movement to a positive GDP gap (as in 2004 and 2005) puts upward pressure on prices. Despite the effort to keep inflation down, rising energy prices during 2004 helped inflation bounce back to 3.5 percent.

## The Great Recession of 2007–2009

The so-called Great Recession began in December 2007 and ended in June 2009. It was the United States' worst economic downturn in the past 80 years. The reasons given for the downturn are varied. Often the recession is linked to the bursting of a "bubble" in the housing market. Why did such pressures build up in the economy? Although other factors were at work, many people believe that one key element was low borrowing costs, brought about by the Fed's low interest-rate policy.

In response to and for some time after the 2001 recession, the Federal Reserve reduced nominal interest rates to historically low levels. As a result, the real rate of interest (the nominal rate adjusted for inflation) fell and was effectively kept near zero. Meanwhile, the U.S. government increased its spending. Both actions—the Fed lowering real interest rates and an increase in government spending—were meant to push the economy back to operating at its long-run potential.

The two actions worked. The economy expanded, and employment increased. A side effect was that the ultra-low interest rates made it extremely inexpensive for everyone to borrow money, many of whom did so to buy homes. Moreover, banks were willing to give even risky borrowers mortgage loans because they could be bundled together and sold to investors, who were largely unaware of (and unconcerned about) any inherent risks of default (nonpayment). Not surprisingly, the demand for houses rose sharply, and the prices for them inflated rapidly. Speculators also began buying houses hoping to sell them at large gains in the future.

Concerned that the rate of inflation might begin to increase to undesired levels, the Federal Reserve started raising interest rates (nominal and real) in early 2004. The problem? Many banks and other lenders had offered home buyers low "teaser" interest rates which were set to increase sharply after a few years if interest rates in the economy went up, which they did. These buyers found themselves in trouble: their payments jumped dramatically upward, and a huge number of them began defaulting on their loans. Foreclosed, vacant houses began to flood the market, and house prices plummeted, taking a serious toll on economic activity. In fact, by mid-2011 the housing market was still mired in an excess supply of houses.

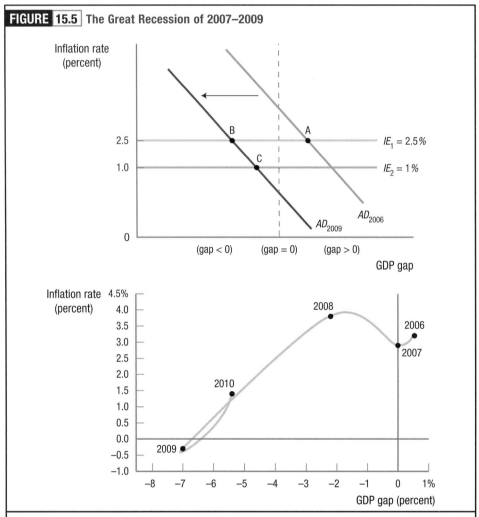

**FIGURE 15.5** The Great Recession of 2007–2009

The Fed began to increase the real rate of interest to keep the aggregate demand curve from increasing beyond the 2006 level (point A). Over the next few years, this action, along with the implosion of housing prices and a subsequent financial crisis in the banking industry, significantly reduced aggregate demand and took the economy from operating at point A toward point B in the figure. In the bottom panel, you see that starting in 2006, when the economy was operating essentially at potential, the GDP gap went from slightly positive to significantly negative in response to the Fed's policies. The further decline in aggregate demand stemming from the problems in housing and other markets led to a large negative GDP gap. As the model predicts, the rate of inflation declined. In 2010, the GDP gap began to close, and inflation remained low.

*Source:* Federal Reserve Bank of St. Louis; author calculations

**Figure 15.5** shows that the increase in the real rate of interest brought about by the Fed's actions was designed to dampen aggregate demand—that is, to keep the aggregate demand curve around its 2006 level (point A). If the Fed guessed right, its policy would have kept the economy operating at potential with no change in inflation or inflation expectations. However, the implosion of housing prices and a subsequent financial crisis in the banking industry led instead to a massive fall in aggregate demand.[5] Not only did consumers curtail their consumption spending as the values of their homes dropped, but business investment also fell sharply as lenders became unwilling to make loans. The combined effect is shown as the large, leftward shift of the aggregate demand curve in Figure 15.5. These events reduce aggregate demand and, with no change in inflation expectations, the economy moved from operating at point A toward point B.

The bottom panel of Figure 15.5 shows that, starting in 2006, the economy was operating slightly above its potential. Following the Fed's interest rate increases, the problems in the housing market and banking industry became more pronounced, and the economy began to slide. You can see that between 2006 and 2008, the GDP gap went from slightly positive to significantly negative. By 2009, the gap had expanded to −7 percentage points, a deviation of actual real GDP from potential GDP that the United States hadn't experienced since the Great Depression of the 1930s. And as the AD-IE model suggests would occur, there was a significant decline in the rate of inflation over this period. The rate of inflation in 2007 was about 3 percent and fell to essentially 0 (−0.3 percent) in 2009.

Before leaving this historic episode, it is useful to make two points. First, why in our story did we ignore the inflation *increase* in 2008? Is it because it doesn't fit neatly into our narrative? No. The increase in inflation in 2008 was a reaction of the CPI to a temporary though very substantial increase in the price of oil. Between July 2007 and July 2008, oil prices surged to $150 a barrel from $60 a barrel. The price effects were short-lived, however: during the last half of 2008, oil prices plummeted, falling back to $40 by year's end. This relative-price event explains the temporary jump in the CPI inflation rate in 2008.

Second, in what direction did the economy head after 2009? The 2010 point in Figure 15.5 shows that the GDP gap remained substantial: hence the observation that it was an anemic recovery. At the same time, the model predicts that with such a large negative GDP gap, inflation expectations would remain subdued. As shown in the bottom panel of Figure 15.5, the rate of inflation during 2010 remained low, about 1.5 percent. Although this is slightly higher than the 2009 number, this low rate of inflation also is consistent with the story our model tells. In the upper panel of Figure 15.5, the 2010 outcome is indicated by point C.

The growth in real GDP resulted from several factors, not the least of which was a huge government-spending program that began late in the Bush administration's term and was expanded by the Obama administration in early 2009. The Fed's actions to lower short-term interest rates to near zero also explain the nascent turnaround. The fact that inflation was restrained in 2010 reflects the fact that the economy still was operating below its potential, putting little upward pressure on prices.

## The 1973–1975 Recession

The recession that occurred from November 1973 through March 1975 was something of a puzzle to economists at the time. For one thing, it looked much different than any of the four previous recessions since 1950. The biggest single difference

· · · · · · ·

[5]We do not want to leave you with the idea that the recession was due *solely* to problems in the housing market. Many other factors, such as the incorrect assessment of investment risk, the extended and some say improper use of new financial investments (with such names as mortgage-backed securities and collateralized debt obligations), and the rapid rise of commodity prices in the summer of 2007, all played some role in triggering the economic decline. We'll have more to say about some of these in Chapter 18.

was that the 1973–1975 recession was not only deep and prolonged, but during the downturn, the expected and actual rates of inflation actually *increased*. According to our economic model, economic slowdowns should lead to falling, not rising, rates of inflation. Why was this downturn so different compared to others?

There are several answers to this question. In October 1973, the Organization of the Petroleum Exporting Countries (OPEC) embargoed oil shipments to many countries, including the United States. The oil embargo substantially increased the price of oil and, consequently, gasoline. A lot of economic resources were spent simply trying to get gas as long lines developed and gas shortages were not uncommon.[6] The OPEC oil-price shock also made it more costly to manufacture products because petroleum is an input in the production of most goods. It became more costly to transport the products from the factory to stores, and more costly for families to drive to the mall and elsewhere. The immediate effect of the price shock can be shown as an upward shift in inflation expectations. The increase in oil prices led many to believe that inflation was going to be higher now and in the future.

The upper panel of **Figure 15.6** shows the model's depiction of the economy in the early 1970s. The economy was enjoying rapid economic growth, and the rate of inflation was fairly moderate, about 4 percent. By 1973, the economy was operating well above its potential, and, as predicted, the rate of inflation was rising. For our analysis, let's locate this situation as point A. In 1973, the expected rate of inflation, which does not fully reflect the effects of the oil-price increase in October of that year, was about 6 percent. The OPEC price shock occurred in October 1973, so what explains the increase in inflation between 1972 and 1973? One explanation is the lifting of wage and price controls that the Nixon administration imposed in 1971. Originally supposed to last 90 days, the controls remained in place—though to lessening degree—until April 1974. As the controls were unwound, the rate of inflation increased. We depict this state of the economy by the aggregate demand, $AD_{1973}$, and inflation expectations, $IE_1(6\%)$, lines intersecting in the positive GDP gap region at an expected inflation rate of 6 percent.

In the fall of 1973, the OPEC price shock hit. We show this by the upward shift in the $IE$ line in the model, to $IE_2(10\%)$. Now the aggregate demand curve ($AD_{1973}$) and the $IE$ line intersect at point B. The model predicts that such a price shock, by itself, would lead to a reduction in the GDP gap *and* an increase in the expected and actual rates of inflation. This simultaneous increase in the rate of inflation and reduction in economic activity is indicative of stagflation. In fact, it is estimated that the price shock itself reduced real GDP growth by two percentage points in 1974 and even more in 1975.

This is what surprised economists at the time. This puzzle arose largely because most economists had not considered the fact that a recession could be caused by something other than changes on the demand side of the economy. The accepted wisdom of the time was that recessions and expansions arose only because of shifts in aggregate demand. Obviously, that view was wrong.

The price shock, while significant, isn't the only factor that explains the 1973–1975 recession. At first, the Fed thought it best to offset the negative output effects of the price shock by undertaking an expansionary policy to boost aggregate demand.

· · · · · · ·

[6]William K. Stevens, "Gasoline Shortages Are Forcing Suburbanites to Readjust Their Life-Style; 7-Year-Old Now Commutes." *New York Times*, February 7, 1974. Compare this with the events of the summer of 2008: Robbie Brown, "Frustration in the South as a Gasoline Shortage Drags On." *New York Times*, September 30, 2008.

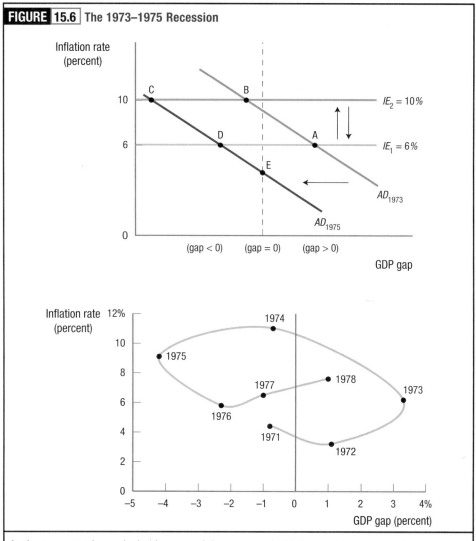

**FIGURE 15.6** | The 1973–1975 Recession

In the upper graph, we depict the state of the economy in 1973 with the aggregate demand ($AD_{1973}$) and inflation expectations [$IE_1(6\%)$] lines. In the fall of 1973, the OPEC oil-price shock shifted the $IE$ line upward. This increase predicts a negative GDP gap *and* an increase in the rate of inflation. The Fed reacted to this surge in inflation by undertaking a policy to boost aggregate demand. When inflation began to increase even higher, policy makers altered course and switched to a contractionary policy instead. This "second stage" of the recession is shown in the upper panel as the further leftward shift in the aggregate demand curve. With higher inflation expectations already in place, the policy of reducing aggregate demand aggravated the economic decline. As shown, this moved the economy from operating at point B to point C. The bottom panel of the figure shows that the model's predictions are consistent with actual outcomes. The price shock and the Fed's aggregate-demand-reducing policy produced a significant negative GDP gap in 1975 along with a high rate of inflation. As the effects of the oil-price shock abated, and the impact of such a large negative GDP gap took hold, the rate of inflation began to diminish, and the economy returned closer to a zero GDP gap.

*Source:* Federal Reserve Bank of St. Louis; author calculations

The idea was to adopt a monetary policy that would cushion the shocks to spending. When prices began to rise even faster, policy makers changed course. In the fall of 1974, worried that maintaining such an expansionary policy would only make inflation worse—the rate of inflation was already in double digits—the Fed switched to a contractionary policy instead. That is, the Fed wanted to *reduce* aggregate demand.

This "second stage" of the recession is shown in the upper panel of Figure 15.6 as the leftward shift in the aggregate demand curve to $AD_{1975}$. Notice that with the higher inflation expectations already in place—the public expected that inflation would simply continue to be as high as 10 percent—a policy of reducing aggregate demand would do nothing to reduce inflation in the near term. As the model predicts, it would only aggravate the decline in economic activity: it would make the GDP gap even more negative.

As we've illustrated it, this reaction should move the economy from operating at point B to operating at point C, which it did. The condition of the economy was so bad in late 1974 that the *Time* magazine cover for December 9, 1974 read "Recessions Greetings" and showed a bedraggled Santa Claus with an empty bag of toys. The lead article in this issue was titled "Gloomy Holidays—and Worse Ahead."

The model predicts that the combination of these two factors will lead to a decline in economic output relative to its potential—a negative GDP gap—and an increase in the rate of inflation. To see if these predictions are an accurate portrayal of what occurred, look at the bottom panel of Figure 15.6. The model does pretty well. Its predictions are consistent with what happened between 1973, when OPEC raised the price of oil, and 1974. Add to this the Fed's demand-reducing policy actions, and you should get an even larger drop in economic activity. The GDP gap became significantly more negative in 1975. Over the next few years, the effects of the oil-price shock abated, the rate of inflation began to diminish, and the economy returned to operating closer to a zero GDP gap by 1977 and 1978.

One thing to notice about this recession is that the rate of inflation (expected and actual) actually remained at a higher level after the 1973–1975 recession. This suggests that the economy drifted to a point more like D in the upper panel of Figure 15.6 than to E, the long-run outcome. Higher oil prices surely contributed to higher rates of inflation from 1973 through 1975. But after these prices stabilized at the higher level, they had no lasting effect on the rate of increase in the general level of prices. As you learned in Chapter 6, this is because the increase in oil prices is a relative price change. Think of it this way: if the price of some good (such as oil) doubles in a month, and all other goods' prices are fixed, the percentage change in the CPI for that month will be large. If all prices remain at their new levels from that month onward, the percentage change in the CPI—the measured inflation rate—will be zero.

So why didn't the rate of inflation drop back to the pre-OPEC rates? Although there continues to be some debate over this, one explanation for continued higher rates of inflation following the recession is that monetary policy remained expansionary until 1980. Although not shown in Figure 15.6, the rate of inflation continued to rise through the rest of the 1970s, matching up with the continued expansion in the supply of money (as predicted in Chapter 12).

## Recap

We have used these recessions in the United States to see how well our model performs. In most respects, the model passes muster. The AD-IE model predicts that we should observe a fall in the expected and actual rates of inflation when the GDP gap is negative, and we should observe an increase in expected and actual inflation when it is positive. Except for special factors that make every recession unique, that is basically what we see in the data.

## 15.5 Explaining Economic Fluctuations: Some Case Studies from Abroad

The model thus seems to fit the facts, at least as they pertain to U.S. recessions. Does it also work to explain economic fluctuations and inflation in other countries? To answer this question, let's use it to analyze recessions in Mexico and Canada.[7]

### Mexico

At the beginning of 1994, things looked rosy for the Mexican economy. The North American Free Trade Agreement (NAFTA) was scheduled to take effect, thus increasing trade between Mexico and the United States. It also led to increases in foreign investment in Mexican businesses. The Mexican government also had taken a number of reforms, which should have led to improved economic conditions. These reforms led to sharp reductions in the government's budget deficit and to the rate of inflation.

Although increased economic activity is normally a good thing, there were problems. Investment by businesses jumped to about 40 percent of GDP in 1994. Because many of the banks were not well equipped to properly screen borrowers, many overly risky businesses loans were made. In addition, Mexican bank regulators simply did not have the resources to adequately oversee the lending activities of the banks. These two factors led many Mexican banks to take inordinate risks when making loans.

The year 1994 also saw much political turmoil in Mexico. The ruling party's presidential candidate, Luis Donaldo Colosio, was assassinated in March. A bloody uprising occurred in the state of Chiapas. These events created the perfect storm of economic and political factors that culminated in a financial crisis. First, interest rates in Mexico jumped significantly on the news of the assassination. Because interest rates were increasing so rapidly and to much higher levels, this increased the likelihood that borrowers would default—cease to pay—on their loans. The rising interest rates also had an adverse effect on the Mexican stock market. Throughout 1994, the Mexican stock market was battered.[8]

The worsening political and economic conditions led foreign investors holding Mexican pesos to dump them as fast as they could. Because the Mexican government tried to keep the peso-dollar exchange rate in a fairly narrow band, it tried to intervene but simply could not stem the tide. On December 20, 1994, the Mexican central bank devalued the peso. By spring 1995, the peso was, relative to the U.S. dollar, worth about half as much as in late 1994. As a result, the rate of inflation spiked in early 1995. The economic and political events of 1994 led to a sharp reduction in economic activity in 1995, along with an increase in the rate of inflation.

Let's boil down the preceding set of events in terms of our AD-IE model. First, the sharply rising interest rates led to a reduction in consumer spending. After loans started to fail, banks curtailed lending to businesses, thus reducing investment. Given the anxiety over the stock market and financial markets in general, many households and businesses significantly reduced their spending. On both counts, this scenario

........

[7]We also have applied the model to recessions in the United Kingdom and Germany. It works there, too: we simply chose Mexico and Canada to keep the discussion manageable.

[8]"Stocks Drop Sharply with Mexico Strife." *New York Times*, January 4, 1994; Anthony DePalma, "World Markets; In Mexico, a Case of Political Jitters," *New York Times*, July 31, 1994.

predicts a drop in aggregate demand. Second, the devaluation of the peso made many goods and services more expensive, which led to a sharp increase in the rate of inflation. This description suggests that there would not only be a sharp decrease in aggregate demand but also an increase in the expected rate of inflation.

In the upper panel of **Figure 15.7**, we map out these effects using the AD-IE model. We start with the Mexican economy operating at point A. Because of the reduction in consumer spending and investment, the aggregate demand curve shifts to the left, from $AD_{1994}$ to $AD_{1997}$. At the same time, the inflation expectations increased, shifting the inflation expectations line upward, from $IE_1(10\%)$ to $IE_2(30\%)$. This moves the economy to point B. Unlike the oil-price-initiated increase in inflation expectations that occurred in the United States during the mid-1970s, however, Mexico's "price shock" came largely from the devaluation of its peso. The combination of these effects should be seen in economic activity falling below potential—a large, negative GDP gap—and an increase in the rate of inflation. Over time, we'd expect the economy to return to point C, a zero GDP gap and a lower rate of inflation.

The bottom panel illustrates just how the economic events played out. Between 1994 and 1995, the Mexican economy suffered a significant decline in output—the GDP gap dropped to over −5 percent. At the same time, the rate of inflation more than tripled, from less than 10 percent in 1994 to over 30 percent in 1995. As the crisis subsided, economic activity picked up, and the rate of inflation declined. By 1997, the Mexican economy had returned to operating at potential, although the rate of inflation remained slightly higher than it was in 1994. The events leading up to and after the 1995 recession in Mexico are consistent with the predictions of the model.

## Canada

The Canadian economy suffered a slump in economic activity that began in 1990 and continued throughout 1993. After a brief period of growth, the economic expansion slowed significantly beginning in 1995. This extended period of negative or low real GDP growth is sometimes called the "Great Canadian Slump." We focus on the initial stages of this period to further test drive our model.

A number of possible explanations have been offered to explain the slump in Canada's economy. Some people argue that the 1989 Free Trade Agreement (FTA) put Canada at a competitive disadvantage with its major trading partner, the United States. The data, however, do not support the notion that the FTA (and later the extension to Mexico via NAFTA) fueled the decline in Canadian economic activity. However, Canadian exports actually increased after 1989.[9] Other potential explanations include technology changes that led to increased unemployment in Canada, political uncertainty, and increases in the nation's minimum wage.

An important player during this episode was the Bank of Canada, the Canadian equivalent of the Federal Reserve. Beginning in 1989, the Bank of Canada began to focus its policies on one objective: lowering the rate of inflation as close to zero as possible. To achieve this objective, the Bank began to raise interest rates. By now you probably can guess what the outcome of this policy was. As interest rates rose, spending by consumers and investment spending by businesses dropped. As our model predicts, a reduction in these two components of expenditures should have led to a decline in aggregate demand and economic activity, with no immediate change in the rate of inflation. Is this what happened?

· · · · · · ·

[9]Clyde H. Farnsworth, "Canada's U.S. Trade Experience Fuels Opposition to the New Pact," *New York Times*, October 3, 1993.

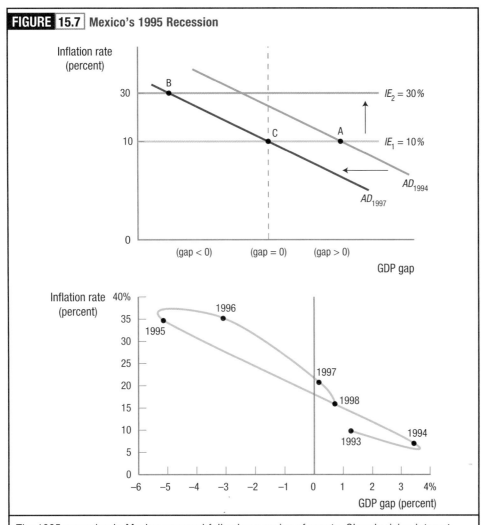

**FIGURE 15.7** | **Mexico's 1995 Recession**

The 1995 recession in Mexico occurred following a series of events. Sharply rising interest rates reduced consumer spending. Banks faced increased loan failures and curtailed lending, thus reducing businesses-investment spending. With households and businesses significantly reducing their spending, aggregate demand fell. At this time, the Mexican peso was devalued, increasing the rate of inflation. The upper panel maps this out. The economy is above its potential and is operating at point A. Reduced spending is captured by the aggregate demand curve shifting to the left; the increases in inflation and expectations of inflation are shown by the upward shift in the inflation expectations line. These move the economy to point B. Over time, the economy would tend toward point C: lower inflation and a return of real GDP growth to potential. The bottom panel shows that this prediction is fairly accurate. Between 1994 and 1995, the Mexican economy suffered a significant decline in output, and the rate of inflation more than tripled. As the crisis subsided, economic activity picked up (the gap closed), and the rate of inflation declined. By 1997, the Mexican economy was operating a little bit above its potential and, although the rate of inflation remained higher than it was in 1994, it was much lower than in 1996.

*Source:* Ebrima Faal, "GDP Growth, Potential Output, and Output Gaps in Mexico." IMF Working Paper (1993); and author calculations

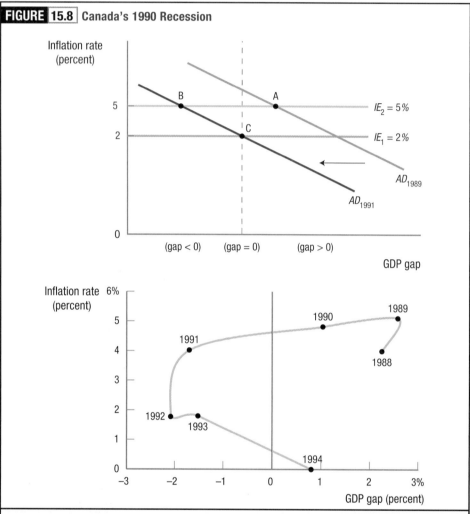

**FIGURE 15.8** | Canada's 1990 Recession

Beginning in 1989, the Bank of Canada focused on lowering the rate of inflation. The Bank began to raise real interest rates to reduce consumer spending and business investment. Starting from its condition before the slump, designated as point A in the upper panel, the Bank's policy should have lowered aggregate demand, which we show as a leftward shift in the aggregate demand curve. As the economy moved from point A to point B, the GDP gap would became negative and the inflation rate—actual and expected—would not be immediately affected. Over time, the economy would shift to point C, with the GDP gap back to zero at a lower rate of inflation. The lower panel of Figure 15.8 indicates that this predicted outcome is very close to what actually occurred in Canada. During the 1990–1991 period, the recession was associated with a negative GDP gap and a slight moderation in inflation. The negative gap put downward pressure on the rate of inflation such that, by 1994, the rate of inflation approached zero while the economy had returned to operating close to its potential.

*Source:* International Monetary Fund; author calculations

The upper panel of **Figure 15.8** shows the Canadian economy before the slump, say, point A. In 1989, it was operating with a positive GDP gap; inflation—both actual and expected—was about 5 percent. The Bank of Canada's policy to increase interest rates should have lowered aggregate demand, which we have illustrated by the leftward shift in the aggregate demand curve from $AD_{1989}$ to $AD_{1991}$. This moved the economy from point A to point B, in the short run. The output of goods and services should have declined, economic activity should have fallen below potential GDP, and the economy should have entered a recession. At first the expected inflation rate would be little affected. Over time, the expected rate of inflation should fall and the economy resume operating closer to its potential. Over time, the prediction is that the economy should return to operating at something like point C in the figure.

The lower panel of Figure 15.8 indicates that this predicted outcome is very close to what actually occurred in Canada. The slump that began in late 1990 was sharp and reduced the level of economic activity with little effect on expected inflation. The decline in economic activity put downward pressure on the rate of inflation. By 1994, the rate of inflation in Canada reached zero as economic activity had once again returned to potential. As with the other examples, the model seems to be a pretty useful tool in terms of analyzing the onset of the Great Canadian Slump.

**ECONOMIC FALLACY**  Recessions occur naturally.

**False.** Common wisdom states that recessions just seem to happen. Sometimes people argue that a long-running economic expansion just runs out of steam. There is even some evidence to suggest that policy makers took this view as the economic expansion of the 1990s continued. Of course, by now you know that this is not true. Expansions end and recessions begin because of some change in aggregate demand, some shift in inflation, or both. The fact that recessions can occur because of policy missteps makes understanding policy actions extremely important. The weather and the pricing policy of oil-producing countries can't be controlled. Nations can, however, try to manage their fiscal and monetary policies to avoid mistakes that lead to economic downturns.

## 15.6 A "Real" Theory of Economic Fluctuations?

Our examples provide a fairly strong case for why most economists believe that economic fluctuations stem from changes in aggregate demand. But you have learned, too, that sometimes recessions are associated with significant price shocks. The oil-price shocks that impacted the U.S. economy (and others) in the 1970s stand out in this regard. Some economists believe, however, that economic fluctuations usually are due to shocks on the production side of the economy. This view, called the **real business cycle theory (RBC)**, is based on the idea that changes in productivity, not in aggregate demand, explain observed fluctuations in the economy's production of goods and services.

**REAL BUSINESS CYCLE THEORY (RBC)** The theory that fluctuations in real economic activity occur because of shocks to productivity, not because of changes in aggregate demand.

Recall that increased productivity is a key factor that explains economic growth *over time*. RBC theorists argue that changes in productivity also can explain *short-term* economic fluctuations. The story goes like this: an economy is expanding along its potential growth path. This economic growth is due to some combination of labor, capital, and, most importantly, advances in knowledge (or technology), which fuel productivity growth. When productivity increases faster than its long-term trend, more factories are built, more workers are employed, and more income is generated. This in turn leads the economy to grow faster than its potential. According to RBC theory, if an increase in productivity can cause real GDP growth to increase faster than potential, then a decline in productivity growth can cause economic activity to slow relative to potential. That is, a negative productivity shock can cause a recession.

At this point, you might be wondering the following: Because productivity growth is based on an increase in knowledge, shouldn't a decline in productivity growth be associated with a *decrease* in knowledge? In other words, do we stop using computers and go back to using manual typewriters or pencils and paper? This literal interpretation pushes the boundaries of reality, of course. However, it is the question that RBC theory has failed to completely answer, which has left the theory subject to debate.

## 15.7  Do Government Actions Stabilize the Economy?

The questions raised by RBC theorists have caused economists to reassess the validity of the aggregate-demand-based approach to explaining economic fluctuations. Think of it: If economic fluctuations really do stem from changes in productivity, what role do government policies aimed at stabilizing aggregate demand play? Are the economic stimulus packages that governments initiate during recessions really effective, or are they just political window dressing with no lasting impact on economic activity? In other words, should the government intervene any time the economy is operating above or below its potential GDP?

One way to answer these questions is to gauge whether or not policy actions by, say, the U.S. government has reduced economic fluctuations. Most modern governments try to manage their economies. This statement does not necessarily mean that more government intervention is preferable, however. For example, before 1980, the Fed's policy efforts focused on keeping the economy growing and unemployment rates low, even at the expense of higher rates of inflation. The success of this policy is questionable: *nine* recessions occurred between 1945 and 1984. Since 1985, however, the Federal Reserve has focused more on keeping inflation low. Until the recent events of 2007–2009, the number and depth of recessions had declined dramatically, compared to the pre-1980s.

Consider this twist. RBC theory, as you have just learned, is based on the idea that economic fluctuations are caused by changes in productivity. The theory assumes that the economy behaves like a perfectly competitive market. That is, prices and quantities freely and rapidly adjust to changes in market forces. We know that this just isn't true. Contracts keep wages from adjusting instantaneously to changes in the labor market, for example. Still, for the sake of theory, it is a simplifying assumption and must not be dismissed out of hand. The RBC model, and variations of it, suggests that there really isn't any need for governments to intervene. If prices and quantities are quickly moving toward their equilibrium outcomes, the economy will cycle around its potential output because of changes in productivity. Because it is arguable that the government has little control over productivity, government intervention will not help stave off these fluctuations.

Here is the interesting part of the story: RBC models actually do a fairly good job of mimicking the behavior of the economy. That is, they are able to map out the economy's ups and downs fairly well even though they don't acknowledge that changes in monetary or fiscal policy affect the pace of economic output. Putting it slightly differently, RBC theories seem to "work" even though they take no government policy actions into account. Nobel Prize-winning economist Robert Lucas, Jr. suggests that this outcome is because government policies in the postwar period, and maybe even more since 1980, have not been as intrusive as they used to be, and those making policies have learned a great deal more about how the economy works.

The behavior of the economy over the past 50 years provides clues to which policy actions were taken and their economic costs. The scenario of trying to maintain a positive GDP gap—trying to push real GDP above its potential—is not a bad depiction of the period from 1960 to 1980. Perhaps not too surprisingly, during this era, the rate of inflation rose from a couple of percent in the early 1960s to double-digit rates by 1980. As policy makers tried to sustain the economy's expansion, they appeared willing through their actions to accept higher rates of inflation as the trade-off of maintaining economic growth and low unemployment rates.

The inflationary outcome of this policy reached its apex in 1980. As we have explained, from this point onward, policy actions seemed to be more directed toward lowering the rate of inflation and keeping it low.

## WHAT YOU SHOULD HAVE LEARNED FROM CHAPTER 15

- That decreases in aggregate demand have important effects on real GDP growth.
- That, if large enough, such decreases in aggregate demand can lead to recessions.
- That negative GDP gaps tend to be associated with reductions in the inflation rate.
- That positive GDP gaps tend to be associated with increases in the inflation rate.
- That price shocks (sometimes called supply shocks) can create a negative GDP gap and a recession.
- That the AD-IE model provides a good approximation of economic fluctuations in many situations, both in the United States and in other countries.
- That a challenge to the aggregate-demand-based view of economic fluctuations comes from the real business cycle theory (RBC), which views economic fluctuations as caused by changes in productivity.
- That government intervention may not always stabilize economic activity.

## KEY TERMS

Recession, p. 396

Expansion, p. 396

Real Business Cycle Theory (RBC), p. 417

## QUESTIONS AND PROBLEMS

1. A rule-of-thumb definition of a recession is six months (two quarters) of negative real GDP growth. Is this the definition that the NBER uses? Why or why not?

2. Some people argue that recessions are a naturally occurring event. Based on your reading of this chapter, do you agree? Explain your answer, and give evidence to support it.

3. During the Great Depression, it was thought that the economy was "stuck" in a condition where the GDP gap was negative. What would need to occur for this to be true?

4. It is fall 2009, and the economy is showing signs of recovery from the recession. It appears that the fiscal stimulus spending and the lowering of interest rates have done their job of increasing aggregate demand. Looking forward a couple

of years, if you are the chairman of the Federal Reserve, what are you starting to worry about? What would be your policy response today? Do you think this policy will be popular?

5. The fiscal stimulus package helped shorten the recession of 2007–2009. Based on this success, politicians call for even more government spending to raise GDP growth permanently. As an advisor to Senator Smart, use the AD-IE model to explain to the senator why this may not be a good idea.

6. As the economy recovered from the 2001 recession, some claimed that it was a "jobless recovery." By that, they meant that even though real GDP was increasing, it wasn't increasing fast enough to cause firms to rehire laid-off employees or to create new jobs. The unemployment rate didn't decline very rapidly. Is it possible to have positive economic growth but not have the unemployment rate decline to its prerecession level? Use the AD-IE model to explain your answer. Also, think about this situation within the context of the production possibilities frontier (PPF).

7. In the 2006 volume of the publication *World Economics*, one of the articles claims that the United Kingdom had entered a period of macroeconomic stability. The author claims that this stability stems from the policy decisions made by the European Central Bank (ECB). Find economic data for the United Kingdom for the period since 2006, and determine whether the author was correct.

8. Your parents' friend Bill believes (and constantly reminds you, the economics student) that the recession of 2001 occurred because of the 9/11 attacks. Is he correct? Could he be correct if the focus was on the recovery from the recession?

9. Why does it take the NBER so long to date the beginning and the end of a recession? To assist you in forming your answer, visit the www.NBER.org Web site, and click on the link to the NBER Business Cycle Dating Committee.

10. Given the makeup of aggregate demand, can a noneconomic event lead to a recession? Think of the aftermath of the 9/11 attacks or the political turmoil in Mexico during 1994. Be sure to explain the spending channels through which such events can affect aggregate demand.

11. In footnote 2, we refer to the 1982 *New York Times* article "The Fed vs. the White House: A Collision Is Brewing over the Course of the Recovery." Basically, the Fed was following a policy to reduce inflation, and the White House was worried about upcoming congressional elections. Use the AD-IE model to illustrate the conflict between these two positions. Which side would you take, and why?

12. The idea behind the real business cycle theory (RBC) is that changes in productivity give rise to recessions and expansions. If such productivity "shocks" show themselves in shifts in the inflation expectations line, should policy makers try to use fiscal or monetary policy to offset such shocks? Does your answer depend on which economic variable—the GDP gap or inflation—is the measure you are attempting to influence?

# PART 5

## Policy Debates

**P**art 5 discusses how government policies can affect the economy, and the role the government should play in an effort to do so. We scrutinize various policy measures to see if they actually worked or not. You will learn that macroeconomic policy prescriptions are not set in stone but are constantly evolving. This means that the government sometimes implements the wrong policies. We also examine the rationale for why governments and central banks—fiscal and monetary policymakers, respectively—might find it difficult to fine-tune the macroeconomic activity of economies.

# Fiscal Policy

*"There are $10^{11}$ stars in the galaxy. That used to be a huge number. But it's only a hundred billion. It's less than the national deficit! We used to call them astronomical numbers. Now we should call them economical numbers."*

*Richard Feynman,*
*noted U.S. physicist*

People often argue about taxes and government spending, or just how big the U.S. government's deficit is. Starting in 2008, it seemed like everyone had an opinion about how big the government's stimulus plan needed to be to push the economy out of the Great Recession. During the 2010 election, taxes were the hot topic. All this arguing is about what we call *fiscal policy*. Fiscal policy relates to the government's policy actions when it changes taxes and spending. These actions include passing legislation to enact stimulus packages, extend unemployment benefits, raise or lower taxes, and so on. Although the decision makers in the city and state you live in also make decisions on spending and tax issues, in this chapter we will focus on the fiscal-policy actions taken by the federal government.

The federal government changes its fiscal policies from time to time to achieve some social goal, such as increasing health-care coverage for those at lower levels of income or the elderly. It also changes policies when trying to cushion the effects of a recession. An example of using fiscal policy for this purpose is the series of stimulus packages designed to keep the economy from sliding further into the recession that began in late 2007. The first stimulus, announced by the Bush administration in early 2008, amounted to about $170 billion in funds distributed to individuals through tax rebates. A year later, the Obama administration was pushing through another stimulus package. That package of tax cuts and government spending totaled more than $800 billion.

We already have used the term fiscal policy in earlier chapters when we derived and used aggregate demand. There we analyzed how changes in government spending affect economic fluctuations. In those chapters, we mostly talked about government spending. In this chapter, we will dig a bit deeper. We now want to see just what fiscal policy is and how it works or doesn't work. You will learn about federal budget deficits, how these are related to the government's overall debt, the theory behind fiscal-policy actions, and just how effective they are in terms of altering economic activity. Having you understand what fiscal-policy actions can and cannot achieve is the objective of this chapter. By the time you finish reading this chapter, you will be better informed about the issues that surround government spending and taxes.

## 16.1  A Common Misconception about Fiscal Policy

Before we get too deep into the various aspects of fiscal policy, let's deal with a popular, though incorrect, notion of how the government operates. The federal government's finances are not just like those of any business or your family. Yet you sometimes hear people say "The government has to balance its books just like any business." Or, "You cannot run a negative balance in your checkbook and neither can the government." Unlike a business, the government's spending decisions are not affected by the constraint of making a profit or going out of business.

If a government spends more than it takes in, it can finance the difference by borrowing. Businesses (and individuals) also do this, but they cannot keep borrowing if they ever hope to turn a profit. Unlike businesses, however, governments have another avenue other than borrowing to raise funds: they can raise taxes. So, for the most part, governments finance their activities by borrowing, by taxing, or both. Sources of these funds include individuals, corporations, and even foreign entities. While the U.S. government cannot tax the citizens of Canada or China, individuals there may opt to lend money to the U.S. government by purchasing U.S. Treasury bonds.

If governments can simply borrow and tax, would they ever run into financial difficulties? If businesses can go bankrupt, can governments? Although most governments do not go out of business, some do "fail" in the sense that no one is willing to lend them money. In 1998, for example, the Russian government defaulted on its outstanding debt. In other words, if you owned a Russian savings bond, you would not be able to redeem it.[1] The situation was resolved, and the Russian government was able to borrow in financial markets. The state of California faced a similar crisis in 2008. Because of poor economic conditions, the government's revenues fell sharply relative to spending commitments. The real possibility that California might default on its debt led to a substantial increase in the interest rate charged by potential lenders.[2] The Greek debt crisis of 2010 and 2011 is yet another example of how even governments should not live beyond their means. Although these governments did not shut their doors, there were cutbacks in government services, so they did "fail" in one sense of the word.

## 16.2  Federal Budget Deficits and Surpluses

The federal **budget deficit** is, by definition, the gap between what the U.S. federal government spends and the revenues it takes in. A budget deficit occurs when the government's outlays are greater than its receipts. When the government's outlays are less than its receipts, there's a **budget surplus**.

· · · · · · ·

[1]Paul Blustein, "Russia's Financial Crisis Worsens." *Washington Post,* June 2, 1998: A1.

[2]Micahel B. Marois, "California Bond Yields Rise to Four-Year High on Budget Impasse." Bloomberg.com, December 26, 2008.

**BUDGET DEFICIT** A budget deficit occurs when government outlays exceed government revenues.

EXAMPLE In 2009, the federal government's outlays were $3.52 trillion, and its receipts were $2.11 trillion. The difference, –$1.41 trillion, was the budget deficit for the year.

**BUDGET SURPLUS** A budget surplus occurs when government receipts exceed government outlays.

EXAMPLE In 2000, the government's outlays were $1.79 trillion dollars, and its receipts were $2.02 trillion. The difference, $230 billion, was the budget surplus for the year.

Did you notice that we used the word "outlays" instead of "spending" to define these two key terms? Recall from Chapter 13 that government outlays include the government's purchases of newly produced goods and services along with the transfer payments it makes for programs such as Social Security, the interest payments it makes to people and businesses that have loaned it money, and so on. For this discussion, outlays better reflects entirely how the government uses the money it takes in.

Have you noticed that almost everyone talks about federal budget *deficits* rather than federal budget *surpluses*? This is because the federal budget has been in surplus in only 6 of the past 50 years, four of which occurred in the late 1990s. **Figure 16.1** shows

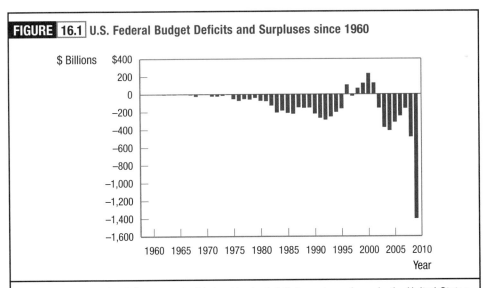

**FIGURE 16.1** U.S. Federal Budget Deficits and Surpluses since 1960

This figure shows the dollar amount of federal budget deficits and surpluses in the United States since 1960. The deficits steadily worsened (became more negative) in the 1970s and 1980s. Although the deficits shrank and turned to surpluses by 2000, the reversal was short-lived. Beginning in 2002, budget deficits returned. Notice that major increases in the deficit usually occur in conjunction with an economic downturn. This is true for the increase in the deficits that occurred in the mid-1970s, the early 1980s, the early 2000s, and obviously in 2009.

*Source:* Council of Economic Advisers

the federal budget deficits and surpluses in the United States since 1960. You can see that the deficit steadily worsened (fell further into negative territory) in the 1970s and 1980s. Although the deficits shrank and eventually turned to surpluses in the late 1990s, this reversal was short-lived. Beginning in 2002, budget deficits returned.

Figure 16.1 shows that major increases in the deficit usually occur in conjunction with an economic downturn. The increase in the deficits that occurred around the recessions of the mid-1970s, the early 1980s, and the early 2000s are examples of this link. Although the deficits shrank during the latter half of the 1980s, a period of sustained economic growth, they again began to grow during the 1990 recession and persisted until 1995.

The 1990s stand out as a rather unique period when you look at budget deficits in the United States. After the economy began to recover following the recession of 1990, deficits began to decline (became less negative) and eventually turned into a surplus for the first time in more than 25 years. There was much political rhetoric about the return of budget surpluses. This political rhetoric was not matched by what eventually happened, though: deficits returned to the United States by 2002, in part because of the 2001 recession. Since then, because of increased outlays relative to receipts, the budget has stayed in the red.

The deficit surged in 2009, increasing to well over $1 trillion. This increase in the deficit stems from the effects of the Great Recession, which occurred between December 2007 and June 2009. Because of the severity of that downturn, government revenues from taxes levied on workers and corporations declined sharply. Combined with the massive increase in federal spending to fight the recession's economic impacts, the deficit swelled.

Looking at Figure 16.1, you might argue that the deficits of the past decade were much worse than ever before. After all, isn't a $400 billion deficit worse than a $200 billion deficit? Such a comparison is often made, and, technically, it is correct: 400 *is* bigger than 200. But from an economic point of view, the *absolute* size of the deficit can be very misleading. What's important in economic analysis is the size of the deficit *relative to* the overall size of the economy. Think of it this way: you are a doctor and asked to prescribe a dietary plan for a patient you haven't met. If you are told the patient weighs 300 pounds, would you consider that person obese and in need of a low-calorie diet? This absolute number could mislead your decision. Shouldn't your prescription depend on whether the person is 5 feet tall or 7 feet tall? Similarly, a $500 billion deficit has very different policy and economic implications for a $1 trillion economy than a $10 trillion economy.

Let's put the deficit into a useful perspective. **Figure 16.2** shows the deficit *as a percent* of GDP since 1960. The general pattern of the deficit measured in this way is similar to that in Figure 16.1. Note, however, that the puny absolute deficits of the 1960s now look fairly sizable when measured relative to the overall size of the economy. The deficits in the 1980s again stand out as large by modern standards, reaching a high of 6 percent of GDP in 1983.

What about the size of recent deficits? The 2004 deficit was about $413 billion. In dollar terms, this was a record for the period after World War II. When measured as a percent of GDP, however, the 2004 deficit becomes only the eleventh largest deficit over the past 50 years. As is obvious from Figure 16.2, however, the deficit of 2009 is (so far) the largest, in dollar terms or in percentage terms, than any in the last half century. Although the deficits in this century have been large in dollar terms, until 2009, they actually were not unprecedented when measured relative to the overall size of the economy.

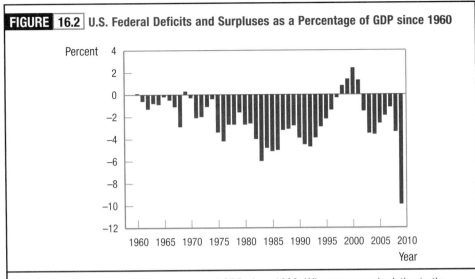

**FIGURE 16.2** | U.S. Federal Deficits and Surpluses as a Percentage of GDP since 1960

This figure shows the deficit *as a percent* of GDP since 1960. When measured relative to the size of the economy, the "small" deficits of the 1960s now look fairly sizable. The deficits in the 1980s again stand out, reaching a high of 6 percent of GDP in 1983. The deficit of 2009, measured in dollar terms or as a percent of GDP, is the largest since 1960.

*Source:* Council of Economic Advisers

## 16.3 Federal Outlays and Federal Receipts

Explaining why the federal budget deficit has changed over time requires that we look into what makes up the deficit numbers. To understand why the deficit grew or shrank, we need to consider how and why the government's outlays and receipts changed over time and the effect this had.

**Figure 16.3** shows the U.S. government's outlays and receipts, both measured relative to GDP, since 1960. Beginning in the 1960s, outlays began to increase relative to receipts. The growth in government outlays, in other words, was faster than the growth of the overall economy. The increase in outlays reflects the fact that the federal government was expanding its social-insurance programs, such as Medicare and Social Security. The expansion of these programs slowed in the 1980s when the federal government shifted some of the responsibility for financing social programs to the states. Although the switch actually began in the Carter administration, the Reagan administration accelerated it. In the late 1970s, the federal government provided about 25 percent of the funding for state and local programs such as housing, education, and mass transit. By the end of the 1980s, federal funding to the states had fallen to 17 percent.[3] Note that receipts, which had hovered around 17 percent of GDP for several decades, also began to increase sharply in the 1990s. This sharp increase in receipts and the slowing increase in outlays explain the budget surplus of the late 1990s.

The sharp divergence of outlays and receipts in 2009 again reflects the impact of the 2007–2009 recession. Government outlays rose sharply as increased federal

. . . . . . .

[3]Michael deCourcy Hinds and Erik Eckholm, "80's Leave States and Cities in Need." *New York Times,* December 20, 1990.

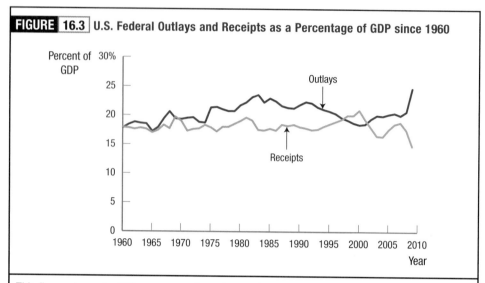

**FIGURE 16.3** | U.S. Federal Outlays and Receipts as a Percentage of GDP since 1960

This figure shows the U.S. government's outlays and receipts, both measured relative to GDP. Beginning in the 1960s, outlays began to increase relative to receipts. The increase in outlays reflected the federal government's expansion of social-insurance programs, such as Medicare and Social Security. Receipts, which were around 17 percent of GDP for several decades, began to increase in the 1990s. This sharp increase in receipts and the slowing increase in outlays led to the budget surplus of the late 1990s. The recent divergence between outlays and receipts reflects the 2007–2009 recession.

*Source:* Council of Economic Advisers

spending was used to help dampen the effects of the downturn. At the same time, receipts—mostly tax revenues—fell due to the sharp decline in personal and business income. These two counteracting forces explain the bulge in the deficit shown in Figures 16.1 and 16.2. With this look at the history of outlays and receipts, let's take a quick look at more specifically what both outlays and receipts consist of.

## Federal Outlays

As you learned in Chapter 13, federal outlays consist of both the government's purchases of goods and services and its transfer payments to individuals. Transfer payments, however, are not payments for goods and services used by the government. Instead, they are payments the government makes to individuals that essentially reallocate the income among them. Social-insurance programs such as Social Security and Medicaid are programs that involve transfer payments. In addition, government-retiree pensions, unemployment-insurance payments, social-welfare programs, subsidies to farmers, and benefit payments to veterans are all lumped under the heading of transfer payments.

**Interest payments** are another component of government outlays. When the government borrows funds to finance its activities, whether for purchases or for transfer payments, it must compensate those who loan it the funds. This compensation is in the form of interest payments on the bonds that the government sells to investors. Interest payments are not a small part of government outlays. The large deficits, the need to fund them, and high interest rates during the inflationary 1970s and early 1980s combined to raise the net-interest payment portion of government outlays.

Why worry about net-interest payments? According to Nobel Laureate in economics James Tobin, paying interest on the funds borrowed "absorbs private saving that otherwise could be channeled to investments that will benefit Americans in the future—homes; new plants and modern equipment; education and research; schools, sewers, roads provided by state and local governments; and income-earning properties in foreign nations."[4]

**INTEREST PAYMENTS** The interest paid by the government to holders of its outstanding debt.

**EXAMPLE** In July, Barbara bought a U.S. Treasury bill with a three-month maturity. She paid $9,000 for the government security. At the end of three months, she received a check for $10,000. The difference is counted as an interest payment by the government.

**EXAMPLE** If the Japanese government holds $600 billion in U.S. government securities, and the average interest rate is 5 percent, the U.S. government will make an interest payment to the Japanese government of $30 billion.

To see how priorities have changed, **Figure 16.4** shows the distribution of the major components of the government's outlays in 2009 and in 1960. In 2009, the largest single component—nearly two-thirds—was spent on *human resources*. This piece of the

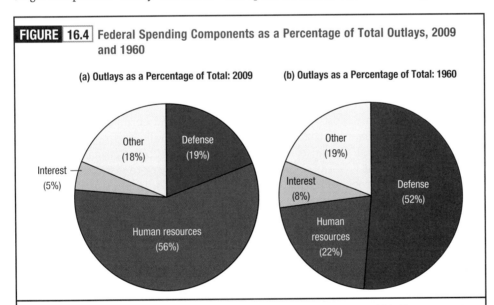

**FIGURE 16.4** Federal Spending Components as a Percentage of Total Outlays, 2009 and 1960

**(a) Outlays as a Percentage of Total: 2009**

- Other (18%)
- Defense (19%)
- Interest (5%)
- Human resources (56%)

**(b) Outlays as a Percentage of Total: 1960**

- Other (19%)
- Interest (8%)
- Defense (52%)
- Human resources (22%)

The major components of the government's outlays in 2009 are shown in panel (a). The same components for 1960 are shown in panel (b). The largest single component in 2009 was money spent on human resources (56 percent), one-fifth of which went to meeting Social Security payments. National defense was the second largest category (19 percent), the government's interest payments were 5 percent, and "other" payments, such as those for physical resources (energy, natural resources, and transportation), international affairs, and general science and technology, make up the rest. In 1960, defense spending was more than one-half of total outlays. In contrast, outlays for human resources were about one-fifth percent of the total. However, in 2009, spending on human resources was the single largest component, and defense spending accounted for less than a one-fifth of spending.

*Source:* Council of Economic Advisers

· · · · · · ·

[4]James Tobin, "How to Think about the Deficit." *The New York Review of Books* (September 25, 1986).

spending pie includes spending on health benefits, Medicare, Social Security, and income-security payments, such as veterans' benefits. Of these components, over one-fifth of total government outlays went to meeting Social Security payments. The outlays for a program such as Social Security are often referred to as intergenerational transfers. When you work and pay into the Social Security system (the deduction is listed under FICA on your paycheck), your "contribution" helps pay someone's monthly check. If we assume that the majority of Social Security recipients are elderly, then the funds are being transferred between generations. *National defense* is the second largest category (19 percent). The government's *interest payment* to those who have lent it money accounted for about 5 percent of total outlays. Payments for physical resources (energy, natural resources, and transportation), international affairs, and general science and technology, are captured in the catchall *other* category, which amounted to nearly 18 percent of outlays.

How has the size of the major components of federal outlays (measured as a percent of GDP) changed since 1960? There are two conspicuous changes. One is the dramatic decline in defense spending; the other is the equally dramatic increase in outlays for human resources. In 1960, defense spending chewed up more than half of total outlays. In contrast, outlays for human resources were about 22 percent of the total. This marked increase in the proportion of outlays going to social programs started in the 1960s when many social-insurance programs were created by Congress, and the coverage of existing programs, such as Social Security, was expanded. Today, outlays for human resources represent the single largest component of government expenditures. The bottom line is that over the past 50 years, the government's spending priority has shifted toward redistributing funds between individuals in the economy.

## Federal Receipts

**Federal receipts** come mostly from the taxes citizens and corporations pay. However, the economic reality is that the federal tax burden falls disproportionately on individual citizens. That's because, in a sense, corporations do not pay taxes: the taxes they pay is money that is not used to build up the company or to distribute to owners of the corporation (stockholders) in the form of dividends. In a sense, it ultimately is the people who are their employees or own the stock of corporations who bear the economic burden of corporate taxes.

**FEDERAL RECEIPTS** The total of federal taxes and other fees collected by the government.

**EXAMPLE** On April 15 each year, many people file their federal income taxes. Along with the forms, they mail in a check to the federal government. Those tax payments are a receipt to the government.

**Figure 16.5** shows which groups account for most of the federal government's tax receipts in 2009 and in 1960. The *individual income taxes* paid by people like you in 2009 amounted to 43 percent of the total receipts taken in by the federal government. The other major component of the government's receipts is the taxes paid by firms and employees to fund social-insurance programs, listed in the figure as *Social Security*. Receipts from *corporate income taxes* come in third, followed by the ever-present *"other"* category. The other category includes excise taxes, which are federal taxes on alcohol, tobacco, telephone service, and gasoline. The "other" category also includes receipts from estate and gift taxes and customs and duties fees, among others. Of these, estate

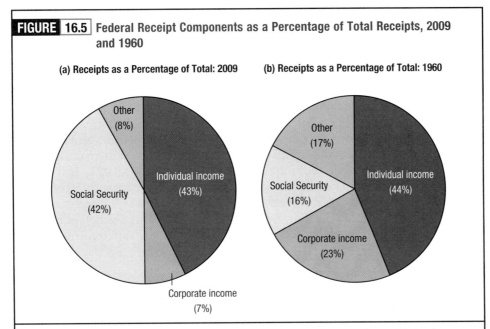

**FIGURE 16.5** Federal Receipt Components as a Percentage of Total Receipts, 2009 and 1960

**(a) Receipts as a Percentage of Total: 2009**

Other (8%)
Social Security (42%)
Individual income (43%)
Corporate income (7%)

**(b) Receipts as a Percentage of Total: 1960**

Other (17%)
Social Security (16%)
Individual income (44%)
Corporate income (23%)

Panel (a) shows that individual income taxes amounted to 43 percent of the total federal government receipts in 2009. The second major source of tax income came from firms and employees funding social-insurance programs. Other taxes (estate and gift taxes, customs and duties, etc.) and corporate income tax receipts came in a close second and third, respectively. The share of total receipts accounted for by individual income taxes has been fairly steady since 1960. However, corporate tax receipts have fallen over time: in 1960, they were almost 25 percent of total tax receipts, compared with just 7 percent in 2009. The most dramatic change has been Social Security. Since 1960, Social Security taxes have increased from 16 percent to 42 percent as a proportion of total tax receipts.

*Source:* Council of Economic Advisers

taxes—sometimes called "death taxes"—often get a lot of press. Supporters of such taxes often point to equity issues: the rich and their heirs should pay their "fair" share on wealth passed between generations. Detractors argue that such taxes lessen the incentive for individuals to leave an estate for their heirs.[5]

Like Figure 16.4, Figure 16.5 shows that there have been some major changes in where the federal government collects taxes over time. Although different presidents have altered marginal tax rates since 1960, the share of total receipts accounted for by individual income taxes has remained fairly steady over the past 50 years. In 1960, individual income taxes accounted for 44 percent of total receipts, and, in 2009, they were about 43 percent. In contrast, corporate tax revenues have fallen over time. In 1960, they were almost a quarter of tax receipts; in 2009, they were 7 percent.

The most dramatic change has occurred in receipts associated with Social Security. Between 1960 and 2009, Social Security taxes collected as a proportion of total tax receipts has more than doubled, increasing from 16 percent in 1960 to 42 percent

· · · · · · ·

[5]Edward Prescott, "Death and Taxes." *Wall Street Journal*, June 1, 2006.

in 2009. Today, this category rivals individual income taxes as a fraction of overall tax receipts.

Not only do some economists consider the overall tax burden an important issue, but an important concern also is whether a tax is progressive or regressive. The individual income tax is an example of a **progressive tax**. As your income rises, there are break-points where you shift into a higher tax bracket. To illustrate this idea, suppose you make $8,000 during the summer working at the local mall. If this income is subject to a tax rate of 10 percent, you would pay $800 in income taxes. If you made $9,000, however, you would pay $800 plus 15 percent on each dollar between $8,025 and $9,000. This 15-percent tax is called the marginal tax rate. It is the tax you pay on each additional dollar of income over $8,025. This type of tax scheme is progressive because the marginal tax rates increase with higher levels of income. In recent years, the highest marginal tax rate was 35 percent, which was paid on each additional dollar made over $357,700. (This example is based on you filing as a single individual. The marginal tax rates are different for married couples.)

> **PROGRESSIVE TAX** A tax that takes a larger percentage of your income as your income rises.

> **EXAMPLE** Debra received a pay raise. Because of this, she was pushed into a higher tax bracket and now pays more in taxes on each extra dollar earned.

What is a **regressive tax**? We mentioned that excise taxes are part of government receipts. A good example of an excise tax is the tax levied on alcohol and tobacco products: the so-called sin taxes. Such taxes are often viewed as regressive. To see this, think of two individuals who purchase a six-pack of beer every week. One person has an income of $100,000 a year; the other makes $10,000. Suppose that the tax on beer increases from zero to $2 per six-pack. Because both individuals buy the same amount of beer every week, the additional $104 tax-caused increase in annual beer expenditures hits the lower-income individual harder than the higher-income person. For the lower-income individual, the additional $104 now being spent on beer is 1 percent of his annual income. For the higher-income person, however, it is only 0.1 percent of her annual income. A tax is regressive, then, if it affects lower-income individuals proportionately more than it affects those with higher incomes.

> **REGRESSIVE TAX** A tax that requires you to pay proportionally more as your income falls.

> **EXAMPLE** Some states have sales taxes on groceries. The sales tax is regressive because Janet, who makes $20,000 a year, pays the same tax on a loaf of bread as Don, who makes $200,000.

Leaving aside the issue of regressivity, how does the "burden" of taxes compare across countries? That is, where does the United States stand in comparison with other countries? To give you an idea, the Organization for Economic Cooperation and Development (OECD) compared tax burdens across countries by measuring the percent of labor costs paid in income and social security taxes by an average single worker with no children. The OECD found that in 2008 these two taxes amounted to about 23 percent of labor costs for the U.S. worker, placing the United States in about the middle of the pack of 30 countries studied. Who had the highest tax burden? In Denmark, these two taxes amounted to over 40 percent of labor costs. In Mexico, however, income and social security taxes paid by workers amounted to less than 5 percent of labor costs.

## Summary

Why have tax receipts increased over time? The simple answer is to pay for increased government outlays; that is, to fund government programs. The increase in federal government outlays indicates that the government has taken on a bigger role in the economy than in the past. In some instances, this arguably is best. Examples where the government is probably better suited to provide the goods or services are the building and maintenance of roads and bridges, and in providing national defense.

To a greater extent than in the past, many individuals in the economy prefer that the federal government, rather than the private sector, provide them with certain goods and services. Although it is easy to point fingers at "special interests" and blame "them" for this change, we all are part of some special interest. Farmers receiving payments not to produce certain crops, those receiving Social Security or Medicare payments, federal government retirees, students on subsidized student-loan programs, and university professors getting federal research grants do not want to have their government-based benefits reduced. Remember that governments do not act in a vacuum: the actions of governments usually reflect politically acceptable outcomes. Otherwise, those outcomes would not occur, or they would be changed. Notice we say "usually." The amount of government corruption and poverty in countries around the world, as we documented in Chapter 11, shows that the political will of a nation's citizens doesn't always prevail.

More often than not, what people debate is the extent to which the government should provide goods and services, such as Medicare, social programs for the elderly and the poor, and even education. In recent years, this has become known as the debate over "entitlements." Recall that we first talked about entitlements in Chapter 7. Are you *entitled* to health care, *entitled* to a college education, and *entitled* to a guaranteed income in retirement? Simply increasing taxes to pay for some government program, however beneficial it may seem, has economic costs and consequences that must be recognized.

Trade-offs, as you learned in Chapter 2, are involved in any decision, whether it's a personal decision to buy a car or a national decision made by elected policy makers. An increase in taxes on labor, for example, negatively affects people's economic decisions in terms of how hard or how many hours they work. Would you take on that second job to pay for a new car if, after paying the taxes, you couldn't afford the car you want, or it takes many more hours of work than you expected? Instead, you might decide to cut your spending, or maybe you will take more leisure time by retiring earlier than you originally planned.

Business owners react this way, too. So that their businesses remain profitable, instead of expanding production and hiring more employees, a tax increase might lead business owners to reduce workers' hours or cut their benefits. Higher taxes can adversely affect those activities that create income and improve economic growth. At the state level, this debate sometimes revolves around the question of whether to have a state income tax or not. As of 2011, nine states, including Texas, Tennessee, and Florida, do not collect personal income taxes. They do collect other taxes to fund their programs. The economic question is whether substituting other taxes creates incentives that lead to better (or worse) economic outcomes. The economic problem for the government to solve is how to fund the programs that the public desires without raising taxes so high that people's economic incentives to work, and therefore provide the funding for those programs, evaporate.

## 16.4 How the Federal Deficit and the Federal Debt Are Related

A budget deficit occurs when the government spends more than it collects. When your parents spend more than they earn, what do they do? Of course, they are not able to tax the neighbors, so they probably borrow the needed funds from family or a bank. When they borrow, they become indebted to the lender. A loan from the bank means that they must sign a contract that requires payment on some future date, with some additional cost—the rate of interest—for the current use of the money.

Unlike your parents, when the government spends more than it gets in tax revenue, it *can* raise the needed money by taxing you and your neighbors. Because raising taxes every time more funds are needed is often politically unwise, the government also borrows from the public by selling financial assets, such as U.S. Treasury notes and bonds. These securities represent promises by the U.S. government to pay the buyer (in effect, the lender of the funds) a certain interest rate, and specify a future date on which the security can be remitted for payment.[6] When you got that $25 savings bond for graduating from high school, the person who bought it was lending money to the government with the agreement that you will get paid a specific amount in the future.

The **federal debt** is the total amount of outstanding loans that the federal government has obtained to fund its activities. The debt is directly related to changes in the budget deficit. When the budget deficit increases, this means that more borrowing will take place. Consequently, the federal debt increases. If the government runs a budget surplus, as it did in the late 1990s, the debt can be reduced by the amount of the surplus, if those funds are used to pay down the debt. Thus, the federal debt is perhaps best thought of as the accumulation of outstanding loans that the government has obtained over the years to finance its deficits.

> **FEDERAL DEBT** The total amount of outstanding loans that the federal government has obtained to fund its activities.

> **EXAMPLE** Over the past year, you have borrowed money for a car and to pay for tuition. The car loan was $3,000, and the loan for tuition was $10,000. Until you start paying these loans off, your total debt is $13,000.

**Figure 16.6** shows the relationship between the federal budget deficit and the federal debt since 1960. The debt measure used here, federal debt held by the public, ignores debt purchased by other government agencies. What you see is that when deficits began to turn more negative in the mid-1970s, the debt began to increase more sharply. When the deficits shrank and turned into surpluses in the 1990s, the increase in the debt slowed and even began to decline because the

· · · · · · ·

[6]You may want to revisit Chapter 4 and review the section on the loanable-funds model to see how government borrowing can affect interest rates.

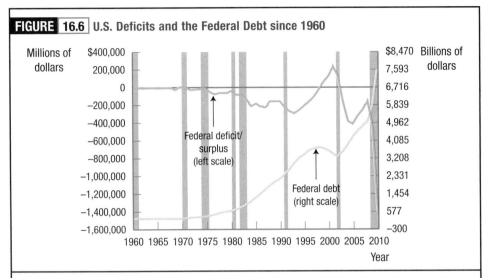

**FIGURE 16.6** | U.S. Deficits and the Federal Debt since 1960

Figure 16.6 shows the relationship between the federal budget deficit and the federal debt since 1960. (Shaded areas indicate U.S. recessions.) When deficits increased in the 1970s, the debt also began to increase. When the deficits shrank and became surpluses in the 1990s, the increase in the debt slowed, and the debt even began to decline. The return of budget deficits in the early 2000s led to increases in the debt once again. Because of the large increase in the federal deficit in response to the 2007–2009 recession, the debt jumped from $5 trillion in 2007 to $7 trillion in 2009 and topped $12 trillion in 2010.

*Source:* Federal Reserve Bank of St. Louis

surplus allowed the government to pay down its outstanding loans. This was short-lived, however.

When deficits returned in the early 2000s, the debt once again began its upward climb, reaching nearly $5 trillion by 2007. Because of the large increase in the federal deficit caused by the 2007–2009 recession, the debt will continue to increase in the near term. Does that mean that the debt will never be paid off? You can see that between 1995 and 2000, it actually fell: the government was paying off its debts. Even so, for the most part, the debt has increased, and is projected to increase in the future.

## 16.5 The Debt Relative to the Size of the Nation's GDP

As frightening as a $5 trillion or $14 trillion debt might seem, remember that the overall size of the economy has increased, and this should be taken into account. After all, if you owe $5,000 to your bank for the purchase of that used car, this has much different implications if your income is $10,000 than if your income is $100,000. To put the federal debt into perspective, **Figure 16.7** shows the debt measured as a percent of GDP over the past 50 years. The debt measure is the same as the one used in Figure 16.6; that is, federal debt held by the public.

Notice that the ratio of debt to GDP starts at a very high level (close to 45 percent) in 1960 and declines until the late 1970s. After reaching a low point in the late 1970s, the ratio began to increase, continuing its climb until the mid-1990s. This

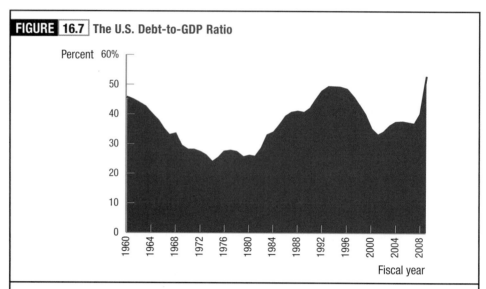

**FIGURE** 16.7 The U.S. Debt-to-GDP Ratio

This figure shows the debt measured as a percent of GDP since 1960. After declining throughout much of the 1960s, in the mid-1970s, the ratio leveled off and then increased sharply from the early 1980s and into the early 1990s. This mirrors the increased deficits of the 1980s and early 1990s. Although the ratio of debt-to-GDP fell in the 1990s, it once again increased as budget deficits reappeared in the 2000s. The events of the past few years have pushed the debt ratio even higher than the 1990s.

*Source:* Council of Economic Advisers

pattern mirrors the increased deficits of the 1980s and early 1990s, stemming in part from economic recessions and in part from changes in the makeup of government spending. The ratio fell in the latter half of the 1990s, reflecting the emergence of budget surpluses. Even so, this decline was short-lived. As budget deficits reappeared in the 2000s, the debt-to-GDP ratio began to increase. As you can see, however, the events of the past few years have pushed the debt ratio higher than any previous level in the past 50 years. In fact, in early 2010, the ratio of debt held by the public to GDP was projected to rise to nearly 70 percent of GDP and to continue increasing in future years.

How does the U.S. debt-to-GDP ratio compare to other countries? **Table 16.1** provides the answer. As a point of comparison, in 2007, the U.S. federal debt held by the public was about 36 percent of GDP. Compared with other industrial economies, the United States had the lowest debt-to-GDP ratio in 2007. The country with the ratio closest to the United States is Sweden. What jumps off the table are the sky-high debt ratios for Italy and Japan. In both countries, the government's debt is more than the country's GDP. Although there is much discussion about the federal government debt in the United States, when you compare our debt with that of other countries, it is not out of the ordinary. Of course, that doesn't mean it should not be a topic of concern.

Recent estimates of the debt-to-GDP ratios—those following the economic downturn that began in 2007—are also included in Table 16.1. Notice that the high debt-to-GDP countries in 2007 remained so in 2009. Given the small window of time, this should not be too surprising. It takes time for a country to reduce its debt. Second, and more important, notice how the debt-to-GDP ratios for most of the

| Table **16.1** Public Debt as a Percentage of GDP: A Cross-Country Comparison | | |
|---|---|---|
| Country | Debt as Percent (%) of GDP | |
| | 2007 | 2009 |
| Belgium | 86.4 | 99.0 |
| Canada | 64.0 | 72.3 |
| France | 66.6 | 78.7 |
| Germany | 65.3 | 77.2 |
| Italy | 105.6 | 115.2 |
| Japan | 194.4 | 192.1 |
| Netherlands | 47.7 | 62.2 |
| Sweden | 41.9 | 43.2 |
| Switzerland | 50.2 | 43.5 |
| United Kingdom | 43.3 | 68.5 |
| United States* | 36.2 | 53.0 |

*This is debt held by the public.

How does the ratio of debt to GDP for the United States compare to other countries? In 2007, the U.S. federal debt held by the public was about 36 percent of GDP. Compared with other industrial economies, the United States had the lowest debt-to-GDP ratio at that time. This is noticeably different from Italy and Japan, which had very elevated debt ratios in 2007. Following the onset of the 2007–2009 global recession, most countries experienced significant increases in their debt-to-GDP ratios.

**Source:** CIA *Factbook* (2010)

countries increased between 2007 and 2009. This occurred as a result of the enormous amounts of money the governments of these countries spent to rescue their faltering economies in the wake of the global financial crisis and worldwide economic recession.

# 16.6 Fiscal-Policy Actions and Economic Activity: The Theory

You now have a better idea of what people are talking about when they argue over the budget deficits and the debt. Now let's turn our attention to how changes in government outlays and taxes—fiscal policy—are used to achieve certain policy goals. To analyze the effect of the government's fiscal-policy actions, we will use the AD-IE model developed in earlier chapters. We already have touched on the role that increases and decreases in government spending play in explaining changes in the level of output in the economy. Here we want to look a bit deeper into the topic by distinguishing between two types of fiscal-policy actions: automatic stabilizers and discretionary policy actions.

## Automatic Stabilizers and How They Work

**Automatic stabilizers** are government-spending programs that automatically kick in when economic conditions worsen. Think of how other automatic stabilizers work. For instance, one type of automatic stabilizer is the automatic pilot. When the pilot of a passenger jet engages the autopilot, the computer system controls the flight of the plane. It adjusts the elevators and the rudder to ensure that the plane flies true to some preset course. Your everyday life is actually full of automatic stabilizers. The thermostat in your dorm room or apartment is an automatic stabilizer: in the winter, it tells your furnace to increase the heat when the temperature falls below your desired level. The cruise control on your car acts like a plane's autopilot, except that cruise control changes only one variable: it increases or decreases fuel to the engine to maintain some desired speed.

What automatic stabilizers are associated with fiscal policy? Perhaps you've heard someone talk about getting unemployment compensation after being laid off from a job. The government's unemployment-insurance program is one example of an automatic stabilizer. When people get laid off, the government (often some combination of state and federal) pays them some fraction of the earnings they have lost. Because the unemployment rate rises during economic downturns, unemployment compensation is designed to stabilize people's incomes. This cushions the effects the economy would otherwise experience due to a drop in consumer spending resulting from job loss.

**AUTOMATIC STABILIZER** Changes in taxes and expenditures that occur to offset changes in economic activity. Automatic stabilizers are counter-cyclical.

**EXAMPLE** Because they are based on income, revenues from individual income taxes increase during economic boom times and fall during recessions. This helps reduce the tax pressure on families during bad times.

**EXAMPLE** During economic downturns, the government's expenditures on food stamps and unemployment compensation rise. This spending is aimed at offsetting the effects of the economic downturn.

The tax structure in the United States also serves as an automatic stabilizer. Recall that the individual income-tax structure is progressive: the higher your income is, the higher the tax rate you pay on each additional dollar you earn. Consequently, if you lose your job, or your working hours get reduced during an economic downturn, the taxes you pay automatically fall, too. This also helps reduce the decline in consumer spending by households during recessions. This means that the current federal tax system dampens the effect of downturns on GDP. Research into this area suggests, however, that the responsiveness of taxes and spending to changes in the economy may in fact vary over time.[7]

We can use the AD-IE model to see how automatic stabilizers work. Suppose the economy experiences a "shock," and, as a result, investment spending falls. This is what happened at the beginning of 2000 when many dot.com companies failed and more recently beginning in 2007 when the housing industry took a nosedive. In both cases, the decline in business-investment spending reduced aggregate demand, shifting the aggregate demand curve leftward from $AD_1$ to $AD_2$ as shown in **Figure 16.8**. With no other changes, this would lead to a short-run decline in output and create a negative GDP gap, nudging the economy from point A to point B.

· · · · · · · ·

[7]Jeff Madrick, "Let's Hear from Those Who Feel Government Has a Role in Stabilizing the Economy." *New York Times*, August 8, 2002.

---

**FIGURE 16.8** | How Automatic Stabilizers Cushion a Decline in Aggregate Demand

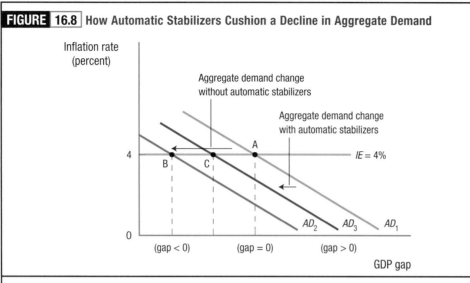

The economy experiences a negative spending "shock" that results in a decline in aggregate demand. This shock leads to a leftward shift in the aggregate demand curve, from $AD_1$ to $AD_2$. With no intervention, this would lead to a short-run decline in output and create a negative GDP gap. However, instead of falling to $AD_2$, automatic stabilizers theoretically mute the reduction in aggregate demand so it falls to, say, just $AD_3$.

---

The purpose of automatic fiscal stabilizers is to reduce the magnitude of the decline in aggregate demand and output. Instead of dropping all the way to $AD_2$, aggregate demand might fall to, say, $AD_3$ (point C) if automatic stabilizers are at work. As you can see, even though the GDP gap is still negative with $AD_3$, the automatic stabilizers—unemployment insurance, reduced income tax payments, and so on—lessened the effect on the economy that originally stemmed from the decline in investment spending. Did you recognize that government outlays tend to increase when the economy slides into a recession and decrease when the economic picture brightens? This partly explains why the budget deficit tends to increase during recessions and declines during economic expansions.

**ECONOMIC FALLACY**    Larger automatic stabilizers would lessen the severity of economic downturns.

**False.** When an economic downturn occurs, automatic stabilizers—increased unemployment compensation, for example—should protect more people from lost income and lost purchasing power and thereby lessen the severity and length of the recession, right? Perhaps not. In 2008 and 2009, many European countries suffered recessions, as did the United States. The share of government spending devoted to automatic-stabilizer programs—unemployment, welfare, and so on—in those countries is generally higher than in the United States. For example, total spending on automatic-stabilizer programs in the United States, as a share of GDP, was 1.6 percent for 2008–2010. In Great Britain, these programs amounted to 2.5 percent of GDP; in France, this spending was 2.4 percent of GDP. But the recession doesn't appear to have abated to a greater extent in those countries than it did in the United States. In contrast, in China, where spending on automatic stabilizers amounted to only 0.6 percent of GDP, the downturn was less severe.

Let's be clear: some level of automatic stabilizers help cushion the economic effects of a downturn. The fallacy is to believe that by increasing the spending on such programs, you can automatically insulate your economy from severe recessions.

## Discretionary Fiscal Policy

Let's continue with our analogy of a pilot flying a modern jetliner. When the pilot engages the autopilot, she gives up discretion over the course of the flight. Disengaging the autopilot means that the pilot now controls the plane's course, its altitude, and the stability of the flight. Similarly, when you turn off the cruise control in your car, you now determine whether you will proceed at 25 or 75 miles an hour. You, like the pilot, have *discretion* over your speed.

**Discretionary fiscal policy** refers to the *deliberate* (as opposed to automatic) policy actions that the government actively takes to change spending or taxes. When Congress passes legislation to expand the coverage of a social-insurance program or to fund a new fighter jet, it is making a discretionary fiscal-policy decision. Congress deciding to decrease the tax rate it imposes on your income is also a discretionary fiscal-policy decision. When the Obama administration pressed for passage of the economic stimulus package in 2008, they were attempting to use discretionary fiscal policy—both in terms of increased spending and tax reductions—to offset the economic effects of the deep recession.

> **DISCRETIONARY FISCAL POLICY** Legislative or administrative actions taken by the government to alter the level of government spending or the tax structure.

> **EXAMPLE** Originally proposed by President John F. Kennedy, in 1963 Congress passed the Revenue Act, which aimed at reducing taxes by $13.5 billion. It was enacted in 1964 by the Johnson administration.

> **EXAMPLE** In 2008, Congress passed and President George W. Bush signed the Economic Stimulus Act. The Act provided for tax rebates to individuals and tax incentives to businesses. The total cost of the Act, in terms of forgone revenue, was estimated to be $152 billion.

There are many other examples of discretionary fiscal-policy actions. Fiscal-stimulus packages that combine tax cuts with increased spending often are proposed to counteract economic downturns. Presidents George H. Bush and Bill Clinton both tried to get fiscal-stimulus packages through Congress in the early 1990s to spur economic activity. However, not all economists believe that stimulus packages, whether via tax cuts or increased government spending, are good for the economy over time.[8] Let's use as a case study a recent attempt to increase economic activity with discretionary fiscal policy. After we establish the basis for the action, we will use the AD-IE model to predict the effects of such discretionary-spending packages.

In 2008, even before the NBER officially dated it, the economy obviously was sliding into a recession. A confluence of negative events occurred, including a collapsing

· · · · · · ·

[8]Daniel Altman, "Pop Quiz: Did the Tax Cuts Bolster Growth?" *New York Times*, May 13, 2007; or Steven E. Landsburg, "Why the Stimulus Shouldn't Stimulate You." *Washington Post*, January 27, 2008.

housing market and a crisis in the credit markets, which, in many ways, was linked to the problems in the housing market. In the fall of 2008, the problems of the financial markets came to a head: several large financial institutions failed, most notably Lehman Brothers. Problems in the financial markets led to government intervention, but the infusion of funds did not restore significant lending (or confidence) in the credit markets. What occurred is often called a *credit crunch*.

The credit crunch, the continued problems in the housing market, and the international spread of economic adversity led to the severe downturn. Officially dated as beginning in December 2007, the recession gained significant momentum in 2008. Unemployment soared to levels not seen in 25 years, and by late 2008, the growth rate of real GDP was significantly negative. The economy was in the midst of a full-blown, deep recession.

Starting from this dire economic situation, the immediate policy objective of newly elected President Obama's administration was to push a massive fiscal-stimulus package through Congress. The idea was to use discretionary fiscal policy, through huge increases in federal government spending and in large tax cuts for individuals, to offset the decline in consumer and business spending that arose from the previously mentioned problems. The stimulus would, in theory, offset the decline in aggregate demand that had already pushed the economy into the worst recession in 80 years.

**Figure 16.9** illustrates how the stimulus package should have worked. Aggregate demand had fallen from $AD_1$ to $AD_2$, and the economy had sunk into recession: it went from point A to point B. The stimulus package would increase government spending—a significant component of aggregate demand—and encourage consumer spending through tax cuts. The aggregate demand curve would shift from $AD_2$ back to, say, $AD_3$ in Figure 16.9 (back to point C). The goal was to reduce the size of the

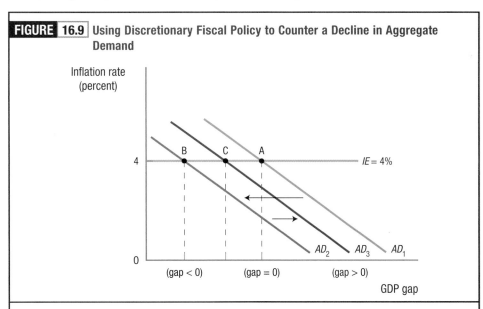

**FIGURE 16.9** | **Using Discretionary Fiscal Policy to Counter a Decline in Aggregate Demand**

This figure illustrates how a fiscal-stimulus package to fight a recession is intended to work. Suppose aggregate demand falls from $AD_1$ to $AD_2$, and the economy sinks into a severe recession. A fiscal-stimulus package of increased government spending and reduced taxes should, according to the model, counteract this decline and increase the demand for goods and services. The aggregate demand curve potentially would shift from $AD_2$ back to $AD_3$ or even to $AD_1$ if the stimulus spending were large enough.

negative GDP gap and get the economy back to its potential rate of output growth. Was it successful?

What about discretionary fiscal-policy actions that are not aimed at offsetting the effects of a recession? For example, the so-called Kennedy tax cuts of 1964 were not enacted because of a recession but because policy makers wanted to boost economic activity. What is the effect of a fiscal policy that lowers taxes? Suppose tax rates are halved for all individuals. Everything else equal, people now have a greater incentive to work more hours: the opportunity cost of *not* working has increased. Thus, if you get to take home more income for the same number of hours of work, you might decide to work full-time or get a second job to buy that motorcycle or car you've been wanting.

We can use the fluctuations model to show the effect of such a policy. Initially, the economy is operating at its potential, so the GDP gap is zero. Cutting tax rates increases consumption spending because people's disposable incomes increase. This shifts the aggregate demand curve to the right from $AD_1$ to $AD_2$ as **Figure 16.10** shows. Notice that this discretionary fiscal policy quickens the pace of economic output. It moves from point A toward point B. At point B, the economy is now operating above its potential—in the positive GDP gap region. As you know, when economies operate in the positive GDP gap region, this puts upward pressure on actual and expected inflation rates. The economy's output remains above its potential only for as long as it takes for inflation and inflation expectations to adjust. As they adjust upward (from B to C in the figure), real GDP returns to its potential until the GDP gap is once again zero.

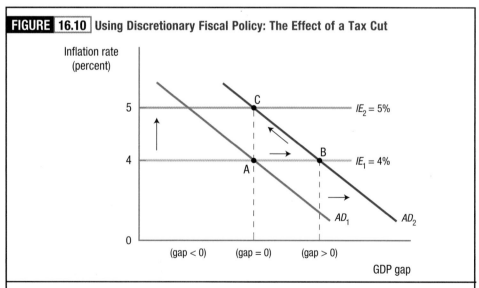

**FIGURE  16.10**  Using Discretionary Fiscal Policy: The Effect of a Tax Cut

The AD-IE model can be used to show the effect of discretionary fiscal-policy actions that are not used to offset the effects of a recession. The economy initially is producing at its potential and with some expected rate of inflation, say, 4 percent. This is illustrated as point A in the figure. Now the government passes legislation to cut taxes to increase consumption spending. This policy action increases aggregate demand, shifting the aggregate demand curve from $AD_1$ to $AD_2$. The economy moves from point A toward point B because inflation rates and inflationary expectations haven't yet adjusted. Because the economy is operating with a positive GDP gap at point B, there is upward pressure on inflation. As inflation and inflation expectations adjust upward, the economy moves toward point C. Over time, real GDP returns to potential, and the rate of inflation, actual and expected, remains higher.

## SOLVED PROBLEM

**Q** Lower taxes or raise spending?

The economy is sliding into a recession. As the economic adviser to the president, you have been asked how to use fiscal policy to avert the decline. Your policy choices are simple: lower taxes, raise government spending, or both. The problem is deciding which one delivers the most bang for your policy buck.

**A** To answer this question, let's use the algebraic version of the consumption function introduced in Chapter 13. There you learned that consumption spending (C) is related to disposable income, defined as income (Y) minus taxes (T). We can write this as

$$C = a + b(Y - T)$$

where $a$ is autonomous consumption, and $b$ is the marginal propensity to consume (MPC). Recall that the MPC has been found to be between zero and one. Let's make it 0.8 for this problem. If we simplify matters and concern ourselves only with household spending and the government—leaving out investment and net exports—then equilibrium between spending and income can be written as

$$Y = C + G$$

where G is government expenditures. To find the equilibrium, substitute into this equation the consumption function, and you get

$$Y = a + b(Y - T) + G$$

Solve for income (Y), and the answer is

$$Y = (a - bT + G)/(1 - b)$$

The effect on income from a change in taxes is measured by the term $[-bT/(1 - b)]$. With an MPC of 0.8, if you advise the president to lower taxes by a dollar, your best guess is that income will increase by $-0.8(-\$1)/(1 - 0.8)$, or $4. The effect of a change in government spending is measured by the term $G/(1 - b)$. Now, if you advise the president to increase G by $1, your projected increase in income is $\$1/(1 - 0.8)$, or $5. This means that in this model, an increase (or a decrease for that matter) in government spending can have a greater effect on income, dollar for dollar, than a decrease in taxes. Can you explain why? For an answer, you must solve Question 17 at the end of this chapter. We also leave for the end-of-chapter questions the issue of whether it is better for long-run economic growth to lower taxes or to raise government spending.

One obvious question is "Why intervene at all?" What if, facing a recession like 2007–2009, Congress and the president allowed the natural adjustment process of the economy to work? **Figure 16.11** shows the theoretical outcome.

The economy begins in an initial state of equilibrium, say point A. Inflation and expected inflation are equal at 2 percent. Consumers decide to dramatically reduce their spending, and businesses cut back on investments in new machinery, computers, and so on. These two reductions in spending act to lower aggregate demand, shown as the shift from $AD_1$ to $AD_2$ in Figure 16.11. The economy shifts from point A to point B. If nothing occurs, what is the economy's natural tendency? First, in the short run, the level of economic activity will decline: the economy will operate below its potential in the negative GDP gap region. Output is affected first because

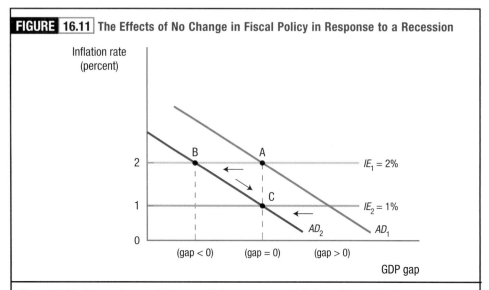

**FIGURE 16.11** The Effects of No Change in Fiscal Policy in Response to a Recession

Figure 16.11 shows what would happen if the government failed to take any fiscal-policy measures during a recession and just allowed the economy to adjust naturally. With the economy in an initial state of equilibrium (point A), consumers decide to dramatically reduce their spending, and businesses cut back on investments in new machinery, which lowers aggregate demand, as shown by the shift from $AD_1$ to $AD_2$. If there is no intervention (assume no automatic stabilizers are at work) in the short run, the GDP gap will be negative. However, over time, inflation and expectations of inflation will adjust downward until the economy moves to a lower rate of inflation consistent with a zero GDP gap (point C).

inflation and inflation expectations are slow to adjust. Over time, however, inflation and expectations of inflation will decline. Theoretically, this adjustment takes place until inflation and expectation of inflation fall to say a rate of 1 percent (as shown in Figure 16.11). The economy moves from point B to point C. At that lower rate of inflation, which becomes the new expected rate of inflation, the economy will have returned to producing at its full potential: the gap is once again zero.

So why intervene? One thing that economists don't know is how long the adjustment process—moving from A to B to C—in Figure 16.11 takes. One reason why the Great Depression remains such an important event is because it lasted for so long. This gives pause to many in authority (and those who advise them) who must decide whether to incur a bigger federal deficit and try to increase aggregate demand, or to do nothing and hope that the natural adjustment process back to full employment is quick. There is no doubt that increased unemployment brought about by a recession is a drain on the economy's potential to produce. More importantly, it also leads to significant human costs. Lost jobs often translate into lost opportunities: lost homes, broken families, or not being able to send your children to college. It is perhaps for such reasons that fiscal policy—run by individuals who must be elected—is so often used to fight recessions.

## 16.7 Fiscal-Policy Issues

So far, you have learned about the deficit and the debt of the U.S. government, and how fiscal policy—in the form of automatic stabilizers and discretionary policy—works. In this section, we examine a few issues in the debate over the usefulness of fiscal policy.

## Do Fiscal-Policy Actions Always Work?

The AD-IE model predicts that an increase in government spending leads to an increase in aggregate demand and, albeit temporary, in real GDP. This knowledge has been used to justify the use of discretionary fiscal policy to combat recessions: if the economy is operating with a large negative gap, increased government spending will increase output and close the gap. But is fiscal policy a viable tool to fight economic downturns? What does the evidence say?

**Figure 16.12** shows the actual relation between the GDP gap and fiscal-policy actions in the United States between 1960 and 2001. The horizontal axis measures the GDP gap. The vertical axis measures changes in discretionary fiscal policy using the cyclically-adjusted deficit; that is, the deficit that would occur without spending changes associated with recessions and expansions. Each point in the chart is a different year. For example, locate 1965 in the figure. The year was characterized by a positive GDP gap equal to about 2 percent and a change in the deficit (relative to potential GDP) that was about 1 percent. If discretionary fiscal policy is always used to offset economic fluctuations, then the points in the chart would be aligned along a line from the southwest quadrant to the northeast quadrant. This would reflect the fact that expansionary fiscal policy (a negative value on the vertical axis) was used when the GDP gap was negative, and that contractionary fiscal policy (a positive value on the vertical axis) was used when the GDP gap was positive.

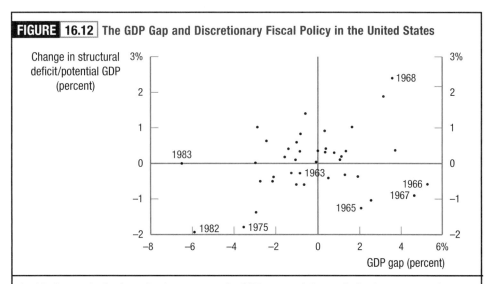

**FIGURE 16.12** The GDP Gap and Discretionary Fiscal Policy in the United States

In this figure, the horizontal axis measures the GDP gap, and the vertical axis measures changes in discretionary fiscal policy. Each point represents these two values for a specific year. If discretionary fiscal policy has been used to offset economic fluctuations, the points should lay along a line from the southwest quadrant to the northeast quadrant. This would reflect the fact that expansionary fiscal policy was used when the GDP gap was negative and that contractionary fiscal policy (a positive value on the vertical axis) was used when the GDP gap was positive. Although the array of points suggests that fiscal-policy actions have sometimes been used to counter economic fluctuations, the fact that many of the points lie in the southeast and northwest quadrants suggests that discretionary fiscal policy in the United States was too often expansionary when it should have been contractionary, and vice versa.

*Source:* Matthew B. Canzoneri, Robert E. Cumby, and Behzad T. Diba, "Should the European Central Bank and the Federal Reserve Be Concerned about Fiscal Policy?" *Rethinking Stabilization Policy*, Kansas City Federal Reserve Symposium (August, 2002).

The relation captured in Figure 16.12 suggests that this characterization isn't too accurate. Sometimes fiscal-policy actions successfully counter business fluctuations. Most economists agree that the government's stimulus spending program that began in 2009 helped slow the economy's downturn. The question, though, is at what cost? The concern is that stimulus spending permanently increased the size and role of government in the economy. The fact is, however, that many of the points in Figure 16.12 lie in the southeast and northwest quadrants, which raises doubts about whether stimulus programs are successful. This suggests that discretionary fiscal policy in the United States generally has *not* been very successful in terms of stabilizing the economy. That is not to say that the fiscal-spending programs won't help a faltering economy. What the results of studies such as this one suggest is that, in general, fiscal policy is not the best tool to use if keeping the economy operating at or near its potential is the objective.

Why would this be true? For one, changes in most discretionary policy actions occur with a significant time lag. By the time legislators recognize the problem, debate the issues, pass the legislation, and the government spends the money, the economy is often out of the recession that prompted their actions. For instance, in early 2009, some argued that spending out of the stimulus package will likely occur only after the recession had bottomed out. This was true because much of the stimulus money was being spent into late 2010, even though the recession ended (at least officially) in mid-2009.

Also, after a fiscal policy is passed, it takes time for the stimulus to "hit the road." Additional time delays are inherent in implementing any fiscal program: where spending will occur and what amount, cutting the checks, distributing the tax rebates, and so on. And only after these events have occurred will individuals' spending habits be affected. Such lags help explain why discretionary fiscal-policy actions are often not viewed as very effective in fighting economic fluctuations.

## Can Deficits Increase Economic Growth?

Our treatment of discretionary fiscal policy indicates that although it impacts aggregate demand, it may not have any positive affect on long-term economic growth. (Leaving aside the issue of who pays for government debt.) Our examples show that fiscal policies shift aggregate demand in the short term but do not lead to lasting changes in real GDP growth. Is there some fiscal-policy action that could lead to long-term economic gains?

Some economists argue that the answer is yes, especially if the action is to reduce taxes. Such an economist believes that by lowering taxes, even if it increases the deficit, the government will increase the incentives for individuals to work more hours and produce more goods than if the government raises taxes. A lower tax structure gives people an incentive to produce goods more efficiently, which increases productivity and leads to higher long-term economic growth. Firms facing lower taxes also have more of an incentive to purchase more machinery and increase worker productivity. Changes in tax policy can lead to long-term gains, but only if they permanently impact the combination of labor, capital, and knowledge available in the economy.

There is some evidence to support this idea. A number of studies have shown that states whose marginal personal income-tax rates are higher, all other factors held constant, are more likely to have slower rates of income growth. There also is evidence suggesting that countries that have lowered their marginal tax rates experience an increase in the growth of output per person relative to those countries that have increased their marginal tax rates. This remains a controversial area of study, but the evidence does not reject the notion that decreasing taxes promotes economic growth.

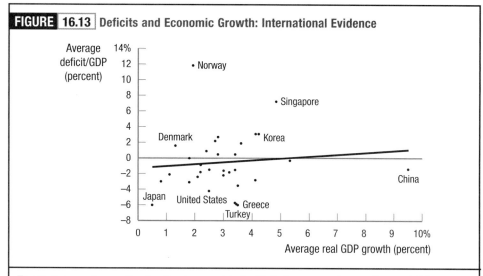

**FIGURE 16.13** Deficits and Economic Growth: International Evidence

To see if expansionary fiscal policy is associated with faster economic growth, we plot the average growth rates of real GDP for a number of countries along with their deficits as a percent of the GDPs. If higher-deficit spending leads to increases in output growth, countries with large deficits should also experience faster rates of economic growth. The figure shows just the opposite is true: countries with larger deficits relative to their GDPs tend to be economies that grow at relatively slower rates.

*Source:* Federal Reserve Bank of St. Louis

What about the overall relation between the outcome of fiscal-policy actions and economic growth? To address this question, let's look at the relation between one result of fiscal policy—measured by government deficits—and economic growth across a number of countries. In **Figure 16.13**, we plot the average growth rates of real GDP along with the average deficit/GDP ratio for a sample of 32 countries. Each is measured for the period 1997–2009. If deficit spending increases output growth, countries with large deficits should also experience relatively faster rates of economic growth. Figure 16.13 shows that this is not true: a number of countries averaged larger deficits relative to their GDP (e.g., Japan, Greece, and Turkey) and expanded at comparatively slower rates since 1997. At the same time, some countries ran large budget surpluses (Norway and Singapore) yet experienced very different rates of growth in output. The lack of a "reliable" relation—the points are widely scattered around the nearly flat trend line—suggests that this analysis should not be pushed too far. Figure 16.13 does suggest, however, that the road to faster economic growth is not likely to be paved with substantially larger government deficits.

## Does Deficit Spending "Crowd Out" Private Investment?

Critics of budget deficits often argue that when the government borrows from the public to finance its spending—when it sells government bonds—its demand for funds competes with those of private industry. Think of the government, Ford Motor Company, and Starbucks all competing for a given investment dollar. Unlike Ford and Starbucks, however, the government doesn't have to be profitable to stay in business. Because the government only wants to get the funds necessary to finance its programs, it can keep bidding up the price it pays you—the interest rate—to borrow the funds. This competition between the government and the private sector for finances is often called **crowding out**. In other words, the government is thought to crowd out private firms in the market for investment funds.

> **CROWDING OUT** Crowding out occurs when the government and private individuals compete for the same investment dollar. The private individuals are crowded out by the government because the government can outbid them for the funds.

> **EXAMPLE** ZZZ Motor Company offered its 10-year bonds with an interest rate of 4 percent. The government offered bonds of the same maturity at 6 percent. Because ZZZ could not raise the rate it pays, investors purchased the government's bonds and ZZZ could not raise funds needed to expand its business.

If crowding out exists, then we should see interest rates rising when deficits get bigger. The government simply bids up the interest rate it is willing to pay lenders until private firms are pushed out of the market. It often is assumed that financial markets are "forward looking." That is, they react to what they perceive might occur in the future. If budget deficits are predicted to increase in the future, people in the financial markets might believe that the increased demand for funds by the government will put upward pressure on interest rates. If they believe that this will happen—if crowding out is happening—these investors should act today, pushing interest rates higher. Crowding out, in its most basic version, thus suggests that announcements of rising deficits should be associated with rising rates of interest.

We can see if crowding out exists by looking at the relation between projected deficits and interest rates. Twice a year, the Congressional Budget Office (CBO) projects what it thinks the deficit will be over the next ten years. The number is reported widely in the financial news and is used by individuals in financial markets to reappraise their personal forecasts of the deficit. If crowding out is an economic phenomenon to be worried about, a CBO forecast of higher future budget deficits should match up with an increase in interest rates. Because the budget forecast is for the next ten years, it makes sense to see how it is related to the interest rate on a ten-year security. If financial markets expect that rising deficits will cause crowding out to occur, they should start pricing this possibility into current interest rates on ten-year government securities.

**Figure 16.14** shows the relation between the CBO's federal deficit forecast and the interest rate on the ten-year government security. The interest rate, the yield on the ten-year Treasury Inflation-Indexed Securities (TIIS), not only reflects market expectations over a time frame consistent with the budget projection, but it also embeds the market's expectation of inflation. You can see that the two economic measures are not related in a way that is consistent with crowding out. During the late 1990s when the CBO projected surpluses—government receipts exceeding outlays—the interest rate should have declined, but it actually increased. When the CBO projected a return of deficits, the interest rate should have risen, but it didn't. As this simple comparison suggests, the conventional wisdom about deficits and interest rates is not supported by the facts.[9]

Should we just ignore the effect of deficits on interest rates? Of course not. For one, we have not taken into account the possibility that the source of buyers of our government debt might change. Currently a significant portion of U.S. federal debt is purchased by foreign entities. Some have raised the legitimate concern that if these

· · · · · · · ·

[9]Robert Eisner, "The Great Mirage: Deficits and Interest Rates." *Wall Street Journal*, August 3, 1994; and Kevin Kliesen "Die Another Day: Budget Deficits and Interest Rates." Federal Reserve Bank of St. Louis *National Economic Trends* (December 2002).

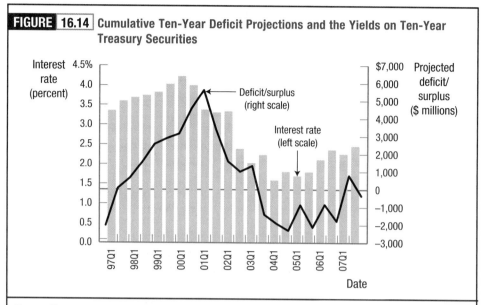

**FIGURE 16.14**  Cumulative Ten-Year Deficit Projections and the Yields on Ten-Year Treasury Securities

If crowding out exists, interest rates should increase when deficits increase. To test this, this figure plots the ten-year deficit forecast of the Congressional Budget Office (CBO) against the yield on ten-year Treasury securities that are indexed to inflation. The figure shows that when the budget surpluses were forecast, the interest rate should have declined, but it didn't. Likewise, when budget deficits were forecast, the interest rate should have risen, but it didn't. The conventional wisdom about deficits and interest rates is not supported by the facts.

*Source:* Federal Reserve Bank of St. Louis

foreign buyers were to reduce their demand for U.S. government securities, there would be a greater burden on the U.S. financial market to absorb the government's debt. This could lead to interest-rate effects that are different from those experienced thus far.

Some evidence also suggests that some longer-term interest rates may increase relative to shorter-term rates when forecasts indicate that budget deficits will increase in the future. Such disparate effects can have important implications for economic activity: if budget deficits increase long-term rates (although our evidence does not lend much support to this idea), this can have negative effects on business-investment spending. One reason is because some business investment is more sensitive to increases in the level of longer-term interest rates. When building a factory, the financing is very long-term and may be based more on interest rates for 20-year securities than for 3-month securities. Similarly, investment in housing by individuals may be affected because mortgage rates are often tied to government interest rates for 5- and 10-year securities.

Finally, if deficits do adversely affect interest rates, this could influence the monetary policy decisions made by the Federal Reserve. For example, suppose a rising deficit causes long-term interest rates to increase, and this in turn reduces business-investment spending, which slows economic growth. If maintaining economic growth is a policy objective of the Federal Reserve—a topic that we will address in the next two chapters—then the larger deficit may make the monetary policy makers' attempts to keep the economy operating at full employment more difficult. But it can get even more complicated: What if deficits raise interest rates, and higher interest rates are not desired by those making monetary policy? Attempts to adjust interest rates through monetary policy may affect economic growth even more. Although there is little monetary policy makers can do about fiscal policy, this potential link helps explain why they often speak out about the interaction between the two.

## The Fiscal-Spending Multiplier

You graduate and get a job in the president's administration as an economic adviser. A recession hits, and your job is to tell the president just how much the government needs to spend to achieve a zero GDP gap. How do you come up with an answer to that question?

During the discussion over the size of the 2009 fiscal-stimulus package, economists debated that exact question. Some of those favoring the plan argued that a spending tax-cut package of $800 billion just wasn't big enough to return the economy to full employment. How did they come to that conclusion? First, they estimated (a calculated guess at) what the size of the GDP gap was. Second, they used something known as the **fiscal-spending multiplier**, or just the multiplier for short.

> **FISCAL-SPENDING MULTIPLIER** The multiple by which GDP is increased for a given increase in government spending.

> **EXAMPLE** The government increased spending on pencils by $1 million. That additional $1 million to ABC pencil company allowed it to hire additional workers who in turn spent more on food. The food store owners spent their extra income on houses. In total, the initial $1 million spent by the government increased total spending (GDP) by more than $1 million.

The multiplier is a measure of how much an additional dollar of government spending impacts the economy. Recall from our discussion of the consumption function that for each additional dollar you get in income, you spend, say, 80 cents of it. Your marginal propensity to consume (MPC) is 0.80. That means that when your income rises by $1, you increase someone else's income by spending 80 cents. If they behave similarly, they will spend a portion of their additional income (your 80 cents), thus increasing another person's income. And so it goes until there is nothing left to spend. If we knew, for example, that everyone in this chain of spending had an MPC equal to 0.80, then an additional income of $1 via the federal government would eventually raise income in the economy by $5.[10]

Let's use some real numbers to illustrate this process. In the last quarter of 2008, actual real GDP was $11.6 trillion. Potential real GDP for that quarter was estimated to be $12 trillion. This means that actual real GDP was $400 billion below potential. (The GDP gap was negative.) If you knew the MPC is 0.8, your policy recommendation would be to increase government spending by $80 billion (= $400/5) to make up the $400 billion gap between actual and potential GDP. If you thought the GDP gap for the coming year was going to be $2 trillion, then your proposed policy would be to increase government spending by $400 billion.

This seems straightforward, but here's the problem: What if you don't know how big the MPC is and, therefore, how big the spending multiplier really is? Even if you have a pretty good estimate of the MPC, your policy prescription ignores the possible effects of taxes, assumes that everyone has the same MPC, and assumes that everyone participates in the spending process until the final dollar is spent. These are very strong assumptions.

· · · · · · ·

[10]The multiplier is essentially equal to $1/(1 - MPC)$. If the MPC is 0.8, then the multiplier is $1/(1 - 0.8) = 5$. As used in the Solved Problem, increase government spending ($G$) by $1, and the multiplier effect predicts a $5 increase in income ($Y$).

Because policy makers—and some economists—rely so heavily on this multiplier relation to make decisions, in 2008, the International Monetary Fund (IMF) extensively surveyed available analyses to see just how big the fiscal-spending multiplier might be. Based on their review of the many studies, they concluded that the fiscal-spending multiplier probably varies between a little less than 1 to as high as 4. They also concluded that multipliers tend to vary over time and across countries. The IMF study also found that the spending multipliers even vary depending on different types of government spending.

During the debate over the fiscal-stimulus package in 2009, the spending multiplier for payments to individuals, such as increased unemployment compensation and health-insurance subsidies, was estimated to be somewhere between a low of 0.8 to a high of 2.2. At the low end, this means for every dollar spent by the government, the eventual impact on GDP is *less than* a dollar. This helps explain why economists had diverging opinions about the size or even the necessity of the fiscal-stimulus package.

## 16.8 Can We Ignore the Deficit and the Debt?

As you can probably tell, the role of fiscal policy and its effect on the economy remains a topic of continued study and debate. It might seem like there's not much evidence to support the idea that the deficit is bad and should be reduced. You should not, however, take this to mean that we should simply ignore the deficit.

One reason is because even though it appears that the deficit doesn't seem to have crowded out private investment and had much of an effect on interest rates, that doesn't mean it couldn't happen. Maybe it did not occur because for years the U.S. economy was the bellwether economy in the world. The stature of the U.S. economy made buying U.S. government securities one of the safest investments around. If foreign investors, especially foreign governments, were willing to continue to purchase U.S. government securities even when deficits became large, then the deficit's effect on U.S. interest rates might have been muted. In other words, foreign demand for these securities (foreign supply of funds) helped keep U.S. interest rates lower than what they otherwise would have been.

But this position could be challenged if the U.S. fiscal situation were to become more like that of, say, Spain or Greece in recent years. Countries, even countries as large as Russia and Argentina, default—fail to pay—on their sovereign debt. As noted earlier, the financial crisis set off by the failure of the Russian government to pay on its outstanding debt in 1998 illustrates that countries, like firms and people, can get into serious financial difficulties. And although the United States has not experienced such extreme difficulties, if future deficits and debt were to significantly expand, we also might begin to experience trouble in selling our debt to investors and face higher interest rates as a result. In fact, in 2011 it was announced that some companies that rate U.S. bonds—the ratings give investors an idea of how reliably they can expect to be repaid—had raised questions about future ratings if the deficit and debt picture were not improved.[11]

Even while the evidence relating the deficit to the economy is debated, ignoring fiscal policy is not a good idea for other reasons. The taxing and spending choices made by the government affect you personally. Changes in tax rates on income affect your labor market decisions, both in terms of how many hours to work and the hiring decisions made by potential employers. If you get less take-home pay for the same (or more) amount of work, you may decide to work fewer hours. If the government decides to increase its spending on government-backed programs, such as national health care, this also affects you. The fact is that the funds spent for the government's provision of health

· · · · · · ·

[11]Damian Paletta and E.S. Browning, "U.S. Warned on Debt Load: S&P Signals Top Rating Is in Danger, Stoking Political Battle on Deficit," *On-Line Wall Street Journal*, April 19, 2011.

care must come from somewhere. The government must increase tax receipts, borrow more, or reduce spending in other areas to meet the funding needs of health care.

In the end, the debate over fiscal policy also is a debate on the size of government: or, perhaps more correctly, what citizens want the role of government in the economy to be. To see this, consider two economies, both with a zero deficit. In one economy, the government accounts for one-third of total output. In the other economy, the government accounts for three-fourths of total output. Because individuals in the former economy probably face a lower tax burden than the latter, only focusing on the deficit will be misleading. The economic consequences of the two governments are much different, even though you could argue, based on their deficits, that each affects their economy in a similar way. Instead of debating deficits, a more useful debate is over how big the government is—its outlays and its receipts—relative to the economy.

## WHAT YOU SHOULD HAVE LEARNED FROM CHAPTER 16

- That governments fund their activities by borrowing or by raising taxes.
- That budget deficits occur when the government's outlays exceed its receipts.
- That budget surpluses occur when the government's receipts exceed its outlays.
- That increases in the deficit lead to increases in the government's outstanding debt.
- That it is best to measure the deficit or debt as a ratio to the size of the economy.
- That the major component of government outlays is for human-resource programs.
- That the major component of government receipts is individual income taxes.
- That automatic stabilizers increase government spending and reduce government receipts during economic downturns and the reverse during economic booms.
- That discretionary fiscal policy, a change in government outlays or taxes, can be used to affect aggregate demand, which, in the short run, can be used to offset economic fluctuations.
- That there is uncertainty over the long-term effects of discretionary fiscal policy, although there is a greater consensus that tax cuts have positive long-term effects on economic growth.

## KEY TERMS

Budget deficit, p. 424

Budget surplus, p. 424

Interest payments, p. 428

Federal receipts, p. 430

Progressive tax, p. 432

Regressive tax, p. 432

Federal debt, p. 434

Automatic stabilizer, p. 437

Discretionary fiscal policy, p. 440

Crowding out, p. 448

Fiscal-spending multiplier, p. 450

## QUESTIONS AND PROBLEMS

1. What is the difference between a budget deficit and a budget surplus? How does each affect the outstanding level of government debt?

2. Governments have the power to print money and therefore to pay off investors. Could there ever be an instance where a government is unable to borrow? Why might investors be unwilling to purchase government debt (and therefore lend money to the government)?

3. If governments increase their need to borrow, common wisdom has it that interest rates will rise. Is this what actually occurs? Can you provide some reasons why the common wisdom might be incorrect?

4. Explain why budget deficits appear to be "cyclical." That is, why do deficits get bigger during recessions and smaller during expansions?

5. A pundit was heard to exclaim that the budget deficit in the United States is much larger than in Belgium and therefore threatens public welfare. Is this a valid comparison? What do you need to know to determine if the commentator is correct?

6. Which component of federal outlays has become the largest over the past 50 years? Which component has declined the most? Which is most likely to increase further in the future?

7. If interest rates are low, that is good for the budget deficit. Explain why this might be true.

8. Most new presidents announce that they will change the structure of the federal tax system, such as close loopholes, increase coverage, make sure everyone pays their fair share, and so on. Suppose you get the job of revising the current system.

   a) Would you focus more on taxing income or taxing sales of goods and services?
   b) Would your new tax system be more progressive or regressive?
   c) If you opted to replace income taxes with sales taxes, can you think of ways to reduce the regressivity of the tax?

9. In July 2007, *The Economist* magazine ran a story titled "How to Deal with a Falling Population." In a world where the population isn't increasing, the workforce is aging, and the general desire is for expanded entitlement programs, design a fiscal policy that would deal with the conflicts that may arise in the future.

10. Explain how the federal debt is related to the federal deficit. Why is the debt sometimes thought to be the accumulation of past deficits?

11. Some people argue that if the government just did away with programs such as unemployment insurance, recessions would be shorter and less severe. Using the AD-IE model:

    a) Provide an economic argument to refute that idea.
    b) Provide an economic argument to support that idea.

12. It is sometimes argued that fiscal policy is ineffective in fighting economic downturns because it takes too long for it to work. Explain this argument.

13. Contrast discretionary fiscal policy with the automatic stabilizers that are built into the government's fiscal policy.

14. The economy is slipping into a recession. As the fiscal-policy expert on the president's Council of Economic Advisers, how would you counsel the president to respond if the president's focus is:

    a) on keeping inflation as low as possible.
    b) on keeping the unemployment rate as low as possible.
    c) to get reelected.
    d) to keep the economy growing close to its potential.

15. The famous British economist John Maynard Keynes championed the idea of using expansionary fiscal policy—running large budget deficits—during economic recessions. He also did not, however, consider expansionary fiscal policy as a means to increasing economic growth over time. Use the AD-IE model to explain his position.

16. Use the loanable-funds model in Chapter 4 to explain why crowding out may not occur.

17. Use the algebraic model in the Solved Problem to answer this question. Assume that autonomous consumption (*a*) is $200 billion, current government spending (*G*) is $500 billion, taxes (*T*) are $50 billion, and the MPC is 0.5.

   a) Based on these values, what is the equilibrium income for this economy?

   b) The economy is predicted to slide into a deep recession. It is estimated that real GDP will fall by $800 billion. Using the preceding values and your answer in (a), how much should government spending increase to make up this gap?

   c) Suppose your estimate of the MPC is incorrect, and it is 0.8 instead of 0.5. How does this affect your estimate of the increase in government spending needed to close the $800 billion shortfall in real GDP?

   d) What are the inflationary implications of using an MPC of 0.8 in making your calculations if in fact the true MPC is 0.5?

18. Economists and policy advisers in many undeveloped countries do not have reliable estimates of the MPC. How does this affect the usefulness of fiscal policies aimed at minimizing deviations of real GDP around potential GDP? Consider short-term and longer-term implications in your answer.

# 17

# Money, Banking, and the U.S. Federal Reserve System

> *"It is not by augmenting the capital of the country, but by rendering a greater part of that capital active and productive than would otherwise be so, that the most judicious operations of banking can increase the industry of the country"*
>
> *Adam Smith,*
> *eighteenth-century philosopher*
> *and economics pioneer*

It's been said that "money is the root of all evil." However, money also is the lubricant that keeps modern economies going. You already have seen how important money is. Increases and decreases in the growth rate of the money supply are directly associated with changes in the rate of inflation. There's never been a hyperinflation without a hyper-increase in the money supply to fuel it.

The problem is that up to now, we really haven't provided you with a real description of what we mean by *money*. Money today is much more than pieces of paper you carry around. It also includes the electronic balances in your checking and savings accounts. Is your credit card money? No, and we will explain why later in the chapter, but it acts a lot like money. Because money includes deposits at banks, it is important to understand how money and banks are related. Banks play a starring role in the money-supply process. They affect the money supply by making loans. Actions taken by the Federal Reserve, the central bank of the United States, affect how much money banks are willing to loan and at what interest rates.

In this chapter, we close some of the gaps left open in previous chapters. After you are finished reading it, you will know what money is (and isn't), how banks "create" it, and how policy makers at the Fed affect its growth. You will also see how these actions simultaneously affect the level of interest rates in the economy. This is important because, as you learned in Chapter 13, changes in interest rates have a big impact on the spending decisions households and businesses make.

## 17.1 Money

People demand money like they demand other goods. In modern societies, money usually takes the form of paper currency (cash) or electronic accounts, neither of which affords much in the way of creature comforts: we can't eat money, and it does not provide adequate shelter against the elements. Yet having money permits us to buy food, housing, clothing, and transportation, and otherwise survive in the world. This makes money an important topic in economics. In Chapter 12, we talked about how the demand for money and its supply together affect prices. In Chapter 13, we showed that a change in the money supply can affect aggregate demand and economic activity in the entire economy. In both instances, we really did not get into any detail about what money really is. So let's now close that loophole and settle on some accepted notions of what money is and is not, and how it is measured.

## Money: What It Is and What It Does

Throughout history, money has taken on a wide variety of shapes and forms. Across the varied cultures of the world, items that have served as money include dog teeth, cattle, precious metals, human beings, bronze plates, and, more recently, pieces of paper with colorful pictures of birds or politicians. In World War II, even cigarettes served as money in prisoner-of-war camps.[1]

How in the world can so many different things be money? The answer is that people agree that one of these physical goods will be readily accepted in exchange for other goods. This means that a plumber might be willing to exchange his services for some dog teeth because he believes that he can exchange the teeth for something he wants, like a pizza. As the title of this section suggests, although it seems silly, the best answer to the question "what is money" is "money is what money does." Let's now discuss what money does to figure out what money is.

**Money as a Medium of Exchange.** Let's return momentarily to our plumber. If the plumber doesn't think that he will be able to exchange dog teeth for a pizza, then he may not accept the teeth as payment for fixing your sink. When this occurs, the monetary exchange system based on dog teeth breaks down, causing one of two outcomes. One is that an alternative form of money arises. The other is **barter**.

---

**BARTER** Barter is an exchange system where goods trade for goods.

**EXAMPLE** You agree with your dentist that you will paint her house in exchange for two checkups and one whitening.

**EXAMPLE** You agree with your neighbor to trade lawn mowing for vegetables from his garden.

---

Barter, the exchange of goods for goods (or service for service), is really inefficient in terms of resources used. Sure, it may work in a household setting where members "trade" services. But suppose you have shovels to trade, and you want to acquire a new laser printer. Barter requires you to find someone willing to trade a printer for shovels. This can be very time-consuming, even if you use eBay or Craigslist, which posts thousands of barter-related ads a month. This inefficiency limits the widespread use of barter. Nonetheless, bartering remains one avenue of exchange. One reason it persists is that because no money changes hands, people can trade goods and services without any tax implications.[2]

· · · · · · ·

[1] For a discussion of one such episode, see R.A. Radford, "The Economic Organization of a P.O.W. Camp." *Economica* 12 (November 1945): 189–291. For a more modern twist, see Stephanie Simon, "Cash-Strapped California's IOUs Just the Latest Sub for Dollars." *Wall Street Journal*, July 25, 2009.

[2] "No Wallet Necessary," *New York Times*, March 21, 2010.

In most societies, bartering gives way to monetary exchange. Regardless of its physical shape, using money significantly lowers the economic cost of trading goods and services. As long as everyone agrees to accept certain coins, pieces of paper, or dog teeth in exchange for goods, switching from barter to monetary exchange frees up time people once spent finding someone to trade with to produce more goods or engage in more leisure. Thus, the most important distinguishing characteristic of a good that becomes money is that it serves as a **medium of exchange**.

**MEDIUM OF EXCHANGE** A good that is used to facilitate trade.

**EXAMPLE** Instead of bartering dental visits for house painting, you pay for your checkups with pieces of colored paper. Your dentist accepts the colored paper because she knows her grocer will too.

To be an effective medium of exchange, the good that is serving as money must possess certain attributes. For instance, suppose we use chickens as money. To be a successful medium of exchange, we must be able to distinguish a chicken from, say, a goose. That isn't too hard. But what if only a special kind of chicken is used as money, say, a certain breed of American chicken versus an Andalusian chicken? How good you are at telling the difference between the two may mean the difference between trading your classic 1970 Mustang for chickens that everyone will accept in exchange and having a flock of chickens that are only useful in other ways.

As you can see, it is critical that whatever is used as money must be easily verifiable and homogeneous. Put another way, a successful medium of exchange should be recognizable and not easily counterfeited. You have probably noticed that the design of U.S. currency has been changing in recent years. Today, the U.S. Treasury is printing the bills with more colors, watermarks, magnetic strips, and so forth.[3] This is an attempt to make the bills harder to duplicate because improved photocopying technology has made it easier to counterfeit money.

Continuing with our chicken-as-money scenario, what happens if you and your dentist agree that the "chicken price" of extracting your molar is 1.5 chickens? That payment could get messy. Other items, usually goods that are storable and more easily divisible than a chicken, often become preferred forms of money. For centuries, gold, silver, bronze, and other metals were fashioned into coins and used for money. Even though various competing monies may have circulated, the government, whether it was Roman emperors, European kings, or modern democracies, often stepped in and produced some form of money that became, by law, the only viable medium of exchange. In the United States, for example, that dollar in your pocket says that it is "legal tender," which means it is accepted in exchange. It also is illegal to try and counterfeit that dollar. So, in effect, the government controls (it has a monopoly over) the production of money. Under these conditions, such money, referred to as *fiat* money, serves the role of a medium of exchange because the government says it does.

As long as buyers and sellers are willing to accept the government's backing of the money—to ensure its value in exchange—then fiat money serves as a medium of exchange. And it does so without any store of gold in a vault somewhere backing its value. When that social contract breaks down, as it did during the hyperinflations we

· · · · · · ·

[3]Steven Heller, "Anatomy of a Benjamin." *New York Times*, April 23, 2010.

talked about in Chapter 12, then acceptance of fiat money stops, and people search for other means to exchange goods and services, even barter.

**Money as a Unit of Account.** If something serves as a medium of exchange, need it have any other features that help identify it as money? Whatever is considered money usually acts as a **unit of account**. This means that the prices of goods are stated in units of the money. For example, a car in the United States is priced in terms of U.S. dollars; in Europe, the price is stated in euros; and in China, renminbi.

> **UNIT OF ACCOUNT** A unit of account is the standard of measurement used to state prices.

> **EXAMPLE** In the United States, prices are stated in terms of dollars. In Mexico, prices are stated in terms of pesos.

This aspect of money enormously reduces the cost of making a trade. To see this, first think about an economy in which there are just two goods: cans of soda and iPods. If the "soda price" of the iPod is 300 cans of soda, then the iPod price of 1 can of soda is 1/300 iPods. Calculating one price—the price of one good in terms of the other—automatically provides the other. Now think of an economy in which there are five different goods. With five items, the number of price-pairs—the price for one good stated in terms of another good—increases to 10. For simplicity, suppose the five goods are denoted by the letters A, B, C, D, and E. By price-pairs, we mean the pair-wise combinations AB, AC, AD, AE, BC, BD, BE, CD, CE, and DE.

Although you might initially be able to keep the 10 price-pairs straight while out shopping, what would happen if there were suddenly 40 different goods to choose from in the economy? This isn't too far from the number of individual items offered for sale in many fast-food restaurants. When there are 40 goods, the number of price-pairs jumps to 780. If there are 100 items, there are 4,950 price-pairs.[4] Comparison-price shopping just got a whole lot harder. Clearly, having some good serve as the unit of account—the standard unit for measuring prices—dramatically lowers the economic cost of assessing relative prices and making trades.

**Money as a Store of Value.** The other attribute of money is that it can serve as a **store of value**. In other words, money can be used as a "temporary abode of purchasing power." This catchy phrase describes our actions when we put dollars, drachmas, or pesos in a cookie jar with the intent of using them to buy things in the future; or when we deposit our paychecks into bank accounts with the intention of saving for next year's tuition. The bank account in this case serves as the store of value function of money.

> **STORE OF VALUE** A good that can be stored and traded later.

> **EXAMPLE** If you put $10 a week into an envelope to save for an iPod, you are using money as a store of value.

· · · · · · ·

[4]The standard formula used to calculate the number of price-pairs is $N(N - 1)/2$ where $N$ is the number of goods. Thus, if there are 10 goods, the number of price-pairs is $10(10 - 1)/2 = 45$. If there are, say, 5,000 items in an average grocery store, calculate how many price-pairs there are. See why it's nice (and economically efficient) to have a unit of account?

Money as a store of value can be problematic, though, especially if the purpose is to save for an expenditure in the future. Suppose you stuff $1,000 under your mattress with the idea that it will pay for tuition next year. What if ten months from now, your university announces that due to inflation the university must impose a tuition increase? That $1,000 will buy less education in the future. Another way of stating this is that today's money lost its tuition "purchasing power" in the future. If you had known this in advance, you should have put the money into an investment. Putting your money in a bank account that pays interest would have increased the $1,000 over time. As long as the return from the investment (the interest earned on the bank deposit) matches the rate of increase in tuition, then using money as a store of value was a good idea.

There have been times in a number of countries when the purchasing power of money fell so dramatically—prices rose so fast—that people reverted to barter. As you saw in Chapter 12, there is an inverse relation between how much money is circulating in an economy and its purchasing power. Hyperinflation reduces money's exchangeability to the point where it becomes worthless. In less-dramatic inflation episodes, such as that experienced by the United States during the 1970s, people sometimes have used nonmonetary assets, such as artwork, real estate, and even baseball cards, as substitutes for money as a store of value. They used these real things because while money was losing its purchasing power, it was hoped that the value of the assets purchased would rise along with other goods' prices.

## Why and How Do Economists Actually Measure Money?

In modern times, economists measure money by combining different financial assets that meet the functional characteristics of money we just described. To do this, we must figure out which existing forms of money—currency, checking accounts, savings accounts, and so forth—fit the different characteristics just described. That is, if a savings account is used only as a temporary abode of purchasing power, should those dollars on deposit be considered money in the same way currency is? Wouldn't you think that currency is more of a medium of exchange than it is a store of value? These distinctions actually are very important—so important, in fact, that the world's central banks (such as the Federal Reserve in the United States and the Bank of England) create and monitor several money measures. Why? These banks control the supply of money in their countries, and the supply of money relative to the demand for it has an impact on inflation and economic activity. You have seen that increases in the money supply in excess of money demand can lead to rapidly rising rates of inflation. Also, it is widely believed that policies that dramatically reduce the supply of money are one cause of recessions.

If you were going to devise a method to measure money, how would you begin? One factor to consider is the money's **liquidity**. The liquidity of money refers to how easily the thing chosen to serve as money—whether its chickens, pieces of paper, or your house—can be converted into another good. After all, isn't that really the key purpose of money, to facilitate exchange?

**LIQUIDITY** The relative ease with which money can be converted into a good or service.

**EXAMPLE** The attendant at a convenience store will accept a $10 bill for the items you purchase but will not take a personal check. Cash is more liquid than checks.

You can think of liquidity as a scale that runs left to right like a dial on an antique radio. The left-hand side of the dial is highly liquid assets. As you move across the dial, liquidity declines. Over on the left-hand side of the dial is cash, the most liquid type of money. What business do you know of that doesn't accept cash? (Remember what we mentioned earlier, that cash is legal tender? If you don't believe us, have a look at some ones or fives.) If cash is the most liquid form of money, next on the liquidity dial is probably checking accounts. You can usually write checks to purchase items and pay your bills but not always. Not all businesses accept checks. In addition, businesses that do accept checks rarely accept checks written against out-of-state bank accounts. So, if you are going to school in Boise and are visiting the Florida beaches over spring break, forget about writing a check on your Bank of Boise account to pay for dinner at the local restaurant. In response to such needs, financial innovations, such as debit cards, have increased the liquidity of checking accounts.

Moving further to the right on the liquidity dial, you hit savings accounts. Even if you have $1,500 in your savings account, proving that to that South Beach restaurant's cashier won't help you pay for dinner. In that sense, savings is less liquid than the money held in checking accounts and as cash. After savings accounts come certificates of deposits, then financial assets such as bonds and stocks, and if we move far enough to the right, maybe even your house. As you move further up the dial—into the illiquid range—exchanging your "money" for the good you want to buy becomes increasingly difficult.

What about credit cards, you might be wondering. Why didn't we discuss them? Because credit cards aren't money: the charges you put on your credit card are debts you owe to the credit card company. If you don't believe this is so, read the upcoming ECONOMIC FALLACY.

Economists use the idea of liquidity to measure the amount of money in the economy. In the United States, the Federal Reserve uses data collected from banks and other financial institutions to calculate several money measures. What they are trying to do is to group together those financial assets—cash, checking accounts, savings accounts, and so on—to provide real-world counterparts to the liquidity concepts described earlier. The most widely followed measures of money circulating in the economy are called **M1** and **M2**. **Table 17.1** provides a breakdown of the amount of money included in M1 and M2.

The M1 measure includes currency in the hands of the public (outside of bank vaults), traveler's checks and checking accounts at banks and other financial institutions (such as credit unions). M1 is the most liquid money measure that most closely captures money's function as a medium of exchange. The M2 measure expands on M1 by adding savings accounts and other financial assets. M2 is, therefore, less liquid than M1.

**M1** A "narrow" measure of money, which includes financial assets that serve mostly as a medium of exchange.

**M2** A "broad" measure that expands on M1 by adding in savings accounts and other financial assets thought to have a store-of-value function.

It is important to mention that neither is *the* correct measure of money. So why have two? The answer is that each provides information that might be beneficial to policy makers. For example, there is evidence that narrower measures of money, such

| Table 17.1 | Two Measures of the U.S. Money Supply: M1 and M2 (in billions of dollars, January 2010) |
|---|---|
| Currency | $861.1 |
| + Traveler's Checks | 5.1 |
| + Demand Deposits | 435.0 |
| + Other Checkable Deposits | 375.3 |
| = M1 | 1676.4 |
| + Savings Deposits | 4856.5 |
| + Small-Denomination Time Deposits* | 1139.9 |
| + Retail Money Funds | 790.7 |
| = M2 | $8463.5 |

*Small-denomination time deposits are those issued in amounts less than $100,000 at commercial banks and thrift institutions.

**Note:** Figures may not sum due to rounding.

The Federal Reserve uses data collected from banks and other financial institutions to calculate several money measures in the economy. The most widely followed measures of money are M1 and M2. The M1 measure includes currency in the hands of the public, traveler's checks, and checking accounts at banks and other financial institutions (such as credit unions). The M2 measure expands on M1 by adding savings accounts and other financial assets. M2 is, therefore, relatively less liquid than M1.

**Source:** Federal Reserve Board of Governors, Statistical Release H6

as M1, are more closely related to changes in prices than the broader measures of M2. However, changes in M2 have been shown to affect economic activity in a more predictable way than M1. Consequently, the Federal Reserve publishes (and economists follow) both measures.

If they are less liquid, why do individuals hold so much money in savings-type accounts compared to checking accounts or as cash? The answer is opportunity cost. Credit cards make it easier for people to reduce their holdings of transaction-oriented money (think cash) and hold more of their "money" as a store of value (think savings account). That is, over time, the public has shifted from holding money in a form that pays no return (cash and noninterest checking accounts) to holding it in a form that pays interest.

Only a generation ago, many people often cashed their weekly paycheck (direct deposit was not yet available) and used that cash until their next paycheck arrived. Some people deposited the money in banks, but others merely stashed the cash in safe places in their homes. Direct deposit and electronic bill paying emerged only as a result of improved computer technology and the widespread use of the Internet.

You have experienced an evolution in terms of how people use money and how it is measured. For example, many of us use debit cards to buy gasoline: we swipe our cards at the pump, get authorization, fill our tanks, and go. As a result, we do not need to carry around cash—just our debit cards. The currency that you would have used sits in a bank account that earns interest—at least until your account is debited for the gas you bought. And if you really need cash, just insert your card at a nearby ATM, whether you are in Minneapolis, Miami, or Milan.

**ECONOMIC FALLACY**   Credit cards are money.

**False.** Even though people use credit cards to buy everything from books to bubble gum, economists don't consider the cards to be money. Rather, a credit card is considered to be a *money substitute*. This might seem like splitting hairs, but the distinction is important, and we make it because we want to measure money as accurately as possible. Using a credit card to buy gas generates a loan from the credit card company to you: the card company pays off the gasoline company for you. You have incurred a debt to the credit card company, which is why it bills you at the end of the month. This means that the money used to purchase the gas comes from the credit card company's bank balance, which already is included in M2. Counting your card balance *and* the credit card company's bank deposit would incorrectly inflate our measure of the actual supply of money. So, just like outstanding balances on home mortgages or student loans are not counted as money, neither are your credit card balances.

Technology allows you to economize on your cash holdings. This not only reduces the cost of trading but also motivates us to hold more of our money in savings-type accounts rather than in cash or in noninterest-paying checking accounts. Technology also allows us to better protect the purchasing power of our money holdings by putting it to work earning interest. Put another way, because technology raises the opportunity cost of holding cash, you are less likely to do so.

The upshot of this is that the definitions in Table 17.1 are not fixed in stone. In fact, the definitions have changed several times in the past 20 or so years. As technology and the way in which we conduct our transactions change, the specific components comprising M1 and M2 will change, too. In other words, although economists' *functional* notion of what money is won't change, the actual items included in the measurement of money have and will continue to evolve. Electronic currency—so-called E-money—may dominate the next generation of what economists measure as money.[5] Just as coins and dollar bills have given way to paper checks, paper checks are being replaced by online-payment systems. In the future, it is not unlikely that digital money will become the most widely used form of money. Maybe one day, cash and coins will be relegated only to collectors and museums.

## 17.2 Banks and Money

Modern banks are a far cry from what they were centuries ago.[6] Both then and now, banks exist to facilitate exchange. Think about it. You get your paycheck, spend most of it, and have some left over at the end of the month. What do you do with this excess income? You could advertise that you are willing to lend it out. But then you'd have to do background checks on potential borrowers, make sure that they use the money for what they borrowed it for, and monitor their payments. This hassle is one role that a bank takes on.

You put your excess income into the bank, and it pays you an interest rate on your deposit. The bank then takes your money and lends it out at some other interest rate that is higher than your deposit rate. The difference is the bank's source of

· · · · · · ·

[5]Peter Spencer, "E-money: Will It Take Off?" *World Economics,* January-March, 2001.

[6]If you are interested in the history of money and banking, a good introduction is Niall Ferguson's *The Ascent of Money: A Financial History of the World* (New York: Penguin Press, 2008). Or, download the PBS series based on the book.

income. Banks thus serve as an intermediary between savers and borrowers. This makes the banks' role in the economy much different than, say, sandwich shops. If banks stop lending, they still can generate income by buying interest-bearing assets, such as government securities. As we vividly saw during and after the recession of 2007–2009, when banks (and other lenders) think it is just too risky to make loans, it becomes difficult for firms to borrow money to continue operating. Business grinds to a halt. Consumers also find it difficult to borrow money to buy houses and cars. The home construction industry suffers, as do automakers. The people who work for these types of businesses then spend less money on other products, which, in turn, affects more companies and people. This is why the government has a special interest in keeping banks operating (even if it's not popular to do so).

## How Banks "Create" Money

Have you seen the classic 1946 movie *It's a Wonderful Life,* starring Jimmy Stewart? In one scene, all of the people with deposits at the Bailey Building and Loan Association want to withdraw all of their money at once. George Bailey (played by Jimmy Stewart) explains to them that he can't give all of them all their money because he doesn't have it. As he explains, their deposits have been loaned out to their neighbors to buy homes, open businesses, and so forth. He offers to pay each person some part of their deposits but not all. The fact that the Bailey Building and Loan holds some deposits but uses most of them to make loans exemplifies what banks do. As you will see, banks affect the supply of money in an economy by making loans, and this in turn affects the expansion and contraction of deposits. This is how banks create money.

Let's simplify reality and think of deposits as just deposits instead of checking accounts that earn interest, small-time or jumbo savings accounts, and so on. This makes the discussion less complicated: a deposit is a deposit. Banks have learned how to manage their deposits. They manage their inventory of deposits, just as a retail manager in a bed store knows how to manage the number of mattresses he has on hand. The difference between mattresses and deposits is that the bank knows that customers make deposits and withdrawals from these deposits on a fairly predictable basis. For example, customers withdraw more cash on the weekend, around holidays, and so on. The bank also observes how many checks are written against existing accounts and predicts how much it will need to cover those payments. Because customers do not request or use all of their deposits, the bank holds only a fraction of the total deposits it needs to meet these periodic withdrawals. The fraction of deposits held back by the bank is called **reserves**.

> **RESERVES** Money that banks hold as a fraction of their deposits to meet their customers' withdrawal needs.

> EXAMPLE Bank reserves are like benchwarmers on sports teams: they only come into play when a team (bank) is in a pinch.

The tricky part for banks is figuring out just how much money to hold as reserves. One bank might be very conservative and keep nearly all of its deposits on hand. This bank wouldn't make loans or buy securities with your money, just keep it safe for you. Its profits would come only from charging you a fee for keeping your money safe from people who might want to steal it. Another bank might take your deposit, keep a small portion of it on reserve, and loan the rest of it out. Taking the risk of loaning out the money could make this bank more profitable than the other bank. The process of lending money out is also the means by which the bank creates money.

Let's see how this works. You have $1,000 in currency, stuffed in your sock drawer. You decide to enter the modern age and open a new checking account at the local bank. When you make the deposit into your checking account, the M1 money supply in the economy—currency plus deposits—does not change because you are just moving the $1,000 from one component of M1 to another. Suppose your bank thinks it prudent to hold 10 percent of all deposits in reserve. This is the bank's **reserve ratio**.

**RESERVE RATIO** The percentage of deposits held as reserves by a bank.

Of your $1,000 deposit, the bank puts $100 safely away in the vault. What about the remaining $900? The bank makes a loan of $900 to your cousin Sue to buy a used Vespa motor scooter. Sue takes the $900, buys the scooter, and the motorcycle shop deposits the $900 into its checking account at the bank. Out of this new deposit, the bank takes 10 percent, $90 in this case, and places it in the vault. Now it has $810 to lend out, which it does to someone else. This person then spends $810 on rare comic books from a dealer, which creates another deposit of $810. The comic-book seller's bank, in turn, holds back 10 percent of this new deposit ($81) as reserves and now has $729 to loan out to someone else. We could go on and on, but you get the idea.

Table 17.2 shows the chain reaction of deposits and lending that your initial deposit of $1,000 set off. It sets off increases in lending because the bank wants to hold as reserves just a fraction of your initial deposit. The bank lends out the rest to other people, who use it to earn money and then make more deposits themselves. Because deposits are part of the money supply, the bank "creates" money as deposits grow. In fact, in just the first five steps, your deposit of $1,000 increased the money

| Table 17.2 | The Deposit Expansion Process with a 10-Percent Reserve Ratio: An Example | |
|---|---|---|
| **Deposits ($)** | **Change in Reserves ($)** | **Loans ($)** |
| 1,000 | 100 | 900 |
| 900 | 90 | 810 |
| 810 | 81 | 729 |
| 729 | 72.90 | 656.10 |
| 656.10 | 65.61 | 590.49 |
| 590.49 | 59.05 | 531.44 |
| 531.44 | etc. | etc. |

Because deposits are counted as part of the money supply, the expansion of reserves that results from them helps banks "create" money. This table shows the chain reaction of deposits and lending from an initial deposit of $1,000. Deposits lead to more lending because the bank holds only a fraction of each new deposit. In this example, of the initial $1,000 deposit, the bank puts $100 into reserve. This frees up $900 with which it can make loans. This loan creates another deposit, of which 10 percent, or $90, in this case, is placed in reserve. The bank now has another $810 to lend out, which it does to someone who buys something from a seller, who makes another deposit, and so on. In the first five steps shown, the initial $1,000 deposit increased the money supply by over $4,095. The process continues until there are no more reserves to lend out.

supply by over $4,095. The process isn't over either: the bank continues to loan out money until it has no reserves to lend out.

## Banks and the Money Supply

The previous example captures the money-creation process pretty well. What you should notice is that the process proceeds not because of the initial deposit, but because the bank desires to hold only a fraction of its deposits in reserve. In any **fractional-reserve banking** system, the impact of a change in the banking system's reserves will have a magnified effect on the nation's money supply. As you will soon see, central banks use reserve levels to change the level of the money supply in their economies.

**FRACTIONAL-RESERVE BANKING** A banking system in which banks are required to hold a certain percentage of their deposits as reserves.

**EXAMPLE** Bill found ten $100 bills on the street and deposited them into his checking account. The bank credited Bill's account for $1,000. It kept one of the $100 bills (10 percent of the deposit) in its vault as required by law. It loaned out the remaining nine.

Let's expand our example a bit and make our bank a bit more realistic. **Table 17.3** shows a balance sheet, which is sometimes referred to as a T-account because of its shape. The balance sheet indicates that First National Bank has more than just deposits and reserves. Among its assets are loans and securities valued at $4,500. Loans and securities (such as U.S. Treasury bills) are assets to the bank because they are the bank's source of income. Against these assets are the bank's liabilities; in this example, the liabilities are deposits totaling $5,000. They are a liability to the bank because the bank owes them to you. (Deposits are your asset.) Against these deposits, First National Bank holds 10 percent in reserve—hence the $500 listed as "desired" reserves. First National is holding no more reserves than desired, so its **excess reserves** are zero.

**Table 17.3** First National Bank's Balance Sheet

| Assets | | Liabilities | |
|---|---|---|---|
| Loans and Securities | $4,500 | Deposits | $5,000 |
| Reserves: | | | |
| Desired | $500 | | |
| Excess | --0-- | | |
| Total Assets | $5,000 | Total Liabilities | $5,000 |

This is a simplified example of a bank's balance sheet, sometimes referred to as a T-account. The balance sheet indicates that First National Bank has assets, in the form of loans and securities, valued at $4,500. These are assets because they are the bank's source of income. The bank also has liabilities, in this case, deposits, which total $5,000. Deposits are a liability to the bank because the bank owes them to depositors (you), should they wish to withdraw them. First National holds 10 percent of these deposits in reserve, which is the $500 listed as "desired" reserves. First National is holding no more reserves than desired, so its excess reserves are zero. Because this is a balance sheet, total assets equal total liabilities.

**EXCESS RESERVES** Excess reserves are the difference between total reserves and desired reserves.

EXAMPLE In August 2001, excess reserves in the U.S. banking system were $1.2 billion. In response to the uncertainties surrounding the events of September 11, excess reserves increased to over $19 billion in September. In October of that year, they fell back to $1.3 billion.

EXAMPLE In August 2008, excess reserves in the U.S. banking system were $1.9 billion. The investment bank Lehman Brothers declared bankruptcy on September 15, 2008. By December 2008, excess reserves had risen to over $767 billion.

Let's assume that the bank tries to keep its excess reserves at zero. Only in cases of increased uncertainty, such as a financial panic, does the bank want to hold excess reserves. Finally, because Table 17.3 is a balance sheet, the bank's total assets equal the bank's total liabilities.

For the sake of this example, let's assume that the amount of currency in the economy is zero. This would mean that the money supply consists only of the $5,000 in deposits. Another way of thinking about this is that the money supply is just a multiple of the reserves being held by First National. With First National's reserve ratio equal to 10 percent, you can see that the amount of money (deposits in this case) is equal to ten times the reserves.

The relation between reserves, the reserve ratio, and the money supply can be written as

$$M = (1/rr) \times R$$

where $M$ stands for the supply of money, $R$ is reserves in the bank, and $rr$ is the reserve ratio. The term $(1/rr)$ is referred to as the **money multiplier**. In reality, the money multiplier is much more complicated than the ratio shown. Even so, for our purpose, the multiplier is used to illustrate the link between changes in reserves and changes in the money supply.

**MONEY MULTIPLIER** The money multiplier is the multiple by which the money supply changes given a change in bank reserves.

EXAMPLE If the desired reserve ratio ($rr$) is 5 percent, the money multiplier is (1/0.05) or 20. A $1 increase in reserves will eventually lead to a $20 increase in the money supply ($M$). If the reserve ratio is 20 percent, the money multiplier is only 5.

Let's use First National's balance sheet in Table 17.3 to focus on how a change in securities sets off a change in the money supply. (Remember from Chapter 12 where we said that the Federal Reserve controls the growth of money by enticing the public to buy or sell government securities? This extends that discussion.) Some of First National's assets are in securities. For example, First National might hold short-term government securities, which are very safe. Now suppose that the government offers to buy some of those securities back. The bank and the government negotiate, agree on a price, and the bank sells $1,000 worth of the securities back to the government. This is shown in **Table 17.4** as a reduction in the bank's "loans and securities" entry. The government pays for the securities by increasing

## Table 17.4 How the Purchase of Securities by the Government Creates Money

### (a) First National's balance sheet following the sale of securities

| Assets | | Liabilities | |
|---|---|---|---|
| Loans and Securities | $3,500 | Deposits | $5,000 |
| (−$1,000 sale of securities) | | | |
| | | | |
| Reserves: | $1,500 | | |
| Desired | $500 | | |
| Excess (+) | $1,000 | | |
| Total Assets | $5,000 | Total Liabilities | $5,000 |

### (b) First National's balance sheet after initial loan

| Assets | | Liabilities | |
|---|---|---|---|
| Loans and Securities | $4,500 | Deposits | $6,000 |
| ($1,000 loan to Ron) | | ($1,000 deposit by motorcycle shop) | |
| | | | |
| Reserves: | $1,500 | | |
| Desired | $600 | | |
| Excess | $900 | | |
| Total Assets | $6,000 | Total Liabilities | $6,000 |

This table illustrates the effect of a government purchase of securities from First National Bank. In panel (a) the government's purchase of $1,000 worth of the securities is shown as a reduction in the bank's "loans and securities" entry. The government pays for the securities by increasing the bank's reserves by $1,000. Because the bank's deposits did not change, its desired reserves are still $500, but its excess reserves increased by the $1,000 from the sale of securities. Because the bank wants to keep its excess reserves at zero, it will loan out the $1,000. Panel (b) shows what happens following the loan—how it leads to additional deposits, then more loans, and yet more deposits. Because of fractional-reserve banking, this initial sale of securities and increase in excess reserves will lead to a multiple expansion of deposits and, therefore, the money supply.

the bank's reserves by $1,000. (How do they do this? We'll explain this "sleight of hand" shortly.)

The bank's exchange of some of its securities for reserves increases its total reserves over and above the bank's desired amount. Because the bank's deposits did not change, its desired reserves stay at $500. However, its excess reserves increase by $1,000 from the sale of securities. What will the bank do? Because it wants to keep its excess reserves at zero, it will loan the $1,000. The bank makes the $1,000 loan, maybe to your friend Ron, who wants to buy a Vespa similar to Sue's. The motorcycle shop owner puts the $1,000 into his account, and deposits increase. In the first "round" of this expansion, the bank loans out the $1,000, which, when deposited, increases the money supply by $1,000. Of the $1,000, the bank increases its desired reserves by $100, leaving another $900 in excess reserves to be loaned. And away the process goes, as shown earlier in Table 17.2, until there is nothing left to loan.

As you can see, the outcome is the same as your making a deposit of cash into your bank account. What is the total effect on the money supply of the government's purchase of securities from the bank at this point? The initial $1,000 increase in reserves will cause the money supply to increase by $10,000. Because of fractional-reserve banking, this initial change in reserves will lead to a *multiple* expansion of the money supply.

So far we've only talked about an increase in deposits or reserves and the money supply. What happens if deposits fall? Instead of depositing $1,000, you decide to withdraw cash from your account. The bank pays you the $1,000, so its liabilities decline by that amount. But because balance sheets must balance, the bank's assets must also fall by the same amount. Part of this shows up as a reduction in the amount of reserves the bank holds. Because we've been assuming that the reserve ratio is 10 percent, the reserves will fall by $100. Now the bank has to find $900 more, and it finds it by reducing its loans outstanding. The bank could do this by asking Sue to pay up her loan: it "calls the loan," in other words. With this reduction in loans, a multiple contraction in the money supply is set into motion.

Banks do not want to reduce their loans if they don't have to. After all, loans pay interest, which is revenue to a bank. In reality, banks might draw down on their excess reserves (if they have any) to meet the withdrawals of their depositors. Or, they may sell some of their securities to do so. As you can imagine, it doesn't take much in terms of customers withdrawing their deposits for the bank to start retrenching its lending activities.

What you have just seen is that the multiple expansion (and contraction) of the money supply can start with one deposit of currency into a checking account. Or, it can occur when a bank sells its government securities back to the government. In the United States, the Federal Reserve buys and sells government securities to change the money supply. This process also is used to affect the level of real interest rates in the economy. We will delve into those topics later in this chapter. First, let's describe what the Federal Reserve is and explain a little more about how it works.

## 17.3 The Federal Reserve System

After nearly 100 years of experimentation and several failed attempts, Congress passed the Federal Reserve Act in 1913. The Act authorized the formation of the central bank we have in the United States today. The Federal Reserve Act was signed by President Woodrow Wilson on Christmas Eve of that year. (A brief history of the events leading up to the creation of the Federal Reserve System is provided in the Appendix.) By creating a central bank, Congress sought to remedy the recurrent problems from which the U.S. economy and banking system suffered. Today, the Fed is responsible not only for directing monetary policy but also for supervising and regulating the banking system, overseeing the payments system between banks, and dealing with foreign-currency operations and consumer and community affairs.[7]

The Federal Reserve Act reflects as much political compromise as it does economics. For example, to gain the support of representatives of the western and southern states, proponents of the central bank agreed to a system of 12 district banks that are geographically dispersed. **Figure 17.1** shows the Federal Reserve districts, along with the district bank cities. You can see that the districts vary greatly in size. This reflects the fact that when drawn up, the districts were established using a formula based on population and business activity. The western districts are much larger than their eastern counterparts because 100 years ago, the West was not as populated nor as commercially prosperous as it is today.

The Federal Reserve map mirrors the politics of the early 1900s. In many aspects, the layout of the Federal Reserve System was a conscious attempt to disperse the power of the central bank. In the late 1800s and into the twentieth century, there was considerable

· · · · · · · ·

[7]For more information on the functions of the Fed, visit the Board of Governors Web site and access the publication *The Federal Reserve System: Purposes and Function*.

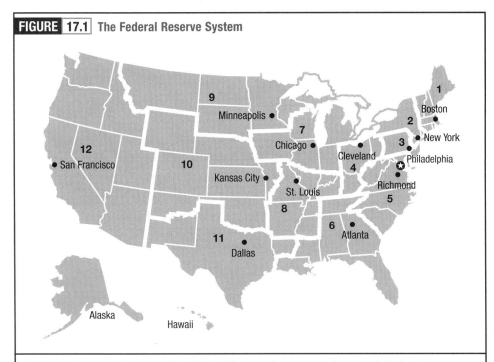

**FIGURE 17.1**  The Federal Reserve System

The Federal Reserve Act created the Federal Reserve System, a collection of 12 district, or regional, banks that are geographically dispersed. This map shows the 12 districts and the city in which each district bank is located. The Board of Governors of the Federal Reserve System is located in Washington, D.C.

*Source:* Federal Reserve Board of Governors

economic and political friction between the agrarian southern and western states and the relatively more urban eastern states. It has even been suggested that L. Frank Baum's classic story, which appeared in 1900, turned-popular 1939 movie *The Wizard of Oz* is really an allegory about the economic and political strife of the times. Economist Hugh Rockoff has suggested that the story is about the debate between those advocating the use of gold to back the money supply versus those wishing to use silver and gold, and about the conflicting interests of eastern bankers and western farmers.[8] When the Federal Reserve System was being established, this kind of parochialism and populism greatly influenced how the system was structured. Incidentally, sentiments such as these still persist. How often during the past few years have you heard talk-show hosts, politicians, or people around your dinner table expound on the issue of "Wall Street versus Main Street"?[9]

· · · · · · ·

[8]Hugh Rockoff, "The Wizard of Oz as a Monetary Allegory." *Journal of Political Economy* (1990). Consider just a few clues: Dorothy and her intrepid group (each member representing a part of society or some political figure of the day) follow the "yellow brick road" (gold is stored in brick-like ingots) to the Land of Oz (gold is measured in ounces, or oz's), and Dorothy is from Kansas (an agricultural state) and transported to the East where she must try to find a way home. And in the original story, Dorothy's slippers were silver, not ruby red. Thus the reason that they were coveted by the Wicked Witch of the West: she wanted control of the production of silver.

[9]Nina Easton, "Main Street Turns against Wall Street." CNNMoney.com (September 28, 2008). The sub-headline is perhaps even more revealing: "A populist backlash is changing America's political climate. Inflamed by the financial crisis and bailouts, a form of class warfare could haunt business leaders for years to come."

## The Board of Governors of the Federal Reserve

The Federal Reserve Act created a central bank that, unlike its counterparts elsewhere in the world, was set up not only to disperse power but also to operate largely independent of the political process. The process of appointing members to the **Board of Governors**, located in Washington, D.C., illustrates this desire for an independent central bank. The Board of Governors is the governing body of the Federal Reserve and consists of seven members.

**BOARD OF GOVERNORS** The governing body of the Federal Reserve System.

The appointment process for board members (governors) and for the presidents of the 12 district banks is designed to minimize influence from the political sphere. The president appoints the seven governors, who must also be approved by the U.S. Senate. Each governor is appointed for a 14-year term, a period longer than any president can serve and longer than the term for any other elected officeholder in the United States.

The fact that the governors' terms are staggered—one term expires on January 31 in every even-numbered year—theoretically limits the ability of a single president to appoint a majority of the board in a four-year presidential term. Today, however, most governors do not serve their entire 14-year terms. Many find themselves in demand by financial and consulting firms. This means that some presidents have been able to appoint all members of the board. In addition, the 12 district bank presidents are appointed not by politicians but by his or her district bank's board of directors and must be approved by the Board of Governors.

The person who guides monetary policy in the United States is the **chairman of the Board of Governors**.

**CHAIRMAN OF THE BOARD OF GOVERNORS** The head of the U.S. Federal Reserve.

**EXAMPLE** Ben Bernanke is the current chairman of the Board of Governors. The previous chairman was Alan Greenspan.

The chairman of the Board of Governors is appointed by the president of the United States and confirmed by the Senate. The chairman is one of the governors of the board and serves a renewable 4-year term. Because the chairman also is a governor, the maximum time this person can serve is the same as the term governors can serve— 14 years. Some chairmen have served longer than 14 years because when they were first appointed, they completed someone's unexpired term and then began a 14-year term of their own. The two longest-serving chairmen (so far) have been William McChesney Martin (April 2, 1951 to January 31, 1970) and Alan Greenspan (August 11, 1987 to January 31, 2006).

Although partly in jest, it sometimes is said that the Fed chairman is the second most powerful person in the United States, second only to the president. How is it that this individual, unelected by voters to this position, wields such power? The reason lies in the fact that policy actions taken by the Federal Reserve have a tremendous impact on our daily lives. Every time the Fed takes a policy action, financial markets react. The Fed's decisions affect how much your car loan is or the interest rate on you student loan. In fact, it is well-documented that public statements made by the chairman sometimes cause large swings in financial markets, both here and abroad.

## The Federal Open Market Committee (FOMC)

Even though the chairman of the Board of Governors technically has no more power than any of the other governors, this is misleading. Most chairmen influence policy in very direct and meaningful ways. The chairman's power stems from the fact that he chairs the meetings of the **Federal Open Market Committee (FOMC)**. The FOMC is the policy-making arm of the Federal Reserve System.

> **FEDERAL OPEN MARKET COMMITTEE (FOMC)** The policy-making arm of the Federal Reserve. The FOMC decides the direction of monetary policy.

The FOMC consists of the 7 governors and the 12 district bank presidents. Although each president is a member of the FOMC, only 5 of the presidents vote on policy decisions at any one meeting. Thus, for each policy decision, there are 12 voting members of the FOMC: the 7 governors and 5 of the 12 bank presidents. Of the bank presidents, the president of the Federal Reserve Bank of New York sits as a permanent voting member of the FOMC. The other presidents serve one-year terms as voting members in a rotation that is set by law. Nine of the Reserve Bank presidents vote one year out of every three, whereas the presidents of the Federal Reserve Banks of Chicago and Cleveland vote in alternate years.

How does this arrangement compare to the policy-making branches of other central banks? The size of the policy-making group—the equivalent to the Fed's FOMC—varies across banks. The Bank of England and the Bank of Japan both have 9 members on their policy committees, and the European Central Bank (ECB) has 18. A small number of central banks have as few as 5 members on their policy-making committee.

The FOMC meets eight times a year in Washington, D.C. In comparison to other central banks, the majority (including the ECB and Bank of England) meet monthly, and a number of banks' policy makers even meet weekly. Sometimes the FOMC holds special, unscheduled meetings. Such meetings are rare and usually occur in response to some unexpected event that could impose serious consequences for financial markets and the economy. For example, the FOMC held a special meeting on September 17, 2001, in wake of the September 11 terrorist attacks on the Pentagon and the World Trade Center.

You now have the foundation to understand the mechanics of monetary policy making. The FOMC sets monetary policy in the United States. The FOMC determines whether to raise or lower interest rates to increase or decrease the growth rate of the money supply. How it tries to bring about such changes is our next topic. What underlies the Fed's decision process is a question we'll explore in the next chapter.

## 17.4 How the Fed Operates

The Fed attempts to control the supply of money and to affect the level of short-term interest rates in order to influence short-term economic activity and inflation by using several policy tools. One is to change the amount of reserves banks must hold against their deposits. The other, and the one most often used, is buying and selling U.S. government securities in the open market.[10]

· · · · · · ·

[10]The Fed also has another policy option at its disposal: changing the interest rate that the Fed charges financial institutions for loans. If a bank needs a short-term infusion of funds, it may borrow from the Fed. The rate that the Fed charges for such a loan is called the *discount* or *primary credit rate*. Our focus reflects the fact that this tool is not a key policy lever.

## The Fed's Reserve Requirements

Earlier, we talked about banks' *desire* to hold some portion of their deposits on reserve. History suggests that some bankers overextend their lending and hold too few reserves to meet unexpected withdrawals of deposits. When this occurs, if the bank is unable to re-call loans or sell assets fast enough to meet customer demands, the bank may experience a "bank run." If the word gets out that your bank is not meeting depositors' withdrawal demands, you and other customers may try to close out your accounts. Such a demand for deposits may not be met because banks operate in a fractional-reserve system.

The Federal Reserve tries to avoid such banking calamities by requiring most banks—actually all depository institutions, which includes banks, credit unions, and savings and loan associations—to hold at least a minimum percentage of their depos-its on account at the Fed, or as currency in their vault (sometimes called vault cash). This minimum amount is the bank's **reserve requirement**.

> **RESERVE REQUIREMENT** The percentage of deposits a bank must hold as reserves, either as cash in its vault or on account with the Fed.

> **EXAMPLE** When you were young, your parents gave you a weekly allowance of $10. Out of that they required you to put $4 into savings. The "reserve require-ment" they imposed on you was 40 percent.

Table 17.5 shows the reserve requirements on transaction accounts that were in effect beginning in 2010. Reserve requirements are not uniform across banks. Earlier in the chapter, we said that the Fed requires most banks to hold reserves, but you can see from Table 17.5 that small banks, those with deposits less than $10.7 million, do not have to. After a bank's deposits exceed this level, however, reserve requirements are imposed. Between $10.7 and $55.2 million, a bank is required to hold 3 percent of its deposits on reserve (as vault cash and deposits at the Fed). For deposit amounts greater than $55.2 million, the reserve requirement increases to 10 percent. And if you think this seems complicated, historically reserve requirements varied across the size of the bank and depending on where the bank was geographically located, that is, whether the bank was a country bank or one located in a major metropolitan area.[11]

| Table 17.5 Reserve Requirements for U.S. Banks | |
| --- | --- |
| Bank Deposits | Required Percentage (%) |
| $0 to $10.7 million | 0 |
| More than $10.7 million to $55.2 million | 3 |
| More than $55.2 million | 10 |

The reserve requirements on transaction accounts that became effective at the begin-ning of 2010 are shown in this table. Reserve requirements are not uniform. Banks with lower amounts of deposits aren't required to hold as much, if any, in reserve, whereas banks with higher amounts of deposits must maintain higher reserves.

**Source:** Federal Reserve Board of Governors

· · · · · · ·

[11]Joshua N. Feinman, "Reserve Requirements: History, Current Practice, and Potential Reform." *Federal Reserve Bulletin*, June 1993.

Altering the level of reserve requirements has two effects. First, it helps the Fed regulate banks' lending activity. Requiring most banks to hold reserves gives the Federal Reserve funds that it can use to help offset the negative effects in case depositors decide to empty their accounts. Second, as you have learned, the Fed can change reserve requirements to alter the money supply. We can show the power of changing reserve requirements by using the money supply equation. If the required reserve ratio is 10 percent, the money multiplier is 10 (or 1/0.10). That means $500 in reserves is the base for a money supply of $5,000; or

$$\$5,000 = (1/0.10) \times \$500.$$

Leaving reserves ($500) unchanged, what happens if the Fed doubles the reserve requirement from 10 to 20 percent? This halves the money multiplier to 5 (or 1/0.2). If reserves do not change, the money supply decreases from $5,000 to $2,500 [$= (1/0.2) \times$ $500]. A decrease in the reserve requirement has an equally powerful effect on the money supply in the opposite direction: for a given amount of reserves, a decrease in the reserve requirement increases the money supply. Because changing its reserve requirements has such a significant impact on the money supply, the Fed does not use this policy tool very often.

In October 2008, the Board of Governors announced a new policy whereby the Fed would pay interest on required and excess reserves held by banks. The interest rate the Fed pays, which is determined by the Board of Governors (as opposed to the FOMC), was initially set at 0.25 percent on both types of balances. What will this change accomplish? Because it lowers the opportunity cost of holding reserves, all else the same, banks should be willing to hold more of them. As we will discuss in the next chapter, the Fed's action was taken to try and soak up the massive amount of reserves created by its policy actions during the financial crisis that began earlier that year (called *quantitative easing*, which we will deal with later in this chapter). The idea is that by paying interest on reserves, some of them will not be used to make loans and create deposits, which could eventually impact the rate of inflation should banks decide to convert their excess reserves into what eventually would become money.

## SOLVED PROBLEM

**Q** Can you change the reserve requirement without affecting the money supply?

**A** You know that the money supply ($M$) is affected by the Fed changing reserve requirements ($rr$). You also have learned that the Fed can affect the money supply using open-market operations. Can the Fed change reserve requirements and not have any effect on the money supply?

As a policy maker, you have the following information: the current reserve requirement ($rr$) is 10 percent, and the amount of reserves ($R$) in the banking system is $500. Given these values, the money supply is

$$M = (1/rr) \times R$$
$$= (1/0.10) \times \$500$$
$$= \$5,000$$

Suppose, because of increased economic uncertainty, you want to make banks increase their reserve holdings. To do this, you could double the reserve requirement to 20 percent. But suppose at the same time, you do not want the money supply to be reduced. Is there some way to achieve both policy objectives? Looking at the money equation, if we raise reserve requirements, what must we also do so that the money supply doesn't decline?

If you said increase reserves, you are absolutely right. But by how much? Using the equation, we can solve for the answer.

If reserve requirements are 20 percent, and reserves are $500, you know that

$$M = (1/rr) \times R$$
$$= (1/0.20) \times \$500$$
$$= \$2,500$$

So, if we set $M = \$5,000$, we can solve for what reserves ($R$) should be. That is

$$\$5,000 = (1/0.2) \times R$$
$$0.2(\$5,000) = R$$
$$\$1,000 = R$$

When the Fed raises the reserve requirement, it can offset its effects by increasing the reserves in the banking system by engaging in open-market operations, specifically, buying securities. When the Fed undertakes such an action, it is called *sterilizing* the effect of the reserve-requirement change.

## Open-Market Operations Conducted by the Fed

Many people think that the Fed simply announces what it wants the level of interest rates or the growth of the money supply to be, and it just happens. This is not the case. To raise or lower interest rates or to increase or decrease the supply of money, the Fed adds or subtracts reserves from the banking system by using what is called **open-market operations**. Although the Fed could accomplish this by changing its reserve requirements, constantly tweaking them would create uncertainty among banks about the amount of reserves they need to hold. As a result, they might engage in less lending, which could negatively affect the economy. Instead, open-market operations are most-often used.

**OPEN-MARKET OPERATIONS** The Fed's buying and selling of government securities.

**EXAMPLE** On May 21, 2008, the Fed sold $4.999 billion in Treasury securities to government securities dealers.

**EXAMPLE** On December 3, 2010, the Fed purchased $6.81 billion in Treasury securities to government securities dealers.[12]

Open-market operations are perhaps the most powerful policy tool the Fed has in its arsenal to affect interest rates. Each time it meets, the members of the FOMC decide on a path for the nation's monetary policy. For example, the policy makers might decide that monetary policy should be more expansionary; that is, the FOMC might want to lower real interest rates to stimulate economic activity. Or they may want to increase the amount of money in circulation. To bring about such changes, the FOMC instructs the manager of the System Open Market Account (SOMA) at the Federal Reserve Bank

· · · · · · ·

[12]These figures come from the Federal Reserve Bank of New York's Web site: www.newyorkfed.org. Click on the link "Markets" to find a history of the Fed's open-market activity.

of New York to take the appropriate actions to achieve these policy goals. The manager, who oversees the people staffing the New York bank's Trading Desk (referred to as the Desk), instructs them to purchase or sell U.S. government securities (historically, Treasury securities) in the open market—hence, the phrase "open-market" operations.

Before describing how open-market operations work, let's take a minute to explain just what the Fed is trying to accomplish from such actions. First, open-market operations are aimed at changing the amount of reserves in the banking system. You already know that changes in a bank's reserves can directly affect the bank's desire to increase or decrease deposits. If open-market operations change reserves in banks, one effect is to change the level of the money supply in the economy.

A second, and some would argue more important, outcome of an open-market operation is a change in the level of short-term interest rates. Sometimes you read headlines like "Fed Trims Interest Rate" or "Fed Raises Rate Sharply." The "rate" being referred to is the **federal funds rate**.

> **FEDERAL FUNDS RATE** The interest rate that banks charge each other for short-term (usually overnight) loans.

The federal funds rate is the interest rate that banks charge each other for short-term (usually overnight) loans. How is it determined? Recall that the Federal Reserve requires banks to hold a certain percent of their deposits (your checking account balances, for instance) in reserve, either at the Fed or in their own vaults. If the required percentage is, say, 5 percent, then for every dollar in deposits, your bank must hold 5 cents in reserve. How are banks' reserves and the federal funds rate related? On any given day, there are banks in the United States that are unable to meet their reserve requirements. On the same day, there are banks that at day's end have more reserves than they need to meet reserve requirements. Banks short of required reserves can borrow from banks with excess reserves. This loan of reserves usually lasts for a day or two until the borrowing bank can make the changes it needs to meet the reserve requirement. The market-determined price to borrow the funds is the federal funds rate. The federal funds rate is determined by the interaction of the supply of and demand for reserves in the U.S. banking system.

## Open-Market Operations and the Federal Funds Rate

Let's now look more closely at how open-market operations work. When the FOMC wants to lower the federal funds rate, it instructs the Desk to buy government securities in the open market. (Although we will refer to lowering the federal funds rate, remember that what the Fed is really trying to lower is the *real* federal funds rate.) The Fed *buys* government securities from a group of "primary dealers," which consists of about 18 large banks and securities broker-dealers.[13] The Fed pays for the securities it purchases by electronically depositing funds in the dealers' bank accounts. This transaction increases the amount of reserves that the dealers' banks are holding, in effect creating excess reserves. The immediate increase in the banks' reserves, given the demand for them, causes the federal funds rate to fall. *By buying government securities in the open market, the FOMC is trying to lower the federal funds rate.*

We can illustrate the effect of this open-market purchase using supply and demand. **Figure 17.2** shows the hypothetical supply of and demand for reserves in

· · · · · · ·

[13]The dealers change periodically. A list of the current dealers can be found at the New York Fed's Web site.

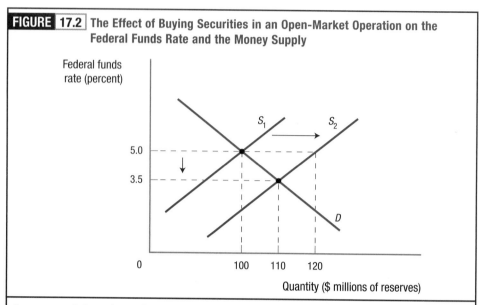

**FIGURE 17.2** | The Effect of Buying Securities in an Open-Market Operation on the Federal Funds Rate and the Money Supply

An open-market purchase of securities by the Fed from dealers shifts the supply curve of reserves to the right, creating a surplus of reserves in the banking system at the original federal funds rate (5 percent). The surplus puts downward pressure on the federal funds rate, which declines until it reaches the new, lower equilibrium rate (3.5 percent). This action also increases the equilibrium amount of reserves in the system, from $100 million to $110 million. To raise the federal funds rate, the Fed would conduct an open-market sale of securities, which reverses the shifts shown here.

the banking system before the Fed purchases the securities. The original intersection of supply and demand determines the equilibrium federal funds rate (5 percent) and the equilibrium quantity of reserves in banks ($100 million).

When the Fed purchases securities in the open market, this shifts the supply curve of reserves to the right, from $S_1$ to $S_2$. At the original federal funds rate, there is now a surplus of reserves in the banking system. At a federal funds rate of 5 percent, the quantity of reserves supplied ($120 million) is now greater than the quantity demanded ($100 million). A surplus of any good causes its price to fall, and the same effect arises in the market for reserves. The increase in reserves given the demand for them puts downward pressure on the federal funds rate, which declines until it reaches the new equilibrium. In Figure 17.2, the Fed's open-market operation lowered the federal funds rate to 3.5 percent and increased the amount of reserves in the banking system to $110 million.

What if the FOMC wants to increase the federal funds rate? To raise the federal funds rate, the manager of the Desk is asked to do exactly the opposite of what she did to lower the rate. Instead of buying government securities from the primary dealers, the staff on the Desk sells government securities owned by the Fed to the dealers. The dealers pay for the securities, which reduces their deposits and, therefore, reserves in the banking system. Given the demand for reserves, this reduction in the supply reserves puts upward pressure on the federal funds rate. *By selling government securities in the open market, the FOMC is trying to increase the federal funds rate.*

The open-market sale of securities shifts the supply curve ($S_1$) in Figure 17.2 to the left. (We leave it for you to draw in the supply-curve shift.) Starting from the original equilibrium of 5 percent, the Fed's action initially causes disequilibrium in the market for reserves. The reduction in the supply of reserves causes a shortage (quantity demanded exceeds the quantity supplied) at the original federal funds rate. This results in an increase in the federal funds rate as the market adjusts to its new equilibrium.

---

**ECONOMIC FALLACY**   The Federal Reserve sets interest rates in the economy.

**False.** You might read or hear someone refer to the Fed or its policy-making arm, the FOMC, as the body that sets interest rates. The Fed has no legislative power to set interest rates or even the federal funds rate. It does, however, have the ability, through the use of open-market operations, to affect the amount of reserves in the banking system, which in turns influences the level of the federal funds rate. And increasing or decreasing the federal funds rate may then influence other rates. Does this seem semantic? Perhaps, but it is important not to engage in such loose thinking. Interest rates are affected by market forces, and while the Fed can try and nudge rates up or down, it cannot overpower the financial market into keeping rates at any specific level without significant economic costs.

---

## Open-Market Operations and the Money Supply

When the Fed wants to lower the federal funds rate, it instructs the Desk at the New York Fed to buy government securities from the primary dealers. This purchase increases brokers' deposits at their banks and initially raises these banks' reserves. That is, $R$ in the money-supply equation rises. (This is the increase in the quantity of reserves shown in Figure 17.2.) In the first instance, this creation of excess reserves leads to a reduction in the federal funds rate. In most situations, banks find it more profitable to make new loans instead of continually lending their excess reserves in the federal funds market. This process of making new loans creates new deposits, as we noted earlier. Given some reserve requirement, banks will use the excess reserves to create more loans and deposits, and expand the money supply.

Suppose the original amount of reserves ($R$) was $10 million, and, due to the Fed's open-market purchase, they now are $15 million. The increase in reserves can potentially increase the supply of money from its original value of $200 million to $300 million. This comes from the following money-supply equation: $300 million = 1/0.05 \times $15 million. This is the money multiplier at work. The increase in reserves (equal to $5 million) brings about an increase in the money supply of $100 million, which is equal to $1/0.05 \times $5 million. Whether you focus on the final number ($300 million) or the change in the money supply ($100 million), *an open-market purchase of securities increases the money supply in the economy.*

What if the Fed's open-market operations are aimed at *increasing* the federal funds rate? In this case, everything is thrown into reverse. When the Fed wants to raise the federal funds rate, you know that they sell some of their government securities to the primary dealers. To pay for these securities, the dealers draw down their deposits, which has the direct effect of lowering deposits in the banking system. It also reduces reserves, which, as you have just seen, has a multiplier effect on the money supply. If, for example, an open-market sale of securities reduced reserves to, say, $8 million, our money-supply formula indicates that the new value of the money supply would be $160 million ($1/0.5 \times $8 million). This $40 million reduction in the money supply comes from the multiplier effect of the $2 million decline in reserves. So, *an open-market sale of securities decreases the money supply in the economy.*

We must add a caveat to this description of open-market operations. Notice that we often use the word "can" instead of "must" in describing the bank's reaction to the Fed's purchase or sale of securities. For example, even though bank reserves might increase due to the Fed's purchase of government securities, banks are not required to turn around and loan them out. In response to the Fed's actions to lower the federal funds rate following the financial crisis of 2008, many banks simply chose to hold more excess reserves than normal and did not make new loans. As of mid-2011, this was still the case. Simply put, the Fed cannot force the money multiplier to work if banks do not wish to cooperate.

**ECONOMIC FALLACY**   The Fed prints money.

**False.** During the recession of 2007–2009, the Federal Reserve undertook policies that lowered the (nominal) federal funds rate nearly to zero. This was accomplished by a massive injection of reserves into the banking system. The consequence was that the money supply increased rapidly. But this is not the same as the Fed printing money. The Fed's actions increased the supply of money by increasing the amount of deposits in the banking system. The Fed did not print more dollar bills. That is the job of the U.S. Department of the Treasury. Even though the outcome may be similar, it simply is incorrect to say "the Fed is printing money."

## A Summary of Open-Market Operations Conducted by the Fed

We've covered a lot of ground. **Table 17.6** summarizes the effect of open-market operations on both the federal funds rate and on the supply of money. When the Fed buys securities, it is trying to lower the federal funds rate and increase the supply of money. This can be thought of as an **expansionary monetary policy**. Conversely, when the Fed sells securities, it is trying to raise the federal funds rate and reduce the supply of money. This can be thought of as a **contractionary monetary policy**.

**EXPANSIONARY MONETARY POLICY** A policy action aimed at lowering the federal funds rate and increasing the growth rate of the money supply.

**EXAMPLE** Following a meeting of the FOMC, the Desk was directed to *purchase* securities in the open-market in much larger quantities than before. The goal was to reduce the real federal funds rate by one percentage point and to increase the growth rate of the money supply from 3 percent to 4.5 percent.

**Table 17.6** How Open-Market Operations Affect the Federal Funds Rate and the Money Supply

|  | Purchase of Securities by the Fed | Sale of Securities by the Fed |
|---|---|---|
| Federal funds rate | Decrease | Increase |
| Money supply | Increase | Decrease |

This table summarizes the effect of open-market operations on both the federal funds rate and on the supply of money. When the Fed buys securities, it is trying to lower the federal funds rate and increase the supply of money (expansionary monetary policy). When the Fed sells securities, it is trying to raise the federal funds rate and reduce the supply of money (contractionary monetary policy).

> **CONTRACTIONARY MONETARY POLICY** A policy action aimed at raising the federal funds rate and decreasing the growth rate of the money supply.

> EXAMPLE Following a meeting of the FOMC, the Desk was directed to *sell* securities in the open market in much larger quantities than before. The goal was to raise the real federal funds rate by two percentage points and to decrease the growth rate of the money supply from 4.5 percent to 3 percent.

Open-market operations are a powerful tool used by the Fed to accomplish its monetary policy objectives. These operations are so important that financial firms, banks, bond traders, and brokerage houses often employ individuals whose main job is to interpret the Fed's buying and selling of government securities. These "Fed watchers" dissect the Fed's securities purchases and sales in an effort to predict whether it is changing its policy course—becoming more expansionary or more contractionary—or simply adjusting reserves for some technical reason. Knowing if and how monetary policy is changing has important consequences on interest rates, the economy, and, ultimately, inflation.

You now know how the Fed, through the banking system, influences the real rate of interest and the money supply. In Chapter 12, you saw that the rate of inflation is related directly to changes in the growth rate of the money supply. This means that monetary policy makers must concern themselves with the longer-run, inflationary consequences of their decisions. And you learned in Chapter 13 that changes in real interest rates impact aggregate demand. This means that policy makers must also be mindful of the short-term output effects of their actions. The success with which monetary policy makers have balanced these short-term and long-term policy consequences is the subject of the next chapter.

## 17.5 When Open-Market Operations Are Not Enough

So far, you have learned that the use of monetary policy, especially when it's conducted using open-market operations, is really aimed at manipulating the real federal funds rate and, in turn, the supply of money. The broader economic goal is to keep the economy operating near its potential GDP while keeping the rate of inflation low. But what if the Fed's policies don't work?

During the Great Recession, which began in 2007, the Federal Reserve (and other central banks around the world) faced a serious problem: it had already lowered the nominal federal funds rate essentially to zero, so there was no way to further lower real interest rates in the economy to increase aggregate demand and fight the recession. To get around the problem, the Fed adopted a policy of **quantitative easing**.

> **QUANTITATIVE EASING** The purchase of assets by the central bank to increase the amount of funds in the financial market.

> EXAMPLE The Fed had already lowered the nominal federal funds rate nearly to zero. With that avenue of expansionary policy closed, it sought to expand reserves in the banking system by purchasing assets (non-Treasury securities, mortgage loans, etc.) directly from banks.

The Fed extended its use of quantitative easing in late 2010 (dubbed QE2) when it announced a six-month program to buy over $600 billion in nontraditional financial assets to help spur the economic recovery. That program ended in June 2011. Just what is quantitative easing, and how does it differ from the Fed's normal use of open-market operations?

When the Fed engages in quantitative easing, it purchases financial assets over and above those bought in normal open-market operations. For example, in an expansionary open-market operation, the Fed purchases short-term securities issued by the U.S. Treasury. A primary goal of such an action, as you know, is to lower the real federal funds rate. But what was the Fed supposed to do when the nominal federal funds rate was already effectively zero? In this case, the Federal Reserve can purchase from banks and other financial institutions (such as mutual funds and insurance companies) other assets such as consumer- and small-business loans, and even home mortgages. By doing so, the Fed's quantitative easing program was intended to inject funds directly into the credit market. With the increase in funds available, banks should have found it easier to increase their lending. As we will detail in the next chapter, during the first round of quantitative easing, banks did not cooperate. They unloaded a lot of questionable assets (e.g., bad mortgages) to the Fed and simply held much larger amounts of reserves than they had in the past.

The first round of quantitative easing was not without its critics. One reason why is because the Fed invoked a little-known provision in the Federal Reserve Act called Section 13(3). Section 13(3) allows the Fed to purchase assets from anyone, not just the banks it regulates. The Fed could, for example, buy your car from you under the provisions of 13(3) to increase the funds you have available for spending. By invoking Section 13(3) the Fed was able to go on a buying spree unlike any it had undertaken before. For example, it bought billions of dollars of "toxic" financial assets, including risky mortgages from banks, money-market mutual funds, and the insurance giant American International Group (AIG). The goal was not only to remove these assets from the institutions' books, thus restoring their financial stability (not to mention profitability), but also to inject liquidity into the banking system to keep lending from drying up.

After a year, it was not clear that the policy was successful: reserves remained unusually high and there was little lending taking place. Although most people hoped that the Fed wouldn't need to use quantitative easing again to keep money flowing in the economy, that hope was dashed when the Fed announced in late 2010 that round two would begin. In this version, the Fed sought to purchase longer-termed securities than usual. And when QE2 ended in June 2011, the economy still had not fully recovered from the effects of the 2007–2009 recession. We will examine the controversy surrounding quantitative easing in the next chapter.

## WHAT YOU SHOULD HAVE LEARNED IN CHAPTER 17

- ■ That money can be thought of as any good possessing the characteristics of being a medium of exchange, a unit of account, and a store of value.

- ■ That economists construct different empirical measures of money to capture these characteristics.

- ■ That the United States has a fractional-reserve banking system wherein banks hold a fraction of their deposits on reserve.

- ■ That the central bank of the Unites States, the Federal Reserve System, is comprised of 12 district banks located around the country and is governed by a 7-member Board of Governors from which a chairman is appointed.

■ That the policy-making arm of the Federal Reserve is called the Federal Open Market Committee (FOMC). The voting members consist of the 7 governors and 5 of the 12 district bank presidents.

■ That the FOMC, through the buying and selling of government securities in the open market (open-market operations), influences the level of interest rates and the money supply in the economy.

■ That an open-market purchase of securities is intended to lower short-term interest rates and increase the supply of money in the economy.

■ That an open-market sale of securities is intended to increase short-term interest rates and lower the supply of money in the economy.

■ That in times of extreme conditions, the Fed can resort to extraordinary policy actions—such as quantitative easing—to help increase the money supply.

## KEY TERMS

Barter, p. 456

Medium of exchange, p. 457

Unit of account, p. 458

Store of value, p. 458

Liquidity, p. 459

M1, p. 460

M2, p. 460

Reserves, p. 463

Reserve ratio, p. 464

Fractional-reserve banking, p. 465

Excess reserves, p. 465

Money multiplier, p. 466

Board of Governors, p. 470

Chairman of the Board of Governors, p. 470

Federal Open Market Committee (FOMC), p. 471

Reserve requirement, p. 472

Open-market operations, p. 474

Federal funds rate, p. 475

Expansionary monetary policy, p. 478

Contractionary monetary policy, p. 478

Quantitative easing, p. 479

## QUESTIONS AND PROBLEMS

1. Most of us engage in barter at some time. For example, "If you'll take notes for me in Econ, I will help you with your calculus homework." If it is so common, why isn't barter the main exchange mechanism in modern economies?

2. In the following list, determine which items are and are not money by our definition.
   a) A cowrie shell
   b) A 500-euro note
   c) A U.S. $20 bill
   d) A Visa card
   e) A British pound note
   f) A debit card
   g) A personal I.O.U. to your pal Joe
   h) A cow

3. In the following list, determine which items serve the role of medium of exchange.
   a) The coins in your sock drawer
   b) The balance in your savings account
   c) The wad of $20s that you carry around
   d) The current value of your stock portfolio
   e) The savings bond you got as a graduation present

4. It seems that older people always say "Put your money in the bank." Is this always a good idea? When wouldn't it be? (And your answer has nothing to do with the bank being robbed.)

5. Why do economists make a distinction between money measures such as M1 and M2? If you wanted a money measure related to how individuals pay for goods and services, which one would you favor? How would your finding have implications for which measure policy makers watch?

6. What is the opportunity cost of holding cash? To answer, think of alternative ways to hold your money.

7. In the period immediately following the September 11, 2001, attacks, banks' total reserve holdings increased sharply. Can you explain why total reserves increased? Was it a sensible reaction?

8. Most modern banking systems are characterized as fractional-reserve banking systems.
   a) Explain what is meant by fractional-reserve banking.
   b) If the holding of reserves against deposits wasn't mandated by the government, would banks do so anyway? Explain.

9. The equation that describes the money supply ($M$) is $M = (1/rr) \times R$, where $rr$ is the reserve ratio, and $R$ is total reserves in the banking system.
   a) If the reserve ratio is increased, all else the same, what happens to the money supply?
   b) When the Fed buys securities from banks, it increases reserves in the banking system. This in turn reduces the money supply. True or false? Explain.
   c) How can the Fed offset a decrease in the reserve ratio to keep the money supply unchanged?

10. What is wrong with the following statements: "The Federal Reserve Board of Governors consists of 12 individuals who serve life appointments. The governors are chosen by popular vote and may be replaced by the president of the United States as the president sees fit. The head of the Board of Governors is the governor with the most seniority on the job. The Board meets weekly throughout the year."

11. The so-called money multiplier increases as reserve requirements increase. Yes or no? Explain.

12. The Fed would like the money supply to increase by $200 million.
   a) If the reserve requirement is 10 percent, by how much should it try to increase reserves through open-market purchases?
   b) If the reserve requirement is 20 percent, by how much should it try to increase reserves through open-market purchases?

13. Use the reserve supply-and-demand diagram in Figure 17.2 to answer the following questions.
   a) Starting from an initial equilibrium, what will happen to the federal funds rate if the Fed engages in an open-market purchase of securities?
   b) Starting from an initial equilibrium, what will happen to the federal funds rate if the Fed engages in an open-market sale of securities?
   c) Starting from an initial equilibrium, what will happen to the federal funds rate if banks reduce their demand for reserves?

14. Use the reserve supply-and-demand diagram in Figure 17.2 to consider the following. If, as many people argue, the Fed can set the federal funds rate at whatever rate it wants, what does this imply about the behavior of bank reserves when:
   a) demand for reserves increases?
   b) demand for reserves decreases?
   c) If the Fed sets the federal funds rate and the demand for reserves changes, what does this imply about the behavior of the money supply?

15. Can you supply a rationale for why some of the district bank presidents are included as voting members of the Federal Open Market Committee?

16. The Fed's open-market operations are conducted daily and accomplished by purchases and sales made through each of the 12 district banks. True or false? Explain.

17. The federal funds rate reflects the interest rate that banks charge each other for short-term loans.
    a) Explain why it is referred to as the "federal" funds rate.
    b) At the federal funds rate of 5 percent, reserves available for borrowing fall short of demand: there is a shortage. Would you expect the federal funds rate to rise or fall? Why?
    c) At the federal funds rate of 5 percent, there are more reserves available for borrowing than demanded: there is a surplus. Would you expect the federal funds rate to rise or fall? Why?

18. Policy makers are trying to increase aggregate demand to fight a recession. Which of the following should they do to accomplish this goal?
    a) Increase reserve requirements
    b) Decrease reserve requirements
    c) Open-market purchases of securities
    d) Open-market sale of securities

19. Now policy makers are trying to decrease aggregate demand to fight inflation. Which of the following should they do to accomplish this goal?
    a) Increase reserve requirements
    b) Decrease reserve requirements
    c) Open-market purchases of securities
    d) Open-market sale of securities

20. The Fed used quantitative easing, the purchase of assets from banks and other financial institutions, during the financial crisis of 2008 and again in 2010 and 2011.
    a) Why did it resort to this policy and not simply purchase Treasury securities in the open market?
    b) How did quantitative easing affect banks? That is, how did the Fed pay for these assets?
    c) What did the Fed assume banks would do with the newly acquired funds?

21. In October 2008, the Fed announced that it would begin paying interest on banks' required and excess reserves. From an opportunity-cost perspective, explain how this may affect the amount of reserves banks are willing to hold. Would you be surprised if excess reserves in the banking system are, on average, greater after this change than before? Explain.

## Appendix 17A The Origins of the Federal Reserve[14]

The Federal Reserve System was created when President Woodrow Wilson signed the Federal Reserve Act into law on December 24, 1913. The Federal Reserve Act represents the culmination of almost a century of experimenting by the U.S. government in an effort to establish a central bank. Although other countries already had central banks, the U.S. was somewhat of a late-comer in this regard. The First Bank of the United States was the nation's initial attempt to establish a central bank. It was created in 1791, and it closed in 1811. Many people in the United States were worried that the Bank would give the federal government monopoly control over the nation's supply of money. They believed that the amount of money in circulation should be determined by the changes in the country's supply of gold and not left to the whims of government officials. In other words, people didn't believe that the government should be allowed to print money when it felt like it. Such a commodity-based monetary system makes it much more difficult for government officials to manipulate the money supply for their own political gain.

Without a central bank, the U.S. government found it difficult to finance the War of 1812. A Second Bank of the United States, created in 1816, was set up to operate as the government's fiscal agent and to provide a uniform currency. The Second Bank was almost immediately embroiled in controversy. A financial panic that some people attributed to the Bank struck the country in 1819. Even though the Bank weathered that storm, it remained in near-constant turmoil. Andrew Jackson attacked it and banks in general during the presidential campaign of 1828. With his presidential victory in 1832, Jackson made good his promise to rid the country of central banking and its policies that, he argued, favored wealthy easterners over the agrarian West. Political support for the bank waned, and in 1836, its charter was not renewed.

Between 1836 and 1913, no central bank existed in the United States. From 1839 until the Civil War, the United States entered what is known as the "free banking era." Basically, free banking gave states more control over banking and created a competitive banking environment. Banks produced their own currency with notes carrying the name of the bank. If a bank was noted for trustworthiness and good management, its notes would trade for a premium relative to others.

With the demise of free banking, the federal government began to assert more control over national monetary policy. The National Banking Act, passed after the Civil War, initiated some aspects of modern banking. National banks were required to hold reserves against their deposits at reserve city banks located in New York, Chicago, and St. Louis. The problem was that in times of financial crisis, customers were not able to access their funds quickly—they were off in one of these cities—leading to fears of bank failure. As some noted, what was needed was an agency that could provide an elastic currency; that is, an agency that could change the money supply to meet the needs of the economy.

The Panic of 1907 is sometimes viewed as the economic event that brought about the creation of the Federal Reserve. In the spring of 1907, the United States experienced a series of stock-price declines along with a reduction in gold inflows. These events triggered a reduction in the supply of money. By the fall of 1907, the economy was in a full-fledged recession, bank customers were trying to withdraw their funds, and, given existing regulations, bank runs occurred. Banks closed, the supply of money declined, and with it, so did economic activity.

· · · · · · ·

[14]The source for this discussion is R. W. Hafer, *The Federal Reserve System: An Encyclopedia* (Westport, CT: Greenwood Press, 2005).

Following the Panic of 1907, the movement to reform the banking industry and create a central bank began with passage of the Aldrich-Vreeland Act of 1908. This act created the National Monetary Commission, which was given the task of studying and analyzing the banking system of the United States and other countries to see if a "best practices" model could be developed. The legislation that created the Federal Reserve Act evolved out of the work done by the National Monetary Commission.

The election of 1912 then set into motion the final push for the passage of legislation that created the Federal Reserve System. The Democratic candidate Woodrow Wilson was elected president, and Democrats controlled both the Senate and the House. After extensive political debate and compromise, the Federal Reserve Act was signed on December 24, 1913.

# Monetary Policy

> *"A good rule of thumb is to try to look as if you know what you're doing even if you're not entirely sure."*
>
> Ben Bernanke,
> Chairman of the
> Federal Reserve Board
> of Governors

**M**onetary policy is widely recognized as the key policy area used by governments to affect the pace of economic activity and the rate of inflation in their countries. Because policy decisions are based on imperfect information, however, the best decisions (at least with 20/20 hindsight) aren't always made. This means that making monetary policy decisions is much like parenting: policy makers (like parents) generally try to follow some basic guidelines and try to adapt to changing circumstances. Still, there is no perfect course of action to follow with every child or every economic situation.

Having a rock-solid, predictable framework upon which monetary policy decisions can be made might improve a central bank's track record, but such a framework doesn't exist. Setting monetary policy is based partly on historical experience—how policy variables have been related to economic variables such as real GDP growth and inflation over time—and partly on the "art" of interpreting changing economic situations.

Some policy decisions have sent economies into a tailspin and put many people out of work. Other policies have led to significant increases in the rate of inflation. But the overall record is not as dismal as this might suggest. Earlier in this century, many economists argued that the decisions made by U.S. monetary policy makers during the past two decades have helped stabilize the economy around its long-run potential GDP better than at any time in the past. And this record of achievement was accomplished with fairly low and stable rates of inflation. Of course, the economic downturn that began in 2007 has significantly tempered those rave reviews.

The melding of both science and intuition means that policy decisions today are different from those made 20 years ago and will probably be different from those made 20 years from now. Even so, what you will see in reading this chapter is that certain core principles lie at the heart of good policy making. In the final analysis, monetary policy makers have become keenly aware that their decisions affect not only short-term economic growth and the level of employment but also the rate of inflation over time. How they balance their actions to achieve the twin goals of stable growth and low inflation is often thought to be the "art" side of policy making. As the opening quote from Fed Chairman Bernanke, made at a 2004 meeting of the FOMC, suggests, making monetary policy evolves as our understanding of the economy changes.

In the previous chapter, you learned the "hows" of monetary policy: the economic measures that are watched and how the Fed tries to control both the supply of money and the federal funds rate. With this foundation, and your knowledge of the AD-IE model, we now want to turn to thinking about the "whys" of policy decisions.

## 18.1 Monetary Policy and the Economy: What Is the Fed's Main Focus?

Economists today generally agree that monetary policy cannot permanently increase the rate of growth of real GDP above its potential without creating serious inflationary consequences. In the long run, most economists agree that monetary policy affects only the rate of inflation. This "consensus" is a relatively recent phenomenon, however. According to the Full Employment Act of 1946, Congress specified that the Fed should act to keep inflation low (prices stable) and the economy growing at a reasonable pace. These dual goals were reinforced by the Federal Reserve Reform Act of 1977, which assigned the multiple policy objectives of "maximum employment, stable prices, and moderate long-term interest rates."

Can monetary policy makers, whether they are at the Fed or any other central bank, be expected to achieve these objectives? And if not, why not? To answer that question, it is useful to recall how monetary policy actions can affect the economy. **Figure 18.1** shows the AD-IE model developed in previous chapters. From an initial condition of equilibrium where the GDP gap is zero and the expected inflation rate is 4 percent (point A), let's suppose that the Fed undertakes an expansionary monetary policy by lowering the federal funds rate and increasing the money supply.

The Fed's expansionary policy initially increases aggregate demand: lower interest rates increase consumption spending and investment spending. As Figure 18.1 shows, this policy leads to a rightward shift of the aggregate demand curve, from $AD_1$ to $AD_2$. In the short run, before inflation expectations have changed, the Fed's policy creates a positive GDP gap (point B). A positive gap, as you have learned, is associated with upward pressure on inflation expectations. Over time, the rate of inflation and inflation expectations begin to increase. As shown by the shift in the *IE* line, inflation expectations and actual inflation drift upward until the economy settles in at a new equilibrium with a rate of inflation (both actual and expected) that is higher (6 percent) and with the economy once again operating at a zero GDP gap (point C). As we will discuss, the lesson learned from decades of policy experience is that constantly trying to make the economy grow faster than its potential rate will lead to persistent and increasing rates of inflation.

The fact that, over time, an expansionary monetary policy does not *permanently* increase real economic growth does not mean that in the short run policy makers ignore the economic conditions around them. During times of economic distress, like the 2007–2009 recession, the Fed usually lowers the federal funds rate to spur consumer spending and investment spending, increase aggregate demand, and keep

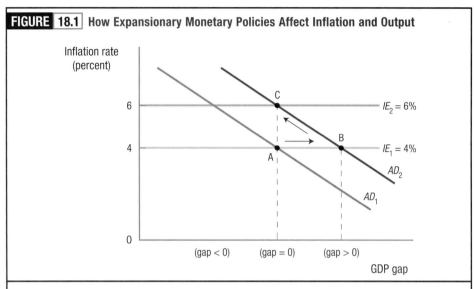

**FIGURE 18.1** **How Expansionary Monetary Policies Affect Inflation and Output**

The AD-IE model is used to illustrate an expansionary monetary policy. From an initial equilibrium of a zero GDP gap and an expected inflation rate of 4 percent, the Fed's expansionary policy increases aggregate demand and shifts the aggregate demand curve to the right. Before inflation expectations have changed, the Fed's policy creates a positive GDP gap. Over time, the rate of inflation and inflation expectations increase. As inflation rises, the GDP gap shrinks, and the economy reaches a new equilibrium at a higher rate of inflation (6 percent) with a zero GDP gap. (In contrast, a contractionary policy shifts the aggregate demand curve to the left.)

the economy from sinking further into recession.[1] To illustrate how the Fed reacts to changes in the economic environment, let's use the past decade as a case study in monetary policy making.

## Monetary Policy, 2000–2010

Figure 18.2 shows the federal funds rate and the rate of inflation over the past decade. The inflation rate used is the CPI less food and energy, the so-called core inflation rate. We use it because many observers felt that it was the rate that the FOMC focused on. The vertical shaded bars, as always, mark recessions. In the late 1990s, the policy makers at the Fed were concerned about several aspects of the economy. One was that the stock market was overheated: stock prices were rising rapidly, and major stock price indexes, such as the Dow Jones Industrial Average, were nearing historic highs. Another was that inflation was likely to rise because the economy was operating with a positive GDP gap. Given this information, the FOMC decided in 1999 to raise the federal funds rate, pushing it as high as 6.5 percent in 2000. As you can see in Figure 18.2, the Fed's contractionary policy—the increase in the federal funds rate—*preceded* the rise in inflation, reflecting the Fed's attempt to keep inflation closer to the presumed target rate of 2 percent.

· · · · · · ·

[1]Paul R. LaMonica, "Fed Slashes Key Rate to 3.5%: Citing Weakening Economic Outlook." CNNMoney.com (January 22, 2008); Barbara Hagenbaugh, et al. "Fed's Move Reflects Worries over Economy." USAToday.com (January 1, 2008). It also is obvious that individuals, who also can see the economic information, start to expect policy changes. Chris Arnold, "Sluggish GDP Growth May Bring a Rate Cut." National Public Radio, Morning Edition, April 30, 2008.

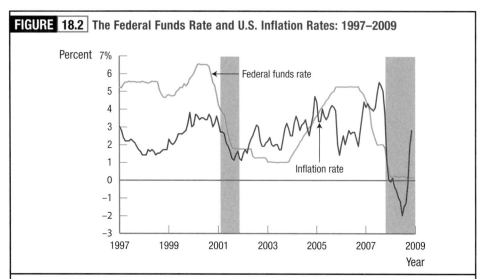

**FIGURE 18.2** | The Federal Funds Rate and U.S. Inflation Rates: 1997–2009

Figure 18.2 shows the federal funds rate and the core rate of inflation over the past decade. (Shaded areas indicate U.S. recessions.) In the late 1990s, Fed policy makers were concerned that the stock market was overheated and that inflation was likely to rise. With this information, the FOMC began to raise the federal funds rate in 1999, pushing it as high as 6.5 percent in 2000. As you can see, the increase in the federal funds rate *preceded* the rise in inflation. In most instances, including this one, we would expect the Fed to increase the federal funds rate when higher than desired inflation is anticipated and to lower it when the economy is not expanding fast enough.

*Source:* Federal Reserve Bank of St. Louis

A series of events that started in 2000—the stock market crash being the most prominent—began to weigh on the economy. Even though inflation continued to rise, the FOMC reversed its contractionary policy in 2001 to fight the downturn in economic activity. As economic growth slowed, the Fed switched policy gears and lowered the nominal (and real) federal funds rate. Although the ensuing recession ended in November 2001, the Fed continued to lower the federal funds rate for the next several years. This action is still being debated. Some people argue that keeping interest rates too low for too long helped fuel the housing "bubble" that burst in 2007.

As the economy recovered from the 2001 recession, inflation began to reassert itself. In Figure 18.2, you can see that inflation moderated during the downturn (as predicted by our AD-IE model) and began to increase in 2004. Although the increase may not look like much, at the time, the Fed was attempting to keep (core) inflation around 2 percent. Increases above that, especially if they were thought to be sustained increases, were met with a proactive response. So, as the rate of inflation was expected to break through the 2-percent target, the FOMC started to raise the nominal federal funds rate by more than the expected increase in inflation. This policy lasted until mid-2007, when, with the economy once again showing signs of faltering, and serious strains in financial markets beginning to appear, the Fed rapidly reduced the federal funds rate by injecting massive amounts of reserves into the banking system. You can see that the timing of the recession's beginning (December 2007) closely corresponds to the start of the Fed's policy switch to reduce interest rates. The reduction in the federal funds rate continued throughout the next couple of years until it reached the historic low of 0.15 percent. (As of mid-2011, the Fed has kept the nominal federal funds rate near zero.)

This description of Fed policy over the 1997–2009 period illustrates just how difficult policy making is, especially if two policy objectives—keeping inflation low and maintaining economic growth—are being sought simultaneously. How does the Fed decide which policy objective to focus on? Does it adhere to specific rules that describe what it should do? Answering questions such as these lies at the heart of many policy debates, but history does provide some answers. In the next section, we'll think about whether policy actions should be guided by rules or discretion. Then we will look at how the Fed approached policy decisions over the past half century to understand how policy evolved.

**ECONOMIC FALLACY**   The Fed knows what the federal funds rate should be.

**False.** When the monetary policy makers at the Fed act to raise or lower the federal funds rate, they do so because they expect those actions to affect the economy in a predictable way. Does that mean they know exactly when to stop raising or lowering the rate, or exactly what the federal funds rate should be? No. The complexity of the economy is such that policy actions are meant to achieve some (real) interest-rate level that policy makers believe, based on available information, is most likely to keep the economy growing at a reasonable pace and to keep inflation low. The fact that interest-rate changes often take place in graduated steps (a quarter percentage point increase or decrease is most common) indicates that the Fed is searching for a rate that is neither too high nor too low. If the Fed knew the appropriate interest rate, it would simply change the federal funds rate once.

## 18.2 Should the Fed Rely on Policy Rules or Discretion?

How would *you* decide whether to increase or decrease the federal funds rate? When would *you* increase or decrease the growth rate of the money supply? Back in the 1950s and 1960s, members of the FOMC often relied on the "tone and feel" of the financial markets—that is, members' instincts based on previous experience—to establish policy. As recently as 1994, one Fed governor said: "I get a feel for what I think is going on based on the information—not only the anecdotal information in the press and the statistical information assembled and compiled by the staff here, but also from the general tone of the market."[2]

If you are thinking that this doesn't seem like a very scientific or reliable way to make decisions, you are right. But think about how you make decisions. How did you decide on your major? Did you research the job prospects of various professions before signing up for all those chemistry or history courses? Or was it that you liked the English courses in high school, so you thought that they might be fun in college, too? Or did your parents simply tell you what your major should be?

You're probably familiar with the phrase, "rules are made to be broken." However, keep in mind that rules create some useful parameters that make people's behavior more predictable. For one, rules (like habits) lower the cost to you of making a decision. If your "rule" is eating the same food at every meal or wearing the same clothes every day, then that rule removes the burden of deciding what to eat and wear. Arguably, it frees up the time spent making such mundane decisions and lets you apply that brainpower to more enriching pursuits.

· · · · · · · ·

[2]Attributed to Fed Governor John P. LaWare by Keith Bradsher, "Fed Relying on Intuition in Setting Rate Policy." *New York Times,* February 28, 1994: C1.

Rules also mean that your behavior is more predictable to others. A rule that most of us obey is to stop at red lights. That means you can feel comfortable driving through an intersection when your traffic light is green. If you thought no one was following the stop-on-red rule, it would affect your driving habits. The breakdown of that rule would lead to traffic snarls at every intersection because drivers would stop at green lights to see if other drivers were going to run the red lights.

Let's apply this logic to policy making. First let's think of **discretionary monetary policy** as an approach where the Fed takes whatever action it deems necessary and appropriate under the circumstances.

> **DISCRETIONARY MONETARY POLICY** Policy actions central bankers take that are not based on underlying rules or guidelines.
>
> **EXAMPLE** Board Governor Jones, when asked to defend his policy decision, stated that lowering the federal funds rate just seemed like a good idea.
>
> **EXAMPLE** Even with inflation running at 10 percent, the members of the FOMC voted to increase money growth because they thought the current unemployment rate of 5.2 percent was too high.

There are many examples of discretionary responses even with established policies in our everyday lives. Here are just a couple: your dog really did eat your term paper, so your professor decides to give you an extra day to finish the project even though the syllabus states that late papers will not be accepted. Or, you get pulled over for driving 65 in a 35 mph speed zone, and your excuse is that you are trying to get to the hospital because your wife is about to deliver a baby. If the police officer gives you a "siren-on" escort to the hospital and not a ticket, that is discretion on her part. Discretionary policy can occur even if there are existing rules. The problem for policy watchers, however, is if discretionary policy takes over. Then there really is no predictable behavior because decisions are made at the whim of the policy maker, and those policies are hard to predict.

Now let's define a **policy rule**. A rule is something that leads to predictable behavior but not necessarily a set mode of behavior. For example, you might develop a rule to wear the same clothes every day no matter what. Or you might develop a rule to wear shorts when the temperature is above 80 degrees and pants when it is below 80 degrees. They are both rules. Just because the second rule is more flexible than the first rule doesn't make it less of a rule.

> **POLICY RULE** An established set of actions to be taken under a given set of conditions.
>
> **EXAMPLE** As a vegetarian, your dietary rule is not to eat meat. When offered a hot dog, even though you are really hungry, you decline it.
>
> **EXAMPLE** The golden rule is to do unto others as you would have them do unto you. You follow this rule and never speak ill about your friends, even when they are not around.

To use previous examples, a policy rule could be the conditions in your course syllabus regarding term papers or the rule regarding speeding. Establishing policy rules for central banks has been a long process. Why? A major reason is that central banks are bureaucracies, and bureaucracies survive in part by maintaining some secrecy in terms of their activities and decision making. This is partly because decisions are sometimes made more efficiently when fewer people are involved. (Think about trying to decide which restaurant to go to when there are two people as opposed to ten.) Also, establishing and announcing a policy rule means that if you do not follow it, everyone knows. And if you break the rule enough times, people will doubt how serious you are about abiding by the rule. Speed by a cop many times without getting a ticket, and you begin to think those speeding laws don't apply.

Economists have studied the use (and abuse) of monetary policy rules. Two key areas of concern are whether rules increase transparency of policy decisions and whether policy decisions are consistent over time.

## 18.3 Policy Transparency

When people behave in an unpredictable manner, you're not likely to believe anything they tell you about what they will do in the future. Remember when you faced a midnight curfew and came home at 2 A.M.? If your parents enforced the midnight curfew by grounding you for a month, this probably led to more predictable behavior on your part: you came home on time. But what if sometimes you were grounded, and at other times your parents didn't say a word about your being late? When rules for being grounded are ambiguous or their enforcement unpredictable, then you do not know how to respond. (More than likely, you tested the boundaries of the curfew rule by staying out past midnight more often.) When we are trying to understand why and how the Fed responds to certain economic events, we do so because ignoring what the Fed does can be very costly. That is, we compare the marginal benefits to the marginal costs of keeping tabs on Fed policy actions.

As recently as the 1980s, central bankers believed that instituting policy rules to guide their decisions would be too confining. Nevertheless, most economists and policy makers have come to recognize the importance of policy rules if only for the fact that they increase **policy transparency**. Transparency simply means that those affected by policy decisions understand why they were made.

> **POLICY TRANSPARENCY** The extent to which individuals can understand and predict policy actions.

> **EXAMPLE** Due to numerous defaults on mortgages, lenders are now required to make the terms of loans more understandable to borrowers.

> **EXAMPLE** Your university catalog clearly states the set of courses students must take to major in economics.

If we all know that a stated policy rule leads to predictable policy actions, then these actions do not come as a surprise. Policy transparency reduces the uncertainty and the costs associated with a change in monetary policy. Not correctly anticipating a change in the direction of policy may mean significant losses for your company. For example, if the Fed is about to undertake a contractionary policy to slow economic activity, it may not be a good time to expand your business. If you knew that in advance, you wouldn't suffer the losses associated with guessing incorrectly and building three new stores, hiring staff, and ordering merchandise.

The Fed and other central banks have significantly increased the transparency of their policy actions in recent years. The move toward increased transparency originated from outside pressure. When Congress passed the Full Employment and Balanced Growth Act of 1978, usually called the Humphrey-Hawkins Act in recognition of its sponsors, it required the Fed chairman to testify before Congress twice a year (February and July) about the Fed's policy objectives and its outlook for the economy. Even though the Humphrey-Hawkins Act has expired, the chairman continues to outline the nation's monetary policy and the economic outlook in testimony before House and Senate banking committees.

Another move to increase transparency is that the FOMC now releases its policy decisions immediately following each meeting. In the past, it provided this information with a long time delay. The minutes of each FOMC meeting are released following the FOMC's next scheduled meeting (the minutes of the March meeting are released following the FOMC's April meeting, for example).[3] Similarly, the Bank of England releases its minutes two weeks after its meetings. In contrast, neither the European Central Bank (ECB) nor the Bank of Canada releases the minutes of their policy deliberations.

Although it's not the case for the Fed, other central banks have established more transparent policy objectives by which their policies can be judged. Based on a survey conducted by the Bank of England, only a few central banks have either no statutory goals or goals not aligned with "monetary stability." The phrase "monetary stability" is somewhat vague, so are there many central banks that operate using specific policy goals? Of the 94 banks surveyed, 55 reported that their policies are directly influenced by an explicit inflation target. Of these 55 banks, all used an inflation target that was set by the bank (31 percent), by the government (27 percent), or by some agreement between the bank and the government (42 percent). The others use some sort of exchange-rate target or money-growth target.

Is policy transparency always good? There's an ongoing debate about whether a central bank should actually announce a specific goal, such as a target rate of inflation. As we noted, some central banks, including the central banks of Canada, the United Kingdom, Australia, and New Zealand, announce specific inflation targets. Could such transparency create problems for policy makers? Suppose a central bank states publicly that its policy objective is to keep inflation low. What happens if the bank announces that it is suspending its inflation objective to focus on a more immediate problem, such as plunging economic growth and rising rates of unemployment? This *announced* policy shift might increase uncertainty among the public—and financial markets—because now people do not know which policy objective will take center stage in the future. Although some people argue that setting inflation targets makes policy makers more accountable, other people believe that targets tie the hands of policy makers in undesirable ways. For example, knowing that the deliberations will become public may deter individuals around the table from taking appropriate, though publicly unpopular, actions.[4]

## 18.4 Time Inconsistency

Economists believe that the policies of central banks should be more consistent in their actions because inconsistent policies often lead to bad economic outcomes. For the past 30 years, the Fed's monetary policies have been more consistent with the organization's stated objective of keeping inflation low. As a result, most people believe the Fed is sincere about keeping inflation low and stable. The Fed has earned credibility.

As we stated earlier, many believe that the Fed's unofficial target for inflation (core inflation) is around 2 percent. During the early 1980s, when expected inflation was

· · · · · · ·

[3]In April 2011, policy transparency took another step forward when Fed Chairman Ben Bernanke held a live press conference following the FOMC's meeting. This was the first time such a press conference had been held by a Fed chairman.

[4]Joseph Stiglitz, "The Urgent Need to Abandon Inflation Targeting." BusinessDay.com (May 8, 2008).

somewhere around 10 percent, the Fed's inflation target (if they really had one at all) was anyone's guess. Once the public believes that the Fed's actions are credible, people's expectations about inflation get factored into their economic decisions. Changes in the expected rate of inflation show up in many areas: banks adjust the interest rates charged for loans, workers and employers revise their expectations of what wage increases to expect, and so forth. In other words, people alter their expectations of inflation in a rational manner, based on information that is made available to them.

What if it becomes clear that the low-inflation policy that the Fed *announced* it would follow is not the policy it *actually is* following? The Fed's decision not to implement its announced policy in order to pursue an alternative policy leads to a **time-inconsistent policy**.

**TIME-INCONSISTENT POLICY** A policy that is not followed consistently over time.

**EXAMPLE** A politician promises one thing in the campaign and does the opposite once in office.

**EXAMPLE** Your professor announces that the midterm will cover Chapters 4 and 5. You respond by reading Chapters 4 and 5, but the test covers material in Chapter 7.

**EXAMPLE** Your parents promised that if you graduated from high school in the top 5 percent of your class, they would buy you a new car. You did, and they gave you an iPhone instead. They made the same promise for your college graduation. What do you expect to get when you graduate?

The idea of time-inconsistency is applicable in many areas. Many of us make personal resolutions—go on a diet, become more organized, and so on—that we intentionally break at some later date. What seems like a good idea now is likely not to be followed in the future. Nobel Prize-winning economists Finn Kydland and Edward Prescott pioneered the idea of applying time inconsistency to monetary policy. They showed the potential outcomes of time-inconsistent policies, and then showed that their predictions explained the actual behavior of monetary policy makers during the 1960s and 1970s. During that time, even though they said keeping inflation low was a priority, Fed officials focused more on the short-term objectives of keeping the economy expanding and lowering unemployment rates than on keeping inflation low. The Fed's policies were time inconsistent.

You have learned that expansionary monetary policy can *temporarily* increase the growth of real output. What if policy makers think they can maintain output growth that exceeds the economy's long-run potential? To keep the GDP gap at some elevated, positive level, the Fed would need to pursue ever more expansionary policies.

One aspect that must be considered is that policy makers do not immediately react to economic changes, nor do their actions immediately impact the economy. Think of it this way: you are eighth in a line of cars stopped at an intersection, and the light turns green. Given the speed of light, everyone sees the change at the same time. Do all cars immediately move forward? No, because not everyone has the same reaction time, not everyone is paying as close attention, and it takes time to push the accelerator down and for the car to move forward. Add this up across several cars and you, sitting back in the line, do not move immediately.

The same kind of lagged effect occurs when the Fed decides to alter its policy. It may take time for the FOMC members to reach a consensus that the economy is in decline and that they need to lower interest rates. After all, GDP data is not known immediately, nor is the unemployment rate. There also will be a lag between the time when the Fed actually changes interest rates or the money supply and when individuals and firms in the economy react. For example, even though the Fed lowered the federal funds rate to near zero in early 2009 and left it there through 2011, the effects of the recession did not end abruptly. The lag occurs because not everyone is able to take advantage of the policy change, or perhaps they are unwilling to given their uncertainties about the future. Even at a low rate of interest, would you be willing to buy a home if you put a fifty-fifty chance on being laid off in the next six months?

**Figure 18.3** shows the effects of a time-inconsistent policy. Starting from an initial equilibrium with an actual and expected inflation rate of 3 percent, policy makers introduce expansionary policies that shift the aggregate demand curve ($AD_1$) to the right. In the short run, this has the desired effect of a positive GDP gap and no change in inflation expectations. As you know, however, over time inflation expectations rise, and the gap returns to zero. But what if the Fed does not realize—or it chooses to ignore the fact—that the GDP gap has returned to zero? Suppose that because of the lagged response, the Fed undertakes yet another round of expansionary policies with the hopes of keeping the gap positive and lowering the unemployment rate even further. These policies again increase aggregate demand, as shown by the shift from $AD_2$ to $AD_3$. Over time, however, the gains are unsustainable: the economy returns to its potential. The only lasting effect is an increase in the expected and actual rate of inflation, as shown by the upward climb of the *IE* lines.

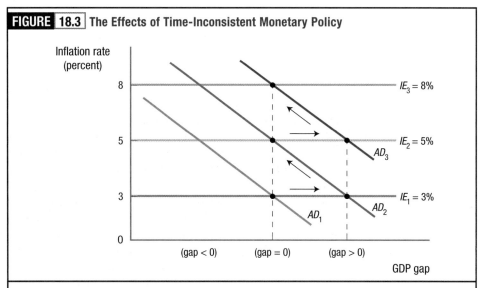

**FIGURE 18.3** The Effects of Time-Inconsistent Monetary Policy

To show the effects of a time-inconsistent policy, we start from an initial equilibrium with inflation (actual and expected) at 3 percent and a zero GDP gap. Policy makers introduce expansionary policies that shift the aggregate demand curve from $AD_1$ to $AD_2$. In the short run, this creates a positive GDP gap with no short-run change in inflation. Over time, inflation and inflation expectations rise, and the gap returns to zero. However, if the Fed prefers faster GDP growth to that associated with a zero GDP gap, it undertakes another round of expansionary policies. This new expansionary policy increases aggregate demand yet again, shifting it from $AD_2$ to $AD_3$. Over time, however, the output gains are unsustainable, and the economy returns to a zero gap. The lasting effect of this policy is a higher rate of inflation and inflationary expectations.

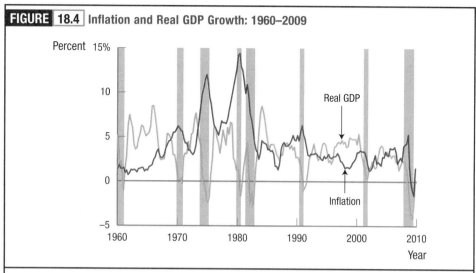

**FIGURE 18.4** | Inflation and Real GDP Growth: 1960–2009

This figure shows the rate of inflation along with the rate of growth in real GDP. (Shaded areas indicate U.S. recessions as determined by the NBER.) If the Fed follows a time-inconsistent policy, the rate of inflation rises over time while real GDP growth fluctuates around its long-term potential. Such an approach explains economic outcomes during the 1960s and 1970s. Consistent with a time-inconsistent policy, the rate of inflation continued to trend upward (the inflation spikes are associated with oil-price increases) while the rate of real GDP growth hovered around its long-run growth of about 3 percent. Although the policy generated short-term gains in output growth, these short-term gains came at a cost of persistently higher rates of inflation. Since 1980, however, it appears that Fed policy has become more focused on lower inflation. At the same time, real GDP growth continues to fluctuate around its long-run growth rate.

*Source:* Federal Reserve Bank of St. Louis

If the Fed follows the policy rule we just explained, we should see the actual rate of inflation rise over time while real GDP growth bounces around its long-term potential. In fact, such a policy approach helps explain the U.S. economy during the 1960s and 1970s. Look at **Figure 18.4** where we plot the rate of inflation along with the rate of growth in real GDP. As you can see, between 1960 and 1980, the rate of inflation continued to rise over time while the rate of real GDP growth fluctuated around an average growth rate of about 3 percent. The notable short-term increases in inflation during the mid- and late 1970s were associated with oil-price spikes. Aside from these temporary causes, expected and actual rates of inflation were definitely trending upward. So, although the policy may have generated short-term gains in output growth, any short-term gains came at a cost of persistently higher rates of inflation. During the period since 1980, however, it appears that policy has more actively sought to lower inflation. Average rates of inflation are much lower than in previous decades, and real GDP growth continues to fluctuate around an underlying average growth rate of about 3 percent.

## 18.5 The Rise and Fall of Monetary Policy Rules

What kind of rules has the Fed used in setting policy? In this section, we briefly look at three rules that the Fed has employed during the past 50 years. As you will find, even though "policy rule" sounds quite official, it is often just a rule of thumb to guide policy makers' decision processes.

## The Phillips Curve

The **Phillips curve** is the name given to the relationship that exists between an economy's inflation rate and its unemployment rate. The relationship, originally between wages and unemployment, was introduced in the 1950s by the British economist A. W. Phillips. The modern version was initially suggested as a policy tool by two Nobel Prize-winning economists, Paul Samuelson and Robert Solow. They found that unemployment and inflation were negatively related: when inflation increased, unemployment fell; conversely, when inflation fell, unemployment increased.

> **PHILLIPS CURVE** A curve that characterizes the inverse relationship between an economy's unemployment rate and inflation rate.

> **EXAMPLE** When the rate of inflation rose from 5 percent to 10 percent, the unemployment rate fell from 8 percent to 4 percent.

The points in **Figure 18.5** are the inflation and unemployment rate pairs for each year between 1960 and 1982. The heyday of the Phillips curve was the 1960s. You can see in the figure that the trace of points for the 1960s suggests a definite negative relation between the two. Policy makers in the 1960s believed that the relation

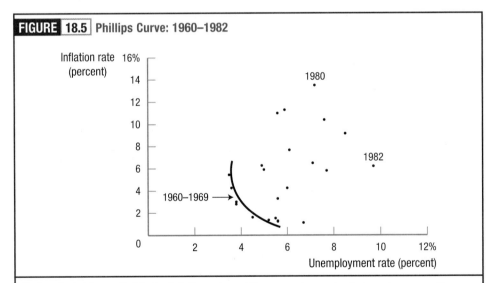

**FIGURE 18.5** Phillips Curve: 1960–1982

Each point in Figure 18.5 is the inflation rate and the unemployment rate in a given year. You can see in the figure that the trace of points for the 1960s suggests a definite negative relation between the two. Policy makers in the 1960s believed the relation was so reliable that they could fine-tune their policies to move the economy back and forth along the curve. However, there is no reliable level to which the rate of inflation gravitates. An expansionary policy to permanently lower unemployment below its full-employment rate will fail. As the economy moves back to its potential rate of growth, the unemployment rate reverts to its full-employment level, and the rate of inflation rises.

*Source:* R. W. Hafer and David C. Wheelock, "Darryl Francis and the Making of Monetary Policy, 1966–1975." Federal Reserve Bank of St. Louis *Review* (March/April 2003): 1–12.

provided an exploitable trade-off. In other words, if they pursued policies that raised the rate of inflation, they could increase economic activity and lower the unemployment rate. The relation highlighted in Figure 18.5 was thought to be so reliable that policy makers believed that their actions could move the economy back and forth along the curve. Expansionary monetary policies to further lower the unemployment rate would produce predictable increases in the rate of inflation. Given the relatively low rates of inflation in the early 1960s, many members of the FOMC voted for policies aimed at lowering and keeping low the unemployment rate. As one member of the Board of Governors put it, "A conscious decision must be made as to how much unemployment and loss of output is acceptable in order to get smaller prices rises." If creating more jobs and getting the extra output "cost" only a percentage or two higher inflation rate, some believed that this trade-off was worth it.

The problem was that reality did not cooperate. The inflation–unemployment relationship that underlies the Phillips curve, which had been reliably observed during the 1960s, was not stable. For one, look at where the economy ended up by 1980 and 1982. You can see in Figure 18.5, there seems to be no discernible level to which the rate of inflation gravitates: it varied between less than 2 percent in the 1960s, and got as high as nearly 14 percent in 1980. This suggests that there is no long-run rate of inflation around which it fluctuates.

That is not true, however, when you look at the unemployment rate. It appears that the points cluster (albeit loosely) around an unemployment rate of about 6 percent. This occurs because when economic activity closes the GDP gap, the unemployment rate also tends to move toward some level associated with full employment. Recall from Chapter 8 that full employment is a level of unemployment consistent with the economy operating on its production possibilities frontier (PPF), that is, at its potential. And, that "full-employment" unemployment rate is believed to be around 6 percent.

Why is that a problem? Suppose, and this actually occurred, that policy makers wanted to keep the unemployment rate at, say, 4 percent. But what if, even when the economy is operating with a zero GDP gap, the unemployment rate is 6 percent? In terms of our AD-IE model, a policy to lower the unemployment rate below its full-employment rate would need to increase aggregate demand and create a positive GDP gap. This is a temporary outcome because, over time, output and unemployment return to their potential levels. But what if the policy is sustained? What if policy makers keep trying to increase aggregate demand to achieve that elusive 4 percent unemployment rate, even though it means operating with a positive GDP gap? As you may have guessed, the answer to both questions is that when the public catches on there will be upward pressure on the expected inflation rate.

You can see the results of such a policy in Figure 18.5. Look at the 1960s. The economy moves up along the Phillips curve as lower unemployment generates higher inflation. Continued expansionary policy lowers unemployment but increases inflation. However, as economic forces are pushing the economy back to its potential rate of expansion and the "correct" unemployment rate, the policy is simply pushing the rate of inflation higher and higher. This explains why in the figure, even though the unemployment rate seems to "hover" around 6 percent, the rate of inflation ranges upward to nearly 14 percent. As policy makers kept trying to keep the unemployment rate below its natural rate, the higher they pushed the rate of inflation.

The outcome of this policy also is shown in **Figure 18.6**. There we plot the growth rate of the money supply (*M*1) and the rate of inflation from 1960 through the early 1980s. Because of the time-inconsistent policies followed by the Federal Reserve, policies that were largely based on the Phillips curve, the decades of the 1960s and

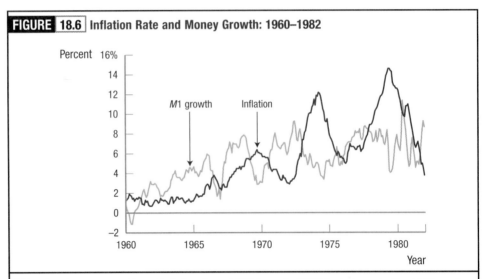

**FIGURE 18.6 | Inflation Rate and Money Growth: 1960–1982**

This plot of money growth and inflation from 1960 through 1982 illustrates why the 1960s and 1970s became known as the Great Inflation. The persistent increase in the rate of inflation occurred primarily because of the time-inconsistent, expansionary policies followed by the Federal Reserve. By the late 1970s, it was widely agreed that the Phillips curve was not a trustworthy rule for making policy decisions and that using it helped produce the upward trend in inflation observed in the figure.

*Source:* R. W. Hafer and David C. Wheelock, "Darryl Francis and the Making of Monetary Policy, 1966–1975." Federal Reserve Bank of St. Louis *Review* (March/April 2003): 1–12.

1970s have become known as the Great Inflation in the United States. Even though the inflation-rate spikes in 1973 and later in 1979 were due to oil-price increases, the underlying inflation rate—mirroring the upward trend in the growth rate of the money supply—continued its upward climb until early in the1980s. By this time, it was widely agreed that the Phillips curve was not a trustworthy rule for making policy decisions. In the long run, the observed short-run trade-off between inflation and unemployment simply isn't there.

### Monetarism

The policy approach called **Monetarism** increased in popularity as policy actions based on the Phillips curve gave rise to higher rates of inflation during the 1970s. Those who adhered to Monetarism, called Monetarists, believed that the Fed should adopt a policy rule aimed at keeping the growth rate of the money supply low and as constant as possible. Although the Fed never truly adopted Monetarism as a formal policy rule, it was thought to provide a viable alternative to the Phillips curve. What made the Monetarist approach attractive at this time was that it focused on inflation. It was becoming increasingly clear to most economists that gyrations in money growth were not responsible for GDP growing permanently faster or slower than its underlying potential. But, as you have learned, inflation is tied to excessive money growth. So, in the face of rising inflation rates, it seemed logical to consider a monetary policy rule that focused on keeping inflation low.

**MONETARISM** The idea that changes in the money supply dominate other policy actions in determining short-run output growth and long-term inflation.

The economist most often associated with pushing the Fed and other central banks to adopt money-growth targets is Milton Friedman, the recipient of the 1976 Nobel Prize in economics. Friedman believed that as well-meaning as policy makers might be, the complexities of modern economies make it impossible for them to fine-tune their policy actions to always achieve their dual policy objectives of economic stability (low unemployment rates) and low inflation. If output growth is, over time, being determined by real factors such as changes in the labor force, capital, and technology (knowledge), then monetary policy really affects only inflation. The challenge of Monetarism ultimately changed the way the FOMC thought about the role of monetary policy in trying to stabilize the economy. Beginning in the 1980s, policy makers switched their long-term focus from maintaining low rates of unemployment to maintaining low and stable rates of inflation.

How does the Monetarist policy rule work? Recall from Chapter 12 that the Quantity Theory of Money states that there is a direct relation between changes in the supply of money and in the price level. Written in its rate-of-change (growth rate) form, the Quantity Theory can be stated as

$$\boldsymbol{M} + \boldsymbol{V} = \boldsymbol{P} + \boldsymbol{y}$$

where $\boldsymbol{M}$ is the rate of growth of the money supply, $\boldsymbol{V}$ is velocity, $\boldsymbol{P}$ is the rate of inflation, and $\boldsymbol{y}$ is the growth of real output in the economy. If output growth ($\boldsymbol{y}$) is, in the long run, determined by economic factors unrelated to monetary policy (i.e., labor, capital, and knowledge), then we can let $\boldsymbol{y}$ be the growth rate of potential GDP. Recall from our earlier discussion that the velocity of money ($\boldsymbol{V}$) captures the institutional and behavioral aspects of a monetary economy. If how people are paid and how they hold their money relative to their incomes doesn't change very much, then this relation may be relatively stable over time. In fact, the presumed stability of velocity is a key element to implementing the Quantity Theory as a policy guide for the short-run. As you will soon see, it turned out that this assumption was the approach's undoing.

If you are willing to surrender control over real output growth—even in the short run—then this version of the Quantity Theory provides the policy maker with enough information to create a policy rule that focuses on the behavior of inflation. Suppose the economy's long-run growth of real output ($\boldsymbol{y}$) averages 3 percent. And suppose that, based on past observation, velocity ($\boldsymbol{V}$) increases at a fairly steady rate, say, 2 percent. After the FOMC (or any other central bank) decides on its target rate of inflation ($\boldsymbol{P}$), the growth rate of the money supply needed to realize that inflation objective is simple arithmetic. If the desired rate of inflation is 5 percent, then under the conditions just stated, the target rate of money growth ($\boldsymbol{M}$) should be

$$\boldsymbol{M} + \boldsymbol{V} = \boldsymbol{P} + \boldsymbol{y}$$

or

$$\boldsymbol{M} + 2\% = 5\% + 3\%$$

Solving for money growth, you get $\boldsymbol{M} = 6\%$. Therefore, the Fed's actions—open-market operations, for example—should be aimed at achieving a money growth rate of 6 percent year in and year out. Over time—assuming that output growth and velocity maintain their average growth rates and that the FOMC does not change its target rate of inflation—using this policy rule would allow the Fed to (on average) hit its target rate of inflation. It also, if announced in advance, is a transparent and time-consistent policy rule.

A variation of Monetarism was used by the Fed as a policy rule from 1979 through 1982. Like the Phillips curve, however, it didn't jive with reality. The facts underlying the rule weren't wrong: over time, money growth and inflation *are* directly related. But the problem with using the Quantity Theory as a short-run policy rule is that it assumes that the growth of velocity is stable. It isn't. The velocity of M1 from 1960 through 1999 is shown in **Figure 18.7**. Notice that up until 1980, M1 velocity followed a relatively smooth, predictable upward path. It fluctuated, but not much. That's great for a policy rule based on the Quantity Theory.

In 1980, things changed. Many financial products that are ubiquitous today were financial innovations of that time—such as the introduction of interest-bearing checking accounts, ATMs, and later such innovations as debit cards (no, they have not existed forever)—and were changing the way people held their money. These new products also dramatically changed the behavior of the velocity of money, as you can see in Figure 18.7: after 1980, it deviated sharply from its pre-1980 trend. The once predictable relationships among money, income, and inflation became less predictable—especially over the short term.

Targeting the money supply to achieve the twin objectives of a stable economy and low inflation therefore fell out of favor. In addition, the "inflation first" constraint of the Quantity Theory meant that little could be done to fight shorter-term economic problems, such as a stalling economy and rising unemployment rates. In

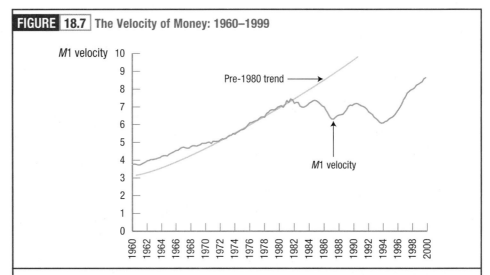

**FIGURE 18.7**  The Velocity of Money: 1960–1999

A problem with using the Quantity Theory as a policy rule is that it assumes that the growth of money velocity is stable. As shown in the figure, the velocity of money from 1960 through 1980 followed a relatively predictable path. After 1980, it not only deviated significantly from that path but also became more variable. Financial innovations that began in the early 1980s changed the way people hold their money and caused velocity to become more unstable. The once predictable relationships among money, income, and inflation became less so after that, and the Monetarist policy rule fell out of favor.

*Source:* R. W. Hafer and David C. Wheelock, "The Rise and Fall of a Policy Rule: Monetarism at the St. Louis Fed, 1968–1986." Federal Reserve Bank of St. Louis *Review* (January/February 2001): 1–24.

other words, the Monetarist's money-growth rule was not flexible enough for policy makers who could not afford to wait five or ten years for the economy to adjust back to its long-run potential. So, in its place came along a rule that provided this flexibility.

## The Taylor Rule

In the early 1990s, economist John Taylor developed a simple shorthand rule to capture the two factors he thought explained why the FOMC raised and lowered the federal funds rate. He argued that in keeping with the AD-IE model, policy makers should respond to higher-than-desired inflation rates by increasing the nominal federal funds rate by more than the increase in inflation; that is, by raising the real federal funds rate. If the economy is expanding too rapidly, that, too, would alert policy makers to increase the federal funds rate. If inflation were too low, or the economy was growing too slowly, then the Fed should consider lowering rates. This approach to policy was dubbed the **Taylor rule**.

> **TAYLOR RULE** A policy rule describing how the Fed should change the federal funds rate. This decision depends on the values of inflation and real GDP growth, relative to predetermined targets.

The Taylor rule is described by the formula:

$$FFR = Inf + 0.5(y - y^*) + 0.5(Inf - Inf^*)$$

This may look imposing, but it really isn't. It is a framework describing how the Fed should change the federal funds rate, a decision that depends on the values of inflation and real GDP growth.[5]

Let's see how the Taylor rule suggests policy makers should act. First, the term $(y - y^*)$ is just the GDP gap. When actual GDP ($y$) is greater than potential GDP ($y^*$), the GDP gap is positive, and the economy is operating at some level above its long-run potential. When this occurs, the rule says the Fed should *raise* the federal funds rate (*FFR*). If the gap is negative, then the rule suggests that the Fed *lower* the federal funds rate. What about inflation? The term $(Inf - Inf^*)$ is the difference between actual inflation (*Inf*) and the FOMC's desired rate (*Inf\**). (Think of *Inf\** as the expected rate of inflation in the AD-IE model; that is, the rate that the Fed would like to occur at a zero GDP gap.) If actual inflation exceeds desired, then the rule prompts the Fed to raise the federal funds rate. The numbers in the equation (0.5) were Taylor's original guess about how much of each deviation—GDP gap or inflation—should be made up by the change in the federal funds rate. Taylor originally assumed that the "desired" rate of inflation was 2 percent, which was pretty much what the FOMC was actually using. So, when the actual rate of inflation is higher than the desired rate of 2 percent, the rule calls for the FOMC to raise the federal funds rate.

The Taylor rule boils down to this: If the economy is expanding too fast, raise the federal funds rate. If the rate of inflation exceeds the target or desired rate,

[5]Specifically, given that *Inf* appears on the right-hand side of the equation, what the Fed really is doing according to the Taylor rule is changing the real federal funds rate, that is, changing *FFR − Inf*.

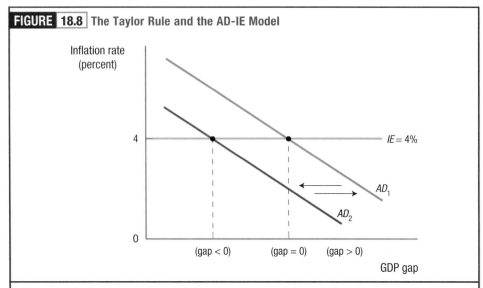

**FIGURE 18.8** The Taylor Rule and the AD-IE Model

The AD-IE model is used to show how the Taylor rule might be implemented. Suppose aggregate demand falls, which is shown as the shift from $AD_1$ to $AD_2$. With actual real GDP now below its potential (a negative GDP gap), and the rate of inflation unchanged, the Taylor rule indicates that the Fed's response should be to lower the federal funds rate enough to get the GDP gap back to zero. This policy response should increase aggregate demand, shifting the curve back toward $AD_1$.

raise the federal funds rate. Conversely, if the economy is expanding slower than its potential, or if the rate of inflation is below the desired rate, lower the federal funds rate.

Let's use the AD-IE model to see how the Taylor rule might be used. Suppose housing values drop, creating problems in the financial sector and causing many businesses and consumers to drastically reduce their spending. This mix of bad economic factors causes a sharp decline in aggregate demand shown by the leftward shift in the aggregate demand curve from $AD_1$ to $AD_2$ in **Figure 18.8**.

With actual real GDP falling below its potential—a negative GDP gap—the Taylor rule indicates that the Fed should lower the federal funds rate. The aim of such a policy response is to shift the curve $AD_2$ back to the right, pushing the economy back to operating at its potential. If done properly and in a timely fashion, this response should at least prevent the economy from contracting further.

During an economic downturn, the Taylor rule provides a clear signal: lower the (real) federal funds rate. But what if economic activity is sagging *and* inflation is rising above the desired rate? As you learned in Chapter 15, such stagflation conditions prevailed in the mid-1970s when inflation was rising *and* the economy was sliding into recession. How should policy be conducted in the face of such conflicting signals? In such situations, using the Taylor rule requires policy makers to decide which objective—maintaining economic growth and full employment or lowering inflation—is more important, how long the policy action they are prescribing should be followed, and when to shift gears to tackle the other problem.

## SOLVED PROBLEM

**Q** The Taylor rule gives policy makers guidance on how to manipulate the federal funds rate. Suppose you are given the following information: actual and potential output ($y^*$) are growing at a 3-percent rate; actual and desired inflation ($Inf^*$) are 2 percent. What should the (nominal) federal funds rate be using the Taylor rule?

**A** Using the earlier equation, the answer is

$$FFR = 2\% + 0.5(3\% - 3\%) + 0.5(2\% - 2\%)$$
$$= 2\%$$

Now suppose there is an economic slowdown. All else the same, what if actual output growth ($y$) falls to zero. What should the federal funds rate be? Substituting the values into the Taylor rule suggests

$$FFR = 2\% + 0.5(0 - 3\%) + 0.5(2\% - 2\%)$$
$$= 2\% + 0.5(-3\%)$$
$$= 0.5\%$$

In other words, if inflation is unchanged, and economic growth slows relative to potential, the rule calls for the Fed to lower the federal funds rate.

What if the economy is slowing *and* inflation is rising? That is, what if stagflation is occurring? To see the outcome, let's suppose that the actual inflation rate increases from 2 percent to 5 percent. Now what does the Taylor rule suggest policy makers should do?

$$FFR = 5\% + 0.5(0 - 3\%) + 0.5(5\% - 2\%)$$
$$= 5\% + 0.5(-3\%) + 0.5(3\%)$$
$$= 5\%$$

Under these conditions, the Fed would raise the federal funds rate. Even though the economy is faltering, the rise in inflation would nudge the Fed to increase the federal funds rate. You can see that when output growth and inflation are moving in opposite directions, this can lead to some surprising actions by the Fed.

Taylor's rule of thumb for policy decisions offers predictable and transparent reactions to economic events. **Table 18.1** summarizes the policy response as dictated by the rule. You can see that when inflation exceeds the desired rate and when the output gap is positive, the unambiguous policy is to raise the federal funds rate. In contrast, the Fed should lower the federal funds rate when the opposite conditions

| **Table 18.1** Summarizing the Taylor Rule | | |
|---|---|---|
| (Cell contents indicate direction of change in federal funds rate: Inflation and then output) | | |
| | Output Gap $< 0$ | Output Gap $> 0$ |
| | Change in Federal Funds Rate: | |
| Inflation $>$ Desired | Increase/Decrease | Increase/Increase |
| Inflation $<$ Desired | Decrease/Decrease | Decrease/Increase |

Taylor's policy rule offers predictable and transparent reactions to economic events. This table summarizes the policy response as dictated by the rule. When inflation exceeds the desired rate *and* when the output gap is positive, the unambiguous policy is to raise the federal funds rate. In contrast, the Fed should lower the federal funds rate when the opposite conditions prevail. When the two economic conditions are in conflict, however, the rule provides an ambiguous signal on whether the Fed should raise or lower the federal funds rate.

prevail. But you also can see that when the two economic conditions are in conflict, the rule is silent on whether the Fed should raise or lower the federal funds rate. In such conditions, discretion—and sometimes political pressures—guides policy decisions.

Although the record on policy rules is mixed, unlike pure discretion, the application of a rule leads to greater predictability in the decision-making process. If the Fed adheres to a stated rule, the public can better predict policy actions based on observations of inflation and output growth. When the Fed doesn't follow a rule or changes the rule without notifying anyone, it can be damaging to the economy.

**ECONOMIC FALLACY**    Policy rules should *always* be followed!

**False.** Economists are often chastised for answering questions with the response "it depends." However, it's true for this fallacy. Policy rules should be followed because they give observers of policy actions some idea of how policy makers will react. If the rule says that they will raise interest rates when inflation rises, then not doing so creates uncertainty.

But suppose your policy rule is to raise the federal funds rate whenever inflation increases. Does this mean you should raise rates even when the increase in inflation stems from factors unrelated to monetary policy? According to your rule, the Fed should have raised the federal funds rate, for example, during the summer of 2008, when commodity prices increased, especially the price of oil. The price hikes increased short-term inflation and people's expectations of inflation. Did the Fed then follow the rule? No.

One reason why it didn't was because the inflation increase stemmed from sources outside of its control, including the spiking of oil and gasoline prices. The other reason why is because even though expected inflation was rising, the economy was sliding into a recession. In this case, the Fed decided not to follow the inflation component of its rule but instead focused on fighting the recession by lowering the federal funds rate.

## 18.6 Can the Independence of a Central Bank Affect Its Policy Actions?

The structure of the Federal Reserve System and how the board members are selected reduce the central bank's ties to the political process. The Treasury-Federal Reserve Accord of 1951 marked the official separation of Federal Reserve policy from the U.S. Treasury, making the Fed's monetary policy decisions even more independent of the political system. In contrast, the selection of central bankers in other countries is often more political because they change as does the administration in power. Much evidence suggests that monetary policy decisions are often made that are consistent with the policy (political?) objectives of the sitting government.

Is there any evidence that having a politically independent central bank is better for the economy? Some people argue that the more independent a central bank is, the lower the rate of inflation its country is likely to experience. If central bankers do not have to answer to voters and politicians who are upset by policies taken to reduce inflation—which, as in the early 1980s, raised unemployment rates—will lower average rates of inflation be the norm?

**Figure 18.9** provides some evidence to see if, in general, the independence of a central bank is related to lower average rates of inflation. (The averages are based on data covering the 1970s and 1980s.) In the upper panel, you can see that countries

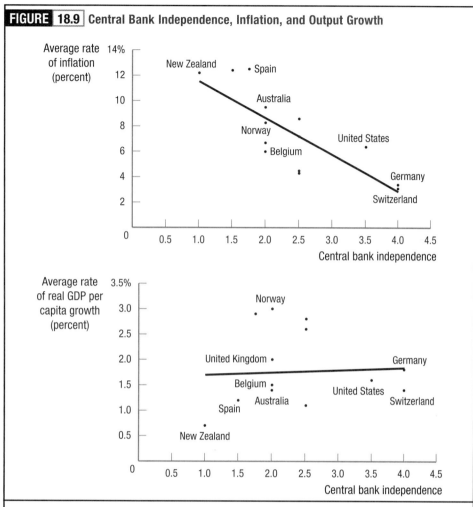

**FIGURE 18.9** Central Bank Independence, Inflation, and Output Growth

The upper panel of this figure shows the relation between central bank independence and infla-tion. It appears that the more independent a central bank is from its government, the lower is the average rate of inflation. The lower panel shows the relation between central bank independence and output growth. There you see basically no discernible relationship between the two mea-sures. Although a government's closer control over the actions of its central bank might result in higher inflation, there is no evidence that doing so results in faster economic growth.

*Source:* Alberto Alesina and Lawrence H. Summers, "Central Bank Independence and Macroeconomic Performance: Some Comparative Evidence." *Journal of Money, Credit, and Banking* (May 1993): 151–62.

with relatively more independent central banks, such as Germany and Switzerland, tend to experience lower average rates of inflation. Although the average relation indi-cates that having a more independent central bank is associated with a lower rate of inflation, it doesn't guarantee it. Look, for example, at the inflation rates of the Belgium, Norway, and Spain. Even though these central banks have about the same level of independence, their average rates of inflation are quite different. Even so, the evidence suggests that an independent central bank may be able to pursue a more credible low-inflation policy if it isn't being buffeted by political considerations.

But inflation is only one side of the policy coin. What is the relation between central bank independence and output growth? The bottom panel of Figure 18.9 plots average real GDP per capita growth along with central bank independence. There you see that there is basically no discernible relationship between how independent a country's central bank is and its average rate of output growth. This result gets back to our point that, over time, output growth is determined by the combinations of labor, capital, and knowledge in an economy and not by the policy actions of the central bank. The figure suggests that government bureaucrats and politicians who think they can generate sustained economic growth—and therefore votes for their reelection—by increasing their control over their nation's central bank are simply wrong.

Finally, note that the independence of a central bank can change over time. In 1989, the government of New Zealand gave its central bank more political independence with the stipulation that price stability (low inflation) would be its stated, publicly known policy objective. Such independence and policy transparency meant that the public would know if the policy makers in New Zealand's central bank did not meet their policy objective. Following this change, New Zealand did in fact achieve a much lower average rate of inflation.[6] Another example is the development of the European Central Bank (ECB). Because of the way it is organized, the ECB is much more independent from the countries' governments than the countries' own central banks used to be. An outcome of this independence is that ECB has taken a much stronger position on meeting its stated long-term goal of keeping inflation low. This focus has increased debate among member countries over the policies taken.[7]

## 18.7 Monetary Policy in a Global Economy: Can the Fed's Actions Affect Exchange Rates?

The policy decisions made by some central banks affect not only their own economy but may also impact the economies of other nations. For example, it is widely believed that before the creation of the euro zone, policy actions taken by the central bank of Germany—the Bundesbank—had a widespread influence on surrounding economies. The same is true for the U.S. Federal Reserve. That's because when the Fed raises or lowers the federal funds rate, this can affect the foreign-exchange rate of the dollar. Recall from Chapter 9 that the exchange rate fluctuates with changes in the demand for and supply of dollars. All else the same, if the Fed reduces the federal funds rate to a level below another country's comparable interest rate, the dollar tends to depreciate in value. Conversely, when the Fed pushes the federal funds rate higher than comparable foreign rates, the dollar appreciates in value.

When members of the FOMC make policy, how their actions will impact foreign-exchange rates often is one consideration in the decision-making process. To use just one example, the following excerpt is taken from the FOMC's minutes of September 16, 2008:

> Despite concern that recent high inflation readings suggested that price pressures could persist, participants [members of the FOMC] generally thought that the outlook for inflation had improved, mainly reflecting the recent declines in the prices of oil and other commodities, the stronger foreign exchange value of the dollar, and the weakening of the labor market.

Even though it may not be the FOMC's biggest concern, the dollar's foreign-exchange value and how it affects domestic inflation and economic activity is

· · · · · · ·

[6]Michael Hutchinson, "Central Bank Credibility and Disinflation in New Zealand." Federal Reserve Bank of San Francisco *Weekly Letter*, February 10, 1995.

[7]David Marsh, "The Euro's Lost Promise." *New York Times*, May 18, 2010.

watched closely by the FOMC. Think about what policy actions the Fed might take if the economy is sliding into a recession. With mounting signs of a recession, the Fed historically lowers the federal funds rate. Taken to avert a domestic economic decline, this policy also affects the exchange value of the dollar. As experienced in the 2007–2009 recession, as U.S. interest rates fell below comparable rates of our trading partners, the dollar declined in the foreign-exchange market.

The Fed's actions to keep our economy from recession can spill over into international trade. First, the decline in the value of the dollar makes goods imported to the United States more expensive relative to goods produced domestically. So, if Fed actions cause foreign exchange value of the dollar to decline, it would take more dollars to buy a British wool sweater than previously. Given this relative price change, not just for sweaters but across a large array of goods, consumers will shift from buying imported goods to buying domestically produced goods. Net exports (the difference between exports and imports) should rise (or at least become less negative). The increase in net exports also occurs because the depreciation of the dollar makes U.S.-produced goods relatively cheaper to foreign consumers. Foreign consumers will alter their buying habits and purchase more U.S. goods. In this case, the improvement in net exports will provide a boost to economic activity in the United States.

But the decline in the value of the dollar can have another effect. Take the events of 2008 as an example. The price of crude oil, a globally traded good, is stated in dollars. That means that if the price for a barrel of crude is $50, a fall in the exchange value of the dollar means that oil producers are getting less purchasing power *in terms of non-U.S. goods* than before. Getting paid $50 per barrel means that it takes more barrels of oil to buy the same amount of goods produced elsewhere in the global economy. Because the purchasing power of "oil dollars" was falling with the exchange value of the dollar, oil producers increased the price of oil to make up the difference. This is, at least in some measure, an explanation for the steep run-up in oil prices during the summer of 2008. This increased the prices we paid for gasoline, which had an adverse consequence on the economy. The Fed must consider consequences such as these when it's debating policy decisions.

Reaction to the Fed's changes in the federal funds rate is possible because of the **flexible exchange-rate** policy followed by the United States for many years. A flexible exchange-rate policy recognizes that sometimes the exchange value of the dollar will rise and sometimes it will fall in reaction to domestic (and foreign) monetary policy actions. Although increases and decreases in the exchange rate of the dollar often spark heated debates, the weight of evidence suggests that, at least for a country like the United States, controlling the exchange value of the dollar is not only very difficult but is not consistent with the Fed's long-term policy goals.

**FLEXIBLE EXCHANGE RATE** A situation in which currency exchange rates fluctuate with market forces.

EXAMPLE You leave for a trip to Paris, and the exchange rate is US$1 to €1. You plan to spend no more than US$1,000. While you are gone, the exchange rate changes to US$2 to €1. In other words, now it takes US$2 to buy just €1. As a result, your dollars don't go as far, and you must be more frugal while you are in Paris.

Is there a circumstance in which it would be wise to abandon a flexible exchange-rate policy and try to fix the exchange value of your currency? Suppose you live in a country that is historically plagued by rampant inflation. Because the main source of inflation is an overly expansionary monetary policy, one avenue to curtail such bad policy decisions is to tie the hands of the central bankers. A **fixed exchange-rate** policy might achieve this objective.

**FIXED EXCHANGE RATE** A situation in which currency exchange rates are not determined by market forces but are set by the government.

**EXAMPLE** During your trip to Paris, the exchange rate never varies from the officially announced rate. You are able to spend your allotted US$1,000.

When a central bank operates under a fixed exchange-rate policy, it must work to keep the exchange value of its currency fixed relative to another country's currency. To keep the currencies' exchange rates constant, the country that adopts the fixed exchange rate must undertake policies that mimic the country to which it has tied its currency. This usually means that the adopting country loses much of its monetary policy independence. However, that is exactly what is desired if the central bankers cannot be trusted to keep inflation at bay.

One example of adopting such a policy is Argentina, which tied the value of its currency—the Argentine peso—to the U.S. dollar in 1991. Argentina did this to counter the country's persistent and high inflation. The move worked quite well, at least for a while. As interest rates fell in the United States during the 1990s, so too did they fall in Argentina. Both countries experienced economic expansions. In 2000, however, the Fed decided to enact a contractionary policy to fight potential increases in inflation. To do this, the Fed raised the federal funds rate. Even though Argentina did not face the same inflation problem, its central bank mimicked the Fed's contractionary policy actions to maintain the peso-dollar exchange rate. The Argentinean central bank's policy caused Argentina to suffer an economic downturn. If it weren't for the fixed exchange-rate policy, the economic downturn might not have occurred.

Should a central bank follow a flexible exchange-rate policy or a fixed exchange-rate policy? Should a central bank consider only domestic issues when setting policy, or must it take a broader, global view of how its actions may impact others? Such questions get mixed responses, partly because the answers depend on the central bank being considered. For a country the size of the United States, monetary policy often is conducted with an eye more toward domestic issues than international issues. For a smaller open economy, however, the choice is not so clear. As the case of Argentina suggests, losing policy independence can be both beneficial and costly.

## 18.8 The Financial Crisis and Great Recession of 2007–2009: A Case Study in Monetary Policy

This section looks at the events that led to the government's drastic actions during what could be the most significant economic event in your lifetime: the economic and financial crisis that began in 2007. We covered the government's fiscal-policy actions in Chapter 16. Now we will focus on the actions of the Federal Reserve.

### Cheap Credit, Housing, and the Credit Crunch

Coming out of the 2001 recession, the U.S. economy did not expand at the pace many economists thought it should. Even with expansionary monetary and fiscal policies in place, the recovery was weak compared with most previous recoveries. As Figure 18.2 shows, following the recession, the Federal Reserve pushed the federal funds rate to an extremely low level—well below the level many economists thought it should be. With this action, the Fed set into motion policies that lowered the opportunity cost of borrowing, and, as basic economic theory predicts, a borrowing boom occurred. As we have touched on earlier in this book, nowhere was this more apparent than in the housing market.

Why focus on the housing market? First, the stock market began to decline in 2000 and did not hit bottom until 2003. After that ride, many investors were not too thrilled about putting money back into the stock market and looked for investment alternatives, one of which was real estate. Second, with credit so cheap, one was foolish not to borrow. This was the attitude many investors—individuals and institutions alike—took. Consequently, huge numbers of people refinanced existing home mortgages, and many others bought new homes. In many instances, home buyers hoped to turn a quick profit by "flipping" their houses. In this environment, many builders started new developments—not only of homes but also of shopping centers and office complexes.

An increasing amount of the borrowing for housing occurred in what's called the *subprime market.* In the subprime market, borrowers have lower credit scores and must pay higher interest rates.[8] To give you some perspective on the magnitude of lending in this segment of the mortgage market, in the late 1990s, subprime loans accounted for about 13 percent of new loans being made. By 2006, that proportion had risen to more than 20 percent of all mortgage loans, or over $600 billion.

In most circumstances, lending in the subprime market is perfectly sensible, provided the rates charged to borrowers reflect the risk to the lender. However, this time around, the increased lending in the subprime market was problematic for two reasons. First, lenders did not do their utmost to make sure borrowers were capable of repaying their loans. Second, most lenders did not hold the loans they originated. Instead, they bundled the loans together and sold these newly created financial assets to investors.

These investors do not want people's loans; they only want the interest income that is generated when people make their monthly payments. The financial assets created with mortgages are known as *mortgage-backed securities*, just one of many "exotic" financial instruments that have become such a hot topic of discussion, and of concern to policy makers, over the past few years.[9] The investments were thought to be less risky for a number of reasons. For one, the bundling and selling process got the sometimes more risky original mortgage loans off of banks' books. Even the government got caught up in the market for these financial products. To promote home ownership in the United States and lessen their lending risks, Congress compelled the government agencies Fannie Mae and Freddie Mac to increase their lending activity in the subprime and mortgage-backed security markets.

Unfortunately, many subprime loans were made at ultra-low teaser rates designed to get people to borrow money. But these rates lasted only a few years, requiring borrowers to refinance their loans later. When interest rates in the economy increased, the rates at which these subprime mortgages were refinanced were higher, sometimes significantly higher than the initial rates paid.

And this is where the Fed's policies come in. You saw in Figure 18.2 that beginning in 2003 and lasting through 2006 the Fed increased the federal funds rate from 1 percent to 5.25 percent. The Fed's action increased other interest rates, including those

· · · · · · ·

[8]Luke M. Shimek, "Subprime Mortgage Lending." *Liber8*, Federal Reserve Bank of St. Louis, September 2007.

[9]Janet Yellen, "The Financial Markets, Housing and the Economy." Federal Reserve Bank of San Francisco *Economic Letter*, April 18, 2008.

on risky subprime mortgages. Borrowers soon began to find themselves facing newly adjusted, higher loan rates they couldn't afford. The housing boom began to unravel.

In early 2007, subprime lenders, many of whom were subsidiaries of large banks, were reporting declining earnings. Companies that rate the safety of investments, such as Moody's and Standard & Poor's (S&P), began to lower their ratings on the securities backed by subprime mortgages. More and more the market was coming to grips with the idea that the risk of the loans not being repaid, what economists call *default risk*, was increasing, and fast. Then, in the fall of 2007 (shortly after the stock market reached an all-time high), the economy suffered a severe credit crunch. The housing bubble burst, and home prices sharply tumbled.

**Figure 18.10** shows a widely used measure of home prices in the United States, the Standard & Poor's/Case-Shiller Home Price Index. The value of the index, reflecting housing prices averaged across 20 cities, more than doubled between 2000 and early 2006, the time of low interest rates. Then, beginning in late 2006, housing prices began dropping. On average, housing lost about 25 percent of its value before leveling off in late 2009, a level from which they had not recovered well into 2011. This decline in home values in turn reduced the value of the mortgage-backed securities purchased by investment groups and sharply reduced the market's valuation of the securities themselves.

Once thought to be great investments (the mantra was "home prices don't fall, so neither will these securities"), mortgage-backed securities turned out to be lousy ones. Even though funds were available, banks and other financial institutions became unwilling to lend, even to each other. Everyone became worried that any so-called toxic securities on the books of borrowing institutions would send them into bankruptcy, and the loans would never be repaid.

The confidence of investors and lenders throughout the financial market, here and abroad, was shaken. The stock prices of several large financial institutions

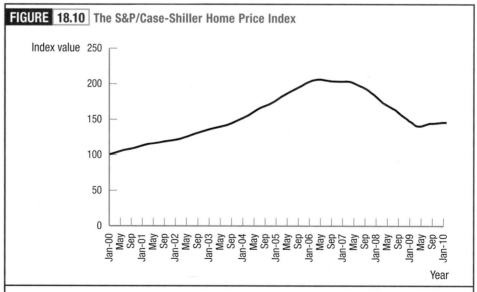

**FIGURE 18.10**   The S&P/Case-Shiller Home Price Index

A widely used measure of home prices in the United States, the Standard & Poor's/Case-Shiller Home Price Index is plotted in this figure since 2000. The value of the index, reflecting average housing prices in 20 cities, doubled between 2000 and early 2006. Within a few short years after that, the average home had lost about 25 percent of its market value before leveling off in late 2009.

*Source:* Standard & Poor's

plummeted, and some failed outright. By March 2009, the value of the stock market dropped to less than half of its 2007 peak. Even with interest rates at record lows, lenders stopped lending, and the economy ground to a halt. The difficulties in the financial market not only intensified the recession here, but the effects spread to countries around the world.

## The Fed's Reaction

Let's use the AD-IE model to analyze the Fed's reaction to this economic catastrophe. In **Figure 18.11**, we start with the economy in 2006, represented by the aggregate demand curve $AD_{2006}$ and with inflation expectations ($IE$) at about 2 percent (point A). The shift in the aggregate demand curve to $AD_{2009}$ shows the reduction in aggregate demand stemming from the problems in the housing and financial markets. With inflation expectations unchanged, the economy slid to point B. The Fed responded by lowering the nominal federal funds rate to near zero, and, when this did not achieve the desired result, it increased funds to banks and other financial institutions using quantitative easing. (Quantitative easing is explained in Chapter 17.) Despite the expansionary monetary and fiscal policies undertaken, the economy suffered the most severe recession since the Great Depression. As we documented in Chapter 15, the GDP gap, which was slightly positive in 2006, by 2009 had fallen to a negative 7 percent.

These combined policy actions of the Federal Reserve and the federal government continued well into 2011. As you can see in Figure 18.11, these combined policy actions shifted the aggregate demand curve rightward. Nonetheless, into 2011, the GDP gap was still negative (point C). With inflation expectations around 2 percent in 2011, the GDP gap remained much larger than anyone wanted. And, consequently, the unemployment rate remained above 9 percent. How much of the rightward shift

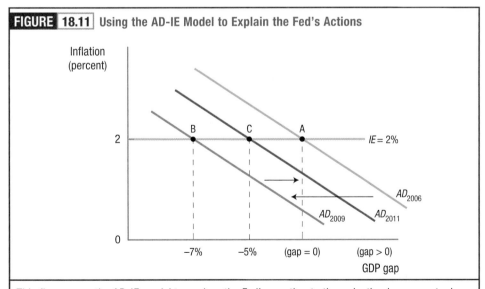

**FIGURE 18.11** Using the AD-IE Model to Explain the Fed's Actions

This figure uses the AD-IE model to analyze the Fed's reaction to the reduction in aggregate demand (the shift from $AD_{2006}$ to $AD_{2009}$) stemming from the problems in the housing and financial markets. The Fed responded initially by lowering the federal funds rate, and, when this did not achieve the desired result, it increased funds to banks and other financial institutions using quantitative easing. Despite the expansionary monetary policies taken, the economy suffered the most severe recession since the Great Depression.

was due solely to the Fed's policies and how much of it was due to the government's fiscal policies is still being debated. Most people believe intervention by the Fed was a major element in preventing an even larger downturn in the economy. Nonetheless, the Fed's actions taken before and after the onset of the recession are considered controversial for several reasons.

**Controversy 1: Interest Rates Were Too Low.** The Fed lowered the federal funds rate and kept it too low for too long after the 2001 recession ended. Many economists believe that the Fed's lowering of interest rates and keeping them low for several years sowed the seeds for the housing boom and its eventual bust. On the other side of the debate are economists who argue that pushing the federal funds rate so low was necessary because the economy was not expanding fast enough to bring unemployment rates down. With actual and expected inflation low, the choice of acting to lower unemployment rates prevailed.

A related effect of this action was the lowering of the foreign-exchange value of the dollar. As we noted earlier in this chapter, the depreciation of the dollar helped cause the massive run-up in oil prices during the summer of 2008. With the dollar falling in value, the purchasing power of a barrel of oil was, likewise, falling for foreign producers. To recoup this loss in purchasing power, there was an incentive to raise prices. That effect, coupled with an increase in the world demand, sent the price of a barrel of oil to nearly $150.

**Controversy 2: Intervention in the Financial Market.** Another controversy relates to the timing and the nature of Treasury-Fed joint intervention into financial markets. In September 2008, the government allowed the investment bank Lehman Brothers to fail. Some people believe this event sent a chill though the financial markets and worsened the fermenting credit crunch. Others suggest that markets actually did not overreact to this particular decision, however. Instead, when Congress passed the Emergency Economic Stabilization Act in October 2008, it committed $700 billion to bail out failed financial institutions. Once passed and endorsed by the Treasury and the Fed, fears of a deepening financial crisis spread quickly. Investors and banks saw it as a sign that it was time to seek safe investment opportunities and stop borrowing and lending funds.

**Controversy 3: Quantitative Easing and Its Aftermath.** Beginning in late 2008, the Fed's actions to keep the nominal federal funds rate to near zero was accompanied by actions to increase the amount of reserves in the banking system. The Fed was able to accomplish this through its first quantitative-easing program of buying up financial assets from banks, insurance companies, and other financial institutions. Through a variety of special programs, the Fed purchased everything from mortgage-backed securities to short-term loans by businesses.

To see the effects of quantitative easing, **Figure 18.12** shows the major components of the Fed's balance sheet (its holding of government securities) over the period of the recession. In normal times, the Fed's portfolio consists mostly of short-term Treasury securities, those that the Fed buys and sells during open-market operations. Look at how the components changed in September 2008, the month Lehman Brothers filed for bankruptcy. Not only did Treasury securities become a much smaller component of the balance sheet, but the sheer size of the Fed's balance sheet increased several fold, and it remained in this lop-sided state through 2010.

One aspect of this controversy is that some argued the Fed should not be making such purchases in the first place. Others raised concerns that when the Fed bought its newly acquired securities from troubled financial institutions, it was placing money in their accounts at the Fed—that is, increasing banks' excess reserves. (As you learned

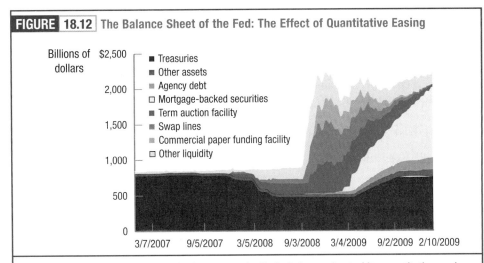

**FIGURE** **18.12** The Balance Sheet of the Fed: The Effect of Quantitative Easing

Billions of dollars

Legend:
- Treasuries
- Other assets
- Agency debt
- Mortgage-backed securities
- Term auction facility
- Swap lines
- Commercial paper funding facility
- Other liquidity

y-axis: $2,500, 2,000, 1,500, 1,000, 500, 0

x-axis: 3/7/2007   9/5/2007   3/5/2008   9/3/2008   3/4/2009   9/2/2009   2/10/2009

This figure graphically illustrates the impact on the Fed's balance sheet of its quantitative-easing policy. The major effect of quantitative easing appears as increases and changes in the major components of the Fed's balance sheet. In normal times, the Fed's portfolio consists mostly of short-term Treasury securities, which the Fed buys and sells during open-market operations. The relative size of the components changed markedly beginning in September 2008, the month Lehman Brothers filed for bankruptcy. Treasury securities became less than 50 percent of the balance sheet, while other components associated with the Fed's quantitative-easing program increased. In addition, the absolute size of the Fed's balance sheet more than doubled.

*Source:* Alan S. Blinder, "Quantitative Easing: Entrance and Exit Strategies." Federal Reserve Bank of St. Louis *Review* (November/December 2010): 465–79.

in the previous chapter, reserves are the base upon which banks can make loans and create deposits.) The magnitude of this program was historic. In the summer of 2007, excess reserves in the banking system were less than $2 billion. By early 2010, they had swelled to $1,120 billion where they remained into 2011.

The outcome of this policy action has not been fully realized. In fact, beginning in late 2010, the Fed instituted yet another round of quantitative easing, nicknamed QE2. At the time of its announcement, the Fed stated that it would purchase $600 billion in long-term U.S. government securities. The program ended in June 2011. An ongoing concern is that the Fed's continued low-interest-rate policy and injection of reserves into the banking system could lead to inflation after the economy begins to expand at a more rapid rate. With the economy emerging from the recession in 2009, and inflation remaining low, many argue that the inflationary effect of Fed policy was far overshadowed by the need to promote an adequate recovery and a lower unemployment rate. By the time you are reading this, you will know the answer to the question: How did the Fed do?

## WHAT YOU SHOULD HAVE LEARNED FROM CHAPTER 18

- ■ That the objectives of monetary policy are low inflation and steady economic growth and that sometimes these goals lead to conflicting policies.
- ■ That policy rules are preferable to discretionary policy.
- ■ That transparent policies are preferable to policies made in secrecy.
- ■ That switching between short-term policy goals and long-term policy goals is time inconsistent.
- ■ That policy actions take time to affect the economy.

- That once interest rates are near zero, one way to engage in expansionary policy is to increase the money supply via quantitative easing.

- That, in general, countries in which central banks are independent of the political process have lower rates of inflation.

- That a country's exchange-rate regime can alter the effect of monetary policy actions, especially by large economies, both domestically and internationally.

## KEY TERMS

Discretionary monetary policy, p. 492

Policy rule, p. 492

Policy transparency, p. 493

Time-inconsistent policy, p. 495

Phillips curve, p. 498

Monetarism, p. 500

Taylor rule, p. 503

Flexible exchange rate, p. 509

Fixed exchange rate, p. 510

## QUESTIONS AND PROBLEMS

1. In February 1994, the *New York Times* ran an article with the title "Fed Relying on Intuition in Setting Rate Policy." In the article, it talked about the Fed justifying its cut in interest rates, referring to a weak economy. Explain why "intuition" and not a "rule" is often applied to making policy decisions.

2. If people form expectations of future economic activity based partly on Fed actions, would you prefer the Fed to adjust policy more often? What are the pros and cons of such policy changes?

3. You have learned that nominal interest rates tend to move with the rate of inflation. If there is a price shock that increases inflation, and interest rates rise, how would you respond if you were the chairman of the Fed? Does your answer depend on which policy objective—steady economic growth or low inflation—influences your decision?

4. In 1991, two congressmen introduced the Federal Reserve Reform Act. One component of the bill was that the Fed would be required by law to immediately announce any changes in monetary policy. Although the law did not pass, since then, the Fed has become much better at announcing policy plans on a more timely basis. Explain how such increased transparency can benefit economic decision making by the public.

5. A number of central banks publicly announce an inflation target as their main goal for monetary policy. What is the opportunity cost if your central bank announces such a policy objective and sticks to it, no matter what?

6. You have learned that rational expectations are formed by individuals acquiring information up to the point where the perceived marginal cost is equal to the marginal benefit of doing so. Based on this idea:

   a) Should a central bank announce one policy objective and secretly try to achieve another?

   b) How can a central bank achieve policy credibility?

   c) How does announcing a specific policy objective, such as a target inflation rate, limit policy decisions?

7. In 2008, oil prices surged, and inflation expectations were on the rise. At the same time, there were mounting signs that the economy was slipping into a recession. Using the AD-IE model, show and discuss what policy action you would pick if:

   a) your goal was to keep inflation low.

   b) your goal was to keep the economy operating at potential GDP.

   c) How did the Fed actually respond? Does this raise questions about the time inconsistency of their policy?

8. The Phillips curve is based on the observed negative relation between the rate of inflation and the unemployment rate. That is, decreases in the unemployment rate tend to be associated with increases in the rate of inflation.

   a) Given what you know about the relation between the unemployment rate and the GDP gap, restate the Phillips curve in terms of inflation and the GDP gap.
   b) Based on the AD-IE model, and given your answer in (a), explain why the Phillips curve is not likely to be stable over time. Why is it that trying to lower the unemployment rate below its full-employment level results in higher inflation?
   c. Using the AD-IE model, explain how a condition of stagflation—rising inflation and a negative GDP gap—falsifies the underlying principle of the Phillips curve.

9. At a recent family reunion, your cousin Scott starts lecturing you about the benefits of using a money-growth target for monetary policy. All he talks about is the evidence showing that, over time, money growth and inflation are positively related. Although you agree with him on that point, you suggest to him that there are possible downsides to using such a policy rule. What are they?

10. Look at Figure 18.7. Between 1960 and 1980, the velocity of money increased at an annual average rate of 4.3 percent. Suppose in 1980, you also knew that real GDP increased at an annual average rate of 5 percent over the past 20 years. Using that information:

    a) If your desired rate of inflation for the next few years was 5 percent, what would you suggest money growth should be?
    b) Between 1980 and 1985, the velocity of money drops from 7 to 6. Calculate the average rate of change of velocity. Using this new number for velocity, if the growth of real GDP growth remains at its average, and your desired rate of inflation hasn't changed, what should money growth be?
    c) It is 1980, and you do not know that velocity is going to decline over the next five years. If you keep the growth rate of money at the level determined in (a), what would be the rate of inflation?
    d) It is now 1995. As you can see in Figure 18.7, velocity has been declining, on average, for most of the past 15 years. Let's say that the average growth of velocity during this time is −3 percent. If you continue to target money growth to achieve a desired 5-percent rate of inflation and real GDP continues to grow at a 5-percent rate, what is going to happen to actual inflation over the next few years?

11. The Federal Reserve Bank of New York published an article in 2008 titled "Divorcing Money from Monetary Policy."

    a) Explain how this can be done using the Taylor rule.
    b) Now explain why this may not make sense given the process used by the Fed to raise or lower the federal funds rate. (Hint: think open-market operations.)

12. Some argue that use of the Taylor rule for determining monetary policy leads to a reduction in policy credibility. Explain how this might happen.

13. Fixing the price of a good is equivalent to having a horizontal supply curve at that price. If a government fixes its exchange rate, explain the effects of changes in the demand for its currency.

14. There are two countries in the world. One decides to fight its inflation problem by raising its interest rates. The other decides to fight its rising unemployment problem and lowers its interest rates. What are the implications for each country's foreign-exchange rate if they follow such policies? What are the economic implications if they do so?

15. The evidence in Figure 18.9 suggests that increased central bank independence is associated with lower average rates of inflation, but there is no apparent relation with output growth. Based on this evidence:

a) Are lower rates of inflation a necessary outcome of increased independence?

b) If the central bank is independent, and its policy objective is to increase the growth rate of output, would you expect to see the same pattern as in the figure?

c) Could the observed relation in Figure 18.9 be more a function of policy credibility than independence?

**absolute advantage** The ability to produce more output than others, using the same amount of resources.

**accounting costs** Explicit costs, or monetary outlays, incurred in the course of doing business as well as costs considered expenses under the law.

**accounting profit** Total revenue less *accounting* costs.

**aggregate demand curve** A line showing the negative relation between the rate of inflation and the level of real output.

**automatic stabilizer** Changes in taxes and expenditures that occur to offset changes in economic activity. Automatic stabilizers are counter-cyclical.

**autonomous consumption** The level of consumption spending that is independent of your level of income.

**barter** An exchange system where goods trade for goods.

**base year** The reference point used to compare price changes over time. The value of the price index in the base year is 100.

**Board of Governors** The governing body of the Federal Reserve System.

**budget deficit** A budget deficit occurs when government outlays exceed government revenues.

**budget surplus** A budget surplus occurs when government receipts exceed government outlays.

**central bank** The monetary authority of a country; the part of a country's government that determines and carries out monetary policy.

**Chairman of the Board of Governors** The head of the U.S. Federal Reserve.

**comparative advantage** The ability to produce a particular good or service at a lower opportunity cost than other producers.

**complementary goods** Goods that are usually used in conjunction with one another.

**consumer price index** The CPI is a type of price index. It measures the change in prices for goods and services frequently bought by households. It is reported monthly by the U.S. government's Bureau of Labor Statistics.

**consumer surplus (CS)** The difference between a person's willingness to pay for a unit of a good and the amount that she actually pays.

**consumption function** The consumption function shows a positive relation between consumer spending and the level of income.

**contractionary monetary policy** A policy action aimed at raising the federal funds rate and decreasing the growth rate of the money supply.

**convergence** The observation that real income per person in a poor country grows at a faster rate than in a rich one. If it continues, the level of real income per person in the poor country will converge—or catch up to—that of the rich country.

**crowding out** Crowding out occurs when the government and private individuals compete for the same investment dollar. The private individuals are crowded out by the government because the government can outbid them for the funds.

**cyclical unemployment** The rise and fall of the unemployment rate that occurs due to changes in business activity.

**deadweight loss** The sum of consumer and producer surplus lost when an artificial price and quantity are imposed on a market.

**deflation** A sustained *decrease* in the general level of prices.

**demand** The quantity of a good a person is willing and able to purchase at any given price during a specified time period (day, week, month, and so forth), *all other factors held constant.*

**demand curve** A graphic representation of an individual's demand schedule. The demand curve plots all of the price–quantity combinations an individual is willing to accept.

**demand schedule** A table that shows the price of a good and the number of units a buyer is willing to purchase at that price during a specific time period.

**diminishing marginal benefit** A situation in which the economic benefit generated from an additional unit of a good or activity is less than the benefit derived from the preceding unit.

**diminishing marginal returns** The condition where the adding of one more unit of some input such as labor, holding capital and knowledge constant, leads to a smaller increase in output compared with the last unit of labor added.

**discouraged worker** The term applied to an unemployed individual who stops searching for employment. As a consequence, they are no longer counted as part of the labor force.

**discretionary fiscal policy** Legislative or administrative actions taken by the government to alter the level of government spending or the tax structure.

**discretionary monetary policy** Policy actions central bankers take that are not based on underlying rules or guidelines.

**disequilibrium** A situation in which the quantity demanded of a product does not equal the quantity of it supplied at the current price.

**disinflation** A reduction in the rate of inflation. Prices are rising at a slower rate.

**disposable income** Income available for spending after taxes are subtracted.

**division of labor** The concentration of a worker's full work effort on a subtask that contributes to the production of a specific good or service.

**economic environment** Prices, wages, laws, and social norms that serve as external constraints on the choices that we make; external factors that dictate the trade-offs we face.

**economic good** Any scarce resource, product, service, or other source of well-being.

**economic growth** A *sustained* increase in real income *per person* over time.

**economic profit** Total revenue less *economic* costs.

**economic rationality** A decision process whereby individuals make choices they believe will advance their own well-being.

**economic standard of living** Measured as the average person's command over goods and services produced in an economy measured using real GDP or income per person.

**efficiency wages** Wages paid above the market-equilibrium wage to attract the best workers, achieve higher worker productivity, reduce worker turnover, and improve morale.

**employment-to-population ratio** The ratio of those individuals employed to the working-age population.

**endogenous growth model** A model of economic growth in which the development and spread of knowledge (technology) plays a central role.

**equilibrium price** The price at which the quantity demanded in the market is exactly equal to the quantity supplied; the market-clearing price.

**equilibrium quantity** The quantity bought and sold at the equilibrium price.

**excess reserves** The difference between total reserves and desired reserves.

**expansion** The period of positive economic growth between the end of one recession and the beginning of the next.

**expansionary monetary policy** A policy action aimed at lowering the federal funds rate and increasing the growth rate of the money supply.

**explicit cost** The monetary cost of a choice.

**federal debt** The total amount of outstanding loans that the federal government has obtained to fund its activities.

**federal funds rate** The interest rate that banks charge each other for short-term (usually overnight) loans.

**Federal Open Market Committee (FOMC)** The policy-making arm of the Federal Reserve. The FOMC decides the direction of monetary policy.

**federal receipts** The total of federal taxes and other fees collected by the government.

**final goods approach** The final goods approach to measuring GDP is based on adding up the dollar value of final goods and services sold in the economy in the current period.

**fiscal-spending multiplier** The multiple by which GDP is increased for a given increase in government spending.

**fixed exchange rate** A situation in which currency exchange rates are not determined by market forces but are set by the government.

**flexible exchange rate** A situation in which currency exchange rates fluctuate with market forces.

**foreign exchange market** The international market in which foreign currencies are traded.

**foreign exchange rate** The price of one currency in terms of another currency.

**foreign exchange rate appreciation** An increase in the foreign exchange value of a currency.

**foreign exchange rate depreciation** A decrease in the foreign exchange value of a currency.

**fractional-reserve banking** A banking system in which banks are required to hold a certain percentage of their deposits as reserves.

**frictional unemployment** Unemployment that occurs because individuals are constantly moving between jobs.

**GDP deflator** The GDP deflator measures prices of all new goods and services produced in the economy.

**GDP gap** The percentage deviation of actual real GDP from potential GDP.

**GDP per capita** The value of GDP per person. This measures a nation's GDP proportional to the size of its population.

**government purchases** New goods and services purchased by federal, state, and local governments.

**gross domestic product (GDP)** The market value of all final goods and services produced in an economy during a given period.

**human capital** A person's physical and mental capabilities, including his or her health, education and skills, entrepreneurial ideas, and risk tolerance.

**hyperinflation** A condition when the general price level is increasing at a rate of at least 50 percent *per month*.

**implicit cost** The forgone opportunity cost of a choice.

**income approach** The income approach to measuring GDP adds up all of the incomes earned from people and businesses producing and selling goods and services.

**indifference** A situation in which a person doesn't care whether an alternative is chosen or not because it yields zero net benefit.

**inferior good** A good an individual is willing to buy less of at each and every price as her income increases and more of as her income declines.

**inflation** A sustained increase in the general level of prices.

**inflation expectations line** A horizontal line showing the expected rate of inflation in the economy.

**inflation tax** The economic cost imposed on holders of money caused by inflation.

**input price** The price paid for a unit of a resource used in the production of a good.

**interest payments** The interest paid by the government to holders of its outstanding debt.

**intermediate good** Something that is used in the production of another good.

**investment** The purchase of final goods by businesses that are used in the production of other goods plus the purchase of new homes by individuals.

**labor force** Everyone in the working-age population who either has a paying job or is looking for one, excluding working-age individuals who are in school and not working, retired individuals who are not working, institutionalized individuals, and individuals working in the home but not being paid for these services.

**labor force participation rate** The percent of the working-age population (16 years and older) in the labor force.

**law of demand** The observation that when the price of a good rises (falls), the quantity demanded of it falls (rises). Changes in price and quantity demanded are inversely related.

**law of supply** When the price of a good increases, suppliers are willing to produce more units of the good, all else being the same. Conversely, when the price falls, suppliers cut back on the number of units they are willing to produce.

**liquidity** The relative ease with which money can be converted into a good or service.

**loanable funds** Funds that are available for borrowing. They are supplied by savers and demanded by borrowers.

**M1** A "narrow" measure of money, which includes financial assets that serve mostly as a medium of exchange.

**M2** A "broad" measure that expands on M1 by adding in savings accounts and other financial assets thought to have a store-of-value function.

**macroeconomics** The study of economy-wide events, such as economic growth, inflation, and business cycles.

**marginal analysis** Comparing the net benefit resulting from allocating an additional unit of a scarce resource to one alternative versus another.

**marginal benefit (MB)** The incremental increase in an economic benefit that results when an additional unit of a scarce resource is allocated to a particular activity.

**marginal benefit curve** A graphic representation of the incremental economic benefit we

receive from consuming an additional unit of an economic good.

**marginal cost (MC)** The incremental increase in an economic cost that results when an additional unit of a scarce resource is allocated to a particular activity.

**marginal cost curve** A graphic representation of the incremental economic cost we incur to consume an additional unit of an economic good.

**marginal propensity to consume (MPC)** The marginal propensity to consume (MPC) measures how much consumption changes for a given change in income.

**marginal rate of transformation (MRT)** The rate at which two outputs can be traded off for one another. The *opportunity cost* of producing one more unit of one good in terms of forgone units of the other good.

**marginal willingness to pay** The reservation price a consumer is willing to pay for each incremental unit of a good.

**market** A location—physical or virtual—where buyers and sellers interact, directly or through representatives, to voluntarily exchange economic goods.

**market demand** The total number of units of a good demanded at each and every price in a particular market. Market demand is the sum of the individual quantities demanded at each and every price.

**market supply** The total number of units of a good supplied at each and every price in a particular market during a particular period of time. Market supply is the sum of the individual quantities supplied at each and every price.

**medium of exchange** A good that is used to facilitate trade.

**microeconomics** The study of how individuals, households, and producing organizations choose to use their scarce economic resources to maximize their own well-being.

**Monetarism** The idea that changes in the money supply dominated other policy actions in determining short-run output growth and long-term inflation.

**money multiplier** The multiple by which the money supply changes given a change in bank reserves.

**natural rate of unemployment** An estimate of what the unemployment rate would be if the economy were operating at its potential.

**net exports** The value of exports minus the value of imports.

**nominal price** A price expressed in current dollars.

**nominal rate of interest** The stated interest rate, unadjusted for inflation.

**normal good** A good that a person is willing to buy more of at each and every price as her income increases and less of as her income declines.

**normative analysis** The evaluation of a situation based on a person's values, religious beliefs, and opinions.

**open-market operations** The Fed's buying and selling of government securities.

**openness** The extent to which goods, services, capital, labor, and ideas flow into and out of a country.

**opportunity cost** The opportunity cost of a decision is the satisfaction or well-being you forgo from not engaging in the next-highest-valued alternative.

**outsourcing/offshoring** The act of shifting employment to another provider or to another location; the terms are usually used to refer to sending jobs to another country.

**Phillips curve** A curve that characterizes the inverse relationship between an economy's unemployment rate and inflation rate.

**physical capital** Land and other natural resources, machinery, and technology.

**policy rule** An established set of actions to be taken under a given set of conditions.

**policy transparency** The extent to which individuals can understand and predict policy actions.

**positive analysis** The evaluation of a situation based on facts and theories, leading to testable implications and validation.

**potential GDP** An estimate of what real GDP would be if the economy were operating at full production.

**preferences** Individual tastes based on how a person subjectively ranks alternative choices.

**present value** The price of some future payment stated in its current price equivalent.

**price ceiling** The maximum price at which a good can be *legally* traded in a market.

**price floor** The minimum price at which a legal trade can occur in a market.

**price index** An index allows one to measure changes in a numerical series. A price index shows how prices, in general, change from a reference year. If the index value is 110, this means that prices are 110 percent of the base-period level.

**price shock** A significant change in the price level, usually caused by the change in the price of an important commodity.

**principle of increasing marginal cost** A situation in which the opportunity cost of consuming additional units begins to rise.

**producer price index** The PPI measures changes in prices from the perspective of the seller. It measures the prices of raw materials, for example.

**producer surplus (PS)** The difference between the price a supplier receives for a unit of output and her marginal cost of producing that unit.

**production function** A relationship that shows the amount of output that can be produced using various combinations of labor, capital, and knowledge.

**production possibilities frontier (PPF)** A graph showing the maximum combination of outputs that can be produced from a given amount of scarce resources and technology over a specified period of time.

**productivity** Production of goods and services per hour of work, or per worker.

**productivity curve** A relation showing the amount of output produced for a given amount of capital per worker, holding knowledge constant.

**progressive tax** A tax that takes a larger percentage of your income as your income rises.

**property right** The legal or social right to use a scarce resource in a particular way.

**purchasing power** The amount of goods and services a unit of money can buy. Purchasing power moves in opposite direction to changes in the price level.

**purchasing power parity (PPP)** A way to compare the relative purchasing power of currencies by comparing the amount of each needed to buy a common bundle of goods and services.

**quantitative easing** The purchase of assets by the central bank to increase the amount of funds in the financial market.

**Quantity Theory of Money** A theory that links changes in the price level directly to changes in the supply of money.

**quota** A quota sets limits on the amount of a good that can be imported.

**rational expectations** Expectations that are based on available and relevant information.

**real-business-cycle theory (RBC)** The theory that fluctuations in real economic activity occur because of shocks to productivity, not because of changes in aggregate demand.

**real GDP** Real GDP is calculated by adjusting nominal GDP for changes in the price level.

**real rate of interest** The nominal interest rate minus the rate of inflation people expect.

**real wage** The nominal wage adjusted for changes in the price level.

**recession** A significant downturn in economic activity, usually measured by negative real GDP growth and rising unemployment.

**regressive tax** A tax that requires you to pay proportionally more as your income falls.

**relative price** The relative price of a good is its nominal price adjusted for changes in the general level of prices.

**reserve ratio** The percentage of deposits held as reserves by a bank.

**reserve requirement** The percentage of deposits a bank must hold as reserves, either as cash in its vault or on account with the Fed.

**reserves** Money that banks hold as a fraction of their deposits to meet their customers' withdrawal needs.

**scarcity** A situation in which only limited resources are available to meet people's unlimited wants.

**shortage (excess demand)** A situation in which quantity demanded exceeds quantity supplied at the current price.

**social infrastructure** The rules, regulations, and institutions that affect decisions to invest in capital, both human and physical.

**specialization** Allocating a person's scarce resources to a limited range of productive activities based on her comparative advantage.

**stagflation** A situation of high or increasing inflation and low or negative real GDP growth.

**store of value** A good that can be stored and traded later.

**structural unemployment** The type of unemployment that occurs due to a mismatch between workers' skills and those demanded by employers.

**substitute goods** Goods that are related in such a way that an increase in the price of one increases demand for the other; conversely, a decrease in the price of one decreases demand for the other.

**sunk cost** Costs that cannot be recouped following a decision.

**supply** The quantity of a good that a supplier is willing and able to provide at any given price during a specified time period (day, week, month, and so forth), with *all other factors held constant*.

**supply curve** A graphic representation of a supplier's supply schedule. The supply curve plots various price–quantity combinations an individual producer is willing to accept.

**supply schedule** A table that shows the price of a good and the number of units a producer is willing and able to supply of it at different prices during a specified period of time, *all other factors held constant*.

**surplus (excess supply)** A situation in which the quantity supplied of a product exceeds the quantity of it demanded at the current price.

**switching costs** The explicit and implicit costs people incur when they change brands, providers, or products.

**tariff** A tax levied on an imported good.

**Taylor rule** A policy rule describing how the Fed should set the federal funds rate. This decision depends on the values of inflation and real GDP growth, relative to predetermined targets.

**time-inconsistent policy** A policy that is not followed consistently over time.

**total expenditures line** The relation between the four spending components and total income or output.

**total factor productivity** The growth in output not explained by growth in capital and labor.

**trade deficit** A situation in which a country's exports are less than its imports.

**trade-offs** Opportunities we pass up when we make one choice versus another choice.

**trade surplus** A situation in which a country's exports exceed its imports.

**transactions costs** The costs people incur when exchanging goods and services. Transactions costs include search and information costs, bargaining costs, and payment and enforcement costs.

**transfer payments** Payments made to individuals by governments that are not related to the production of goods and services.

**unemployment rate** The unemployment rate measures the percent of the *labor force* that is not employed.

**unit of account** A unit of account is the standard of measurement used to state prices.

**valued added** Value added is the increase in market value of an item as it progresses through stages of production. The sum of value added is reflected in the final price of the good.

**well-being** A person's happiness, benefit, or pleasure.

**willingness to pay** The maximum amount of money a person is willing to pay for a good.

# INDEX